How To Be Your Own Booking Agent

THE Musician's & Performing Artist's Guide To Successful Touring

JERI GOLDSTEIN

EDITED BY KARI ESTRIN

CHARLOTTESVILLE, VIRGINIA

Copyright ©2006 by The New Music Times, Inc.
All rights reserved
Manufactured in the United States of America

Sixth Printing   April, 2006
Revised 2nd Edition
Updated

Library of Congress Control Number: 2003115754
ISBN: 978-0-9606830-4-8
ISBN: 0-9606830-4-6

The products mentioned in this book are the trademarks of their respective companies.

The owner of this book may make copies of the forms contained within for their own use without asking permission of the publisher. Other portions of this book may not be reproduced in any form without permission from the publisher.

Editor: Kari Estrin
Copy Editor: Deborah Liv Johnson
Copy Editor: Libby Post
Original Front Cover Design: John Odam Designs
New Cover Montage: Communication Services
Book Design: Rosie Smith/Bartered Graphics
Index: Juniee Oneida

Published and distributed by:
The New Music Times, Inc.
P.O. Box 1105
Charlottesville, VA 22902
Phone: 434-591-1335
Fax: 1-866-874-9321
E-mail: jg@performingbiz.com
Web: http://www.performingbiz.com

To my parents, Renee and Sheldon,
who have always encouraged me to exercise my imagination
and blaze my own trail to endless possibilities.
Thank you for your love and support.

In Loving Memory Of
Freyda Epstein
1956–2003

Friend, *musician, voice, violin, Alexander Technique teacher and choral director.*

Freyda Epstein was an extraordinary musician, period! As an original member of the band Trapezoid and leader of Freyda and Acoustic AttaTude, she toured the world and touched people's lives with her music and gentle spirit. Dying in a car accident in the early morning on May 17, 2003, Freyda never reached her favorite music gathering in Charlottesville, VA.

To honor her life's work, the Freyda Epstein Memorial Scholarship Fund has been established to help young musicians study voice and violin at the Augusta Heritage Center each summer.

For information or contributions:
http://www.augustaheritage.com

Freyda Epstein Memorial Scholarship Fund
Augusta Heritage Center
Davis & Elkins College
100 Campus Drive
Elkins, WV 26241

In Memory Of
Lena Spencer
1922–1989

In 1960, she opened the doors to Cafe Lena
in Saratoga Springs, NY
along with her husband Bill.
She offered countless numbers of young performers
their first chance to perform in a listening room
before a cappuccino-drinking audience.
Lena embodied the true spirit of the coffeehouse empressario.
She inspired me to dedicate my life to the performing arts and its creators.

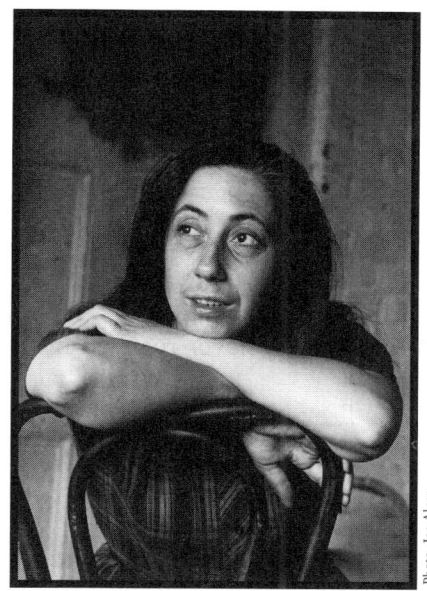

Photo: Joe Alper

Table of Contents

Foreword xiv
Introduction xv
Acknowledgments xvi
How To Use This Book xviii

Chapter One: Road Map To Success 1
    Exercise One: Dream List 2
    Dreams Lead To Goals 4
    Long-Term Goal Setting Affects Today's Booking Strategies 4
    Exercise Two: Long Term Goals Setting—Where Will I Be In Ten Years? 6
    Exercise Three: Five Year Goals 8
    Exercise Four: Two Year Goals 8
    Exercise Five: One Year Goals 10
    Resources 14
        Books to Organize and Enhance Your Business and Life

Chapter Two: Preparing To Do Business 15
    Assessing Your Current Situation 15
    Setting Up Your Workspace—Getting Down To Business 17
    Planning Tools 18
    Getting Organized And Stocking Up 19
    Assessment Form 27
    Resources 29
        Daily Planners, Long-Distance and Cell Phone Service, Magazines, Mail-Order Catalogs, Office-Supply Stores with Mail-Order Catalogs, Postal Meters, Shipping Carriers, Software, Telephone Headsets and Accessories, Warehouse-Club Stores

Chapter Three: You Are A Small Business Entrepreneur 31
    Clarify Your Structure 31
    Five Types Of Business Entities—What Kind of Business Are You? 33
    Create Your Team of Professionals 34
    Creating A Business Plan 35
    Taxes 37
    Chart: Sample Meal-Allowance Rates 40
    Chart: Sample IRA Savings for 30 Years 41
    Resources 43
        Accounting Software, Business-Plan Software, Music Business Books, Organizations and Businesses, Websites for Tax Information

Chapter Four: First Encounters 45
    Composing Scripts 45
    The Art Of Asking Questions 47
    Script For A New Venue—The Cold Call 48
    Calls To Familiar Promoters 51
    Telephone Techniques 52
    Venue Information Form 58
    Resources 59
        Books and Audio Cassettes about Telephone Sales

Chapter Five: The Promotional Package 61
Elements Of A Promotional Package 62
The Photographic Experience 67
Fees And Photographic Rights 70
The Difference Between Custom Prints And Economy Quantity Prints 71
The Overall Package 76
Tips To Keep Printing Costs Down And Information Current 78
Working With A Graphic Artist 79
The One Sheet 79
Electronic Press Kit 80
Working With A Copy Writer 82
Working With A Printer 82
Sample Press Releases 85
Resources 88
   Audio Duplication Companies, Directories, Electronic Press Kits, Graphic Artists, Photographers, Photo Reproduction Companies, Photo Retouchers and Hand Coloring

Chapter Six: The Art Of Negotiating 91
Negotiations In Your Daily Life 91
Building Relationships 92
Win-Win Negotiating 94
Three Main Steps to Every Negotiation 95
Negotiating Techniques 100
Negotiating Gambits 109
Know Your Bottom Line 113
Types Of Deals 115
The Offer 120
Tour Budget Form 122
Resources 124
   Negotiation Books and Cassettes

Chapter Seven: Contracts 125
Write It Down For Clarity 125
What Every Contract Should Include 126
Send Your Own Contracts 127
Read All Contracts Carefully 128
How To Deal With Questionable Items On A Contract 129
Keep Track Of Your Contracts 130
Types Of Contract Agreements 131
Letter of Intent 131
Letter of Confirmation 133
Performance Contract 137
Explanation of Specific Clauses 143
Contract Riders 148
Budget 149
Technical Rider 154
Hospitality Rider 154
Union Contracts 156
When There Is A Breach Of Contract 157
Blank Contract Forms 160
Resources 182
   Books about Music Business, Legal Resources, Unions

Chapter Eight: The Art Of Touring 185
- Reasons For Touring..186
- Creative Tour Planning 187
- Building A Home Base Of Support..190
- Audience Development 194
- Regional Touring 195
- Venue Booking Time Frames 199
- Booking Different Venue Types..200
- The Role Of Festivals, Contests, Battle Of The Bands, And Showcasing In Regional Touring 202
- Block Booking To Build A Regional Presence....................................206
- National Tours...206
- House Concerts...210
- Touring The College Market...210
- Sharing The Stage—Opening Acts, Support Acts, Co-Bills, Tour Exchange, Multi Act Tours, Open Mics 212
- Niche Marketing—Creative Touring Alternatives................................218
- New Performance Venues 224
- Market Your Act For Success 225
- Resources...227
  Books, Chain Store Venues, Contests, Database Disks, Festivals and Venues Online, Organizations with Venue Lists, Road Maps Online, Showcases, Tour Directories, Trade Magazines with Directories, Websites

Chapter Nine: U.S./Canada Crossing Borders 235
- Immigration Regulations 236
- Helpful Advocates 236
- U.S. Artists Planning To Tour Canada 238
- Work Permits/Canada..238
- Crossing The Borders..240
- Chart: Ports Of Entry (Inspection Stations Across The U.S./Canadian Border....242
- Contacting The Canadian Consulate/Embassy 243
- Canadian Money Versus U.S. Dollars..244
- Canadian Artists Planning To Tour The U.S. 244
- Applying For A Work Permit/U.S. 244
- Resources...247
  AFM Offices U.S. and Canada, Canadian Embassies in the U.S., Commercial Bonding Agents, Internet Currency Exchange-Rate Sites

Chapter 10: Managing The Road 249
- The Road Manager's Role 249
- Life's Details On The Road..250
- Road Stories..254
- Touring Check List 269
- Travel Savvy..271
- Working With A Travel Agent 271
- Information You Must Know About Travel 274
- Discount Travel Programs..277
- Car Rental 278
- Hotels 280

  Resources 283
   Discount Programs, Discount Airlines, Frequent-Flyer Programs, Instrument Insurance Providers, Merchandisers, Services, Software, Travel Agents, Travel Websites

Chapter 11: Conferences 285
 A Variety Of Conferences To Attend 285
 Expanding Your Markets..286
 Two Types Of Conferences 287
 Enhancing Your Conference Experience 289
 Showcasing 289
 Exhibiting 293
 Networking At Industry Events 296
 Additional Promotional Tools..298
 Resources 301
  Books on Networking, Display Manufacturers, Membership Organizations Presenting Conferences, Non-Membership-Driven Conferences

Chapter 12: Funding Sources 307
 Funding Resources 307
 Grants 308
 The Application Process...310
 The Canada Council For The Arts 313
 Meet The Composer 314
 Sponsorships 315
 Record Company Tour Support..320
 Resources 322
  Foundations Centers and Resource Organizations, Government Funding Sources, National Funding Organizations for the Arts, Regional Arts Organizations, State Arts Agency Directory, Canadian Funding Resources, Canadian Provincial Arts Councils, Sponsorship Directories

Chapter 13: Marketing Your Act..329
 Marketing And Business 329
 Your Marketing Plan 330
 You Are Your Own Publicist 333
 Working With A Publicist 336
 Follow-Up 338
 Mailing Lists 339
 Interviews..341
 Getting Previews and Reviews 343
 Resources 344
  Marketing Books, Publicists

Chapter 14: Accessing The Media—Print.......................................345
 Magazines—Genre Specific 345
 Trade Papers And Magazines...347
 Major Market Newspapers 348
 Local Daily Newspapers 349
 Arts And Alternative Papers 351
 Wire Services..353
 Newsletters 353

Resources 356
   Directories, Genre Magazines, Newspaper, Radio and Television Directories, Organizations with Targeted Media Lists, Print Trade Magazines, Wire Services

Chapter 15: Accessing The Media—Radio 363
Radio Formats 363
Commercial and Non-Commercial Radio 367
College Radio 368
Public Radio 370
Nationally Syndicated Radio Shows 371
Local And Regional Shows 373
Community Radio 373
Resources 375
   Radio Lists and Directories, Radio Trade Magazines and Online Sites,

Chapter 16: Accessing The Media—Television 377
Educational Access 377
Public Access 378
Public Television 379
Cable Television 381
Local Network Affiliates 383
National Networks 385
Television Contests 385
Resources 388
   Television Networks and Shows

Chapter 17: Internet Marketing 389
Get Hooked Up And Logged On 390
E-Mail 391
Websites 393
Resources 396
   Internet Website Registration, Internet Magazines, Internet Marketing Books, Internet Music Sites, Internet Software, Auto Messaging Software, Site Marketing Companies

Chapter 18: Working With Your Record Label 399
Working With A Team 400
Sales, Publicity and Promotional Tools 402
Radio Promotions 406
Marketing Your Recordings To Specialty Stores 408
Resources 411
   Directories of Record Labels, Internet Lists of Labels, Master Tape Restoration, Music Business Books, Online Independent Music Sales, Song-Plugger Companies, Websites

Chapter 19: Working With Professional Agents And Managers 413
Definitions 413
Carefully Consider Who You Invite Into Your Business 414
The Courting Stage 415
Which Comes First—The Manager Or The Agent? 417
Experience Versus Inexperience 419
Working With A Manager 420
Working With An Agent 423
The Agency's Cost To Represent An Artist 427

    Looking For An Agent 428
    Resources 433
        Books on Management, Directories, Organizations with Agency Lists,
        Organizations for Agents and Managers

Chapter 20: Hiring Help 435
    Remain In Control 435
    Where To Find Help 437
    Working With An Assistant 438
    The Co-Op 439
    Resources 442
        Books and Audio Cassettes on Managing Employees

Chapter 21: The One-Year Plan 443
    Target Date Format 444
    Jessie's One-Year Plan 447
    Exercise: One-Year Plan 454
    Resources 456
        Time Management Books

Chapter 22: When To Quit Your Day Job 457
    How Are Your Doing? 458
    Yearly Evaluation 458
    Planning To Quit Your Day Job 460
    When Your Business No Longer Feeds You 462
    Resources 464
        Books on Career and Personal Change

Chapter 23: Ethics And Attitude 465
    Ethics 466
    Honesty 466
    Loyalty 470
    Attitude 472
    Situations Where Attitude Makes A Difference 472
    Resources 476
        Books about Ethics in Business, Organizations Governing Business Conduct of
        Agents and Managers

Chapter 24: Epilog 477
    Be Creative In Both Business And Art 477
    Resources 479
        Books about Creativity and Success

Appendix 480
Index 484
About The Author 490
Manager-In-A-Box® 491
The Performing Biz 491
About The Editors 492

Foreword

Sadly, you can't learn to be a great *musician* or *performing artist* exclusively by reading a book. No matter how unfair it seems, I think we all understand that this type of greatness can't just be "studied up on" and learned logically with very much success—it's too strongly determined by some inscrutable combination of heredity, early childhood experience, hands-on teaching by great teachers, and other elusive ingredients.

On the other hand, you can learn a lot about *business*, including the music and performing arts business, from books. It's easy to learn enough from books like **How To Be Your Own Booking Agent** to actually begin involving yourself in the music and performing arts business professionally. And from there, you can learn as you go.

I know this because it happened to me: Nobody in my family was in business—let alone the music business. I never took a single business or music business class—let alone pursue a degree in the subject.

I got my initial education in the music business from *books*.

And thank goodness for Jeri Goldstein, because she's written one of the truly indispensable books about the music and performing arts business.

The way I read this book was with pen in hand, underlining and writing, "so true, so true!" and, "key point!" over and over in the margins. I bet you'll wind up doing that, too.

Some of Jeri's insights are going to be immediately and obviously crucial (don't quit your day job until you've worked out a way to keep your health insurance). Other parts of the book, like the excellent sample contracts, may not prove their value until you suddenly need them months from now, but you'll be incredibly grateful at that time to have them.

Some items in this book can even lead you on paths you never imagined. I would like to draw your attention in particular to the resources Jeri's flagged for your attention at the end of each chapter. These include a selection of the most helpful books and resources you'll ever find on related subjects—already thoroughly hand-picked for you. Similarly, be sure to enjoy the anecdotes throughout the book from others who have "been through it all"—they're fascinating.

Happy gleaning!

Micah Solomon

Micah Solomon (micah@oasisCD.com) is President and CEO of Oasis CD Manufacturing, often considered one of the companies most devoted to the success of independent musicians. Through Oasis CD, Micah has given thousands of independent musicians their first significant chances at radio play through the OasisSampler™ CD series which is regularly distributed to all major niche radio stations nationwide, and he has pioneered various other outstanding distribution opportunities for independent artists. For more information about Oasis CD, see the inside back cover of this book or visit www.oasisCD.com.

Introduction

I have written this book with the notion that a performing career needs to be approached from a holistic perspective—one aspect of your career cannot develop successfully without other aspects being given equal attention. The art cannot flourish without the business.

The following pages demystify the business of booking, touring and promotion and place at your fingertips the means with which to create a successful performing career of your own design.

As an artist, you may already possess a natural talent for handling the business side of your art or you may struggle to get the job done. There is a tension between the tasks of booking and performing. You want to perform and practice your art, yet you must become proficient at business in order for your art to thrive. In resolving the need to incorporate both jobs, you inevitably will find this book invaluable. The new resources, hot tips and insightful comments from industry professionals will be helpful in making your days flow more smoothly as you fine-tune your skills and increase your business savvy. As you become more efficient at taking care of the business, the business will allow you the time to focus on your art.

At some point during the evolution of a performing career, artists may find themselves in a working relationship with a professional booking agent or, at the very least, someone who assists with booking performance dates. Until that time, or if that time never arrives, there is a void—a void of information, of resources and of accessible contacts. This book attempts to fill the gaps, answer the questions, offer solutions and methods, and a reality-based step-by-step road map to fashion a career as a touring performer.

I made my first foray into the world of agenting as a student, coordinating The Side Track Cafe, a small coffeehouse at the State University College in Oneonta, New York. While booking acts for this venue, I discovered that I could create a local circuit with a few nearby colleges. By linking together a number of dates, I put more money in the artist's pockets while lowering the fees for each date individually and stretching my budget. The musicians were happy to have more work, the colleges were happy to present quality performances and I was happy to make it all come together. This was truly the beginning of my booking career. I met other presenters, began working with a few artists and successfully created a few tours. I felt that I had provided a valuable service and I enjoyed the results.

Many agents I have known have similar tales to tell. Some had been performers but felt compelled to help other artists with bookings rather than tour themselves. Some are artists who had less than satisfactory experiences with their own agents and found it necessary to take charge. In other instances, the members of a band simply assigned one member to do their booking.

However you may come to the position, whether it is out of love of the arts and the artists or simply as a matter of your own creative survival, performing this agenting job well is a fundamental requirement for a successful performing career.

Let me set the record straight. Booking agents are essential to the movement of the cultural and popular arts around the world. This book is a tribute to the hard working people behind the scenes who connect artists and presenters in an effort to quench a demanding public's thirst for live entertainment.

In 20 years of working as both a manager and a booking agent, I have gathered a wealth of information while developing many life-long business and personal relationships within the entertainment industry. In these pages, I offer you the benefit of my self-directed schooling with the hope that your successes will be many and your career long-lasting.

Jeri Goldstein
Charlottesville, Virginia
e-mail: jg@performingbiz.com

Acknowledgments

There are so many people and events that have influenced the writing of this book over the course of my 20 years in the entertainment business. This book would not exist without their help, their experiences and their support. To all of those with whom I have worked, this book pays homage to your dedication to the arts and the artists who touch so many people's lives.

This project seemed to be my destiny because so many circumstances fell into place at exactly the right time. It is no wonder that I was able to find absolutely the right people to join with me to make this project come to fruition. To my long-time friend and editor Kari Estrin, whose expertise in the entertainment business as a promoter, a manager, a tour manager, agent, magazine publisher and editor, enhanced her commitment to take this project to a higher ground. She challenged me gracefully to stretch my boundaries and reach for answers beyond my grasp until all that needed to be said, was said. To my new friend and copy editor, Deborah Liv Johnson, who helped me find my writer's soul. As a touring musician and label owner, her business savvy and reactions to my writing were an invaluable litmus test. Her years as editor for Adventure 16's *FOOTPRINTS Magazine* helped attend to the details and add guiding light. Thanks to my dear friend Libby Post, who joined the team as final copy editor. As owner of Communications Services, her copywriting and graphic design expertise were fully appreciated as she helped bring the project to its conclusion. I appreciate their incredible efforts on my behalf in the face of their own projects, jobs and lives. Their support and partnership are so much a part of this book.

To all the industry professionals, whether long-time relationships or new acquaintances, thanks for sharing your wit and your wisdom to adorn these pages. You graciously responded to my requests for comments and found time to search your vaults filled with years of experiences for stories and insights that would uplift and educate. Without your contribution, this book would only tell a small fraction of the whole story.

Special thanks to all the folks at *A Prairie Home Companion,* Sugar Hill Records, Warner Bros. Records, Red House Records, Music For Little People and Columbia Artists Community Concerts with whom I shared a vision for some very special artists. Our working together, often day-in and day-out, gave the world some terrific music.

To Irene Young, who shared her 20 years of photographic expertise and enriched the book as well as my life. To Leslie Berman, whose contacts, knowledge and experience as a writer in the music business, coupled with her legal expertise, proved invaluable when writing about contracts. To Nina Gorin and Airway Travel, who has helped move my acts, my friends and relatives around the world and shared her travel savvy and her friendship. To Tracey Lake, whose enthusiastic support and encouragement allowed me to see this project to its end. To Barbara Karol who opened her home to provide me with a writer's retreat and whose friendship continues to feed my soul.

And there are those people who have been a part of my life and have encouraged me in my endeavors. Their influence can be felt on every page. My thanks to Jackie Alper, Phyllis Barney, Betsy Bartholomew, Stevie Beck, Nancy Boyer, Linda Clark, Sarah Drenan, Dan Griffin, Valerie L'Herrou, Mary Huey, Steven Kravitz, Paul Kurland, Russ and Elise Kushigan, Pat McFarland, Kate McKee, Nancy Michon, Billy Murphy, Ken Olsen, Jill and Donald Person, Barry Poss, Jeanne Rizzo, Andrea Rounds, Ruth Pelham, Margreta Hartje-Swanson, The Folk Alliance and The IBMA.

Thanks to Juniee Onieda for the index and John Odam for the cover design. To Rosie Smith for creating and executing the book design. Her easygoing manner and incredible patience lasted through all of my changes and whims.

And, my heartfelt thanks goes out to all of the artists who allowed me to participate in their lives and their businesses. Without these artists, I would not have had the experiences that I share with you here. Without these artists, the world would not be as rich. Thanks to Robin and Linda Williams, with whom I shared 20 years of career building, family gatherings, celebrations and challenges. We helped each other grow, accomplish and find our way. To Dan Crary, whose music opened new doors and broadened horizons. During our 10 years, we challenged them to open their minds and go in fresh new directions. To Freyda Epstein, who truly spoke with a unique and creative voice. Her music moved me as it did so many. My growth from our association is immeasurable. To Garrison Keillor and The Hopeful Gospel Quartet, thanks for inviting me to be part of something so many could enjoy. To Ferron, although our time together was brief, we faced the challenges of transformations with honesty and commitment. Thanks for including me on the team. To Cathy Fink and Marcy Marxer, who expanded my business know-how in what seemed to be an instant. They continue to inspire me to get the job done. To Byron Berline and all the boys in the California band, who pushed the musical envelope—together we lit a few fires. To Eileen Carson and The Fiddle Puppet Dancers, who trusted me to go where I had not been before in an effort to bust open the world of dance. To Cathy Winter and Betsy Rose, who ushered in a whole new era. To Julie Kabat and Carole Friedman who taught me to enjoy fundraising for classical music events.

A very special thanks to Phyllis Kurland who is responsible for introducing me to the entertainment business and without whose guidance, friendship and creativity, I might have become an art therapist.

How To Use This Book

Reading this book from beginning to end offers a concrete, step-by-step approach to developing and enhancing a performing career. Each chapter builds upon the last, expanding your knowledge of proven techniques and giving you methods to create a work style that will help you achieve your performing career goals.

Or, you may find yourself drawn to specific topics which will answer particular and immediate questions with which you are currently dealing. Each chapter holds its own and can be used as a reference when you reach that particular phase of your career development. Access each subject as your needs dictate.

No matter how involved you are with performing—full time, part time, a novice or a long-time veteran, reading Chapter One and completing each of the exercises will impact how you proceed with the rest of your performing experiences. Once you have read a majority of the other chapters, reading Chapter 21 and completing the exercise will provide the immediate career boost necessary to motivate you throughout the next year.

What You Will Find

The Quotes
Take inspiration from the comments offered by professionals in the business who work in the field every day. Their years of experience will, quite simply, make you more effective and more efficient in a shorter amount of time. Their quotes fill every sidebar with insights into their specialized field.

Some professionals wear many hats. Quote credits reflect each person's position in relation to the topic they are discussing and, in some cases, will be different if they have commented on a variety of topics. When someone is quoted more than once in a chapter, their first credit appears in full while subsequent credits may be shortened.

The HotTips:
Found in the upper right or left corners of a page, the HotTips in each chapter will save you time and money while providing insights into proven methods or resources which you can use to your immediate advantage.

The Resources
At the end of each chapter, you will find a resource section. This is the information I wish I had when I began. The resources provided are pertinent to that specific chapter. I have always wanted a book which offered resources appropriate to what I was reading right then and there. When I find a book that does that, it makes a profound difference in my personal and business growth. Once I have finished a book, looking through the resources offered at the end of the book had less impact. I wanted to know what I needed to know right after reading the information. This book puts the appropriate resources in front of you right when you need them. When you finish reading about touring, the touring resources are right there for you. It is the same with every other chapter.

You will find a listing of available gig directories, festival directories, media resources, funding sources, lists of books, tapes and current websites to help advance your skills and provide immediate access to the information you need. There are lists of photographers, photo reproduction companies, directories of radio stations, records labels, managers, agents, merchandisers, newspapers, magazines and newsletters. For those newly introduced to grants, lists of local, state, national and provincial arts councils are included as well as lists of organizations to join and conferences to attend with showcasing opportunities, band contests, song writing contests and performance competitions.

I have gathered product resources, mail order catalog information and product websites so that you may organize your business efficiently while keeping your costs down.

These resources are provided so your time working at developing your career is not spent seeking out the tools you need but is spent making the calls needed to make a living. Utilize them at the time you need them. As you proceed through the book, you may find one or a number of the recommended resources are appropriate to enhance a current project or the particular phase of your development. Many of the resources may be found repeated in a number of chapters because different aspects of the resource may be important to each of the chapters. For instance, you will find a listing for *Pollstar* in Chapter 8, Touring; Chapter 13, Marketing Your Act; Chapter 18, Working With Your Record Label and again in Chapter 19, Working With Professional Agents and Managers. In each case, *Pollstar* prints different directories which are an important reference for that specific chapter.

A Note About The Resources

I have included them because they will make a difference in your life. For some, the resources may be the most important part. Some of these resources and books can be found in your local libraries, college or university libraries, in local book stores or in one of the online book stores. They may be found in the business or personal growth sections. They may also be ordered directly from the publishers or organizations listed. You may want to browse through the resource sections for reference books that you would like to access immediately. Many of the suggested books, listings and subscriptions may be added as your business grows.

Some resources are free or available with a subscription or a membership. Others may sport a prohibitive price tag. You may find them important in the future or when your budget allows. I have included them so you will know what is out there.

Area Codes, Addresses And Websites

The resources have been meticulously researched and verified for accuracy. During the last year, there has been a massive revamping of the telephone area code system. Find current area codes on the Internet: http://www.melissadata.com.

If you call a number and the area code has been changed, you may get a wrong number message. In most cases the number is correct and the area code needs to be updated. Check with the operator or the web address above.

People and businesses move. Always phone ahead and confirm each address before mailing any of your materials to a resource listing. Similar to street address changes, website addresses also change. Many will leave a forwarding address on their old home page, some do not. Some websites may only be accessible by using a specific search engine. The websites listed have been checked on Microsoft Excite, Netscape Navigator and Yahoo.

Updating The Information

The resources will be updated periodically with new versions available in future editions of the book. I invite your input. If you encounter a resource which is outdated or some aspect of the contact information has changed or is incorrect, please contact me via e-mail, jg@performingbiz.com. In our fast-paced, technological world, your help to keep the resources as current as possible is invaluable. I will post particularly important changes on the performingbiz.com website on the Resources page regularly.

New And Noteworthy Resources

If you find a resource which you feel will be of value and would like to share your discovery, please forward your information via e-mail. It may be included in future editions of the book as a HotTip or on the Resource page on the nmtinc.com website.

This book will be your guide. Return to it time and again with new questions as you tackle each phase of your career development.

Let's begin the adventure. Take charge of your career and shape your own success.

CHAPTER ONE
Road Map To Success

"A person with great dreams can achieve great things."

Bob Rotella
sports psychologist, author

We all have dreams that crystallize our hopes for our greatest achievements, happiest moments or desired pleasures. Most of us find our dreams at the end of sentences beginning with "If only . . ." Sometimes our passion makes us bold enough to live out one or two. The challenge for all of us is to place our dreams within the "big picture"—the overview of our lives—and believe that we can fulfill them. Our dreams are the chunks of coal from which we will cut our diamonds.

Given the importance of dreams in determining our life's direction, a discussion about planning your future would be the most logical place to begin. In order to do this, you need to give some thought to what you would like your future to look like. This chapter is designed to get you thinking beyond the moment and working towards designing the successful career that you have envisioned for yourself.

This chapter is probably the most important one in this book and I will refer to it often. If you do nothing else but read this section and complete the suggested exercises, you will be on your way to succeeding in whatever you choose to

"Imagination lays the tracks for the reality train to follow."

Caroline W. Casey
astrologer, author

> "This business is a long, slow business. It's about growing organically through playing and people liking you. You have to do your part by getting the message out there, but it doesn't just happen all at once."
>
> **Amy Kurland**
> owner,
> The Bluebird Cafe

> "Whatever you vividly imagine, ardently desire, sincerely believe, and enthusiastically act upon, must inevitably come to pass!"
>
> **Paul J. Meyer**
> self-improvement author, motivator

> "First say to yourself what would you be, and then do what you have to do."
>
> **Epictetus**
> Greek philosopher

> ". . . and nothing is worse, than a dream deferred."
>
> **Nikki Giovanni**
> author, poet

do. Unfortunately, most performing artists, musicians, dancers and actors are usually in survival mode—living from one gig to the next, or if they are particularly adept at this booking business, living from one tour to the next. However, if you begin to view your career on a larger scale, you will have more control over your life, your performing career and of your choices along the way.

A successful touring career does not just happen. Most artists who seem to prove the "overnight success" theory have really been steadily plugging away at the details of their businesses to make their dream their reality. Magic plays no part in these successes—hard work, persistence and a vision of what lies at the end of the long path do.

Transitioning Dreams Into Reality

Last summer I remember sitting at my kitchen table reading a book about publishing. In a momentary day dream, I saw myself writing a book that would gather the information I had learned through the years and making it available to performing artists. Something compelled me to write down the time, the date and the dream.

My dream looked like this:

I will write a book about how to effectively create a successful performing career.

This dream was so clear that I used the term *I will write* instead of *I would like to write*. There was simply no doubt in my mind that I would do this. It was just a matter of figuring out how to do it, not whether it would get done. To integrate our dreams into the "big picture" of our lives, we must first identify our dreams and write them down.

Exercise One: Dream List

Now it is your turn to find your passions and articulate your dreams. To accomplish this, you might want to have a notebook or a loose-leaf binder on hand. This will be your planning book. I have provided many areas within this book to begin each exercise immediately. Begin your dream list on page 3 and expand on it in your planning book. I've found that having a planning book keeps all of my project ideas in one place, and not on scraps of paper which are easily lost.

Set aside an hour of quiet time by yourself. If you have a career partner or a life partner, encourage them to begin this exercise as well. Once you have both completed individual dream lists, you might consider working on a list together. List as many dreams as you can think of. Let your fantasies flow. Do not stop at 25 dreams if you can list 100. Allow your imagination to be limitless. This exercise is to get you to think big, think wild, go for the extreme. Do not be practical. Do not think about whether it is possible or not, or how you will ever do it.

It is *your* dream list. Right now have fun with this. You can include personal dreams, family dreams, or business and career dreams; it doesn't matter. Dreams help form the foundation of our life goals. Dreams are the substance that fuels our plans.

Some dream examples are to:
- Travel to Europe within the next five years
- Learn how to play a particular sport or instrument
- Make your first recording
- Perform in Carnegie Hall

Refer to your dreamlist occasionally. Once you reach a dream on your list, check it off, but don't remove it. This will serve as a reminder of your accomplishments throughout your life. As you look back on your list, you will feel a sense of satisfaction as your dreams become realities.

"What you can do, or dream you can, begin it; Boldness has genius, power and magic in it."

Goethe
German poet

Dream List

_____
_____
_____
_____
_____
_____
_____
_____
_____
_____
_____
_____
_____
_____
_____
_____

Now that you have identified and recorded your dreams, you have begun to think beyond the moment—beyond the tasks looming before you. So many of us get caught up in the details that we rarely make time to view our careers or our lives from a distance. Our vision for the future impacts upon the decisions we make today.

Here is an analogy that illustrates how identifying the dream allows us to plot the steps leading to it. Let us say you are about to take a road trip from New York City to Denver. In preparation for the trip, you spend some time reviewing a

"Go confidently in the direction of your dreams. Live the life you've imagined."

Henry David Thoreau
American author

road map to decide which routes are best. This overview provides you with such useful information as estimated times and distances, projected costs and even possible attractions to visit along the way.

In short, you will make up your travel schedule with the confidence that you *will* reach your destination. Unless you had unlimited time and money and were simply out for a joy-ride across the country, you would not think of beginning this trip without your map. *So, why would you start a performing career without a plan?* I invite you to view the rest of this chapter as your personal road map to help you define your future.

Dreams Lead To Goals

Now you are prepared to embark on the next exercise—identifying your long-term goals. Use the dream list you have created as a catalyst. Within this list of dreams, you have begun to lay the groundwork from which you will build your goals. If you have lived with a particular dream tugging at your imagination, now is the time to acknowledge it.

One of the benefits of setting long-term goals is that it enhances your ability to make thoughtful decisions about new opportunities that are presented to you. With your life's dreams and goals before you, you are able to calculate how a new opportunity will fit into your plans. Will it take you off on some tangent that does nothing to move you closer to your dreams, or will it offer you some new way of advancing to your goals? You will be able to make those kinds of decisions more effectively once your goals are in place. Long-term goals are not rigid—they are a flexible guide that moves with the flow of your life. As a guide, they offer you a focal point, a tool, by which you can set your sights and move forward to achieve your dreams.

Therefore, long-term goal setting is not as overwhelming as it sounds. You probably have gone through this process in your mind at one time or another and simply haven't written down your thoughts. The act of writing them out, and committing your thoughts to paper is a very powerful one. It challenges you to stretch the boundaries of the way you presently view your life. Enjoy the process!

Long-Term Goal Setting Affects Today's Booking Strategies

Long-term goals place you on a path. They help to determine which direction your career will move in over the next few years. As performing artists, here are just some of the decisions that your long-term goals will influence:

❖ The types of venues you choose

"One thing you have to be prepared for is that other people don't always dream your dream."

Linda Ronstadt
singer

"The person who makes a success of living is the one who sees his goal steadily and aims for it unswervingly. That is dedication."

Cecil B. De Mille
film director

"When you start walking your true path, amazing things start to happen."

Debra Russell,
Certified Life Coach
www.artists-edge.com

- Whether you perform full time or part time
- When you make the move to full time or back to part time
- Whether you book yourself, hire an assistant or look for an agent
- Whether you decide to seek management
- What type of business entity you become
- Where your home base of operation will be
- What type of marketing plan you will follow
- Whether you tour solo or with a band
- Which touring markets you choose

For example:

Those wanting to establish mainstream media and industry recognition must tour certain markets, perform in specific venues and attract the attention of specific media outlets. Therefore, you would:

- Select to perform in major markets like New York City, Boston, Philadelphia, Los Angeles and Chicago.
- Prepare to play in showcase clubs like The Bottom Line, Tramps, Hard Rock Cafe, House of Blues, The Troubadour and The Bluebird.
- Pursue the writers and critics at papers like *The Boston Globe, The Washington Post, Los Angeles Times, The Philadelphia Inquirer, The New York Times,* and *The Chicago Tribune.*
- Target radio formats and stations to receive airplay on AAA, Americana, Adult Contemporary, Country and College Radio stations.

For those wanting to develop a lasting performance career without focusing on recognition from the mainstream industry or media, you would:

- Play in any region you choose and in performance situations most suited to your performance.
- Create your own niche markets.
- Establish a loyal regional following without regard for hitting specific regional and national media and industry-heavy markets.
- Practice creative tour planning on your own terms.

Without your long-term goals to guide your steps from day to day and keep you from getting distracted, you have less of a chance of fulfilling your dreams. Your long-term goals ultimately influence who you will call tomorrow morning. For example: If you have determined that your goal is to play Carnegie Hall within the next ten years, all of the steps you take from tomorrow on should move you toward that goal. Start performing at small community arts centers and then

HotTip:

When you plan for the long term—you have a road map by which you can chart your progress.

When you write out your plan—you make a commitment to it.

"I have a broad appreciation for, and experience with, lots of different kinds of music and I can play many different kinds of music. Secondly, having been the MC for Hot Rize for years, I felt very comfortable speaking to an audience. Lastly, I had been energized by the live media experiences we had, particularly live radio. As I looked at my life and my desire to make a contribution, I thought I could capitalize on those three aspects of my experience. I came up with the idea of a variety show that would include music, conversation, information and that would try to build community on the air. That's what I set out to do."

Nick Forster
musician, creator of
E-Town radio show

move to larger community theaters to develop a local and then regional following. Your first step toward that Carnegie Hall performance would be to identify all of the local community arts centers in your immediate area and contact them. Your first call tomorrow might be to the community arts center in your hometown. If you had not identified the goal to perform in Carnegie Hall, you might be focusing your attention in many different directions and not targeting your energy towards your specific goal.

> *"Whereas your goals are the stepping-stones toward your dreams, your objectives are the lampposts that illuminate the path to each goal."*
> — Charles J. Givens
> author, entrepreneur

Exercise Two: Long-Term Goal Setting—Where Will I Be In Ten Years?

To complete this exercise, set aside at least one hour of free time. Having someone else write down your thoughts as you speak may be more effective. If not, simply use the space provided at the end of this chapter on page 11 or write directly in your planning book.

To Set Your Long-Term Goals, Ask Yourself

What do I see myself doing over the next ten years? As you spend time fantasizing about this, let your wildest dreams flow.

> *"The ten-year planning exercise helped me put my life into focus. I was able to gain an overall perspective and, as a result, my efforts were much more directed and organized. This process allowed me to envision projects that I had previously dismissed as being beyond my grasp."*
> — Freyda Epstein
> performer, teacher of violin, voice and the Alexander Technique

A contemporary musician's possible long-term goals:
1. My goal is to perform in the U.S. as well as in many other countries so that I might mix my desire to travel with my desire to explore the art of other cultures.
2. I want to gain enough expertise in my art to be invited as a presenter at festival workshops as well as on college and university campuses.
3. I would like my career to develop to the point where major festivals invite me to perform on their main stage.
4. I would like to have ample financial resources to enable me to make a new recording every eight months to two years.

A classical musician's possible long-term goals:
1. My goal is to be a soloist invited to perform with various orchestras.
2. I would like to have a recording contract with a premier classical record label.
3. I would like my career to develop to the point where I play Carnegie Hall, Lincoln Center and the great venues in Europe.

> *"Make no little plans; they have no magic to stir men's blood . . . Make big plans, aim high in hope and work."*
> — Daniel H. Burnham
> architect, city planner

These are just two ways in which you can shape your long-term goals. Whatever your specific art form or genre of music, allow yourself to see into your future and shape your plans—do not stop yourself with practicalities. We are filled with so many project ideas. This exercise will allow you to articulate them. By writing down these ideas, you unclutter your thoughts. Be limitless, always keep in mind that this is what you want to be doing in ten years. It is not set in stone. Once you see your goals written out before you, you gain a sense of direction and are motivated to see them actualized.

Actualizing the Ten-Year Goals

I will use a hypothetical musician, Jessie, to demonstrate how to create long-term goals. Her goal is to perform internationally. This is the practical part. There are skills that Jessie must use in conjunction with other professionals and resources which must eventually be incorporated into her plan. At this point in her career she may not know which players can assist her, but she may realize that she will need some outside help. Here is a list of practicalities that Jessie may incorporate into her long-term view.

- Ten years from now Jessie will work with a number of contacts in Europe to book her performance dates overseas. She will have a personal assistant to arrange her appointments and manage the details of her career.
- Jessie will have had multiple feature articles written about her innovative seminars generating numerous international speaking and festival invitations.
- Her press kit will be filled with her most current reviews from *The New York Times* and *Billboard* as well as other major trades and newspapers.
- She will have been signed to a record label several years earlier whose publicity department arranges all of her interviews and promotional appearances.

These are just some of the practicalities that will be part of this musician's life in the long term. Each goal requires the accompaniment of very specific events and/or people in order for it to be realized. When goals are broken down, piece by piece, they become less overwhelming and more easily accomplished.

With these steps, you place yourself on a path. From now on, everything you do will relate to your long-term goals. All of your plans for action have a focal point leading toward them. Now, the rest is relatively easy. Once you know where you are going, the details of how you get there are simply a matter of taking it one step at a time. Once you have set the goal, many of the details seem to fall into place. Every time I have done this exercise with artists during a consultation, their reaction has been one of pure relief. Relief in knowing they now have a direction—a path to follow—and that they can handle the details.

The next step is to work your way back from ten years and repeat this same exercise for your five-year goals. Why

> "Musicians often avoid the 'business hat,' but if you can wear it, your career will move forward tenfold. Set goals and have fun with them."
>
> **Deborah Liv Johnson**
> singer, songwriter,
> label owner,
> Mojave Sun Records

> "To follow, without halt, one aim: there's the secret of success."
>
> **Anna Pavlova**
> Russian ballerina

> "Opportunities are usually disguised as hard work, so most people don't recognize them."
>
> **Ann Landers**
> journalist

work backwards? When you have a vision to work towards, it determines all of the steps necessary to achieve your goals. Many corporations begin with a vision of the completed business—how they want to operate in the corporate community. Then they put the company together to match their vision. That is what we are doing here. By working backwards from your ten-year goals, you can more easily fit the appropriate steps in place to achieve *your* long-term vision.

Exercise Three: Five-Year Goals

As you begin thinking about your five-year goals, refer often to your ten-year goals. Prompt yourself by stating each ten-year goal first. Again, we will use our international performer as an example.

She states: "If I want to be able to tour successfully on an international level in ten years, then in five years I must have established a successful touring career in the U.S. and have begun sending material to some festivals in Canada and Europe. Once I have played a few Canadian and European festivals and have begun to build an audience, I will return to each of these areas for short tours in the regions where I had previously played the festivals."

Using this example, write your five-year goals on page 12.

Actualizing The Five-Year Goals

The practicalities required to actualize Jessie's five-year goals become easier to picture as the future comes into view more clearly.

❖ In five years, Jessie will have a solid touring base in the U.S.
❖ She has received print media recognition with one or two feature articles written in some of the smaller trade papers and tour press in area newspapers.
❖ She has produced three recordings on her own label and has recently sold over 15,000 combined units by placing displays in small regional gift shops.

Exercise Four: Two-Year Goals

You can begin to see your career take shape as you establish these sets of long-term goals. As you continue to backtrack to your two-year goals, the details of your business become easier to imagine. Continue to prompt yourself by now stating your five-year goals as you work on your two-year goals.

For example:

Our international performer would say: "If I have begun touring some festivals in Canada and Europe in five years, then in two years I must establish myself in multiple regions throughout the U.S. I will have been invited to a number of

---

"Whatever thy hand findeth to do, do it with all thy might."
The Old Testament

*"Bite off more than you can chew,
Then chew it.
Plan more than you can do,
Then do it."*
Anonymous

"Write your goals down and ask yourself everyday, 'What have I done towards these goals?' This takes self-discipline and it works!"
**Dick Renko
manager,
Trout Fishing In America,
Muzik Management**

major festivals performing on some of the side stages as well as participating in a few workshops. My first recording should be reviewed in a few of the industry trade magazines and I should begin receiving airplay on a few stations in each of the regions in which I perform."

With this example in mind, write out your two-year goals on page 12.

Actualizing The Two-Year Goals

There are many events that must take place in order to reach your two-year goals. These events are much closer to current reality and are more easily imagined. For instance, Jessie would include some of the following in order to accomplish her two-year goals:

- Attend a few booking conferences where she could meet the festival directors and presenters she is specifically targeting. Hopefully, they will see her showcase.
- Have a part-time assistant sending promotional packages to prospective presenters or calling various print and radio media in order to set up interviews for media coverage.
- Formally create a new record label which will produce her future recordings. Jessie also needs to establish a business entity so that she can conduct the label's business legally.

As you can see, the closer you get to your immediate future, the tasks which you must complete become very clear.

One-Year Goals Become Clear

Having completed the ten-year, five-year and two-year goals, you are now able to look at your immediate future with concrete ideas for your goals during the next year. Stating your one-year goals now becomes a logical exercise, with less guesswork or sense of enormity. Shaping your career is now a series of easily accomplished tasks. With Jessie's goals for the long term clearly defined, her one-year goals fall into place.

One-Year Goals For Our Musician, Jessie:

Hypothetically it is now January.
1. Set up a workspace this winter.
2. Develop a promotional package.
3. Book a regional fall tour.
4. Begin booking a spring tour of club dates.

Jessie's goals will strategically move her through her year leaving little doubt about her direction. These four goals essentially divide her year into four distinct projects. Each

---

"Begin; to begin is half the work. Let half still remain; again begin this, and thou wilt have finished."

Ausonius
4th century Roman poet

"If you doubt you can accomplish something, then you can't accomplish it. You have to have confidence in your ability and then be tough enough to follow through."

Rosalyn Carter
former First Lady

"Ah, but a man's reach should exceed his grasp or what's a heaven for?"

Robert Browning
Victorian English poet

> "We need objectives. We need focus and direction. Most of all, we need the sense of accomplishment that comes from achieving what we set out to do . . . ."
>
> Leon Tec, M.D.

project will require a specific amount of time. Within each time frame, Jessie will have to list and define the tasks that will be necessary in order to complete each project. By breaking down each project and goal into smaller tasks which can be accomplished in a finite amount of time, Jessie can now create a one-year plan to help her reach her one-year goals. (See Chapter 21.)

Now you are ready to work on *your* one-year goals. All of the information and the exercises within this chapter will help set you on your career path. This is the doorway to your future. Take your time to complete this process and have fun with it. The work you do now sets the tone for the rest of your career. Incorporate these planning tools into your life and you can accomplish anything you choose to do.

Exercise Five: One-Year Goals

Working back from your ten-year goals, review each exercise—ten-year, five-year and two-year. Now envision your goals for your first year, step by step, and write them down on page 13.

With your goals in place and the information provided in the remainder of this book, you will have the tools with which to create a one-year plan of action. Chapter 21 offers a guide.

> "Be really clear and honest with yourself about your objectives and your motivations for setting those objectives."
>
> Sue Trainor
> musician, publicist

> "It's magical what starts to happen when you get specific and real about what you want to accomplish. I've seen this happen over and over again. It's one of the reasons why I really demand that my clients get specific. People say, "I want this goal, but I don't know how to get there." I say, "Let's just start working on it." Opportunity just starts to happen."
>
> Debra Russell,
> Certified Life Coach
> www.artists-edge.com

Summary

- ⟡ A dream list is a list of your fantasies for your business and personal life. Add to your dream list throughout your life.
- ⟡ Long-term goals affect the decisions you make for the short term and give you more control over your life. Long-term goals provide an overview of your career then give you both the flexibility to adjust your direction when necessary and a series of benchmarks to keep you on track.
- ⟡ Tools for long-term planning are:
    Ten-Year Goals
    Five-Year Goals
    Two-Year Goals
    One-Year Goals

My Long-Term Goals—Ten Years
Date Recorded _____

My Five-Year Goals
Date Recorded _____

_____
_____
_____
_____
_____
_____
_____
_____
_____
_____
_____
_____

My Two-Year Goals
Date Recorded _____

_____
_____
_____
_____
_____
_____
_____
_____
_____
_____
_____
_____

My One-Year Goals
Date Recorded _____

Resources

A Goal Is A Dream With A Deadline: Extraordinary Wisdom For Enterprising Managers And Other Smart People
Leo B. Helzel, Friends Helzel
McGraw-Hill
ISBN: 0070282625

Golf Is Not A Game Of Perfect
Bob Rotella
Simon & Schuster
ISBN: 068480364X

First Things First
Stephen R. Covey
Fireside
ISBN: 0671864416

Master Strategies For Higher Achievement (audio cassettes)
Universal Laws of Success and Achievement (audio cassettes and workbook)
Thinking Big (audio cassettes)
Brian Tracy
Available from Nightingale Conant
Phone: 1-800-525-9000
Ask for free catalog.

Peak Performance
The Power Of Innovative Thinking
Available from National Seminars Publications
Phone: 1-800-258-7248
Ask for free catalog

SuperSelf: Doubling Your Personal Effectiveness
Charles J. Givens
Simon & Schuster
ISBN: 0671700979

Take Charge Of Your Life (audio cassettes)
Jim Rohn
Available from Nightingale Conant
Phone: 1-800-525-9000
Ask for free catalog.

The 7 Habits Of Highly Effective People
Stephen R. Covey
Simon & Schuster
ISBN: 0671663984
ISBN: 0671708635 pbk.

The Seven Spiritual Laws Of Success
Creating Affluence: Wealth Consciousness in the Field of All Possibilities
Deepak Chopra
Amber-Allen Publishing & New World Library
ISBN: 1878424114
ISBN: 1880032422
Phone: 1-800-227-3900

Turn Your Great Idea Into A Great Success
Judy Ryder
Peterson's/Pacesetter Books
ISBN: 1560794623

Unlimited Power
Personal Power II (audio cassettes and books)
Anthony Robbins
Available from Nightingale Conant
Phone: 1-800-525-9000
Ask for free catalog.

CHAPTER TWO

Preparing To Do Business

"It is necessary to surpass oneself always; this occupation ought to last as long as life."

Christina
Queen of Sweden, 1629-89

Welcome to this moment. You have come to this point with a life full of experiences leading you here. Feel proud of all of the accomplishments you have achieved up to now because they are the building blocks for everything to follow.

Assessing Your Current Situation

Now is the time for a reassessment of your career and to implement a plan of action. Take stock of what you have already got going for yourself by making a list. This chapter gives you a concrete starting point from which to assess how to use your existing skills and resources. You will also identify your needs and priorities. To accomplish this exercise, I have provided a worksheet on page 27 to use as an aide when evaluating what you need to work more efficiently.

When listing your business skills, remember to consider typing, creative writing, sales, graphics, photography, bookkeeping, etc. When listing your equipment include computers and software, typewriters, office furniture, and touring vehicle.

When this list is completed, evaluate it. You may decide to learn a database or bookkeeping system or even hire a

"I will accept the present as it is, and manifest the future through my deepest, most cherished intentions and desires."

Deepak Chopra
author, philosopher

"We must not stay as we are, doing always what was done last time, or we shall stick in the mud."

George Bernard Shaw
British playwright

My List of Necessities

_____

_____

_____

_____

_____

_____

_____

_____

_____

_____

_____

_____

_____

_____

_____

bookkeeper. You may also decide to buy a portable computer and specific software. Keep in mind that as you work on this list, you will rediscover areas of expertise long buried. You will refer to your list over and over. The list is your tinker-toy—it takes the guesswork out of finding the tools with which to build your individual career.

Fill out the questionnaire on pages 27 and 28 to begin your assessment process. If you need more room, continue your list in the additional space provided.

Determine Your Necessities

Once you have worked through the assessment questionnaire, identify some skills and items necessary in order to plan your performing career more seriously. For instance, if you determine that creating a promotional package is one of your first priorities, but your financial situation is limited, develop the basics. Have a good promotional photograph taken. Have a biography written. Create stationery and business cards. Buy some inexpensive pocket folders in which to send your packet. Any other items to include in your promotional arsenal, like a color slide or a video, can wait until your finances are more secure. With this example in mind, write out your list of necessities in the space provided.

As you examine the list, determine what items are needed immediately and which ones can wait until next year—or perhaps even longer. Now, revisit this list and prioritize the items which need your immediate attention.

Skills Versus Time Versus Cost Assessment

This exercise will also give you some clear indication about how you want to spend your time.

Once you have a clear picture of your talents and skills, you can make more effective choices, like whether or not to design your own promotional materials or hire a graphic artist. If you are comfortable speaking on the phone, making your own booking calls may be easy. Otherwise, you may want to hire someone to make those calls. Whether you are adept at bookkeeping or computer programming, accounting or people management, assessing your situation before making important business decisions will help you make the right choices to run your business effectively and efficiently. Your time will be spent working on the things you do best.

For example:
I realized how to utilize my time and talents efficiently, over ten years ago when I purchased my first full database program to create my contact and contract databases. I had been using a very simple mailing list program to keep track of all of my contacts and I was about to outgrow its capabilities.

I felt it was time to transfer my contacts into a program that could more easily manipulate the information.

At the time, database programs were fairly cumbersome to work with. Designing my own database from an "off-the-shelf" product was a baffling chore. After reading the manual, I quickly realized that it would take me the better part of a year to create the program of my dreams. Since my goal was to book performance dates and not to become a computer expert, I hired a representative from the software company to create what I needed.

The cost to hire a consultant was minimal compared to the amount of time it would take me to create the program. In the end, I booked more dates, which paid for the two weeks of consultation. I got what I wanted and needed to reach my goals.

Be aware of what you take on and how it impacts your goals. I was able to quickly identify this computer project as one that stretched beyond my skill level since I had previously assessed my strengths and weaknesses. I was also able to place a real value on my time and where it would best be spent.

Compare Assessment With Goals

When you compare the assessment list with your list of goals, you will quickly identify areas that match your own expertise and areas that do not.

As we move through the book, your goals and this list will form a base from which many of the important decisions about your career will be made. Use these lists to maintain a clear path towards obtaining the results that you have defined for yourself. By knowing what skills you possess, you are able to make decisions regarding your best interests efficiently. This is particularly important when the time comes to find other professionals who may become members of your career team, such as an agent, a manager, a lawyer, an accountant, a publicist or a graphic artist.

Setting Up Your Workspace—Getting Down To Business

To do our most creative work, we need our surroundings to be comfortable according to our individual needs. Comfort comes in many forms. For some, it is a desk in front of a window looking out to the garden. For others, it is a room filled with gadgets and equipment; and still for others it might be a phone, a desk and a swivel chair. It is important to identify those things that allow you to do your best work and set up a space that invites you to accomplish your tasks each day. It is important to be comfortable in your space so you use it to your best advantage. In the rest of this chapter,

"Consider well what your strength is equal to, and what exceeds your ability."

Horace
Roman poet, satirist, literary critic

My List of Priorities

_____

_____

_____

_____

_____

_____

_____

_____

_____

_____

_____

_____

_____

_____

> "Really know what kind of resources are available to you. What am I going to use to keep up on hot new tips? How am I going to gauge where I need to be taking my business over the next year, over the next three years, five years?"
>
> **Andrew McKnight**
> singer, songwriter

> "The life of an artist is, in relation to his work, stern and lonely. He has labored hard, often amid deprivation, to perfect his skill. He has turned aside from quick success in order to strip his vision of everything secondary and cheapening. His work is marked by intensive application and intense discipline."
>
> **John Fitzgerald Kennedy**
> U.S. president
> *New York Post*, 1963

> "Disorganization costs time and money. The way you design and organize your office ultimately affects your professionalism and productivity."
>
> **Lisa Kanarek**
> author,
> *Everything's Organized*

I offer some specifics to help make your workspace/creative space more efficient, more cost-effective and more suited to your own work style.

Many of us began our businesses in our homes using the dining room table or spare bedroom. That worked for many years and still works for many. Those of you that have access to a completely separate space are indeed fortunate. Wherever you find a workspace to your liking, it is helpful to have some or most of the following supplies in your office. I have selected some of the most commonly used items and recommended some specific brands as well as purchasing methods for optimum efficiency and least expense. Much of what is listed below can be purchased at your local office-supply store or from a discount catalog. See the resource list at the end of this chapter.

Planning Tools

In Chapter One, you created your long-term and short-term goals. The planning tools below will help keep track of your yearly, monthly and daily plans as you work toward attaining your goals.

1. A Yearly Planner:

Available in any office-supply store. The laminated washable type allows you to write in the year so you do not have to buy a new one each year. This wall-mounted planner is a constant reminder of weekly and monthly activities, yet it provides an at-a-glance overview of the entire year. The yearly planner prevents you from getting lost in the details of the moment. It keeps you looking outward and allows you to keep your future goals guiding you forward.

2. A Daily Planning Book:

Get one that has room for note-keeping as things come up during the day. It should include a place where you can write a daily "to-do" list and have a place where the hours of the day are broken down for appointments. Your daily planning book will include both business and personal appointments, plans and "to-do" lists. *This intertwining of your daily personal and business life serves as a reminder to nurture them together.* Since your personal life was included within your ten-year plan, you now need to include it within your daily plans. For example, include everything from phone calls to the west coast to lunch and dinner appointments, contracts you need to issue, your children's ball games and recitals, your practice and rehearsal sessions, your family's doctor and dentist appointments, press releases to prepare, as well as your exercise and workout times.

There are many systems available at office-supply stores or by mail order. Get something to carry with you and that you enjoy working with. Keep the system simple. Some have so many components that you become overwhelmed by them. The Day Timer system is a compact package that includes very tidy additions like an address book, work books, a full-year calendar along with a six-year calendar. Many of my friends and colleagues use Franklin Planners for all of their daily, monthly and yearly planning.

3. A One, Two or Three-Year Calendar:

Use this calendar to keep track of tour planning and confirmed dates. These are also available at local office-supply stores. The "Month-at-a-Glance" administrator type by Keith Clark is well suited to booking. It has the current year in the front of the book and the next year at the back of the book. This year-at-a-glance overview again keeps you looking ahead and able to keep the "big picture" in mind. Within the body of the calendar, each month has large boxes where you can make notes.

Getting Organized And Stocking Up

Shipping Supplies:

1. # 10 Envelopes for Letters

Have these preprinted with your logo and return address at the local quick-copy printer.

2. Jiffy Bags and Bubble-Type Shipping Envelopes

Both items can be purchased in many sizes. For example, use #0 for a single cassette and use # 6, which is 12" x 13", for large posters. You will use lots of shipping envelopes so purchase a case to save money. Compare the cost of a single large #6 envelope at $1.20 with the cost of a single #6 envelope when purchased in a case at $.34. A case of large #6 envelopes contains 100 envelopes and costs approximately $34. A case of the smaller-size envelopes contains 250 envelopes, again reducing your costs. Save time by shopping through a catalog—and remember, they deliver it to you!

3. Priority Two-Day Mail Envelopes and Boxes

Free from the post office, these will hold up to one and two pounds of anything that fits inside and the postage remains a set rate. Exceed two pounds and you will be charged accordingly. These are great for contracts, photos, promotional packets, etc. You will be surprised at what can fit into one of these envelopes.

4. Manila Envelopes, 9" x 12" or larger

Available 100 to a box and should last for a while. They are also fine for contracts and mailing printed material that needs to stay flat.

"The more organized you are about your business, the more time you will have for your music."

Cathy Fink
musician, songwriter, producer

"A daily planner also gives you the flexibility in planning your schedule and work flow . . . things that need to be done today as well as those tasks that need to be done in the future."

Jeffrey J. Mayer
author,
Time Management for Dummies

"Ninety percent of failure is due to lack of organization."

Henrietta C. Mears
minister, educator

> **HotTip:** 🌶
> Buying office supplies in bulk or by the case can save money. Assess your needs once or twice a year and stock up. Save time and money by not running to the office supply store at the last minute and paying premium prices.

"Order is heaven's first law."
　　　　　Alexander Pope
　　　　　British poet

5. Strapping Tape or Shipping Tape and Dispenser

Available from office-supply stores, but much more economical from mail-order catalogs.

6. Postage Scale

Purchase a two-pound scale from an office-supply store unless you go the postal meter route. The scale comes with the meter in most rental deals. But if you purchase your own scale, the meter rental deal is less expensive.

7. Postal Meter (optional)

This item is usually rented from either Pitney Bowes or IMS Hasler. Assess the volume of mail you will be sending. The biggest factor to consider when thinking about renting a meter is how much time you will save waiting in line at the post office. If you are mailing five or more pieces per day that need to be metered at the post office, you may want to consider renting the meter. Count on approximately $80 to $100 in rental fees per three-month period, depending on the style and size of the meter. The smallest meter with a two-pound scale will probably do the trick at this point. This is a huge time saver and is certainly something to be considered in your office plans. If you plan on offering your merchandise in a mail-order catalog, a meter is a must. A representative from either company can help you decide the most appropriate meter for your needs. They will also equip you with the necessary supplies like meter strips and ink rollers. Meters must now be refilled electronically. Contact the meter company for details. Once you think of yourself as a small business, waiting in line at the post office is not an effective use of your time.

8. Preprinted Mailing Labels

These labels can be mail ordered with your return address on fan-fold computer sheets to print directly from your computer's database. The peel and stick variety is the most efficient.

9. Self-Sticking Stamps

If you do not have the postal meter, sheets of self-sticking stamps make quick work of preparing tour itinerary mailers.

10. UPS/Federal Express Account

In order to sell your CDs and cassettes through your own mail-order catalog, you may also want to set up an account with UPS or Federal Express. For a nominal weekly fee, they will stop by your office every day to pick up your shipments and supply you with all of the necessary books, charts and a scale. If you do volume mailings of bulky items like tapes, CDs, videos or books, this may prove to be a huge savings in time and money. UPS and Federal Express also have prepaid overnight letters at a discount.

"Remember that time is money."
　　　　　Benjamin Franklin
　　　　　U.S. statesman, inventor

Computer and Supplies:

This is an optional investment which you may already have made. With so many discount stores and mail-order catalogs available along with used computers, it is certainly an item that should be seriously considered. There is no question that it will make life easier. A portable computer may better fit your travel and home office environments.

When deciding which computer to get, assess:
- Portability
- Weight
- Memory size
- Disk drive size
- Modem capabilities and speed
- Screen size
- Operating system

Software types to consider are:
- Database or contact management programs
- Word processing
- Desktop publishing
- Spreadsheet
- Bookkeeping or checkbook programs
- Music programs compatible with instruments
- Calendar
- Organizing programs

Your computer may already have been loaded with valuable software at the factory that fulfills many of the above necessities. Perhaps your new computer will come with some version of a database or a contact manager such as ClarisWorks, which Macintosh provides in many of its computers. (See resource section.)

Software Programs:

Types of programs to help you accomplish your booking tasks:

1. Contact Manager

These programs were designed for salespeople and have built-in modules to help you close the sale. Contact managers are a form of database that holds many thousands of records. They can sort your data on a variety of fields which can be created to your own design for optimum data input and retrieval. A contact manager has capabilities already set up and designed for the specific purpose of keeping in touch with your contacts with greater ease and efficiency.

The contact manager has a "notes" area directly under the contact information. While you are talking on the phone, you can keep extensive notes about that conversation. It will stamp your notes with the time and date. When you call

---

HotTip: Federal Express and Quickbooks have partnered to offer discounts to Quickbooks users. http://www.fedex.com

"I really think it's essential that anybody who is going to be a touring performer have portable computer capability so they can stay in touch with their e-mail correspondence."

Paul Schatzkin
former president,
Songs.com

"The whole idea of using a computer is to help you get more work done in less time. And with a contact manager you can coordinate the basic components of your planner with a single software program."

Jeffrey J. Mayer
author,
Time Management for Dummies

Notes:

back, you have the information handy and can refer to "our conversation of such and such date." They also have a "recall" field which allows you to set an alarm or tickler date to remind you to call back. Contact managers come with a word-processing program within the program, many of which are compatible with some of the more popular word-processing systems. A report generator interfaces with your contact information and can automatically generate specific information in particular formats. For instance, a tour itinerary can be generated from the contract database portion.

The word-processing module allows the creation of your own reports and documents which can interface with the contact manager. This capability is perfect to create and mail contracts and press releases thereby streamlining your work time. Some programs also come with an "order entry" module that can be used to keep track of your CD sales as well as print invoices or interface with your bookkeeping or checkbook program. In short, these programs help you to be more productive, keep track of your contacts, keep track of your time and the discussions you have had.

2. Database Programs

Database programs come in two forms, flat file and relational. A flat-file database has the capability of accommodating a finite number of fields into which data may be input. Most contact managers are actually flat-file databases. A relational database has the capability of allowing data in one field to interact with data in another field, creating a possible comparative relationship between fields and even between multiple databases. File Maker Pro or Microsoft Access are examples of relational databases.

3. Booking Programs

One would think that with all of the booking agencies around the world, someone would have developed a generic booking program. In fact, the reality is that many agents have developed their own programs from standard database packages, adapting them to their own work styles and specific data entry methods. They were created with the developers' interests in mind.

Some agents offered their programs for sale to other agencies. Many of them required that you adapt your method of working to their program or your data to their mode of input. Some of these programs were inflexible and could not be changed to suit personal needs. Even though the developers thought of most of the questions and solved most of the problems that might be encountered, the maintenance and support of these programs proved difficult for the developers. Unfortunately, most of the programs that I researched were no longer in use by the agencies. They had outgrown them or were no longer being offered for sale. Many agencies have moved to contact management programs and are once again recreating their dream program to suit their own needs. (Check this chapter's resource section for programs currently available.)

Printers:

Printers are available through mail-order catalogs or in computer and office-supply stores. The variety is endless and the prices are very reasonable. My suggestion is to examine where you will be doing most of your printing—on the road or at the office. You may want to purchase a more portable printer if you are only able to buy one. These compact bubble-jet types are great to have on the road and will help with multiple set lists, words to new songs, or preparing upcoming mailers in your hotel. You will need ink cartridges and some machines may require additional font cartridges.

Modems/DSL/Cable/T1 Lines:

High speed, providing quick access to your on-line necessities is the key. With the volume of information you want to download from the Internet or e-mail, you will want the fastest modem speed you can afford at the time. The prices are coming down rapidly and on-line time is precious, so you do not want to be spending it on lengthy download times. Mail-order catalogs will save a bundle on this item.

Fax Machines:

This may be an avoidable investment at first if your computer is equipped with a fax/modem along with the software to receive and send faxes computer-direct. However, the prices on dedicated machines have also come down considerably. Mail-order catalogs or office-supply stores offer a wide variety. If you plan on using your fax machine as a copy machine, consider getting a plain paper fax machine.

Stationery and Supplies:

1. *Letterhead* and *envelopes* can be printed at a quick copy printer. More information is included in Chapter Five, The Promotional Package.
2. *Post-it notes, phone-message pads, file folders, staples and stapler, paper clips, computer paper, computer labels* are all available at office supply stores or through mail-order catalogs.

Phone and Supplies:

1. *A One-Line or Two-Line Phone with Hold Button.*

If you only have one line and you share that line with business and personal calls or with other family members, you might consider getting a distinctive ring feature, a numbered voice mailbox system (push 1 for family matters, push 2 for

> **HotTip:** Combination fax/printer/copier machines save money up-front, but if one element breaks, you lose the use of the whole machine while it is being repaired.

"The only way that you can be successful today is to become more productive, efficient, and effective, not just busy. When productivity increases, the quality of your work improves, you get things done on time, and best of all you accomplish more tasks with less effort."

Jeffrey J. Mayer
author,
Time Management for Dummies

"Try to handle each piece of paper only once. Every time you pick up a piece of paper needing your action, failing to act only means you'll have to double your time and energy spent on it by picking it up again."

Michael LeBoeuf
American professor
of management, writer

> **HotTip:** 🌶
> Many online phone services are available. Skype.com and Vonage.com are two cost-saving plans.

booking) or another line to be kept separate for booking purposes. If you are going to be using a fax or modem consider having two separate lines for these tasks. If you use one line mostly for long-distance outgoing calls and rarely for local calls, like a fax line, ask your local phone company for the very basic program which costs between $6.00 and $10.00 instead of the regular charges of $20.00 plus. You will be charged so many cents per local call. But if you do not use that line for local calls, you will only be charged by your long distance carrier for your outgoing long-distance calls at whatever low rate you have been able to get.

2. Headset

One of the great accessories available is the headset. There are many varieties from very cheap to very, very expensive. The cheap ones unfortunately tend to have poor sound quality, making your long-distance conversations difficult. They are also often clumsy and cumbersome to wear. There are some very good headsets in the $100 to $150 range that will let you maneuver through lengthy phone sessions with ease and comfort. Many of these headsets have a headband apparatus. The most comfortable one I have found weighs only a few ounces and has an earpiece that slips over your ear with a small adjustable mouthpiece. Some headsets are wireless and will allow you to roam your workspace accomplishing two or three things at a time. (See resources for order information.)

3. Cellular Phone

A cellular phone is an essential business tool for a touring artist. It offers security and comfort on long stretches of empty roads should a situation beyond your control cause delays. You simply have the ability to continue to do your business anywhere, anytime. Your cell phone plan will reduce the need for a regular home phone and phone plan. Free long distance is included in most cell phone plans.

Long-Distance Phone Service:

There are many options to choose from with many discount possibilities. I will not suggest particular phone companies here, although I have my favorite; but I will suggest options that will reduce your phone bill.

1. Six-Second Billing

While most personal long-distance services bill in one minute increments, business services bill in six second increments. Just think of all the phone machine messages you have left this year that only lasted 12, maybe 15 seconds, and you were billed a full minute. Faxes often take less than 30 seconds. You will immediately notice a tremendous savings in your phone bill with this option. This is where you can save many hundreds and thousands of dollars each year. The phone is your number one communication tool and it makes sense to scrutinize your billing options.

2. A Low Per-Minute Rate

Many services are waging a rate war getting your per minute rate. Check with each company and ask them for their lowest current promotional rate. Do not settle for only a low per-minute rate. Often this low rate covers up poor service in other areas. Check with others who also have that service to get an idea of the quality provided in all areas. If the company won't give you a per-minute rate, but quotes a discount percentage off your entire bill, insist that they make a comparison with your previous bill. Discount percentages can be deceiving and often end up costing more money.

3. Account Coding

This option will allow you to create a series of codes that you can apply to clients or vendors or specific tours. If you are an agent working with a number of artists, assign an account code to each artist. Your monthly bill will separate the number of calls and costs for each code. As a single artist, assign a code number to each specific tour to tally costs and assess profits. There is a minimal charge for this service depending on your monthly billed totals.

4. Charitable Donations

Some services will also donate a percentage of your total bill to one or a number of organizations that you designate or with whom they are associated. (i.e., Working Assets)

5. Monthly Minimum Contract

Once you determine the volume of calls you make within a year, additional discounts are available with a one-year contract where you guarantee that your bill will reach a minimum monthly amount. Inquire about the various options. This option can reduce your per-minute rate, give you free account coding or any number of other discounts.

6. Award Programs

Ask about joining the phone company's award program. Many services offer points per minute of phone time which can add up. Some awards may be frequent-flyer miles or other items like printers, computers or hotel stays. I have received multiple round-trip airline tickets, a microwave, a stereo and numerous other items from my phone points.

7. Promotions

Ask if they are offering any promotions. Some will offer free calls on a specific day for one or more years, others free

> **HotTip:** Ask about special international calling programs. Some companies offer discount rates and frequent-flyer mileage points.

hours. Your inquiry will save you money. The phone companies all want your business and are willing to pay you for it. Find out what they offer before accepting one company over another. There are valuable savings to be had in this one area of your business.

Stocking Up Tips

As you set up your office, establish relationships with various vendors, especially local office-supply stores. Let them know you would like to continue doing business with them as you need to replenish your supplies. Ask for any discounts they might offer to long-term customers. Often a 15 percent savings on cases of shipping materials or other supplies can add up.

Warehouse clubs offer great savings in this area as well as on office furniture and office equipment. A one-year membership in one of the nationwide warehouse clubs can do wonders for your budget during this initial phase of purchasing.

National chain discount office-supply stores and mail-order catalogs will offer the best discounts on supplies and equipment. I've ordered most of my computers, printers, fax machines and supplies from mail-order catalogs and have never had a problem. Delivery is always prompt and some catalogs pick up the shipping costs depending upon the price of the item ordered.

"People want economy, and they will pay any price to get it."

Lee Iacocca
former CEO,
Chrysler Corporation

Summary

- Assess your current skills and resources.
- An efficient work space promotes effective work habits.
- Take advantage of bulk buying for savings on office supplies.
- Mail-order catalogs can often offer better deals.
- Inquire about current promotions and savings programs when shopping for services and supplies.
- Research long-distance phone services thoroughly for your best options and lowest rates.

Assessment

1. Are you working at your performance career full time? ____ or part time? ____

    a. Would you like to perform more than you do? ____ or less? ____

2. What are your personal skills? _____

    _____

    _____

3. What are your business skills? _____

    _____

    _____

4. What office equipment do you own or have access to? _____

    _____

    _____

5. Do you have available materials with which to promote yourself?

    ____ Yes   ____ No (Refer to Chapter Five, The Promotional Package.)

    a. What promotional materials do you have?

    Black and White Photos ____   Color Slides ____

    Press Packet ____   Posters ____   Flyers ____

    Recording ____   Video ____

    b. What do you need immediately that you do not have? _____

    _____

6. In what areas do you wish to develop your skills? _____

    _____

7. In what areas would you hire a professional or seek assistance? _____

    _____

8. What personal contacts do you have who can assist you with your performing career?

    _____

9. What mode of transportation do you use to get to performances?

    Your Own Car ____   Van ____   Rental Vehicle ____

    Air Travel ____   Other Public Transportation ____

a. What is your desired mode of transportation for touring if different from above?

_____

10. Do you have a lawyer or know one from whom to seek occasional advice?

    ____ Yes   ____ No

11. Do you have an accountant or someone with whom to consult?

    ____ Yes   ____ No

12. Does your current financial situation allow you the freedom to pursue your performing goals?   ____ Yes   ____ No

    a. If No, have you determined how much capital you need to get started or make the changes you desire?   ____ Yes   ____ No

    b. If No, have you considered finance sources that might be available to you?

       ____ Yes   ____ No

    c. What are they? (i.e., family, bank loans, savings)_____

    _____

    d. What changes would you need to make in your current situation to allow you to consider your performing career more seriously? _____

    _____

Continue your list below if you need more room.

My Assessment List—continued

_____
_____
_____
_____
_____
_____
_____

Resources

Books:

Everything's Organized
Lisa Kanarek
Career Press
Phone: 1-800-CAREER-1
ISBN: 156414254X

Feng Shui at Work: Arranging Your Office Space to Achieve Peak Performance and Maximum Profit
Kristine Lagatree
Villard
ISBN: 037575010X

Organizing from the Inside Out
Julie Morganstern
Owl Books
ISBN: 0805056491

Time Management for Dummies
Jeffrey J. Mayer
IDG Books Worldwide
ISBN: 1568843607

See Chapter 21 for more time management books.

Daily Planners:

Day-Timer
Available at office supply stores or call for catalog
Web: http://www.daytimer.com

Day Runner
Available at office supply stores or call for catalog
Web: http://www.dayrunner.com

Franklin/Covey
Available at office supply stores or call for catalog
Web: http://www.franklincovey.com

Long Distance and Cell Phone Service:

Alltel
Web: http://www.alltel.com

AT&T
Consumer Marketing Sales: business or home
Web: http://www.att.com

Sprint
Web: http://www.sprint.com

Sprint PCS
Web: http://www.sprintpcs.com

Verizon
Web: http://www.verizon.net

Working Assets
Web: http://www.workingassets.com
(Leases their lines from Sprint.)
(Donates 1% of your monthly bill to various non-profit organizations which you can select.)

Online Phone Service

Skype.com
Web: http://www.skype.com

Vonage VoIP Phone Service
Web: http://www.vonage.com

Magazines:

Mac World
Web: http://www.macworld.com

PC Magazine
Available in bookstores, libraries, magazine stands.
Web: http://www.pcmagazine.com

Mail Order Catalogs:

BrownCor International
Office supplies, shipping supplies
Web: http://www.browncor.com

Computer Discount Warehouse CDW
Web: http://www.cdw.com

Mac Mall
Hardware and software
Web: http://www.macmall.com

PC Mall
Hardware and software
Web: http://www.pcmall.com

Quill
Office supplies, equipment and furniture
Web: http://www.quill.com

Robbins Container Corp.
Shipping supplies, boxes, envelopes
Web: http://www.cornellrobbins.com

Tiger Direct
PC hardware and software
Web: http://www.tigerdirect.com

Office Supply Stores With Mail Order Catalogs:

Office Depot
Office supplies, equipment and furniture
Web: http://www.officedepot.com

Staples
Offices supplies, equipment and furniture
Web: http://www.staples.com

Postal Meters:

IMS Hasler
Web: http://www.mailingsolutions.com

Pitney Bowes
Web: http://www.pb.com

...ing Carriers:

Airborne Express
Web: http://www.dhl.com

Federal Express
Phone: 1-800-238-5355
web: http://www.fedex.com

United Parcel Service
Phone: 1-800-742-5877
web: http://www.ups.com

Software:

Contact Managers:

ACT!
Windows/MAC
Symantec Corporation
175 West Broadway
Eugene, OR 97401
Phone: 1-800-441-7234 or 541-334-6054
Fax: 541-984-8020
Web: http://www.symantec.com
IN CANADA:
Symantec Canada LTD.
895 Don Mills Road
500-2 Park Centre
Toronto, Ontario M3C 1W3
Phone: 1-800-441-7234 or 416-441-3676
Web: http://www.symantec.com

Gold Mine
Windows
Phone: 1-800-654-3526
Web: http://www.frontrange.com

Tour Manager
Music Business Store
Web: http://musicbusinessstore.com

Databases:

ClarisWorks
Address book, calendars, database module, word processing, paint, draw, communications bundle packaged with new computers.
Web: http://www.clarisworks.com

File Maker Pro
Multi-user-relational database
PC/MAC
Available from office supply stores and catalogs
Web: http://www.filemaker.com

Telephone Headsets and Accessories:

Radio Shack Headsets
Available at local Radio Shack stores

Plantronics Executive Systems
Web: http://www.plantronics.com

Warehouse Club Stores:

Memberships required for discounts

BJ's Club
Web: http://www.bjs.com

Costco Wholesale
Web: http://www.costco.com

Sam's Warehouse Club
Web: http://www.samsclub.com

CHAPTER THREE

You Are A Small Business Entrepreneur

"You've got to be a good business person if you are going to do this. Have your business wits about you—that means having systems and infrastructure in place so that you can concentrate on your art."

Andrew McKnight
singer, songwriter

Whether you work at a performing career full time or part time, you are creating a small business. As such, there are certain steps you will need to follow to make sure that your small business is properly maintained.

The tools to identify your long-term and one-year goals were discussed in Chapter One. Chapter Two assessed your current career situation. Now you are ready to create your own business structure. This chapter will provide suggestions on how to clarify your business structure, who to turn to professionally for assistance with your business, what types of business entities you can consider and how to keep your performing business legal.

"Entrepreneurs are participants, not observers; players, not fans.

Joseph Mancuso
author, founder,
Center for Entrepreneur
Management

Clarify Your Structure

Be very clear about the structure in which you operate your business. If you are the group's or band's leader, then structure

> "Once you get immersed in business, don't confuse doing good business with doing good music. Leave enough time in a day to continue developing as an artist. Getting caught up in the business and forgetting about making art is a trap, just as much as doing good art and ignoring business is a ghetto."
>
> Ken Brown
> songwriter, composer

> If you want a thing well done, do it yourself.
>
> proverb

> "The first rule in the opera is the first rule in life: see to everything yourself."
>
> Nellie Melba
> Australian soprano

your situation to reflect that. Own the responsibilities that come with leadership. When the band is doing well, you will reap the benefits. When group leaders diffuse their role, the group structure becomes clouded and members become unsure of their role. If you start a band, decide whether it is your band or whether you want the band members to be equal participants. Be clear about your goals before looking for members to join the group. Your advanced structure decisions will save you a great deal of stress once you are up and running.

Business Strategies For Solo And Duo Performers

Solo performers have several business structures from which to choose. They most often act as the sole proprietor of their business unless they have decided to take on a business partner for financial reasons. I will explain each of the legal business terms later in this chapter, but for now, a simple definition will suffice. Solo performers are likely to be in complete charge of all of their business transactions, therefore, a sole proprietorship would work well for their legal business structure. Solo performers may also choose to incorporate their business giving them extra tax advantages.

Duos, on the other hand, may select a few different legal structures—a partnership, a limited liability company (LLC), or an incorporated business. Acting as equal partners, their financial commitment, the responsibilities for conducting all aspects of the business, and the benefits derived from the business, are shared equally.

Business Strategies For Performing Groups

Performing groups larger than two members are often challenged with deciding the best method of structuring the group to take care of business effectively. Here are some alternatives. Once you examine these options, your decision as to which business entity to form legally may be clarified.

A Single Leader Within A Group

Within this structure, there is clearly one group leader or band leader. The business, the group or band name, the expenses, and the income, are the sole responsibility of the leader and owned by the leader. Group or band members are paid a salary or hired on a per-date basis. Sidemen or group members should also be paid a per diem (daily amount for meals) when touring as well as have all of their expenses taken care of by the leader. The leader sets the rate of pay and per-diem amount based on the tour's budget. If any group member takes on responsibilities or tasks that help the leader run the group's business, that person should be paid an additional fee for the work. This method of leadership offers the leader multiple choices for deciding on an appropriate business entity. A sole proprietorship would work well in this case as would an LLC or an S corporation.

Equally Shared Leadership Within A Group
Another possible group scenario is when all members of the group or band share the ownership and responsibilities of the group's business equally. Each member would invest in the group with equal shares and would reap any profits equally as well. Expenses for the business are divided among members. If any one member takes on additional responsibilities, they should be paid accordingly. One such situation may occur when one person takes on the task of booking the group. That person should be paid an additional fee above their regular share of group income. By taking 10% or more off the top of any booking (before expenses and shares are paid out), the group demonstrates their appreciation for that member's efforts and the additional compensation helps prevent job burn-out. All phone bills and shipping costs are the group's expense, not the individual's. This structure is well suited to become an S corporation.

Five Types Of Business Entities— What Kind Of Business Are You?
You have a few options when deciding what type of business entity to select.

1. Sole Proprietorship
A sole proprietorship is an unincorporated business that is owned and operated by one person who receives all the profits and is personally responsible for all the losses.

If a sole-proprietor business suits your needs apply for a "d.b.a., Doing Business As" certificate. (It is sometimes called a "Fictitious Name Certificate.") Each state may differ, but in most states you can file this form at the county or city clerk's office. If you are doing business in a specific county, check the county clerk's office. Some cities require the certificate be filed with the city clerk's office and not the county. Check with the clerk's office nearest you to determine where to file your application. The cost is often under $10, again, depending upon your local municipality.

2. General Partnership
A general partnership joins together two or more people in a relationship to carry on a trade or business. Each partner contributes money, property, labor, and/or skills, and agrees to share in the profits or losses of the business.

3. Limited Liability Company (LLC)
A limited liability company is an unincorporated association of two or more members who own membership interests

> **HotTip:** Select a few potential names when filing a Fictitious Name Certificate in case one is already taken by another business. Consider filing a few names at the same time, one for your main business and one for either your record label, your publishing company and perhaps one to form your own advertising agency which entitles you to advertising discounts.

"We need to adopt policies and structure that we're precise and clear about and that we hold ourselves accountable to."
Ben Cohen, Jerry Greenfield
Ben & Jerry's Double-Dip

"Being in your own business is working 80 hours a week so that you can avoid working 40 hours a week for someone else."
Ramona E. F. Arnett

based on their capital contributions. It will be taxed as a partnership while limiting the personal liability of all of its owners.

4. C Corporation

A C corporation is an entity with a legal existence apart from its owners. In a C corporation, the number of shareholders is unlimited. The corporation may continue even though the shareholders may change. Start-up fees, record keeping costs, required board meetings, tax liabilities and other regulations make corporations the most expensive business entity. Legal deductions for health insurance, health care and retirement planning may offset the general start-up and operating disadvantages. Corporations must comply with both state and federal laws.

5. S Corporation

S corporations are a hybrid form of the C corporation. After the 1996 tax law changes, S corporations are allowed up to 75 shareholders who must be legal residents of the U.S. Like the general partnership, all profits and losses pass directly through to the shareholder. Unlike the C corporation, the S corporation is a simpler business to set up and operate and costs less at tax time. However, many of the benefits and deductions are unavailable to the S corporation. Health insurance and retirement contributions are greatly limited.

There are advantages and disadvantages to each type of business entity. Depending on the structure of your group, you may find yourself benefiting from one over another. I suggest you consult a lawyer to help determine what business entity will work for you. The setup costs for creating any of the business entities other than a sole proprietorship can be expensive. Each of the other business entities will also require additional record keeping for legal and tax purposes. In addition to consulting a lawyer, speak with an accountant to help understand the tax implications of each of these structures. By consulting an accountant and lawyer, how the responsibilities of any one of these structures will affect the way you conduct your business will become clear.

In order to register your business with your local and state government, call the city or county clerk's office or the Secretary of State's office for a business registration guide for your state. Many states will provide you with a complete packet of forms.

Create Your Team Of Professionals

Along with a lawyer and an accountant, there are other business consultants that can help you create your business by sharing their expertise. There are small business service centers

> "There are over 13 million small businesses in this country..... A sole proprietorship is the easiest form of small business to start up."
>
> **Bernard Kamaroff**
> C.P.A., author,
> *Small-Time Operator*

> "Success in business requires training and discipline and hard work. But if you're not frightened by these things, the opportunities are just as great as they ever were."
>
> **David Rockefeller**
> businessman

available to help in addition to the following organizations. The resource section at the end of this chapter has a list of suggested books along with addresses and phone numbers. By using these resources, you can find assistance with accounting, consulting, finance and legalities.

Small Business Administration (SBA)
A branch of the Small Business Administration or Small Business Development Center is located in most major cities. By contacting one of these offices you can often get valuable, free advice at these crucial beginning stages. (See resources at the end of this chapter.)

SCORE (Service Corps of Retired Executives)
This organization matches you with a retired executive who can offer their vast expertise in many areas of organizing and maintaining a business.

University Graduate Business Programs
If you are near a college or university that offers a Masters in Business Administration (MBA), you may be able to get free counseling with a graduate student. MBA students often take on independent projects for credit. Contact the independent- or directed-studies department at the school offering the MBA. You can offer the department a proposal for a specific project or a specific time period that may incorporate the student into your business. The MBA placement office can also help contact an MBA student looking for a part-time paid position. Students are often looking for interesting opportunities and your business may provide experience in an area of interest to them while keeping your costs down.

University Graduate Special Interest Groups
Special interest groups are often formed by a group of students in MBA programs to explore subjects not normally covered within the curriculum. For example, there may be a number of students interested in the music business. As a musician, with a certain amount of information and expertise about the music business, you may offer to work with this interest group and share your information in exchange for their expertise in general business operations, marketing, etc.

Creating A Business Plan
Are you asking yourself, "Why would I need a business plan if I have done all of the long-term planning in Chapter One?" If so, the answer is simple. A business plan helps you answer very specific questions about who is running your business, how it will operate, and what your projected goals are.

Creating a business plan does not have to be a daunting task. All businesses, including performers, should have a

---

"Once you recognize that your life is not your business, but something your business must serve, you can begin to work on your business, rather than in it."

Michael E. Gerber
author,
The E Myth

"Working with MBA students is a wonderful way for self employed people and small businesses to explore new avenues of business growth. It's a great win-win situation. At the Darden MBA program, the music and entertainment special interest group generated several projects; from musicians starting labels to marketing projects to a CD manufacturing business analysis. The work I did in special interest areas was the most exciting part of my MBA curriculum. It's not what you learn, it's what you do!"

Tracey A. Lake,
MBA graduate,
Darden School of Business

"Work smarter, not harder."
Ron Carswell

"Drive thy business or it will drive thee."
Benjamin Franklin
U.S. statesman, inventor

"First, your plan is a road map to success. It guides you as you make decisions that affect both creative and financial results. Second, your plan is essential for securing financial backing of any kind. The funding source—even if it is your rich uncle—will ask for details about your business which are included in the plan."
John Stiernberg
business consultant,
Stiernberg Consulting
author, Succeeding In Music:
A Business Handbook for
Performers, Songwriters,
Agents, Managers, and
Promoters

"You can fly by the seat of your pants, but you will probably get torn pants. Successful business owners are usually those who have taken the time to evaluate all the aspects of their businesses and to map their plans for the future."
**Linda Pinson and
Jerry Jinnett**
authors,
small business consultants

business plan if they intend to be successful. However, most small business owners do not take the time to create one. I know of only a handful of performers who have created business plans. Those who have are attaining their career goals at a rapid pace and are doing very well.

Whether you are a solo performer or a rock band, creating a business plan to accompany your long-term goals sets down concrete information which describes exactly how you intend to operate your performing business. Once you have your business plan, you will truly have the road map to control the success of your business. Along with your lawyer and your accountant, your business plan will also help you to determine the type of business entity that will best serve your business and the type of tax liabilities for which you are responsible. You know your business better than anyone else. You are the perfect person to write your own business plan.

The Benefits of Having a Business Plan Are:
1. It is a valuable tool that helps to guide you through the life of your business. When kept up to date, your plan helps you analyze the growth and value of your business.
2. It is essential if you choose to apply for loans or seek investments to finance individual projects or purchases to "grow the business." Your investors and lenders will need documentation outlining your financial needs and methods of repayment. The business plan includes your credit history and your business' credit worthiness.
3. It will help you define how to market your product and exactly who to target. It will provide an investor or lender with valuable information about your position within the market and give realistic projections of the demand for your product or service in that market.

A Business Plan Includes:
1. A description of the business
2. The products and/or services you offer
3. The management and personnel in the business (whose business is this and what is their background)
4. The legal structure of the business (refer to page 33, Five Types Of Business Entities)
5. A statement of purpose or the goals of the business (partially taken from your ten-year goals in Chapter One)
6. The needs of the business (taken from your "Assessment List" in Chapter Two, what you need to operate)
7. A budget and other financial documents (this can be for the entire business and for specific projects)
8. A marketing plan (an overall plan to market the performers, including promotional package design, and then specific marketing plans for individual tours, recording projects and special performances)

Taxes

Let's face it, no matter what type of business you decide to operate, you will need to be concerned with paying your taxes in accordance with the rules that govern that particular type of business entity. By working with an accountant, you can set up a system that can help keep track of all of your receipts, quarterly and yearly payment schedules for city, state and federal taxes and a plan for all of your allowable deductions. For a monthly fee, many accountants offer a monthly bookkeeping service that can relieve you of some of the paperwork. I strongly suggest establishing an ongoing relationship with one accountant who will maintain a history of your business. Your accountant will be in an informed position to help determine appropriate business decisions and weigh their tax implications based on your history and your goals.

Allowable Deductions

No matter which business entity you select, keep all of your receipts for your business' operating expenses. Some purchases, like computer equipment, furniture or a touring vehicle, may be depreciated over time to give you a tax benefit for a number of years instead of only in the year you purchased the item. Your accountant will help you determine the best way to keep track of your expenses to give you the most tax relief. Here is a list of the categories for allowable deductions so you may keep the appropriate receipts.

Travel

1. Airline tickets
2. Taxi, commuter bus and limousine fares
3. Car rental or operating your own car
4. Lodging
5. Baggage and shipping costs
6. Cleaning and laundry (for stage use only or only while on tour)
7. Tips
8. Meals on the road

The standard meal deduction for most areas of the country is $30. See Figure 1 on page 38 for locations eligible for higher meal deductions. If you travel outside the continental United States, the rates may be higher. You may access current daily rates by calling the IRS at FedWorld, 703-321-8020 or go to http://www.policyworks.gov/perdiem on the Internet.

Auto (if it is your touring vehicle)

1. Insurance
2. Gas and tolls
3. Car repairs and maintenance

HotTips:

IRS Publication 463 Travel, Entertainment and Gift Expenses, details methods of deducting expenses.
IRS Forms:
1-800-829-3676
http://www.irs.gov/pub/irs-pdf/p463.pdf

There are two methods of keeping track of auto expenses:
1. Regular—Keep a record of all actual costs and keep receipts.
2. Mileage—Maximum cents per mile. Each year the IRS increases mileage amount by one cent.

"Remember you are running a business, and you should keep track of every tank of gas, meal, toll, Xerox copy, and every CD you sell or give away. It's an hour a day of paperwork at least to be a musician."

Harvey Reid
musician, label owner,
Woodpecker Records

> **HotTip:**
> IRS Publication 587
> Business Use of Home
> IRS Forms:
> 1-800-829-3676
> http://www.irs.gov/
> formspubs/index.html

Figure 1. *Selections from Publication 463 for 2006: Appendix A-1. Locations Eligible for Higher Standard Meal Allowance for Travel*

KEY CITY	COUNTY/LOCATION	AMOUNT
California		
Fresno	Fresno	$54
Los Angeles	Los Angeles, Kern, Orange, Ventura, Edwards AFB	$64
Monterey	Monterey	$64
San Francisco	San Francisco	$64
West Sacramento	Yolo	$44
Colorado		
Aspen	Pitkin	$64
Boulder	Boulder	$54
Denver	Denver, Adams, Arapahoe, Jefferson	$49
Fort Collins	Larimer	$44
Connecticut		
Hartford	Hartford, Middlesex	$49
New Haven	New Haven	$64
District of Columbia		
Washington, D.C.	Virginia counties of Arlington, Loudon and Fairfax	$64

"Talk to an accountant, talk to an attorney. I found somebody who deals with independent work-at-home-type people and knows me and my music. He is able to point me in the right direction regarding my taxes and planning for the future."

Andrew McKnight
singer, songwriter

Office

1. Rent

If you have an office in your home, consult with your accountant to determine what percentage of your house you are using for business purposes. The rules for home-office deductions are very strict and this deduction may raise a red flag to the IRS if you are not careful. For example, only items used for business may be kept in the home office. Personal items, like clothing and personal files, may not be stored in the closet in the office.

2. Utilities—Heat and Electric

For in-home offices, a percentage can be deducted from your total utility bill for the portion used for business.

3. Phone

Basic service charges may not be deducted unless you have a dedicated business line. If your business shares your personal line, you may only deduct the long distance business calls.

4. Insurance

You can purchase separate business insurance if your office is not in your home or deduct a portion of your homeowner's or renter's insurance if you do have a home office. Check to make sure that whichever insurance you carry, it covers your equipment while on the road. However, many policies require you to purchase a separate policy for your instruments and electronic equipment.

This would result in another deduction. (See resources, Chapter Ten, for instrument insurance providers.)
5. Office Supplies
6. Office Furniture
7. Office Equipment

Shipping
1. Postage, Fed Ex, UPS
2. Meter rentals

Stage Clothes
   These may not be worn off stage.

Research and Development
1. Costs related to preparing for a recording project
2. Seeking a record label, agent or manager
3. Hiring band members

Entertainment
1. Costs related to dining with clients, representatives from prospective recording labels, promoters
2. Purchase of new recordings or books in your field, etc.

Self-Produced Recording Projects
1. All expenses associated with the project
2. All costs to you associated with selling the finished product

Printing

Advertising

Salaries

Sales Tax

Employment Taxes
1. If you have any full-time employees or are yourself taking a salary
2. Social Security taxes
3. Self-employment taxes

Memberships, Union Dues and Subscriptions

Conferences

Pension Plans

Retirement Plans

Types Of Retirement Plans
Check with your accountant about setting up a tax-deferred retirement plan. There are numerous types of plans available some of which will suit you better than others. Consult with a financial planner and set up an investment plan along with your tax plan.

> **HotTip:** Work with a financial planner to determine higher interest-bearing savings vehicles than normal bank savings accounts—ways to keep your money accessible and liquid for recording projects, equipment and instrument purchases, and general business growth.

"The avoidance of taxes is the only pursuit that still carries any reward."

John Maynard Keynes
British economist

> **HotTip:**
> Additional catch-up retirement fund contributions are allowed if you are 50 or older.
> http://www.irs.gov

1. Individual Retirement Account (IRA): You can contribute up to $3,000 tax free up to age 50 until 2010 and $3500 after age 50. Funds are taxable at the time of withdrawal after age 59 1/2. Penalties are applied for early withdrawal.
2. Roth IRA: Contributions to a Roth IRA are taxable in the year they are contributed. When money is withdrawn at retirement, it is tax-free. The Roth IRA contribution limit amount is currently $3000 up to age 50 and $3500 catch up contribution after age 50. The limit will increase for inflation over the next few years.

   If you need to withdraw money from a Roth IRA prior to age 59 1/2, you may do so without penalty. It can pass to a non-spouse or family member as an inheritance at its current value without taxes due from the beneficiary, since the taxes have been paid already. This makes a Roth IRA an excellent savings vehicle for artists who may need to use some of the funds for emergency situation or special projects.
3. Savings Incentive Match Plane for Employees (SIMPLE IRA): Beginning in 2002 the deductible contribution was $7,000 per year with a required employer matching contribution ranging from 2% to 3%. Annual contribution increases in $1,000 increments are set until the limit of $10,000 in 2005.
4. Keogh Plan or Simple 401(k) Plan for sole proprietors or partnerships: These plans allow deductions expressed as a percentage of your net self-employment earnings up to $9,000 for 2004. A corporate retirement plan increases the percentage of W-2 wages. Be aware that these plans become more complex if you have employees. Those over 50 may make additional catch-up contributions-the amount of the catch-up contribution will increase each year.

Sample Tour Savings Plan
Here is a sample of a two-week tour with low-paying fees. If you had an agent who received 10% of this fee, the following illustrates a possible scenario for ten gigs.
   5 dates @ $500 = $2500
   3 dates @ $350 = $1050
   2 dates @ $700 = $1400
Total tour: $4,950 x 10% = $495.00 payable to your agent

"In this world nothing is certain but death and taxes."
Benjamin Franklin
U.S. statesman, inventor

"The taxpayer is someone who works for the federal government but doesn't have to take a civil service examination."
Ronald Reagan
actor, politician, U.S. president

If you did not have an agent, you could take that $495.00 and deposit it into a retirement plan. If your plan was an IRA, you would be allowed a tax-deferred contribution of up to $3,000 per year for an individual. Greater contributions may be allowable depending on your business type, the retirement plan you have established, your age and your marital status.

Let's assume that you were able to complete 10 tours in one year similar to the one above earning you $49,500 in performance fees. 10% of that is $4,950. If you make a contribution to an IRA of $250.00 after each tour (approximately once per month) you would have met the maximum contribution of $3,000 for an individual and would have $1,950 extra to place in an additional investment or savings plan for future projects.

Your money can begin to work for you right away. I have included a chart, Figure 2, below, that demonstrates the benefits of making a contribution to your IRA after each tour instead of waiting until the end of the tax year. The biggest advantage to making these smaller contributions is that they are more manageable than one large $3,000 contribution. The likelihood is that if you have not saved it during the year you might not have it at the end of the year. Remember, you would have to pay

> **HotTip:**
> Take the 10% you would have to pay an agent and pay yourself with savings into your own retirement plan. Make a deposit after each tour and watch your retirement savings grow! Don't wait until the end of the tax year.

Figure 2. I.R.A. Savings Interest Accrual at Different Percentages of Interest

Interest Rate		6%	Annual	Monthly
Amount of payment			−$ 3000	−$ 250.00
Number of periods:				
years	months			
1	12		$ 3,000	$ 3,099
5	60		$ 13,911	$ 17,530
10	120		$ 36,542	$ 41.175
15	180		$ 66,828	$ 73,068
20	240		$ 91,524	$ 98,172
25	300		$ 161,594	$174,115
30	360		$ 234,175	$252,384
Interest Rate		**8%**	**Annual**	**Monthly**
Amount of payment			−$ 2000	−$ 166.67
Number of periods:				
years	months			
1	12		$ 3,000	$ 3,133
5	60		$ 14,600	$ 18,492
10	120		$ 40,460	$ 46,041
15	180		$ 78,456	$ 87,086
20	240		$ 134,286	$148,237
25	300		$ 216,318	$239,342
30	360		$ 336,850	$375,074
Interest Rate		**10%**	**Annual**	**Monthly**
Amount of payment			−$ 2000	−$ 250.00
Number of periods:				
years	months			
1	12		$ 3,000	$ 3,168
5	60		$ 15,315	$ 19,521
10	120		$ 44,812	$ 51,638
15	180		$ 92,317	$104,481
20	240		$ 168,825	$191,424
25	300		$ 292,041	$334,473
30	360		$ 490,482	$569,831

> "As a small business person, you have no greater leverage than the truth."
>
> **Paul Hawken**
> author, founder,
> Erewon Natural Foods,
> Smith & Hawken

> "It is essential that musicians understand the importance of securing their future financially by paying themselves first. The creative person who takes 10% off the top of the money they earn and invests it in a ROTH IRA can use the compounding of time to leverage even a small amount of dollars into a comfortable retirement. That money when invested early in your career will help secure tax free income during your 'golden' years."
>
> **Margreta H. Swanson**
> Financial Advisor with
> Securities America

> **HotTips:**
> The tax laws change often. Get the most current information from the IRS or your accountant each tax year.
>
> Get valuable tax information specifically created for music industry professionals IRS Audit Technique Guides: MSSP Entertainment-Music Industry 3153-101; TPDS 83411J, TPDS 84150P
> http://www.irs.gov/pub/irs-mssp/music.pdf

"The hardest thing in the world to understand is income tax."

                  Albert Einstein
                         physicist

your agent after each tour. So, pretend that your IRA is your agent and send it a check as soon as the tour is over.

Income To Be Reported

The terms gross income, adjusted gross income and taxable income are often misunderstood. Below are descriptions of each and how they are different.

Gross Income: The total income from all of your sources whether it is performing, royalties, merchandise sales, wages from jobs other than performing, investments, interest, rental properties, dividends and savings accounts. Whether you are a full-time performer or not, you must keep accurate records of all of your sources of income.

Adjusted Gross Income: The total income after you have taken allowable business and pension deductions but before your personal deductions.

Taxable Income: The adjusted gross income less personal deductions, which are the itemized deductions, plus your personal exemptions.

Music Business Professionals

As a performer you may also wear many hats in your business. You may be a songwriter, publisher or producer. There are specific tax regulations that may apply to each of these roles which entitle you to certain tax benefits. The Internal Revenue Service has printed a music industry booklet detailing information with you in mind. Although this booklet was designed for accountants preparing music industry clients for an audit, it gives you the information you will need to be prepared and act within legal guidelines. To download IRS Audit Guide MSSP Entertainment-Music Industry 3153-101; TPDS 83411J you need Adobe Acrobat Reader available for free from: http://www.adobe.com. Then download the 65 page document from the IRS site: http://www.irs.ustreas.gov/prod/bus_info/mssp/index.html.

Summary

- ✧ Think of yourself as a small business.
- ✧ Develop a team of professionals whose long-term relationship to you and your business will provide legal, accounting and general business expertise.
- ✧ Create a business entity that will suit your business goals and organization.
- ✧ Write a business plan that helps drive your business and reinforces your goals.
- ✧ Organize an effective bookkeeping system and save all of your receipts.

Resources

Books:

Anatomy Of A Business Plan, 5th Edition
Linda Pinson
Dearborn Trade Publishing
ISBN: 0793146003
Other related books by the authors:
Keeping the Books
The Home Based Entrepreneur
Steps To Small Business Start-Up
Target Marketing for the Small Business
The Woman Entrepreneur

Creating A Winning Business Plan: A No-Time-For-Nonsense Guide to Starting a Business and Raising Cash
Gregory I. Kravitt
Joraco Inc.
ISBN: 1557384711

How To Start, Finance and Manage Your Own Small Business
Joseph R. Mancuso
Prentice Hall Press
ISBN: 0134348613

Money Smart Secrets For The Self Employed
Linda Stern
Random House
ISBN: 0679777113

Pond's Personalized Financial Planning Guide For Self Employed Professionals And Small Business Owners
The New Century Family Money Book
Johnathan D. Pond
Bantam Doubleday Dell Publishing Group
ISBN: 0440504783

Succeeding in Music: A Business Handbook for Performers, Songwriters, Agents, Managers and Promoters
John Stiernberg
Backbeat Books
ISBN: 087930702

Small-Time Operator
How To Start Your Own Small Business, Keep Your Books, Pay Your Taxes, and Stay Out Of Trouble, 27th Edition
Bernard Kamoroff, C.P.A.
Bell Springs Publishing
ISBN: 0917510186

This Business Of Music: The Definitive Guide to the Music Business, 9th ed.
William M. Krasilovsky and Sidney Shemel
Billboard Books
Watson-Guptill Publications
ISBN: 0823077284

The E Myth
Why Most Small Businesses Don't Work and What To Do About It
Michael E. Gerber
Harper & Row Publishers, Inc.
ISBN: 088730362

The Kitchen Table Millionaire:
Homebased Money Making Strategies to Build Financial Independence Today
Patrick Cochrane
Prima Publishing
ISBN: 0761509291

The Legal Guide For Starting & Running A Small Business
Fred S. Steingold, Attorney
Nolo Press
ISBN: 0873371747

The Musician's Business & Legal Guide, 3rd ed.
Mark Halloran, Esq.
Prentice Hall
ISBN: 0130316814

The NAFE Guide To Starting Your Own Business
A Handbook For Entrepreneurial Women
Marilyn Manning and Patricia Haddock
Irwin Professional Publishing
ISBN: 0786304081

The S Corporation Handbook
The Complete Book of Corporate Forms:
How To Form Your Own Corporation Without a Lawyer for Under $75
The Executives' Business Letter Book
Ted Nicholas
Enterprise Dearborn
Dearborn Financial Publishing

Your First Business Plan
The Complete Book of Business Plans
Joseph Covello and Brian Hazelgren
Sourcebooks
ISBN: 1570710449

Accounting Software:

Peachtree
1505 Pavillion Place
Norcross, GA 30093
Phone: 1-800-247-3224
Phone: 770-724-4000
Fax: 770-564-5888
E-mail: sales@peachtree.com
Web: http://www.peachtree.com

Quicken
Quickbooks Pro
Intuit
web: http://www.intuit.com

Business Plan Software:

Available at office supply stores, bookstores and from mail-order catalogs

Business Plan Pro
by Palo Alto Software

BizPlan Builder
by Jian

PlanMaker
by POWERSolutions

Organizations and Businesses:

National Association For Female Executives (NAFE)
NAFE's Business Basics Center
BBC, NAFE
260 Madison Avenue, 3rd floor
New York, NY 10016
Phone: 1-800-634-NAFE
Web: http://www.nafe.com
Three free report booklets:
The Small Business Financial Guidebook
The Small Business Resource Report
The StartSmart Small Business Adviser

Canada Business Service Center
Web: http://cbsc.org

Interactive Business Planner
Web: http://www.sb.gov.bc.ca

Small Business Administration
SBA Business Management Courses
The Office of Management Information and Training
Management Assistance, Small Business Administration
1522 K Street, N.W., Room 636
Washington, DC 20416
Phone: 202-724-1703

SBA Online
Web: http://www.sbaonline.sba.gov/

SBA Development Center
Web: http://www.sbaonline.sba.gov/SBDC/

SBA Regional and State Resources
Web: http://www.sbaonline.sba.gov/regions/states.html

Office Women's Business Ownership
Web:
http://www.sbaonline.sba.gov/womeninbusiness/

SCORE: Service Corps of Retired Executives
Call the National Headquarters for regional offices:
Phone: 1-800-634-0245
Web: http://www.score.org

The Company Corporation
Form your own corporation legally
Web: http://www.corporate.com

Internal Revenue Service (IRS)—Forms
Phone: 1-800-TAX-FORM (1-800-829-3676)
Fax: 703-487-4160 dial from your fax machine
Personal Assistance
Phone: 1-800-829-1040 (9:00 a.m.-5:00 p.m.)
Web: http://www.irs.ustreas.gov
Telnet: Iris.irs.ustreas.gov
FTP: ftp.irs.ustreas.gov

Umbrella Organizations for 501(c)3

Folk Alliance
Phone: 901-522-1170
Fax: 901-522-1172
Web: http://www.folkalliance.net

CDSS
Phone: 413-268-7426
Fax: 413-268-7471
Web: http://www.cdss.org

Websites For Tax Information:

Essential Links To Taxes
Web: http://www.el.com/elinks/taxes

Center for Financial & Tax Planning
Web: http://www.taxplanning.com

1040.Com
Web: http://www.1040.com

FedWorld
Web: http://www.fedworld.gov

Small Business Taxes and Management
Web: http://www.smbiz.com

Revenue Canada
Web: http://www.ccra-adrc.gc.ca

CHAPTER FOUR
First Encounters

"The state of alertness—your preparedness in the present, in the field of uncertainty—meets with your goal and your intention and allows you to seize the opportunity."

Deepak Chopra
author, philosopher

Now, your office space is set up and you are ready to begin making phone calls. Every phone call you make can unlock the door to new opportunities. Preparation is the key which enables each booking session to provide you with daily successes and a visible momentum to your tour planning.

Composing Scripts

For those of you who are uncomfortable with originating new booking calls, consider using a list of questions or a script to remind you of all the points you would like to cover in the initial conversation. Composing a script or a number of different scripts helps to anticipate the promoter's questions and keeps the conversation flowing. Actually, having a script to refer to may be helpful until you incorporate the questions you want answered into the flow of your conversation naturally. It will serve as a prompt—allowing you to get the information you need.

You can compose scripts for all the various performance situations you anticipate wanting to play. For example, create tailored scripts for festival calls, club calls, performing art center calls, etc. Each script will focus on the individual performance environment and enable you to zoom in to your intended promoter's specific scenario.

"Develop good telephone skills. If you rehearse your own songs in order to deliver them with the most impact, do the same with your telephone rap."

Dick Renko
manager,
Trout Fishing in America,
Muzik Management

> **HotTips:**
> Most venues provide general information on their website. Check the upcoming performance schedule, technical specifications and booking contact before calling.

Rehearse your script until it feels natural. It is not something that needs to be memorized. With time, however, you will find yourself covering all the questions you have scripted in conversations with prospective presenters. I find myself composing simple scripts in my head prior to most calls. Once I have thought through the main points that I want to make during the conversation, I write out a list of talking points as a reminder. Preparation will allow you to present yourself more professionally. You will sound more knowledgeable about yourself, your needs and how you want to be presented. You will accomplish more in one phone call and avoid a second or third call with questions that you initially forgot to ask. After some practice, you will not sound like you are reading prepared questions. The information gained from these prompts is worth a few practice calls while you get the hang of it.

Know Something About The Venue

As with most successful conversations, people enjoy speaking with someone who shows an interest in the things they care about. Know the basics about the venue or promoter before you call. Find out the kind of shows they book, the size of the hall, who has played there recently and, if possible, what kind of budget they work with. Knowing the specifics can help eliminate venues that are not suitable for you and provide you with additional conversation starters that demonstrate your interest in the venue and the promoter.

Two Minutes To Hook Them

You may only have two minutes to hook someone into your conversation. In other words, you need a good opening. For example: "Hi. I'm Jane Smith with the TuneSmith's Trio. We perform country-flavored originals and will be in your area during the week of September 23rd to promote our new release on XYZ label. We still have a few dates open. Our recording has been out only three weeks and we are receiving airplay on over 40 east coast radio stations."

You need to capture a promoter's attention and hold it as you develop the flow of your patter. Fielding as many calls in a day as a promoter does, your call needs to be as succinct and to the point as possible. In the beginning, a script may help to introduce yourself and get a conversation going. Along with your introduction, include some piece of information that implies urgency or time lines. This will usually prompt some questions for more details. Now you are into the conversation and can continue with your agenda. By having information on hand, you begin to win them over. Remember, talking points should include venue size and type of presentation, as well as annual budget, hall specifications, budgets spent on specific kinds of performances and a variety of contact personnel.

> *"Cold calls are the most intimidating because there is a high probability that the person you are calling will not respond with interest or enthusiasm."*
>
> Laura J. Lovgren
> author,
> *Techniques of Effective Telephone Communication*

The Art Of Asking Questions

How you phrase a question can make or break your conversation. Questions should always prompt conversational answers or be open ended. Keep in mind that this is your information-gathering stage to be used later during your negotiations. The goal is to ask these questions in order to gather as much information about the promoter and the venue as possible without sounding like an interrogator.

Ask Questions To Get Positive Responses

When asking a question, a good technique is to phrase your question to elicit a positive response. Avoid any opportunity for them to answer with a no. This technique will get them used to responding positively to you and eventually get them used to saying yes.

Question: I understand you have a very successful jazz series each season.
Possible Answer: Yes, we are very pleased with the turnout in past years and all indications are that it is continuing to grow.

Ask Open-Ended Questions

Similarly, avoid any questions that can be answered with a simple yes or no answer. Your goal is to engage in a conversation. Asking open-ended questions helps you to accomplish that goal. This subject is discussed in greater detail in Chapter Six, The Art of Negotiating. But for now, let me offer an example of an open-ended question.

Question: How often do you present performances? (This question can certainly be answered simply, yet it cannot be answered with a yes or a no.)
Possible Answer: We have a number of different series which run throughout the year. Each series offers multiple performances.

This demonstrates how to get your conversation flowing. By asking an open-ended question, you have prompted a response which provides you with much more important information from which to continue your conversation. Had you asked, "Do you present concerts?" the response could have been a simple one-word answer, yes or no, and your conversation would be stalled.

Goals For A Cold Call

Assuming you are calling a venue that you have never played before and do not know very much about, you need to:

1. Get as much information about the venue as you can in this first conversation.

HotTips:
Emails may not be the best introductory contact. Your well-crafted message may be deleted if the person has not received a phone introduction first.

"He or she will need to be comfortable with making 'cold calls' at all hours of the day and night. Some club/concert hall owners are up early, others don't start work until after 6 p.m. Be persistent and learn what they want, when they're in, and what you can offer them (beer sales, college friends who will come to the gig, mailing list and followers, Internet following, etc.)"

Chris Daniels
recording artist,
former executive director,
Swallow Hill Music Association

2. Find out the name and direct number of the person who has the authority to book you. Make sure you get the proper spelling of their name.
3. Find out when they present your type of performance.
4. Get some indication of their budget.
5. Find out their scope of presentations (concerts, festivals, coffeehouses, theater, dance, storytelling, lectures, poetry readings). You may find yourself fitting into more than one category giving yourself more than one performance opportunity to discuss.
6. Ask when they do most of their booking. Many performing arts centers book their entire next season during the preceding fall—some clubs book as tightly as six weeks before the date. (See Chapter Eight.)

Below is a list of sample questions to help you fine-tune your scripts. You will find that some presenters are amenable to answering your questions while others will be quite relieved to end the conversation after question number two. Presenters have more invested in speaking with you once they have determined they have some interest in your act. The more compelling your opening statement, the more likely you will get most of your questions answered.

Script For A New Venue—The Cold Call

1. Greeting To The Person Answering The Phone:
"Hello, I would like to speak with the person coordinating the bookings for concerts. May I have their name and direct line? Let me make sure I have the correct spelling. When is the best time to reach them?"

2. Your Opening To The Presenter:
"Hello, I'm Bill Jones and I represent The Sound Project, an acoustic jazz trio. We are setting up a CD release tour in the fall and will kick it off in the Northeast. We would like to include a date in Northampton."

This will include your name and the group you represent. It will also include a short descriptive sentence about what you do. You should throw in a hook, a statement of urgency, something to excite the promoter—like a new release. You might be kicking off the tour in their area or have something newsworthy happening that they will not want to miss.

3. Frequency Of Presentation:
"How often do you present concerts?"
You can substitute whatever type of performance you present. Refer back to the example of the open-ended question.
"What is your general performance season?"
Some performance seasons are year-round, some only during the summer or October-May. (More in Chapter Eight.)

> "Whether one makes a living at this depends only on the number of hours per week one devotes to making phone calls . . . the more phone calls you make, the less emotional freight each individual phone call carries. At some point, when speaking to a presenter, you begin to realize and take responsibility for the fact, that it really is your responsibility and not theirs whether you make a living. At that point you are free to treat the presenter with some compassion, and at that point folks will stop dreading your phone calls."
>
> **Bob Franke**
> songwriter, performer

4. Booking Time Period:
"When do you do most of your booking for your season?"

This is an important piece of information. Chapter Eight, page 199 and 200, details the various time frames when presenters book various performance venue types.

5. Hall Size And Seating:
"How large is the hall and what is your seating configuration?"

Some clubs will be mostly standing room with a few tables even though they may say seating capacity is 300 and standing is 700. This means they may not even have 300 seats in the house and may not suit your performance style. Performance spaces are varied. Auditoriums may be set up in the round. They may be in gyms with bleachers and a dance floor or be a cafeteria transformed into a coffeehouse.

6. Presentations In Other Venues:
"Do you use performance venues other than your own?"

College campuses often have more than one venue and a promoter may present in more than one performance space in town or even out of town.

7. Performance Variety:
"What other kinds of performances do you present?"

Here's where you find out if they present concerts, festivals, coffeehouses, theater, dance, storytelling, lectures, poetry readings, etc.

"What other acts have you presented recently?"

This will give you an idea of the kind of budget they work with as well as the scope of their performance schedule. This will also help you determine if this is a venue suitable for your presentation and the budget you require.

8. Technical Information:
"What kind of in-house sound system do you have or do you hire a professional sound company?"

This immediately gives you an idea of their professional level. You can continue with this in as much detail as you may need, offering some of your technical requirements up front.

"What kind of lighting system is available and do you have an in-house designer and technician?"

9. Ticket Pricing:
"What is your general ticket pricing policy?"

Depending on the presenter, this information can vary. They might always charge one specific ticket price or their ticket prices may change according to the act. This gives you an indication of their flexibility—again helping you determine whether this is a suitable venue for you.

> *"Don't waste a potential buyer's time by attempting to tell them how awesome you are over the phone. It doesn't work. Get something in front of that person like a CD or video, if they haven't actually seen your performance."*
>
> **Mike Drudge**
> agent,
> Class Act Entertainment

> **HotTips:**
> Send an Electronic Press Kit as follow-up to your first phone call to provide immediate information for their review.

The above questions will get you the information you need to make an educated decision about playing this date. Once you have decided this is a suitable venue for your performance, you can get more specific and detailed about your desire to perform there and what you will need. You will also have ample information to decide if you want to send any of your promotional materials or save your money for another venue. Getting the answers to many of the above questions will also help you to quote your fee appropriately.

Although negotiation is covered in Chapter Six, I suggest you hold off quoting your fee until after you have gotten the answers to most of the above questions and they have had an opportunity to review your material. Some promoters may be very blunt and ask your fee right up front. Quoting your fee early in the conversation may shorten your call and immediately let you know that this venue could not have afforded you. These questions are also a way of stalling—allowing you to quote your fee when you are better educated about their venue. Being better informed allows you to make better decisions about your bottom dollar. As we will discuss in Chapter Six, the fee is not always the most important issue.

The Closing
1. Review Information:

Reiterate the time frame when you will be touring through the area. Ask what would be helpful to them in getting to know your act. Some may want a full press packet, others just a bio. Some presenters ask for a CD, some a cassette. Often they want a written letter about your upcoming tour dates and fees. Others want to see reviews from other dates and want to know the size of the crowd you drew on the last few dates.

2. Share New Information:

This is the time that you can share some additional information about yourself, the tour and the promotion that you expect to do for each date. It is your opportunity to generate some enthusiasm and demonstrate a bit of your personality, talk about the support that your record company will provide and perhaps something about the band or troupe members. Your excitement for your work is infectious. When they receive your information, it may remind them of your enthusiasm and they will look at your materials in a more positive light.

3. Offer To Send Promotional Materials:

Suggest to the promoter that you will send information and then call in a week to make sure they have received it. Ask what time of day would be best to contact them. Make a note of your call-back date and time (this is where contact management software can be very useful) and CALL THEM AT THAT TIME. This gives the promoter a sense of your

---

"Always be on time, be easy to deal with, making the presenter's life as easy as possible. A lot of people forget about these very basic things."

David Holt
traditional musician,
storyteller

professionalism and lets them know that you care about your business. This also demonstrates some insight into the care and follow-up they can expect from you once a date is booked.

4. Close The Conversation:

A good close is as important as a good opening. Be respectful of the time that the presenter has spent with you and thank them for sharing all the information. If everything has gone well, you can very sincerely mention that you are looking forward to speaking with them after they have received your materials and that you are also looking forward to working with them.

If you are not able to reach the main booking person on this first call, attempt to get as many of the first nine questions answered as possible by the person you have reached. You may only find out who the right contact person is, the best time to reach them and their direct line. Don't be discouraged—these are incredibly valuable pieces of information. Consider yourself successful and move on to the next call.

An information form is on page 58, which you may copy directly from the book or use as a model to create your own information-gathering device. This can easily be included on a computer database program.

Calls To Familiar Promoters

Once you have established your initial relationships, you may find yourself using your scripts less often. I have found that having my list of questions handy serves as a welcome reminder. Once you have performed for a promoter, the revenues your performance generates becomes a factor in your relationship. If your performance went well, your future conversations will likely lead to additional dates. If your interactions with the promoter continue to be pleasant, even though the performance was not as successful as anticipated, you still have a relationship to build upon for future dates.

You may continue to create and utilize a script as a reminder once you have established an ongoing relationship. The tone of the questions will change to incorporate new performance opportunities.

For example you may discuss these topics:
1. *Audience Development:*
   Explore opening act possibilities or shared bills to increase your audience. This is also something to suggest when making cold calls to venues in areas where you are unknown. (More in Chapter Eight.)
2. *New Performance Situations:*
   Discuss festival possibilities now that you know this venue also does a summer festival. Suggest this as another

> **HotTip:**
> Always follow up with a phone call within 5 to 10 days of sending promotional materials unless you have sent them overnight or by Electronic Press Kit. Waiting longer will cost you money. Your package has more time to get lost and they have more time to forget your initial conversation.

"The artist's timing is important. It can be a matter of luck. The presenter may be juggling the acts that will sell with the number of uncertain nights. The presenter needs to keep his options open until there is a deadline to complete the current calendar for confirmation from "in-demand acts." The response an artist gets from a presenter depends on when they call.

Tim Mason
booking manager,
Club Passim

> **HotTip:** 🌶
> Keep notes about past performance dates—number of tickets sold, total revenue, product sales. Refer to your notes before making calls to familiar presenters. Your notes will influence the questions you ask and the flow of conversation.

method to increase your audience in the area. Your name recognition can also help to increase festival draw.

3. *Interest In Success:*
   Emphasize how much you enjoyed playing their venue and that you are interested in helping make this a successful date for both of you.

Telephone Techniques

The telephone remains the primary communication tool for booking. Whether you are successful with Internet communications, direct mail or letter writing, at some point you will find it necessary to communicate by phone. Phone skills for booking are similar to some types of phone sales and telemarketing skills. Adopting a few general practices early on in your booking career will make your phone time more pleasant and more effective.

Your Telephone Personality

Not everyone has the gift of gab and not everyone is comfortable speaking on the phone. You may be surprised to discover that while you are very comfortable performing on stage, a one-on-one phone conversation can be stressful. However, you are now a sales representative for your own act and may need to adopt a new persona suited to the tasks at hand. Incorporate the following simple practices before every phone-calling session and you will improve your chances of success.

For a successful phone call, remember to be:

❖ *Enthusiastic*—Your enthusiasm for your project is infectious and will leave a lasting impression.
❖ *Prepared*—Have all of your notes, pens, paper, calendar and computer ready before you call.
❖ *Knowledgeable*—Do your homework about the venue and about your show's performance needs.
❖ *Courteous*—Respect the promoter's time, be succinct but friendly.
❖ *Confident*—Projecting confidence instills promoter confidence in you and your act.
❖ *Focused*—Knowing your goals allows you to roll with the conversation and be alert to new opportunities.
❖ *Positive*—A positive attitude promotes positive action by the promoter on your behalf.
❖ *Professional*—Maintaining your highest level of professionalism promotes respect for you and your act.

Any good salesperson understands the value of these goals. As we discussed earlier, you must prepare yourself for each phone session. Similar to preparing for your performances, preparing for a phone session can involve a series of rituals to get yourself ready. Warming up for a phone session

"There is only one rule for being a good talker—learn how to listen."

Christopher Morley
American author

increases your effectiveness. These simple suggestions are just that, simple. Yet they are often forgotten by most people launching into a day of booking calls. However, they can make the difference between a successful day and a day full of frustrations.

Preparing For A Phone Session

1. *Be well rested:* A tired voice comes across as being bored and uninterested. It is hard to muster enthusiasm when you are about to yawn. Maintaining focus is difficult and your perceived level of professionalism drops significantly when you are tired. You might consider doing paperwork instead.
2. *Eat light meals:* Heavy meals make you sleepy.
3. *Do something active:* A brisk five-minute walk will help you to focus your attention. Keep physically fit. Exercise keeps your mind alert and enables you to concentrate on the details.
4. *Leave your personal problems aside:* You do not bring your personal problems on stage with you and you definitely do not want to bring them to a phone session. Being friendly is extremely valuable. However, allowing your personal troubles to influence your phone personality is unprofessional.
5. *Smile:* I learned this valuable lesson while studying to be a commercial DJ. You can actually hear when someone is smiling. It is much easier to project a positive attitude and enthusiasm for your art while you are smiling. This technique works on the radio and it really works on the phone. Practice in front of a mirror placed by the phone next time you make a call to a friend. Catch a glimpse of yourself every once in a while to see if you are smiling. Make a call while smiling and you will notice a difference.
6. *Plan short breaks:* Take a few short breaks to stretch and refocus your attention. This keeps you alert and your enthusiasm level high.
7. *Plan the number of calls per session:* Keep the number of phone calls reasonable. Trying to book the whole tour in one session is unrealistic. A reasonable number of calls for one person may be too many or too few for someone else. You are your best judge on this one. Once you are on a roll, you can always add to your list. Adding to a short list increases your sense of accomplishment much more than only making it through one third of a long list.
8. *Stand while speaking:* It is often helpful to stand up during some of your calls. You become more animated and much more focused. While sitting, the tendency to slump into your chair manifests itself in a slumping tone to your voice as well as your focus and attention. Your level of enthusiasm decreases as the day wears on. A

"Make sure you have a quote sheet in front of the presenter so they'll remember what you said by seeing it in print."

Peter Wernick
former banjo player with
Hot Rize,
former President, IBMA

"Artists should respond quickly to an inquiry and make sure their contact number and address is on all of their material."

Coleman "Spike" Barkin
festival, special events
promoter,
Lincoln Center Out-Of-Doors

"Call first, be professional, be persistent (without being annoying), come through with materials promised and do follow-ups."

Hariette Kyriakos
agent,
Bookin'

> **HotTips:**
> Keep call lists manageable—add to them if you have completed the original list. This promotes feelings of success and motivates you to make calls.
>
>
>
> If you have *call waiting*, know how to use it every time. Your level of professionalism drops significantly the first time you disconnect someone.

> "Modesty is not going to accomplish anything when you are in the 'agent mode.' One thing you can do is rely on quotes. Preface reading some choice quotes with a statement like, 'This makes me uncomfortable to even say, but I'm going to make a presentation to you. I owe it to my band to let you know. The Washington Post says we are "The finest group to come along in a long time," and I'll read you the direct quote.' Admit that it makes you uncomfortable and the buyer won't go away thinking you are a swelled-head person."
>
> Peter Wernick
> former banjo player with Hot Rize,
> former President, IBMA

portable headset allows for mobility and keeps you slightly active and enthusiastic. Many DJs stand for their entire shift because they are more animated. Having a chair that encourages healthy posture is the next best thing to standing. Keep your head up and your attention out.

9. *Know your phone equipment:* Be very familiar with all of the gadgets and systems you have acquired to make your phone calls more efficient, such as *call waiting* and the hold button on a two-line phone. You are obliged to return a disconnected call, costing you money. I have been disconnected more times than I care to remember by people placing me on hold or answering their *call waiting*.

10. *Return calls promptly:* Foster a reputation for returning calls. Develop a system for returning calls at a particular time of day. This allows you to stay focused on your plans for outgoing calls. It is likely that some of these messages are responding to your mailings or cold calls. It is to your advantage to get back to these callers as soon as possible, certainly within 24 hours. Your prompt response will be appreciated and will enhance your professional reputation.

11. *Be pleasantly persistent:* Keep your name in front of the promoter. Follow-up calls must be prompt. Be sure to call at the time you suggested. Check in on your status of consideration as often as once a week. They may not be thinking about you every minute but your persistence to keep in touch will demonstrate your professionalism and your commitment.

12. *Create a booking persona:* Some artists have found they can more effectively represent themselves when they are detached from their artistic persona and create an alter ego, "The Booking Agent." It is a technique that allows some artists to essentially become the person that does the booking and not the artist. Although an extreme measure, some may find it becomes easier to deal with promoters if the promoter thinks they are speaking with an agent. For those of you that really find it impossible to talk about and sell yourself, this can serve you well until you build up your phone confidence. I always advocate honesty in building your relationships and encourage you to find your booking voice as the artist representing yourself and your act. Nevertheless, the job needs to be done and someone has got to do it.

13. *Remind yourself this is business—not personal:* Sometimes you will be faced with rejection. Do not take it personally. It becomes more difficult to detach yourself when you, as the artist, are making the booking calls. After all, you are representing what you have worked most of your life to develop—your talent. Having someone say they are not interested in hiring you, for whatever

reason, can still play on your emotions. I have had moments when my close relationships with my artists influenced my emotions when a promoter rejected one of them. It is even more difficult to remain objective when you are the artist and a promoter turns down the opportunity to present your act. Being rejected is not always a comment on your ability. More often than not, it has more to do with the promoter's taste or whim. Do not let it reflect on your opinion of yourself.

14. *Keep a lighthearted attitude:* Do not take yourself too seriously. Call upon your sense of humor. Nothing breaks the ice like a good joke to start off your conversation. Your call will be more memorable when appropriate humor is incorporated into the conversation. It puts everyone in a positive frame of mind.

15. *Treat each promoter as though they are special:* Your caring for each person comes across in your phone attitude and the attention you give to each individual. Make the most out of each call while you have got their attention. Since you have worked hard to get this person on the phone speaking, do not jump to another incoming call and place the first caller on hold. You lose the momentum of the conversation. For all you know, the incoming caller may be someone trying to sell you something. Be aware, however, that many promoters will put you on hold—often.

> **HotTip:**
> Use *call forwarding* instead of *call waiting*. The *call forwarding* feature, from your phone company, will forward an incoming call to a mailbox on the same line or a phone machine on another line. This reduces the number of busy signals the incoming caller gets. You get your messages and have given your full attention to the caller with whom you are currently speaking. The cost is just a few dollars per month, and presents a much more professional image.

Practice each of these techniques and you will be better prepared to make all of your dealings on the phone more pleasant and effective. Adopting many of these suggestions early in your booking career will be helpful as you begin to deal with more experienced promoters and larger performances. These methods form the foundation of the skills you will need during all of your negotiations.

Be Creative In Your Attempts To Reach The Booking Person

As a performer and a creative individual, there are many opportunities to introduce a creative flare into your business. One area where your creativity can come into play is when you search for the person who actually is responsible for the bookings for each organization. This can sometimes become a frustrating experience. Often the number listed in a directory may be the concert line or the information number for the organization. This is often the case when you are booking tours at smaller venues, folk clubs and with many nonprofit organizations. The result is too many phone messages being left that are not returned. Do not let that deter you.

> **HotTip:** When emailing the booking person, create an email that is well written, informative and includes hot links rather than invitations to visit your website.

The Back Door Method
When the phone number listed in a directory continually gets you no further than an answering machine, do not give up. Go around to the back door. Start thinking creatively and begin doing some local area research. Here are some back-door suggestions:

1. Ask any of the other artists you know if they have performed at this venue, and if so, the name of their contact.
2. Check with some of the other presenters and venues in the area. They may have a direct contact.
3. Check with a local newspaper or radio station in the area. Find out who writes about your type of performance or which radio DJ presents your type of music. Ask them for the local contact for the presenting group. They are more than likely to at least have the publicity contact. From there you can get the booking contact.
4. Check with a local music store—they often have contact with local presenters.
5. Cross check the directory you are using with other directories for that area. Another directory may list an alternative number.
6. Call some of the listed booking agencies that represent acts similar to your genre of music or performance type. They may have dealt with this presenter and may have a direct contact. In most cases, many agents will be happy to help you with this one resource.

Reach Anyone In Business Within Four Phone Calls
I once heard that you can reach anyone you want to in approximately three or four phone calls, missing persons excluded. I have tried this many times and am now a firm believer in this theory. It takes 70% creative thinking, 20% belief in your objective, and 10% persistence. After all, anyone in business, especially in the entertainment arena, is usually sitting in an office doing a job. No matter who it is you are attempting to reach—the head of a record company, a television network executive, a manager, an agent, a performer, or a presenter—they are all people sitting in an office doing their jobs. Remove the mystique from their persona and it is much easier to make a phone call and speak with whomever you desire.

When I was booking acts, my favorite example of this occurred the year that Larry McMurtry's novel, *Lonesome Dove*, was being made into a television movie. Robin and Linda Williams asked me to find out who was making the movie and attempt to get some of their music to the producers.

Loving a good challenge, I was determined to test the three-call theory and get to the music producer. There are probably very well-traveled routes to take if you are on the

"Press on: Nothing in the world can take the place of perseverance. Talent will not; nothing is more common than unsuccessful men with talent. Genius will not; unrewarded genius is almost a proverb. Education will not; the world is full of educated derelicts. Persistence and determination alone are omnipotent."

Calvin Coolidge
U.S. president

inside of the television/movie business; I was not. However, I had previously worked for an NBC affiliate television station and was still in touch with the programming manager. This was my first call. I asked them which network was producing the movie and the number of the production department of the main network. I found out the network and the number, and on the second call, I was speaking with a secretary in the production department. She gave me the name of the production company making the movie and the set location phone number. My third call was to Texas, where I spoke with a production assistant on the set of the movie. They gave me the name and number of the music producer and the address to send the music. I decided to make a forth and final call to the music producer, who said he would look for the package. I sent my material Fed Ex and it was in his hands the next day.

What could have been a daunting project, turned out to be fun and fruitful when approached with the spirit of solving an Agatha Christie mystery. Your attempts to contact any presenter for whom you would like to perform can echo this example. Use some of your creative energy that is reserved only for your art and apply it to aspects of your business. It will make those details of your day-to-day business take on a whole new energy.

Summary

- Create a script of talking points to help keep your conversation flowing and serve as a prompt to get all of your questions answered.
- Ask questions that require open-ended, conversational answers.
- Stay focused and alert to new performance opportunities.
- Develop an effective telephone personality. Rehearsing your script with a partner can be a tremendous help in developing your telephone personality.
- Prepare for each phone session to remain alert, focused and efficient. This allows you to make the most out of each booking session.
- Incorporate these important phone techniques early in your career to prepare you for more involved phone negotiations.
- Use the fill-in form provided or develop your own form to fill out while talking with a promoter.
- Be a creative researcher when attempting to find the contact person for the venues you want to play.

VENUE INFORMATION FORM

State _____ Venue _____ Time Zone _____
(Time Zones: E, C, M, P, Other)

1. Address _____ Website: _____

2. City, State, Zip _____

3. Booking Contact _____

4. Phone _____ Direct Line /Extension _____

5. Fax _____ E-Mail _____

6. Name of Assistant _____ Direct Line /Extension _____

7. Best Times to Contact _____

8. Performance Types _____

9. Performance Frequency _____

10. General Performance Season _____

11. Booking Time Frame _____

12. Recent Acts Presented _____

13. Venue Capacity 1._____ 2._____ 3._____

14. Alternate Venues _____

15. Sound and Lights Systems _____

16. Ticket Pricing Policy _____

17. General Working Budget _____

Call Date _____ Comments _____

_____
_____
_____
_____
_____
_____

Resources

Books and Audio Cassettes:

Getting Through: Cold Calling Techniques To Get Your Foot In the Door (cassette)
Stephen Schiffman
Simon & Schuster
ISBN: 0671866427

Power Phone: How To Make The Telephone Your Most Profitable Business Tool
George R. Walther
Mass Market Paperback
Berkley Publishing Group
ISBN: 0425104850

Relationship Selling: Building Trust To Sell Your Service
Karen Johnson and Jean Withers
Self-Council Press
ISBN: 0889085293

Selling By Phone: How To Reach and Sell To Customers
Linda Richardson
McGraw Hill
ISBN: 0070523762

Selling With Honor: Strategies For Selling Without Selling Your Soul
Lawrence Kohn and Joel Salzman
Berkeley Press
ISBN: 0425157040

Selling With Integrity: Reinventing Sales Through Collaboration, Respect and Serving
Sharon Drew Morgan
Barrett-Koehler Publishers
ISBN: 1576750175

Telephone Tips That Sell: 501 How-To Ideas and Affirmations To Help You Get More Business By Phone
Art Sobczak
Business By Phone
ISBN: 1881081052

Telephone Sale and Motivation Made Easy
Valerie Sloane
Business By Phone
ISBN: 1881081044

Teleselling Techniques That Close The Sale
Fred L. Penoyer
AMACOM
ISBN: 08814479391

Guides:

Techniques of Effective Telephone Communication
National Seminars Publications
P.O. Box 41907
Kansas City, MO 64141-6107
Phone: 1-800-258-7246
Fax: 913-432-0824
In Canada:
National Seminars Publications
Phone: 1-800-258-7246

CHAPTER FIVE
The Promotional Package

"Put it before them briefly so they will read it, clearly so they will appreciate it, picturesquely so they will remember it and, above all, accurately so they will be guided by its light."
                                         Joseph Pulitzer

The promotional package is the artist's main sales and marketing tool. It can also be referred to as a press kit or simply as "promo." Developing an effective and attractive promotional package should be at the top of your priority list and can make a huge difference in your career. It is your act's first introductory piece that any promoter or media person will see. A good press kit will evolve as your career does.

Each update of your promotional package should reflect your current career status. If you are just getting started, you may not have the capital to invest or want an expensively designed and printed package. It is also unlikely that you will have the history as an artist to include numerous reviews from prestigious media. Therefore, the key to making the most effective and attractive package is to work with the resources you have at hand.

As you begin to identify what information will be included in your promo, and what form it will take, keep in mind that your promotional package serves three main functions:

"Your first appearance . . . is the gauge by which you will be measured."
                            Jean Jacques Rousseau
                            18th-century Swiss philosopher, author

> **HotTip:** 🌶
> "Press kits should be designed to answer the six (and often first) most-asked questions:
> What is your genre of music or type of performance?
> What is your performing experience?
> In what region of the country do you have an audience base?
> How large is your audience base?
> What is your recording experience?
> What sets your music apart from other groups of this genre?
> The more straightforwardly you can answer these questions, the more you set yourself apart as a professional."
>
> Diane Rapaport
> author, publisher

1. Introduces

Your promotional package is your introduction to a prospective promoter. It has to make a significant impression to stand out among the thousands of other promotional packages received. It serves as your representative. These first impressions must sell you and your act to the promoter. From your package, a promoter can immediately tell a number of things about you.

It reveals whether you are:
- Organized
- Creative
- Experienced
- Professional
- Effective in communications
- Unique
- Viable as an act in their market

2. Informs

Your promotional package is the informational resource which the promoter will draw material from to help publicize your appearance once it is booked. How the information is organized is just as important as what it says. The effort you put into designing a "user friendly" package will increase your chances of being hired and, then, promoted successfully. If important information is buried in either poorly written or designed materials, I guarantee most promoters will not take the time to search for it. Make it concise, make it accessible, make it interesting and make it work.

3. Markets

The promoter will send elements of your packet to the press to market the act and entice the audience to buy tickets. A well-designed kit contains elements that the press find informative and interesting—elements which entice them to schedule preview articles and interviews. A well-written press release or bio may find its way into a preview column—lifted from the press kit, word for word. This is especially true in smaller, "local" papers.

Elements Of A Promotional Package

With this in mind, let us examine the individual items that your press kit should contain to fulfill these three functions adequately and simply. If you are just beginning to develop your career, you may not have some of these items. Your package builds with time. When planning your press kit, design it to allow for new press clippings and items to be added and updated easily.

> *"Your visual image must work for you when you are not there in person. Consider every printed piece from posters to mailing labels your ambassadors. Make sure they all work together to reinforce your image."*
>
> Patrice McFarland
> graphic designer,
> New York State Museum

Biography

A biography is your performance resume. It should concisely provide information about your related career. A well-written biography will effectively incorporate the following:

1. *Performance Description:* Descriptive information about the performance type, style or genre. (i.e., blues, classical, country, folk, hiphop, rap, jazz, percussive dance, cowboy poetry)
2. *Performer Background:* Information about the performer and other important members of the band, troupe or cast. If it creates a unique point of interest, include nationality or childhood regional influences. Birthplace becomes important when it impacts upon the performance; otherwise, you may need the space for more pertinent information. Your group may include a list of two or more individuals whose bios would be important to include separately. This adds impact and importance to the group as a whole.
3. *Special Performances:* Meaningful performance experiences such as awards, special radio or television appearances, unique events or touring situations.
4. *Recordings:* Recent recordings and production credits can be included in the bio. It is not necessary to list everything—only the most recent and most important. A discography would be the appropriate place to include all of your previous recording credits.
5. *Quotes:* A few choice quotes from some of the more prestigious papers and promoters, or even from other artists are appropriate and desirable.
6. *Notable Venues:* Notable performance venues or festivals can be worked into a short paragraph. This provides a window into your performing experience and can serve as a reference point for prospective promoters. Choose your venues carefully. The promoter may call these venues to see how well you did.

If you have trouble describing yourself artistically, ask a friend or perhaps a newspaper contact who knows your music to help you out. You may also consider hiring a professional writer who specializes in bios to spice up your writing. A well-written biography can make a difference. It has to entice the reader to want to know more about you, to hear you, to see you perform and then to hire you. It is often quoted from, and as I mentioned earlier, if well written, whole paragraphs might be extracted for use in articles, newsletters, flyers and mailings. Bebe Harton, a publicity director from the Carpenter Center in Richmond, Virginia once commented that one of my artist's packages "read like a good book, it held my interest from

"Clarity is the key. Tell us who you are and what you do. Include a tape or CD. Additional materials (clippings, photo) are helpful."

Stevie Beck
former associate producer,
A Prairie Home Companion,
Minnesota Public Radio

"Send just enough but not too much—a well-written bio, an article, a list of places you've played, live performance reviews and some music."

Nancy Carlin
agent,
Nancy Carlin Associates

"When reading a promo kit, a critic wants nouns, not adjectives. We don't want to read how great your act is; we can decide that for ourselves. We want to know when she was born, where she grew up, and who did the original version of that cover tune."

Geoffrey Himes
music critic,
The Washington Post

> **HotTip:** Short, interesting paragraphs that are well written are the key. If your bio doesn't hold the promoter's interest, they probably won't make it through the rest of your packet. The writing has to sparkle in order to hook them and keep them reading.

"Put together a great press kit. You only exist on paper to most of the media and presentation tells it all."

John McCutcheon
singer, songwriter,
reprinted from
International Musician, 1992

"Assuming you're an unknown, no fancy writing tricks will make your bio work better than a simple, easy-to-decipher, factual account of yourself. If you have such credentials as songwriting credits or performance credits on records or gigs by well-known performers, that might help."

Mike Boehm
pop music writer,
*Los Angeles Times/
Orange County Edition*

cover to cover." I knew from that comment that she would be able to use most of my artist's packet effectively to promote the concert. Her statement also told me that everything that went into designing it—the layout, copy, colors, and paper choices—all played a part in making the package accessible and useable.

Your bio should be short enough to be typeset onto one page in a typeface large enough to be read easily. Anything smaller than 10 point is too small. In the case when the information in your bio is necessary to be included but cannot fit on one page, it is better to go to a second page than to set the type too small. However, whenever possible, edit your bio to fit onto one page. This will increase the chances of having it read completely and you will also save money every time you have it reprinted.

General Information Sheet

This sheet can list information that is not necessary to include in the bio. Items often included are: places you have performed by category (festivals, concert halls, clubs, radio and television shows), special workshops or projects, and a discography or videography (listing of all your recordings or videos). This should be kept current on a yearly basis. Add new information as your career grows. It is optional at the beginning.

Quote Sheets

Quote sheets are simply excerpts of some of the best lines taken from larger, full-length articles, reviews and interviews. Pick out the flashiest and most descriptive lines that really capture the flavor of your act. You may design a sheet with quotes about your recordings and a separate sheet with quotes about your performances. This allows the promoter to easily access the information most important to them. Quote sheets do the work for the promoter. If you have already read through the articles and pulled out the best material, it makes an immediate impact when first read in quote form. You will find the promoter and the media pulling from these sheets since it is a time-saver.

Reviews, Interviews And Preview Articles

As a developing artist, newspaper articles may be hard to come by at first. Any good article that you get is worth including. It tells promoters that you are out there working and drawing a reaction from the media.

1. *Reviews* track your history and development. When you have many of these from which to choose, you can begin selecting the reviews that really say something extraordinary or were written in a major paper from a

major market. To those reading your press kit, a review from *The New York Times* means more than a review from a smaller paper. Select three to five from the cream of the crop (too few may not make enough of an impact; but too many will never be read). This is one area that requires frequent updating especially when you receive your first hot review from *The Washington Post* or *The New York Times*.

2. *Preview articles* are often written by snatching whole paragraphs directly from your own bio or press release. Unless the writer has added their own commentary about you, your recording or performance, you should consider carefully whether the inclusion of a preview article will enhance your packet. You may decide to combine the preview article and the review from the same paper to create an interesting page. (Chapters 13 and 14 will discuss the importance of getting preview articles and how to increase your chances for advance coverage.)

3. *Interviews* are in a class by themselves. When you are developing your career, it is difficult to interest prestigious writers to do an interview. However, once there is a "buzz" about you, you need to find time to fit in as many of the requests as possible. Including an entire interview within your packet may give the reader more details about you and your career. If the interview is written in a prestigious magazine, like *Rolling Stone*, it speaks volumes about your position within the industry. If you do not think you are ready for *Rolling Stone* or *Billboard* yet, then look at your own field to decide which magazines and newspapers matter within your industry. (This will be discussed further in Chapter 14.) An interview presents a new way of looking at your accomplishments.

Press Release

A sample press release is always great to include. Again, it makes your kit very useable and professional and, as we discussed earlier, a well-written press release will often be used "as is." It cuts down on the work a promoter or newspaper writer needs to do. It also says exactly what you want it to say about yourself. A press release should be short and succinct. Leave some blanks in the first and last paragraphs for the particular information about the local promoter and the gig itself, like who, what, where, when, why and how. Start with that information and end with the same information. The middle paragraph or two could include facts and descriptive wording about your act. The writing needs to entice people to your show while giving them some background information

---

"I look for a one-page bio, an 8 x 10 photo, preferably with the act's name and representative underneath, a brief cover letter, two or three reviews/interviews (not a raft of them!), and a demo cassette or CD. I don't care if it's a demo cassette; but have the label printed in a professional manner. If the goods are there, it will come out."

Michael Jaworek
Chesapeake Concerts

"What I look for in press kits is clarity and focus. I want something right up front that says very clearly just who this person is and why they are interesting."

Larry Kelp
host, *Sing Out*, KPFA,
freelance music writer,
The San Francisco Chronicle,
East Bay Express,
Contra Costa Times

"I look for . . . reviews which describe the performance and audience reaction."

Coleman "Spike" Barkin
festival, event promoter,
Lincoln Center Out-of-Doors

"Create your own press release with 'fill-in-the-blanks' for the presenter. Don't expect them to know how to describe your act or be aware of your recent accomplishments. Make their job easy."

Liz Masterson
singer, songwriter

"Fill-in-the-blank, well-written press releases are essential. Press people love it, promoters love it. It'll get you press, it'll get you work."

John McCutcheon
singer, songwriter,
reprinted from
International Musician, 1992

about the personnel in the group and the performance they can expect. Once you have your bio written, most of your work is done. You can pull the most descriptive sentences from the bio to create your middle paragraph(s) for the press release. A sample press release follows.

Who, What, Why, When, Where, How (must include) →

Descriptive paragraph (must include) →

Informative optional paragraph →

Added interesting paragraph (optional) →

More information (optional) →

Final repeat necessary info →

Necessary info →

THE NEW MUSIC TIMES, INC.
Artist Management
P.O. Box 1105, Charlottesville, VA 22902
804-977-8979 • FAX 804-977-6914

PRESS RELEASE
ROBIN & LINDA WILLIAMS & THEIR FINE GROUP

Robin & Linda Williams and Their Fine Group will appear in concert at (Venue Name) located at (Venue Address) on (Day and Date) at (Time). Tickets are (ticket price optional). The concert is a production of (promoter or producer, optional).

Robin & Linda Williams are joined by Their Fine Group, Jim Watson and Kevin Maul. Jim was a founding member of the Red Clay Ramblers and has toured with Robin and Linda for eight years playing bass and adding his distinctive harmony vocals. Kevin Maul, a full-time member of the group for six years, joins in on dobro and harmony vocals.

The group released their first all-gospel album on February 15, 1995. Titled *Good News,* the CD showcases the group's outstanding vocal harmonies and tight musicianship. Released on the Sugar Hill label, *Good News* features a variety of styles from the Appalachian and African-American traditions to the Williams' own distinctive originals. It has garnered rave reviews and received extensive air play. *Good News* was nominated for Gospel Album of the Year in 1995 by the International Bluegrass Music Association.

The Williams' contributed their harmony vocals to the opening cut of Mary Chapin Carpenter's Grammy-award winning album, *Stones In The Road.* In the summer of '93, they opened 16 concert dates around the country for the three-time Grammy Winner and "CMA Female Vocalist of the Year."

Robin & Linda Williams are familiar favorites of listeners to Garrison Keillor's radio program, *A Prairie Home Companion.* They have also appeared on *Mountain Stage, The Grand Ole Opry, Austin City Limits* and *Music City Tonight.*

Join Robin & Linda for an evening of entertainment at (Venue Name and Address) on (Date) For reservations and information call (Phone Number).

For Information and Bookings: (Include Name and Phone)

To Schedule Interviews, Contact: (Include Name and Phone)

Press release used by permission of Robin & Linda Williams

This press release, written and used in 1995, is an example of how to incorporate current items of interest along with attention-getting information while promoting a current concert date. The third, fourth or fifth paragraphs could be eliminated, leaving only the concert information and band composition to satisfy the announcement requirements of this press release. By adding any combination of the other three paragraphs, the press release becomes more enticing to the audience and the media deciding to print it. See page 85 at the end of this chapter for sample press releases created by professional promoters and publicists.

The Photographic Experience
Written with Irene Young, Photographer

Conceiving an effective promotional photo can either be a wonderfully creative and self-affirming endeavor or it can be one of the most frustrating and costly tasks of your performing life! Careful planning will pay off in the long run. Avoid the last minute "this will have to do" approach and your career will be better off for your attention. Celebrity photographer, Irene Young, suggests, "The ideal result is a promo photo at least as good as your performing art." What any performer has to offer will initially be judged by their visual materials. Your photo should say something great about you!

Finding A Photographer

Generally speaking, you won't find the photographer you are looking for in your local *Yellow Pages*. One effective method of finding a photographer is to check out other artists' photos that you may see in the entertainment section of the paper and ask about their experience with the photographer they used. *The Black Book-Photography* is a national directory of photographers, available in many bookstores and at some libraries. (See this chapter's resource section.) You can also check local and national trade publications appropriate to your field of performance for display ads. The resource sections of this book will list many of these publications as well as recommended photographers around the country.

Your photo will often be the most-used tool in your press kit. It will be used in newspapers, on flyers, in season brochures and in newsletters. If you are unknown, people often make judgments about whether or not to attend your show simply by the way your photo represents you. An intriguing photograph on posters plastered around town is bound to pique the audience's curiosity.

Goals For Your Photograph
1. Create interest in the act.
2. Motivate the viewer to buy a ticket.
3. Make a visual statement about your performance.

> "Be on time with releases, make them clear, concise, easy to use. Put yourself in the position of the person on the receiving end. Try writing a short, but interesting, news article about yourself using only your own original press materials. Do it in ten minutes."
>
> **Sue Trainor**
> performer, publicist

> "I like a really good first impression. . . . I like everything to be in order, creative yet businesslike. Packaging really makes a difference to me in marketing."
>
> **Stuart Ungar**
> Cheney Hall, Manchester, CT

> "Quality photographs make quality promotions. Great design rarely saves a lousy photograph."
>
> **Patrice McFarland**
> graphic designer,
> New York State Museum

With this firmly in mind, it is best to hire a photographer who specializes in promotional photos, not the portrait photographer at the mall or your brother-in-law the wedding photographer. Those photographic styles do not accomplish the above goals. Your visual image is at stake. This is one time when your investment in time, energy and finances can impact the future of your career. Whether you take your friend up on the freebie or hire a pro, here are a few tips to help make the session more successful:

Choosing A Photographer

1. Choose a photographer who is interested in conveying your art first and the art of the photography second.
2. Choose a photographer who is experienced with performers and genuinely committed to conveying the essence of the artist. Enthusiasm is catchy and can make the difference between a high-energy or tiresome shoot.
3. Choose a photographer who will help you stretch and exaggerate if you are going for that lively look. A good photographer will not let you cross the line into the "realm of overdoing it." However, do not be afraid to try something new if the photographer or stylist makes a suggestion. On the other hand, if your gut tells you "absolutely not," listen to it. For example, if you do not like your makeup, speak up! You want to take pride in mailing out your image and voicing your thoughts after the session is too late.

Framing

1. Your image should fill the frame. Do not leave excess space above your head. For instance, you would not want to stand in a field at a distance from the camera.

Backgrounds

1. Use simple solid backgrounds and avoid overly-busy environments. They can prevent you from being seen as the focal point of the shot.
2. Avoid overly-busy clothing and colors that are identical to the background in tonal quality. For example, do not wear a white shirt against a white wall.

Tell A Story

1. Convey something about your act, or the music, or the show. When appropriate, let the instruments or props in the photo help tell a story about you.
2. Provide the photographer with some of your music prior to the session, so he or she can become familiar with your art. Similarly, a video of your performance is helpful for other art forms such as dance or theater.

"The CD's got to have a good cover. The photo of the band has to say something about the music and really look interesting, not just four guys standing in front of a brick wall with their arms crossed, wearing leather jackets."

Greg Haymes
music writer,
Albany Times Union

"We get artsy *photos with a minuscule performer in an oceanic field all too frequently. Creative is fine, but the more of you in the picture, the better. Use as much of the photo frame as possible."*

Mark Moss
editor,
Sing Out! Magazine

Location Shoots

1. Shoot in the late afternoon when the light is best for on-location sessions. Initial morning light is nice but performers rarely want to try and look their best that early.
2. Do not let anyone photograph you in direct overhead midday light! You may shoot in midday shade but it is usually best to combine this with a diffused flash.

Time

1. Be prepared to spend three to five hours if you are shooting a CD cover and two to three hours if you are shooting promotional pictures.
2. If you are shooting a CD booklet cover, try to leave enough time and energy to shoot one roll of black and white. You will need black and white photos to promote the CD.
3. Group shots may take longer.
4. Get a good night's rest before your session and eat something before you arrive so your body does not have to run on empty.

Dress And Focal Point

1. Hire a stylist, if you can afford it. It can be a relief to have help with your hair, makeup and clothing.
2. Bring a variety of *pressed* clothing so the photographer can help you choose your best look.
3. When shooting a group, make sure people are not wearing too many busy patterns unless it is part of the group's look.
4. Consider whether you need black and white photos, color or both. Bring appropriate clothing choices to shoot both types of film.
5. Your eyes are a focal point of the photo. If your look includes your glasses, please bring frames without lenses or non-glare lenses.
6. Pretend each person in a group is the only one in the photo. This helps to focus the subject's attention on the photographer so that one person is not visually wandering, thus making an otherwise great photo into a reject.
7. Do not cut your hair right before a photo session. If you don't like the cut, you won't like your photos.

Share your ideas with your photographer. If you do not have any, it is the photographer's job to direct you. If you are working with a graphic artist, they may have specific ideas that will compliment your overall project and will work directly with the photographer. A photographer is doing a good job when they create a comfortable environment in which you are moved to express yourself and deliver your best image. Once

---

"For any serious major publication, you have to think in terms of the quality of the photo—what's going to be reproducible and what are the correct parameters for it so you don't run something too big, too small, too stupid—looking too overly posed. I'm amazed at how many bad pictures I get."

Richard Harrington
pop music critic,
The Washington Post

"Love yourself the day of your session, and every day of your life! Throw any self-judgment and criticism about your visual image out the window! Use your photo session as a time to get to know your own exquisite nature. We all have one . . . just waiting to be summoned."

Irene Young
photographer

"One of the things that we try to do in an artist's photo session, whether it's for People *magazine* or for an album cover, is to have some fun. Sometimes we have guidelines from an art director or editor about what they'd like to see. That's always helpful and we make sure we cover those bases. The fun comes after that, when we can be spontaneous."

Will and Deni McIntyre
McIntyre Photography Inc.

you have developed a good ongoing relationship with a photographer, use them for all of your future photo sessions.

If you are preparing to take a leap professionally, but have been using amateur photographers, it is time to seek an experienced professional photographer. I favor using a professional since I have endured too many sessions done by well-meaning friends, that caused time delays and a frustrating outcome. Save your money for a professional session. It will be well worth it.

Fees And Photographic Usage Rights

When you pay a photographer for a session, you are usually paying for a particular usage. For example, if it is a promo session, you cannot use the photo on a CD cover without further negotiations. It is best to ask up front what the fee includes. For instance, if a magazine wants to use your photo as cover art, the use exceeds promotional use. The photo is now helping to sell the magazine and is clearly being used by a third party. The magazine needs to call the photographer and negotiate a one-time usage fee. If they fail to do so, they are breaking copyright laws. (See copyright section.) To clarify, promotional use includes press packets, posters, and publicity. It does not include t-shirts, songbooks, CD booklets, video covers, postcards or posters that you intend to sell. If you are going to sell it, then call the photographer and negotiate an additional fee.

Professional photographers are generally paid at the end of the session unless they have agreed to bill a third party, i.e., a record company, or a publisher. They may, however, ask for an advance to cover their expenses. You can expect to pay for the session expenses which are above the quoted shooting and usage fee. They might include: cost of the film and processing, assistant and stylist, shipping charges, proof sheets and custom final prints.

"It's important to have a professional product. Whether or not your photo gets published in papers often depends on how good the photo is. The cost depends on time, the amount of film that is shot and processed, whether you shoot just black and white or black and white and color, and how many final prints you get. If you have a group it's going to cost more. In the end, using a professional will not only save you money but it will earn you money."

**Susan Wilson
photographer**

A Copyright is a right that the federal government gives an author of original works of expression to exclude others from copying or commercially using the works without proper authorization. Some examples of works of expression are photographs, books, articles, computer programs, drawings and sculptures.

A Copyright is deemed to exist the moment that the work is "fixed in a tangible medium of expression" or completed.

Copyrights are of critical importance to photographers and to those who buy and sell images, in particular in the digital age. Copyrights provide the legal framework that allows the photographer to negotiate a fair price for her work. Computer technology has made it possible to make copies that are actually better than the originals. However, copyright law applies in the on-line world with equal force and authority. Thus, the photographer can protect herself from "digital infringement" without additional legal formalities.

*Frederick N. Samuels, Esq.
Intellectual Property Law and
The Photography Industry*

Reprinted with the author's permission

Copyrights And Photography

The copyright is the property of the photographer. It is exactly like the author of a song owning that copyright. *This is why you will need a release form signed by your photographer in order to copy your photos for the agreed upon uses.*

Crediting Your Photographer

It is usual to credit the photographer on your black and white copies and your color slides. If you do not give credit, you could liken it to your not being credited for one of your original songs. In addition, if your photographer has already been published in major publications, it can only help you when your photo, with a recognizable name on it, hits the arts editor's desk.

Choosing a Photo

It is crucial to use a magnifying glass or loupe when viewing proof sheets (also called contact sheets). You can obtain a viewing loupe from a photographic or art supply store. One that magnifies 8 times is sufficient and costs under $10. You will need this tool throughout your career so it is a good investment. There is no way to see the subtle differences between expressions without magnification.

When examining different frames, pay most attention to your facial expression and the visual message you are sending. Any dust spots or scratches are usually *not* on your negatives but, instead, on the glass or plastic sleeves used while contact printing. Some labs will take the negatives out of their sleeves for printing contact sheets. If they do not, your photos will appear less crisp (sharp) because the plastic sleeves diffuse the image. Do not worry about this. The plastic protects your negatives and your final prints will be printed with the bare negative. Also, minor exposure differences are dealt with during the printing of your final custom prints. Contact sheets are exposed for an average time. Custom prints are created individually and printed repeatedly until they meet professional standards.

The Difference Between Custom Prints And Economy Quantity Prints

A custom print is your carefully created final print from which you make all of your reproductions. They should meet standards such as correct exposure and general sharpness (unless purposefully diffused). A quality custom print should not have an isolated area too light or too dark. Good detail should reign throughout and, at the same time, the tonal range should be from well-defined blacks to grays to whites. Your mass-produced quantity photographs will pick up contrast during duplication. The lab or your photographer will print the custom original with a little less contrast to compensate

"When my group's CD was released, The Washington Post *opted to use a lively photo of another group with a well-known photographer's credit. Our review ran without a photo and I learned an important lesson."*

Jennifer Cutting
producer, songwriter,
instrumentalist,
Sun Sign Records and Productions

"Invest in the very best promotional material you can afford. Your promotional materials should reflect the quality of your show. When your materials are professional, presenters get the message that you care enough about your career to make the investment and that you view yourself as a professional."

Dianne de Las Casas
professional storyteller,
director, Story Ballet Magic,
president, Independent
Children's Artist Network

> **HotTips:**
> You will find a list of reproduction companies in the resource section at the end of this chapter. All those listed have come highly recommended by artists and agents who use them regularly.
>
>
>
> Most newspapers can download your photo if it is in JPEG or TIFF format. When providing digitized photos on a CD, include only a high resolution, 300 dpi photo for the reprint quality required. A low resolution, 72 dpi image, is not suitable for reproduction in newspapers or brochures and should not be sent for those purposes. Discuss resolution and format requirements with your end-user for optimum printing results.

for this later development. Also, your custom original should be printed on a *pearl surface*. This gives you the luster of a glossy print, yet enough texture to be able to retouch the photo if necessary. Use a professional photographer and you won't have to think about all of this.

Quantity Prints

Quantity prints, also called multiple prints, are made by copying your original custom print. They will not equal the quality of a custom print. Usually, a large negative (8x10) is made from your custom print. A strip that identifies your act and contact information is added. Then, quick contact prints are made from this large negative. This reduces the price from $20.00 per custom 8x10 to a quantity print costing anywhere from $.50 to $1.00 per print. Expect a minimal one-time set-up fee for the 8x10 negative and the stripping in of your name or logo. An option to the traditional 8x10 is the composite format of two different 5x7's printed on an 8x10 sheet. This offers the press a choice without doubling the cost to you. Only a composite set-up fee is charged.

Litho Quantity Prints

Many reproduction companies also print large quantities using a method of litho printing on a printing press. These copies have a dot pattern or screen on them and do not reproduce well in newspapers or brochures. The low price ($90 per 500) may get your attention but the uses for these prints are limited. For example, they are perfect for autographing at concerts or to use in an introductory packet.

Digital Images

Computer technology, digital cameras and the use of PhotoShop software has made the transmission and manipulation of photographic images instantaneous and easy. Yet, technology cannot replace the talent and years of experience of a professional photographer, professional photo lab or photo reproduction shop. In the hands of these professionals, these advances in digital technology can help to make your photographic image the highest quality possible.

In the past, color slides and prints from film were the norm. Prints from film offer benefits to users as they can be easily scanned on a flatbed scanner for a number of reprint uses. Professional photographers still prefer the quality that film offers and shoot film in most photo sessions, rather than shooting with a digital camera. A CD of digital images can then be produced during the film development process, providing both digital images and prints, offering the client the maximum flexibility. Prints can then be reproduced in quantity and the digital images can be used in the following ways:

❖ A CD of high resolution, 300 dpi TIFF images can be burned and mailed to media and promoters for marketing.

- High Resolution Images can be emailed in JPEG format for reprint purposes. Some files may be too large, even after ZIP compression, to e-mail and must be sent on a CD.
- High Resolution JPEGs can be downloaded from your website and converted to TIFF format for printing.
- Low Resolution Images are appropriate for online and onscreen viewing only.

Photo Retouching

The art of retouching has taken quantum leaps with computer technology, specifically PhotoShop software. Imperfections in a photographic image can now easily be corrected and refined. It is best to discuss corrections with your photographer and allow them to oversee any image manipulation for the best final results.

Makeup

Using a makeup artist can help the darker areas under your eyes. But, if this is too much of a stretch for you, do not use one. A really good makeup artist can place some makeup on a man and no one would ever know it. Women have more latitude with the amount they wear. The best rule is probably this: If you can afford it, and you or your photographer know a good makeup artist, then go for it. If not, do not worry. A good photographer can use lighting and strategic camera angles to make your photo great. Unless your act requires a more intense makeup look, subtlety is the key. A little makeup can help a lot but it is not necessary.

8½" x 11" Flyer Slick

A flyer slick is a master sheet which includes a photo and the name of the act and provides a blank space for the promoter to add information about an upcoming performance date. You might even include a quote or two from recognized sources. This is an optional piece to your kit. However, when you supply one or two flyer slicks to the promoter, they can reproduce it at their own cost in their desired quantity. Ask the printer or designer to use an 85 line screen when reproducing the photo on the flyer. This creates a dot pattern that will enable the promoter to either print or photocopy directly from this "slick." All they need to do is add the information relating to their event. The beauty of the slick is that you can have 100 of these printed up on light-weight, slightly-glossy paper, *inexpensively*. Then, you only need to send one or two to each promoter. They can then print as many as they need on whatever color or kind of stock they prefer.

Posters

If you have a small budget with which to create your entire package and already have the slick, then printing posters is

> # HotTips:
> A flyer slick saves you money when you produce it and then saves the promoter money when they reproduce it.
>
> Sending the promoter your self-designed flyers and posters insures that your image will be represented as you determine it should.

> **HotTip:**
> When printing posters, size them 11 inches by 17 inches to fit into a # 6 Jiffy bag and ship flat.

optional. The advantage to printing a poster is that it will be of a design that you choose and represents you exactly as you want to be represented. The poster can be incorporated into your overall press-packet theme. Posters are generally much larger than the flyers, often running from 11" x 17" to 18" x 22". Leave some blank space for additional promoter information to be inserted.

Posters give you more creative room for color use and an interesting design although these factors can also raise the cost of producing your concept. Promoters will generally ask for between two and 50 posters and the poster size often dictates how many places it can be displayed. Therefore, considering these factors, printing a poster, especially in two to four colors, can add to your overall promo kit budget. When deciding to add a poster to your package, estimate the number of performances for which you will use these posters. You may embark on a thematic tour for which this poster was specifically designed. If so, print just enough to cover your needs for the tour or the time frame. However, posters can always be reprinted if you run out or more dates are added to the tour. But keep in mind that the cost per piece drops as you print larger quantities. If you do not need five thousand, do not spend the additional money and then throw away a few thousand, even though the per-piece cost is less.

Posters add impact to your overall promotional package and when used in conjunction with the flyer slick, present you in a very professional light. However, printing and shipping posters will cost you more money. In the long run you will be very glad you chose to design and print your own—especially when you see them posted around the various cities on your tour. Considering some of the "interesting" designs that the promoters have come up with, you will appreciate having control over your image.

Logo
Designing a logo is not a necessity but I strongly recommend it. Simply selecting a particular typeface for your name can serve as a logo. When you select that type or actually design a logo, keep in mind what kind of statement you want to make and how that logo will represent you. Include it on your stationery, photos, posters and flyers, t-shirts and other merchandise. A well-designed logo can have a lasting impact on your audience long after you are gone. The choice of colors in your logo and the graphic design of your logo should be incorporated into the rest of your packet, making your promotional package unified and cohesive.

Business Cards
A business card is your calling card and as such it is a must in your promotional package. Keep it simple but informative. The

graphic artist will incorporate the design elements that went into the stationery within your business card. One clever idea that I have seen was printing an artist's list of recordings on the back of their card. One could also use the back to list books, performance titles and other credits of interest. Business cards can be printed cheaply at any of the quick-copy printers. When printed as part of the overall package printing project, they can be printed along with posters or pocket folders using otherwise wasted space on the larger sheets of card stock. (See Figure 3.)

Demo Recording Or Video

With the variety of formats available to present your

> **HotTips:**
> CD-ROM technology makes it possible to create state-of-the-art, multi-media press packets and business cards.
>
> *Your Name*
> o
> *Contact Info*

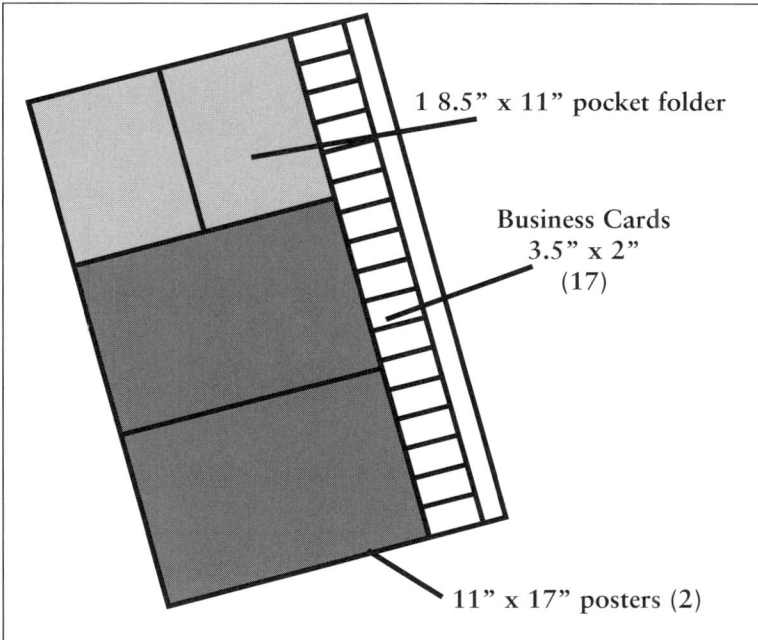

Figure 3. Press Sheet Possibilities

recorded demo, consider your costs very seriously. There are reproduction companies that can provide you with a demo cassette tape format for an extremely low price. Considering that the promoter is likely to only listen to snatches of your demo and will not likely listen to an entire tape or CD, sending a small sampling would be more cost effective. Anywhere from three to five representative cuts would be ample. However, note that promoters find CDs especially efficient as they can quickly sample a number of cuts. Still, there are promoters who find cassettes convenient because they often listen to promo material in their cars. Ask the promoter for the preferred format before sending your packet.

If you are signed to a label, you can negotiate the price of promotional CDs and cassettes. This price will often be well below the artist purchase price. As a performance act other than musical, a video demo is often required and is the

> "The cassette (and everything else you send out!) should include name and contact information. This is an absolute must because the materials in press kits often get separated."
>
> **Jim DeRogatis**
> former pop music editor,
> *Chicago Sun Times*
> former senior editor,
> *Rolling Stone*

> "Business cards are only reminders—if your imagination limits you to that usage. But they also can be powerful selling tools, marketing vehicles that set you apart from your competition."
>
> **Jay Conrad Levinson**
> author,
> *Guerrilla Marketing Weapons*

> **HotTip:** Dress appropriately for any television production. Coordinate with group members to avoid clashing patterns or colors. Avoid loud patterns, very bright colors, and bright whites.

best method of representing your act. Production costs can be sizable. Always ask the promoter what format they would like. Here are a few ideas to help you produce a demo video.

Video Production Tips
1. Prepare to have an upcoming performance taped in one of the better venues.
2. Propose your taping project to a local college broadcast department for independent credit.
3. Check with students of public access classes.
4. Check with producers at local commercial or public television stations. They may be interested in taping a show and creating a production that can fulfill your promo needs and perhaps be suitable for a broadcast project on their station.
5. Ask a record company. They may be able to tag onto another production already in progress for a larger group. While the crew is assembled, your video can be produced at a fraction of the cost if the concept is simple to execute.

A Cover Letter

A cover letter should always accompany any promotional package sent. If you are using a computer, it is a simple task to have a general cover letter already prepared that enables you to add a paragraph of specifics. It is certainly not necessary to write lengthy cover letters which include items that will eventually be covered in some form of contract agreement. The cover letter's first paragraph might simply restate some feature points of your conversation and what you have included in the package. If you have been asked to provide specific fee and performance date information, include that in the second paragraph. The concluding paragraph should state when you will contact them again and that you are looking forward to working with them. The letter may be that simple. The more you have pre-written, the less time you will spend creating cover letters. They should be informative and demonstrate your organization and commitment to your business.

The Overall Package

How you put all these pieces of your packet together varies. Your intended use will also influence what method of packaging you choose. The five main methods are: The brochure, the pocket folder, file folder, the one sheet and the Electronic Press Kit. Let's examine each method more closely.

The Brochure

A well-designed brochure can creatively incorporate a photo, a biography, some quotes and selected general information. Brochures are perfect in some instances. I have found them very useful for finite, time-sensitive situations such as a specific direct mailing to a targeted audience. The quantity will be determined by the number receiving the mailing. Or, a brochure can be very useful as an introductory piece of promotion. I would tend to keep this type very general. When writing copy for a brochure, use dates only for events that have already taken place. (i.e., Our first CD was released in the spring of 1995.) Including statements about events that are about to take place immediately dates the brochure. It becomes obsolete as soon as that date occurs. You want your material to be as current as possible. In the interest of saving yourself money and a trip to the paper recycling center, keep your writing timeless in brochures used for this purpose.

Pocket Folders

I have been a long-time advocate of some sort of pocket folder. Preassembled, colorful folders can be purchased cheaply at office-supply stores. If you go to the added expense of having one made from a particular paper and color, you can also print them with a logo and/or photograph. The cost for having a printer fold, glue and print your folders will add a sizable amount to your budget but may be worth the expense to accomplish your overall graphic look. Depending on the number you print, the paper you choose and the number of colors of ink you select, the cost will vary. It is usually more cost effective to have a larger number of pocket folders printed at one time (1000). If you decide to print folders, I suggest not printing your address and phone numbers directly on the folder in case of an unexpected move. Your business card will fit nicely into the die-cut slots in the pocket. The great thing about the pocket folder is that it neatly holds all of the various elements of your packet together. It presents a unified, professional, visual representation of your act. On the down side, the pocket folder does not always fit into a standard-size file cabinet. Some recipients will toss the folder and separate the elements in order to file the information in their storage system.

The File Folder

Many promoters and individuals in the media find that materials sent in a simple file folder with your name on it is the most efficient way for them to deal with an artist's material. Once they have read through the packet, it can easily be stored in a file cabinet. Those folders fit comfortably and materials won't be lost in the transfer from the original packaging. It is even more important to have contact information on every sheet when using this method. Without the pockets, individual sheets can slip out of the file. File folders come in many colors. Although using a color folder is more expensive, it will stand out and be more attractive than a plain manila folder.

> # HotTips:
> Avoid including upcoming dates when writing copy for a general brochure. Once a future date passes, the brochure is dated and obsolete.
>
> Use colors, labels and printed designs on folders and file folders to create a promotional package that stands out among the hundreds of other packages promoters receive.

Brochure

Pocket Folder

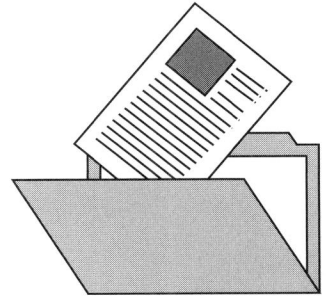

File Folder

> **HotTips:** 🌶
> Replace your photograph from a newspaper review with a correctly sized 85 line screened photo mechanical transfer or linographic output of your photograph before reproducing copies for your press kit. The photo will always reproduce well, copy after copy.

Sample Basic Sheet

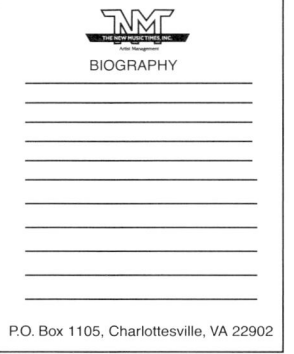

Basic Sheet printed with Biography

Pocket And File Folder Inserts

The inserts are the biography, general information sheet, quote sheets, reviews, interviews, sample press releases and photos. The pocket folder now affords you the opportunity to add or delete any one insert of your package. Any individual element can easily be changed or updated at low cost and as often as needed. One technique that has been very cost effective is to design a basic sheet that includes the logo, address and phone numbers. This sheet can be printed in a large quantity. You can use more than one color and can even print on a variety of colored papers to fit your color scheme. Once you have this printed, use small quantities of it to add the information from each of the various elements onto the basic sheet.

Tips To Keep Printing Costs Down And Information Current

1. Print 2500 basic sheets. These sheets will serve as your stationery as well. Use 100 basic sheets upon which the printer inserts (crashes in) or prints the biography on the blank portion of the sheet. Use another 100 sheets to crash in the quotes and so on. You end up with a full set of inserts, 100 copies of each insert that are assembled in an order of your preference into the pocket folder. You may decide that printing more than 100 at a time suits your needs, but a short run insures the current information is used up before it becomes obsolete.
2. Print inserts at a quick-copy type of printer at a fraction of the cost of a full offset printing operation.
3. Print copies so they are clean and crisp and done on light, colored paper or white so that the promoter can easily photocopy or print as many copies as they need.
4. Use lighter colored paper for sharper faxes.
5. Keep design elements like type, graphics and photos sharp. Avoid placing type over other graphic elements in the text body if it will be photocopied or faxed. The copies tend to reproduce poorly.
6. Use black ink for body copy for sharper reproductions. Red ink will reproduce as black or dark gray. Blue inks are harder to reproduce.
7. Let your color and paper choices add to your overall design of your packet. There are lots of paper varieties available including recycled stock. Remember, every aspect of your promotional packet should reflect who you are and how you want to be represented—right down to the kind of paper you use.

Insert Design Strategies

If you choose to use the pocket folder to hold your package contents, there are a number of interesting methods of arranging the elements within the pockets to place emphasis on the important aspects of your act. Work with your graphic artist and your printer to accomplish these ideas.

1. *The Full Sheet Method:* Place full sheets one sheet behind the other in the left and right pockets. Using this method, only the front sheets are visible upon opening the folder. Depending on whom your intended recipient may be, you can arrange your information to specifically target that person. For instance, print media appreciate having all of the factual information, like biography and info sheet, together in the right-hand pocket, and photo, reviews and quotes together in the left-hand pocket. A presenter seeing your packet for the first time would benefit from having the information arranged so that the most interesting, attention-grabbing aspects of your career that are particularly interesting to their venue are in the front.

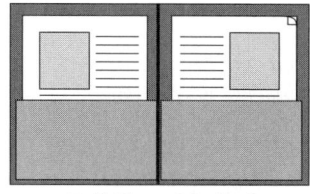

Full Sheet Method

2. *The Horizontal Stepped Method:* I am a huge fan of this printing method. Instead of each sheet remaining 8 1/2" x 11", they are cut in increments of your choosing to accommodate the number of sheets necessary. For instance the last sheet is 8 1/2" x 11", next sheet is 8 1/2" x 9", next sheet is 8 1/2" x 7". This method allows a portion of each sheet to be displayed upon opening the folder. It affords the artist an opportunity to place immediate emphasis on many different aspects of their career at a single glance. This works well for bands whose members as individuals are important to the makeup of the group. In other words, the group would not exist if not for each of the individuals. Example: The Highwaymen—Willie Nelson, Kris Kristofferson, Waylon Jennings and Johnny Cash. Who would you place on the first page of that press kit while covering up the others? Another interesting way to use this method is to emphasize different aspects of your performances. Perhaps you perform for children, conduct workshops, are available for residencies, are eligible for grants, perform for dances or work with symphonies, etc. This stepped method allows you to print one sheet describing each of those various and important aspects of your career and display them prominently all at once. Other information such as reviews, info sheets and quotes may be printed in full sheet format and placed behind the stepped sheets or in the other pocket.

Horizontal Stepped Method

3. *The Vertical Stepped Method:* The vertical stepped method accomplishes the same goals as the horizontal method. This method affords you slightly more sizing options should you have many categories needing to be emphasized.

Vertical Stepped Method

The Versatile One Sheet

Most clubs and certainly radio stations have little need for extensive press packets. A One Sheet is perfect for these situations. Using the front and back of a single letter size page, a one sheet can incorporate succinct, critical information targeting your intended audience.

Create Specific One Sheets Adaptable To:
- Radio Campaigns
- Club Dates
- Special Projects
- Workshops
- Booking Conferences

The One Sheet Should Include:
1. Short Bio Paragraph
2. Photo/CD Cover/Project Poster
3. Logo/Name/CD Title/Show Title
4. Related Critical Acclaim Quotes
5. Specific Theme Information
6. Contact Information

The One Sheet is an inexpensive promotional tool that keeps your shipping costs low, can be reproduced in small quantities, makes your point quickly and provides minimal reading material for the recipient.

The Electronic Press Kit (EPK)

All of the previously suggested elements to include in your promotional package, can be incorporated into an Electronic Press Kit that can be either emailed or downloaded from your website. The content of an EPK can also be burned to a CD and mailed or included with a printed press package. An EPK provides additional advantages to present video and audio in one professionally created package. It can include PDF forms to use as posters, flyers and press releases. MP3 sample audio files of your music along with video clips, offer the recipient an immediate preview of your performance. JPEG and TIFF files of promotional photographs provide the recipient with user friendly tools for marketing your act.

Working With A Graphic Artist

If visual art is not your forté and you have determined not to attempt designing your own promotional package, seek the aid of a graphic artist. I have been fortunate to have had the opportunity to work with some excellent artists. There are exceptionally talented people everywhere. I suggest you examine other performer's promotional packets and ask them who they have used if you have not yet worked with one. Ask to see portfolios. This becomes a matter of taste and the ability to communicate with each other. When you hire a graphic artist, you can negotiate the scope of their job. The designer often serves as the point person overseeing the various aspects of producing your entire package, from design to printing.

"Electronic Press Kits (EPK™) are quickly becoming the new standard that both the professional and independent music industry is using to communicate the value and marketability of an artist. Real-time updates, richer information, cost-efficiency and increased effectiveness give the EPK™ a significant advantage over traditional paper press kits."

Panos Panay
founder & CEO,
Sonicbids

"The same way you would choose a mechanic, a carpenter or a therapist, you will want to find the right designer for you and your project. Find someone capable and experienced who understands your passion."

Patrice McFarland
graphic designer,
New York State Museum

Their job may include all of the following:

1. Consult with the artist about overall package.
2. Design the overall package: including logo, stationery, envelopes, business cards, insert sheets, pocket folder, brochure, poster, flyer; possibly work with you on your photo session and any other clever items that help promote you.
3. Oversee design and production.
4. Consult with various printers for best price and production quality.
5. Prepare all elements of design for printer.
6. Examine printer proofs.
7. Examine final print job.

Before consulting with your chosen graphic artist, it would be to your advantage if you could present them with a general concept of how you would like to be represented. I was taught the following exercise by one of the exceptional graphic artists with whom I have worked. This exercise really helps you to hone in on your image.

Exercise:

1. Make a list of adjectives which describes you (your act).

_____

_____

2. Make a list of adjectives which describes how you want your act to be seen.

_____

_____

3. Make a list of favorite colors that you feel represent your act.

_____

_____

4. Make a list of images that your act, your music, your performance brings to mind.

_____

_____

_____

5. Describe your act in three words or less.

_____

"To find a designer, ask friends whose materials you like. You can usually find designers in the Yellow Pages under 'graphic design' or ask a local printer for some recommendations. Sometimes printers will refer you to designers they like—which usually means designers who have a practical understanding of the printing process. They'll often end up costing you less than a designer who designs things that are 'cool' but costly to produce. Always ask to see samples, and show them samples of things you like. Don't be afraid to say what you want but remember that the designer is a professional with a trained understanding of what works and what doesn't."

Valerie L'Herrou
graphic artist

"Graphics are far more strategic than most people realize. They involve quality ideas and planning. They are an important and personal part of your relationship with the public. They are you on paper. Make wise choices and invest in your image."

Patrice McFarland
graphic designer,
New York State Museum

HotTip: Establish ongoing relationships with a few printers in town. Find an offset printer for the big jobs and a quick-copy printer for the small jobs.

"You can have price, quality, speed—pick any two."

Anonymous

Your graphic artist will truly be impressed if you present these lists at your first meeting. They will be able to work on the graphic representation of your image with more awareness of what you are trying to accomplish with your packet.

Working With A Copy Writer

A copy writer is someone who can take the factual information you provide and transform it into well-written copy for your bio, press release and any of the other pieces in your kit. The benefit to using a copy writer is their ability to take the dry facts and add flare to the writing. The biography needs to generate some excitement and a copy writer, especially one who knows and enjoys your performance, can more adequately organize the factual information in a manner that will accomplish that task. A copy writer with experience in promotional pieces can manipulate your information so that it flows well and presents an organized, informative and enticing portrait of your act.

When looking for a copy writer, first, seek out a reviewer who has previously written something favorable about your act. If you have not yet been reviewed, check with reviewers in your local paper who write about your type of performance. If you like their writing style, approach them with a proposal for a freelance project.

To Find A Copy Writer:
❖ Check with writers for trade magazines in your field.
❖ Ask a publicity person from previously played venues.
❖ Contact local college English or marketing departments.
❖ Contact local advertising or marketing agencies.

Working With A Printer

Your graphic artist will be the direct link to the printer with whom you finally work. There are many good printers and some really great printers. For some of the printing tasks, such as inserts, it is more cost effective to use a quick-copy printer like Kinko's or Copy Cat. Use an offset printer, who has the printing presses to print large format sheets, if you are printing posters or pocket folders.

Cost

Consider your bottom line in producing the materials in your promotional package as well as the cost to the promoter when they use your materials. (Do they have to create their own posters using your photo or have you sent a flyer which can be reproduced cheaply?) The reality is that your promotional package may be the largest initial investment that you make in your career, next to a recording, video or touring vehicle. It certainly is one of the most important investments to help spread the word about you early in your career. There are methods of creating a high-quality package without spending exorbitant prices.

Budget Helpers

1. *Quick-Copy Printers:* Use a quick-copy printer to insert text copy in black ink on all your insert sheets.
2. *Light-Colored Paper and Black Ink:* Print full page review copies on a white or light-colored paper stock in black ink at a quick-copy printer. Reviews don't need to be copied onto basic stationery sheets since they may require the full page. However, make sure your contact information is prominent on the page.
3. *Ink Color:* Decide which elements of your package will be printed in the same color and on the same paper stock. If you want everything to match, choose a paper line that comes in both text and cover weights. Ask your graphic artist for swatchbooks of paper samples. Posters, business cards, pocket folders may all be printed on the same stock. If so, the printer can "gang" (place on one large sheet) these elements together and print them on larger sheets of paper on a large press. They then cut the paper into the separate elements. This makes the best use of the paper size, and saves you money. Using an offset printer will cost more, but they are equipped to do more complicated printing projects with multiple colors and in larger-size paper formats. (See Figure 3, page 75.)
4. *Budget:* Ask questions of either the graphic artist or the printer who quotes the job. Let them know that you want to make the most efficient use of paper size to stay within your budget.
5. *Multiple Quotes:* Get quotes from a variety of printers before settling on one.
6. *Samples:* Ask for samples of their work.
7. *Recommendations:* Check with friends for printer recommendations.
8. *Discount Paper Stores:* Purchase reams of paper at discount paper stores and bring your paper to the printer for some additional savings. Volume discounts are available if you purchase a case or more. When you find a paper that you like and think you will use for a while, buy in bulk. Papers are often discontinued. If your design incorporates a specific paper, make sure you have an adequate supply to last a while. Most printers are not open to the customer supplying their own paper because the printer makes a large percentage of their profit from the paper price markup. Check with your printer first.
9. *PDF Proofs:* Get PDF proofs of all graphics e-mailed to check the work prior to printing. A PDF attachment makes your review fast and easy.
10. *Inferior Printing:* Do not settle for an inferior printing job. If you are not satisfied or if any mistakes are the fault of the printer, insist that they make corrections—even if it

HotTip: PDF proofs are your insurance that all copy and digital images are correct.

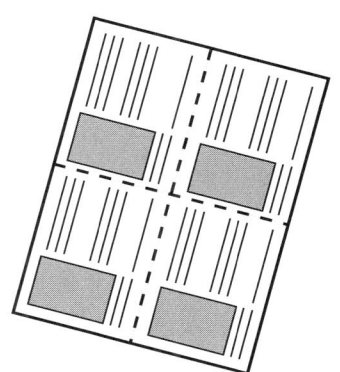

Dotted lines indicate cuts which will result in four postcards from one 8.5" x 11" sheet.

> **HotTip:** Check online sources for postcards, e-mail campaigns, newsletters. (See resource section, page 90.)

means reprinting the whole thing. You should not be charged for a mistake by the printer.

11. *Printer Loyalty:* Once you find a printer whose work quality is satisfactory and with whom you enjoy working, use them for your other printing projects. They will begin to know your printing needs and help you achieve the best results at the best price for your budget.

12. *Postal Requirements:* Check with the post office or the mailing house with whom you work for specific size and weight requirements prior to designing your mailing pieces. The post office will reject oversized pieces or charge you additional postage. Surprises like that adversely affect your budget.

13. *Itinerary Post Cards:* When printing tour-itinerary postcards, the graphic designer can size each postcard at 4 1/4" x 5 1/2" and the printer will fit four (4) on an 8 1/2" x 11" sheet of paper. This is a legal size for shipping at the lowest postcard rate as specified by the post office and saves a considerable amount of money. The printing term for this is "four-up."

Summary

✧ The promotional package is your main sales tool. It introduces, it informs and it markets.

✧ The elements to include in your promotional package are: a cover letter, a biography, general information, quote sheets, reviews, interviews, previews, press release, black and white photos, color slides, poster, flyer slick, business card, demo recording or video.

✧ Design your promotional package to reflect your developing career and keep your package current.

✧ Develop relationships with a graphic artist, a photographer, a copy writer and a number of printers to effectively execute the production of your promotional package.

✧ Investing in the creation of a high quality promotional package is a priority in your career development.

Sample Publicity Releases

Sandy Goldfarb Public Relations
12741 Pacific Avenue #8
Los Angeles, CA 90066

Phone/Fax: (310) 391-3139
sandy_goldfarb@hotmail.com

SCOTLAND'S BATTLEFIELD BAND PERFORMS IN CONCERT AT THE ARK IN ANN ARBOR APRIL 21

The Battlefield Band will present music in the Scottish tradition live in concert at The Ark, 925 Sunnyside in Ann Arbor, Tuesday evening, April 21st at 8:00 p.m. Tickets are $15 in advance, $18 at the door. Advanced tickets can be purchased at The Ark box office. For information phone (313) 761-1800.

Under the banner *Forward With Scotland's Past,* the Battlefield Band has been performing throughout the world for almost thirty years. Inspired by their rich heritage of Celtic music and fired by the strength of the modern Scottish cultural scene, Battlefield Band mixes the old songs and tunes with self-penned material. They play on a unique fusion of ancient and modern instruments: bagpipes, synthesizers, fiddles, flutes and whistles, guitars, citterns, accordion and bodhran (drum). During these years there have been many line-up changes, with individuals going on to play in other bands and pursue other interests and new members joining, bringing with them new ideas, attitudes and influences. The smooth organic way in which these changes take place enables the Battlefield Band's music to constantly change and evolve, while still presenting the traditional Scottish sound for which they are known.

Battlefield Band and its members have twenty CDs and two videos, all on the Temple Records label in Scotland. The most current CDs are <u>ACROSS THE BORDERS</u>, a live recording with many of Scotland's finest musicians and singers joining in as guest performers, and three solo albums by the band members: <u>JOHN McCUSKER</u>, a self-named album of original fiddle tunes, <u>THE SUNLIT EYE</u>, by keyboardist singer-songwriter Alan Reid, and <u>CHASING SHADOWS</u>, by new vocalist, guitarist and songwriter, Davy Steele. Rounding out the current line-up is Mike Katz, whose bagpipes can be heard on albums by his previous band, Ceolbeg. A new band recording featuring the current line-up will be available in March, 1998. All Temple Records products are available in the U.S. from Rounder Records in Cambridge, MA and in Canada from Danon in Toronto.

#

**Press Contact:
Sandy Goldfarb (310) 391-3139**

Reprinted with permission of Sandy Goldfarb

IMMEDIATE RELEASE
SWEET HONEY IN THE ROCK at ZELLERBACK AUDITORIUM
Jan. 24, 1998   **8:00 PM**

JR Productions, in association with Cal Performances, is proud to welcome back to the Bay Area **Sweet Honey in the Rock** for their annual black history month concerts. The January 24 show will be at Zellerbach Auditorium on the campus of UC-Berkeley. For ticket information, please call 510-642-9988. Tickets are $25 and showtime is 8:00 PM.

Sweet Honey in the Rock is a community-based cultural organization of African American *a capella* women singers who continue to challenge, surprise and uplift audiences world wide. They are a Grammy award-winning group with deep musical roots in spirituals, hymns, gospel, jazz and blues. Performing with their voices and hand percussion instruments, this electrifying ensemble creates a deeply personal, yet universally evocative sound.

Founded in 1973 by Bernice Johnson Reagon out of her vocal workshop of the SC Black Repertory Company, 22 women have participated in this singing ensemble. Their current ensemble includes: Bernice Johnson Reagon, Ysaye Maria Barnwell, Nitanju Bolade Casel, Aisha Kahlil, Carol Maillard and Sign language interpreter, Shirley Childress Johnson.

With the current release of their newest 34 song compilation CD, *Selection, 1976-1988,* Sweet Honey in the Rock explores the sound they have created over the last 25 years, including: *Ella's Song, Rivers of Babylon, Biko, State of Emergency, Crying for Freedom in South Africa,* and two previously unreleased songs, *As Long As I Have Breath In My Body* and *Cape Fear River Chant.* "The sound of Sweet Honey in the Rock is a wide-open sound, one that invites you in….And it is music without boundaries in a broader sense as well, sources in the tradition of unaccompanied congregational song…" Richard Harrington, *Washington Post Magazine.*

Tickets for the Zellerback performance can be purchased through all BASS ticket centers. Charge by phone 510-762-BASS or mail order by sending a SASE and a check for $25 to JR Productions, 433 Town Center, Box #604, Corte Madera, CA 94925.

Sweet Honey in the Rock will also be appearing on January 23 at the Luther Burbank Center, 50 Mark West Springs Rd., Santa Rosa, CA. For ticket information, please call 707-546-3600.

For further media information, please contact JR Productions at 415-789-8878 or by fax at 415-789-8883. For other ticket information and group sales, please contact JRTX at 415-789-0188.

▼

Jeanne Rizzo
433 Town Center, Suite 604 ▼ Corte Madera, CA 94920
Tel: 415.789.8878 ▼ Fax: 415.789.8883 ▼ Email: JRProds@aol.com

Reprinted with permission of JR Productions

Contact: Kari Estrin
(617) 491-4435

FOR IMMEDIATE RELEASE!

DE DANANN & MAURA O'CONNELL and the ANDY STATMAN KLEZMER ORCHESTRA plus BELA FLECK AT THE BERKLEE PERFORMANCE CENTER

Date: March 20, 1985

Place: Berklee Performance Center, Boston, MA

Time: 7:30 p.m.

Tickets: $10.50 reserved seating, on sale at Berklee Box Office, Strawberries, Out of Town Tickets, Ticketron Concert Charge (617) 497-1118, Teletron (617) 720-3434

CELTIC MEETS KLEZMER AT THE BERKLEE!

Kari Estrin and Black Sheep Concerts will present a rare and exciting combination of musical styles on Wednesday, March 20th when Ireland's DE DANANN and the ANDY STATMAN KLEZMER ORCHESTRA take the stage at the Berklee Performance Center.

DE DANANN, one of Ireland's most popular traditional groups, is well known for energized arrangements of material ranging from fast-paced reels, Music Hall tunes and pop songs. The band's current line-up features outstanding musicianship on a variety of instruments. FRANKIE GAVIN, the leader of the group, is considered the best Irish fiddler in the world. ALEC FINN plays a wide range of string instruments, including steel string guitar, mandocello, mandolin, and the Greek bouzouki. MARTIN O'CONNOR plays button accordion and JOHNNY "RINGO" McDONAGH adds rhythm on the bodhran (a goatskin hand drum) and the bones. For this performance, MAURA O'CONNELL will rejoin the group with her dynamic soprano vocals.

ANDY STATMAN is a multi-instrument virtuoso who blends his knowledge of many musical traditions into his own brand of klezmer music. Klezmer, a kind of traditional Jewish jazz, borrows from other European music, including waltzes, Russian marches, and gypsy fiddle music. STATMAN's magic lies in his ability to inject this Old World music with fresh contemporary energy, using his background in jazz, bluegrass, ethnic and classical music.

STATMAN, a native of New York City, studied mandolin with Dave Grisman and was part of the Greenwich Village folk scene in the early Sixties. Later he became interested in jazz and ethnic music. He was fortunate to be able to study clarinet with Dave Tarras, the last great living European klezmer master. STATMAN was a member of Breakfast Special, a progressive bluegrass band, and has recorded with the Doug Sahm Band. In his KLEZMER ORCHESTRA, his masterful clarinet is backed by BOB JONES on guitar, MARTY CONFURIOUS on acoustic bass and DAVID STEINBERG on trumpet and French horn.

After DE DANANN and THE ANDY STATMAN KLEZMER ORCHESTRA perform their individual sets, the two groups will fuse their musical talents in a climactic joint set. Another highlight of the evening will be a special appearance by BELA FLECK, who will demonstrate his banjo prowess as he performs his own brand of Irish and New Acoustic Music. A member of the NEWGRASS Revival, FLECK is well known for his progressive banjo style.

Tickets are available at the Berklee Box Office, Strawberries, Out of Town Tickets, Ticketron, Concert Charge (617) 497-1118, Teletron (617) 720-3434. For more information, call (617) 876-0099.

One Camp Street   **Cambridge, MA 02140**   **617-491-4435**

Resources
Audio, CD-ROM & DVD Duplication Companies:

Digital Brothers
1125 Victoria St., Suite C
Costa Mesa, CA 92627
Phone: 949-645-9702
Fax: 949-642-7249

Disc Makers
7905 N. Rt. 130
Pennsauken, NJ 08110-1402
Phone: 1-800-468-9353
Fax: 856-661-3458
Web: http://www.discmakers.com

Oasis CD & Cassette Duplication
Phone: 1-888-296-2747
Fax: 540-987-8810
E-mail: info@oasisCD.com
Web: http://www.oasisCD.com

Groove House Records
5029 Serrania
Woodland Hills, CA 91364
Phone: 1-888-GROOVE-8 (476-6838)
Web: http://www.groovehouse.com

I.D. Rom
Rompus Interactive Corp.
510 Front St., 4th floor
Toronto, Ontario M5V 3H3
Phone: 416-217-1364
Fax: 416-217-1378
Web: http://www.idrom.com
Interactive business cards combining CD-ROM and the Internet

Shape CD
875 Avenue of the Americas, Suite 1811
New York, NY 10001
Phone: 212-279-2929
Fax: 212-279-0909
Web: http://www.shapecd.com
CD interactive business cards combining CD-ROM and the Internet

Electronic Press Kits

Sonicbids
580 Harrison Avenue, Fourth Floor
Boston, MA 02118
Phone: 617-275-7222
E-mail: info@sonicbids.com
Web: http://www.sonicbids.com

Directories:

Musician's Atlas
38 Porter Place
Montclair, NJ 07042-2036
Phone: 973-509-9898
Fax: 973-655-1238
E-mail: info@musiciansatlas.com
Web: http://www.MusiciansAtlas.com
Lists duplication manufacturers, graphic designers, photographers

The Black Book—Photography Directory of Photographers in the U.S.
Available in some libraries, bookstores or for purchase.
740 Broadway, 2nd floor
New York, NY 10003
Phone: 1-800-841-1246
Fax: 212-673-4321
Web: http://www.blackbook.com

The Recording Industry Sourcebook
Artist Pro Publishing
ISBN: 1931140235
Web: http://www.recordingindustrysourcebook.com

Graphic Artists:

Graphis Design
Directory of Graphic Artists
Available in libraries and bookstores.

Graphic Artists Guild
90 John Street, Suite 403
New York, NY 10038
Phone: 212-791-3400
Phone: 212-791-0333
Web: http://www.gag.org
By subscription
Weekly newsletter—free ad placement for those seeking artists.

Graphic Artists Guild Chapters

Atlanta	Northern California
Boston	Southern California
Chicago	Seattle
Maryland	Portland, OR
Indianapolis	Vermont
New York City	

Photographers:

Those listed below were recommended by agents, artists and record companies for their expertise in promotional and CD cover photography. Listed by region.

Irene Young
41 River Terrace, #304
New York, NY 10282
Phone: 1-800-863-9323
Email: iy@ireneyoungfoto.com
Web: http://www.ireneyoungfoto.com

Susan Wilson
87 Bristol Street, Suite 2B
Cambridge, MA 02139
Phone: 617-547-5457
Fax: 617-876-9050
Email: swilson@susanwilsonphoto.com
Web: http://www.susanwilsonphoto.com

McIntyre Photography Inc.
Will and Deni McIntyre
3746 Yadkinville Road
Winston-Salem, NC 27106
Phone: 336-922-3142
Fax: 336-924-0345
Email: info@macfoto.com
Web: http://www.macfoto.com

Denise Grant
Suite 102, 183 Bathurst St.
Toronto, Ontario M5T 2R7
Phone: 416-406-6100
Fax: 416-703-0297
E-mail: andoff@interlog.com

Beth Gwinn
P.O. Box 22817
Nashville, TN 37202
Phone: 615-385-0917
Fax: 615-269-5754
Email: BethGwinn@aol.com
Web: http://www.bethgwinn.com

Jim McGuire
711 8th Ave. South
Nashville, TN 37203
Phone: 615-244-1947
Email: mcguire@nashvilleportraits.com
Web: http://www.nashvilleportraits.com

Marc Norberg
711 West Lake Street, #419
Minneapolis, MN 55408
Phone: 612-340-9863
Fax: 612-340-9252
Email: mail@marcnorberg.com
Web: http://www.marcnorberg.com

Brenda Ladd Photography
1700 South Lamar Blvd.
Suite 322
Austin, TX 78704
Phone: 512-707-0070
Web: http://www.brendaladdphoto.com

Marc Tule
627 8th Ave.
San Diego, CA 92101
Phone: 619-234-9634
Fax: 619-232-4818
Web: http://www.marctule.com

Anne Hamersky
1188 Noe Street
San Francisco, CA 94114-3744
Phone: 415-695-1723
Fax: 415-695-1700
Web: http://www.annehamersky.com

Photo Reproduction Companies:
U.S.:

Black and White Photo Lab
295 Huntington Ave., Suite 205
Boston, MA 02115
Phone: 617-266-2641
http://www.blackandwhiteinc.com

Modernage
1150 Avenue of the Americas
New York, NY 10036
Phone: 1-800-997-2510
Phone: 212-997-1800
Fax: 212-869-4796
Web: http://www.modernage.com

Sukolsky-Brunelle
908 Penn Ave.
Pittsburgh, PA 15222
Phone: 412-391-6440
Fax: 412-391-9401
Web: http://www.sbi-online.com
Fast turnaround for color slides.
Rates differ depending on time.

A & B Photography
650 W. Lake Street
Chicago, IL 60606
Phone: 312-454-4554
Web: http://www.A-BPhoto.com

Chromatics
625 Fogg Street
Nashville, TN 37203
Phone: 615-254-0063
Fax: 615-242-2334
Web: http://www.chromatics.com
Image archiving, image management.

Star Photo
38 Music Square East
Nashville, TN 37203
Phone: 615-242-1883
Web: http://www.starphotoservice.com
Original negatives kept on file.
Phone in reorders.

ABC Pictures
1867 E. Florida Street
Springfield, MO 65803
Phone: 1-888-526-5336
Web: http://www.abcpictures.com

Producers & Quantity Photo
6660 Santa Monica Blvd
Hollywood, CA 90038
Phone: 323-462-1334
Web: http://www.pqphoto.com

Action Reprographics, Inc.
2550 Wyandotte St., Suite A
Mountainview, CA 94043
Phone: 650-968-7226
Fax: 650-623-0103
Email: info@actionreprographics.com
Web: http://www.actionreprographics.com

Canada:

Galbraith Photodigital Inc.
24 Carlaw Ave.
Toronto, ON M4M 2R7
Phone: 416-531-6913
Phone: 1-800-561-5466
Web: http://www.galbraithphotodigital.com

E-mail Marketing Websites:

Constant Contact
Web: http://www.constantcontact.com

Topica
Web: http://www.topica.com

Vertical Response–ibuilder
Web: http://www.verticalresponse.com

CHAPTER SIX
The Art Of Negotiating

"We are negotiating every day. Anytime you are eyeball-to-eyeball, nose-to-nose, belly button-to-belly button, kneecap-to-kneecap, toe-to-toe with another person, you are negotiating."

Roger Dawson
The Secrets of Power Negotiating: You Can Get Anything You Want

Negotiating is truly an art. Those skilled in its techniques have the opportunity to create the lives they have always dreamed about. Your knowledge of negotiating will not only serve you in your booking business, but also in all things personal and interpersonal. Most of us only think of negotiating in relationship to large deals like purchasing a car or a house. Those are the times when we picture ourselves winning the advantage over the car salesperson or real estate agent to get the best possible deal.

Negotiations In Your Daily Life

What we do not often realize is that real estate agents and car salespeople are highly skilled negotiators practicing their negotiation techniques every day with a variety of individuals. We may not think of ourselves as skilled negotiators but, in reality, we negotiate several times a day—with our children about an appropriate bedtime, with our friends when deciding at which restaurant to dine, at PTA meetings, and at board

"To be persuasive, we must be believable.
To be believable, we must be credible.
To be credible, we must be truthful."

Edward R. Murrow
radio broadcaster, television producer, former director of United States Information Agency

meetings. We also negotiate with the service person at the garage, the hotel desk clerk for room rates, the car rental agent and our significant other when considering just about anything. If we all had a little more knowledge of negotiating techniques, we could make all of our daily interactions with people much more pleasant and rewarding.

The Experts

There are experts in the field of negotiation who have written volumes on the subject. Leading lecturers have recorded a number of valuable tape series. You can study negotiation techniques by employing the resources listed at the end of this chapter. These experts will provide you with an in-depth study of the art of negotiating as well as all the techniques and personality traits to be aware of as you negotiate. You will discover that most of the negotiations discussed, and many that you will encounter, take place face-to-face.

Interestingly though, booking negotiations are rarely conducted face-to-face. Most negotiations take place on the phone; faxing and e-mail have become a mainstay. This necessitates some very specific negotiation skills. Although booking will mainly involve phone, fax and e-mail contact, I will go over some of the more important techniques that are necessary when you find yourself negotiating face-to-face. However, I encourage you to explore the wide world of negotiations, in more depth, under the tutelage of the experts. It is a fascinating study that will make a difference in your everyday life and not just when you are working on the "Big Deal."

Most businesses, and certainly the entertainment business, depend on individuals interacting with one another. All of these interactions eventually result in some form of negotiation to arrive at some type of an agreement. As a performer, you will be faced with booking agreements, recording contracts, licensing contracts, publishing contracts, performing rights licenses, endorsement deals, travel deals, equipment rental contracts, personnel and crew contracts, management and, perhaps eventually, an agent contract. All of these will require negotiation skills and it is critical to learn them well.

Building Relationships

Individuals interacting together form the basis of your business relationships. The ease with which you move through any of your negotiations will depend upon how well you have nurtured your relationships.

Good Relationships Are Key to Your Business

As you begin making calls to presenters, keep in mind that you are only one of many performers and agents calling that presenter on that particular day. Also keep in mind that many presenters work regular office hours and some, just like you,

"The answer to good business is not in the mechanics; but the answer is in handling people."

Roger Dawson
negotiator, lecturer

"Relationships are the stuff of life."

Eric W. Skopec,
Laree S. Kiely
co-authors, *Everything's Negotiable When You Know How To Play The Game*

work out of their homes. They have families and personal lives; their job or hobby is to book performances for their venue or organization. Awareness of this factor will help you create the tone of your conversation and allow you to present a more personable attitude. After all, these are people with whom you will develop a relationship.

Developing a good relationship with your presenter is your number one priority if you are to be successful. The relationships you develop will help you stand out from all the others attempting to book the date that you want and will be the foundation of your business. A good relationship will get your phone calls answered most of the time even if you do not get the date every time.

Nurture Your Relationships

One of the main reasons booking agents are so valuable to the development of a performer's career is the relationships they have nurtured for years with presenters, managers, record companies and the media. These long-term relationships afford a booking agent and their performers many opportunities that performers booking themselves will find hard to compete with.

Your only recourse is to make a serious commitment to nurturing your own relationships with presenters. No longer should you only be concerned with getting the "one-time" gig. You want your relationship with the promoter to progress to the point where you have an opportunity to get the gig next year and the year after that. Or, that they will recommend you to other promoters when possible. Competition is stiff, with a majority of dates going to the known ticket sellers. If your act hopes to have any chance of being considered, you need to develop your relationships carefully and maintain them if you are in it for the long haul. Once again, having a clear picture of your long-range goals will help you determine the amount of time you will invest in nurturing these relationships.

The Benefits Of A Good Relationship
❖ Promoter will answer your calls more often.
❖ Promoter will think of you for specific events or multi-bill performances.
❖ Promoter will recommend you to other promoters when appropriate.
❖ You will have a more pleasant negotiating experience.
❖ It will extend your longevity on the circuit.

Developing your relationships will take time and effort. You are the one who needs a favorable relationship—so it is really all up to you. Your livelihood depends on it. Developing your presenter/performer relationships will result

> "A working relationship where trust, understanding, respect and friendship are built up over time can make each new negotiation smoother and more efficient. . . . the ongoing relationship is far more important than the outcome of any particular negotiation."
>
> Roger Fisher &
> William Ury
> co-authors, *Getting To Yes*

> "Whether you are booking yourself or booking other artists, it is important for a presenter to feel free to bounce ideas off you. A comfortable, cooperative working relationship can lead to creative bookings and expanded opportunities for all concerned."
>
> Stevie Beck
> former associate producer,
> *A Prairie Home Companion*

> "... that's my concept for making conflict work in which parties summon all their imaginative skills and resources to provide each other with an array of benefits that neither would realize were it not for the other."
>
> Fred E. Jandt
> co-author,
> Win-Win Negotiating

> "I truly believe that this is a partnership between all parties involved, which can be as simple as artist to promoter directly. . . . If only the artist and the agent walk away from a show feeling good about it because they made their money, then something is wrong."
>
> Jim Fleming
> agent,
> Fleming & Associates

> "This isn't about winning, it's about both sides receiving appropriate compensation. I've negotiated when I've had the upper hand and when the artist held all the cards."
>
> Jim Hirsch
> former executive director,
> Old Town School
> of Folk Music

in contract negotiations that consider the best interests of each party. This is the goal to strive for in every negotiation. We will examine win-win negotiating in the next section. In preparation to become a win-win negotiator, here are some suggestions to help you build good relationships.

Five Steps To Building Good Relationships

1. *Treat each person with respect.* Respect their time and their position.
2. *Show interest in the things that interest them.* Make a point of inquiring about their lives. Some likely topics are health, family, recent shows, outside hobbies or interests, a recent vacation.
3. *Have compassion for them as an individual.* Everyone has their good and bad days. Be flexible if *now* is not the most opportune time to talk.
4. *Understand their position, their limitations and advantages.* If they are a presenter, they may have hall constraints or budget limitations. Or, they may have multiple performance opportunities that are to your advantage. By educating yourself, you are in a better position to make a favorable proposal that will work for you both.
5. *Maintain an awareness of their booking schedule.* Do they book a year in advance, six months in advance or six weeks before a performance date? Must they comply with grant deadlines? Your knowledge of their specific situation demonstrates your professionalism.

Use these five steps as you develop each booking relationship. They will help to shape your professional reputation.

Win-Win Negotiating

I have always conducted my negotiations with a win-win philosophy. By caring for the other party's concerns and objectives, I have been able to achieve my goals as well as assist the other party to obtain their objectives. As a booking agent, my main concern is for the artists that I represent. I need to make certain that their interests are primary. However, throughout my career, I have worked to insure that all of the promoters' concerns are addressed as well. Whenever I can help them get more from the performance, it is in my artist's best interest to do so.

A win-win attitude should prevail in all of your negotiations and, in particular, all of the booking negotiations you encounter. Each performance date that you negotiate partners you with the promoter to present the most successful performance possible. Therefore, your contract negotiations must create an atmosphere of cooperation, not competition. That is why it is so important to negotiate with a win-win philosophy.

Five Standards Of A Win-Win Negotiation
The Secrets of Power Negotiating by Roger Dawson,
Produced by Nightingale Conant Corporation, Copyright © 1987 by Nightingale Conant Corporation. All rights reserved.

1. Everyone involved in the negotiation feels like a winner.
2. Each cared about the objectives of the other.
3. The belief is held by each side that the other was fair in the way they conducted the negotiations.
4. Each negotiator should feel that they would enjoy negotiating with the other at some time in the future.
5. The belief is held by each party, that the other party is determined to keep the commitments made in the contract.

A win-win negotiator is a negotiator who can get what they want in the negotiation and still bring themselves up to the standards held in these five benchmarks.

As you move through each negotiation, ask yourself how you are holding up to these benchmarks. Have you worked hard to get everything you set out to accomplish? Have you been concerned with the other party's objectives as well as your own? When you can answer "yes," you have built a strong foundation for your relationship and your negotiating experience will be a fulfilling one.

Three Main Steps To Every Negotiation
Any negotiating situation should have three main steps to be a successful negotiation.

1. *Establish Criteria:* What does the other party want? What do you want? Can each of you provide what the other is asking for? What can you provide, if not everything?
2. *Gather Information:* Get as much information about the other party as possible. It is important to have information prior to the actual negotiation; but be very alert to gain any additional information possible. The more information you have, the greater advantage you have during the actual negotiations. Information is key to establishing your position.
3. *Come To A Resolution:* This is the stage where you both fine-tune each point being considered and come to a final agreement. The criteria from step one and the information from step two impact the resolution of each point to create a mutually positive agreement.

"In every good negotiator there must be the desire to achieve, to aspire, to take that sensible but extra measure of risk that represents a commitment to one's strivings."

Chester L. Karrass
author,
The Negotiating Game

Important Points When Beginning A Performance Negotiation
Every negotiation will include these three steps. The criteria, information and resolution stages will vary depending on the type of agreement you are negotiating. For instance, the

> *"Remember, you are working for two customers:*
> 1. *The promoter, who is paying the freight.*
> 2. *The audience, who is buying the ticket.*
>
> *The audience is the promoter's customer as well—working together we can give our customers a memorable experience."*
>
> Christine Risatti
> director,
> Downtown Presents

preparation you will have to do before negotiating a record contract will be very different from that of a performance contract. Let me outline the important points to consider in each of these three steps when beginning a typical performance negotiation.

1. Establish Criteria For Booking Situations

- ❖ What would the presenter like from you? Are you the performer that can provide them with the performance that addresses their presenting concerns?
- ❖ What do you want from the presenter? Does this presenter have the venue, the technical requirements, the budget, the date and the audience that will fulfill all of your performance needs?
- ❖ How can each of you help to satisfy each other's goals?

Ask these questions to explore each other's needs as they relate to the possible performance. Your approach to booking any date should always be one that is concerned with how your performance will benefit the presenter along with fulfilling your touring goals. This way, you will create a better deal that will benefit each of you.

2. Gather Information

You may recall in Chapter Four that we spent time establishing a list of questions that would help you determine if this promoter and venue were right for you. Those answers will be the base from which we build our information during the negotiations. Remember, the more informed you are, the greater advantage you have in negotiating. But, having the advantage does not mean that you will "take advantage" of the presenter during your negotiations. Instead, it means you have provided yourself with every possible means of making the best decisions.

> *"Vigorous let us be in attaining our ends, and mild in our method of attainment."*
>
> Lord Newborough

While you are gathering your information, the promoter will be doing the same about you and your performance. Along with your list of questions from Chapter Four, page 48, you will want answers to some of the following questions:

About the Promoter
- ❖ Is this a reputable promoter?
- ❖ Do they pay their bills?
- ❖ How do they treat their performers?
- ❖ Do they promote their shows effectively?
- ❖ Do they return phone calls?
- ❖ Is this a promoter with whom other artists enjoy doing business?
- ❖ Does the venue have a good reputation?
- ❖ Is the venue known for the quality of their production? (sound, lights and staging)

- Does the promoter provide quality hospitality? (meals, refreshments backstage, hotel)
- Does the promoter have a good reputation with the local media? (Can they get coverage?)
- Does the promoter have any quirks that would be good to know about in advance? (abrupt or soft speech, inability to make timely decisions, offers false hope in booking you and then doesn't book you, delays return of contracts)
- Will this promoter and this venue be an asset to your career development?

About the Artist
- Is the artist easy to deal with?
- Do they follow up and send materials when needed?
- Do they show up on time for performances?
- Do they make unreasonable requests in their hospitality rider?
- Have they performed in the area before and what was the revenue?
- What has the revenue been on the last few tour dates?
- Can the venue handle the technical rider? Will production costs rise due to technical requirements?
- What do other promoters have to say about working with this act?
- Does the artist have a good reputation with the media?
- Will the artist relate well with your audience? Do they relate well to audiences in general?
- What is the artist's reputation for relating to staff and technical crew?
- Does the artist have any quirks that would be good to know about in advance? (tardiness, drinking, rudeness, shorter show than contracted for, invites too many guests, never available for promotional efforts, often does not show)
- Will this artist be an asset to the promoter's presentations?
- Can the promoter sell this artist in their market?

These sample questions are some of the most important. You may have a few of your own to add to the list. Many of these questions may be answered by the promoter or artist themselves during your conversations, but it may require some research on your part to acquire this information elsewhere. Having the answers to these questions will establish some advantages for each side. Not knowing what information the other side has is what makes this negotiating game so interesting. Now, you have the opportunity to use this information either to create a deal that suits both parties' needs or to determine that the performance is not worth pursuing. Let me give you an example of the latter.

> **HotTip:**
> Gather as much information as possible about the promoter, the venue and the event. Thoughtful decisions can be made during a negotiation when you are informed.

"Never sell yourself short. Decide what you are worth and then charge it. Asking for more money is always risky but it's the difference between living to make ends meet and making a living."

Dianne de Las Casas
professional storyteller, director, Story Ballet Magic, president, Independent Children's Artist Network

> *"Most poorly-negotiated deals center on just stating a fee and watching the date either be rejected with no discussion, or even worse, confirmed quickly, leaving you to wonder if you settled for too little."*
>
> **Jeff Laramie**
> president,
> SRO Artists, Inc.

Example:

You are beginning negotiations with a promoter. While speaking with another performer, you mention that you might perform at the promoter's venue. You ask the other performer if they have ever worked at this venue or know anything about the promoter. The response is, "Yes! And I will never work for him again. We never got paid and neither did the sound crew." This is an extreme example, yet not unheard of. Knowing this information, would you continue to negotiate with this promoter? Perhaps. However, you would make sure that you establish some safeguards in your contract to protect you. You might get a larger deposit in the form of a bank or certified check, or make sure their business check clears by the date established in the contract. You might request payment in cash upon arrival, before you perform. No money up front—no performance. You might decide not to continue negotiating with this promoter and forego this date. You can walk away. Because you gathered valuable information, you have the ability to weigh your options.

3. Come To A Resolution

Once you have established criteria and gathered all the information necessary, it is time to finalize your agreement and resolve as much as possible. This is when you will realize the benefit of all of your preceding work. Use whatever information is on hand, along with the established criteria, to create a mutually acceptable agreement. Keep in mind that each of you may want something different, and that the negotiation may not be about price alone. There are many points to be considered in arriving at a successful agreement. Fees are just one of these points. You will see all of these questions again in Chapter Seven when we discuss contracts.

Here is a list of questions that will need resolution:

- *Travel:* Who pays for it?
- *Accommodations:* Will it be provided and where?
- *Percentage points after the split point:* What percentage over the expenses does the artist get? (See pages 119-120.)
- *Expense budget:* Do you agree with the expenses indicated and the amounts allocated?
- *Hospitality:* What refreshments or meals will be provided by the promoter?
- *Ticket prices:* Is it one set price or are there discounted prices or subscriptions; how does this affect your fee or percentage?
- *Opening act and act's performance time:* Will there be an opener; who is it; who decides the act and how much time do they get?
- *Main act's performance time:* How long do you perform? If there are any breaks, how long?

- *Billing:* Are you the only act, and if not, who gets top billing?
- *Advertising and promotion budget:* What will they spend on advertising and what will they do to promote the show? This item often requires adjustment depending on the market and the promoter. Consider it carefully.
- *Technical requirements:* What do you need and what are they prepared to provide?
- *Technical support:* Who are they getting to provide the support? Do you have someone to recommend or do you bring your own?
- *Number of complimentary tickets:* How many tickets can you have for your guests?
- *Merchandise percentage, if any, taken:* Do they take a percentage of your merchandise sales? If so, how much?
- *Deposit amount:* How much will they send to hold the date and when will you receive it? (*Note:* Usually a deposit is included when the contract is signed and returned.)
- *Number of stage or crew hands:* Some halls pay their hands by the hour. This will factor into your expense budget. Your set-up may not require the number designated or you may require more.

Price Is Not The Only Issue

In many booking negotiations, the fee is not always the most important issue and it certainly will not always be the only issue. Many other factors influence the outcome of a negotiation. From the list above, you can see how many other factors need to be considered when booking a date. Any one of these can tip the negotiation scale in one direction or the other. Here is an example where the fee was secondary to the promotional benefits and the need to fill an empty date.

Example:
You are booking a tour and happen to have one date during the week that you have not been able to fill. Your goal is to schedule the date and use the concert to establish a better presence in a particular city. You call a prospective venue and explain your situation. It is not necessary to get your normal fee because you need to fill the date. You reach the promoter and to your surprise, your type of performance is exactly what their audience has been requesting. The promoter has money available but had not gotten around to booking your type of act yet. You explain that you are in the area and that date would work out perfectly for your routing. The promoter sees this as an opportunity to fulfill a presentation goal. While the presenter's budget is below your normal fee, you have already established the necessity for filling the date to use it to build your reputation in the area. On one hand,

HotTip:
The fee is only one aspect of a negotiation. Consider all of the issues that influence the decision to accept a date or agree to an offer.

"... be clear and sensibly flexible when negotiating the details of essential guarantees, housing, food, travel, sound equipment and technical support for the contract."

Judith-Kate Friedman
singer, songwriter

the promoter has the open date and can help develop your audience while providing many of your required criteria. On the other hand, you can help the promoter fill a presentation slot and satisfy a segment of their audience. You both are looking for something different. However, you are able to create a situation that is mutually beneficial, where price did not play a major role.

This may also be one of the times when performing for a percentage of the door and having your hotel accommodations and meals provided helps keep your on-the-road, out-of-pocket expenses down while still performing.

Negotiating Techniques

There are a number of techniques you should practice that are crucial to becoming an effective negotiator. After all, you are negotiating for your own benefit or the benefit of the group you represent. It stands to reason that you would want to use these skills to create the best deal for both parties to a negotiation.

Ask Open-Ended Questions

As discussed in Chapter Four, ask open-ended questions in your quest for information. Create a flow of conversation by asking questions that cannot be answered with yes or no or with numerical answers. Ask questions that require a feeling response or a descriptive response.

Here are some examples:
Do not ask: Do you present concerts?
Possible answers: Yes or No

This kind of question establishes a flow that will continue to provide short, uninteresting answers. This is not engaging for either of you. Avoid it as much as possible.

Ask: What are the varieties of programs you present during the year?
Possible answer from a university presenter: We present a concert series that includes some jazz, some folk, some popular acts and at least one classical event. Each year we have a small coffeehouse series presenting acts that are small enough to perform in our 130-seat venue. During the summer we work with the theater department to present a touring Broadway musical and we have a music festival each August.

This is a great deal of information and, in reality, you might not get such an extensive response. For the sake of this example, you now know that they have multiple venues for presentation, they have a budget that can support theater and music and they work with other departments on campus. You also know that their program incorporates some year-round presentations. This provides you with momentum to

---

"Try to get some guarantee just so you know you have gas money, hotel money, food money, and money to pay the musicians. Go more for the overage points—that's really where you negotiate. Promoters like it, it's fair to them, and they're happy to hand you the money if they sold the house."

Charlie Dahan
in-house agent, A&R,
Shanachie Records

"How you phrase the question determines the answer. . . . In other words make it open-ended. Preface your questions with how, why, why not, what, or who."

William Ury
author,
Getting Past No

"Know how to ask. There is nothing more difficult for some people, nor for others easier."

Baltasar Grecion
Spanish author

continue asking for more specific information based upon this answer.

Do not ask: Did you have a successful season last year?
Possible answer: Yes or No or Somewhat, and you have not nudged them into a conversation.
Ask: How did you feel about last year's season?
Possible answer: In general, it was very successful. We found that the jazz series worked very well as did the summer festival. We had a hard time selling some of the smaller shows but then again, we did not have that much money tied up in them.

Again, this gives you more to work with. You now know that jazz works well and they probably spent a large amount of their budget on that series. You also know that if you were attempting to fit into the coffeehouse series, they do not have much money allocated for it and you may not get your desired fee. Now, you have an opportunity to ask about the type of festival they produced and some of the specific acts they used throughout their season.

Asking the right question is a very effective technique for gathering information. Form your questions carefully—your goal is to involve the presenter and allow them to enjoy telling you as much about their series and themselves as possible.

Ask Questions That Result In Positive Responses

This technique works well in tandem with the previous one. Form your questions so that the response is always positive and often results in a "Yes" answer along with some additional conversation. In this instance you will be gathering information related to how they operate and do business.
Ask: I understand you have three performance venues. That must require a very efficient technical crew?
Possible answer: Yes, in fact we have one staff member coordinating a team of technical people that could range from a crew of two up to 15, depending on the show.

Do Not Be The First One To Mention Price

Earlier, I discussed that it is to your advantage to be as knowledgeable as possible about each venue and promoter before you quote your fee. By having most of the information that you have gathered from Chapter Four, page 48, you will be better prepared to determine your value at this venue with this promoter.

For instance, after you question the promoter, you know they present ten concerts per year similar to your type of performance. They have $10,000 to spend and they divide it evenly among each concert spending $1,000 per show. If you

> "There's a fine line: On the one hand, we'll never get any respect for our music if we don't demand significant fees; on the other hand, what persuades the other person is not what's important to me, but what's important to her or him. Somewhere in the middle is a territory called, "I-don't-work-for-nothing-but-I'll-work-with-you-so-we-both-win."
>
> **Dan Crary**
> guitarist, professor

> "Ask a lot, but take what is offered."
>
> **Russian proverb**

> "Create a 'yes momentum.' Once the person gets used to saying yes to you, it's much easier to conclude a successful negotiation."
>
> **Ted Nicholas**
> publisher, author

> **HotTips:**
> Be definite when quoting fees. Use precise numbers and say for example, "My fee is $1,000." If you state a range of fees such as $1,000 to $1,500, you are suggesting that your fee is negotiable.

had quoted your fee lower than $1,000, before finding out the way they disperse their budget, you would have undervalued your act and perhaps not even gotten the date. On the other hand, they may have also determined they were getting a deal and could have applied the additional money from your fee to another act that asked for more than $1,000.

Some promoters want to get to the bottom line quickly, and before you get the conversation moving they've asked you bluntly, "What's it going to cost me?" Do not be thrown off your agenda. This is a perfect opening for you to begin asking your scripted questions.

1. How many seats are in the hall?
2. What is your ticket pricing policy?
3. Who else have you presented in this category?

These are questions you need to know before answering with your fee. Your counter may also be, bluntly, "What is your budget for this type of act?" Be aware that they are well informed of the going performance fees in their market. They are also knowledgeable about what they can expect from their audience. You may be at a disadvantage in this area. These probing questions educate you and give you a better foundation from which to quote a reasonable fee.

Establishing Value

Most car salespeople and real estate agents know that they need to establish the value of their product with the prospective buyer. You will always find a list of items and their associated costs. Each item adds to the total value of the entire product or package. As an artist, it is important to establish your value within each market so that each promoter considers your act appropriately.

Factors that establish your value include:
- Recording credits
- Venues previously performed
- Your history
- Reviews
- Past box office sales
- Product sales
- Media attention including airplay
- Previous performance fees

These factors impact each new negotiation. Even when entering a new market, presenting these past performance reports allows you to add leverage to the negotiation. If, for instance, you have consistently sold out 900-seat venues and received upwards of $5,000 in the Boston market, a promoter in another city may be inclined to offer a slightly higher

---

"You don't want to talk about money first. You first want to talk about what you are trying to accomplish together. Do you have a team? Can you find common ground? Then talk about money. The person will come to you more honestly, more openly, more willing. Give the information they need to be secure that they are not going to lose money on this show."

Jeanne Rizzo
promoter, manager,
JR Productions

"Find out the capacity of the club and the ticket price. Figure you'll sell half the house and then 75% of that should be the guarantee and after that go for the best bonus points possible."

Charlie Dahan
in-house agent, A&R,
Shanachie Records

guarantee than if you had only played to 150-seat venues. The fact that you have no track record in a new market will have more influence on the promoter's offer the first time. Once you have established a consistent value in some markets, you have an effective negotiating tool.

Put It In Writing
The next effective technique is to put your requirements in writing. If you have determined what you want out of this negotiation and put it in writing, it is a much more convincing argument and appears as though it is less negotiable.

Example:
You have established a set fee for your performance at $2,500. You create a form or letter that states your fee and other specific requirements for your performance. This letter accompanies any promotional material sent to prospective promoters after an initial conversation. It also is used as a handout at conferences. Any promoter receiving this letter will view these requirements as being less negotiable because they were written out rather than verbally quoted. The promoter will not necessarily buy the act at that price, but you now have a starting point from which to negotiate. Some promoters, however, will not attempt to negotiate if the fee is too high. They may feel that their time is better spent working with an artist who seems more approachable from the start.

By presenting your needs in writing, they are perceived to be official. They are negotiable, but the perception is more concrete and unchangeable. This is one reason that, when possible, you should always send your own contract once the negotiations are complete instead of accepting the presenter's contract. By doing so, you have the opportunity to control the manner in which the agreements are stated. If there is something questionable to the other party, it is up to them to notify you that changes are needed. We'll discuss this more in Chapter Seven, Contracts.

Be Able To Walk Away
It is very important to maintain a certain distance from the desired outcome and be able to walk away from any deal if it really does not meet your goals. Once you let the other side know you are committed to getting the gig, or a contract with that particular record company or that licensing deal, you have weakened your negotiating position dramatically. The other party can then assume they have control over the negotiation. It is very difficult to stay detached enough to walk away from something that you may have worked hard at and invested a great deal of time and money in. If you have established your bottom line and determined what your goals are for this

> **HotTip:** A good example of "putting it in writing" is used in many arts council touring directories listing the artist's current performance fee. Once printed in the directory, presenters rarely challenge the quoted price.

"While we should expect promoters to take the risk with us in developing an artist in their market, we should not ask them to assume the total risk. It is far better to play the market for a low, or no guarantee, than to pass through the market. How the show does, all things being equal, will begin to establish the artist's 'value' in that market and then you have a starting point when you return."

Jim Fleming
agent,
Fleming & Associates

"Value in the marketplace ultimately comes down to a popularity contest translated into the number of folks that are willing to plop $8, $10, or $15 to hear you do your thing for an evening. Record airplay can reinforce your sell, as can strong print media attention in a given market, but ultimately it comes down to tickets sold."

Mike Drudge
agent,
Class Act Entertainment

> **HotTips:** 🌶️
> Developing "walk-away power" may strengthen your negotiating position.

negotiation, walking away from a situation that neither meets your goals nor fulfills your bottom line may be the only action you can take. Be prepared to make that call with any deal you are negotiating. You may be surprised at the response when you exercise "walk-away" power.

Benefits Of Walking Away From A Deal:
1. You get out of a deal that was not in your best interest.
2. You exhibit a strength to hold to your convictions.
3. The other party may respect you more and offer to make some concessions to keep the negotiations going. They have also invested their time and do not want to lose any momentum gained to this point.

Examples:
1. Realize that you can walk away from any deal and still feel good about yourself and your objectives. As you begin making your calls to particular markets where you want to play, make sure that you have a number of presenters in that market that are potential performance venues. Do not get yourself set on playing for one specific presenter. If they are unable to meet your requirements or are taking too long to give you a decision, you will not have committed yourself emotionally to the gig. If you are emotionally attached, you may feel forced into accepting their offer even though it is below your standard. But by remaining detached and leaving your options open, you will not place yourself in a weak negotiating position and then accept the unacceptable.

2. When you have predetermined booking criteria you are able to evaluate each aspect of a negotiation and know when a deal will fulfill your goals. While negotiating the points of a contract with a presenter, you reach a part of the discussion that talks about advertising and billing. Since you have been added to the bill late, your name will not appear anywhere on the advertisements, flyers or posters. As you review your goals for performing in this concert, you realize a key factor was promotion. You had wanted to use the promotion to offset the fact that you are taking a lower-than-usual fee. The lack of promotion for your act now makes this date less desirable. You suggest to the presenter that this situation is not meeting your needs and have decided not to perform after all.

The promoter recognizes your predicament and respects your decision to not do the date. However, before letting you go, they propose to do some additional advertising that includes your act, as well as printing a flyer to be inserted in a special edition of the weekend newspaper distributed to households throughout the city. These are items that they had already planned for

"You have to be willing to walk away."
Mary McFaul
manager, Laura Love Band, McFaul Booking & Management

"Identify the features of your particular product and how it can benefit the presenter."
John Peterson
former artist manager, club owner, promoter

and thus were able to accommodate the addition of your act.

You conducted your negotiations in a manner that compelled them to assist you in reaching your objectives. Your determination to walk away from the date emphasized your commitment to your act and your objectives, strengthening your position. The promoter could have let you walk but they had also invested a great deal in the negotiation and felt your addition to the bill would enhance the show.

Never get past the place in the negotiations where walking away from the deal is not an option. There are many factors that need to be considered in each negotiation. The closer you get to resolving all of the details of each negotiation, the more difficult it becomes to walk away from the deal. You will be involved in many deals for which you have worked hard and perhaps even waited a very long time to realize. Prepare yourself carefully before each negotiation to determine your objectives. Hold fast to those objectives and remember to add this very effective technique to your negotiation skills.

NO Is Just The Beginning

The most wonderful sounding words a booking agent can hear are, "Yes, we want your act!" When we cannot get a "Yes" then "No" is a great relief. What does "No" mean? For some, it means that you now know exactly where this promoter stands. They have given you a direct answer and you can move on. You can save yourself any number of additional phone calls attempting to get a "Yes" when all you get is "Maybe, call back in a week." But even though "No" is clear and sounds final, is it really?

"No" is simply a new beginning, an opportunity for a different approach and a new opening. Never accept a "No" and then hang up. You will miss countless opportunities to start with a fresh perspective. They may have said, "No" in relation to the particular circumstance you had been discussing, but future opportunities abound.

It is at this point that you begin to talk about future dates, future tours and any other interesting points that can keep your relationship building. Remind them that you will return next year at this same time and perhaps they would like to lock in a date now. Use "No" as an opening for new opportunities. I have often had some of the most engaging conversations with presenters after they have turned me down. It was at that point that they felt more at ease to share additional information about their presentations. I was able to learn enough new information to create a more advantageous situation for my artists in the future.

"Leave every conversation with something . . . if you get a no, then get information!"

Mark Laurie
agent,
Skyline Management

"Sometimes 'no' is the best decision. Early on, artists tend to take every gig offer regardless of how low it may be on the ladder. Constantly evaluate what you get out of each gig financially, emotionally, exposure-wise, etc."

Cathy Fink
singer, songwriter, producer

"The longer you have a relationship with a promoter, the easier it is to cut to the quick and ask that promoter for an answer. I can smell a 'no' that is surrounded by a 'maybe' about a mile away. You can't teach that, you have to develop it over the years."

Jim Fleming
agent,
Fleming & Associates

Don't Assume You Want The Same Things

Most people enter into a negotiation assuming that both parties want the same thing. Usually, it is assumed that the best price is the issue. You might think your goal is to get the highest fee you can while assuming the presenter is attempting to get the act at the lowest fee possible. This is not necessarily the case. In an earlier example we talked about promotion providing the major impetus for booking the date. In some cases, the fee may be the overriding issue. The presenter may be concerned with a reasonable guarantee, but filling their date with a particular type of performance may also be of importance. Getting that performance may cost them more than another type of act. They are willing to pay the higher fee because it fits their presentation goal. In this case, price is not the main issue.

As you ask your questions, listen carefully to determine the real objectives of the other side. They will often differ from your own. However, you might be in a position to help them realize their objectives without taking away from your own. This is another way to achieve a win-win deal.

Develop Your Listening Skills

Since most booking negotiations occur on the phone, it is paramount to have good listening skills. Since you cannot read body language on the phone, you must rely solely on what you hear. You can determine a great deal from the tone of their voice, their energy, their silences, the words they choose and the manner in which they phrase their sentences.

For example:
- *They might sound distant or distracted.* Their responses are not quite on target with your comments. Do something to reengage them or you have lost the gig right then. Change your approach, change your topic or ask a direct question about their interests. You might also suggest that it sounds like they are very busy and perhaps it would be better to call another time. This kindly gives them an out and allows you to remain professional with another chance to speak with them at a more favorable time. Do not hang up until you have made your next phone appointment.
- *A tired voice could be bored.* Perhaps they just did not get enough sleep or even are bored. You might take the opportunity to jolt them back into the conversation by simply joking and ask them if they were out late seeing some hot new act. That will alert them to the fact that you are on to their obvious lack of interest and get them more focused on you.
- *A long pause may mean they are waiting for more information.* It may also tell you that they like to consider all

"If you want to persuade people, show the immediate relevance and value of what you're saying in terms of meeting their needs and desires . . . Successful collaborative negotiation lies in finding out what the other side really wants and showing them a way to get it, while you get what you want."

Herb Cohen
author, business consultant

the facts and really think about each piece of information. Be considerate of their process, but do not let the silence last too long. Ask if you can help them with any piece of information you have already discussed or if they are missing additional information that would help them come to a decision. If they were indeed simply daydreaming, this will get them back on track.

- *Don't allow yourself to be rushed.* As much as you want to finalize every contract, slow the conversation down if you sense that they are rushing you. The promoter might want to skip over details leaving them for a later time in an effort to get off the phone. Be pleasantly insistent that you would appreciate finalizing all of the questions important to you. If they are rushing because of previous commitments, do not hang up until you have set another time to complete all of the details. If they speed up, you slow down.

- *They are speaking softly.* This is a technique sometimes used to distract you. However, leave some room for the possibility that the person may simply be soft-spoken. When you are straining to hear the conversation, your concentration is thrown off. Ask the person to please speak up, that you are having trouble hearing them. If they are soft-spoken, they will attempt to correct the situation immediately. However, if they are speaking softly to gain an advantage, they may continue to do so. But, they may also speak slightly louder now that you have pointed it out to them.

> **HotTip:** You must rely on your listening skills. Phone negotiations depend exclusively on how you interpret what you hear.

Avoid Making Important Decisions Under Pressure

Booking tour dates requires accomplishing our calls and negotiations to meet a deadline. Whether the deadlines are self-imposed or whether they are determined by outside influences such as presenters, the media, or the record company, it is in your best interest to make educated decisions. You do not need to make a quick decision because of pressure. You can gracefully work the pressure to allow yourself the time to gather the necessary information or consult with appropriate resource people. I have included the following negotiation techniques to assist you when you are feeling pressured to ink the deal quickly.

Time

Savvy negotiators use time to their advantage. Offering deadlines during a negotiation allows you to complete an agreement by a certain time. Deadlines can work for both parties. When appropriate, the artist can offer a 24- to 48-hour deadline, or a week, etc., to get confirmation on a booking or to clarify a point in the contract in order to prevent

> *"I believe there is positive and negative manipulation. One has to develop, in developing negotiating skills, the ability to manipulate the situation so that a decision is arrived at in a timely manner."*
>
> **Jim Fleming**
> agent,
> **Fleming & Associates**

> **HotTip:** 🌶
> Try not to leave a really sticky issue for last. It can ruin the entire negotiation. Surround it with issues which can be resolved quickly and provide momentum to the negotiation.

a negotiation from dragging on unnecessarily. A lengthy negotiation may cause you to miss other important deadlines such as sending timely promotional materials to the media. This deadline time period allows each party to consider the situation carefully and return to the negotiations with well thought out decisions, ready to finalize the deal. If the presenter is unable to come to a decision by the deadline or has not gotten back to you, you may feel free to move on to pursue another date. In these instances, make one more check-in call to remind the presenter that you need a decision. Inform them that you will be looking for other options on that date. Presenters are busy and your date is not the only one on their mind. But, you had set a deadline. You gain a great deal of respect from a presenter by reminding them of the deadline and offering them another opportunity to finalize the date. More often than not, they will be grateful for your call and will confirm the gig. If, on the other hand, they pass on the date, you have left the situation in good standing and now still have time to find a replacement date.

Any time you are negotiating and feel unsure of a particular point or need time to discuss the issue with band-mates or other career team members, offer your negotiating partner a 24-hour break to consider the facts more carefully. You can simply say something like, "Why don't I get back to you tomorrow, I just want to sleep on this." Or, "Let me think about this tonight and I'll get back to you tomorrow." This gives you the time you need to weigh the facts and make a comfortable decision. You may hear something very similar from the other party when they need to review issues concerning them.

"If your opponent sets a deadline and you can meet it, meet it. If you can't, ask for an extension well in advance of the deadline. If you wait until the last minute, you'll have a lot of anxiety wondering if you are going to get the extra time you need."

John Ilich
author,
The Complete Idiot's Guide To Winning Through Negotiating

The Set-Aside

The set-aside technique allows you to take a particularly sticky issue and set it aside for the moment. You can work on some other issues and make some progress in the negotiations. When there has been some time away from the problem issue, go back to it with a renewed freshness. The progress made on other issues provides a momentum towards a successful negotiation. You can now approach the thorny issue from a new direction with enthusiasm for being able to work out many other details. While having set this issue aside, try not to leave it to the final issue especially if it could prove to be a deal-buster. Have some other smaller issues to return to after making this one work.

For example:

You are stuck on the percentage split after expenses. Set that aside and work on show time, ticket price and the opening act. Come back to percentage after some of these other simpler items are determined. These other details will also influence the percentage split and will clarify the issue. After setting this, continue with a few of the final details to complete the contract negotiation. (See page 115, Types Of Deals.)

The Trade

Generally the trade is used when party One has made a proposal that does not quite meet party Two's full expectations. In some instances where you are feeling pressured to conclude the negotiation, you might accept a less-than-favorable offer. Instead, party Two can counter-propose a trade that would equalize the negotiation. The trade can be used very effectively in booking negotiations.

For example:

The presenter offers you a date to play at their festival on a side stage for one set on Sunday. They suggest a fee that is one-third your normal festival fee. You recognize that performing at this festival would still benefit your act even though you are not getting a prime stage slot or your normal fee. In accepting the offer, you suggest that you would be willing to do that if the promoter would be willing to confirm you now for next year's festival, at your normal fee with a main stage slot. This trade gets the promoter what they want this year and gives you a guarantee for both this year and next. Another win-win deal. Use the trade anytime you find yourself being offered a proposal that falls short of your expectations. You can justify accepting the offer when you know you have gained something in trade that meets with your objectives more closely.

These are some of the most common techniques used during booking negotiations.

Negotiating Gambits

A gambit is a term familiar to chess players. According to *Webster's Dictionary*, a gambit is when one player sacrifices a pawn at the opening of a game of chess to gain an advantage. A gambit, in negotiating terms, is any maneuver to gain advantage. The following are specific gambits used by one opponent to gain the advantage over another. These tactics can be used by both parties in any negotiation. The use of these gambits does not necessarily follow the standards of a win-win negotiator. However, they are used all of the time. You should be aware of them and be able to recognize them during your negotiations so you may effectively counter them.

Higher Authority

This is a gambit that we often encounter in booking. A higher authority can be a husband or a wife, the supervisor,

"Be careful that victories do not carry the seeds of future defeats."

Ralph W. Sockman
American religious leader

> **HotTip:**
> "Find the person with the most authority with whom you can do your business.
> Never alienate the person that stands between you and the person with the most authority.
> Don't give the person who doesn't have ultimate authority the position of ultimate authority.
> Never ask them for a *yes* or *no* if you are not prepared for them to say *no*."
>
> Jeanne Rizzo
> promoter, manager
> JR Productions

the manager, the committee, the board of directors, the accountant, the lawyer or the club owner's partner. In some cases, the higher authority being referred to may be imaginary—a person created simply to stall or place the burden of any final decisions upon someone perceived to have greater power.

Any time the person you are negotiating with says, "Well, let me just check with my partner" or "I will have to run this by the board for approval" or "It looks good to me, let me just check with the club owner and see what she thinks," you are dealing with higher authority. In many booking situations, higher authority entities like boards and committees and the club owner's partner may, in fact, be real and may have the final say. In some instances, though, you are talking to the one who makes the booking decisions and they are inventing a higher authority to give themselves a chance to say "No" and not be responsible for it. I have had many situations when I would be waiting for an answer from the presenter who had to run the date by the club owner. Did he really? No. He just said that so he would have an out.

Remove Their Resort To Higher Authority

So, how do you deal with higher authority? Whenever possible, remove the other party's resort to higher authority right up front. You know you are being considered for the date; you know they like your act. As you begin negotiations, ask them, "Is there any reason why we cannot confirm a date today?" They may say, "No, I think I can make a commitment today." They may also say, "Well, I'll have to run it by the board which meets on Tuesday." In this case they might be meeting with the board, and if so, you should ask them to recommend your act to the board. Get them to go to bat for you. If they agree to do that, you can be fairly sure of the date. If they hesitate, you can be pretty sure they do not really want to hire you. Sometimes you might simply say, "Is it really necessary to run this one by the board—can we come to a final decision now?" If you have built a strong relationship with the presenter, you might feel more comfortable challenging them in this manner.

In many booking situations with organizations run by boards, the board has usually sanctioned someone to do the booking for the organization and they have ultimate authority to make decisions. However, when larger fees come into play, that person may have certain restrictions placed on their authority. In those cases, the booking person is instructed to check with the board. Discovering whether or not the person really must check with a higher authority at the start of your negotiations can save you time and move things along more quickly.

Higher authority can be a way of passing the buck, especially when an unfavorable decision needs to be made or

> "Higher authority is typically used near the end of a long and tiring negotiation—when you think all of the critical issues have been resolved and agreement has been reached."
>
> Eric W. Skopec
> and Laree S. Kiely
> co-authors,
> *Everything's Negotiable When You Know How To Play The Game*

a point in the negotiation is introduced that may not be acceptable. Stay alert in your negotiations so you know when higher authority is being used.

Splitting The Difference

Negotiations will often reach a point when splitting the difference may seem to be an obvious next move. When appropriate, the other party may encourage you to split the difference. Always avoid offering to split the difference yourself. Even though you know you are willing to split the difference, it puts you in the weaker position to offer to do so.

> **HotTip:** Ask the person with whom you are negotiating whether they have the authority to finalize the deal.

For example:
Your asking fee is $2,000 and they have offered $1,000. They want to keep the fee as low as possible. They have some additional funds in their budget and are willing to spend them. They know that if they can get you to suggest splitting the difference then there is no chance to split the difference again. Once you offer to split the difference and the presenter accepts, the fee is final at $1,500. You are the one who wants the higher fee. It is not to your advantage to offer to split the difference.

You can counter this move by talking about how much promotion you do for each date, the posters you supply and what your record company is willing to do. Once you have emphasized how much value they are getting for their $2,000, they might offer to split the difference and come up to $1,500. You are now closer to your objective but do not accept right away. Continue the same discussion explaining how much effort and what resources you add to any date including sending out a mailer to your mailing list throughout the area. You were going to do those promotional items on your list anyway, right?

If they really want the act and really do have the money in the budget, they might once again offer to split the difference offering a final fee of $1,750. At this point you have not conceded anything and are getting much closer to your target fee. If they do not offer to split the difference again, you still end up with $500 more in the guarantee. You might have landed there if you had made the offer but this way there was a chance to get even closer to your target.

You may find that these next two gambits are more manipulative. Again, I include them because you may encounter them during a negotiation.

The Flinch

A flinch is a visible or verbal expression of surprise or dismay at some recently revealed piece of information. The flinch is used to catch the other party off guard and suggest that what

> **HotTip:** 🌶
> Be alert when dealing with two people in any negotiation. They often present a united front. If they resort to good-guy, bad-guy, you can be caught unaware and believe one or the other party is working for you. They are not.

they have just said is so outrageous that it is amazing they even had enough nerve to say it. In face-to-face situations, the audible exclamation is usually accompanied by an extreme look on the person's face. On the phone, a likely reaction could be pretending to choke and saying "Excuse me! Did you say what I thought you said?" This exclamation throws the other person into a defensive mode if they are not prepared and do not understand that a tactic is being used to mentally disarm them. Watch out for this one. I have had record executives and presenters use this one very creatively while working on a deal. If you do not catch on quickly, you will find yourself making concessions and dropping your fee or retracting a request. It takes a certain amount of "chutzpah" to use this effectively. The drama is what is so alarming and tips the negotiation in a favorable direction towards the person flinching.

For example:

The presenter asks for your fee and you say, "$2,000." He immediately flinches in an overtly audible fashion. "You are kidding, right? $2,000! I don't have that in my budget." You are shaken by this exclamation and begin to feel that maybe it is too much. But, you know what he is doing. Do not back down. He is just trying to get you to come down in price by using this ploy to get you off your guard.

Good-Guy, Bad-Guy

Most of us have seen this one played out in the movies and on television. Often referred to as good-cop, bad-cop, the bad cop tries to wrangle the information from the suspect by using threats and even physical intimidation. He gets upset that he's not getting anywhere with the suspect and storms out of the room. Then the good cop steps in, offers the suspect a cigarette and speaks calmly while trying to befriend him. Now, if the suspect is not careful, he might begin answering the questions the good cop asks because he thinks this cop is acting on his behalf. In reality, he is not.

Any time you are negotiating with two people, watch out for good-guy, bad-guy. The most effective way of countering this tactic is to simply identify it and embarrass the two for even attempting to use good-guy, bad-guy in their negotiations with you.

For example:

You might be negotiating a club date and the club is owned by two partners. Instead of one of the partners doing all of the negotiations, they each participate. You could find yourself talking with partner One and having a hard time getting him to agree to anything you need. Partner One likewise presents an unreasonable attitude towards your requests. Partner One finally passes you on to the good-guy, partner Two, who is calm and friendly. Two makes you feel like you are the reasonable one and that his partner was rude and impossible. What is happening? All of a sudden, you begin to feel like this guy is on your side and he is going to bat for you against his partner. You might begin trusting partner Two to actually do your negotiating for you with partner One. They may say something like, "I have known him for a long time—I will try to get him to agree to some of these requests." But remember, this guy is not on your side, he is negotiating against you. You can counter this approach by simply attributing everything the bad-guy says to the good-guy as well. View them as one person, both saying the same thing. You can say, "I know what you guys are up to, using good-guy, bad-guy with me. I will just assume that everything he said, you said as well. Now if you want to discuss the issues, I am willing to do that, but you will have to deal with me fairly." Once you let them know you are aware of their tactic and challenge them to discuss the issues at hand, they will begin dealing with you in a reasonable fashion.

"A wise man will make more opportunities than he finds."

Francis Bacon
English statesman

The above negotiating techniques are the ones that you will most likely experience in your booking negotiations. Once you enter into a higher level of negotiations on larger events or more involved contracts, honing your negotiating skills will be to your benefit. Any time you find yourself involved in contract negotiations that are beyond your negotiating expertise, seek outside help to allow your team to make educated, creative decisions. Remember, you are attempting to create win-win deals that benefit both parties. Your career is at stake in these situations. Learn the techniques and skills that will help you deal with the professionals you encounter every day.

Know Your Bottom Line

Before entering into any type of negotiation, you must know your bottom line. What are you willing to accept in the worst-case scenario? What are your highest expectations? Does your bottom line reflect reality? The answers to these questions will differ with each individual project that you attempt. Your bottom line for a local tour will be very different from your bottom line for a national tour. One of the best methods for determining your bottom line is to create a budget for every project you undertake.

"The bottom line can change for a promoter when a club has bar sales as a backup or a concert series has sponsorship support."

Steve Reichman
promoter,
Showman

Creating A Budget

Creating a budget does not require an accounting degree. It requires a little time and research and some attention to your touring habits and necessities. A budget needs to reflect your projected income and projected expenses. The more time

> "Have time lines for budgeting from the first moment you begin to book dates. First create the big picture with all the tentative budgets from anticipated gross income to anticipated gross expenses before you make your first booking call."
>
> Jeanne Rizzo
> promoter, manager,
> JR Productions

you put into researching costs in advance, the more accurate your budget will be. You will find a list of budget items to be included in a tour budget on pages 122-123. Once you have researched the necessary unknown items such as travel costs, hotels, etc., you will be able to determine the average fee required from each performance date. Assuming that you are not yet in the position of commanding a set fee, having this average pre-date fee allows you to make adjustments while you are booking the tour. You will be able to justify accepting a lower fee in one town knowing that you have made up the difference in another, thus maintaining the projected income for the tour budget.

Another factor to keep in mind is what the market will bear from one city to another and your position in that market. We all must invest in developing our businesses. A tour into an unknown market is an investment in your business. It makes sense, then, that a certain portion of your tour budget in a new marketplace include some investment dollars. View your budget with an open mind towards building your reputation. Deciding not to tour in a new area because the numbers are in the red is similar to a business deciding not to introduce a new product because the advertising costs will outweigh the returns during the first year. You must invest in order to grow. Having the tour budget delineate your exact expenses and projected income can help to seek investors to sponsor part of the tour. Without the budget, there is nothing concrete to judge profit at the end of the tour or growth from one tour to the next.

Budgets Help Define Negotiating Parameters

As you embark on various projects during your career, creating a budget for each will help you define your negotiating parameters. If your tour budget specifies a fee range of $1,000 to $3,000 per date, accepting a series of dates that fall under the $1,000 fee will affect the tour dramatically. The budget helps you meet your financial obligations. Therefore, you would be justified to either turn down multiple offers that fall short of meeting your bottom line or to make necessary adjustments in your projected budget. Adjusting the budget would be a reasonable response to research that establishes your market value at a lower rate than the original budget. If you are unknown to a majority of the presenters, your market value will be lower than if you had a larger box-office appeal. Knowing exactly what it will take to make the budget work will help you negotiate your best possible fee. This way if you are not getting the optimum, you are, however, "making budget." An accurate budget gives you a better handle on your negotiating range.

> "Remember that if a promoter or club is offering you a guarantee of $100 while charging $8 at the door, they aren't planning to have more than 15 people attend."
>
> Cathy Fink
> singer, songwriter, producer

Assess The Bottom Line To Meet Your Needs

Knowing your bottom line helps to determine which offers are most likely to meet your budgetary needs. If offers are falling within a similar range, use that in negotiating with presenters who fall slightly short of that. Apply some pressure to nudge the fee up and ask them to at least meet the minimum to help make the tour worthwhile. If they are only slightly off, they may feel that it is the least they can do. They will naturally be working to maintain their budget as well.

As you begin negotiating larger deals, such as recording contracts, knowing your bottom line when you begin negotiating places you in a more strategic position. Offers falling far short of the bottom line can be considered after the more reasonable ones. Once the budget is figured down to the bare minimum, any offer exceeding that will at least prove to be financially feasible. Consideration of all of the other contract details may favorably set one deal apart from another, making your negotiating decisions easier.

Include Peripheral Factors

The bottom line is not only about price. It can also include peripheral items such as advertising, promotion, hospitality, royalty percentages, merchandise percentages, etc. Including many of these peripheral factors into your bottom line gives you a broad base from which to negotiate. For instance, let us use the aforementioned example where the range of fees was $1,000 to $3,000. Include in your bottom line a percentage of dates that need to take place in certain markets where promotion is a key factor. Some of the lower offers may meet the promotional requirements. If so, those dates are now back in the game plan. Determining your bottom line introduces flexibility. It gives you the ability to compare a variety of factors that contribute to making the best deals.

The Tour Budget form on page 122 includes some items that, on one hand, you may never use or, on the other hand, may eventually be useful. You may also want to supplement the budget by including items that are specific to your act.

Types Of Deals

Now that you have a preliminary understanding of the techniques required to become a savvy negotiator, let us look at some of the varieties of deals you can put together.

Straight Percentage

This is often encountered in the early stages of a performing career. Many club dates and venues that are unfamiliar with your act may offer you a straight percentage. The percentages will vary ranging from 100% of the door on down. If you have a following in an area and will draw well at this venue, sometimes an act can do very well with a straight percentage

> *"We find that more and more of our business is based on evaluating each performance by the ticket price, the seating capacity and resulting gross potential. By looking over the expenses carefully, two parties can arrive at a fee for an artist which appears to be fair for that particular venue with that set of expenses. Deciding whether that fee and overage will work within your fee range then becomes an easier and more concrete set of numbers to evaluate."*
>
> **Jeff Laramie**
> president,
> SRO Artists, Inc.

> *"There are very few things that are not negotiable. Do some soul searching and figure out what your bottom line is and do not cross it. Especially if you've had an independent contract and you know how to run your business. You can always go back to running it yourself."*
>
> **Mary McFaul**
> manager, Laura Love Band,
> McFaul Booking & Management

deal. The presenter has very little to lose on a straight percentage deal and, in fact, may expend very little energy in promoting the date. Since the incentive to draw an audience directly benefits the artist, the responsibility for the bulk of the promotion rests with the artist. If you have determined that your own promotional efforts can bring in a crowd, have worked through your budget and have considered all of the peripheral benefits of playing under these circumstances, the straight percentage deal may work for you.

> **HotTip:** Always have a calculator by the phone when making booking calls. When you see the numbers, you can make educated decisions.

Straight Guarantee

In this situation, you and the promoter agree to a fixed fee for the date. Accepting a deal with a straight guarantee, especially when an act can begin commanding larger fees, can often be very rewarding. While building your career, the guarantees will be low. In new venues where your audience is undeveloped, a straight guarantee assures you of some income. Many situations exist where the venue is fairly confident of selling the show, yet, the seating capacity and ticket price do not leave enough income above the guarantee to warrant an additional percentage split.

For example:

Venue capacity (number of seats)		500
Ticket Price	x	$10
Total Gross Potential		$5000
Artist Guarantee		– $3500
Overage (Promoter's Income)		$1500

Once you begin drawing crowds, it is important to weigh all of the factors that make up the financial picture. In Chapter Seven, Contracts, you will be introduced to the Contract/Budget Settlement Form. By using this form during all of your negotiations, you will be able to view the entire financial picture of each performance date and make a very precise judgment of whether or not striking a deal for a straight guarantee is an advantage. If you are at a point where the guarantees begin to grow, new deal options will emerge when you consider the seating capacity, ticket price and all of the expenses within the overall picture. You may now review how some of the guarantee, plus or versus a percentage deal, may work to everybody's advantage.

Guarantee Plus Percentage

Here a guarantee is determined after carefully considering seating capacity, expenses, the act's draw potential, etc. Once all the budget items have been considered, the gross potential income has been calculated and the amount of income remaining after all expenses is determined, a percentage of that overage can be decided upon. The presenter and the artist will split the net income on a percentage basis. (See page 120 for further definitions of split point percentage deals.) The percentage splits can be anything from 50/50, 60/40, 70/30, 80/20 and many shades in between with the larger percentage usually going to the artist. The percentage will then be added to the guarantee for the total artist's fee.

This type of deal often represents a true win-win scenario. By building in the percentages, everyone has an opportunity to make more money if everyone does their job and the show sells well. The risk of presenting the date is shared more equally in this scenario. Look at the big picture for each deal you negotiate to determine when a guarantee plus a percentage can be advantageous.

Guarantee Versus Percentage

In this case, a guarantee is determined and then a percentage is fixed. The artist receives whichever amount is greater. For instance, the guarantee may be $500 versus 75%. If the total income from tickets is $600, then the artist gets the $500 because 75% of $600 is only $450. If the total income from tickets sales is $1,500, then the artist would get $1,165, which is greater than the guarantee. These types of deals are often encountered when working with smaller organizations, many of whom have low expenses or have not incorporated a line-item budget into their procedures.

Guarantee Plus Bonus

Here a guarantee is set. When a specific number of seats have been sold, a set bonus amount will be added to the fee. If the capacity of the venue is large enough, multiple bonuses can be earned as each seating increment is reached. For example, the guarantee may be $1,500 with a seating capacity of 350. Bonuses can be set to any reasonable dollar amount agreed to by both parties. They can be awarded for any predetermined sales figure reached. For example, once 200 seats are sold, the act receives their first bonus of an additional $250. At 250 seats sold another bonus of $250 is awarded. If 300 seats are sold, there will be an additional bonus of $250. At sell-out, 350 seats, a further bonus of $250 is added to the artist's fee. Four bonuses of $250 equals $1,000 which is then added to the guarantee of $1,500 giving the artist a total fee of $2,500.

Many venues prefer this type of deal over a guarantee versus percentage because of its simplicity. Often, venues that prefer this type of deal are those that are unable to collect all of the ticket income from outside ticket venues the night of the performance. There are many venues that are simply unable to calculate all of their expenses on the night of the show and the guarantee plus a bonus allows the deal to be settled to everyone's satisfaction. The Barns at Wolf Trap in Vienna, Virginia and the Luther Burbank Center in Santa Rosa, California often use this scenario. This type of deal leaves both parties lots of options for creative negotiating.

> "If I'm inclined to book someone, but I'm not sure about their draw, I propose a reverse guarantee. The artist guarantees the club a certain amount of business versus what we would normally pay. If they can deliver the show, they get paid as if it were a standard booking. If they are wrong, the club doesn't suffer and the artist makes up the difference between the actual admissions and whatever the minimum guarantee agreed upon. It is a good reality check for people who I think should spend some money on the act."
>
> Tim Mason
> booking manager,
> Club Passim

Four Sample Deal Scenarios

Here are four scenarios demonstrating each of the deals previously described. Each deal uses the same information from the Givens box. Each of the four scenarios is calculated based on a sold out show. The summary on page 120 analyzes each scenario and shows which deal offers the artist and the promoter their best net fee when the show sells out, sells 400 seats, sells 300 seats or sells 200 seats.

Givens

Number of Seats	S	550
Ticket Price	T	$ 20.00
Gross Potential	(SxT)	$11,000
Artist Percentage	A	65%
Artist Guarantee	G	$ 2,000
Show Expenses	E	$ 2,500
Promoter's Fee	F	15%
Promoter's Percentage	P	35%

Scenario 1: Straight Guarantee

Deal is written: Artist's Guarantee is $2,000.

Artist's Guarantee	(G)	$ 2,000
Gross Potential	(SxT)	$ 11,000
Less Artist's Guarantee	(G)	$ 2,000
Less Expenses	(E)	$ 2,500
Total Promoter's Net	=	$ 6,500

Scenario 2: Guarantee Plus Percentage (of Net)

Deal is written: $2,000 Guarantee plus 65% of Net (after Expenses)

Artist's Guarantee		(G)	$ 2,000
Plus Expenses		(E) +	$ 2,500
Sub Total of Expenses		(G+E) =	$ 4,500
Promoter's Fee		(F)	15%
To Promoter	(15% x $4,500)	+	$ 675
Total Expenses	($675+$4,500)	=	$ 5,175
Gross Potential		(SxT)	$11,000
Less Total Expenses		-	$ 5,175
Equals Overage to Split		=	$ 5,825
Artist's Percentage (65%)		(A)	65%
Equals Artist's Percentage		=	$ 3,786
Artist's Net	($3,786 + G)	=	$ 5,786
Promoter's Percentage (35%)		(P) =	$ 2,039
Promoter Net	($2,039 +$675)	=	$ 2,714

Scenario 3: Guarantee Versus A Percentage (of Net)

Deal is written:
$2,000 Guarantee versus (or) 65% of Net
(If 65% is greater than the guarantee, the Artist gets the 65%, otherwise the Artist gets the $2,000 guarantee.)

Artist's Guarantee		(G)	$ 2,000
Plus Expenses		(E) +	$ 2,500
Sub Total of Expenses		(G+E) =	$ 4,500
Gross Potential		(SxT)	$11,000
Less Total Expenses		-	$ 4,500
Total Net Income		=	$ 6,500
Artist's Percentage (65%)		(A)	65%
Equals Artist's Net		=	$ 4,225
Promoter's Percentage (35% x $6,500)			$ 2,275
Plus Artist's Guarantee		(G) +	$ 2,000

(If the Artist receives the percentage, the guarantee is added back to the promoter's revenue.)

Promoter's Net	=	$ 4,275
Artist's Total Net	=	$ 4,225

Scenario 4: Guarantee Plus Bonus

Deal is written: $2,000 Guarantee plus $1,000 bonus at 400 seats sold and another $1,000 bonus at 500 seats sold.

Artist's Guarantee		(G)	$ 2,000
At 400 seats plus		+	$ 1,000
At 500 seats plus		+	$ 1,000
Total Bonus		=	$ 2,000
Total Artist's Net (Total Bonus +G)			$ 4,000
Gross Potential		(SxT)	$11,000
Less Artist's Net		-	$ 4,000
Less Expenses		(E) -	$ 2,500
Total Promoter's Net		=	$ 4,500

BREAK EVEN EQUALS: 225 SEATS

Artist's Guarantee	(G)	$ 2,000
Plus Expenses	(E)	$ 2,500
Total		$ 4,500
Divided by Ticket Price	(T)	$ 20

> # Summary
>
> Break even in all scenarios is 225 seats. To calculate break even, add Artist's Guarantee (G) + Expenses (E) and divide the total by the Ticket Price (T).
>
> | At 550 Seats Sold | Artist | Promoter | |
> |---|---|---|---|
> | Scenario 1 | $2,000 | $6,500 | If show sells out, then Scenario 2 |
> | Scenario 2 | ✔ $5,786 | $2,714 | is best for Artist but, remember |
> | Scenario 3 | $4,225 | $4,275 | that sellouts are far from certain. |
> | Scenario 4 | $4,000 | $4,500 | |
>
> | At 400 Seats Sold | | | |
> |---|---|---|---|
> | Scenario 1 | $2,000 | $3,500 | If show sells about three-quarters |
> | Scenario 2 | ✔ $3,836 | $1,664 | (75%) then Scenario 2 is best for |
> | Scenario 3 | $2,275 | $3,225 | Artist. |
> | Scenario 4 | $3,000 | $2,500 | |
>
> | At 300 Seats Sold | | | |
> |---|---|---|---|
> | Scenario 1 | $2,000 | $1,500 | If show sells about half (50%) |
> | Scenario 2 | ✔ $2,536 | $ 964 | then Scenario 2 is best for Artist. |
> | Scenario 3 | $2,000 | $1,500 | |
> | Scenario 4 | $2,000 | $1,500 | |
>
> | At 200 Seats Sold | | | |
> |---|---|---|---|
> | Scenario 1 | ✔ $2,000 | $ (500) | If show sells about one third |
> | Scenario 2 | ✔ $2,000 | $ (500) | (33%) then all Scenarios will be |
> | Scenario 3 | ✔ $2,000 | $ (500) | the same for Artist. |
> | Scenario 4 | ✔ $2,000 | $ (500) | |
>
> Understand the terminology used to negotiate booking deals. Use your budget form each time you negotiate a contract and calculate all of the possible options with the hard numbers in front of you. Work with each promoter to negotiate deals that are creative, easy to administer and mutually beneficial.

Basic Budget Terminology

Jeff Laramie, President of SRO Artists, Inc. provides the following information on basic "split point" terminology in an article which originally appeared in *Inside Arts*. A portion of the article is included here with Jeff's permission.

- ❖ *Gross Potential or Gross Revenues or GP:* The total amount of money that can be generated if all tickets are sold.
- ❖ *Net Potential or Net Revenues:* The total amount of money generated by ticket sales, less taxes, restoration fees or discount programs applied to the face value of the ticket price.
- ❖ *Expenses:* The total expenses attributed to the specific performance; can include rent, advertising, stage hands, tickets, catering, ushers, box office, insurance, ticket commissions, production (sound and lights), ASCAP/BMI, etc. (See Contract Budget/Settlement Form, Chapter Seven, page 152.) Figure expenses first, then add in the artist fee for total expenses. Taxes and restoration fees are not an expense. Some promoters amortize advertising for a season of events and allocate a set amount per performance.

- *Break Point:* (Break-even point) The total expenses plus artist fee. Divide this amount by the average ticket price to determine the number of tickets that need to be sold to break even.
- *Promoter Profit or Promoter Fee:* A percentage of the expenses which is paid to the presenter/sponsor/promoter as a return on their investment. Industry standard is 15% of expenses, but can be any amount agreed to by both parties. Multiply your total expenses (including artist fee) by the promoter profit margin (i.e., 15%), then add that amount to the expenses to derive the *split point*.
- *Split Point:* The total expenses plus artist fee, plus presenter/promoter profit margin. The split point will vary with actual expenses at time of settlement. Divide this amount by the average ticket price to determine the number of tickets that need to be sold to break even and generate your required profit margin.
- *Hard Split Point:* This is a fixed expense amount agreed to by both parties. It does not take into account any changes, up or down, in presenter *expenses*. This is used when it is impossible, or undesirable, to calculate the expenses of one event because it is part of a series of events or other related circumstances.
- *Overage:* The amount of money or profit left after you subtract the *split point* amount from the *net potential*. (At settlement, this will be *net revenues* less actual *expenses* plus presenter/promoter profit.)
- *Percentage Amount:* The ratio that the overage will be split. The artist portion appears first, i.e., 70-30 over the *split point* would be 70% of the *overage* to the artist, and 30% of the *overage* to the promoter.

The Offer

Once the negotiation is complete to the point of having most of the details worked out, it is time for an official offer to be made. You can tell the promoter that you will fax them an Offer Sheet that you have filled out, and ask them to read it over, sign it and return it by fax. You can also have these forms in an email file, but they will need to be faxed back with the promoter's signature. I suggest using your own offer sheet, making sure all the details are those you want included. A blank Offer Sheet is included on page 162.

Conclusion

Now that we have discussed many of the techniques, gambits, tour budgeting and types of deals that will make your negotiations more successful, use these techniques on your next booking calls. Listen carefully while speaking with each promoter to determine whether they are using any of these techniques with you. Knowledge is power and your awareness of these techniques will make you a more savvy negotiator. You will sharpen your skills with each new call and your ability to create win-win deals will become easier with every booking.

Summary

- We are negotiating all of the time.
- Knowledge of the art of negotiation can help you in your business and personal life.
- Enhancing your negotiating skills will make your life's negotiations go more smoothly and your deals more profitable.
- Practice win-win negotiations any time you negotiate.
- Negotiation techniques are important skills to possess as you strive for success in all of your deals.
- Although you may not use them, negotiating gambits may be being used against you. It is important for you to recognize them.
- Knowing your bottom line will help you make better negotiating decisions.
- Create budgets for all of your projects to define your bottom line.

Tour Budget

Personnel

_____Leader Fee

_____Band Member Salaries

_____Road Manager

_____Crew

_____Per Diems

Travel

_____Rental Vehicle

_____Rental Trucks

_____Tour Bus and Expenses

_____Owned Vehicle (monthly loan payments, if any)

_____Air Fare

_____Parking Expenses

_____Gas and Tolls

_____Repairs/Maintenance (project expenses prior to and during a tour)

_____Hotel

Contracted Personnel

_____Agent Fees

_____Management Fees

_____Publicist Fees

_____Office Help

Technical

_____Equipment Rentals

_____Sound System

_____Lights Package

_____Stage Props, Set and Decorations

Insurance

_____Liability Insurance

_____Business Insurance

_____Instrument and Equipment Insurance

_____Auto Insurance

Phone

_____Base Monthly Fee

_____Monthly Minimum Contract

_____Special Equipment

_____Special Features

Advertising and Promotion

_____Co-op Ads with Record Company

_____Tour Advertising

_____Release Ads

Shipping

_____Tour Mailing

_____Contracts and Promotional Materials

Printing

_____Mailer

_____Additional Promotional Material

_____**Total Anticipated Tour Expenses**

Income

_____Performance Guarantees

_____Estimated Average Percentages of Split

_____Merchandising

_____Sponsorships

_____Grants

_____**Total Anticipated Tour Income**

_____**Anticipated Fee Range Per Date (The Bottom Line)**

Miscellaneous

_____

_____

_____

Resources

Books:

Everything's Negotiable. . . . When You Know How To Play The Game
Eric Wm. Skopec and Laree S. Kiely
AMACOM a division of American Management Association
ISBN: 0814451616

Getting Past No
William Ury
Bantam Books/ Bantam Doubleday Dell Publishing Group, Inc.
ISBN: 0553072749

Getting To Yes
Roger Fisher and William Ury
Houghton Mifflin Company
ISBN: 0395317576

Give And Take: The Complete Guide To Negotiating Strategies And Tactics
Chester L. Karrass
Harper Business
ISBN: 0887307434

Negotiating For Dummies
Michael C. Donaldson, Mimi Donaldson
IDG Books Worldwide
Web: http://www.dummies.com
ISBN: 1568848676

Negotiate To Close: How To Make More Successful Deals
Gary Karrass
Simon & Schuster
ISBN: 067128860

Power Talking: 50 Ways To Say What You Mean And Get What You Want
George R. Waltham
G.P. Putnam
ISBN: 0399136061

Power Negotiating: Strategies For Success
Mike R. Stark
Tri Mark Publications
ISBN: 0964945304

Smart Negotiating: How To Make Good Deals In The Real World
James C. Freund
Fireside
ISBN: 0671869213

The Complete Idiot's Guide To Winning Through Negotiation
John Ilich and Robert K. Heady
MacMillan General Reference
ISBN: 0028610377

The Negotiating Game
Chester L. Karrass
Harper Collins Publishers
ISBN: 0887305687

25 Role Plays For Negotiation Skills
Sandy Aherman and Ira G. Asherman
Human Resources Development Publishers
ISBN: 0874259975

Win-Win Negotiating
Fred Edmund Jandt w/ Paul Gillette
John Wiley & Sons, Inc.
ISBN: 471882070

You Can Negotiate Anything
Herb Cohen
Bantam Books
ISBN: 0553281097

Cassettes:

The Secrets of Power Negotiating (audio cassettes)
Roger Dawson
Nightingale Conant Corporation
Phone: 1-800-323-5552
Call for a catalog.

CHAPTER SEVEN
Contracts

"A contract is a verbal agreement between two parties. Period. The rest is just paperwork. In a business where we depend on verbal communication, we must have confidence in a person's word. The contract, as follow-up, spells out in black and white what you both agree to. At that level, it is important as an historical physical document representing your agreement."

Jim Fleming
Fleming & Associates

How often have you thought, "If I only had a contract, this wouldn't be happening to me now?" In some instances, you may have worked for presenters who were also your friends and felt it would be insulting to your friendship to issue a contract. Who would guess that that very same friend would not make enough money to cover your guarantee and would impose upon your friendship to suggest that you forego part of your fee!

Write It Down For Clarity

This is a very familiar scenario. Most of these situations could be avoided if there was a contract of some form that finalized the agreement. As we discussed in Chapter Three, as soon as you accept money in exchange for a performance, you are conducting business. Businesses develop operating procedures which allow them to interact efficiently. The procedures you use demonstrate your professionalism to those

"The actual terms of a contract are not as important as the character, abilities and motivation of the party that you're contracting with."

Bill Straw
president, Gift Horse Records, Blix Street Records

> "A written contract cannot anticipate all the circumstances which could arise in real life performance situations. . . . Common sense dictates that we work towards clear and unambiguous communication, and full understanding, in advance, of what everyone expects from the event."
>
> **Rick August, Karen Haggman, Cathy Miller, Susan Casey**
> steering committee, Canadian Caucus

> "Although the music industry is held together largely by relationships and a certain degree of trust, no artist or promoter should ever underestimate the importance of the contract. Should a disagreement arise, the relationship and trust will disappear quickly and all that will be left is a legal document that you've signed. Write them and read them carefully."
>
> **David Lloyd**
> former program events, Luther Burbank Center

with whom you do business. Whether you deal with friends or with strangers, it is to your advantage to create a standard procedure of acknowledging the agreements you make. This demonstrates your respect for your work and demands that those doing business with you take you seriously.

A contract can be a simple written form that clearly expresses the details of an agreement. It can be referred to when questions about specific details arise. In its most formal sense, a contract is a legally binding document that commits the parties that have signed it to follow through with each of the statements contained within the document. In its most useful sense, a contract is a document that explains the mutual obligations of the parties who have signed it and acts as a clear reminder of what everyone has promised to do. When a verbal agreement is left verbal, the details may become confused when recounted or may even be forgotten.

What Every Contract Should Include

1. The final details of the negotiation which have been agreed to by both parties.
2. What will constitute a breach of the agreement.
3. The consequences that will be imposed in the event of a breach, i.e., the details are not followed or the venue closes and the gig is cancelled at the last minute. What action will be taken to resolve a conflict?

Each contract should spell out these three items. The formality with which you delineate these is of less concern than the fact that you have included them. Your forms can be simple and short or laden with clauses filled with legal jargon and long. The true test of a successfully executed contract is whether an arbitrator, a judge or a jury will enforce it if it is contested by one of the parties. The true test of the honest relationship between the signatories remains in the resolve of the parties to honor the contract to each party's fullest capability. Should a problem arise, the document must then withstand the scrutiny of those who will interpret it to its legal result.

Therefore, when creating a contract for your use to finalize performance agreements, consult with a lawyer in the state from which you operate your business. It is worth the consultation fee to have a lawyer check your contract for clarity, legal meaning and the inclusion of any required language deemed necessary by the legal system in your state.

I have consulted with lawyers to create my original contracts and riders and any time significant changes need to be made. My resources for standard contract forms used within the industry are found in the resource section of this chapter. Over the course of the two decades I have issued performance contracts, I added to the standard forms once I discovered items that did not address all of my clients' concerns. You will find a similar discomfort with any standard form you use as the basis for your own contract. And remember, *I am not a lawyer and cannot provide you with legal advice.* Seek a lawyer for that purpose. However, the forms, clauses, and information within this chapter have been well researched and are provided as a starting point from which you can create a contract form suitable for your needs.

This chapter will discuss a variety of written forms that can be used to document your agreements. I have provided sample, blank forms at the end of this chapter for your own use.

Spell Out The Details

Many performing situations may not require lengthy, formal contracts. However, it is to your advantage to have agreements which explain all of your requirements and define every detail discussed with the presenter. In some instances, members of certain unions may find it advantageous to use their own union's contract form, while in other cases a letter of confirmation may be all that is required. No matter what situation you find yourself in, issue a contract that spells out the agreement to your satisfaction.

Send Your Own Contract

In Chapter Six I mentioned the importance of sending your own contract to every presenter. By creating an individualized contract, you can include language that takes all of your needs into consideration. Your contract will outline all the requirements you need to present your best performance, while being clearly worded to your advantage. As I mentioned during our discussion of negotiating techniques, items which are written, especially in a contract form, seem more official and are less likely to be questioned. On the other hand, do not let the official nature of the contracts you receive keep you from questioning anything within them. When the presenter chooses to question any of the language in your contract, they will have to do so in writing. The responsibility for challenging the wording rests with the recipient of a contract. But as was discussed in Chapter Six, anything in a contract is negotiable. Therefore, any of the language you have used in your contract might also be questioned by a presenter.

Create Simple Documents

In most cases, it is best to create a simple document that clearly states the terms of the agreement. Any additional clauses relating to your specific requirements should use uncluttered language that simply states the facts. There are times you will encounter language included in a document that is purposely filled with clauses which will tax your

"If there is no problem, then there should be no problem writing it down."

Cash Edwards
former agent, owner,
Under The Hat Productions

"In the 'battle of the forms,' the person who sends out the contract which they prepared (and sends it first) usually takes the high ground. Surprisingly often, the other party will just sign it without even making changes."

Charles Driebe, Jr.
entertainment attorney,
manager, Blind Boys of
Alabama

> *"Language exists in contracts so that parties to them know their rights, duties, liabilities and entitlements. The document itself, rather than collateral remembrances of who said what, will control when disputes arise. Non-legal English is often imprecise, no matter how careful the drafting. Legal English has technical meaning, i.e., there are words of art which the legal system understands. If the occasion requires, proper drafting of a performance contract, management or agency agreement can, in the end, save rather than cost you money."*
>
> Andrew Braunfeld
> attorney, partner,
> Masterson, Braunfeld,
> Maguire & Brown

knowledge of English. This verbage is not deliberately written to confuse you, but in some cases is expressly included to test you and to challenge your control over the contract negotiations. In most cases, however, the use of legalese in a contract is for clarity of interpretation by attorneys, leaving no doubt about what is meant by the statement within the context of the law. If you miss some important detail because it was concealed by the language, it is not the responsibility of the party issuing the contract to alert you. Many recording contracts will include such language. The complexity and confusing language of recording contracts perfectly illustrate the need for your lawyer to review the contracts before you sign.

When you create your own contract, you may decide to hire a lawyer to help you write the final version. I recommend consulting an entertainment lawyer in your state to make sure you have included any language required by the state in which your business resides. The laws governing contracts made in California differ from the laws governing contracts made in New York. Consult resources that include standard contract forms. Two excellent resources are *The Musician's Business & Legal Guide* and *This Business of Music*. Both are listed in the resource section of this chapter.

When They Issue The Contract

If you have been issued a contract by a presenter, it is up to you to make sure the wording of their contract does not adversely obligate you. It becomes your responsibility to challenge any questionable item. Most clubs and many promoters will be pleased to accept your contract. When you are contracting with larger presenters such as festivals, colleges and universities, state and local government agencies, and many major performing arts centers, they will insist on issuing their own contracts. In these cases, you can attach a copy of your contract and any contract riders to theirs making it part of the entire agreement. Your contract may be disregarded in some instances and in other instances, the intent of your contract may be incorporated into theirs. Once when I was booking a date with Lincoln Center, I issued my contract and they issued their contract. When I asked that mine be attached to theirs, they rewrote their contract to incorporate my clauses in their own language and reissued the newly written, completed document. It was not the easiest route to take, but their legal department insisted. It worked out well for us both.

> *"Never take anything for granted."*
>
> Benjamin Disraeli
> 19th-century British prime minister

Read All Contracts Carefully

Anytime you are issued a contract, READ IT CAREFULLY! Their standard written document may be written for a particular type of performance, for a specific number of days, possibly with unreasonable insurance clauses or requirements. Make sure that all of the clauses beyond those describing your actual agreement meet with the expectations you have of this agreement. DO NOT SIGN until everything has been scrutinized and you are satisfied with what you find or have negotiated and changed.

How To Deal With Questionable Items On A Contract

Remember, everything's negotiable! Do not assume that the negotiations are over because the contract has been issued; in many cases the negotiations have just begun. Recording contracts are often negotiated once a copy of a standard contract has been sent by a label for your review. After negotiating your way through a record label's standard contract, the label will issue a draft of the agreement that you have created during your negotiations.

As you read through each contract, make notes on a separate piece of paper that you keep with the contract. Once you have found all of the questionable items on a contract, phone the presenter and discuss each item. Often, the presenter may have a very good reason for including a specific clause. Many times that particular clause will not pertain to your act. By voicing your objections, the presenter may reconsider the clause and decide it can be deleted. The more contracts you read, the more skilled you will become at negotiating necessary changes. If you find any incorrect details, even misspelled words or names, it is your responsibility to bring it to the presenter's attention and make any corrections. A miscommunication is often discovered while going over the contract carefully. It is preferable to discover mistakes at this stage, rather than when you show up to perform on the wrong night.

Changing The Contract

As you go through the contract with the promoter, you can make any agreed-upon changes directly on the contract in blue or black ink. If a word needs to be changed, cross out the old word once and write the new language above it. Place your initials and the date of the change next to each changed or deleted item. Once all of the agreed changes have been made, sign and date the contracts, make photo copies for yourself, and mail them back. If you are attaching a copy of your contract or riders send them back with the changed contract issued by the presenter. If the presenter has any changes to make to your contract, they will have to repeat this procedure. When you receive your copies of the completely signed and modified contracts, read them over once more. If something was missed, call about it immediately. Do not wait until the day before the show to bring up a contract item that could have been discussed weeks earlier.

"While the contract itself may (hopefully) not be needed in the strict legal sense and won't see the light of a courtroom, we have 'em, use 'em, and recommend 'em. . . . It just helps me to ask all the appropriate questions and clear up any misconceptions we may have about exactly what the agreement is!"

Lou Berryman
singer, songwriter

Keep Track Of Your Contracts

Dealing with your contracts in a timely manner will keep the paperwork from building up and overwhelming you. Be vigilant about your contracts. I have often received contracts back from a presenter who has not even read them, nor even bothered signing them in all of the necessary places. Check your contracts for signatures and dates. Send them back if they are not signed. A missing signature now may mean that all the details outlined within the contract will not be attended to later.

Make sure that all your contracts are returned by the date specified. When a contract is one day past due, call the presenter and remind them of the missed deadline. Most often, it is a simple matter of forgetfulness or of the contract getting buried among piles of other papers; sometimes it is deliberate neglect in order to avoid presenting the date. This can occur when a presenter uses your own contract due date clause against you such as: *This contract will be null and void if not signed and returned with deposit by _____ (specified date).* Your purpose for inserting the clause is to get the presenter to return the contract in a timely manner. If you have not received the contract on time, you have the option of pursuing another performance date after checking with the presenter as to the reason for the contract's tardiness. However, a presenter deliberately trying to get out of the date by not returning the contract would be legally within their rights since your own clause provided them an out. One way to avoid this scenario from occurring would be to use the phrase: *This contract must be signed and returned with deposit by _____ (specified date) or the Artist may cancel this date and seek other performance opportunities.* This clause places the opportunity for cancellation solely on the Artist. By keeping abreast of each contract's due date, you can troubleshoot any problems that arise.

Methods Of Tracking Contracts

If you are using a database or contact manager, it is easy to utilize the "recall date" field to insert a date 10 to 14 days from the date the contract was sent. Set an alarm or a flag to remind you when this contract is due back. If it has been returned prior to the return date, cancel the reminder alarm.

Create a chart that can include all of your contract and promotional mailings as well. The chart provides you with a cross-check system. Should a presenter phone asking for promotional material that had been sent with the contract, there is a record of the date sent and the contents of the package. A handy chart that you can use in your office is on page 182. Add or delete any items to customize your chart.

> *"Return contracts in a timely manner. Pay attention to your business. Don't waste the presenter's time and money making them call you to sign and return contracts or send promo materials."*
>
> Andy Spence
> director,
> Old Songs Festival

Types Of Contract Agreements

A variety of contract agreements may be suitable for use in your office. Creating some standard forms will work nicely in most cases. If you are working on a computer or word processor, creating a series of standard forms that you can access and customize for each presenter is an efficient and quick method of preparing contracts. Contact manager users or database aficionados can create a word-processing document that merges data from the contract database information form with the word-processed contract document. Your final printed version will have all of the contract language along with the details for each specific date. I have created sample copies of each type of contract format using fictitious names and details to demonstrate how each format can be used. In the case of the Budget/Contract Settlement Form, I have included two sample scenarios—a small venue presentation and a large venue presentation. Blank forms are at the end of the chapter. You may re-key these into your computer or make photocopies directly out of the book as a starting point. Consult an entertainment attorney when creating contract forms for your specific needs.

Contracts And Forms Discussed In This Chapter:
1. Letter Of Intent
2. Letter Of Confirmation
3. Contract Information Form
4. Offer Form
5. Contract/Budget Settlement Form
6. Performance Contract, simple
7. Performance Contract, complex
8. Performance Contract Riders
9. Technical Riders
10. Hospitality Riders

Letter Of Intent

This form is useful to hold a performance date with a presenter. Both of you have agreed to the date and both of you will hold this date until a specific time in the future when you will make a commitment and issue a full contract. There are a number of reasons for using the Letter of Intent during the early stages of negotiation.
1. The presenter is lacking confirmation of some of the information pertinent to the performance. If there is a problem confirming any of the following information, the hold on the date can be cancelled. (i.e., available venue, adequate budget, grant awards, agreement to be a cosponsoring organization, time, or actual date availability, etc.)
2. The artist is unsure of supporting tour dates in the area. The time between issuing the Letter of Intent up to the specified confirmation date allows the artist to book support dates. If support dates have not been booked by the specified time, the hold on the date can be cancelled.

> **HotTip:** It is better to have a simply-written letter detailing your agreement rather than to rely on a verbal conversation.

"Just as there really is no 'one size fits all' in clothing, every contract should be carefully tailored to suit specific needs. Don't find a contract and just copy it. It won't fit and if you try to alter it yourself, you risk selling yourself short or worse yet, negating the entire contract or the provisions that should be in your favor. Establish a relationship with an entertainment attorney at the outset of your career to draft your contracts to protect you and your work. It's much more expensive to hire an attorney after the fact to try and get you out of a bad deal."

**Suzette Becker,
entertainment attorney,
Becker Entertainment Law**

> **HotTip:** 🌶
> Issue a Letter of Intent to place a hold on a specific date. There is less chance the date will be given to another act when you provide a written confirmation of your intention to perform.

3. The date in question is so far into the future that many factors surrounding the date need further research before confirmation. However, you do want to have a completed contract on the date.

Issuing a Letter of Intent establishes a commitment from both parties to make the date work. It is entered into with a mutual understanding that there may be circumstances beyond either party's control which prevent confirmation. For example: A presenter may want to present you in May, but will not find out whether they have received this year's grant allocation until January. In this case, the date of the performance is not dependent upon any other factors and you agree on a date that works well for you both. The artist issues a Letter of Intent on November 5. It is signed and returned by the presenter by November 15. Both parties have committed to make this date happen. Once the presenter receives notice about the grant, final negotiations take place and a formal contract can be issued.

The Letter of Intent can be as detailed as you like, including as much information as you have at the time you send it.

Items To Include In A Letter Of Intent
Paragraph One
1. The act's name and the words *intends to*
2. What the act intends to do: perform, lecture, present, etc.
3. The presenter's organizational and/or legal entity name
4. Any specifics known about the intended date, i.e., date, time, venue, length of performance, tickets, fees, etc.

Paragraph Two
5. A specified date to finalize confirmation
6. The method in which the act will be notified
7. What specifics are still needed to confirm the date
8. What action will result if notification is not received by the specified date

Paragraph Three
9. A pleasant closing sentence or brief paragraph
10. A place for a signature of the act's designated officer and for the presenter's signature

Using the above example, there is a copy of the Letter of Intent that might be issued by the artist on page 133.

This example is very businesslike, to the point and is all you need. A Letter of Intent does not have to be lengthy. Just write the facts that explain the intentions of both parties and when both parties expect to finalize the agreement. Two copies of the letter should be sent on your stationery and can be signed by whomever you have designated as the official contract signatory for the act.

> **Figure 4. Letter Of Intent**
>
>
> XYZ Band
> 1234 Main Street
> Anytown, VA 12345
> 800-432-2345
>
>
> Tim Jones
> ABC Community Arts Center
> P.O. Box 1234
> Small Town, KS 56789
>
> Dear Mr. Jones:
>
> The XYZ Band intends to perform for the ABC Community Arts Center in Small Town, KS on Saturday, May 8, 2004 at 8:00 p.m. The performance will take place at the Community Center on Main Street. All other details pertaining to this performance will be finalized upon notification of grant approval by the Kansas State Arts Commission.
>
> If ABC Community Arts Center does not receive its grant award, the hold on this date is no longer valid. The Artist is free to seek other bookings for the above mentioned date. ABC Community Arts Center must notify the Artist in writing by January 31, 2005 regarding the status of their grant application. Failure to notify the Artist by that date releases the Artist from its intended performance date.
>
> Good luck with the application. We are looking forward to working with you in May.
>
> Sincerely,
>
> Jane Smith
> XYZ Band Leader
>
> _____
> Purchaser
>
> _____
> Date

Letter Of Confirmation

This format leaves nothing tentative and can be used instead of a lengthy contract form to present a more informal agreement. You may choose to follow your Letter of Confirmation with a formal contract at a later date. The Letter of Confirmation would include all of the details of the performance date in question and would not include the additional legal clauses that are found in a long-form standard contract. Please use the example on page 134 as a guide.

Figure 5. Letter Of Confirmation.

XYZ Band
1234 Main Street
Anytown, VA 12345
800-432-2345

Tim Jones
ABC Community Arts Center
P.O. Box 1234
Small Town, KS 56789

Dear Mr. Jones:

This letter confirms that the XYZ Band ("the Artist") will perform for the ABC Community Arts Center ("the Purchaser") in Small Town, KS on Saturday, May 10, 2005 at 8:00 p.m. The performance will take place at the ABC Community Arts Center at 431 Main Street. The performance will be partially funded by a grant from the Kansas State Arts Commission. The Artist will receive $1,500 guaranteed flat fee for their performance and the Purchaser will provide 2 double rooms at a nearby hotel for the night of the performance. The performance will include 2 sets of 45 minutes each with a 15 minute intermission. Tickets for this event will be $10 in advance and $14 at the door. All sound and lighting equipment will be provided by the Purchaser. A professional sound and lighting company will be hired. Technical and hospitality requirements have been attached and are made a part of this agreement.

XYZ Band will be the sole act on the bill. The Artist will receive a deposit of $750.00 from the Purchaser made payable to XYZ Band by bank check to be returned with this letter by February 15, 2005 or the Artist may cancel this agreement and seek other performance opportunities. The balance of $750.00 will be due payable in cash on May 10, 2005 at the completion of the performance.

Please sign both copies of this letter and return them with the deposit to the above address. One copy will be signed by the act and returned for your files. If you have any questions, please don't hesitate to call. Enclosed you will also find the promotional materials that you requested. I would be happy to supply any additional materials necessary.

Thank you for your prompt reply. We are looking forward to working with you in May.

Sincerely,

Jane Smith
XYZ Band Leader

_____
Purchaser

_____
Date

Items To Include In A Letter Of Confirmation
Paragraph One
1. Confirm who will be performing, include the act's legal performance name
2. What the act will do: perform, lecture, present, etc.
3. The presenter's organizational and/or legal entity name
4. All of the specifics known about the confirmed date, i.e., date, time, venue, address of performance, length of performance, number of tickets to be sold, fees and percentages to be paid after expenses have been recouped, technical and hospitality provisions, etc.

Paragraph Two
5. Name any additional acts on the bill and length of play
6. Specify the billing (which act is the main act) and the order in which the acts shall perform
7. Method and time of payments, deposit date, to whom payments are made
8. Date when this letter must be returned or the artist may cancel this agreement and seek other performance opportunities

Paragraph Three
9. Directions to the presenter for signing this letter
10. Any information about additional materials being sent with this letter, i.e., promotional materials

Paragraph Four
11. A pleasant closing sentence or brief paragraph
12. A place for signature of act's designated officer and for the presenter's signature

Again, using the above example, a copy of a Letter of Confirmation that the act might have sent appears on page 134.

HotTip: A Letter of Confirmation is a letter that confirms the details of your agreements. It is suitable for many smaller performance situations.

"If you are just starting out and are confused about contracts, do not worry! A Letter of Confirmation with all of the details of your agreement included will serve you well. Make sure there is space for your signature and the presenter's signature. Then have one signed copy returned to you. As you tour more extensively, you will discover specific items and needs that can be drafted into your own contract and/or contract rider."

Kari Estrin
former booking and special events director,
Caffe Milano, Nashville, TN

Contract Information Form
Before we discuss the long form of a standard contract, let us create a Contract Information Form that you can fill out while you are negotiating the final contract. This form will include all of the items that will eventually be written into the contract. If you use a contact manager or database, this form can be recreated as a database field form. Once it has been filled in, the information contained in each field can then be merged with the final word-processed document and printed as your final contract.

This form will allow you to track the progress of your negotiations by indicating the dates that interest was first expressed, when an offer was made, when it was confirmed and when the contract was sent. A sample Contract Information Form has been filled in and provided on page

CONTRACT INFORMATION FORM

<u>The Sound Project</u>
(Group's Name and Contact Information)

Today's Date <u>8/20/2004</u>

Contact Name <u>Jim Smith</u>

Company Name <u>Southern California Productions</u>

Address <u>P.O. Box 1020</u>

City <u>Laguna Beach</u>   State <u>CA</u> Zip <u>92677</u>

Phone Day <u>714-234-4567</u> Phone Night <u>714-234-5923</u> Fax <u>714-234-4568</u>

E-mail Address <u>js@scp.com</u>   Web Address <u>http://www.scp.com</u>

Interest <u>8/20/04</u> Offer <u>9/4/04</u> Confirm <u>9/14/04</u> Contract Sent <u>9/15/04</u>

Type of Engagement <u>Concert</u>
(concert, workshop, festival, lecture, co-bill, opener, etc.)

Performance Date(s) <u>March 2, 2005</u>   Time(s) <u>8:00 p.m.</u>   AM/PM

Number of Sets <u>2</u>   Length <u>45 min. each</u> Intermission Length <u>20 min.</u>

Load In Time <u>4:00 p.m.</u>   Sound Check Time <u>5:00 p.m.-6:00 p.m.</u>

Place of Engagement

Name <u>Pacific Performing Arts Center</u>

Address <u>1234 South Highway</u>

City, State, Zip <u>Laguna Beach, CA 92677</u>

Phone <u>714-245-6565</u>   Fax <u>714-245-6566</u>

Box Office Phone <u>714-222-4000</u>   Back Stage Phone <u>714-222-1001</u>

Capacity <u>1200</u>

Compensation To Be Paid

Fee Guarantee $ <u>2,500 guarantee</u>

Percentage of Gross/Net of Door: <u>plus 65% of net (after expenses)</u>

Deposit Amount Due $ <u>1,250</u>   Date Due <u>9/29/2004</u>

Balance of Guarantee $ <u>1,250 plus % due</u>   Date Due <u>3/7/2005</u>

Additional Compensations

Workshop, Class, Lecture Fee _____

Transportation

　　Ground   <u>Artist arrives in own bus</u>
(taxi, car rental, train, bus, parking, limo)

　　Air _____

Lodging <u>Presenter provides 2 double rooms in nearby hotel</u>

Meals Provided or Buy Out <u>Presenter provides 4 hot meals after sound check, backstage</u>

Ticket Price(s) <u>$15 general advance admission (adv.), $18 day of show (d.o.s.)</u>

Scaled or Discounted Tickets	N/A

Merchandising Percentages Taken by Venue   15%
Additional Act(s) on the Bill ✔ Yes ___ No   Name(s) TBA
Type of Performance TBA   Local Act ✔ National Act ___
Set Length   25 Minutes   Start Time 8:00 p.m.
Technical
Sound Provided by   Laguna Sound & Lights
Lights Provided by   Laguna Sound & Lights
Contact Name and Phone   Bob Powers, 714-244-9789

136-137 to demonstrate its use. A blank copy of this form is included at the end of this chapter on pages 160 and 161.

Some of the above information will be incorporated into a technical rider and a hospitality rider. They are items that need to be negotiated, therefore, it is important to include them on the information form while discussions are in progress.

Performance Contract

A performance contract, whether a simple listing of the agreed-upon details of your agreement, or a more complex document written with many clauses using legal language, needs to clearly represent the details that the two parties have agreed upon.

When You Are Just Beginning

It is just as important for an artist who is beginning a professional career to send a written form outlining their agreements as it is for a seasoned performer. Many of the dates that you will book might have fees ranging from $50 to $500. Often these dates will be in clubs or smaller performance venues where you might play for a small guarantee versus a percentage of the door or just a percentage of the door. Whatever the situations are that you encounter in these early stages of your career, you may not be in a position to ask for some of the amenities that are afforded more established artists. The detailed requirements of more established artists are often described in the clauses contained within the Performance Contract as well as the Performance Contract Rider.

Some of these items are:
1. *Hotel accommodations:* I suggest asking the presenter if they provide hotel or have a deal with a nearby hotel. They

> **HotTips:**
>
> Ask the presenter whether they provide hotel, meals or any travel expenses. By making the inquiry, you increase your chances of getting what you have asked for.
>
>
>
> Some promoters may offer an artist a meal "buy-out." The promoter pays each member of the group a set dollar amount with which the artist may purchase their own dinner. $10 is often reasonable.

may throw in hotel and lower your already low guarantee. Sometimes having accommodations covered is advantageous in the early stages. Although it certainly does not hurt to ask for accommodations, do not expect them.

2. *Meals and hospitality:* In some clubs, a presenter is not likely to provide a meal or drinks in the dressing room, if in fact they even have a dressing room. Be prepared to provide your own meals and pay for your own drinks, perhaps at a discounted rate. Again, ask if there are refreshments or meals provided and be pleasantly surprised and grateful when they are. If not, ask if there is a restaurant nearby that they recommend or with whom they have a discount arrangement.

3. *Travel expenses:* It is very unlikely that any reimbursement for travel of any kind will be paid to you at this point. Depending on with whom you are negotiating and the type of performance you are pursuing, making an inquiry regarding your travel needs is advised. Sometimes travel expenses may be paid in lieu of a portion of your fee especially if the promoter has an airline sponsor. Depending on the performance situation, you may opt for the travel just to get yourself to the date and be seen.

4. *Deposits:* When your fees are low, it is unlikely that deposits will be made. I do, however, suggest you begin asking for deposits once your fees begin to grow beyond $500 and certainly beyond $1,000 dollars.

With these exceptions, a simplified Performance Contract which you may modify for your own needs begins on page 139.

The more complex Performance Contract, which begins on page 141, can be used for all of your performance dates as soon as your level of performance warrants its use.

American Federation of Musicians of the United States and Canada (AFM) or American Federation of Television and Radio Artists (AFTRA) members may consult with the union to modify one of the member's personal contracts in order to incorporate the information necessary from the union, making it acceptable as a legally recognized union contract. Members may download copies of the union contract from their website or call the union's offices to have contracts sent to you. (See resource section for contact information.)

The sample contract included on page 141 is the result of pulling together some of the best clauses from a number of resources as well as from my consultations over the years with lawyers to create my contracts. I have completed this sample contract using the Contract Information Form from page 136, and I will explain some of the clauses which I have included.

PERFORMANCE CONTRACT—Simple

THIS CONTRACT is made this day of <u>September 9, 2004</u> by and between <u>The Sound Project</u> hereinafter called the Artist and <u>Laguna Productions</u>, hereinafter called the Purchaser. This Contract for Artist's personal services on this engagement described below shall consist of all provisions in this Contract, and any attachments. This Contract shall be executed by Purchaser and returned by <u>September 29, 2004</u>. If Artist has not received the Contract as described above, the Artist shall at anytime thereafter have the option to terminate the agreement.

1. Purchaser's Contact Information:
   Contact Name <u>Jim Smith</u>
   Company Name <u>Laguna Productions</u>
   Address <u>P.O. Box 1020</u>
   City <u>Laguna Beach</u> State <u>CA</u> Zip <u>92677</u>
   Phone Day <u>949-234-4567</u> Phone Night <u>949-234-5923</u> Fax <u>949-234-4568</u>
   E-mail Address <u>js@scp.com</u>
   Personal Phone (home, beeper, etc.) <u>949-234-5525</u>

2. Place of Engagement:
   Venue Name <u>High Top Club</u>
   Address <u>1000 South Pacific Hywy</u>
   City, State, Zip <u>Laguna Beach CA 92677</u>
   (Map or directions from nearest highway exit to be furnished by Purchaser)
   Phone <u>949-240-0535</u> Fax <u>949-240-3536</u>
   Box Office Phone <u>949-222-3333</u> Backstage Phone _____
   Capacity <u>120</u>

3. The Performance Date, Times, Length, Load In and Sound Check:
   Performance Date(s) <u>March 7, 2005</u> Time(s) <u>8:00 p.m.</u> AM/PM
   Number of Sets <u>2</u> Length <u>45</u> Intermission Length <u>20</u>
   Load In Time <u>4:00 p.m.</u> Sound Check Time <u>5:00 p.m.-6:00 p.m.</u>
   Sound Check Times of Additional Acts, if any _____

4. Type of Engagement: (specify concert, workshop, festival, opener, co-bill): _____
   <u>Concert</u>

5. Compensation to Be Paid:
   5.1. Fee Guarantee $ <u>$200.00 versus 50% of door</u>
   5.2. Percentage of Gross <u>50%</u> /Net ___ of Door ✓
   (Any percentage of the net will be determined by allowable expenses as indicated on the approved, attached budget.)
   5.3. Additional Compensations:
      5.3a. Workshop, Class, Lecture Fee, etc. <u>N/A</u>
      5.3b. Transportation <u>N/A</u>
      5.3c. Lodging <u>N/A</u>
      5.3d. Meals <u>N/A</u>

5.4. Total Guarantee $200.00 versus 50% of door

6. Tickets Prices $ 8 general adm.

7. Merchandising Policy of the Venue: 10% taken by venue or _____ flat fee.

8. Additional Acts on the Bill _____

9. Set Length of Additional Acts _____ Start time _____

10. Technical Requirements: Purchaser shall provide sound and/or lighting equipment as described in the attached Technical Rider. Purchaser shall provide a copy of the Technical Rider to the sound and lighting technicians no less than two (2) weeks prior to the engagement.

11.0. Cancellation:

11.1. Purchaser agrees that Artist shall have the right to cancel this engagement without liability upon written notice to Purchaser no later than 30 days prior to the date of performance in the event Artist is called upon to render their services for a radio or television appearance, motion picture, or any career advancing opportunity. Artist will attempt to reschedule the date with the Purchaser for a mutually convenient time.

11.2. Should Purchaser have cause to cancel this agreement, notice must be given to Artist in writing no later than thirty (30) days prior to this engagement. Any notice given less than thirty (30) days will require full payment by Purchaser to Artist as described in Contract paragraph 5.4 unless Artist agrees to waive any part of that payment or Purchaser and Artist agree to reschedule the engagement for another time.

12. Force Majeure: This agreement by both parties to perform their obligations herein is subject to proven detention by serious illness, accidents, or accidents to means of transportation, labor disputes or walkouts, acts of God, or any act of public authority, material breach of Contract by Purchaser, or any other condition beyond either party's control. Neither party shall be liable to fulfill the remainder of the Contract nor perform or present any "make-up" date unless expressly agreed to by both parties for a convenient future time.

13. Disputes and Attorney's Fees: Any controversy or claim arising out of or relating to this contract, or the breach thereof, shall be settled by arbitration administered by the American Arbitration Association in accordance with its [applicable] rules and judgment on the award rendered by the arbitrator may be entered in any court having jurisdiction thereof.

14. It is agreed that Artist signs this Agreement as an independent contractor and not as an employee.

In witness whereof, the parties have executed this Contract on the respective dates shown by their signatures.

Laguna Productions	The Sound Project
Purchaser/Organization's Name	Artist
Jim Smith, President	Bill Jones
Name and Title	Name and Title
Jim Smith, President 9/23/2004	*Bill Jones* 9/27/2004
Authorized Signature Date	Authorized Signature Date
94-1234567	123-05-9455
Federal I.D. / Social Security #	Federal I.D. / Social Security #

Please sign and return TWO (2) copies of this Contract. One copy will be returned fully executed for your files.

PERFORMANCE CONTRACT—Complex

THIS CONTRACT is made this day of <u>September 9, 2004</u> by and between <u>The Sound Project</u> hereinafter called the Artist and <u>Laguna Productions</u>, hereinafter called the Purchaser. This Contract for Artist's personal services on this engagement described below shall consist of all provisions in this Contract, and any attachments. This Contract shall be executed by Purchaser and returned by <u>September 29, 2004</u>. If Artist has not received the Contract as described above, the Artist shall at anytime thereafter have the option to terminate the agreement.

1. Purchaser's Contact Information:
    Contact Name <u>Jim Smith</u>
    Company Name <u>Southern California Productions</u>
    Address <u>P.O. Box 1020</u>
    City <u>Laguna Beach</u> State <u>CA</u> Zip <u>92677</u>
    Phone Day <u>949-234-4567</u> Phone Night <u>949-234-5923</u> Fax <u>949-234-4568</u>
    E-mail Address <u>js@scp.com</u>
    Personal Phone (home, beeper, etc.) <u>949-234-5525</u>

2. Place of Engagement:
    Venue Name <u>Pacific Performing Arts Center</u>
    Address <u>1234 South Highway</u>
    City, State, Zip <u>Laguna Beach CA 92677</u>
    (Map or directions from nearest highway exit to be furnished by purchaser)
    Phone <u>949-245-6565</u> Fax <u>949-245-6566</u>
    Box Office Phone <u>949-222-4000</u> Backstage Phone <u>949-222-1001</u>
    Capacity <u>1200</u>

3. The Performance Date, Times, Length, Load In and Sound Check:
    Performance Date(s) <u>March 2, 2005</u> Time(s) <u>8:00 p.m.</u> AM/PM
    Number of Sets <u>2</u> Length <u>45</u> Intermission Length <u>20</u>
    Load In Time <u>4:00 p.m.</u> Sound Check Time <u>5:00 p.m.-6:00 p.m.</u>
    Sound Check Times of Additional Acts, if any <u>6:15 p.m.</u>

4. Type of Engagement: (specify concert, workshop, festival, opener, co-bill):
    <u>Concert w/opening act TBA</u>

5. Compensation to Be Paid:
    5.1. Fee Guarantee $ <u>$2500.00 plus 65% of net (after expenses)</u>
    5.2. Percentage of Gross _____ /Net <u>65%</u> of Door _____
        (Any percentage of the net will be determined by allowable expenses as indicated on the approved, attached budget.)
    5.3. Additional Compensations:
    5.3a. Workshop, Class, Lecture Fee, etc. <u>N/A</u>
    5.3b. Transportation
        Ground <u>Artist arrives in own bus</u>
        Air _____

CONTRACTS 141

5.3c. Lodging   Presenter provides 2 double rooms at nearby hotel.
5.3d. Meals Provided or Buy Out   Presenter provides 4 hot meals after sound check
5.4. Total   2,500.00 plus 65% of net (after expenses)

6. Deposit Amount Due $1,250.00   Date Due 9/29/2004

7. Balance of Guarantee $1,250.00 plus any % due   Date Due 3/7/2005

8. Ticket Prices: 1200   seats @ $ 15 adv.
   _____ seats @ $ 18 d.o.s.
   _____ seats @ $ _____

9. Merchandising Policy of the Venue: 15% taken by venue or _____ flat fee.
10. Additional Acts on the Bill: TBA w/Artist's approval
11. Set Length 25 minutes   Start Time 8:00 p.m.

12. Technical Requirements: Purchaser shall provide sound and/or lighting equipment as described in the attached Technical Rider. Purchaser shall provide a copy of the Technical Rider to the sound and lighting technicians no less than two (2) weeks prior to the engagement.

13. Withholding: Purchaser shall notify Artist of any and all state or local taxes required to be withheld or deducted from the Artist's fee specified in the Contract prior to signing the Contract. If Artist is not so notified, payment of any such withholdings shall be the responsibility of the Purchaser and shall not be deducted from Artist's fee.

13.1. Taxes: No admission tax shall be deducted from the gross box office receipts before computing percentages due unless the amount of tax is stated on the Contract.

14. Insurance and Indemnity: Purchaser agrees to obtain at Purchaser's sole cost and expense any and all necessary personal injury and property damage liability insurance with respect to the activities of Artist on the premises of Purchaser or at any other location where Purchaser directs the Artist to perform. Purchaser shall provide Artist with a copy of the Certificate of Insurance no less than fourteen (14) days prior to the performance in the amount of no less than one million dollars per occurrence with respect to damage to property and no less than one million dollars with respect to death or personal injury. Purchaser's policy shall name Artist and Artist's employees, and representatives as additional insured parties.

14.1 Purchaser shall indemnify and hold Artist and Artist's employees and representatives, and attorneys harmless from and against any and all claims, demands, actions, damages, liability, costs and expenses including attorney's fees arising out of or in conjunction with any personal injury, death, and loss of or damage to property which occurs in connection with any performance by Artist unless caused by the sole conduct of Artist or any employee or representative of Artist.

15.0. Cancellation:

15.1. Purchaser agrees that Artist shall have the right to cancel this engagement without liability upon written notice to Purchaser no later than 30 days prior to the date of performance in the event Artist is called upon to render their services for a radio or television appearance, motion picture, or any career advancing opportunity. Artist will attempt to reschedule the date with the Purchaser for a mutually convenient time.

15.2. Should Purchaser have cause to cancel this agreement, notice must be given to Artist in writing no later than thirty (30) days prior to this engagement. Any notice given less than thirty (30) days will require full payment by Purchaser to Artist as described in Contract paragraph

5.1 unless Artist agrees to waive any part of that payment or Purchaser and Artist agree to reschedule the engagement for another time.

16. Force Majeure: This agreement by both parties to perform their obligations herein is subject to proven detention by serious illness, accidents, or accidents to means of transportation, labor disputes or walkouts, acts of God, or any act of public authority, material breach of Contract by Purchaser, or any other condition beyond either party's control. Neither party shall be liable to fulfill the remainder of the Contract nor perform or present any "make-up" date unless expressly agreed to by both parties for a convenient future time.

17. Disputes and Attorney's Fees: Any controversy or claim arising out of or relating to this Contract, or the breach thereof, shall be settled by arbitration administered by the American Arbitration Association in accordance with its [applicable] rules and judgment on the award rendered by the arbitrator may be entered in any court having jurisdiction thereof.

17.1. Attorney's Fees: In the event that any dispute arises while this agreement is in force that results in litigation or arbitration, all reasonable attorney's fees and costs of the prevailing party will be paid by the losing party.

18. If any term, provision, covenant, or condition in this Contract is held by a court or competent jurisdiction to be invalid, void or unenforceable, the rest of the Contract shall remain in full force and effect and in no way be affected, impaired or invalidated.

19. It is agreed that Artist signs this Agreement as an independent contractor and not as an employee.

20. Jurisdiction: This Contract may not be assigned, modified or altered except by an instrument in writing signed by both parties. This Agreement along with the attached riders and budget constitutes the sole and binding Contract between the parties hereto. This Contract shall be construed in accordance with the laws of the State of _California_ and the laws of that state shall govern its interpretation and effect.

In witness whereof, the parties have executed this Contract on the respective dates shown by their signatures.

Southern California Productions	The Sound Project
Purchaser/Organization's Name	Artist
Jim Smith, President	Bill Jones
Name and Title	Name and Title
Jim Smith, President 9/23/2004	*Bill Jones* 9/27/2004
Authorized Signature Date	Authorized Signature Date
94-1234567	123-05-9455
Federal I.D. / Social Security #	Federal I.D. / Social Security #

Please sign and return TWO (2) copies of this Contract. One copy will be returned fully executed for your files.

Explanation Of Specific Clauses

Points 1-11 are self-explanatory, asking for the detailed contact information of the presenter and the venue and the other items negotiated. These details are taken directly from the Contract Information Form. Several clauses are highlighted to clarify their use and importance.

> **HotTips:**
> Know the exact capacity of each venue. Include discounted, series and scaled ticket prices when calculating the gross potential sales of any venue.
>
> Ask about merchandising fees up front. Be prepared to adjust your sales prices when the venue asks for a high percentage of your fees.

❖ *Clause 2: Place of Engagement (page 141):* The venue address and contact information, including all of the phone numbers, e-mail addresses, backstage and box office numbers, must be correct on the contract so when publicizing the event, your audience knows exactly how to buy tickets and where to go. Also, you and your crew will know how to contact the venue to discuss details of your performance and to periodically check on ticket sales. The capacity of the venue is critical in order to calculate the correct number of tickets sold. Your final payment is based on the number of tickets sold if you are receiving any additional percentages before or after expenses. If your fee is based on a percentage of the door without any guarantee, knowing the correct capacity number can make a tremendous difference in your pay. (Refer back to page 115 for descriptions of types of percentage deals.)

❖ *Clause 8: Ticket Prices (page 142):* In many cases, there will be one ticket price for general sales that applies to the entire theater. In other situations, there will be an advanced sale ticket price and a day-of-show or at-the-door ticket price which is usually a few dollars higher. Many theaters have the capability of dividing the theater into sections such as orchestra, mezzanine, first balcony, second balcony and so forth. In this case, the presenter may scale the ticket prices to offer seats closer to the stage at a higher price. I have often suggested that a Golden Circle of higher-priced tickets, situated close to the stage may be offered as a fund-raising effort. The presenter can tell you how many seats are in each section and what ticket price will be applied to that particular number of seats. The orchestra may seat 400 and the price per seat may be $25.00, whereas the second balcony may seat 150 and the price will only be $12.00. Once you have the numbers of seats and their prices, you can then calculate the gross potential income at that venue. The gross potential or gross ticket sales is the total income from ticket sales before any expenses have been deducted.

❖ *Clause 9: Merchandising Policy (page 142):* Many presenters and venues require a percentage of the artist's product sales. If you forget to ask about this during the contract negotiations, it does not mean they will forget to take their percentage on the day of the performance. It is to your advantage to know in advance if you are expected to pay the presenter or the venue a percentage of your sales. With advance notice, you can adjust your prices accordingly. Some venues ask for a low 5% or 10%, other larger venues can get you for a whopping 35% to 50%. Venues in the city of Chicago have banded together and are all asking for a high percentage. Why do the venues charge a merchandise percentage in the first place? The most reasonable answer I have heard over the years is that as an artist/vendor doing business in a new city almost every night, it is unreasonable to expect the artist to apply for and receive a license to do business in each city. Some venues claim that they are mandated by the city to collect these merchandise percentages because they are providing a place in which the artist can sell their goods in that particular city. The venue is then supposed to use those funds collected to pay the city local taxes.

Smaller presenters have begun to take a cut of the artist's merchandise simply because they also feel that they are providing the artist with a place to sell their product and a small cut of the merchandise will help offset some of the presenter's costs to do the show.

> **HotTip:** Advance your shows. Call ahead to each venue to review your technical requirements. Have copies of your technical needs dispersed to appropriate technicians.

- *Clause 12: Technical Requirements (page 142):* The technical needs of the artists should be taken seriously by the presenter. Optimally, each technician receives a copy of the specific technical requirements necessary to be prepared for the artist's arrival. It is a great comfort to receive a call from the sound technician one or two weeks before your date to discuss the show, knowing they have seen the rider and they have most or all of your requirements. This clause helps to prevent those last minute panic situations because the technician never received a copy of your technical rider from the presenter.
- *Clause 13: Withholding (page 142):* If the state in which you are performing requires the presenting venue to withhold a percentage of income tax from the performer's fee, you want to know about it in advance. You may not encounter this when playing in smaller venues, but once you begin performing in larger venues, the state tax board keeps abreast of the venue's presentations and requires that venue to alert each performer about the possibility of income taxes being withheld from their fee.
- *Clause 13.1 Taxes (page 142):* If the federal, state or local municipality in which the venue does their business requires any tax on the gross ticket sales of any presentation, it should be the venue's responsibility to pay those taxes and it should not affect your guarantee or percentage.
- *Clause 14: Insurance and Indemnity (page 142):* It is very important that you include this clause in your contract. Whether you perform in a public facility or a private club, you want to be sure that the presenter has purchased a liability insurance policy that covers the facility in which the concert is taking place. It should include personal and property damage for the audience, the crew, staff, your group, your staff and your instruments and equipment. You want the presenter to be covered in case any unforeseen accident should occur. This way you will not be held liable

for the damage. There are potential dangers lurking all around a performance venue—a loose theater seat, a misplaced ladder, a blown stage light causing an electrical fire or a stagehand knocking over your instrument and breaking it. Perhaps one of your band members decided to tweak the volume level on the sound board and inadvertently bumped something which blew out an amp. Do you want to pay for that? More famous incidents resulting in death have occurred such as the Rolling Stones concert which was later illustrated in the film *Gimme Shelter*. In short, include this clause in every contract and make sure that the presenter has an insurance policy before stepping into the venue.

❖ *Clause 15: Cancellation (page 142):* An artist needs to incorporate a clause which allows them to cancel a performance in the event a career-advancing opportunity should become available to the artist. Thirty days from a performance date is usually a respectable amount of time in which to cancel an engagement. Many presenters will allow this clause to remain with a longer period of time, like sixty days, and many will cross out this clause completely. Without this clause, you have no recourse when confronted with an opportunity. You can try explaining the situation to the presenter and hope they understand and will allow you to reschedule the date.

If the presenter needs to cancel their date, it is even more important that you have this clause explaining the presenter's responsibilities to the artist. It is often easier for the presenter to replace an artist than it is for the artist to fill a cancelled date on short notice. This clause makes certain that you receive payment if the presenter cancels the date on short notice.

❖ *Clause 16: Force Majeure (page 143):* There are events that occur which are beyond our control. This clause takes all of those situations into consideration. It relieves the artist and the presenter of their obligations set out in the contract if any of these uncontrollable forces prevent either party from performing the duties of the contract. Weather situations are a perfect example. How often has an airport been shut down or a road closed due to snow, preventing you from reaching the gig on time or at all? If you are performing at a union hall and the union members are on strike, this clause releases you both from playing the date at that venue. In most instances, both the artist and the presenter may decide to reschedule the date for a later time convenient to you both. Many presenters attempt to include a "rain date" on a date near the original date. By inserting the last sentence in this clause in your contract, you notify the presenter that you will be unavailable to perform on their rain date, but will consider another date which is more to your convenience, like the next tour through the area. Consider your costs to return to do a "make-up" date when you discuss this situation. It is very likely that you will have other performance obligations already scheduled on the make-up date. You need to consider travel costs and pay to crew and group members—consequently, how does replaying the date affect your entire budget?

❖ *Clause 17: Disputes and Attorney's Fees (page 143):* Earlier we discussed that one of the three main pieces of information to include in a contract is the exact method in which any dispute would be settled. In this case a clause used by the American Arbitration Association (AAA) is included. Recognized by courts across the country, the AAA is a reputable organization whose settlement decisions will be upheld. The cost to use arbitration is much more reasonable than bringing a full suit to court. If you are a union member of the AFM or AFTRA, they will provide free legal assistance should a contract dispute arise and you have issued a union contract. The four methods of dispute settlement are discussed near the end of this chapter. You may decide to use one of the alternatives. Consult with your lawyer to create a clause appropriate to your situation. Acts whose shows regularly generate income over $50,000 per show will need to include a clause which allows you to pursue full litigation.

❖ *Clause 17.1: Attorney's Fees (page 143):* It is also important to state who is responsible for any lawyer's fees or costs once the dispute is settled.

❖ *Clause 20: Jurisdiction (page 143):* This clause simply states that should there be a dispute between the presenter and the artist, and should it be necessary to settle the dispute in court or by arbitration, you want to settle it in your home state, not the presenter's state. This is one clause that you will find being changed often by the presenter. They, of course, want any dispute to be settled in their home state and often cross out your state and insert their own.

> **HotTip:** One benefit of membership in the AFM is access to the Union's free legal services.

I have included clauses 12 through 20 in the main performance contract rather than in the contract rider as a measure of covering yourself legally. Many artists do not send a contract rider. Often, presenters do not recognize artist contract riders. If any of these clauses are covered within the rider and the rider is crossed out, some very important concerns are then out of your control. However, you can include an attachment clause in the beginning of the contract stating, "All riders attached are herein made part of this contract." Unless they cross out that statement, the contents of any attached riders are covered and will continue to remain in force.

Contract Riders

While a performance contract spells out the specific details that the artist and purchaser have agreed to during their negotiations, contract riders explain additional requirements necessary to present your act. Contract riders often become elaborate documents detailing everything from the necessary, such as the manner in which the artist is to be paid, to items that may seem ridiculous, like the famous story of the color and quantity of M & Ms to be included or removed from the bowl in each dressing room. Some requests are unnecessary and other requests, even those that seem silly, are inserted for very good reasons. The M & Ms are a good example of what may seem ridiculous. However, the band Van Halen purposely inserted that clause when they realized their contract rider was not being followed. By inserting this incredibly detailed and picky item, they were able to tell whether or not all of the details outlined in their rider had been followed precisely. Attention to the important details was their real goal in this case. It became a famous story among presenters and artists alike. I am not advocating the use of these items in your riders. Rather, clearly state your needs and check on how they are being dealt with well in advance of each date.

The rider is able to specify personal requirements as well. Sometimes items that may show up in a hospitality rider can be emphasized more strongly in the performance contract rider or included here when a hospitality rider is not used at all. For instance, the world's premier Cajun band Beausoleil Avec Michael Doucet includes the following in their contract rider: "Please, under no circumstances should the band be served Cajun food." Greg McGrath, one of the members of the band, made that request noting that the band would rather sample local ethnic cuisine while touring since they cook some of the best Cajun food around while at home.

Contract riders are the butt of many jokes among presenters. Some presenters do not even acknowledge their existence and will cross out every page of a rider. Once again the artist/presenter working relationship is worth many times more than all the pages of any rider, no matter how necessary you believe your rider to be.

Your objective for attaching a contract rider is to realistically aid the presenter in making your performance run smoothly. When you create your own riders, view them as an extension of your working relationship with the presenter. Up until now you have built a relationship that joins you together with the purchaser to present a successful performance. This is not the time to begin taking advantage of the relationship you have worked so hard to develop. Be realistic when you consider all your rider requirements.

> "The promoter of the festival that I worked for cancelled the festival two weeks before it was to take place. Out of the 17 bands booked, 12 were unable to get replacement gigs. Of those 12 bands, only six of them had written contracts. With those contracts, two of them got 50% of their guarantee, one got 100%, the other three bands got 10%. It was interesting to see that much variation in the cancellation clauses written into each contract. Six bands didn't have any contract and they were just left high and dry."
>
> **Chuck Wentworth**
> director,
> The Big Easy; RI Cajun & Bluegrass Festivals

> "Keep your rider requirements reasonable. I've had artists who sold 150 seats making the most ridiculous demands. I don't appreciate those types of demands under any circumstances. However, if you are selling 2000 seats at $25 each, I will be more inclined to be responsive."
>
> **Jim Hirsch**
> former executive director,
> Old Town School of Folk Music

A copy of the Performance Contract Rider form can be found on page 172 in the forms section of this chapter.

Budget

Within the body of the Performance Contract Rider, paragraph 2.4 mentions that payment will be determined in part by the approved expenses as described in the budget. Most presenters create a budget of expenses for each performance they present. Some of the smaller venues keep their expense budget very informal and often underestimate the cost of producing the performance. It is certainly to your advantage to get the presenter to consider all of their actual expenses and provide you with a complete list of those expenses. When your fee is based, in part, on a percentage of the net, it means you will receive the percentage amount agreed upon of all money left after the presenter has deducted their expenses. Knowing what those expenses will be and keeping them in line will benefit everybody.

Here is a budget form which you can include with all of your contracts. You may not need to be concerned with some items when you work with many of the smaller venues. This form provides you with a method of tracking presenter expenses prior to contracting and at the time of settlement. Use the "estimated" column as you finalize your negotiations and the "actual" column when you settle the box office. When you are provided receipts, check them against the "actual" column for a cross-reference of all expenses.

This budget form was provided by Jeanne Rizzo, former owner/booker of the Great American Music Hall in San Francisco, California. In recent years, Jeanne has managed Canadian artist Ferron and George Winston. As Ferron's former agent, I used this form when negotiating all of her contracts.

The form on page 150 is filled out to illustrate how it might be used when performing at a smaller venue for a community organization or music society.

"We are most interested contractually with the date the artist is to appear, the money deal and to make sure the artist has the right equipment. We do not honor any rider requests. After 23 years of business, we have never had an artist walk away unsatisfied."

Stanley Snadowsky
co-owner,
The Bottom Line, NYC

"A number of facilities have their own riders that refer to unique situations specific to that facility. The most common one relates to sound volume or decibel level). Certain schools, particularly those with religious affiliations, include clauses concerning language used on the stage, and restrictions pertaining to alcohol back stage. This can also be an issue for state schools. Most facilities would have their rider on their web page."

I.B. Dent
interim director,
Gertrude C. Ford Center for
the Performing Arts

CONTRACT BUDGET/SETTLEMENT
(Small Venue)

PERFORMANCE DATE Oct. 1, 2004   CITY, STATE Athens, OH
SUBMITTED BY Jeri Goldstein   APPROVED BY Jim Smith
              Athens Music Society

TICKET SCALE	@		ATTENDANCE	@	
125	$10 =	$1,250	115	$10	= $1,150
___	___ =	___	___	___	= ___
___	___ =	___	___	___	= ___
___	___ =	___	___	___	= ___

HALL CAPACITY 125

DISCOUNTS	@		DISCOUNTS	@	
___	___ =	___	___	___	= ___
___	___ =	___	___	___	= ___
___	___ =	___	___	___	= ___
___	___ =	___	___	___	= ___

TOTAL DISCOUNTS None

GROSS POTENTIAL $1,250   GROSS ATTENDANCE 125

HALL COSTS	ESTIMATED	ACTUAL
Rent	$75	$75
Other %/Gross		
Stage Hands #____ @ $____/hr.		
Loaders #____ @ $____/hr.		
House Manager		
House Staff		
Box Office Fee		
Ticket Commission %		
$____ @ ____%		
Ticket Printing	$35	$35
Day of Box Office		
Security		
Custodial		
House Sound	$100	$100
House Lights		
Spotlights #____ @ $____/hr.		
Spot Operators #____ @ $____/hr.		
Piano		
Tuner		
Equipment Rentals		
Parking		
Other Facility Expenses		
SUBTOTAL HALL	$210	$210

CONTRACT BUDGET/SETTLEMENT CONTINUED: PRODUCTION

Advertising		$185	$185
	Print ads	$50	$50
	Radio	trade	trade
	Graphics	$25	$25
	Printing	$35	$35
	Mailing	$75	$75
	Poster/Flyer Distribution	free	free
	Program Production		
Production Costs			
	Sound Company/Engineer		
	Lighting Rental/Engineer		
	Equipment Rentals		
	Stage Manager		
	Runner/Assistant		
	Additional Box Office		
	Backstage Security		
Artist Hospitality		$75	$75
	Green Room	$15	$15
	Transportation		
	Hotel	$25	$25
	Artist Assistant Misc.		
Insurance @ $0.20 Seat		$25	$25
ASCAP/BMI/SESAC/SOCAN		$10	$10
TOTAL EXPENSES		$470	$470
ARTIST GUARANTEE		$450	$450
SUBTOTAL		$920	$920
Producer's Fee @ 15 %		$138	$138
TOTAL SHOW COST		$1,058	$1,058
GROSS POTENTIAL		$1,250	$1,250
Less Show Cost		$1,058	$1,058
Net Profit/Split		$192	$192
Artist's % of Net @ 70 %		$134.40	$134.40
Producer's % of Net @ 30 %		$57.60	$57.60
Potential to Artist		$584.40	$584.40
Potential to Producer		$195.60	$195.60

    The next budget is for a concert at a large venue presented by an outside promoter. The cost and potential income is much higher. This will give you some idea of what to expect when you deal with more mainstream promoters as your career develops.

CONTRACT BUDGET/SETTLEMENT
(Large Promoter)

PERFORMANCE DATE Oct. 1, 2004   CITY, STATE York, PA
SUBMITTED BY Jeri Goldstein   APPROVED BY Jim Smith
         York PAC

TICKET SCALE	@		ATTENDANCE	@	
1000	$18 =	$18,000	982	$18	= $17,676
500	$22 =	$11,000	435	$22	= $9,570
500	$25 =	$12,500	470	$25	= $11,750
	=			=	

HALL CAPACITY 2000

DISCOUNTS	@		DISCOUNTS	@	
	=			=	
	=			=	
	=			=	
	=			=	

TOTAL DISCOUNTS _____

GROSS POTENTIAL $41,500   GROSS ATTENDANCE $38,996

HALL COSTS	ESTIMATED	ACTUAL
Rent	$2,500	$2,500
Other %/Gross		
Stage Hands # 6 @ $ 8 /hr. #hrs 8	$384	$384
Loaders 4 @ $ 8 /hr. #hrs 4	$128	$128
House Manager	$200	$200
House Staff	$300	$300
Box Office Fee	$500	$500
Ticket Commission % $_____ @ ____ %	$1,660	$1,660
Ticket Printing	$50	$50
Day of Box Office	$160	$160
Security	$300	$300
Custodial	$150	$150
House Sound		
House Lights		
Spotlights # 2 @ $ $125 /hr. #hrs ____	$250	$250
Spot Operators # 2 @ $ $10 /hr. #hrs 2	$40	$40
Piano	$250	$250
Tuner	$85	$85
Equipment Rentals		
Parking	$175	$175
Other Facility Expenses		
SUBTOTAL HALL	$6,882	$6,882

CONTRACT BUDGET/SETTLEMENT CONTINUED: PRODUCTION

Advertising		$6,000	$5,900
	Print ads	$3,000	$2,450
	Radio	$1,500	$1,400
	Graphics	$250	$250
	Printing	$350	$350
	Mailing	$1,600	$1,450
	Poster/Flyer Distribution		
	Program Production		
Production Costs		$2,320	$2,320
	Sound Company/Engineer	$1,500	$1,500
	Lighting Rental/Engineer	$550	$550
	Equipment Rentals		$60
	Stage Manager	$120	$120
	Runner/Assistant	$50	$50
	Additional Box Office		
	Backstage Security	$100	$100
Artist Hospitality		$615	$515
	Green Room	$250	$200
	Transportation	$85	$85
	Hotel	$180	$180
	Artist Assistant Misc.	$100	$50
Insurance @ $0.30 Seat		$600	$566.10
ASCAP/BMI/SESAC/SOCAN		$250	$238
TOTAL EXPENSES		$16,667	$16,381
ARTIST GUARANTEE		$10,500	$10,500
SUBTOTAL		$27,167	$26,881
Producer's Fee	@ 15 %	$4,075	$4,032
TOTAL SHOW COST		$31,242	$30,913
GROSS POTENTIAL		$41,500	$38,996
Less Show Cost		$31,242	$30,913
Net Profit/Split		$10,258	$8,083
Artist's % of Net	@ 70 %	$7,181	$5,658
Producer's % of Net	@ 30 %	$3,077	$2,425
Potential to Artist		$17,681	$16,158
Potential to Producer		$7,152	$6,457

> **HotTip:** Include a sentence in your cover letter to the presenter suggesting that the presenter is responsible for distributing copies of the specific riders to the appropriate personnel.

"Have the artist's riders updated!"
Christina Risatti
director,
Downtown Presents

Technical Rider

A Technical Rider should accompany your Performance Contract and Performance Contract Rider and will include all the specific details of your technical requirements. Copies of this rider can then be distributed to the technical personnel working on each specific performance. I have received many last-minute calls from technical personnel claiming they have never received a copy of the technical rider. Even though one was sent with the original contract, the presenter often forgot to forward a copy to the appropriate technician. The Technical Rider form is on page 175 in the forms section of this chapter.

Hospitality Rider

The hospitality rider provides the purchaser with specific information about your act's eating habits, lodging and transportation necessities. It is here that specific details regarding backstage and on-stage requests are stated. This is the form that may tax your presenter's good nature if you are not reasonable with your requests. As you think about your absolute necessities, be realistic. Ask for what you need to perform your best show.

Consider that you may have been driving for hours to make sound-check time and may not have had time to stop for a meal. Knowing that one will be provided for you after sound check is a welcome thought. While preparing this rider, keep in mind that in most cases, this is a budget item that will be deducted from the gross income as one of the presenter's expenses. The more extravagant you are with your requests, the more money will be deducted before your percentage split.

Depending on the type of venue you are performing in, many of your requests will not present any problem for the presenter. Some venues may not have kitchens to prepare hot meals or even a separate room for eating a meal. Prepare your rider to present your needs. Any item that presents a problem for the presenter can most likely be worked out by finding acceptable alternatives. Your flexibility will be most appreciated by each presenter you work with when it comes to discussing items on your Hospitality Rider. You may simply want to add your act's name to the blank form on page 178.

Information Form

There is one last form that you may want to include with your contract and all of the necessary riders. This information form has proven invaluable when the presenters have filled them out. As you will see, it not only requests information specific to the day of performance, but also requests some local media contacts, directions to the venue and the hotels, day of show contacts and shipping address to pre-ship merchandise if needed.

HOSPITALITY RIDER

Dressing Rooms
__2__ Clean Dressing Rooms, heated or air conditioned with private bath, and secure from audience or staff, labeled with Artist names.
Hand towel for each person
Ironing board
Iron
Full-length mirror
Fresh-brewed coffee, tea, hot water and herb teas, milk (special milk __1%__)
Bottled spring water, any brand, not chilled in individual bottles, enough for Artist and crew with real glasses or cups, no Styrofoam please.
Fresh fruit platter

Dining Area near Dressing Rooms (or in dressing room if large enough)
Hot meal after sound check with real plates, silverware and napkins consisting of:
- salad
- fresh broiled fish or chicken
- fresh steamed vegetables
- rice or potato side dish
- crusty bread
- dessert cake, fruit pie or cookies
- soft drinks, coffee, decaf, teas, milk
- NO Dairy

Artist has some specific dietary needs:
- 1 vegetarian requires vegetable dish with tofu

On Stage
Bottled spring water (unchilled), 1 bottle for each member of act for each half of show if there is an intermission. Preferred brand __Evian__
Hand towel for each person
- 1 cup of tea with lemon for lead singer

Lodging
Artist prefers to stay at __Holiday Inn__ Hotel when possible. Purchaser shall pre-pay for rooms and provide Artist with confirmation numbers and contact, address, phone and fax numbers with the return of this contract. When Artist travels in own vehicle, hotel parking must be paid by Purchaser. Artist vehicle is __25__ feet long.

Transportation
Artist will arrive by __own bus__.
When Artist provides own transportation, parking is required for __1 bus 25' long__ (number of vehicles or size and type of vehicle) near stage door of venue for load-in and load-out and for the duration of the show.
When Artist arrives by means other than own transportation, Purchaser shall provide ground transportation as specified in Contract Rider paragraph 9. Artist may require Purchaser to provide local transportation and driver on day of performance to fulfill media requests and interviews to promote show.

> **HotTips:**
> Access Local 1000 through their website:
> http://www.afm.org/1000/
>
> In the U.S. call AFM at:
> 1-800-ROADGIG
> (1-800-762-3444)
> In Canada call AFM at:
> 1-800-INFOFED
> (1-800-463-6333)

When completed by the presenter and returned with the contract, you are able to begin your promotional campaign with the names and addresses provided. If you have another person working to promote you, this form can easily be copied and sent to your publicist. Because it does not include your compensation or other contract-specific details, this form can also be provided to other members of your team when necessary, i.e., record company publicist, management, other members of the act, etc. A sample copy of the information form can be found on page 180.

Union Contracts

The American Federation of Musicians (AFM) of the United States and Canada

The AFM offers their union members many benefits. If you are a musician performing regularly in one specific geographic area, you might want to consider joining the local in your area. As a touring musician, consider joining Local 1000, which has been created specifically to address the concerns of those musicians who tour regularly outside of their local's area.

Some of the benefits offered by AFM membership are:
1. Free Legal Assistance
2. Contract Guarantee Fund
3. Emergency Travel Assistance Programs
4. Pension and Retirement Funds
5. Approved, Free Legal Contract Forms
6. Health and Disability Insurance
7. Equipment/Liability Insurance
8. Credit Unions
9. AFM Mastercard with Preferred Rates
10. Immigration Assistance (INS work permits)

Once you have become a member of the AFM, they will assist you with the information necessary to prepare and file your contracts for each performance. They have recently implemented an electronic filing system that allows you to complete your contract and file it with your local through your computer. Each contract filed affords you all of the benefits enjoyed by an AFM member. Should a dispute arise with a presenter, your membership benefits will, among other things, provide you with free legal assistance to follow through with the dispute to its conclusion, even if that means going to court. All of these union benefits are supported by membership dues. A percentage of each member's completed performance contract is deducted or charged against the fee.

American Federation Of Television And Radio Artists (AFTRA)

Artists who perform regularly on television or on radio may also become a member of AFTRA. Many radio and television shows on which you may appear will issue you an AFTRA contract. (See the resource section for contact information.)

When There Is A Breach Of Contract

Let us return to the example we first encountered at the beginning of the chapter. Your friend promoted a concert and did not have enough money to pay your guarantee. If you had issued a contract to finalize your original agreement, would things have worked differently? Possibly. By agreeing to the items clearly delineated in the contract and then signing it, your friend might have been more respectful of your business and might have taken his/her obligations to you more seriously.

The concert might still have lost money. But because your contract would have spelled out not only your friend's responsibilities and obligations, but also the consequences and actions that would be taken against him should there be a breach, he might have made backup arrangements to insure that all the obligations would be met. If no arrangements had been made, and you did not get paid, the contract you issued and signed serves as your historical documentation of the agreement. This document can then be used as evidence if you choose to turn to the law to seek compensation for breach of your contract.

Your Options

It is advisable to know the legal options that are available to rectify a breach of contract, prior to designing your contract. Incorporating specific clauses which demonstrate your resolve to have the letter of the contract honored places the other party on alert. It is then up to you to decide whether to follow through with the actions necessary to uphold your rights as outlined in your contract. You should always consult a qualified lawyer before taking any legal action. Most lawyers offer an initial consultation for free or for a minimal fee in order to discuss your options, and to tell you which options, upon being hired, they would be willing to pursue.

The following factors must be considered when deciding to exercise your legal right when your contract has been breached:

1. Which contract item is in question?—i.e., is it money owed, unfulfilled rider requests, insurance liability infringement, etc. The seriousness or monetary value of the item in question may help to determine your commitment to seek resolution.
2. What is the cost to you in both time and resources to rectify the infraction?

"A relationship with an attorney means there is always someplace to go and someone to call when trouble hits. More poignant, however, is the notion that it is easier to prevent a mess than to clean one up after the fact."

Andrew L. Braunfeld
attorney, partner,
Masterson, Braunfeld,
McGuire & Brown

"Discourage litigation. Persuade your neighbors to compromise whenever you can."

Abraham Lincoln
U.S. president

"You shoulda come to me first."

Don Corleone, Esquire

> "If you are a touring musician (in the U.S. and Canada) you've gotta join the AFM. They have a one page standard contract that you can use to get the basics of your deal in writing in advance. If you have contracted a date and have problems getting paid—the union will come to your aid."
>
> John Porter
> manager, The Nitty Gritty Dirt Band, Kris Tyler, Mike Robertson Management

> "Litigation is my own choice of last resort for resolving contractual disputes and breaches, because it's costly, time consuming, and exasperating—and that's when it's going well. If you have a real contractual breach, and it's important enough, review all your options, including dropping the issue, and make the cost versus benefit analysis of each option before you do a thing. Believe it or not, you can always save money by consulting an entertainment law specialist first."
>
> Leslie Berman
> attorney at law

3. Which method of conflict resolution will be the most effective to resolve this dispute given the answers to the first two questions?

For example:

If you were not paid a guarantee of $300 and you have a signed contract, what will it cost you to make the presenter pay the money owed? Weighing the costs of pursuing some of the options below may help you decide where your efforts are best spent. If, on the other hand, the unpaid guarantee is $5,000, the stakes are higher and taking action against the promoter more justifiable. Consider each of the four options below and how their expense and time commitment can impact upon your decision to pursue any one of them.

Methods Of Resolving A Breach Of Contract

Small Claims Court

Ordinarily you represent yourself, fill out simple paperwork and pay a small fee to file the complaint or claim form. Then a court date is set, you bring your evidence and if necessary and possible, a witness, or a notarized statement from a witness. The judge hears both sides of the case and makes a ruling for one of you. If you win, you get a judgment for the amount of money the judge decrees (which might be less than you asked for) which you can then enforce by any one of various collection methods. If the person who owes you fails to show up in court, you win by default. Again, you get a judgment in your favor which you can enforce.

Small claims courts are generally held in local town or village courts rather than in county or state courts. Each state's small claims courts have rules about how much you can sue for, who can sue and what you must do to bring a suit. The advantage to pursuing a claim here is the relative simplicity and speed of the process and the low cost of bringing suit.

Arbitration

Arbitration is an alternative to an ordinary law suit. The arbitrator is usually chosen for her/his familiarity with your industry. But, the arbitrator should not be friendly with either of you and should have no financial connections to either of you. You set a time for the arbitration, meet in a less formal setting than a courtroom and have no rules about what evidence or which witnesses you may bring forward. After each of you has presented your side of the case, the arbitrator decides which of you wins. You can then enforce the arbitration settlement by any of the collection means available. Including an arbitration clause in your contract and agreeing in advance on a specific arbitrator or arbitration resolution organization will speed up your claim considerably. You can agree upon who should pay the arbitrator's fee.

Mediation
A neutral party guides negotiations toward a mutually agreeable and sustainable (i.e., viable) settlement. Parties sign an agreement as to method and time of payment of settlement. Enforcement may be limited in some jurisdictions. It is usual for both parties to share paying the mediator's fee. A clause regarding mediation may be included in your contract.

Litigation
This is a standard law suit. The minimum amount for which you may sue differs from state to state. If you have a very large claim and you and the other party live in different states, you may be able to claim federal court jurisdiction. Usually both a substantial amount, say over $50,000, plus legal residence in different states allows you to qualify. Any judgment can be enforced and the value of judgment and fees are reclaimed from the loser.

Conclusion
If you use a well-written contract, deal with each presenter openly and honestly, and do your research to know with whom you are dealing, the necessity for dispute settlements should be rare during your career. If the occasion should arise, though, make every effort to resolve your differences out of court and with the help of a qualified professional.

Summary
- A contract is an agreement between two or more parties.
- Prepare a written document detailing the items to which both parties have agreed.
- Create your own standard contracts and contract performance riders to clearly outline the specifics of your act's needs.
- Read each contract and any modifications made to the contract carefully before signing it, especially contracts issued to you by the presenter.
- Challenge contract items that are inappropriate for your act and negotiate a change or a deletion from the contract.
- Incorporate a budget sheet for each contract that you negotiate to keep track of presenter expenses.
- Promptly issue and return contracts. Keep track of contract return due dates.
- Investigate the benefits offered by membership in a union appropriate for your act.

If you choose to make photocopies of the forms on the following pages, your printer may ask if you have permission from the author to copy any portion of this book, as required by the 1986 Copyright Law. You may show the printer the boxed statement on page 161 whenever you copy any form from this book for your own use.

Chapter 7 Forms—Contract Information Form (2 pages)
Enlarge this form by 127% to fit 8½" x 11" page.

CONTRACT INFORMATION FORM

_____
Group's Name and Contact Information

Today's Date _____

Contact Name _____

Company Name _____

Address _____

City _____ State _____ Zip _____

Phone Day _____ Phone Night _____ Fax _____

E-mail Address _____ Web Address _____

Interest _____ Offer _____ Confirm _____ Contract Sent _____

Type of Engagement _____
(concert, workshop, festival, lecture, co-bill, opener, etc.)

Performance Date(s) _____ Time(s) _____ AM/PM

Number of Sets _____ Length _____ Intermission Length _____

Place of Engagement

Name _____

Address _____

City, State, Zip _____

Phone _____ Fax _____

Box Office Phone _____ Back Stage Phone _____

Capacity _____

Compensation To Be Paid

Fee Guarantee $ _____

Percentage of Gross/Net of Door: _____

Deposit Amount Due $ _____ Date Due _____

Balance of Guarantee $ _____ Date Due _____

Additional Compensations

Workshop, Class, Lecture Fee _____

Transportation

    Ground _____
(taxi, car rental, train, bus, parking, limo.)

    Air _____

Lodging _____

Meals Provided or Buy Out _____

Ticket Price(s) _____

Scaled or Discounted Tickets _____

I, Jeri Goldstein, the author of *How To Be Your Own Booking Agent and Save Thousands of Dollars,* do hereby grant permission to the book's owner to copy any form provided within this volume in whatever quantities deemed necessary for the owner's express use.

Jeri Goldstein

Enlarge this form by 127% to fit 8½" x 11" page.

Contract Information Form—Page 2

Merchandising Percentages Taken by Venue _____

Additional Act(s) on the Bill   Yes _____   No _____   Name(s) _____

Type of Performance _____ Local Act _____ National Act _____

Set Length _____   Start Time _____

Technical

Sound Provided by _____

Lights Provided by _____

Contact Name and Phone _____

Note: _____

CONTRACTS   161

Chapter 7 The Offer Sheet

Note: Offers should be submitted on letterhead.
Enlarge this form by 127% to fit 8½" x 11" page.

OFFER SHEET

DATE:
TO: FAX #:

FROM   FAX:

AS AUTHORIZED BY _____, PLEASE ACCEPT THE FOLLOWING FIRM OFFER:

ARTIST:

DATE:

COMPENSATION: DEPOSIT:

LOCATION:

LENGTH OF PERFORMANCE:

TICKET PRICE:

VENUE CAPACITY:

MERCHANDISING:

HOSPITALITY:

LODGING:

PRODUCTION: Will be provided as per Artist's technical rider

OFFER EXPIRES:

AUTHORIZED SIGNATOR

_____

Chapter 7 Forms—Letter Of Intent
Enlarge this form by 127% to fit 8½" x 11" page.

Date _____

_____
_____
_____

Dear _____

_____ intends to perform for _____ in _____ on _____, ____ at _____. The performance will take place at the _____ located at _____.
All other details pertaining to this performance will be finalized upon notification of _____.

The Presenter must notify the Artist in writing by _____, ____ regarding the status of the details for this date. Failure to notify the Artist by that date releases the Artist from its intended performance date and the Artist is free to seek other bookings for the above-mentioned date.

Good luck. We are looking forward to working with you.

Sincerely,

_____   _____
Leader   Date

_____   _____
Purchaser   Date

CONTRACTS

Chapter 7 Forms—Letter Of Confirmation
Enlarge this form by 127% to fit 8½" x 11" page.

_____
_____
_____
_____

Date _____
_____
_____
_____

Dear _____,

This letter confirms that _____ will perform for _____ in _____ on _____ at _____. The performance will take place at _____ located at _____ _____. The Artist will receive _____ for their performance. The Purchaser will provide _____ single/double rooms at a nearby hotel within _____ minutes drive and no more than _____ miles away from the venue for the night(s) of _____. The performance will include _____ sets of _____ minutes each with a _____ minute intermission. Tickets for this event will be _____. All sound and lighting equipment will be provided by the Purchaser. A professional sound and lighting company will be hired. Technical and hospitality requirements have been attached and are made a part of this agreement.

_____ will be the sole act on the bill. A deposit of _____ dollars made payable to _____ by bank check will be returned with this letter by _____, ____ or the artist may cancel this agreement and seek other performance dates. The balance of the guarantee _____ dollars plus _____ percent of the _____(net/gross) above expenses will be due on _____ at the completion of the performance.

Please sign both copies of this letter and return them with the deposit to the above address. One copy will be signed by the artist and returned for your files. If you have any questions, please don't hesitate to call. Enclosed you will also find the promotional materials that you requested. If you need any additional materials, please call.

Thank you for your prompt reply. We are looking forward to working with you.

Sincerely,

_____   _____
Leader   Date

_____   _____
Purchaser   Date

Chapter 7 Forms—Contract Budget/Settlement (2 pages)
Enlarge this form by 127% to fit 8½" x 11" page.

CONTRACT BUDGET/SETTLEMENT

PERFORMANCE DATE _____ CITY, STATE _____

SUBMITTED BY _____ APPROVED BY _____

TICKET SCALE   @   ATTENDANCE   @

_____ ____ = _____   _____ ____ = _____

_____ ____ = _____   _____ ____ = _____

_____ ____ = _____   _____ ____ = _____

_____ ____ = _____   _____ ____ = _____

HALL CAPACITY _____

DISCOUNTS   @   DISCOUNTS   @

_____ ____ = _____   _____ ____ = _____

_____ ____ = _____   _____ ____ = _____

_____ ____ = _____   _____ ____ = _____

_____ ____ = _____   _____ ____ = _____

TOTAL DISCOUNTS _____

GROSS POTENTIAL _____ GROSS ATTENDANCE _____

HALL COSTS	ESTIMATED	ACTUAL
Rent		
Other %/Gross		
Stagehands #____ @ $____/hr. ____ #hrs.		
Loaders #____ @ $____/hr. ____ #hrs.		
House Manager		
House Staff		
Box Office		
Ticket Commission % $____ @ ____%		
Ticket Printing		
Day of Box Office		
Security		
Custodial		
House Sound		
House Lights		
Spotlights #____ @ $____/hr. ____ #hrs.		
Spot Operators #____ @ $____/hr. ____ #hrs.		
Piano		
Tuner		
Equipment Rentals		
Parking		
Other Facility Expenses		
Subtotal Hall		

CONTRACTS 165

Enlarge form by 127% to fit 8½" by 11" page.

CONTRACT BUDGET/SETTLEMENT CONTINUED: PRODUCTION		
ADVERTISING	ESTIMATED	ACTUAL
Print Ads	_____	_____
Radio	_____	_____
Graphics	_____	_____
Printing	_____	_____
Mailing	_____	_____
Poster/Flyer Distribution	_____	_____
Program Production	_____	_____
PRODUCTION COSTS		
Sound Company/Engineer	_____	_____
Lighting Rental/Engineer	_____	_____
Equipment Rentals	_____	_____
Stage Manager	_____	_____
Runner/Assistant	_____	_____
Additional Box Office	_____	_____
Backstage Security	_____	_____
ARTIST HOSPITALITY		
Green Room	_____	_____
Transportation	_____	_____
Hotel	_____	_____
Artist Assistant Misc.	_____	_____
Insurance @ _____ /Seat	_____	_____
ASCAP/BMI/SESAC/SOCAN	_____	_____
TOTAL EXPENSES	_____	_____
ARTIST GUARANTEE	_____	_____
SUBTOTAL	_____	_____
Producer's Fee @ _____ %	_____	_____
TOTAL SHOW COST	_____	_____
GROSS POTENTIAL	_____	_____
Less Show Cost	_____	_____
Net Profit/Split	_____	_____
Artist's % of Net @ _____ %	_____	_____
Producer's % of Net @ _____ %	_____	_____
Potential to Artist	_____	_____
Potential to Producer	_____	_____

Chapter 7 Forms—Performance Contract (simple) (2 pages)

Enlarge form by 127% to fit 8½" by 11" page.

PERFORMANCE CONTRACT

THIS CONTRACT is made this day of _____ by and between _____ hereinafter called the Artist and _____, hereinafter called the Purchaser. This Contract for Artist's personal services on this engagement described below shall consist of all provisions in this Contract, and any attachments. This Contract shall be executed by Purchaser and returned by _____. If Artist has not received the Contract as described above, the Artist shall at anytime thereafter have the option to terminate the agreement.

1. Purchaser's Contact Information:

Contact Name _____

Company Name _____

Address _____

City _____ State _____ Zip _____

Phone Day _____ Phone Night _____ Fax _____

E-mail Address _____ Personal Phone (home, beeper, etc.) _____

2. Place of Engagement:

Venue Name _____

Address _____

City, State, Zip _____
(Map or directions from nearest highway exit to be furnished by Purchaser)

Phone _____ Fax _____

Box Office Phone _____ Backstage Phone _____

Capacity _____

3. The Performance Date, Times, Length, Load In and Sound Check:

Performance Date(s) _____ Time(s) _____ AM/PM

Number of Sets _____ Length _____ Intermission Length _____

Load In Time _____ Sound Check Time _____

Sound Check Times of Additional Acts, if any _____

4. Type of Engagement: (specify concert, workshop, festival, opener, co-bill):

_____

5. Compensation to Be Paid:

5.1. Fee Guarantee $_____

5.2. Percentage of Gross _____ /Net _____ of Door _____
(Any percentage of the net will be determined by allowable expenses as indicated on the approved, attached budget.)

5.3. Additional Compensations:

5.3a. Workshop, Class, Lecture Fee, etc. _____

Enlarge this form by 127% to fit 8½" x 11" page.

PERFORMANCE CONTRACT   Page 2

5.3b. Transportation _____
5.3c. Lodging _____
5.3d. Meals _____
5.4. Total Guarantee_____
6. Ticket Prices: $ _____
7. Merchandising Policy of the Venue: _____% taken by venue or _____ flat fee.
8. Additional Acts on the Bill: _____
9. Set Length _____Start Time _____

10. **Technical Requirements:** Purchaser shall provide sound and/or lighting equipment as described in the attached Technical Rider. Purchaser shall provide a copy of the Technical Rider to the sound and lighting technicians no less than two (2) weeks prior to the engagement.

11.0. **Cancellation:**
11.1. Purchaser agrees that Artist shall have the right to cancel this engagement without liability upon written notice to Purchaser no later than _____ days prior to the date of performance in the event Artist is called upon to render their services for a radio or television appearance, motion picture, or any career advancing opportunity. Artist will attempt to reschedule the date with the Purchaser for a mutually convenient time.
11.2. Should Purchaser have cause to cancel this agreement, notice must be given to Artist in writing no later than forty-five (45) days prior to this engagement. Any notice given less than forty-five (45) days will require full payment by Purchaser to Artist as described in Contract paragraph 5.4 unless Artist agrees to waive any part of that payment or Purchaser and Artist agree to reschedule the engagement for another time.

12. **Force Majeure:** This agreement by both parties to perform their obligations herein is subject to proven detention by serious illness, accidents, or accidents to means of transportation, labor disputes or walkouts, acts of God, or any act of public authority, material breach of Contract by Purchaser, or any other condition beyond either party's control. Neither party shall be liable to fulfill the remainder of the Contract nor perform or present any "make-up" date unless expressly agreed to by both parties for a convenient future time.

13. **Disputes and Attorney's Fees:** Any controversy or claim arising out of or relating to this Contract, or the breach thereof, shall be settled by arbitration administered by the American Arbitration Association in accordance with its [applicable] rules and judgment on the award rendered by the arbitrator may be entered in any court having jurisdiction thereof.

14. It is agreed that Artist signs this agreement as an independent contractor and not as an employee.

In witness whereof, the parties have executed this Contract on the respective dates shown by their signatures.

_____   _____
Purchaser/Organization's Name   Artist

_____   _____
Name and Title   Name and Title

_____   _____
Authorized Signature   Date   Authorized Signature   Date

_____   _____
Federal I.D. / Social Security #   Federal I.D. / Social Security #

Please sign and return TWO (2) copies of this Contract. One copy will be returned fully executed for your files.

Chapter 7 Forms—Performance Contract (complex) (3 pages)

Enlarge page by 127% to fit 8½" x 11" page.

PERFORMANCE CONTRACT

THIS CONTRACT is made this day of _____ by and between _____ hereinafter called the Artist and _____, hereinafter called the Purchaser. This Contract for Artist's personal services on this engagement described below shall consist of all provisions in this Contract, and any attachments. This contract shall be executed by Purchaser and returned by _____. If Artist has not received the Contract as described above, the Artist shall at anytime thereafter have the option to terminate the agreement.

1. Purchaser's Contact Information:

Contact Name _____

Company Name _____

Address _____

City_____ State _____ Zip _____

Phone Day _____ Phone Night _____ Fax _____

E-mail Address _____ Personal Phone (home, beeper, etc.) _____

2. Place of Engagement:

Venue Name _____

Address _____

City, State, Zip _____
(Map or directions from nearest highway exit to be furnished by Purchaser)

Phone _____ Fax _____

Box Office Phone _____ Backstage Phone _____

Capacity _____

3. The Performance Date, Times, Length, Load In and Sound Check:

Performance Date(s) _____ Time(s) _____ AM/PM

Number of Sets _____ Length _____ Intermission Length _____

Load In Time _____ Sound Check Time _____

Sound Check Times of Additional Acts, if any _____

4. Type of Engagement: (specify concert, workshop, festival, opener, co-bill):
_____

5. Compensation to Be Paid:

5.1. Fee Guarantee $_____

5.2. Percentage of Gross_____/Net _____ of Door _____
(Any percentage of the net will be determined by allowable expenses as indicated on the approved, attached budget.)

5.3. Additional Compensations:

5.3a. Workshop, Class, Lecture Fee, etc. _____

PERFORMANCE CONTRACT

Page 2

5.3b. Transportation
Ground _____
Air _____
5.3c. Lodging _____
5.3d. Meals Provided or Buy Out _____
5.4. Total _____

6. Deposit Amount Due _____ Date Due _____

7. Balance of Guarantee _____ Date Due _____

8. Ticket Prices: _____ seats @ $ _____

_____ seats @ $ _____

_____ seats @ $ _____

9. Merchandising Policy of the Venue: _____ % taken by venue or _____ flat fee.

10. Additional Acts on the Bill: _____

11. Set Length _____ Start Time _____

12. Technical Requirements: Purchaser shall provide sound and/ or lighting equipment as described in the attached Technical Rider. Purchaser shall provide a copy of the Technical Rider to the sound and lighting technicians no less than two (2) weeks prior to the engagement.

13. Withholding: Purchaser shall notify Artist of any and all state or local taxes required to be withheld or deducted from the Artist's fee specified in the Contract prior to signing the Contract. If Artist is not so notified, payment of any such withholdings shall be the responsibility of the Purchaser and shall not be deducted from Artist's fee.

13.1. Taxes: No admission tax shall be deducted from the gross box office receipts before computing percentages due unless the amount of tax is stated on the Contract.

14. Insurance and Indemnity: Purchaser agrees to obtain at Purchaser's sole cost and expense any and all necessary personal injury and property damage liability insurance with respect to the activities of Artist on the premises of Purchaser or at any other location where Purchaser directs the Artist to perform. Purchaser shall provide Artist with a copy of the Certificate of Insurance no less than fourteen (14) days prior to the performance in the amount of no less than one million dollars per occurrence with respect to damage to property and no less than one million dollars with respect to death or personal injury. Purchaser's policy shall name Artist and Artist's employees, and representatives as additional insured parties.

14.1 Purchaser shall indemnify and hold Artist and Artist's employees and representatives, and attorneys harmless from and against any and all claims, demands, actions, damages, liability, costs and expenses including attorney's fees arising out of or in conjunction with any personal injury, death, and loss of or damage to property which occurs in connection with any performance by Artist unless caused by the sole conduct of Artist or any employee or representative of Artist.

15.0. Cancellation:

15.1. Purchaser agrees that Artist shall have the right to cancel this engagement without liability upon written notice to Purchaser no later than _____ days prior to the date of performance in the event Artist is called upon to render their services for a radio or television appearance, motion picture, or any career advancing opportunity. Artist will attempt to reschedule the date with the purchaser for a mutually convenient time.

PERFORMANCE CONTRACT

15.2. Should Purchaser have cause to cancel this agreement, notice must be given to Artist in writing no later than forty-five (45) days prior to this engagement. Any notice given less than forty-five (45) days will require full payment by Purchaser to Artist as described in Contract paragraph 5.1 unless Artist agrees to waive any part of that payment or Purchaser and Artist agree to reschedule the engagement for another time.

16. Force Majeure: This agreement by both parties to perform their obligations herein is subject to proven detention by serious illness, accidents, or accidents to means of transportation, labor disputes or walkouts, acts of God, or any act of public authority, material breach of Contract by Purchaser, or any other condition beyond either party's control. Neither party shall be liable to fulfill the remainder of the Contract nor perform or present any "make-up" date unless expressly agreed to by both parties for a convenient future time.

17. Disputes and Attorney's Fees: Any controversy or claim arising out of or relating to this Contract, or the breach thereof, shall be settled by arbitration administered by the American Arbitration Association in accordance with its [applicable] rules and judgment on the award rendered by the arbitrator may be entered in any court having jurisdiction thereof.

17.1. Attorney's Fees: In the event that any dispute arises while this agreement is in force that results in litigation or arbitration, all reasonable attorney's fees and costs of the prevailing party will be paid by the losing party.

18. If any term, provision, covenant, or condition in this Contract is held by a court or competent jurisdiction to be invalid, void or unenforceable, the rest of the Contract shall remain in full force and effect and in no way be affected, impaired or invalidated.

19. It is agreed that Artist signs this Agreement as an independent contractor and not as an employee.

20. Jurisdiction: This Contract may not be assigned, modified or altered except by an instrument in writing signed by both parties. This Agreement along with the attached riders and budget constitutes the sole and binding Contract between the parties hereto. This Contract shall be construed in accordance with the laws of the State of _____ and the laws of that state shall govern its interpretation and effect.

In witness whereof, the parties have executed this Contract on the respective dates shown by their signatures.

_____ _____
Purchaser/Organization's Name   Artist

_____ _____
Name and Title   Name and Title

_____ ____ _____ ____
Authorized Signature   Date   Authorized Signature   Date

_____ _____
Federal I.D. / Social Security #   Federal I.D. / Social Security #

Please sign and return TWO (2) copies of this Contract. One copy will be returned fully executed for your files.

Chapter 7 Forms—Performance Contract Rider (3 pages)
Enlarge this form by 127% to fit 8½" x 11" page.

Performance Contract Rider

The parties hereto hereby acknowledge that the following additional terms and conditions are incorporated in and made part of this Contract.

1.0 BILLING:
Artist shall receive one hundred (100%) top line, sole headline billing in all advertising and publicity. No other acts shall receive prominent billing on any advertisement or promotion without Artist's prior written agreement. Artist has the right to approve any additional acts to be placed on the bill and to determine the length of such act's performance prior to their hiring and prior to the release of any publicity. Artist also reserves the right to invite any last minute guests on stage, at their discretion, as long as it does not impose a technical or economic burden on the Purchaser.

2.0. PAYMENT:
2.1. All payments provided for hereunder shall be made by Money Order, Cash, Certified, Cashier's, Business or School Check. Payment shall be made in U.S. currency unless specifically provided herein.
2.2. All payments shall be made to _____ unless otherwise specified. Purchaser shall settle box office and make all payments to Artist in a secured, private area.
2.3. A deposit of fifty percent (50%) of the total guaranteed compensation shown on the Contract shall be due by the date specified on the Contract. The deposit shall be in the form of a certified or cashier's check made payable as described in 2.2. If the deposit is not received by the specified due date, Artist shall have the right to cancel the engagement without liability of any kind to Purchaser.
2.4. When a percentage figure is included in the total compensation due to the Artist, the method of calculating the percentage shall be gross receipts determined by admissions minus expenses as agreed in budget.
(a). All acceptable expenses shall be shown in the budget. Purchaser shall provide net receipts for all items designated and agreed upon in the budget. If there is any difference between the budget and the actual amount spent, Artist shall receive the percentage share of the difference as shown on the Contract. Expenses in excess of the budget shall be borne solely by the Purchaser unless Purchaser obtains Artist's prior written consent to incur excess expense.
(b). Purchaser shall provide all receipts for expenses at the time of settling the box office. If, at that time, Purchaser is unable to provide all receipts for the performance, Purchaser shall furnish such receipts to Artist, within ten (10) days after the Artist's performance, copies not presented at the time of settlement. Any expense not supported by receipts shall not be deductible as such.
(c). All tickets shall be printed by a bonded ticket printer, or if at a college or university, by the official printing department of the institution.
(d). All tickets must be consecutively numbered.
(e). When two or more shows are scheduled, each show shall be a different colored ticket. Tickets of different prices shall be in a separate set for each price.
(f). Artist shall have access to the box office prior to opening for inspection of the ticket manifest provided by the printer.
(g). No tickets shall be offered at a discount or a premium without prior written consent of the Artist. All tickets shall be calculated at the full face value on the ticket.
(h). Artist or Artist's representative shall have full access to all box office sales to determine the gross receipts of the performance.
(i). Purchaser shall not distribute more than ___% of total number of available seats as complimentary tickets. Each complimentary ticket shall be issued as a canceled ticket and may not be resold. Purchaser agrees to supply proper radio, television and newspaper personnel with complimentary tickets from the Purchaser's allotment.
(j). In addition, Purchaser shall provide Artist with _____ complimentary tickets per performance, the unused portion of which shall be placed on sale the day of the performance with the permission of Artist or Artist's representative.
(k). Purchaser shall be fully responsible for any and all counterfeit tickets. Under no circumstance shall Artist absorb any loss as a result of such tickets.

3.0. PUBLICITY AND ADVERTISING:
3.1. Purchaser will use only those current publicity materials provided by Artist or Artist's representative to advertise and publicize this engagement.
3.2. Purchaser agrees to publicize the engagement to its fullest capabilities including display ads in major area newspapers, listings in all available media formats, bill posting, mailings and distribution of circulars as well as

Performance Contract Rider Page 2

any possible pre-promotions on radio and television. Purchaser shall be responsible for all matters relating to the promotion and production of the performance, including but not limited to production costs, venue rentals, security and advertising.

3.3. All television, radio, press appearances and pre-concert phone interviews, must be cleared in advance with _____ at _____.

3.4. Artist requests that Purchaser forward any clippings of original reviews, previews, publicity, advertising, and copies of posters to Artist at the address provided.

4.0. HALL:

4.1. Purchaser will provide personnel to staff the hall with ushers, ticket takers, box office personnel.

4.2. NO SMOKING restrictions will be enforced in the hall, on stage and in the dressing room area during sound check and performance.

4.3. Stage must be accessible to performers by means other than through the audience. Stage, backstage must be swept, and curtains must be clean and in good condition.

4.4. For all indoor performances, hall will be available to sound and lighting company at least four (4) hours prior to sound check, for set up and equipment testing.

4.5. For all outdoor performances, Purchaser must provide a covering over the stage area to protect Artist and all equipment.

5.0. SECURITY:

5.1. Purchaser shall provide an adequate security staff to insure the safety of Artist and Artist's personnel, equipment, instruments, personal property and vehicles from the time of arrival at the venue until final departure. Purchaser shall be responsible for the security of all items in Artist's dressing rooms and shall prevent all unauthorized personnel from entry to dressing rooms or backstage area. Security will prevent unauthorized persons from entering hall during sound check and from coming on-stage during and after performance.

5.2. Purchaser shall provide Artist with _____ backstage passes upon Artist's arrival at venue unless Artist notifies Purchaser of other arrangements. When Artist provides laminate passes, NO backstage passes, stage access passes or guest passes may be distributed by Purchaser without Artist's approval.

5.3. All guest tickets and backstage access passes shall be picked up at the box office and not at the stage door.

6.0. DRESSING ROOMS:

6.1. Purchaser shall provide _____ clean, lockable, dressing rooms, well heated or air conditioned, well lighted with full length mirror and with a private bathroom in or near dressing room(s). Dressing rooms shall be accessible to the stage by separate entrance other than through the audience. All unauthorized people shall be denied access to the dressing room area.

6.2. Purchaser agrees to provide bottled water on stage and refreshments backstage with a hot meal after sound check for _____ Artist's band and crew. Please refer to Hospitality Rider included. Please notify Artist(s) representative of final food arrangements at least 1 week prior to engagement. Please note special dietary requests for allergies/vegetarians.

7.0. LODGING:

7.1. When Purchaser provides lodging it shall be at a AAA-recommended hotel for the night of the performance. Artist requires _____ non-smoking double rooms with two double beds and private bath near the venue. Rooms shall be pre-paid by Purchaser and confirmation numbers, address, phone and fax numbers, e-mail address and contact person provided to Artist at least two weeks prior to the performance.

8.0. TRANSPORTATION:

8.1. Purchaser agrees to provide ground transportation at Purchaser's expense to and from airport, hotel and venue. Artist requires a vehicle large enough to transport _____ people, luggage, equipment and instruments. Please notify Artist of driver's name and phone number two weeks prior to engagement. When Artist is required to use public transportation from an airport, Purchaser shall reimburse Artist the full amount of receipt at time of settlement. Purchaser shall provide time schedules for recommended public transport as well as street maps and directions.

9.0. MERCHANDISING:

9.1. Artist or Artist's licensee shall have the sole right to sell, advertise, promote and distribute prior to, during

Performance Contract Rider — Page 3

and after the performance, any and all merchandise bearing the Artist's name and/or likeness, including but not limited to souvenir program books, pictures, records, tapes, and items of clothing, etc. All receipts derived from the sale of said merchandise belong solely to the Artist excluding any percentage of sales as specified in advance in Contract.

9.2. Purchaser shall provide a 6-foot table set up in a convenient location for display and sale of merchandise.

9.3. Purchaser shall provide at its expense persons to sell Artist's merchandise who will be available in the venue at sound check time to receive and set up merchandise from Artist or Artist's representative unless otherwise specified.

9.4. Artist or Artist's representative will conduct an inventory of all merchandise prior to any sale and again at the close of all sales.

9.5. Purchaser is responsible to provide security for all merchandise and for all moneys from sales. Any percentage due to Purchaser or venue from merchandise sales or starting cash box provided by Purchaser will be settled by Artist or Artist's representative at inventory closeout and deducted from final accounting.

10.0. RECORDING RESTRICTIONS:

10.1. There shall be NO recording, copying, reproducing, or transmitting of any performance by Artist by any means now known or to be later developed, including audio and/or video, without written prior consent of Artist.

10.2. Purchaser shall restrict any audience member from taking any flash photographs at any time during the performance. Purchaser shall further restrict any audience member from recording any and all portions of the performance by any means now known or to be developed including audio and/or video.

10.3. Purchaser shall limit photography by professionals and must check with Artist(s) or Artist's representative prior to granting permission to professionals.

_____
Purchaser/Organization's Name

_____
Name and Title

_____
Authorized Signature   Date

_____
Federal I.D. / Social Security #

_____
Artist

_____
Name and Title

_____
Authorized Signature   Date

_____
Federal I.D. / Social Security #

Chapter 7 Forms—Technical Rider (3 pages)
Enlarge this form by 127% to fit 8½" x 11" page.

TECHNICAL RIDER

This Technical Rider is hereby attached to the Contract for the performance date of _____ between the parties named herein.

1. Purchaser _____
   Address _____
   City, State, Zip _____
   Phone _____ Fax _____ E-mail _____
2. Artist _____
   Artist Advance Contact _____
   Address Advance Contact _____
   Phone _____ Fax _____ E-mail _____
3. Place of Engagement _____
   Address _____
   City, State, Zip _____
   Venue Description (i.e., high ceilings, thrust stage, bare walls, etc.) _____
   _____
   Day of Show Phone _____
4. Type of Performance (i.e., concert, workshop, festival, etc.) _____
   _____
5. Number of Sets and Length _____
6. Audience Capacity _____
7. Load-In to be determined by _____

Hall will be available for load-in and setup by technical crew at _____.
and for Artist load-in at _____

8. Sound Check

Hall will be available for Artist sound check _____(date) _____(time). All sound reinforcement systems shall be in place, in good working order with room EQ'd, prior to Artist's arrival for sound check. Artist requires a _____(hour(s)) setup and sound check period. Artist shall complete setup and sound check _____(hour(s)) prior to performance time provided that all equipment is in good working order and hall was accessible at the times indicated above. Purchaser shall not permit the doors to open to audience until all technical and sound checks have been completed to Artist's satisfaction. Purchaser, technical crew and Artist agree to make every effort to start the performance on time. Purchaser shall pay Artist _____ penalty for starting the performance later than _____ minutes past the contracted start time due to the fault of the purchaser. Any additional expenses, like union overtime charges shall be the sole responsibility of the purchaser when the expense occurs due to a late start.

9. Sound Reinforcement System

Purchaser agrees to provide a professional sound system in good to excellent working condition appropriately sized to cover the entire room. The system shall minimally consist of the following:

House Console
   _____ input channels

Enlarge this form by 127% to fit 8½" x 11" page.

TECHNICAL RIDER Page 2

    4-Band EQ on each channel
    Acceptable Brands _____
    _____

House Rack (Outboard Gear)
    _____ Digital Reverb
    _____ Digital Delay
    _____ Outboard Compressors
    _____ 1/3-Octave Equalizer for stereo setup
    _____ CD Player
    _____ Cassette Player/Recorder set up for record and playback

House Speakers
    Stereo 3- or 4-Way System shall adequately provide coverage for venue
    Artist prefers system to be flown whenever possible.
    Speakers should be angled for adequate balcony coverage when not flown.

House Mix Position
    Stage Right Center or Stage Left Center
    Not more than _____ feet from the stage
    Unacceptable Mix Positions: Behind walls, under balconies, in balcony

Stage Monitor System
    _____ Channel Console
    4-Band Sweepable EQ on each input
    Preferred Brands_____
    _____

    _____ 1/3-Octave EQ's
    _____ Reverb Unit
    _____ Identical Monitor Wedges
    Each wedge should contain _____ woofers plus one _____ horn.
    _____ Separate Monitor Mixes
    1 Monitor Mix Engineer

Monitor Mix Position
    On Stage _____ (left or right): Engineer must have full view of stage with no obstructions.

On-stage Equipment
    _____ Microphones
    _____ Boom Stands
    _____ Straight Stands
    _____ Electric Quad Boxes
    _____ Active Direct Boxes
    _____ Piano (specify) _____
    _____ Stools or benches
    _____ Drum Risers _____ high _____ feet wide by _____ feet deep.
    _____ Drum Throne
    Specific Back-Line Equipment Required: _____
    _____
    _____

All technical questions regarding specific equipment and Artist's requirements must be directed to Artist Representative (Name)_____ (Phone) _____

Enlarge this form by 127% to fit 8½" x 11" page.

TECHNICAL RIDER   Page 3

10. Personnel
Purchaser agrees to hire a professional sound company including sound engineers trained to set up and run the technical equipment specified in this Technical Rider. If technical personnel are provided other than from a professional sound company, Artist must be notified. The name and contact numbers are:

_____

11. Stage Plot
Artist will provide Purchaser with the following when the completed contract (wc) is returned or during sound check (sc):
      _____ A current stage plot and line input chart (wc)
      _____ A set list (sc)
      _____ A list of soloing musicians (sc)
      _____ Special information regarding backup tapes, effects, sampling and computer-generated sounds. (sc)

12. Lighting
Purchaser shall provide a professional lighting system with adequate personnel to operate the house system and any follow spots. When Artist provides a lighting design and plot, Purchaser's designated lighting technician shall contact Artist or Artist's representative at least two (2) weeks prior to engagement. Purchaser's lighting technician contact _____ Phone _____.
Lighting requirements when a light plot is not provided should be simple and enhance the performance. Lighting should frame artists directly. Avoid light spills into the audience or unnecessarily lighting unused portions of the stage.
    Operator must be present during sound check to position and final-focus lights
      _____ Follow Spots with Operator
      _____ Leko's placed and focused one on each player position to highlight solo's
      _____ Par64's for front, rear and side fills to provide general wash with colored gels

Acceptable Flesh Tone Gels: pale lavender, pale pinks and light reds.
Acceptable Mood Gels: reds, blues, purples, ambers.
      _____ Dimmer Board and Operator
Artist shall instruct operator regarding specific light cues or mood changes during sound check. Unless otherwise instructed, lighting and color changes should be kept to a minimum and compliment the performance at all times.

13. Purchaser is responsible for providing copies of this technical rider to the appropriate personnel not less than two weeks prior to the engagement.

_____   _____
Purchaser's Name and Title   Artist's Name and Title

_____   _____
Authorized Signature   Date   Authorized Signature   Date

Chapter 7 Forms—Hospitality Rider (2 pages)
Enlarge this form by 127% to fit 8½" x 11" page.

HOSPITALITY RIDER

Dressing Rooms
   _____ Clean Dressing Rooms, heated or air conditioned with private bath, and secure from audience or staff, labeled with Artist names.
   Hand towel for each person
   Ironing board
   Iron
   Full-length mirror
   Fresh brewed coffee, tea, hot water and herb teas, milk (special milk____)
   Bottled spring water, any brand, not chilled in individual bottles; enough for Artist and crew with real glasses or cups, no Styrofoam please.
   Fresh fruit platter

Dining Area near Dressing Rooms (or in dressing room if large enough)
Hot meal after sound check with real plates, silverware and napkins consisting of:

_____
_____
_____
_____
_____
_____
_____
_____
_____
_____

Artist has some specific dietary needs:
_____
_____

On Stage
   Bottled spring water (unchilled), 1 bottle for each member of act for each half of show if there is an intermission. Preferred brand _____
   Hand towel for each person
   _____
   _____
   _____

Lodging
   Artist prefers to stay at _____ Hotel when possible. Purchaser shall pre-pay for rooms and provide Artist with confirmation numbers and contact, address, phone and fax numbers with the return of this contract. When Artist travels in own vehicle, hotel parking must be paid by Purchaser. Artist vehicle is_____ feet long.

Transportation
   Artist will arrive by _____.
   When Artist provides own transportation, parking is required for _____ (number of vehicles or size and type of vehicle) near stage door of venue for load-in and load-out and for the duration of the show.

HOSPITALITY RIDER Page 2

When Artist arrives by means other than own transportation, Purchaser shall provide ground transportation as specified in Contract Rider paragraph 9. Artist may require Purchaser to provide local transportation and driver on day of performance to fulfill media and promotional interviews to promote show.

_____   _____
Purchaser's Name and Title   Artist's Name and Title

_____ _____ _____ _____
Authorized Signature   Date   Authorized Signature   Date

Chapter 7 Forms—Information Form (2 pages)
Enlarge this form by 127% to fit 8½" x 11" page.

INFORMATION FORM

PLEASE RETURN THIS FORM WITH YOUR SIGNED CONTRACT. THANK YOU.

Artist Name _____
Performance Date(s) _____ Time(s) _____
Venue Name _____
Venue Street Address _____
Name of person filling out this form _____
Your Phone # (___) _____ Your Fax # (___) _____
Setup/Rehearsal Time _____
Artist will have access to venue at what time _____ sound check time _____
Stage Size _____
If you have theater specifications, please return a copy with this form.

IMPORTANT PHONE NUMBERS
Person who booked the show _____ (___)_____
Person to notify upon arrival _____ (___)_____
Technical person (sound/lights) _____ (___)_____
Backstage contact _____ (___)_____
Box Office contact _____ (___)_____
Publicity person _____ (___)_____

In case of emergency contact number day of show _____ (___)_____
Where Artist may be reached at venue day of show _____ (___)_____

Address where record albums and artist merchandise can be shipped (a street address and phone number where someone is present between 9:00 a.m. and 5:00 p.m. weekdays)
Address: _____
Phone: (___) _____

Please give directions to the performance location from a major highway. Add a separate sheet if more room is needed.
_____
_____
_____
_____
_____

PLEASE PROVIDE A MAP OF THE LOCAL AREA
(Please mark venue, parking, lodging, restaurant etc. on map)

Recommended hotel(s) near performance location (name/address/phone number):
_____
_____

Enlarge this form by 127% to fit 8½" x 11" page.

INFORMATION FORM   Page 2

If you are providing lodging, please give name, address, and phone number of Hotel:
_____
_____

Private lodging:
_____

Dinner arrangements or nearby restaurants, grocery stores or specialty markets.
_____
_____

Location _____

Please recommend a local auto mechanic or _____ dealer in case of emergency or routine maintenance checkup.
_____
_____

Please list three local radio and TV stations and contacts, phone numbers, addresses:
_____
_____
_____

Please list local newspapers for interviews, calendar listings, press releases. Contacts, addresses, phone for individuals who deal with each type of service: _____
_____
_____
_____
_____
_____
_____

Please recommend a local (insert your special request. i.e., masseuse, guitar teacher, golf pro, etc.) ____
_____
_____
_____
_____

CONTRACTS

Chapter 7 Forms—Contract & Promo Tracking Form
Enlarge this form by 127% to fit 8½" x 11" page.

Play Date	Venue	City	CONTRACT Send Date	CONTRACT Return Date	PROMO Send Date	Package Contents	SHIPPING Cost	SHIPPING Method

Contract & Promo Tracking Form

Resources

Books:

All You Need To Know About The Music Business
Donald Passman
Simon & Schuster Trade
ISBN: 0684870649

Entertainment Law
Howard Siegel, Esq.
Editor-In-Chief
Albany New York: New York State
Bar Association, 1990

*Get It In Writing: A Musician's Guide
To The Music Business*
Brian McPherson
Hal Leonard Publishing Corporation
ISBN: 0793566991

Law and Business of the Entertainment Industries
Donald E. Bilderman, Martin E. Silfen, Robert C.
Berrz, Jeanne A. Glasser
Watson-Guptil
ISBN: 02759698356

*Legal Aspects of the Music Industry: An Insider's
View of the Legal and Practical Aspects of the
Music Business*
Richard Schulenberg
The definitive guide to contracts commonly used in
the music industry.
Watson-Guptil
ISBN: 0823083276

*Making It In The Music Business:
A Business & Legal Guide For Songwriters and
Performers*
Lee Wilson
Allworth Press
ISBN: 1581150369

Music Contracts.com
Web: http://www.contracts.com
Downloadable contracts and contract packages
priced per item.

This Business of Music
William M. Krasilovsky and Sidney Shemel
Billboard Books/Watson-Guptill Publications
ISBN: 0823077284

The Musician's Business & Legal Guide
Mark E. Halloran, Esq.
A Jerome Headlands Press Book
P.O. Box N
Jerome, AZ 86331
Phone: 520-634-8894
Fax: 520-634-2518
E-mail: jhpress@sedona.net

*101 Music Business Contracts
(CD-ROM included)*
R. Williams
Platinum Millennium
ISBN: 0971339880
Web: http://www.order-yours-now.com

See page 43 for more books.

Legal Resources:

American Bar Association
321 North Clark Street
Chicago, IL 60611
Phone: 1-800-285-2221
Phone: 312-988-5000
Web: http://www.abanet.org
Available: *The Red Book*
List of state bar associations and more.
Call for publication list.

Beverley Hills Bar Association
300 South Beverly Drive, Suite 201
Beverly Hills, CA 90212
Phone: 310-553-6644
Call for publications list.

California Lawyers for the Arts
Fort Mason Center
Building C, Room 255
San Francisco, CA 94123
Phone: 415-775-7200
Fax: 415-775-1143
Web: http://www.calawyersforthearts.org

California Lawyers for the Arts
1641 18th Street
Santa Monica, CA 90401
Phone: 310-998-5590
Fax: 310-998-5594
Web: http://www.calawyersforthearts.org

Music Attorneys, Legal and Business Affairs Registry
The Music Business Registry
7510 Sunset Blvd., Suite 1041
Los Angeles, CA 90046-3418
Phone: 1-800-377-7411
Fax: 1-800-995-7459
E-mail: info@musicregistry.com
Web: http://www.musicregistry.com

Practicing Law Institute
810 Seventh Ave.
New York, NY 10019
Phone: 1-800-260-4754
Fax: 1-800-321-0093
Call for publication list.
Web: http://www.PLI.edu

Volunteer Lawyers for the Arts
918 16th St. NW
Washington, DC 20006
Phone: 202-429-0229
Web: http://www.thewala.org

Volunteer Lawyers for the Arts
One East 53rd Street, 6th Floor
New York, NY 10022
Phone: 212-319-2787
Art Law Line: 212-319-2787, ext. 1
Web: http://www.vlany.org

Lawyers:
See Appendix, page 482.

Unions:

American Federation of Musicians of the United States and Canada (AFM)
New York Headquarters
1501 Broadway, Suite 600
New York, NY 10036-5503
Phone: 1-800-762-3444
Phone: 212-869-1330
Fax: 212-764-6134
Web: http://www.afm.org

AFM—Local 1000
Web: http://www.afm.org/1000/

AFM—West Coast Office
3550 Wilshire Blvd., Suite 1900
Los Angeles, CA 90010
Phone: 1-800-237-0988
Phone: 323-251-4510
Fax: 323-251-4520

AFM—Canadian Office
75 The Donway West, Suite 1010
Don Mills, Ontario Canada M3C 2E9
Phone: 1-800-463-6333 (within Canada)
Phone: 416-391-5161
Fax: 416-391-5165
E-mail: afmcan@ican.net

American Federation of Television and Radio Artists (AFTRA)

AFTRA-New York Office
260 Madison Avenue
New York, NY 10016
Phone: 212-532-0800
Fax: 212-532-2242
Web: http://www.aftra.com

AFTRA-Los Angeles Office
5757 Wilshire Blvd., 9th floor
Los Angeles, CA 90036-3689
Phone: 323-634-8100
Fax: 323-634-8246

CHAPTER EIGHT

The Art Of Touring

"Whether you are working with an agent or booking yourself, you are responsible for making sure your tour is doable, enjoyable and a good career investment. The artistic freedom that you have on stage extends into the booking process. Custom designing your tour with a broad definition of success maximizes your chances for satisfaction and minimizes road burnout."

Judith-Kate Friedman
singer, songwriter

You have planned your future and organized your business throughout the early parts of this book. Since you have increased your business savvy, you now are ready to get down to the nitty gritty and finally book your tours. At the end of this chapter is a resource section which contains lists of directories, magazine references with specific performance venues and contact information, as well as websites offering lists of venues. With the resources provided, you should find enough potential promoters and venues to keep you on the phone and on the road for many years to follow. More importantly, however, this chapter offers some fresh alternatives about how to pursue performance dates. You are the creative source of your successful touring career, therefore, approach booking tours using the same creative nature with which you approach your art.

"The advantages of doing your own booking are having direct contact with the buyer and a better feel for the gig."

Liz Masterson
singer, songwriter

Reasons For Touring

Each artist approaches their reasons for touring with a very individual perspective which may change each time you tour. Examine what you want to get out of each trip and make sure each tour builds on the success of the previous one. In many performers' lives, their determination to craft a successful performing career in their hometowns may preclude them from ever needing to travel. The performers' desire for the warmth and comfort of their own beds night after night might drive their career plans. For those of you who have decided to expand beyond your city's limits and take on the challenge of "The Road," determine your reasons for touring as you consult this list. Feel free to add some reasons of your own in the spaces provided.

> *"I think the most important thing to figure out before you book a tour is why you are doing it—to promote a new product, for exposure and reviews, to make money? These things can influence which gigs make sense and which promoters/venues to approach."*
>
> **Tam Martin**
> owner, agent,
> Beachfront Bookings/Productions

Reasons for touring are to:
- Move beyond the hometown venues which you have outgrown
- Make a living
- Promote a new release
- Promote a new band
- Try out new material
- Practice new material before recording
- Travel and see the world
- Promote a cause (political, charitable, social)
- See friends and family in other parts of the world
- Promote a new show
- Build audience and increase your value in new markets
- Showcase for career-advancing opportunities (for agents, managers, TV or radio, studio work, to join a new group)
- Support a larger act (as opening act or co-bill)
- Support an anchor date (build a full week from one initial date)
- Support a hobby or sport outside of performing (golf, skiing, collecting, antiquing)
- Support another event outside of performing (conferences, weddings, family gatherings, vacations)
- Perform for new audiences simply because you enjoy it and that is what you do

_____
_____
_____
_____
_____

> *"A music tour is not a pleasure cruise, although your friends will often say, "How was your vacation?"*
>
> **Sean Blackburn**
> singer, songwriter

Use this list of reasons for touring along with your additions each time you begin planning a tour. Having a clarity of purpose makes booking each date more meaningful. Having a well-defined purpose for touring also factors into your bottom line when you are negotiating, creating budgets, and planning travel and promotional campaigns.

Remind yourself of the reasons for this upcoming tour prior to each phone session. This will spark your enthusiasm and give you incentive for booking the tour. Each new phone call gets you that much closer to realizing the goal of the tour. With each tour you book, the business of booking will become easier to accomplish. The next step is to make each trip more fulfilling than the last in order to satisfy the original reason for touring.

By applying the reasons for touring to each successive tour, a self-booking artist can add inspiration to opportunity and imagination to the mundane—redefining the meaning of success.

Creative Tour Planning

As creative individuals, artists who book themselves have the opportunity to infuse their tour planning with the same creative energy that drives their art. The artist who plans their own tour schedule can make routing decisions that will incorporate fun, adventure and career-advancing activities within the allotted tour time. These decisions have the benefit of being made without consulting an agent, whose goal is most likely to pack as many commissionable dates within the designated tour time as possible, leaving little or no time for fun and adventure.

Cherish these moments of inspiration as you develop a tour that is a reflection of your whole self—the artist, the entrepreneur, the family member away from home, the publicist promoting a new release, the roller blader, the cyclist, the skier, the golfer, the seeker and the tourist. Review your life's dreams and goals each time you begin planning your next tour. Perhaps it can be a stepping stone to fulfilling one of those dreams. Allow the artist within you to be the overseer of this aspect of your career. Creating an exciting tour that enhances your whole life is one of the advantages the self-booking artist has over an artist booked by an agency.

Enhance your tours with a creative flare by considering each type of date booked and incorporating additional business and personal events into the schedule during the planning process. Each time I began planning a tour for any of my artists, I would ask them about their personal agendas and the specific goals that they would like to accomplish. This shaped much of my creative focus as I reviewed the maps and the time frame allotted to the tour. The overview helped me envision all of my resources for performance venues as well as any target points of interest along the travel route. I was able to consider known friends or family in cities they would be likely to pass through and any other factors that I

> **HotTips:**
> Tour to towns near friends and family to keep in touch and build your fan base. Friends and family can turn a nearly empty venue into a comfortably full room, impressing the promoter.

"After 20-some years of touring, we tired of always seeing 'the place we played at and the place we stayed at.' We now make more of an effort to see more, do more, enjoy time on the road outside of the gig—catch a museum, etc."

Cathy Fink
singer, songwriter, producer

> **HotTips:**
> Check with your accountant, travel to clearly-defined tour dates is deductible even when non-business events are included within the travel time.
>
>
>
> *How To Make Money Performing In Schools* by David Heflick is an excellent resource for those artists performing in school assembly programs. (See resource section of this chapter.)

knew might be of interest to my artist. These next two lists provide some suggestions for creative scheduling and creative use of non-performance days. Keep in mind, however; there are no rules that strictly demand that a tour be conducted in one manner or another.

Booking The Dates Creatively

1. *Higher-Paying Mid-Week Dates:* Use higher-paying mid-week bookings in schools, colleges and concert series to support weekend club dates and showcase venues that are lower-paying, audience-development dates.
2. *Professional Conferences:* Use a preexisting professional conference you are attending as an anchor date for a short tour in a new area or a return tour if the conference is held in the same location annually.
3. *Family Events:* Plan a short tour to surround a scheduled family event. Make the travel and the tax deductions work doubly for you.
4. *Pickup Dates:* Allow yourself to include lower-paying pickup dates into your tour schedule when necessary. Pickup or fill-in dates serve many purposes. They provide some income from an otherwise off night or they can cover your hotel and meals and save you from extra "day-off" expenses. They help build new audiences in an area which might have been passed by on your way to the main date. They can keep a touring group motivated and the performance sharp when an anticipated date falls through in the schedule.
5. *School Assembly Programs:* For those whose tours include school assembly programs, often one district can present an act in a number of schools during one week. Schools can also bus students from different schools to attend multiple performances taking place in one central location. Be attentive to your setup and breakdown times when scheduling multiple schools in one area.
6. *Multiple Performances In One Venue:* When presenting a nighttime adult performance at a venue, a daytime assembly program may be scheduled in the same venue, again bussing the students in. This maximizes setup and sound check times—two events, one setup.
7. *Mix Business With Pleasure:* Schedule tours in areas of the country where the weather is conducive to your special interests or hobbies. For skiers, tour Colorado during ski season. For golfers, tour where it is warm. For sport fishing enthusiasts, tour where it is open season and when your favorite fish are running. Bring your favorite hobby equipment with you if your mode of travel and space permit, i.e., roller blades, ice skates, skis, bicycle, fishing gear, etc.

8. *Check Other Local Venues:* Check other local venues in the towns where you are booked for possible opening act situations to precede your booked date and promote yourself to a new audience.
9. *Check Other Artist's Tour Schedules:* Check upcoming artist tour schedules on the Internet, *Pollstar* and *Performance* (see resource section) before planning a tour for potential tour-support slots.

Creative Off-Day Scheduling—Business

1. *Media Promotions:* Use non-travel open dates to schedule radio station drop-ins to promote new releases.
2. *Consignments:* Use non-travel off days to strategically place merchandise, (CDs, books, videos) in music stores and bookstores for consignment sales.
3. *In-Store Promotions:* Use non-travel off days to schedule promotional in-store performances. Many chain record stores and bookstores like Borders Books and Music, Barnes & Noble Bookstores and Hear Music Stores will sponsor promotional or paid in-store performances.
4. *In-Person Media Interviews:* While planning travel, use off days to arrive early or the day before a performance to take advantage of day-of-show media interview possibilities on radio and TV.
5. *Phone Interviews:* An off day in your hotel can be a productive time to schedule media phone interviews for upcoming tour dates.
6. *Alternative Sales Locations:* Use an off day or very early arrival to visit local restaurants and strategically place promotional listening copies of your CD for use as background music. A well-placed flyer can accompany the CD to promote the upcoming date.

Creative Off-Day Scheduling—Personal

1. *Family and Friends:* Use visits with friends or family as a home base from which to travel to performance dates while on an extended tour far from your own home base.
2. *Sightseeing:* Allow yourself to be a tourist when time permits. Enrich your life and take in a museum, a national park, attend the theater or local events or enjoy ethnic or local cuisine.
3. *Other Acts:* Attend performances of others when you have a night off. Keep abreast of currently touring acts and perhaps the competition. Be inspired by your peers and colleagues. You might pick up a few tips. If there is an opportunity, introduce yourself to the act and the promoter. This act may prove to be a likely one for which to open. Check out the venue for performance compatibility with your show. Drop off your press package in person.

> "I used a free day during a short North Carolina tour to call all the local record stores and find out which ones accepted consignment CDs. Then I went to those stores and dropped off my CDs. The next day I played a radio show and mentioned that my CDs were available at those stores. This supplemented my income for the tour by a couple of hundred dollars."
>
> **Muriel Anderson**
> guitarist, composer

> "Work on your art, work on your stage craft, work on your writing, practice every day."
>
> **Geoff Bartley**
> guitarist, singer, songwriter

> "In New Zealand, we were able to combine one of our favorite hobbies, cycling, with a tour. We took a group of friends there and all cycled together Monday through Friday. On the weekends, we took off for gigs in other places and they kept cycling. We met up with the group again on Monday and hopped on our bikes. The tour paid for the fun and it was a blast!
>
> — Marcy Marxer
> singer, songwriter, producer

4. *Vacation While Touring:* Plan tours to distant lands with an attached vacation. When traveling that far, it would be unfortunate to not schedule some sightseeing time without the concerns of performance. International festivals provide perfect anchor dates for such vacations.
5. *Cooperative Memberships:* Inquire about extended-member courtesies with affiliate gyms in other cities for those of you belonging to gyms or are about to become members. YMCAs and YWCAs have roving membership programs. Other facilities do as well, especially facilities within the same chain. Gold's Gym is one such chain to which many musicians and actors belong because of their reciprocating membership program.
6. *Personal Needs:* Plan ahead to schedule massages, special interest sessions or lessons with specialists who work in the towns where you are touring. Include a question on your information sheet for names and numbers of massage therapists and other specialists of interest to you.
7. *Hobbies and Sports:* Plan a day or a part of a day to enjoy your chosen hobby or sport. Let the promoter know of your interests. They may join you and offer suggested facilities, local contacts and, maybe, even a guest membership at their club for the day. This also takes your artist/promoter relationship to new levels.

> "It's much harder to do your daily things like make phone calls, find food, gas, a post office, beer etcetera, when you don't know where you are."
>
> — Harvey Reid
> songwriter, producer, label owner, Woodpecker Records

The more you incorporate your interests and various aspects of your life into your tour planning, the more whole you will feel during the tour. Keeping your self healthy in mind, body and spirit will aid in the prevention of road burnout and keep your shows fresh night after night. Touring is work. Your actual performances take the least amount of time during a tour than all of the other events leading up to the performance. Traveling away from the support of friends and family, plus missing your daily routines, takes their toll on a touring artist. Use your creativity to maintain yourself solidly while touring. Once again, it takes advance planning and being aware of who you are. The person you are at home does not change when you go on the road—only the surroundings change.

Building A Home Base Of Support

> "I'd say my home fan base, the place where I try everything new and people are supportive of me, is the Freight & Salvage in Berkeley. That place has been invaluable for figuring out who I am musically. I didn't really start getting bookings outside Northern California until I was ready to start touring."
>
> — Laurie Lewis
> musician

Artists that bound onto the scene with a built-in national reputation are few and far between. Most performers get their start in hometown performance situations. Whether your goals are to someday tour internationally or perform regularly in one location, everyone needs to begin somewhere. Building a hometown fan base of support is often a safe way to start your career. Take a few moments and consider your position within your own community. I have provided some fill-in blanks for you to note your progress as well as to include some of your ideas which might be sparked in the process.

Assess Your Home Base Of Support

Use the form provided on page 192 and the answers you have filled in to determine your next steps. For example: If your answers indicate that you still have some room to expand your audience within your hometown, set up a plan of action based on those specific questions. If, on the other hand, you see a trend indicating that you have reached the maximum goals in your hometown then it is time to begin expanding out from that base. Incorporate what you have discovered here into your one-year or two-year plan and strategically build your home base of support.

Why Is A Home Base Of Support Important?

Working in isolation is often a necessity for a creative person. But at some point, a performer has to test their creations on an audience. So many of the artists I have worked with over the years have all valued the benefits of building a home base of support. Here is a listing of reasons why. You may have a few of your own to add.

Build A Home Base Of Support To:
- Build a local reputation from which to expand
- Instill confidence in your performance
- Practice new material in a supportive environment
- Help generate enthusiasm for your career building
- Create a supportive community from which to venture forth on tour and return to for rejuvenation
- Provide a base for your livelihood
- Provide inspiration for your creativity
- Provide stability in your life
- Network with other local artists in order to expand and build a creative support system
- Develop your promotional skills
- Develop your business skills
- _____
- _____
- _____

How To Build A Home Base Of Support

Perform as often as you are able and in as many different performance environments as possible. This is ultimately the most direct route to developing a solid home base of support that you can expand and develop. Not all of the following situations are appropriate for your act, but you may also be missing some local opportunities to perform by prejudging the compatibility of your performance with a specific performance environment. This list of potential performance environments is intended to challenge your concept of appropriate venues for your act. Reconsider a few new venues you may have previously dismissed as unlikely and discover a new audience and a new

> "Be a hero in your own hometown first. If you don't have a good core following in your own area, there is little point in trying to conquer the outside world. Given the odds, hometown heroism is all you may be able to achieve. It is no small achievement."
>
> **Mike Boehm**
> pop music writer,
> *Los Angeles Times/Orange County Edition*

> "There was a real healthy music scene around Iowa City with these two joints, The Sanctuary and The Mill. It was my way of easing back into it. It was low risk and low stress. A lot of times I'd write a song that afternoon and try it out that night at the bar."
>
> **Greg Brown**
> singer, songwriter

> "Developing a home base of support is one of the most important steps a band can take. Not only do you start making a little money on the side, but seeing that people like what you're doing is also a big boost to the band's confidence. Now with the Internet so prominent, the word can spread like mad, even from a small town."
>
> **Andy Deane**
> **Bella Morte**

Assess Your Home Base Of Support

❖ Have you built a local fan base?
　Yes _____　No _____　Somewhat _____
　List three things that you can do, or have done, to accomplish this.
　　1. _____
　　2. _____
　　3. _____

❖ Do you have local media recognition?
　Yes _____　No _____　Somewhat _____
　a) If yes, list three notable media outlets that support you.
　　1. _____
　　2. _____
　　3. _____
　b) If no, list three notable media outlets to target for upcoming events.
　　1. _____
　　2. _____
　　3. _____

❖ Do you have a network of other local performers with whom you communicate? _____
　Yes _____　No _____　Somewhat _____
　b) If not, list three local or regional performers with whom you want to share information.
　　1. _____
　　2. _____
　　3. _____
　List three other performer resources with whom you regularly communicate outside of your performing group or ensemble.
　　1. _____
　　2. _____
　　3. _____

❖ Do you have a steady ongoing local performance venue or venues?
　Yes _____　No _____　How many times per year? _____　How many venues? _____

❖ Can you sell out the smaller performance venues? (50-150 seats)
　Yes _____　No _____　Somewhat _____

❖ If yes to the above question, can you sell out a medium-size performance space in town? (250-500 seats)　Yes _____　No _____　Sometimes _____　Almost _____

❖ If yes to the above question, can you sell out one of the larger performance spaces in town? (500+ seats)　Yes _____　No _____　Sometimes _____　Almost _____

❖ Are you called upon for local community events?
　Yes _____　No _____　Somewhat _____　Often _____　Not often enough _____

❖ List three such community events which you have played.
　　1. _____
　　2. _____
　　3. _____

❖ Can you estimate the distance to which your base of support extends? i.e., 50 miles, the entire county, the three neighboring counties (beyond that it becomes regional).

> *In building the Dave Matthews Band career, we built up a local, home-grown fan base which expanded and spread word-of-mouth, giving us a regular base to venture out from while taking care of the bills. The grassroots method of building early on is the foundation and where you build out from is the key to the whole picture. Building a music career is like building a house—the stronger the foundation, the stronger the house. Without building on the grassroots level, it would be equivalent to putting up a fancy copper roof on a house and everybody talking about how beautiful it looks, although nobody's thought about the foundation.*
>
> Coran Capshaw
> manager, Dave Matthews Band,
> Red Light Management

outlet for product sales. These venues may necessitate some minor adjustments to your performance but the benefits of additional income sources and career growth may prove worthwhile.

Alternative Performance Environments

- Local and state arts council presenting organizations
- Local school assembly programs, colleges and universities
- Residencies and workshops in schools, colleges and universities
- Hospitals, nursing homes, retirement facilities, special care facilities, etc.
- Community groups and clubs (Lions Clubs, Knights of Columbus, etc.)
- Local special events: festivals, fairs, grand openings, ribbon cuttings and other ceremonies (sponsored by local government or businesses)
- Religious group events and celebrations
- Fraternity and sorority parties
- Libraries
- Music stores and bookstores
- Trade organization conferences held in and around town
- Hotels and inns in conjunction with the hotel catering services for weddings, parties and other similar events, etc.
- Local restaurants, bars and performance clubs
- Sporting events, tournaments and contests
- Charitable benefits

_____
_____
_____

This list gives you a broad scope of general performing situations from which to begin building your local performances. They may not be the ideal performance situations but they will give a developing artist a broad audience base of support. Varying your performance situations is the best way to develop that audience fan base. As you hone your performances and become known locally for your particular

> "If you are making waves in Seattle, then talk to people in Vancouver, talk to people in Portland. Meet the people in the press and at the radio stations and start creating something for yourself close to home. Don't worry about playing Boston. If you've got the goods, you'll eventually get to Boston."
>
> Mary McFaul
> manager, Laura Love Band,
> McFaul Booking & Management

> "Ani played the neighborhood bars and went downtown and played every club and open mic that she could. Tour relentlessly. Get out there and keep your costs down. Know who you are and know what you want to do."
>
> Scott Fisher
> manager, Ani DiFranco,
> president, Righteous Babe Records

performance style, performing situations will begin to present themselves. Eventually, a broader audience base creates demand and allows you to become more discriminating in selecting comfortable types of performance situations.

The Most Underused Resources

One of the benefits of developing your career close to home is that one of the main booking resources is already in your house. We often miss some of our greatest treasures because they are right under our noses. The phone company delivers it every year for free. In it, you will find every local, city government office, all of the town's theaters, bars, clubs, restaurants, businesses, social clubs, schools, colleges and universities, and hospitals! Yes, I am referring to the phone book. They are now available on CD-ROM for cities both nationally and internationally. Libraries have phone directories in their reference section. Many cities have gathered their resources and are incorporating them into their own city sites on the Internet. You can access them by clicking on Digital City. (Web: http://www.digitalcity.com)

The local newspapers are also a valuable resource. The entertainment section is not the only section to peruse. Check local-event calendars for fairs, festivals and other events that happen annually and save any listed numbers so you can call them to be booked at next year's event. Local clubs and organizations often list their event calendars on a weekly basis. Get to know your community. Apply your creative nature and rely on the tools close at hand to thrive on the home front.

Calling these local organizations utilizes the same techniques we have already discussed. The only difference is, in some instances, you may end up speaking with your banker, your neighbor or the owner of the restaurant you frequent. If you perform in town at all, many folks may already be familiar with your name, if not your performance. You have a built-in edge—take advantage of it and enjoy the familiarity while you can.

Audience Development

The role the audience plays in the touring artist's career development is important. A large, loyal fan base is what every artist strives for and craves. It is no coincidence that many artists develop an extremely loyal and enthusiastic fan base in their hometowns before touring to other cities. The artists who nurture those fans, who cater to their fans by performing often and being accessible, are rewarded with their support. In many cases, the artist's fan base is one of the major factors that helps to build their widespread recognition. For example, when the audiences fill the performance venues night after night and purchase a lot of merchandise, the mainstream music business takes notice.

"Everybody's a hometown band somewhere. At one time the Rolling Stones were a local band too. Try to work as much as you can, hone your live show and get the word out. If what you've got is good, then the people who know about you will tell others."

Greg Haymes
former member of Blotto,
music writer,
Albany Times Union

"The secret of success is constancy of purpose."

Benjamin Disraeli
19th-century British
Prime Minister

"Go to the doors that are open. You want to push the envelope and start moving past your comfort zone. But if you've been knocking on this door and it's closed, stop worrying about it for a while and take the gigs where they're happy to see you."

Mary McFaul
manager

Any artist that has had a devoted hometown audience will tell you—there is nothing like it! Audiences often feel a sense of ownership which increases their loyalty to the act. They knew you when you just got started which gives them a sense of history with, and commitment to, the act. They watched as the career blossomed and the audiences grew. They were there through it all and are there each time you play in town or in nearby towns.

That loyalty and enthusiasm must be developed with consistent, compassionate nurturing. In the beginning, you must play often and you must keep in touch with your audience. They need to know you appreciate their support and that you care about them. How do you do that?

Nurturing Your Audience
1. Invite them to sign your mailing list and become a part of something exciting. (More about mailing lists in Chapter 13.)
2. Keep them informed about your career and your life in an enjoyable and entertaining manner (Nothing is too personal for a fan but you need to find your own comfort zone of disclosure.)
3. Be accessible at your performances. Be available to sign products, shake hands and get to know your audience.
4. Give back to your community. Doing benefits for hometown organizations shows you really care and want to be considered part of the community. Doing hometown new CD release concerts or a premier of a new production gives the hometown audience, once again, a sense of being special. They are special.

So many artists that I have spoken with who think their careers are beyond their current hometown world, never really value what they can create locally. The thought of being labeled a local artist seems unappealing to many. Garnering the local artist accolade does not preclude you from venturing out. It only means you have viable resources and a wealth of support to return to. Reassess your home base situation and take advantage of some of the suggestions made here to build and expand your base of support.

Regional Touring
When thinking of expanding an artist's career, envision concentric circles created when you drop a stone in a pond. If you imagine yourself expanding your base of support out from the center where that stone first dropped (your hometown), you might be able to envision all of the towns, counties and neighboring states that fall within those circles. As your local artist reputation begins to take hold in and around your town, ripple effects begin to expand outward. You will find that your fan base has some small pockets of supporters in the surrounding

---

"My local fans are the people who have helped me to make a living entirely on my music for the last six years. These are the people who have enabled me to produce my CDs without the help of a record label . . . I know a very large percentage of those product sales were generated by my fans and friends here at home. We have a mutual fondness and respect for one another. A real bond."

Terri Allard
singer, songwriter,
Reckless Abandon Music

"Everybody's gotta be from somewhere. We're proud of where we are from. The people in our immediate geographic vicinity are the ones that made it possible for us to pursue this as our living. We celebrate the fact that we have our focus in our home base."

Bridget Ball
singer, songwriter

"If you wish success in life, make perseverance your bosom friend, experience your wise counselor, caution your elder brother and hope your guardian genius."

Joseph Addison

> **HotTip:** 🌶
> "Playing the right room can mean success or failure for the artist."
> Steve Reichman
> promoter,
> Showman

> "The level of competition for gigs is very high and there are days when you're tempted to just give up. My fans would never let me do that! In their minds I have already 'made it' and that kind of support keeps me going on even the very worst of days . . . . I love touring and plan to tour as much as possible in the future; but for me there's definitely no place like home."
> Terri Allard
> singer, songwriter

> "We started out playing for little more than gas money. Sometimes we played for free as far away as Pittsburgh and New York when we were getting our feet wet on the rest of the east coast. Touring out of state is the first real test for a band. Anyone can get their friends to like their band, or at least act like they like what they're doing, but playing for a crowd of stone-faced strangers can rock the band's confidence. The key is to keep plugging away. We found that people warmed up to us more and more with each trip to a city."
> Andy Deane
> Bella Morte

towns. Your goal in becoming a regionally known artist is to nurture your reputation within those concentric circles.

Once you have established a strong local reputation, select a number of neighboring small towns or larger cities that you can include in your base of support. As you plan your expansion, here are a few suggestions to keep in mind:

Expanding Out

- *Build upon your home-base strengths:* If you have developed a reputation with a specific organization, fraternity or local club, get recommendations and contacts from those presenters to their counterparts in the next town. There is no need to start from scratch.
- *Use your local home-base media contacts:* A recommendation from your hometown media contact can get your foot in the door at other regional media outlets and help score a preview article or a review.
- *Use your network of artists for recommendations:* Get recommendations of good venues and possible opening act opportunities to begin building new audiences.
- *Keep your travel costs down:* Play in towns that allow you to drive home each night. Your guarantees and percentages will probably be low in the beginning. Unless you have invitations for community housing, large hotel bills can be discouraging to your expansion efforts.
- *Use the resources at hand:* The library and the Internet have phone books of every city in the country to aid in your search for new venues. See the resources suggested at the end of this chapter as well.
- *Keep your fans informed:* By expanding close to the home base, your already loyal fans are an audience enhancement. Send regular mailing list and e-mail notifications of your new performances. Those loyal fans can and will travel. Your new venue presenter will be more likely to invite you back when you fill the house.
- *Select media markets:* Select new towns which offer desirable media coverage. This lends added credibility to your growing credentials.
- *Select markets with prestigious venues:* Expand to markets where playing a notable venue would be advantageous.
- *Consult your ten-year plan often:* Incorporate already-established goals into your expansion planning. One city may prove more advantageous over another within your concentric circles depending upon your preset goals.
- *Use the skills learned in your home base:* Incorporate all of the efforts that helped build your local home base of support to any new area in which you choose to expand.
- *Return often to solidify your new fan base:* Once you have developed some performance sites in these other towns, plan frequent return dates to continue building this audience.

Advantages Of Touring By Region

There is comfort and security in the known. The home base of support provides that. Expanding beyond that comfort zone is a challenge to any artist's development. For many, remaining a hometown performer is appropriate to all of their life's goals and dreams, but for others, the lure of the road keeps their performance fresh and artistry at its peak. For the artist whose long-term goal is to develop a national or international career, it is necessary to move out from the comfort zone. One of the best ways to test yourself in a larger pond is to create short regional tours—a further expansion of the concentric circles.

It is interesting to observe artists who have moved along this path. The artist's hometown fan base creates a wave of enthusiastic audience members that follow the group to performance dates throughout the surrounding area. Similar to the domino effect, the excitement generated on the homefront helps to generate new fans in the nearby towns. This in turn generates new fans in towns beyond those, and on and on. If an artist continues to expand in this manner, eventually there is a much larger, more undeniable fan base. We have all seen it happen to one act or another—the excitement is contagious. It is often at this point that many in the entertainment business begin to apply the term "creating a buzz" to the particular act. It is also at this point that many artists begin to garner enough recognition by those in the entertainment industry to boost their careers to the next logical level.

Develop The Surrounding Region

By developing the surrounding region, you build upon your previous efforts and allow each new step to overlap with the last. New audiences are engulfed in the process and your comfort zone expands along with you.

Additional Benefits To Developing Your Career Regionally

- The tour budget for a nearby regional tour remains low.
- Regional tours can be shorter with brief breaks to return home without affecting the budget.
- Shorter distances between dates build your touring road skills in small doses.
- Places may be more familiar within the region, allowing you to adapt to touring more easily. The discomfort of finding yourself in unfamiliar surroundings as you attempt to expand your business takes its toll.
- Regional and state arts-council touring grants may be available to you once you have moved beyond your own town. (More about grants in Chapter 12.)

"Be not afraid of growing slowly, be afraid of standing still."

Chinese proverb

"When I first started playing with the Seldom Scene, we really were seldom seen. We didn't play very much—one night a week in a club. Then we started playing a few festivals. But back in those days, a good portion of dates were played within 100 miles of Washington, D.C., up into Maryland and maybe down as far as North Carolina and that was it. By using the DC area as a start point, we were able to establish a base very easily."

John Starling
lead singer,
The Seldom Scene

"We concentrated on one region, playing the artist every 45 days in different clubs—really working the region. Then we applied the same strategy to the next region; concentrate on one region at a time."

Charlie Dahan
in-house agent, A & R

> **HotTip:** 🌶 Venture into a new region once you have a solid track record in one region.

"Early in our career, we were based in Washington, D.C., and we built a strong circuit of weeknight club gigs there. We used the weekends to travel up and down the East Coast, playing opening acts at showcase venues. We made our income on the weeknights, and we used the weekends to do some serious audience building. Gradually, we were able to expand the strategy nationwide."

Pete and Maura Kennedy,
The Kennedys
touring performers and
recording artists

"Regional airplay provided our entrée into regional markets. With the advent of A3, Americana and college radio you can get some strong regional airplay. Use the Album Network Yellow Pages *or* Billboard *to find the names of local concert promoters and the best local talent agencies. A good regional agent can book you on a string of gigs in the area and gives you a shot at breaking even on your first regional tour."*

Chris Daniels
recording artist

Regional Touring Beyond The Circle

As one expands their concentric circles, it might seem that this process could eventually encompass all of the regions that would fulfill an artist's touring goals. Fortunately we live in a time when the world is made smaller by the technology at our fingertips. It is no longer daunting to also develop specific regions that do not connect with your home base region.

Developing a home base region to its widest possible expansion point also allows the artist to test their stamina for the road, their promotional know-how and their performance consistency. It provides an artist with a credible performance record of audience numbers and merchandise sales to offer to new presenters. These two factors make a statement about your value in the marketplace. One of the main considerations of any presenter is, "Can the artist sell tickets?" An artist's value in the marketplace becomes an integral point influencing fee negotiations. By drawing upon their track record, the artists can use their value as leverage when beginning to negotiate with new presenters.

Selecting New Regions To Develop

There will come a time when a sense of daring pushes you to challenge your newly acquired touring skills by booking dates in a totally new region. When venturing beyond established comfort zones, consider these factors.

Factors To Consider:

- ❖ The distance of travel to and around the region and its potential performance opportunities. Those factors will influence your travel budget.
- ❖ Particular advantages one region holds over another at this time in your career. Prestigious venues and important media outlets (newspapers, radio, television) are two examples.
- ❖ Cities or markets within the region that may provide you with a springboard into your particular industry. For instance, go to New York for theater and music and to Nashville for music and publishing.
- ❖ Connections with other artists in this region upon which to draw for suggested venues, potential opening-act situations or co-bill opportunities.
- ❖ Previous performances, promotion or marketing in this region to provide a base upon which to build.
- ❖ Recommendations from credible sources to specific promoters. Use the contacts you have established in other regions to seek new connections.
- ❖ The challenges you foresee in this particular region.
- ❖ Existing multiple performance situations in close proximity that allow you to develop a regional following in a short time.

- How often you can return to this region given the distance, cost to tour, types of performance situations and media.
- Key performance venues that one must perform at in order to advance their career.
- Other factors influencing your decision to tour in this region. Perhaps someday you might consider moving there, you have friends or family in the region, a family member has a job opportunity, etc. Consider everything!

Timing To Plan A Regional Tour

Planning a tour outside of your region requires plenty of lead time which will vary depending on the multiple factors listed below. The more time you allow yourself for planning, the better prepared you will be as you arrange the details of each of the individual dates—travel arrangements, promotional efforts and how to incorporate outside interests.

Set Deadlines For Confirmation

Even though you might begin to plan a tour six or eight months in advance, some of the venues you are attempting to include in the tour may not be ready to confirm dates that far in advance. Here is where your steadfast adherence to your goals for the tour assist you in making necessary decisions. Are the venues that book six to eight weeks out worth waiting for on this tour or is it more important to concentrate on venues that are prepared to commit within your time frame of a half a year or more in advance? Consider these factors as you set your time line for each regional tour.

Venue-Booking Time Frames

- *Performing arts centers, concert series selling season tickets, festivals, state and city fairs and many arts council organizations:* Those venues dependent upon various grants all require a lengthy booking time. Their lead time to book a date may require from between eight months to as much as 18 months prior to the performance date. Bookings for these types of venues often coincide with regional and national booking conferences. If plans include these types of venues, become familiar with the appropriate conferences and showcases. A listing of conferences is in the resource section of Chapter 11.
- *Bars, clubs and professional concert promoters:* Less lead time is required by these presenters—who often book dates as close as three weeks to three months prior to the performance date. Six weeks is often optimum allowing ample promotion time. It is also in this type of venue that one would be likely to find a pickup date when necessary.
- *Summer festivals:* Festivals are often booked by the preceding December. Many promoters book the following summer's performers at the previous summer's festival allowing only

> **HotTips:**
> Keep records of your audience numbers and merchandise sales to quote to venue buyers and to judge your progress and readiness to move to the next region.
>
> The entertainment industry is one that depends upon people's connections with each other within their field. Use your connections. Ask others to share theirs.

"...Give yourself a minimum of six months, although I prefer a year, to plan a two-week tour outside your region."

Liz Masterson
singer, songwriter

"We plan about a year or a year and a half ahead. We try to confirm our schedule at least six months ahead except for last-minute radio interviews or workshops which might come along. We figure our time on the road will cost us an average of one-hundred dollars a day so it's important not to have too many days off."

Steve Gillette
singer, songwriter

THE ART OF TOURING

a few open slots for new performers. Although many headline acts are booked months in advance, promoters will sometimes fill out their schedule with regional acts closer to the event. Use these summer festivals as anchor dates in a targeted new region.

> "Since most festival bookings are done many months in advance, it is often possible to get one set, and then build other dates around it respecting the festival's restrictions about playing in the immediate area."
>
> **Rod Kennedy**
> founder, producer,
> Kerrville Music Festival

> "Most festival directors need a mix of well-known names (drawing cards), strong support artists, and a small handful of newcomers. The kits, tapes, CDs and so on they get in profusion work as reminders, but they're often NOT very good at getting unknowns on the bill."
>
> **Richard Flohil**
> former artistic director,
> Mariposa Festival

> "I do not move a performer to the next level of performance at our festival, i.e., showcase or main-stage concert unless I see they work to increase the 'buzz' about themselves."
>
> **Fred Kaiser**
> program director,
> Philadelphia Folk Festival

> "Performers should find out when festivals start booking. Even though you may not be selected for that year's festival, check back closer to the festival in case there has been a cancellation or an open slot in the programming."
>
> **Spike Barkin**
> festival and special events producer

Performance Venue Presenting Seasons

Performance Venue	Presenting Season
Festivals and Fairs	Spring, summer, fall mostly
Concert Sheds and Tents	June through September
Performing Art Centers	Fall through late spring
Bars, Music Showcases, Nightclubs	Year round
Colleges, Universities	August through May, some summer
Elementary Schools	September through June
City Events	Summer—depends on climate
Dances	Year round
Camps and Workshops	Summer, occasionally spring or fall
House Concerts	Year round
Churches	Year round, depends on promoter

Booking Different Venue Types

Keeping track of venue booking schedules can be difficult when planning tours that involve more than one performance venue type, but it is certainly not impossible. For the seasoned touring artist, performing at a variety of venue types makes the tour more interesting. However, during the booking process, one must be prepared to deal with many different types of negotiations and a host of details that may be as different as night and day from one phone call to the next.

For those in the dawn of your touring careers, select one type of performance venue in a new region, rather than attempting to book dates at a variety of venue types. By booking one kind of venue, booking schedules, production facilities and the presenters with whom you negotiate are likely to be similar. This similarity allows you to prepare your conversations, promotional materials and performances in a consistent manner. You can develop a familiarity with the format and build confidence in your booking skills.

The comparison on page 201 demonstrates the stark difference between a club date and a performing-arts-center date. It is not always possible or advantageous to perform in one type of venue for an entire tour. But, these differences may help to discern where you would like to place your emphasis.

Booking And Performing In Clubs

Booking Time Frame
A club tour requires an optimum of six weeks to three months planning. Club promoters usually book dates in a tighter time frame since they often allow for a last-minute fill-in for a breaking artist with a "buzz" or an established ticket seller. Club promoters generally advertise on a weekly basis utilizing the popular "strip ad." The strip ad promotes anywhere from three to ten performances in one ad. Attention to promotion and advertising for individual dates varies with the act and the budget agreed upon during negotiations.

The Facility
Most clubs have good-to-excellent sound and lighting equipment and technicians and can accommodate everything from acoustic solos to large electric bands. The stage sizes vary from very small to medium. Often, one wonders how all of the band's gear will ever fit. Dressing room facilities vary from good to cramped to virtually nonexistent. The seating in club venues runs the gamut from standing only, to a few seats and small tables, to tables and seating for the capacity of the club. Often food and bar beverages are available throughout the performance with either table service or self service. This means that extraneous noise will be inevitable throughout the performance along with people moving about. However, it does not preclude a listening audience atmosphere.

The Audience
The audience that is likely to attend a club date is one that is more knowledgeable about popular, contemporary music, new trends and artists. They tend to be a record-buying audience who frequents all types of music stores. Club performances often have later start times with the main act sometimes beginning as late as 10 or 11 p.m. This tends to influence the age demographics of the audience. If an artist is attempting to build a career recognized by mainstream media and the music business, club dates are a necessary venue type to include in your tours.

Booking And Performing In A Performing Arts Center

Booking Time Frame
Booking generally requires eight months to eighteen months lead time. Seasonal promotion and grant applications are driving factors in the lengthy lead time. Promotional efforts generally include season brochures, individual and season posters, programs to each event, individual event and series advertising, mailing to a subscriber list, and advance sales to

> **HotTips:**
> Allow enough research time to find appropriate venues.
>
> As you begin touring regionally, shorter tours are more productive, more cost effective, provide a sense of satisfaction and accomplishment, and are essential preparation for the longer tours in your future.
>
>
> Become familiar with the presenting season of the different types of venues and presenting organizations.

"A key element to an arts center's success is planning ahead. Grant funds are crucial to the operation of nonprofit presenting organizations. Many grant deadlines are March 1 for a season that begins in July and runs through June of the following year. It is imperative that artists representing themselves are aware of this process in order to ensure a successful and ongoing relationship with the presenter."

Mary Leb
artistic director,
Carnegie Hall,
Lewisburg, WV

season ticket buyers. There is very little room for adding a last-minute performance date although cancellations do occur.

The Facility

Most facilities have technical crews or at least a technical director on staff. If they have in-house sound and lights, they are often adequate to excellent, although sometimes there will be a need to supplement with rental equipment. If there is no in-house system, a professional sound and light crew is hired. The facilities usually have adequate to multiple dressing rooms with a green room for artist hospitality and a private bath with showers. The stage, large by comparison to the club stage, often sports multiple curtains, stage wings and raked theater seating. Sometimes there are balconies. If refreshments or bar service is available, it is in a lobby area outside the performance space. This represents the ultimate in listening audience formats.

The Audience

The audience likely to attend performing-arts center performances are supporters of the arts in general and are most likely to be familiar with the "high arts"—Broadway and other theatrical presentations, ballet and modern dance, opera, classical and jazz music. In general, the audience tends to be older than the club crowd. Although this audience will follow niche performers and be well educated, they may be less knowledgeable of the pop arts or the most current musical acts. An artist can expect to do relatively well selling product at the venue because this audience is less likely to frequent record stores on a regular basis searching for new releases. An artist can perform at these venues throughout their career, earn a very good living, yet still not achieve mainstream media or industry notoriety unless coupled with mainstream radio airplay and performances in notable club venues.

This comparison is a simplified theory borne out by a personal study of the industry as it relates to the careers of the artists I have worked with and known in the pop, country, rock, jazz, folk and bluegrass fields. I offer this comparison as a simple starting point as you consider what type of performance venues are suitable for your act.

The Role Of Festivals, Contests, Battle Of The Bands, And Showcasing In Regional Touring

Festivals

Once the decision has been made to tour outside your own area, developing an audience in a new region requires many appearances in the same venues. If an artist is totally unfamiliar with the potential venues, a prime introductory performance situation would be to play a festival held somewhere within the desired region.

> *". . . it has been a joy to have helped many artists receive their first regional exposure, and then watch the performers become widely recognized. . . . A performance by an unknown artist at a major festival can provide an opportunity for dozens of regional concerts otherwise unavailable. A well-received large festival performance can jump-start an artist in any region."*
>
> **Dan DeWayne**
> artistic director,
> Chico & California
> World Music Festivals

> *"We've really been known in the past years for presenting new artists on a regular basis. We push that in the press. We want to be on the upper edge of that. We also always try to get the best regional people on the Newport Festivals."*
>
> **Bob Jones**
> artistic director,
> Newport Festivals

> *"Most artistic directors know the minute their last festival is over, who they want for the next one."*
>
> **Richard Flohil**
> former artistic director,
> Mariposa Festival

In all genres, festivals lend a new act immediate credibility with a large and unfamiliar audience. The individual act alone does not bare the burden of drawing the entire crowd. It has the benefit of the festival's built-in audience's loyalty. Festivals usually draw their audience from within the surrounding region as well as from a distance depending on the festival's reputation. An artist has the opportunity to showcase their act to many more people than any smaller performance venue could offer. Upon reaching this broader audience, the artist has a much better chance of drawing reasonable crowds and getting some media attention on their return tour to that region.

Booking festivals in an intended region needs to be a priority of a developing touring artist. Festivals are a unique presenting opportunity because the promoters understand the advantages of the multi-performer format. They often program their events to cater to a specific genre, i.e., jazz, blues, folk, bluegrass, pop, dance. Yet within the genre, they are open to presenting many varieties of performances. The audiences depend on the promoter to offer a varied program. Given this format, festival promoters are able to include selected unknown and up-and-coming acts within the performance schedule, generally, without compromising their revenues. This gives the developing artist a choice situation in which to win new fans at very little expense.

Booking Suggestion:

As a first attempt in a new region, direct your initial efforts to nearby regions in which festivals you would like to perform take place. Book a number of dates at a local venue to build recognition in the area. Once you begin to have some success, contact the festivals in that region. Festival promoters keep abreast of the artists performing in local venues as well as the attention the artists receive from the media and the audience. The booking period for this first round of festivals should take place while you still have work within your own region and are beginning to expand. When you are ready, be selective and expand gradually. Choose festivals within your home region and in regions nearby. Do not expect to conquer the whole country at once. Be patient! Festival promoters often take time to evaluate an artist's potential contribution before they are ready to include them in the program. Many may keep your materials, tracking your career for a season or two. Festival promoters often look for artists who can add something new to their program or who can fit comfortably within the festival's format while enhancing the overall show. They are keenly aware of keeping their programming fresh with the current trends as well as allowing it to reflect the expectations of their audiences.

". . . Most festival producers attract audition submissions from hundreds, if not thousands, of the best performers in the country. So, you not only need to be among the best, but you also need to be patient. Some festivals have a waiting list of three to four years before a performer can be booked, after they are considered to be what the producer wants."

Rod Kennedy
founder, producer,
Kerrville Music Festival

"The entire festival circuit is a great way to develop an audience, but if there is no comprehensive marketing plan to back this up, then it will only serve a short-term purpose and you may get stuck in this groove."

Rosalie Goldstein
management consultant,
Goldstein & Associates, Ltd.

"The songwriter contest frequently puts emerging songwriters on the fast track to developing an audience. If they place well, they are often invited to perform at the festival. It also allows us to give away prizes and money making it more exciting than a straight showcase. The screening process enables us to hear a lot of up-and-coming artists."

Steve Szymanski
vice president,
Planet Bluegrass,
Telluride Festivals

Contests

In recent years, many festivals have begun to incorporate songwriter contests or instrumental contests into their festival program schedules. Artists must submit a specified number of original songs along with a registration fee. Those selected from the applications are given an opportunity to perform a few songs before the festival audience and a set of judges. Artists appear at their own expense. The winner of some contests may receive a variety of prizes including cash or instruments. The audience-development opportunity is often the most important reason for participating in these contest events. Many artists who have done particularly well with the audience, whether they have won the contest or not, will be invited back to appear at the main festival in years to come. Winners often use the prestige of having won the festival as an additional boost to their promotional campaign.

Battle Of The Bands

This performance opportunity is more often found in the rock, blues and jazz genres and offers bands a regional showcasing situation that is rewarded with some career advancement or money. The media recognition from these events is often widespread. In some instances semifinalists and finalists compete nationwide. The rewards can include opening act slots on a tour, recording contracts or, in the case of songwriters, having their song recorded and released by a main act. The attention given to these events often creates an immediate audience increase for the participating bands and certainly for the winners.

Record companies, publishing companies, performing rights societies, venues, radio stations and newspapers are often the sponsors of such events. Watch local newspapers for announcements or contact the various performing-rights societies like ASCAP and BMI, for upcoming events. (See resource section of this chapter.) There may be a registration fee required. If you are selected to participate, the registration fee is well worth the investment given the publicity and recognition that will be afforded the winning act.

Booking Suggestion:

Once having participated in one of these events, the act should follow up with a tour of club dates in that region. Book the tour soon after the final event to take advantage of recent publicity—especially if you are among the winners.

Competitions

Prestigious competitions are held around the world in the classical arts. One example is the Van Cliburn International Piano Competition which takes place every four years. There are competitions where young artists can be judged among their

---

"ASCAP's showcase programs, which span the various musical genres, have been extremely effective in presenting new and developing talent to industry audiences. ASCAP invites a broad-based industry list ranging from record company A & R executives to publishers, managers, film and television music executives, agents, producers, attorneys and other songwriters. Regularly-scheduled showcases are held in New York, Los Angeles, Chicago, Nashville and London."

Brendan Okrent
sr. director of repertory,
ASCAP

"BMI showcases around the world provide an opportunity for BMI songwriters to be heard and seen by music industry and everyday music listeners at all different stages of their career. These showcases highlight many different genres. Some of the artists we've showcased were Lisa Loeb, Counting Crows, Dogs Eye View, Ani DiFranco, Rod Sexsmith."

Jeff Cohen
senior director,
BMI Writer/Publisher
Relations

"Each year, hundreds of artists from all over the world enter the Young Concert Artists International Auditions in New York to win a place on the Young Concert Artists Roster . . . The winner's prize is, almost literally, a career in hand."

Susan Wadsworth
founder and director,
Young Concert Artists

musical peers for highly sought-after positions on prestigious touring rosters. Young Audiences, Inc. and Young Concert Artists are two such organizations.

Showcase Clubs

Showcasing is often associated with trade conferences as well as some types of performance clubs. Conference showcasing is discussed at length in Chapter 11.

Many clubs offer artists a "pay-to-play" opportunity in their venue. The venue, known for presenting up-and-coming acts is frequented by those in the industry and the media searching for the next hot act. The club owners know they offer a new act many desirable advantages—because they have the club that you need to play in order to build industry, media and audience attention. The clubs charge the artist for their use and to gain access to their very specialized audience. This is clearly a career-advancing opportunity if you are ready to commit yourself to building this particular audience, and can pay the fee which is often somewhere between $100 and $200. These showcase clubs have built their reputations as the premier venue to see important new acts. The audience of industry representatives turns out each day wanting to catch the possible stars of tomorrow.

Not all showcase clubs are "pay-to-play." Some clubs are known for presenting new artists with a "buzz" in some of the major markets. Industry and media representatives frequent these clubs for similar reasons as above. Showcase evenings are set apart from the regular performance schedule in many clubs. Others designate showcase slots in the early evening prior to the main show. These half-hour or shorter slots often begin around 6 p.m. to allow industry representatives to catch one or two sets on their way home from the office. Depending on the audience response, a showcasing act may be invited to open for a main act in the future.

These situations still require a great deal of work on your part. Unlike festivals or battles of the bands, you do need to promote yourself to the local media. It is also to your advantage to send specific invitations to both media and industry personnel. This requires researching the names and addresses of the important people in town. The first step is to ask the club owner if they have a mailing list that you could buy and a media list that they would send you. Then, remember your contacts. It is likely that you are not the first artist to perform at this showcase venue. Check within your network for someone who has played there and has a list of appropriate people. Also, check the resources at the end of this chapter as well as Chapters 18 and 19. Industry magazines like *Pollstar* and *Performance* publish directories of record company A & R representatives, agencies and management companies.

> "Always have a few press kits on hand. Every performance is like a showcase in a way. There are often people in the audience who will be inspired to bring you to their event if you mention the different kinds of things you do either from the stage or in your newsletter on the product table."
>
> **David Roth**
> singer, songwriter

> "We try to offer 30-minute time slots from 6:30 to 9:00 on Tuesday through Saturday for people to come out and play. You want to get a roomful of people so if you have somebody from a publishing company or a record company who comes by and says, 'Oh, look there's some interest in this person,' they'll listen a little more closely."
>
> **Amy Kurland**
> owner,
> The Bluebird Cafe

> **HotTip:** 🌶
> Statewide conferences of presenting organizations offer showcasing acts block- booking opportunities. Check with the state arts council for presenter consortia in your state.

Block Booking To Build A Regional Presence

One of the benefits of attending and showcasing at booking conferences is the possibility of being included in the block-booking process. (More in Chapter 11, Conferences.) Originally this idea was started by a coalition of college, university and performing arts center presenters who banded together in one region to offer artists multiple dates. The dates would be strung together in a short time frame. The artist would have a regional tour virtually handed to them and, in return, would offer the presenters a block-booking fee. If, for instance, the artist's single date fee was $1,500, the coalition might offer a two-date fee of $1,200 per date; a three-date fee of $1,100 per date; and a five-date fee of $1,000 per date. The dates would have to fall within the same week and, since they would be in the same region, the costs to the artists for executing the tour would be greatly reduced.

By instituting this block-booking process, many regional presenters are able to afford nationally-touring artists and major productions. Without the reduced fees, individual presenters would find it difficult to offer their audiences a broad cultural spectrum of events. The artists have the opportunity to develop a regional presence once they are included in a block tour. Many organizations continue to implement this booking strategy.

You may find it advantageous to be the one to suggest this strategy in your own booking process as you contact presenters within any given region. By offering reduced block-booking fees to a series of presenters, you may get them talking among themselves about the benefits of joining together to book your tour.

Exploring any of the above-mentioned methods of expanding your position in the market should be primary in your touring-career goals. Creating successful tours builds upon sound foundations. Each new step needs to rely on the previous one. Remember that every new touring challenge adds considerably to existing budgets, therefore, use the tools you have already discovered along with the new resources offered here. Your successes need not drain your finances or your resolve. Challenge your growth into new regions with finesse, smarts and creativity.

National Tours

The rigors of planning and executing a tour nationally demand that the artist have their business skills and routines well managed. The key factors to a successful national tour are preparation, timing and budgeting.

A national tour joins together a number of regions within a given time frame that target specific markets as tour sites. The choice and number of markets which are determined necessary

---

"We feature a cooperative buying program, on-site and full-time enrollment discounts to get the schools to buy more readily. We feel that the artists are as much a part of what we are doing as the schools themselves."

Eric Lambert
executive director,
Association for the Promotion
of Campus Activities

"When a band is beginning to look at the prospect of touring, you feel excited and look forward to it in the same sense of a kid going off to camp for the first time . . . a bit of anxiety mixed with giddy anticipation. Remember—camp is six weeks, a tour can last forever . . . or seem like it."

Dan Griffin
promoter, manager,
former road manager,
10,000 Maniacs, Leon
Redbone, The Delevantes

to cover during a particular tour will influence the length of time the tour will last. A national tour of the United States could last for an entire year. For our purposes, I have chosen an arbitrary tour starting date (September 4), to illustrate realistic time frames. Splitting the year into sections, a year-long tour could look something like this:

Sample Tour Plan

1. Three weeks to cover the east-coast markets beginning September 4.
2. One week off.
3. Six weeks in the northern and southern midwest beginning October 8.
4. Break for the holidays from November 23 through January 5 with a few performance dates scheduled during that time frame.
5. Six weeks to play markets in the southeast and southwest beginning January 5, hopefully avoiding the harshest winter weather.
6. Two-week break in mid-February.
7. Four-week tour of the southwest, California and the northern west coast beginning March 4 and ending April 3.
8. Two-week break for Passover and Easter holidays.
9. Four weeks to return to some smaller markets in regions already played with individual dates and shorter weekend tours.
10. Two-week break.
11. Three-month tour, nationwide fairs, festivals and shed dates.

This schedule allows the act to play as many major markets as possible throughout the country within a year. There is time to return to some markets and play the smaller ones while incorporating some university dates and clubs. All will reinforce the previous play in the larger markets. The summer months allow an act to play the fair and festival circuit by returning to regions previously played during the year. This enables the artist to hit a different audience.

This tour plan is often the method used by bands releasing new recordings with a major label. Even with label tour support, a tour bus, booking agents, management and the record company's promotional team, undertaking a national tour is grueling for the artist. As a self-booking artist, undertaking this kind of touring requires that your business and touring savvy be at their peak. Having a support team to help with contacts and promotions is necessary to insure the success of a tour of this scope.

> **HotTip:** Suggest a reduced block-booking fee to a number of presenters in one region if they book you within a tight time frame.

"Call home! The most creative part of touring is trying to remain a semi-normal person while being involved in an incredibly abnormal activity. It's lonely on the road and it's lonely at home. Kids grow up fast and no one on their deathbed ever wished they had 'spent just a little more time in the office!' It'll keep you grounded and human."

John McCutcheon
singer, songwriter,
from *International Musician*,
1992

"I devised a three year U.S. touring plan since the 3 Mustaphas 3 lived in Europe and touring had to be efficient. The plan focused on playing the most successful return dates in the region last played, which financially allowed them to develop one or two new regions each tour. At the end of three years, and with the combination of the band's talent, a supportive label and our agent's follow-up, Billboard recognized 3 Mustaphas 3 as one of the top 10 World Music bands and World Music CDs for that year."

Kari Estrin
manager, tour manager,
3 Mustaphas 3

Are You Ready?

Here are some indications of when you might be ready to launch a national tour of this magnitude. Any one or two of the reasons listed below may be enough for you to consider a national tour.

❖ You have a new release which you are starting to send out nationally for review. You want to follow up with live touring.
❖ You have performed at festivals throughout the country and have many pockets of fans from which to draw your audience.
❖ Your record company has offered some financial and promotional tour support. (More in Chapter 18, Working With Your Record Company.)
❖ You completed shorter tours in many of the major markets within most regions of the country and have some following.
❖ Your mailing list has grown to include supporters in markets throughout the country.
❖ You feel that you could book enough dates to at least support the costs of the tour, perhaps make some money, but not lose more than you have determined is a valid amount to invest.
❖ You have booked and completed other successful four-to-six week tours.
❖ You have all of your contact, promotional and computer systems functioning to allow you to remain in touch and keep up with the business while touring, or you have made arrangements for a support team back home.
❖ You have considered the impact that lengthy touring would have upon family relationships and you have their full support. It is always easier to book another tour than to win back bruised and neglected family members.
❖ You have spent the better part of the previous year planning and booking this tour.

Gain A National Presence On Your Own Terms

Once you have accomplished many of the items on the above list, you will be better prepared for a national tour. It is important to note that one does not have to tour as rigorously as mentioned above to develop a national presence. An artist who is tackling one region after another to gain some notoriety at festivals, conferences, and performance venues and strategically markets their product, gaining media recognition, has every bit of an opportunity to have a national presence.

Booking Suggestion:
Again, always return to the goals laid out in the ten-year plan. Do your goals require that you tour intensively

---

"Touring nationally can be a good thing or a bad thing depending on your name recognition and financial resources. In many cases, the revenue generated from gigs alone is barely enough to pay for the tour. Without tour support, a penny saved is truly a penny earned. To build your fan base and perform in the same cities every two to three months, one may have to bite the bullet for a while and bunk with friends, drive long hours, and carry all your own gear. But once the fans are hooked, less frequent visits (twice a year) will keep things rolling."

RAVI,
singer, songwriter,
former guitarist of triple
GRAMMY nominee, Hanson

"Never book a gig on your child's birthday. Never book a gig on your partner's birthday if you can help it."

Bob Franke
singer, songwriter

throughout the country within this time frame? If they do, can you affirm that the above scenarios have all been met prior to launching an extensive national tour? If you again answered yes, then it is time to select the year that you plan to tour in this manner. Allow yourself six months to a year to book the tour dates while you continue to tour in the manner you have been doing locally and regionally.

As you plan a national tour, it is more important than ever to establish the reasons for doing this national tour. Some of the more likely reasons might be to:

- ❖ Promote the release of a new recording nationally.
- ❖ Promote a support slot on a main act's national tour.
- ❖ Promote one of your compositions that has had national media attention on television, radio or film. Touring nationally would solidify your recognition along with the composition.
- ❖ Solidify your connections with your fans nationally since you have built pockets of support around the country.
- ❖ Build the national media recognition at this time in your career development.

> "If you are the booking agent for your band, you are the 'designated driver'—this job has to be done by a person who is not into any kind of abuse—If you screw up and alienate a concert promoter, the whole band suffers."
>
> **Chris Daniels**
> recording artist

Using National Chain Stores To Book National Tours

Earlier in this chapter, I briefly mentioned a few national book and music store chains. Some of these work with individual artists to help them create a national tour of all of their stores. Hear Music is expanding their chain of stores in many major markets around the country. Each of their stores have been specifically designed to include a performance area to spotlight a featured artist. Starbucks and Borders Books and Music are very involved in presenting artists at many of their stores throughout the country. Whether used simply as a promotional stop within a tour or planned as its own tour, dates booked in conjunction with some of these chains are a resource of which to take advantage. While developing a performance presence around the country, these venues also offer a recording artist a viable merchandise outlet for their recordings.

Similarly, hotel chains may offer some artists a consistent source of revenue along with the potential for a nationally-recognized touring venue. If an artist has established a relationship with a hometown chain hotel, use that resource to connect with other hotels within that chain nationwide. This process may provide an artist with necessary anchor dates upon which to build other regional venues. Hotel lounges may not be in your career plans but, strategic negotiations with

> "The remarkable thing about the 2001 cross-country tour was that we went out with another relatively unknown band and stayed out for over two months, making enough money to keep both bands going. After the tour, we saw a massive serge in merchandise sales online and our CD sales more than doubled."
>
> **Andy Deane**
> Bella Morte

> **HotTip:** 🌶
> "House concerts cost so little to produce and the atmosphere is very intimate. They are more like a community gathering with a little music on the side. You get to see an artist in a way you wouldn't in a more formal venue."
> — T.R. Ritchie
> performer, author,
> *Bring It On Home: A Simple Guide to Producing House Concerts*

a national chain may land you some steady gigs and free housing as you make your way across the country.

House Concerts

At one point, the house concert was more of a grassroots undertaking by individuals within a community, caring enough about the music to occasionally present a small concert in their home. The medium proved so appealing to both the artist and the audience that many house concert promoters have created a full-time series of house concerts. The house concert movement has since exploded around the country. Many acoustic artists create an entire national tour of house concerts. For many artists, it is an excellent way to begin building a national presence and develop an intimate, loyal following.

House concert audience size will vary based on the available room in the person's house. Due to room size, these performances are most often presented without sound reinforcement. It may be one of the most intimate settings in which an artist can perform. If your act is compatible with this type of performance venue, these spaces offer you a comfortable national tour.

> "I love house concerts! They're a wonderful way for a musician to be introduced into a new community. Once I find a host, I send them a list of guidelines and we go from there. The money can be good and the intimacy can't be beat."
> — **Deborah Liv Johnson**
> singer, songwriter, label owner,
> Mojave Sun Records

Touring The College Market

Colleges and universities offer the performing artist some very unique performing experiences. There are often a number of possible performance sites on a college campus along with a number of presenting organizations within the campus community. Many campuses include theater-type venues that are recognized performing arts centers. These venues sometimes fall under the auspices of the theater and music departments and have budgets to support their presentations.

Who Books The Shows?

Facility Directors

Presentations are most often booked by the performing arts center director or the faculty head of the respective department. Facility directors belong to organizations that cater to the performing arts center presentation format. In the U.S., the Association of Performing Arts Presenters (APAP) is a national organization with regional subdivisions. This organization hosts a national booking conference held in New York City in mid-January. The regional affiliates also hold annual regional conferences, generally in the fall. The majority of bookings for these performing arts centers are accomplished by attending these conferences and consulting artist touring directories from regional and state arts councils. The Canadian equivalent of APAP is Canadian Arts Presenting Association/L'Association Canadienne Des Organismes

> "A good place for information about any facility is on their website. There, you will find Technical information about stage size(s), lighting, sound, etc. A significant number of student programming boards also have their facilities shown. Calendars of events display the types of programs produced. Some advanced research prevents wasting time trying to book an acid rock group into a facility that presents major symphonies or ballets."
> — **I.B. Dent**
> interim director,
> Gertrude C. Ford Center for the Performing Arts

Artistique (CAPACOA). (More about conferences in Chapter 11.)

The Students

The Campus Activities Office also hosts many other performance events from major concerts in their on-campus arena to dance parties in the cafeteria. Funding for these events comes from the campus activities fees that every student pays. These funds are often dispersed by the student activities board or student council. Most committees that receive budget allocations from this board are headed by students with faculty advisement. Booking performance dates through the activities office provides an interesting challenge to most professional agents. As a self-booking artist, working with student presenting organizations takes perseverance, determination and, often, a commitment to be instructive and to assist the students' booking experience. While student activity programming fosters a student learning experience, professional artists and agents are quick to realize this learning experience may often be at their expense.

Although the financial rewards of booking college campus activities venues can be high, the constant turnover of student committee chairs can prove frustrating and expensive. Within one booking season, you may deal with two different chairs. Your costs to send promotional materials and the percentage of unreturned phone calls attempting to reach a student with fluctuating office hours are high.

Staff Or Faculty Programmers

Some activities offices are staffed by savvy programmers who are solely responsible for booking the entertainment. Discovering which colleges work with a staff director of programming is the more desirable route to building a lasting booking relationship with that college. Many programmers are members of the National Association of Campus Activities (NACA), the primary professional organization partnering entertainment with campus activities. NACA hosts one national booking conference and eleven regional booking conferences each year. Although this organization's membership costs and conference-attendance expenses may be prohibitive for many self-booking artists, some have found their niche in the college market by joining NACA. (More in Chapter 11, Conferences, Trade Shows and Industry Events.)

Working With Colleges

The college-activities market is a fickle one with a tendency to book novelty acts and the current musical fad or trend. The interests of the market change with each new student body. You may have been a hit on campus one year only to find

> **HotTip:**
> "Stay on the phone— find out when the booking student has office hours—try to get a personal email. If after four calls, they don't return your call, ask for the Student Activities Advisor and see what is happening with the student in charge."
> **Chris Fletcher**
> CEO, Coast to Coast Music Booking, manager, promotional consultant, instructor, Music Business

"When you really know the performer, whether it is a speaker or a musician or an artist, then you can really target some unusual kinds of classes and those faculty members will be very grateful to you for offering a very different and unique experience."
Phyllis Kurland
coordinator,
Nassau Community College Cultural Program

"For the most part, the extent of experience relative to the entertainment industry available to a student programmer prior to their first year at the college level, has been to attend their high school prom. It is important to take the time to explain buyer/agent/artist protocol to the student programmer. In a positive way, share anecdotes that will demonstrate to the student the need to handle things in a professional manner."
Charles Steadham
owner, agent,
Blade Agency

yourself old news the next with little or no chance for a return booking.

Working in the college market demands that your professionalism be at its peak during every step of the process. Because you are likely to be dealing with students unfamiliar with the business of presenting, it is up to you to take the lead for their benefit as well as your own. Follow up on all phases of the contract negotiation, promotion, date advance and, even, technical setup rests squarely upon your shoulders if you want to be sure it is done right.

It is difficult to determine how effective the college market is in developing a lasting fan base. Even though college radio has often been at the forefront of breaking new pop artists, many new acts find their performances to be poorly attended by the students themselves. An artist that does their own promotion in local media outlets may find that they draw a more receptive community audience to the campus venue.

By understanding the variety of campus presenting organizations, you can determine where to direct your booking efforts when including colleges and universities in your list of potential performance venues.

Sharing The Stage

Touring careers have often been enhanced by sharing the stage with other artists. Whether by design or by chance, these multi-performer opportunities can have a positive impact on an artist's career. There are six possibilities that I would like to discuss here:

1. Opening Acts
2. Support Acts
3. Shared or Co-Bills
4. Tour Exchanges
5. Multi-Act Tours
6. Open Mics

Opening Acts

The opportunity to open for an artist whose audience draw surpasses your own is one that should be sought after while building your career. Performing before an audience larger than you are normally used to presents challenges that will enhance your performance and business skills, as well as develop your audience more rapidly.

Benefits of performing in opening-act slots:
❖ Perform for and develop a new audience.
❖ Showcase your act to the venue booker.
❖ Be seen by media who have come for the main act.
❖ Use this performance as a reference in your press kit to other presenters.

"Student leadership is very volatile. It changes frequently as students drop out of school, drop out of the organization, come into the organization, graduate, etc. It is very important to be sure that the person you are speaking with is authorized to represent what they say they are representing. Call the director of student activities or the faculty advisor for the organization and check that the students have that authorization."

"College students can hear when people are trying to con them and just sell them anything for the sake of selling them anything. They need to have someone who's sincere, who wants to work with them, who will help them without always trying to get something back for themselves."

Phyllis Kurland
coordinator,
Nassau Community College Cultural Program

"Open for whomever you can. It will increase your exposure and credibility. Also, it will get your songs heard by others who can do you some good."

Greg Trafidlo
songwriter, performer

- Promote an upcoming solo date to the new audience.
- Add names to your mailing list from this new audience.
- Add income and build new audiences when used as a fill-in date during a tour.
- Develop your reputation among other artists as well as promoters.
- Break into prime clubs.

Some of the disadvantages:
- Pay is often not very good.
- Time slots are usually between 20 minutes and 45 minutes long, which may be good or bad depending on the individual act and situation.
- Audience is there to see the main act which makes your job as a performer more challenging in your attempt to win over an ambivalent audience.
- Audience members may arrive later, choosing to miss the opening act.
- Sound check may not be long enough or nonexistent, depending on the length of time of the main act's sound check.
- Main act's sound engineer may not engineer your show, leaving you with a potentially less-experienced engineer or the house engineer (which may work for you).
- The person who books the venue may miss your set and opt to come later.

Even with all of these disadvantages, many opening act slots are a boost to the artist's career and should be included in your tour plans whenever possible. Landing some of these choice opening slots takes persistence and creativity.

Four Methods Of Becoming An Opening Act
1. The promoter initiates the booking of the opening act and uses an opening act slot to test new artists wanting to play their venue.
2. An artist actively offers their act as an opener to prospective promoters while calling for bookings. If you have a hometown reputation, promote yourself to a local promoter who presents larger acts. Inform them of your availability to open for compatible upcoming shows.
3. The main act selects an opening act with whom they feel comfortable and informs the promoter of their choice.
4. The opening act solicits targeted main acts by contacting the act, their agency or their management.

Support Act
An offshoot of an opening act is the support act. Similar in all of the above-listed ways, the support act differs only in the length of time they may open for a main act. Many

> **HotTip:** While booking dates at new venues, always inquire about upcoming main acts already booked into the venue. There may be a compatible artist for whom your act could open.

"Be brief! Play 25 minutes. Unknown openers who play 40-45 minutes are making a mistake. People want to like you but, people want to see who they came to see. People love to be blown away. You ought to be able to do that in five songs."

Charlie Hunter
manager,
Young/Hunter Management

"It is extremely important to have chemistry between the opener and the headliner so the opener can actually pick up some fans and be remembered. I don't think it makes sense to have openers just for the sake of having openers."

Tim Mason
former events coordinator,
Old Vienna Kaffeehaus
booking manager,
Club Passim

"Have an agent with strong relationships. Only approach headliners whom your artist makes sense to support. Utilize your entire team to pitch everyone involved on the other side. Be early."

Tom Chauncey
agent,
Rosebud Agency

> "If you're booked at least one month before the first date, make sure your name is on the tickets, programs and all advertising. You'll only get tiny notices, but it puts the bug in media people's brains in each city for the next time you come through. If you're booked two weeks out, I'd still take the tour, but I'd lower my expectations. Your name won't be on anything. No one will be expecting you."
>
> **Charlie Hunter**
> Young/Hunter Management

> "I used to manage Eric Wood. We were invited to do a couple of dates with Richard Thompson. People would later ask, 'Who have you been out with?' and we would say, 'Richard Thompson,' and heads would snap back around. I would then submit demos to record companies and they would say, 'Now this guy's been on stage with Thompson.'"
>
> **Jordi Herold**
> former manager, Eric Wood, booker, The Iron Horse, Northampton, MA

record labels, in conjunction with an artist's booking agency and management, will vie for a support slot for an entire tour. Artists promoting a new release use the support slot to build audience awareness in the major markets in which the main act is likely to tour. Most of these deals are collaborations between each artist's management and possibly the record label. If you are interested in landing a support slot to help promote a new release, build audience recognition and gain media attention, begin a strategic plan to:

1. Determine the main acts with which you are most compatible.
2. Research *Billboard's* various talent and touring directories as well as *Performance Talent/Personal Managers*, *Pollstar Personal Managers* directories and others listed in the resource section of this chapter. Note artists of interest and their managers.
3. Contact the manager, inquiring about upcoming tours and if they are considering support acts. Many managers have their select list of preferred opening acts they regularly draw from when they need an opener. Ask to be considered for that preferred list after they've reviewed your material.
4. Send your promotional packet and current recording and/or video.
5. Phone them within one week to follow up on your packet.
6. Invite them to attend an upcoming show when you are performing in their area.
7. Plan to explore opening for a number of artists. This process often takes a very long time unless you, yourself, have management making these strategic connections for you.

There are always opportunities for other artists to hear your music and see you perform at venues such as festivals where many performers share the stage(s), showcases, industry events and conferences as well as simply having your music passed along by other artists. Being aware of these choice opportunities to get your music out to artists that don't know you is key to building important relationships within the industry. Passing your music along to a manager at an industry event may land you the next support act slot. Above all, if you begin to target specific artists for opening act and support act slots, remember to keep in touch with the management every once in a while. There are often times when an act, already selected by the main act's management, drops out of the slot and management is in urgent need of someone to fill in. Your check-in call may just get you the gig.

I would always check in with various managers on behalf of my artists. While working with Robin & Linda

Williams, they had developed a number of relationships with artists they enjoyed. I would place a call every now and again to check on the touring status of these artists and always let the managers know how Robin & Linda's tour schedule was shaping up. One such check-in call landed Robin & Linda 16 dates as support for Mary Chapin Carpenter on a cross-country tour. So keep tabs on your connections and make a point of timely check-ins. As the old saying goes, "It is not what you know, but who you know, and it helps to be in the right place at the right time . . ."

Shared Or Co-Bills

This situation places each act sharing the bill on more equal footing. Here the promoter views each artist or group as commanding similar audience numbers even though they may draw from different audiences. The pairing of acts increases audience recognition for each of the acts and potentially doubles the overall audience size. Where one or the other act alone may not suitably fill a venue, the co-bill situation makes it financially viable for the promoter to still present each of the acts, and create an event.

Two methods of creating co-bill pairings:
1. The artists discover a compatibility with each other and find that by joining together, the overall show is stronger. The work in booking the tour is shared as are the costs. Often the co-bill can command higher fees because of the potential for a higher audience draw. The co-bill artists then promote the joint show directly to the promoters.
2. The promoter has had inquiries from various acts that they think would work well together in a co-bill presentation. The promoter then offers a date to each of the artists suggesting they pair the two acts. If the acts are comfortable with the pairing, the promoter negotiates similar fee deals with each artist, although the fees do not necessarily have to be the same. For instance, one of the artists may have a larger draw in a particular area and is duly compensated. While both acts perform for a similar amount of time, one act may be carrying the bulk of the audience recognition. As with the opening act, where the main act helps to introduce the opener to a new audience, the co-bill offers the same advantage to the lesser known act.

Finding compatible pairings has become a valuable method of touring and increases an artist's audience and media recognition. When touring in new regions or internationally, the benefits of sharing the bill are dramatic. Seek out other artists interested in testing this touring style. Each artist

> "Being on tour as the opening act for Shawn Colvin had Vance Gilbert playing the club of record in every single major market over a five-week period. Vance had a very high percentage of invitations to return as a headliner."
>
> Jordi Herold
> former manager,
> Vance Gilbert

> "My artists always report back to me regarding opening acts. We make note of the good and the bad and share that information with talent buyers."
>
> Dick Renko
> manager,
> Trout Fishing in America,
> Muzik Management

> **HotTip:** 🌶️
> Team up with artists you enjoy performing with and create a unique multi-act show to generate interest from new presenters.

brings their own audiences, their years of experience and their contacts to the situation. Attempt a few dates first to test compatibility before launching a lengthy tour. You may be surprised at some of the benefits of simply joining with another artist to accomplish similar touring goals.

Tour Exchange

This touring method has recently been gaining in popularity. Simply put, two artists living in different locations, each having built their own fan base of support, join together in a co-bill situation. For one part of the tour Artist # 1 tours in Artist # 2's home base region and for the other part of the tour, they swap with Artist # 2 touring in Artist # 1's home base region. This co-bill sharing is really serving as an introduction for each of the artists into a brand new region. Each artist is depending upon the other's built-in draw and each makes a commitment to share their base of support with the other in a cultural exchange broadening each of their audiences and venues in the new regions.

Within their own area, each artist takes on the tasks of booking and promoting the tours. What each artist has developed in their own area benefits the newcomer. Tour exchange is a bold and exciting way for artists to network with each other while developing a presence in a new region. Once having toured the new region as partner in the co-bill, the act can attempt a solo return tour to familiar ground. There is no guarantee that one's audience will flourish with one exchange tour but the likelihood of having developed some following is greater than attempting a tour from scratch.

Multiple-Act Tours And Performances

During the last few years, the multiple-act tour has become a mainstay in the entertainment industry. Similar to the co-bill situation, artists join together to create a touring show comprised of three, four or more acts which can be a boon to each of the individual artist's careers. Rallying around some of the more well-known artists, these multiple-act tours present an audience with variety and present a promoter with benefits usually afforded to only festival promoters. Additionally the show, as a whole, sells better than that of the artists individually.

Some promoters have latched onto this format and have created multiple performer shows on their own, joining together compatible artists centered around a theme. Songwriter circles fall into this category and have proven to be very successful for all concerned.

Within this format, an artist participating in a touring show has the benefit of the groups' reputation to help build their own. The group often has a wider selection of venues

> *"Sometimes musicians who want to continue a solo or otherwise independent identity can team up musically and businesswise. Try a two-soloists team; the concert is part solo, part collaboration. Businesswise, when we're in my territory I book us, and he books us in his territory. It avoids the assumption that soloists are weak on stage, and it provides some division of responsibility in the booking."*
>
> Dan Crary
> guitarist, performer

willing to present the tour than the individual might have. The revenues generated from the group as a whole are often much greater than those potential revenues generated by the individual. Because of the multiple-performer bill, ticket prices are justifiably set higher, which adds to the higher revenues generated. The group has an opportunity to draw from each artist's resources once they are pooled together, again, increasing the benefits to the individual and the group. Along with the co-bill, the multiple-performer tour offers an artist another touring method to enhance their career development.

Some tours that have successfully used this method have been Christine Lavin's *A Winter's Night Tour* which first included John Gorka, Patti Larkin and David Wilcox. Christine followed that by touring with a group comprised of talented women artists called *The Four Bitchin' Babes*. Today, that tour is continuing with different artists—Camille West, Debbi Smith, Sally Fingerett and Megan McDonough. The recording artists on Windham Hill Records capitalized on the popularity of their recordings by joining forces around the winter holidays to create *The Winter Solstice Tours*. Over the course of a number of years, a variety of Windham Hill artists performed to large and enthusiastic audiences. The tours would always include a quartet and two solo acts or one duo and a solo act. A few artist configurations were: The Modern Mandolin Quartet, Barbara Higbie and Liz Story; Nightnoise, Barbara Higbie and Phil Auberg; Turtle Island String Quartet, Tuck and Patti, and Michael Mannering. Sarah McLachlan's *Lilith Faire* tour has played to sold-out audiences in the many thousands during 1996 and '97. Some of the participants have been Joan Osborne, Kelly Willis, Jewel, Tracy Chapman and Mary Chapin Carpenter.

Open Mics

With the continually growing talent pool from which buyers can now program their schedules, the market has become overly crowded. Open mic performance situations have cropped up everywhere in an effort to offer performance opportunities to new artists without the promoter risking their budget on undeveloped talent. They have proven to be successful performance experiences for everyone participating. The audience gets a free or very reasonable evening of entertainment by artists within their own community, while the presenter fills the room on an otherwise off-night, and perhaps sells food and drink. Additionally, the artist gets to experiment with new works in front of a supportive audience. Everyone wins! Artists have a chance to initially develop a fan base while testing their performance skills. It is a no-risk opportunity for an artist to see if they want to pursue a performing career in the first place. On a more practical level, the open mic situation

> "It's a good idea to create a theme for the tour and excite the audience with a concept beyond simply presenting a concert. The Three of Hearts tour was a good example of this. We each came from a different musical base, Margie Adam is more from women's music, Liz Story from New Age and I spread between the two. It was exciting for people to experience those worlds coming together. The Winter Solstice Tour *was more the excitement of framing the Christmas holidays as a solstice celebration rather than the classic Christmas concert."*
>
> **Barbara Higbie**
> recording artist,
> Windham Hill/Slowbaby Records

> "We do open mics in clubs and try to do them as concerts. It's really a good way to improve skills and musicians get an opportunity to play as often as they want for a listening audience."
>
> **Chris Lunn**
> Victory Music open mic concerts

> **HotTip:** 🌶
> Consider alternative performance markets to establish and maintain your career. The road to the mainstream venues is not always the most advantageous one for everyone.

can weed out those performers who really are not ready for the stage or who discover this is not their true calling. Every once in a while, a new talent shines brightly. These performance situations are the proving ground similar to the phenomenon started in the comedy field by venues like Catch A Rising Star.

Actively incorporate all of these methods into your touring plans as ways of expanding your audiences and showcasing for new promoters.

Niche Marketing—Narrow Your Focus To Expand Your Market

Target your bookings and your marketing to a specific audience or group of people for another powerful and effective way to build new audiences. The term niche implies restrictive or exclusive and, in a way, it is. In this instance, focus your attention on a few exclusive personal areas of interest in an attempt to find your niche. This section will help you clarify and pair your interests with potential alternative markets. In doing so, you will see how becoming niche-focused opens the doors to new opportunities, new venue possibilities and an alternative way of thinking about booking yourself.

Positioning yourself in a specific market depends on your life's goals. Measure your success as a touring artist by strategically attempting to reach those goals. Face the facts, there are many hundreds of thousands of people making some part of their living performing but only a very small percentage have achieved name recognition by the general public, the entertainment industry and the media. Other artists have gained modest notoriety within a very small circle, and still others fall somewhere in between the two. There is no pre-set plan to follow on your way to this thing called "stardom." There are specific markets one must play to build industry recognition if that is the desired goal. Our current models for success come from that very small percentage of artists who have already achieved international recognition. No wonder most artists define their level of success by measuring it against the mainstream models. You may now be ready to find some new models. Perhaps you are creating one right now with every daring step you take developing your career.

What Is Right For You?

There are some existing, well-traveled circuits where many performers find comfort. Some follow the path to the known venues or festivals which cater to a specific genre of music, dance or theater. Other artists find that performing on the college circuit or the state-fair circuit is a comfortable fit. Your career track may demand that you target venues like the

> *"When you market to groups of people who are interested in things you have a passion for, you multiply the power of everything you do. Your shared interest with the group puts you on the inside instead of the outside."*
>
> Jana Stanfield
> singer, songwriter, author

Hard Rock Cafe, the Philadelphia Folk Festival or Lincoln Center, or your career track may simply demand that you earn a living doing what you love to do, perform. If your goal is to perform and make a living at it, then you must also consider alternative markets that will allow you to accomplish that goal.

Reduce your competition or eliminate it altogether by finding alternative markets. The traditionally-traveled circuits are crowded with performers, similar to yourself, vying for the same venues, the same audiences and the same dollars. Discovering an alternative niche where you shine as the recognized entertainer of note, the one performer to invite when a performer is needed, could be an envious position.

I am encouraged by the stories of performers' creativity in seeking new markets. My consultations and workshops with performers around the country often result in the performer being relieved to hear about these alternative methods of creating an audience without the stress of clawing their way through the mainstream. For many artists, the mainstream holds little interest. Gaining access to an alternative audience, that will appreciate their performance and support them more intensively, breathes new enthusiasm for their continued efforts to pursue their chosen art. Let me share an example that illustrates how niche marketing can enhance your career.

> **HotTip:** Explore conferences, trade events, and gatherings for groups which hold some interest for you.

"The foundation for creating and sustaining a future in the music and entertainment industry is to identify, articulate and create the market niche around on one's own unique portfolio of gifts and talents."

Kevin Asbjörnson, M.I.M.
founder,
principal recording artist,
PianoOne, LLC

The Caregiver Niche

Singers/songwriters Greg Trafidlo and Laura Pole opened an entirely new market for themselves when they incorporated Laura's nursing career into their music. Laura was invited to perform at an upcoming nursing conference. Not only did they get paid for the performance along with travel and accommodations but they found an audience hungry to support their music by purchasing their cassettes and CDs. Greg and Laura's interest in health care prompted them to write and record music specifically about caregiving. Because of Laura's affiliation with the profession, they found a very enthusiastic market for their music and were invited to perform at conferences nationwide. They used these professional conferences as anchor dates for short tours of other more traditional types of venues. Here is Greg Trafidlo's accounting of their development as performers in the "caregiver niche."

" With Laura's work as a cancer nurse in Roanoke, we had the opportunity to play for hospital functions, Christmas parties and patients. Our recognition by the Virginia medical community began after we were flown to Atlanta to perform at the National Headquarters for the American Cancer Society's awards banquet.

Our third release, *To Those Who Feel, A Tribute To People Who Care For People*, remains our best seller—especially in the spring during National Nurses Week and National Hospital Week. Regional and national nursing publications began writing stories about the "Singing Nurse," exposing us to an even greater market.

We were commissioned to write songs for the regional AIDS project, perform for community services banquets, write and perform for a healthcare-related television special and statewide

> meetings of the American Cancer Society. We were also asked to perform on the steps of the U.S. Capital for the American Nurses Association Rally for Health Care Reform.
>
> Our caregiver album found its way to nationally known healthcare speakers who are now using our songs as part of their presentations to even larger audiences. We developed a working relationship with a couple of presenters who are actually distributing our tapes and CDs for us as well as including them in their catalogs.
>
> Today we are regular performers at many national healthcare conferences. Fifty percent of our engagements are healthcare-related and have given us national attention in ways that could not have been achieved through the normal routes."
>
> Greg Trafidlo and Laura Pole
singers, songwriters

As you can see, the artists' involvement within the caregivers' community positions them as the only recognized national performers available. They have created a loyal market virtually free of competition.

Laura's nursing credentials gave her an insider's perspective of the group for which she and Greg were now performing and those attending these meetings viewed Greg and Laura as one of their own. This increased the enthusiasm for their music, future bookings and product sales.

This is just one example of how finding your own niche exposes you to ongoing opportunities. Once entrenched within the niche, there seems to be a self-perpetuating process that carries one deeper into the market. Invitations come to you more frequently from referrals within the market, which increases your visibility throughout the niche. From this example, imagine how targeting your specialty can broaden your own career markets.

Defining Your Alternative Markets

Target potential touring markets by closely examining your interests and hobbies. Earlier we explored ways to include interests and hobbies within a tour's time frame. The beauty of performing for alternative markets is that each performer can define their own optimum market by assessing one's interests. The following list pairs a few interests and hobbies with targeted markets.

> *"Focus on what is working. We ask our contacts or mailing-list people to give us leads of places we might be able to play. We give energy to the places that are appropriate for us like conferences, churches, music festivals, coffeehouses and private parties and ignore the many places that aren't. Suddenly we have a lot of work."*
>
> Kathleen Hanan
singer, songwriter,
Inside Out

Target Market Suggestions

1. *Healthcare:* hospital parties, medical professional meetings, senior facilities, pharmaceutical trade conferences, nursing conferences, etc.
2. *Sailing:* boat shows, races, yacht club events, marina parties, sailing clubs, etc.
3. *Environmental:* Audubon Society meetings, museums, zoos, schools, political events, clubs, etc.
4. *Golf:* tournaments, club events, golf course social programs, golf schools, training meetings, etc.

5. *Cooking:* equipment and appliance trade conferences, demonstrations, cooking schools, country inns, cooking radio and television shows, etc.
6. *Cars:* dealers and dealership events, car shows, race events, auctions, commercials, etc.
7. *Science:* fairs, conferences, schools, trade shows, tournaments, etc.
8. *Children:* hospitals, camps, schools, social clubs raising money for children's needs, etc.
9. *Psychology:* meetings, conferences, university lecture series, etc.
10. *Business (pick a field):* trade shows, office parties, annual events, grand openings, etc.
11. *Religion:* meetings, events, holidays, conventions, etc.

Examine your interests, hobbies and passions in your own life. Include everything from your religious groups and affiliations to the sports teams and leagues to which you belong, and from the causes and charities you care about to the products you buy and the stores you frequent. Consider everything and list your ideas below.

> "When you begin doing concerts for groups of people with a common interest, you are niche marketing.... Marketing to a specific group is the easiest way to get word-of-mouth referrals. You can quickly multiply your name recognition, your demand and your bookings."
>
> **Jana Stanfield**
> singer, songwriter, author

Niche Marketing Ideas

_____
_____
_____
_____
_____
_____
_____
_____
_____
_____

> "The country Americana sound is not as authentically accessible in Europe as it is stateside. Performing for thousands overseas, surrounded by fjords, medieval courtyards, vineyards and alpine views, has been nothing short of thrilling. These successes have instilled new confidence and inspiration to identify and develop another personally meaningful niche market—the movement to stop violence against women."
>
> **Candace Asher**
> singer, songwriter

You now have a base from which to begin targeting your niche markets.

Marketing To A Niche

Creating these alternative markets is certainly one way of enhancing the tour markets you are already working. You may be bold enough to see it as a complete shift in how you think about your touring career. As further proof of how effective niche marketing can be, I suggest reading singer songwriter Jana Stanfield's book, *A Musician's Guide To Outrageous Success, Making and Selling CDs and Cassettes*. Jana is proof of how booking tours into these niche markets can redefine success for a touring artist.

As in the above example, Greg and Laura's experience with niche marketing validates this strategy. Once Greg and Laura were invited to the first nursing conference, they were seen by other professionals in the field who were involved with coordinating other conferences and meetings. Having witnessed the audience's response to their music, Greg and Laura were logical choices, if not the only known choice, for these other events.

David Roth, a singer, songwriter from Seattle effectively markets himself to conferences, workshops and teaching institutes dealing with health, psychology and spiritual growth. Here are some of his niche marketing stories.

"My greatest booking "tool" over the years has been word-of-mouth. I made it a habit to ask my early sponsors (coffeehouses, cafes, churches, etc.) if they would write me a letter of endorsement based on their experience of my work. These letters became my "press kit" and, in the decade-plus since that time, I have accumulated some kind words, articles and reviews that seem to have anywhere from minimal to powerful influence on "uninitiated" producers and promoters.

A good friend was booked to do an audio-visual presentation on a Saturday night at the Omega Institute, Center for Holistic Studies in Rhinebeck, New York. He brought me along to play between shows. There were over 300 people in attendance (including the program director) and my five or six songs went over rather well. Based on that and a couple of phone conversations a few months later, Omega offered me the faculty position of "resident bard." I spent parts of the next four summers there giving concerts, performing in workshops, emceeing evening events, facilitating songwriting and singing lessons/classes, going to work in shorts and sandals, and . . . eating tofu!

Joel Goodman, founder and director of the Humor Project in Saratoga Springs, New York, was in a workshop with me at Omega one summer, and he heard me sing. A few years later he invited me to his wonderful annual conference which is attended by more than 1,000 folks from around the world. After my first appearance in 1995, I received the honor of doing the Saturday night keynote presentation the following year (Bob Newhart was Friday night).

Dr. Bob Schwarz, the director of the Institute for Advanced Clinical Training in Pennsylvania, convenes seminars around the country where psychologists, psychiatrists, and other mental-healthcare professionals study new therapeutic techniques. Since many of my songs (both serious and silly) include a psychological slant we discovered that music was a wonderful stress-reducing element to such proceedings. I have been to half a dozen of his events over the years.

Conferences, retreats and special events have added a wide variety of quotes to my press packet from a range of sponsors unlikely to be found on the resumes of many folk singers. I think this diversity is appealing to someone who may never have considered having live music at a convention or training. In some cases I am the first "music person" ever added to the faculty of these institutes. The budgets are often larger than that of a folk organization or coffeehouse. When they give me an honorarium *and* a plane ticket, I can *then* call the local coffeehouse to see if *they* would like to make use of my presence in the area, if time permits."

—David Roth

The Benefits of Niche Marketing
by Jana Stanfield

- You are performing for people with whom you share a common bond.
- It is easier to get bookings because you are the only musician with any knowledge of the things they are interested in.
- It is easy to become a celebrity among these groups.
- The audiences are appreciative and, in many cases, they are very large.
- These audiences buy more albums. They want to support you because your music relates to them.
- The pay can be five to ten times higher because you are seen as a unique commodity in their field.
- The groups will often pay your travel expenses in addition to your performance fees.
- You can easily start playing for a certain kind of group at a local level and then move up to the state level and national level.
- You can travel around the country to play for these great audiences at the same time that you are pursuing personal interests like vacationing, visiting friends, skiing or beach bumming.

Working In Alternative Markets

As you begin to book these alternative markets, keep in mind that the individuals with whom you negotiate and make arrangements are professionals within their own field. They may have very little knowledge of event planning, negotiations, contracts and performer hospitality. The task of educating them about your requirements remains with you. All of the skills and techniques that you have incorporated into your bookings up until now still apply.

Always present yourself professionally while remaining flexible with your contact and understanding of their situation. They are eager to make a positive impression on you as well as the rest of their organization. Although these individuals are not likely to be professional concert presenters, you will find that their sense of duty and desire to make the event a memorable one will make these concerts some of your most satisfying performances. In some situations you may be fortunate to actually work with an event organizer whose experience in planning and whose attention to detail will make your cooperative relationship an extremely rewarding one.

Examine Your Alternatives

Examine the alternatives that are available to you. We all have such a wealth of experience from which to draw. Our personal histories are filled with experiences from our education years, previous job situations, past artistic collaborations and outside interests that help make our lives whole. For instance, if you once taught science in an elementary school, incorporate your knowledge from that experience into your performance

HotTip:
When working in alternative markets outside the entertainment industry, modify and simplify your contracts and riders. Simple contracts will be appreciated by those not used to dealing with industry standard agreements.

> **HotTip:** 🌶
> Return to your field and put your hard-earned degree to use on your own terms. Consider all the possible niches which can become new markets for you.

and create an elementary school program which combines your music with your education and teaching skills. Perhaps you were a real estate agent. Real estate agents have membership organizations that hold meetings and conferences. Become the entertainer of choice. Think of the insider comments you, alone, could make as you wrap your performance in meaningful patter they can relate to. If you are a trained therapist turned performer, I can only imagine the clever material you might prepare for an audience of therapists.

New Performance Venues

Niches can also be created simply by selecting alternative performance sites. Earlier, I mentioned how some bookstores incorporated a performance space into their facility design and regularly program performances. I have witnessed a number of these gigs while touring with my artists. During setup and sound check we all wondered why we were there since no one would find us tucked upstairs, out of the way. As soon as the music began, people flocked from out of the stacks of books two floors down and filled the folding chairs. The strategically placed coffee bar helped to complete the coffeehouse atmosphere and create a performance environment conducive to listening and introducing the music to a brand new audience.

Cafes and coffee bars, like Starbucks, are creating a circuit of new venue alternatives to the traditional club. Shopping malls offer artists another venue likely to attract an audience that has never been exposed to your performance. Finding shopping malls attractive, Victory Music in Tacoma, Washington, has developed an additional open mic series different from the coffeehouse-concert open mic situation Chris Lunn mentions in his sidebar quote. Although the audiences are often transient, an artist has a unique opportunity to hook new fans who might eventually look for them in a more traditional venue. These listeners may have never discovered the artist had the series not been established in this alternative venue.

I have always been a strong believer in taking the arts to the people instead of waiting for the people to find the arts. I discovered folk music in my first year of college because the activities director programmed the performers in non-traditional venues. I was introduced to old-timey music by the Highwoods String Band playing in my biology lab, blues and gospel by Rev. Dan Smith performing in my photography class and Bessie Jones, one of the Georgia Sea Island Singers, singing gospel in the library. I may have never stumbled into the area where the evening festival was held had I not been intrigued by what I saw and heard during the day as I moved from class to class. This is creative programming using alternative venues to capture new audiences. It helps to explore

"In a mall, people pass by who wouldn't normally listen to that kind of music but who are now getting exposed to it. That wouldn't happen in a club. The malls can draw a wider audience and expose more people to more diverse styles of music. Doing an open mic at a mall with its walk-through audience, an artist also has to learn a different audience approach."

Chris Lunn
Victory Music
open mic concerts

innovative methods of introducing the art to the audience when presenting art forms that stretch the general public's notion of what is popular and, certainly, what is familiar.

An audience is an illusive thing to chase. Audience development plagues all artists and promoters regardless of their level of operation. Solo performers need to consider every angle as do symphony orchestra directors. Major label recording artists continually work with their record companies, agents and managers to devise new touring collaborations to entice their audiences and enable the artists to sell product over a period of years.

Market Your Act For Success

Consider the setting in which your performance takes place, your method of marketing, the staging and, even, your dress. Dress your act for success—place yourself in venues that raise the level of your performance simply by virtue of the setting and the clothes you wear. Here are a few exciting examples that demonstrate my point.

A few years ago a tour was designed for The Masters of Bluegrass. The artists dressed in tuxedos and upscale promotional materials were designed and marketed to major performing arts centers around the country. Ticket prices were scaled in accordance with many of the other season events programmed at these venues beginning at $20 and up. The act's fees increased dramatically. The shows played to sold-out audiences that were mostly unfamiliar with bluegrass music.

Another phenomenon occurred when *Riverdance* made its way to America and toured nationally. Public television presented the original taped performance and audiences around the country became intrigued with percussive dance and traditional Celtic music. American audiences paid big bucks to attend performances in some of the major performance theaters. *Riverdance* provided an introduction to an art form that had it not been presented in a particular setting, would have remained undiscovered by a large audience.

Although percussive dance performances have been part of many dance and folk festivals for years, *Riverdance* producers understood the value of presenting their show in venues traditionally reserved for the "high arts." Audiences who regularly attend the ballet or the symphony at these venues may never find out about the dance or folk festivals in their area. Yet, when *Riverdance* was announced as part of the season programming, the performance was bought by the regular season ticket buyers as part of their package partially because public television sanctioned the performance. This is also true of the popular Irish group, The Chieftains, who for years have been marketed to large classical-music venues, while other equally talented traditional Irish groups play in

> "A good thing to do is to have spot entertainment in various locations on campus, in the lobby of the library or the lobby of the main classroom building. These are ways to bring things to the students as well as have some publicity for a program that you are presenting later in the day."
>
> **Phyllis Kurland**
> coordinator,
> Nassau Community College
> Cultural Program

smaller halls and clubs and are marketed solely through folk music channels. The broad audience base for whom The Chieftains perform is a direct result of the marketing strategy adopted early in their career.

Conclusion

Be creative and explore uncharted territory. There is an audience waiting to appreciate you and support you. Take advantage of these unique opportunities.

Summary

- Establish your reasons for touring before every tour.
- Tour creatively to make the most out of your touring experience professionally and personally.
- Create a home base of support.
- Expand your tours regionally.
- Create a national presence on your own terms.
- Become familiar with venue booking seasons and performance seasons.
- Expand your audience by performing at showcases, battles of the bands, festivals, contests.
- Use shared performance situations to expand your audience.
- Consider niche marketing as a touring alternative.
- Explore alternative venues to expand your market.

Resources

Books About Touring:

Booking & Tour Management for the Performing Arts
Rena Road Show Shagan
Allworth Press
ISBN: 1880559366

Book Your Own Tour: The Independent Musician's Guide to Cost-Effective Touring and Promotion
Liz Garo
Rockport Publishing
ISBN: 1884615198

Bring It On Home: A Simple Guide to Producing House Concerts
T.R. Ritchie
P.O. Box 479
Moab, UT 84532-0479
Phone: 801-259-6230
E-mail: TRRinUTAH@aol.com

Concert Tour Production Management: How to Take Your Show on the Road
John Vasey
Focal Press
ISBN: 0240802357

Gigging
A Practical Guide for Musicians
Patricia Shih
Allworth Press
ISBN: 1581152752

How To Make Money Performing In Schools
David Heflick
Silox Productions
P.O. Box 1407
Orient, WA 99160
Phone: 509-684-8287

Note By Note
A Guide to Concert Promotion
Folk Alliance
962 Wayne Ave., Suite 902
Silver Spring, MD 20910-4480
Phone: 301-588-8185
Fax: 301-588-8186
Email fa@folk.org
Web: http://www.folk.org

The Music Business: Career Opportunities and Self-Defense
Dick Weissman
Crown Publications
ISBN: 0609810138

The Touring Musician: A Small Business Approach to Booking Your Band on the Road
Hal Galper
Watson-Guptil Publications
ISBN: 0823084299

Chain Store Venues:

Barnes & Noble
Web: http://www.barnesandnoble.com
List of stores nationwide.
Contact community relations coordinator at each store.

Borders Books and Music
Web: http://www.borders.com
Web: http://www.borders.com/stores/index.html
List of stores nationwide by state, contact, phone, address, directions.
Contact the community relations coordinator at each store. List of stores available at each store.

Starbucks/Hear Music
Call local store in each town. May have booking coordinator for a number of stores.
Web: http://www.starbucks.com/hearmusic

Contests:

Billboard Song Contest
P.O. Box 470306
Tulsa, OK 74147-0306
Web: http://www.billboard.com/bb/songcontest
Songs may be submitted in Rock, Alternative, Pop, Contemporary/Christian, Traditional Gospel, Jazz, R&B, Rap, Latin, Dance/House, Country, Folk, World. Presented by *Billboard* in conjunction with Oklahoma City University School of Music and Performing Arts, Music and Entertainment Business Program.

Colgate Country Showdown
Special Promotions, Inc.
63 Music Square East
Nashville, TN 37203
Phone: 615-321-5130
Fax: 615-320-1708
Web: http://www.countryshowdown.com
Judged showcases nationwide with prizes

Newfolk Contest for Emerging Songwriters
Kerrville Festival
P.O. Box 291466
Kerrville, TX 78029
Phone: 830-257-3600
E-mail: info@kerrvillemusic.com
Web: http://www.kerrville-music.com
Information, deadline and rules for current year available.

Chris Austin Songwriter's Contest
Merle Fest
Wilkes Community College
N. Wilkesboro, NC 28697-0120
Phone: 1-800-343-7857
Web: http://www.merlefest.org

International Songwriting Competition
211 7th Ave North
Suite LL-20
Nashville, TN 37219
Phone: 615-251-4441
Web: http://www.songwritingcompetition.com

John Lennon Songwriting Contest
Web: http://www.johnlennonsongwritingcontest.com

Telluride Troubadour Contest
Takes place at Telluride Bluegrass festival in June (application deadline late April).
Singer/Songwriter Contest
Takes place at the Folksfest in August (application deadline July).
Planet Bluegrass
P.O. Box 769
Lyons, CO 80540
Att: Steve Szymansky
Phone: 1-800-624-2422
Web: http://www.planetbluegrass.com

Falcon Ridge Artist Showcase
Falcon Ridge Folk Festival
74 Modley Road
Sharon, CT 06069
Att: Anne Saunders/ Howard Randall
Phone: 860-364-0366
E-mail: anne@falconridgefolk.com
Web: http://www.falconridgefolk.com

American Ballet Competition
Dance Affiliates
4701 Bath Street, #46
Philadelphia, PA 19137
Phone: 215-636-9000
Fax: 215-564-4206
Web: http://www.dancecelebration.org

Van Cliburn International Piano Competition
Van Cliburn Foundation
2525 Ridgmar Boulevard, Suite 307
Fort Worth, TX 76116
Phone: 817-738-6536
Fax: 817-738-6534
E-mail: clistaff@cliburn.org
Web: http://www.cliburn.org

World Federation of International Music Competitions
104, rue de Carouge
CH-1205 Geneva, Switzerland
Phone: 011-41-22-321-3620
Fax: 011-41-22-781-1418
Web: http://www.wfimc.org

Young Audiences, Inc.
115 East 92nd Street
New York, NY 10128-1688
Phone: 212-831-8110
Fax: 212-289-1202
Email: ya4kids@ya.org
Web: http://www.youngaudiences.org

Young Concert Artists, Inc.
250 West 57th Street, Suite 1222
New York, NY 10107
Phone: 212-307-6655
Fax: 212-581-8894
Web: http://www.yca.org

Music Competitions
Web: http://www.music.indiana.edu/music_resources/competit.html

Festivals And Venues Online:

Canadian Folk Festivals
Web: http://www.yorku.ca/cstm/festival.htm

Festival Finder
Web: http://www.festivalfinder.com

Festival Network Online
Web: http://www.festivalnet.com

Folk Venues
Web: http://www.folkmusic.org/shows.html

Musi-Cal
Web: http://www.musi-cal.com

Music Links
Web: http://www.yahoo.com/entertainment/music

Opera America
Web: http://www.operaamerica.org

Operabase
Web: http://www.operabase.com
Opera schedules, venues, festivals, reviews, links

Traditional Dance in Toronto
Web: http://www.dancing.org/

U.S. Chambers of Commerce
Web: http://www.uschamber.com

Organizations With Venue Lists:

Association of Performing Arts Presenters (APAP)
1112 16th Street, NW, Suite 400
Washington, DC 20036
Phone: 202-833-2787
Fax: 202-833-1543
E-mail: info@artspresenters.org
Web: http://www.artspresenters.org/
Membership required.
Directory of presenting members, arts agencies.

Canada Council for the Arts/
Le Conseil Des Arts Du Canada
350 Albert Street
P.O. Box 1047
Ottawa, Ontario K1P 5V8
Phone: 1-800-263-5588 in Canada
Phone: 613-566-4414
Web: http://www.canadacouncil.ca
Directory of Canadian Music Festivals.
Jazz, Folk, World Music Presenter's Directory

CDSS Group Directory
Country Song and Dance Society (CDSS)
132 Main Street
P.O. Box 338
Haydenville, MA 01039-0338
Phone: 413-268-7426
Fax: 413-268-7471
E-mail: sales@cdss.org
E-mail: office@cdss.org
Web: http://www.cdss.org
Membership available.
Lists of organizations presenting dances across the country.

Folk Alliance
510 South Main Street
Memphis, TN 38103
Phone: 901-522-1170
Fax: 901-522-1172
E-mail: fa@folk.org
Web: http://www.folkalliance.net
Membership required.
Venue, presenter, media, mailing lists available for sale.

International Bluegrass Music Association (IBMA)
2 Music Circle South, Suite 100
Nashville, TN 37203
Phone: 1-888-GET-IBMA (438-4262)
Phone: 615-256-3222
Fax: 615-256-0450
Web: http://www.ibma.org
Membership required.
Venue, presenter, media, membership mailing lists available.

International Fairs Association
P.O. Box 985
Springfield, MO 65801
Phone: 1-800-516-0313
Fax: 417-862-0156
Web: http://www.fairsandexpos.com
Directory listing county, state and international fairs and events in U.S., Canada, foriegn.
Associate membership available for performers, agent; directory free w/membership.
Early December—annual conference, trade show held in Las Vegas.

International Society for the Performing Arts (ISPA)
17 Purdy Ave.
P.O. Box 909
Rye, NY 10580
Phone: 914-921-1550
Fax: 914-921-1593
E-mail: info@ispa.org
Web: http://www.ispa.org
Membership required.

The Metropolitan Opera Guild, Inc.
70 Lincoln Center Plaza
New York, NY 10023
Web: http://www.metguild.org
Opera related resources
Newsletter: Opera News

National Association for Campus Activities (NACA)
13 Harbison Way
Columbia, SC 29212-3401
Phone: 1-800-845-2338 or 803-732-6222
Fax: 803-749-1047
Web: http://www.naca.org
Membership required.
Directory of college activities programmers available to members.

National Storytelling Network
132 Boone Street, Suite 5
Jonesboro, TN 37659
Phone: 423-913-8201
Fax: 432-753-9331
Web: http://www.storynet.org
Membership available.
Directory of organizations, storytellers, workshops, festivals, production companies, publishers of storytelling works; bi-monthly magazine.
National Storytelling Festival—annually first full weekend in October.

Ontario Council of Folk Festivals
410 Bank Street, Suite 225
Ottawa, Ontario K2P 1Y8
Phone: 1-866-292-OCFF
Fax: 613-560-2001
Web: http://www.ocff.ca

Rhythm & Blues Foundation
100 South Broad Street, Suite 620
Philadelphia, PA 19110
Phone: 215-568-1080
Fax: 215-568-1026
Web: http://www.rhythm-n-blues.org

Western Fairs Association
1776 Tribute Road, Suite 210
Sacramento, CA 95815
Phone: 916-927-3100
Fax: 916-927-6397
E-mail: wfa@fairsnet.org
Web: http://www.fairsnet.org
Listing of fairs, expositions in western states. 150 member fairs in U.S. and Canada.
Membership available.

Road Maps Online:

Map Quest
Web: http://www.mapquest.com/

Map Blast
Web: http://www.mapblast.com/
Road directions door to door.

Showcases:

American Society of Composers, Authors, and Publishers (ASCAP)
ASCAP—New York
One Lincoln Plaza
New York, NY 10023
Phone: 212-621-6240 membership
Fax: 212-724-9064
Web: http://www.ascap.com

ASCAP—Los Angeles
7920 Sunset Blvd., 3rd Floor
Los angeles, CA 90046
Phone: 323-883-1000
Fax: 323-883-1049

ASCAP—Nashville
Two Music Square West
Nashville, TN 37203
Phone: 615-742-5000
Fax: 615-742-5020

ASCAP—Chicago
1608 N. Milwaukee, Suite 1007
Chicago, IL 60647
Phone: 773-394-4286
Fax: 773-394-5634

ASCAP—London
8 Cork Street
London, W1X 1PB
Phone: 011-44-207-439-0909
Fax: 011-44-207-434-0073

ASCAP Showcases:
ASCAP Presents—unsigned bands in U.S. and U.K.
ASCAP Showcases on the Road—held annually around the U.S.
Quiet On The Set—new emerging solo and group singer/songwriters
ASCAP/MAC Cabaret Songwriter's Showcase—cabaret and theater songwriters
The ASCAP Foundation Presents Through the Walls—concert trained composers/performers who cross genres

Broadcast Music Inc. (BMI)
BMI—New York
320 West 57th Street
New York, NY 10019
Phone: 212-586-2000; Fax: 212-246-2163
E-mail: newyork@bmi.com
Web: http://www.bmi.com

BMI—Los Angeles
8730 Sunset Blvd., 3rd Floor
West Hollywood, CA 90069-2211
Phone: 310-659-9109; Fax: 310-657-6947

BMI—Nashville
10 Music Square East
Nashville, TN 37203
Phone: 615-401-2000

BMI Monthly Showcase Events held in New York City/Los Angeles/Nashville:
BMI Acoustic Roundup—last Wednesdays, hosted at The Living Room, NY and second Thursdays at the Sutler, Nashville
Five or six writers in the round.
BMI NY Songwriters Circle Held at the Bitter End. *LA Acoustic Lounge*
Writers network with writers, musicians, managers, publishers.
BMI Open Mic—every Monday night at Baggot Inn
BMI Music Connection Showcase—second Mondays—Nashville
BMI Collaborator's Connection—Second Wednesday, every other month
BMI Pick of the Month—Up and coming bands showcase in LA's best venues. Industry executives attend regularly.
BMI Legal Series—second Thursdays every month at BMI offices (320 W 57th)
Panel of BMI attorneys discuss publishing, record deals, management contracts, etc.

National Academy of Recording Arts and Sciences
3402 Pico Blvd.
Santa Monica, CA 90405
Phone: 310-392-3777
Web: http://grammy.com
Check this site for future showcase opportunities. They have sponsored showcases for unsigned and independent label bands.

Women In Music National Network
31121 Mission Blvd., Suite 300
Hayward, CA 94544
Phone: 510-232-3897
Web: http://www.womeninmusic.com
Membership required. Showcases, networking events, educational seminars, quarterly publication.

Tour Directories:

AustralAsia Music Industry Directory
20 Hordern Street
Newtown, N.S.W. 2042
Australia
Phone: +61-12-9557-7766
Fax: +61-12-9557-7788
E-mail: directories@immedia.com.au
Web: http://www.immedia.com.au
Purchase $50 US or free at international trade fairs like MIDEM
Online directory: $40—6 months; $80—12 months.

Billboard Directories
1515 Broadway
New York, NY 10036
Phone: 1-800-745-8922
Web: http://www.billboard.com
Directories: Print and Online Subscriptions

International Talent & Touring Directory
Listing artists, their management, their agency, record label, performance venues, hotels, and services.

International Buyers Guide
Lists labels, publishers, recording studios, venues, clubs, concert promoters, country artists and managers, and radio stations in US and Canada.

International Latin Music Buyer's Guide
"Yellow Pages" of Latin Music contacts in US, Mexico, Central and South America.

Chamber Music America
305 7th Avenue, 5th Floor
New York, NY 10001-6008
Phone: 212-242-2022
Web: http://www.chamber-music.org

Facilities Directory
650 First Avenue
New York, NY 10016
Phone: 212-532-4150
Fax: 212-213-6382
Conventions, expositions, event management, and large production.
Annual directory: Call for current directory price.

International Folk Dance Directory
International Folk Culture Center
Our Lady of the Lake University
411 SW 24th Street
San Antonio, TX 78207-4689
Phone: 210-436-8888
Fax: 210-436-8889
E-mail: ifolkcultu@aol.com
Web: http://www.folkdancing.org
US, Canada and foriegn folk dance and music groups, camps, festivals, institutes, parties, symposia, tours, weekend centers, college and university folk dance and folklore programs, directories, libraries, museum, organizations.
Call for prices and current directory availability.

The North American Folk Business Directory
Folk Alliance
510 South Main Street
Memphis, TN 38103
Phone: 901-522-1170
Fax: 901-522-1172
Web: http://www.folkalliance.net
Listing U.S. and foriegn folk venues, folk press, radio stations, newsletters, publications, record companies, agents, managers, performers, publicists.

Musical America
400 Windsor Corporate Center, Suite 200
East Windsor, NJ 08520
Phone: 800-221-5488, ext. 7783
Web: http://www.musicalamerica.com
Listing of presenters and festivals for ethnic, folk, children's, dance, Jazz, theater, classical, opera.

Music Directory of Canada
23 Hannover Drive # 7
St. Catharines, Ontario L2W 1A3
Phone: 905-641-3471
Fax: 905-641-1648
Web: http://www.musicdirectorycanada.com
Listings of artists, agents, managers, labels, festivals, presenters, and other music related resources.

Musician's Atlas
38 Porter Place
Montclare, NY 07042
Phone: 973-509-9898
E-mail: info@musiciansatlas.com
Web: http://www.MusiciansAtlas.com
Lists websites for artist development, agents, clubs, press, radio stations.
Annual print directory and atlas online.

The Musician's Guide to Touring & Promotion
Musician
49 Music Square West
Nashville, TN 37203
Phone: 615-321-4295
Fax: 615-327-1575
Web: http://www.musiciansmag.com
Lists agents, bands, clubs, press, fanzines, radio stations, music stores and more.
Semi-annual directory.

Festivals Directory—Northwest
P.O. Box 7515
Bonney Lake, WA 98390
Phone/Fax: 253-863-6617
E-mail: info@festivalsdirectory.com
Web: http://www.festivalsdirectory.com
Festivals in WA, OR, BC, ID

Dance USA
Web: http://www.danceusa.org
Lists of presenters, festivals for dance, theater, dance schools, choreographers, dance teachers, movement arts, yoga.
Updated yearly.

Dance Directory
Web: http://www.dancedirectory.com
Dancers, teachers, merchants, competitions

Talent & Booking Online
P.O. Box 14265
Palm Desert, CA 92255
Phone: 760-779-8056
Fax: 760-773-3568
Web: http://www.talentandbooking.com
The Official Country Music Directory: Lists artists, personal managers, booking agencies.

Theatre Communications Group, Inc.
520 Eighth Ave.
New York, NY 10018-4156
Phone: 212-609-5960
Fax: 212-609-5900
E-mail: tcg@tcg.org
http://www.tcg.org
Theatre Directory—Lists regional theatre companies and organizations around the U.S.

The Dance Gypsy
2518 Sunset Lake Rd.
Dummerston, VT 05301
Phone: 802-257-4478
Fax: 802-257-9933
E-mail: info@thedancegypsy.com
Web: http://www.thedancegypsy.com
Directory of folk dance presenters.

Trade Magazines with Directories:

Bluegrass Now
P.O. Box 2020
Rolla, MO 65402
Phone: 1-800-736-0125 or 573-341-7336
Fax: 573-341-7352
E-mail: bgn@fidnet.com
Web: http://www.bluegrassnow.com
Festival calandar in each issue. Subscription: Call for rate

Bluegrass Unlimited
P.O. Box 771
Warrenton, VA 20188-0771
Phone: 1-800-258-4727
Fax: 540-341-0011
E-mail: info@bluegrassmusic.com
Web: http://www.bluegrassmusic.com
Bluegrass festival directory once a year plus itinerary listings. Subscription: Call for rate.

Dirty Linen
P.O. Box 66600
Baltimore, MD 21239-6600
Phone: 410-583-7973
Fax: 410-337-6735
E-mail: info@dirtylinen.com
Web: http://www.dirtylinen.com
Online Gig Guide—click on "Gig Guide;" then click on "Events/Festivals."
Includes tour schedules in each issue listing venues and contact information. Subscription: Call for rates.

Jazz Times Magazine
8737 Colesville Road, 9th Floor
Silver Spring, MD 20910-3921
Phone: 301-588-4114
Fax: 301-588-5531
E-mail: info@jazztimes.com
Web: http://www.jazztimes.com
Club Guide: September Issue; night clubs, managers, booking agents
Subscription: Call for rates.

Performer (Northeast, Southeast, Southwest)
285 Washington Street
Sommerville, MA 02143
Phone: 617-627-9200
Fax: 617-627-9930
E-mail: info@performermag.com
Web: http://www.performermag.com

Performance Magazine
International Touring Talent Weekly Newspaper
1203 Lake Street
Fort Worth, TX 76102-4504
Phone: 817-338-9444; Fax: 817-877-4273
Web: http://www.performancemagazine.com
Subscription: Includes 51 weekly magazines and ten yearly directories. Individual directories also available separately.
Weekly magazine: Artist tour itineraries, news features, box office reports, international news and market reports.
Performance Series of Directories:
Talent/Personal Managers
Clubs/Theatres/Colleges
Concert Productions
Facilities
Talent Management
International
Talent Buyers
Transportation/Accommodations
The Black Book (phone and fax guide)
Equipment and Personnel

Performing Arts Yearbook for Europe
27 Wilfred Street
London SW1E 6PR
UK
Web: http://www.api.co.uk

Pollstar
4697 W. Jacquelyn Avenue
Fresno, CA 93722
Phone: 1-800-344-7383
In California: 559-271-7900
Fax: 559-271-7979
E-mail: info@pollstar.com
Web: http://www.pollstar.com
Subscription: Includes weekly magazine plus five bi-annual directories. Individual directories also available separately.
Weekly magazine: Tour itineraries, music industry news, box office summaries, Concert Pulse Charts for album sales and radio airplay in nine formats.
Directories:
Talent Buyers & Clubs
Concert Venues
Concert Support Services
Agency Rosters
Record Company Rosters
ConneXions
Mailing labels available for additional fee.

SingOut! Magazine
The Sing Out Corporation
P.O. Box 5460
Bethlehem, PA 18015-0460
Phone: 610-865-5366
Fax: 610-865-5129
E-mail: info@singout.org
Web: http://www.singout.org
Annual directory of folk festivals.
Subscription: Call for current rates.

U.S. and Canadian Regional, State, Local and Provincial Arts Councils:

For lists of presenters who book acts through state arts council touring directories, see Resources, Chapter 12, Funding.

Websites for Touring and Career Assistance:

Folkmusic.org
Web: http://www.folkmusic.org
Venues, shows, house concerts, business databases, folk radio list, folkDJ-L

Getsigned.com
Web: http://www.getsigned.com
Career development information

Gig Swap
Web: http://www.gigswap.com

Indie-Music.Com
Web: http://www.indie-music.com
Online newsletter, career development info, news and more.

Indie Contact Bible
Web: http://www.indiebible.com
Websites, links, to promote your music

Music Contracts.com
Web: http://www.musiccontracts.com
Forms of music industry contracts

Music Dish
Web: http://www.musicdish.com
Articles, musicians's assistance site

Music Moz
Web: http://www.musicmoz.org
Directories, links, resources

Musician's Exchange
Web: http://www.musicians.about.com

The Music Review
Web: http://www.musreview.com
Lists promoters, agents, managers, radio stations, TV and other music resources.

Powergig
Web: http://www.powergig.com
Booking resource for gigs of every variety

CHAPTER NINE

U.S./Canada Crossing Borders

"Develop a relationship with the people at immigration and at the border. Keep officials in the loop by sending them all the paperwork they require so that no last minute surprises arise or that they are unprepared."

Pierre Guerin
former executive director,
Winnipeg Folk Festival

Although there is plenty of work to keep a touring artist performing within the United States, there are many performance opportunities for those interested in branching out beyond our borders. One of the most accessible and popular choices for a foray across the border is Canada. Information regarding immigration regulations for U.S. artists touring in Canada and Canadian artists touring in the U.S. is included in this chapter.

Cultural exchange between the U.S. and Canada has enjoyed a comfortable flow over the years. Artists have demonstrated enough interest in exploring the touring possibilities of each country and promoters have had enthusiasm for presenting culturally-unique performances to make these exchanges viable. However, there are regulations which each country has established regarding immigration in an effort to

"Be prepared, be polite and be honest. Anything else is a gamble. Know what paperwork is required and have it all in a file. You're asking permission to enter that country as a guest. Be as honest and straightforward as you can and you'll usually have no problem."

Ken Brown
songwriter, composer

> **HotTip:**
> Since 9/11, USCIS regulations have become more involved and costly.
> Leave 90-120 days prior to the first U.S. date to file appropriate visa applications.

protect their own country's cultural survival. The main obstacle remains the paperwork. Although initially daunting, it is not insurmountable and, once you have worked with the system, each successive round becomes as simple as filling out familiar forms, filing properly and paying the appropriate fees.

Immigration Regulations

Each country has its own immigration regulations for artists entering that country for the purpose of working as an entertainer. Whereas some countries' regulations have become more relaxed, like those in Europe, others, like Canada and the U.S., have tightened their regulations. This makes entry into the countries both expensive and time-consuming.

The immigration regulations in the U.S. and in Canada change frequently and with very little notice or fanfare. Those planning tours to either country must allow enough time to have the appropriate applications processed and mailed. Changes in application procedures, costs and forms occur in both countries on an annual basis. Therefore, please call to verify all information before mailing materials.

Helpful Advocates

When dealing with government agencies, it is to your advantage to develop a working relationship with key individuals. If you reach someone at an agency, get their name and direct number and always call that person when dealing with a problem or simply asking a question. The following agencies and organizations offer valuable assistance when you are working on immigration applications.

American Federation Of Musicians Of The U.S. And Canada

The benefits of membership in the American Federation of Musicians' Union includes the assistance of a knowledgeable staff member to shepherd you through the application process when applying to the United States Citizenship and Immigration Service (USCIS), for a visa to tour in the U.S.

The union can supply all of the necessary visa forms along with union contracts. If you are an agent, a promoter or a friend helping to bring a foreign performer into the U.S., you will appreciate the union's assistance. Contact the main office in New York City at 1-800-ROADGIG (1-800-762-3444).

The AFM of Canada is also extremely helpful and knowledgeable about the immigration process and will assist Canadian members of the Musician's union with their visa applications when planning to tour the U.S. All of the Canadian union offices are listed later in this chapter as well as in this chapter's resource section.

> *"I would suggest that Canadians join the Musician's Union and take advantage of their membership. The union can give you advice and assistance on what has to be done when applying for visas."*
> **Rosalie Goldstein**
> management consultant,
> Goldstein & Associates, Ltd.

> *"Contact the staff at your local AFM for assistance with any problems with the visa application process."*
> **Corina Robidoux**
> supervisor,
> Artist Immigration,
> Canadian Office,
> American Federation of Musicians of the United States and Canada

Human Resources Development Canada

Contact with this office can detail information for specific employment permits for musicians and others seeking temporary employment in Canada. It is the intent of the Canadian government to employ Canadian artists first. When applying for work in Canada, it is important to indicate that you are a culturally unique performer. Supporting documentation from the presenter hiring the act, along with your promotional materials describing the act, will be necessary. Your Canadian employer will be your contact to HRDC for specific information and forms required by those needing to apply for a Work Permit.

United States Citizenship And Immigration Services

The USCIS has offices throughout the United States. Any foreign artist planning to tour in the U.S. must apply for a visa from the USCIS. All of the necessary forms and a current information packet can be obtained from any of the regional USCIS offices or call:

- ❖ USCIS Ask Immigration: 1-800-375-5283—Addresses and phone numbers
- ❖ Forms Request Line: http://www.uscis.gov form I-129
- ❖ Passport Agency: 202-647-0518—Passport applications and information http://travel.state.gov/passport_services.html

When you call the USCIS for the application packet of forms, you will receive the current addresses and phone numbers of the regional USCIS offices. Allow enough time to receive all the forms, gather your supporting documents, submit the application and wait for approval. Allow ninety to one hundred-twenty days from when you submit the completed applications to receive your visa. The earlier you begin the process, the sooner you will be able to finalize the details of the tour.

Local And State Politicians

There are officials in congressional offices whose expertise in USCIS regulations can assist you should an application be delayed or denied. Check with your local representative before calling your state representative.

The Promoters

Most festival and foreign promoters will assist with immigration applications and necessary tax papers. Festival promoters experienced with including foreign performers in their programs send most of the necessary forms along with their performance contracts. When you finalize an agreement with a foreign promoter, issue your contracts promptly unless they routinely issue their own, as is the case with most of the Canadian festivals.

HotTip:

The INS has become the Unites States Citizenship and Immigration Services under the U.S. Government's Department of Homeland Security. For current news related to touring: http://www.nepama.org/new pages/new_immigration.asp

"Local congressional representatives are incredibly helpful with USCIS matters. They want to help their constituents in areas where they can affect the outcome regardless of political affiliations. Use their expertise."

Robyn Boyd
agent,
Wooden Ship Productions

> **HotTip:**
> For extensive information on Work Permits and Confirmation in Canada, visit: Citizenship and Immigration Canada
> http://www.cic.gc.ca

U.S. Artists Planning To Tour Canada
Work Permits/Canada

Artists and their crew who are U.S. citizens and reside in the U.S. do not need a Work Permit as long as the artists are only performing in Canada for a limited period and are not performing in a bar or a restaurant. Under the new regulations, when performing for most festivals, concert venues, universities, non-profit presenting organizations or private events such as weddings, you will no longer need a Work Permit. If you are a film and recording studio user for a limited time period or a guest speaker on Canadian television or radio broadcasts, a Work Permit is not required.

U.S. Artists Requiring A Work Permit:
- Bands performing in bars, clubs and restaurants.
- Actors, singers and crew in Canadian theatrical productions.
- Individuals involved in making film, television, Internet and radio broadcasts for extended periods of time.
- Any performer who will be in an employment relationship with the organization or business contracting their services in Canada.
- A performer in a Canadian-based production or show that extends for a lengthy period of time.

If you find yourself fitting into one of the above categories requiring a Work Permit, you must work with your Canadian employer to file your application. The Canadian employer will contact Human Resources Development Canada who will supply them with all of the pertinent application forms for the Work Permit and Confirmation. Your Canadian employer is the conduit through which all contact with HRDC will be conducted. Even if you work through the Canadian Consulate in the states, you will still need the assistance of your Canadian employer to file the appropriate forms for the Work Permit.

Entertainers Requiring A Work Permit AND Confirmation

Both Confirmation and a Work Permit are required when entertainers are coming to establishments where the performance is secondary or incidental to the establishment's commercial activity and is used to attract the public for a purpose other than simply to view or listen to an art form. For example, bands playing as background music in restaurants or bars need to obtain Confirmation and Work Permit.

Work Permit Fees

Work Permit fees for solo performers requiring one are $110. US and $150. CND. For a group of three or more people, artists and crew included, the Work Permit fee is $330. US and $450. CND. Fees may be paid in either US dollars or Canadian dollars.

"Since the criteria for admission to either country is specific and often undergoes modification, the touring performers who are best prepared are those who have access to a practicing immigration lawyer or those who are members of the musician's union."

George Balderose
agent,
Music Tree Productions

Work Permit applications may be obtained at the Canadian consulate nearest you. It is easier, though, to fill out the permit papers at the Immigration Office when crossing the border. It is suggested that the first promoter you are contracted with notify the Customs and Immigration Office at your intended point of entry if you are driving or at the airport where you will first enter Canada. I also suggest that you call ahead to that port of entry.

Crossing The Borders

When Crossing The Border You Must Have:

- Copies of all signed contracts for the duration of your tour in Canada.
- Your Confirmation (if you've gotten one from the Canadian consulate).
- A list of all of your instruments and equipment that includes their original cost and serial numbers. (Bring any receipts available for cost verification. Border officials refer to this as "carnet.")
- A current passport or a valid original or good copy of your birth certificate or a valid driver's license along with a picture I.D.
- A current rabies certificate if you travel with pets. You will be refused entry without it.
- Cash for the correct amount to pay the permit fee.
- Cash to pay for any possible duty on merchandise you intend to sell in Canada.
- Cash to bond your instruments and equipment (not always necessary). This is a deposit to insure that you do not sell your instruments or equipment in Canada. There are commercial bonding agents that one can hire to handle this detail for you. There will be a charge for the bonding agent. If you carry large, expensive equipment, it is suggested that you contact a commercial bonding agent prior to your tour departure. Immigration can put you in touch with a reputable agent. (See the resource section of this chapter for commercial bonding agents.)

Know Your Point Of Entry

For any artist driving across the U.S./Canadian border, you need to know which border crossing you intend to use. I have found it helpful to call ahead to that inspection station in an effort to avoid any last-minute surprises. Inform them of your approximate time of arrival, how many are expected to cross with you and in how many vehicles. If you are expecting work permits or visas to be at the station, it is to your advantage to call ahead to make sure they have arrived. If you have not applied for a work permit from the Canadian consulate prior to the tour, you can fill out an application at

> **HotTip:**
> The fee paid for one work permit can include all of the contracted Canadian dates within one year's time, even if the dates are not consecutive. You must have a contracted date once every 30 days to apply for the permit for the entire year.

> "Prepare a manifest of all the equipment that you are taking into the States and have it notarized. This will save you lots of time at the border (especially if you are going by car).
> THE GOLDEN RULE—
> PLEASE NO DRUGS!"
>
> Rosalie Goldstein
> management consultant,
> Goldstein & Associates, Ltd.

> "When crossing any border, it is always good to know the laws and how they apply to you. Border guards are not always as well informed as you might think and so it is wise to know the score and be able to defend your rights in a CALM and COOL, but knowledgeable fashion."
>
> Rob Lutes
> Canadian musician

> "If you plan on telling the officials that you're just coming through to visit friends, don't expect to be able to breeze through carrying a whole sound system, recordings, promotional material and newsletters advertising your gigs in that country."
>
> Ken Brown
> songwriter, composer

the border crossing. I have found the border officials to be very helpful when they have advance notice of your crossing. A complete list of the the northern border ports of entry and their phone numbers, begins on page 241.

Immigration Versus Customs Stations

Plan your routes to cross the border at an inspection station designated for immigration. Not all border-crossing inspection stations are able to conduct involved immigration inspections nor do they have the appropriate forms or personnel to deal with work permits or visa problems which may face many touring artists. When crossing at inspection stations that mainly deal with customs inspections, you may find that your crossing takes much longer, and in some cases, you may be directed to travel to another inspection station many miles out of your way. However, all stations that are set up for immigration inspections also have customs officials on duty.

While speaking with every one of the inspection stations listed on pages 241-242, the inspectors agreed that they would appreciate an advance call notifying them of an approximate crossing time. They also reiterated the importance of crossing at a port of entry with immigration services to insure a speedy and successful crossing. The list of ports of entry begins on the Pacific coast and moves east. Most of the boldface listings are positioned on main travel routes.

Contacting The Canadian Embassy/Consulate

The Canadian Embassy in Washington, DC can provide you with application forms for work permits. You must have an application in hand if you plan on applying for a work permit in person at the Canadian Embassy/Consulate. Interviews for work permits are only scheduled on Tuesday through Friday from 2 p.m. until 4 p.m. They can be reached at:

The Canadian Consulate in Washington, DC
Visa Section
501 Pennsylvania Ave., NW
Washington, DC 20001
Staff Assistance: 202-682-1740
Web: http://www.canadianembassy.org

Canadian Embassies/Consulates are located in the following U.S. Cities:

New York	Minneapolis
Boston	Los Angeles
Buffalo	San Francisco
Chicago	Seattle

Should you have any specific questions or problems consult an embassy staff member. They can help to determine

http://www.customs.ustreas.gov/xp/cgov/toolbox/contacts/ports

Ports Of Entry

Bold Type: Immigration services available. Regular Type: Customs services with limited or no immigration services

US

Seattle, Washington District
- **Pacific Hywy Truck Crossing**....360-332-6091
- **Peace Arch at Blain, WA**...........360-332-8511
- Lynden, WA 360-354-6661
- **Sumas, WA** 360-988-4781
- Sea-Tac Int'l Airport........................
- Oroville, WA 509-476-3132
- **Eastport, ID** 208-267-2183
- Danville, WA.............................509-779-4862
- **Metaline Falls, WA** 509-446-2572
- Laurier, WA...............................509-684-2100

Helena, Montana District
- Morgan, MT..............................406-674-5248
- Opheim, MT   406-724-3212
- **Piegan, MT**...............................406-732-9297
- Raymond, MT 406-895-2620
- Roosville, MT............................406-889-3737
- Scobey, MT...............................406-783-5372
- **Sweetgrass, MT** 406-335-9559
- Turner, MT 406-379-2651
- Willow Creek, MT....................406-398-5512
- Whitetail, MT...........................406-779-3531
- Wild Horse, MT 406-394-2371

St. Paul, Minnesota District
- **Portal, ND** 701-926-4411
- **Pambina, ND**............................701-825-6722
- Noyes, MN 218-823-6212
- Pinecreek, MN 218-463-1952
- Roseau, MN 218-463-2054
- Warroad, MN 218-386-1676
- Baudette, MN............................218-634-2661
- International Falls, MN 218-283-8611
- Duluth, MN (sea only)..............218-720-5201
- Grand Portage, MN 218-475-2494

Detroit District
- **Sault Ste. Marie, MI**...................906-632-8822
- **Port Huron, MI** 810-982-0493
- Algonac, MI...............................810-794-3321
- Detroit and Canada Tunnel 313-568-6019
- Detroit–Service Port 313-442-0368
- **Detroit Metro Airport**...............734-941-6180

Buffalo District
Niagara Falls Bridges:
- Rainbow Bridge, NY 716-282-3141
- Lewiston Queenston Bridge 716-285-1676
- Whirlpool Bridge 716-282-5920
- Peace Bridge..............................716-885-6375
- Thousand Island, NY 315-482-2681
- Alexandria Bay, NY 315-482-2472
- Ogdensburg, NY........................315-393-0770

Canada—Information 888-242-2100

- Pacific Hywy 604-535-5450
- Douglas, BC........................604-535-5450

- Osoyoos, BC.......................250-495-6545
- **Kingsgate, BC** 250-424-5424
- Carson, BC..........................250-442-5551

- Calgary Airport..................403-292-6380

- Carway, Alberta 403-653-3077

- Coutes, Alberta 403-344-3744

- N. Portal, Saskatchewan 306-927-2335
- **Emerson, Manitoba**............204-373-2197

- Piney, Manitoba 204-423-2153
- South Junction, Manitoba..204-437-2266
- Sprague, Manitoba.............204-437-2361
- **Rainey River, Ontario** 807-852-3968
- **Ft. Frances, Ontario** 807-274-9780

- Pigeon River, Ontario 807-964-2095

- **Sault Ste. Marie, Ontario** ...705-941-3115
- Sarnia, Ontario 519-464-5000
- Walpole Island, Ontario.....519-627-4242
- Windsor, Ontario 519-257-7780
- Windsor, Ontario 519-257-6900

- Niagara Falls, Ontario 905-354-6043
- Lewiston Queenston Bridge.416-973-4444

- Landsdown, Ontario..........613-659-2313

- Prescott, Ontario................613-925-3221

Massena, NY	315-764-0310	Cornwall, Ontario	613-932-7410
Champlain, NY	518-298-7900	Toronto Internat'l Airport	905-676-2563

Portland, Maine District

Highgate Springs, VT	802-868-3349	Philipsburg, Quebec	514-248-2411
Richford, VT	802-848-7766	Abercorn, Quebec	514-538-2334
Derby Line I-91, VT	802-873-3316	Rock Island, Quebec	819-876-5777
Norton, VT	802-822-5222	Stanhope, Quebec	819-849-9135
Fort Kent, ME	207-834-3223	Claire, NB	506-992-2124
Madawaska, ME	207-728-4565	Edmundston, NB	506-737-1050
Van Buren, ME	207-868-2202	Saint Leonard, NB	506-423-6282
Limestone, ME	207-325-4760	Gillespie, NB	506-473-3536
Fort Fairfield, ME	207-473-7396	Perth-Andover, NB	506-273-2073
Bridgewater, ME	207-425-4502	Centreville, NB	506-276-3519
Jackman, ME	207-668-3771		
Hamlin, ME	207-868-0966	Grand Falls, NB	506-473-3553
Houlton, ME	207-532-2906	Woodstock, NB	506-325-3160
Vanceboro, ME	207-788-3813	St. Croix, NB	506-784-2225
Calais, ME	207-454-2546	St. Stephens, NB	506-465-2120
Lubec, ME	207-733-4960	Campobello Is., NB	506-752-2091
Portland, ME District Office	207-780-3622		
Bangor, ME	207-945-0334	Fredericton, NB	506-452-3711

> *"What we do from our end is make sure that immigration has a copy of the contract and has a copy of all the relevant paperwork. We even go to the extent of calling Immigration ahead of time to let them know what is coming, why it's coming and how it's going to be happening. Not taking anything for granted really made a difference."*
>
> Pierre Guerin
> former executive director,
> Winnipeg Folk Festival

what type of work permit you need and if you may be eligible for any exemptions.

Canadian Money Versus U.S. Dollars

When planning a Canadian tour, realize that most Canadian presenters will want to negotiate the fee in Canadian dollars rather than U.S. dollars. On any given day, the Canadian dollar fluctuates. For example, if your fee in the U.S. is $1,000 and you negotiate a fee of $1,000 with your Canadian promoter, make sure that you are both talking the same currency. If you are a U.S. artist, you want U.S. dollars. $1,000 Canadian will eventually equal approximately $760 U.S. dollars after the exchange. To achieve $1,000 U.S. you must get paid approximately $1,400 Canadian, and even then the final amount may not equal $1,000 U.S., depending on the exchange rate and where you exchange the money. If you want to get $1,000 in U.S. dollars, state that in your negotiations. (See the resource section of this chapter for currency exchange websites.)

Canadian Artists Planning To Tour The U.S.

Applying For A Work Permit/U.S.

A Canadian artist planning to tour in the U.S. is required to apply for a I-94 Departure Record under the P-2 Classification. If you are working with a U.S. agent or one of the U.S. presenters, they can obtain the application papers online from USCIS and apply for you. If you are applying from Canada, applications may be requested from your musician's union local office or the USCIS office in Vermont and then returned to that office.

U.S. Immigration Office, Vermont
75 Lower Weldon Street
St. Albans, VT 05479-0001
Phone: 1-800-375-5283
Web: http://www.uscis.gov Downloadform I-129

The AFM-Canada will supply union members with applications and will also process them.

The Application Process:

1. Request application forms from the AFM local nearest you.
2. Complete all forms. You will be provided with:
   a. Checklist—P2 Application - AFM Canada
   b. Application Cover Letter - Application and Information required to obtain Class 'P2' Non-Immigrant Work Permit
   c. P2 Application—Musician Personal Information - Part 1(A)
   d. P2(s) Application—Technician/Crew Personal Information - Part 1(B)
   e. P2 Application—Traveling Information - Part 2
   f. P2 Application—Policy of Indemnity - Part 3
   g. Expedited Processing—P2-AFM Canada
3. Send a tour itinerary including promoter contact, venue, city, and state. Send all materials to the AFM local or directly to the main AFM office in Ontario. Applications being filed by an AFM local will eventually be sent to the main union office in Ontario. From there the application is sent to the Vermont office of the USCIS for processing and approval.
5. An approval notice, I-797, will be mailed or faxed to each applicant.
6. Take the approval notice with you to the point of entry. For example: A performer flying from Winnipeg to Minneapolis will go through immigration at the Winnipeg International Airport. That is the first point of entry. If you are driving from Winnipeg to Minneapolis, your first point of entry is Pambina, ND.
7. Present your approval notice to the immigration officer. They have final approval to issue your I-94 Departure Record (P-2) and allow you entry into the United States. There is a $6.00 USD permit fee.
8. A valid passport is the best form of identification to present at the port of entry.

HotTip:
Premium Processing is available for $1,000 fee plus the application fee, $190.00 per application. Check www.artistsfromabroad.org for latest news and updates on immigration requirements for touring artists.

"Foreign artists other than from the U.S., planning to tour in Canada, must have their visas sent to the Canadian Embassy/Consulate in their home country."

Nancy Carlin
agent,
Nancy Carlin Associates

"It's best to always have a return ticket in your hand back into Canada so as to avoid problems. People on trains seem to be hassled less than those on busses, and those in cars fare best of all. Finally, try to avoid looking like a bum!"

Heidi Fleming
agent,
Fleming Artists Management

> **HotTip:**
> Include a list of musicians and technicians:
> 1. Name
> 2. Job description
>
> Submit with application on a separate sheet of paper.

You must provide:
- One completed application for every musician (Part 1a, Part 2 and Part 3) and one completed application for every technician (Part 1b, Part 2 & Part 3)
- Submit a listing of all musician(s) and/or Technician(s) names along with their job descriptions on a separate sheet of paper.
- All musicians names in the application must be members in good standing of the AFM, and Part 2) must be completed or membership verification provided.
- A Money Order must be attached in U.S. Dollars payable to USCIS (United States Citizenship and Immigration Services) in the amount of $190.00 (flat fee regardless of the number of musicians).
- If applying for technician/crew members, and additional U.S. Dollar Money Order payable to USCIS in the amount of $190.00 (flat fee regardless of number of technician/crew members) must be attached. One Money order for band and technician/crew may be attached in the amount of $380.00 U.S. Dollars.
- Enclose $20.00 in Canadian funds payable to AFM for administrative processing fees.
- Include copies of all employment contracts and verification of employment for any member of the technical crew. Utilize the Traveling Engagement Contract -Form T2 included with the AFM P2 packet of forms.
- If any members of band or crew are landed immigrants, contact AFM Canada for further information and procedures.
- Designate a Port of Entry for all applicants and have confirmation from travel agent for air travel and Pre-Flight Inspection Information.
- If you choose Premium Processing, contact AFM Canada for its arrival

"The previous visa situation with the P3's was a dream! Often, if you are trying to break into a market, you may get a last-minute call for a really good gig, because someone better known than you had to cancel—we could get those permits in virtually 48 hours through the union. Now, we are back to the old, situation which can take from 90 to 120 days."

Heidi Fleming
agent

"The benefit of working with the AFM is that it will take its members by the hand and make sure the paperwork on either side of the Canada-U.S. border is completed properly, so there will be no surprises."

George Balderose
agent

The entire application process can be executed at your AFM local. If you have an existing relationship with your local, it is advantageous to make all applications through that office. Their personal knowledge of your history will be helpful should a problem or delay arise during the application process. You may, however, submit your application to any of the AFM local offices including their main location in Ontario. Applications and contract forms are available from any of their branches. I have had the opportunity to work with staff in each of the following offices and found their assistance invaluable.

AFM Canadian Offices
- Ontario Office: 1-800-463-6333 (within Canada) 416-391-5161; Fax: 416-391-5165; E-mail: afmcan@afm.org
- Winnipeg Office: 204-943-4803; Fax: 204-943-5029
- Vancouver Musicians' Association: 604-737-1110; Fax: 604-734-3299

Contracts

AFM members applying for a work permit through the AFM must submit all of the completed contracts for an entire tour as are available at the time of submission. The AFM contract form requests specific information on each member of the group. If you use a contract form other than from the AFM, it is to your advantage to attach the AFM's contract forms to your contract when submitting an application for a work permit and when sending it to the presenter for their signature.

> **HotTip:** Revenue Canada recently changed their rules requiring the artist or agent to file tax forms directly to the appropriate Revenue Canada office and not through the event promoter. The promoter will send the forms to you with your contract. The Revenue Canada form will have the appropriate return address.

Conclusion

When sharing the culturally-unique talent which exists in both the U.S. and Canada, both countries are enriched by the exchange. Do not let the government regulations and application fees prevent you from exploring a touring career which extends across the borders. Your newfound audience will be richer for their knowledge of your artistic gift and you will expand your career opportunities.

Summary

- Cross the U.S/Canadian border and take advantage of new touring opportunities.
- Become familiar with the government regulations regarding immigration and customs when crossing international borders.
- USCIS and AFM personnel are available to assist with forms and information to make border crossings go smoothly.
- Leave enough lead time to prepare applications for visas and work permits.
- Select travel routes that place you at ports of entry with appropriate immigration services.
- Have all of the necessary papers with you when crossing the border.
- Advance your crossing with the appropriate port of entry immigration office.

"The assumption is that performers will also do their homework from their end because there are things that we can't help with. If you're going across the border with a van full of equipment and some product, you have to have an equipment manifest, a list of everything you've got and you have to appear professional and organized."

Pierre Guerin
former executive director,
Winnipeg Folk Festival

Resources

American Federation of Musicians (AFM) of the United States and Canada

New York Headquarters
AFM
1501 Broadway, Suite 600
New York, NY 10036-5503
Phone: 1-800-ROAD-GIG
Phone: 1-800-762-3444
Phone: 212-869-1330
Fax: 212-764-6134
Web: http://www.afm.org

AFM—West Coast Office
3550 Wilshire Blvd., Suite 1900
Los Angeles, CA 90010
Phone: 1-800-237-0988
Phone: 213-251-4510
Fax: 213-251-4520

AFM—Canadian Main Office
75 The Donway West, Suite 1010
Don Mills, Ontario
Canada M3C 2E9
Phone: 1-800-463-6333 (within Canada)
Phone: 416-391-5161
Fax: 416-391-5165
E-mail: afmcan@ican.org

AFM—Vancouver Musician's Association
925 West 8th Avenue, Suite 100
Vancouver, BC V5Z 1E4
Phone: 604-737-1110
Fax: 604-734-3299

AFM—Winnipeg Musician's Association
180 Market Ave. East, Room 201
Winnipeg, Manitoba R3B 0P7
Phone: 204-943-4803
Fax: 204-943-5029

AFM Local 1000—Touring Artists New Local
1501 Broadway, Suite 600
New York, NY 10036-5503
Phone: 1-800-ROAD-GIG
Phone: 1-800-762-3444
Phone: 212-869-1330
Fax: 212-764-6134
Web: http://www.afm.org/1000/

Artists From Abroad
Web: http://www.artistsfromabroad.org

United States Citizenship and Immigration Services
Vermont
75 Lower Weldon Street
St. Albans, VT 05479-0001
Phone: 1-800-375-5283
Web: http://www.uscis.gov

USCIS Information
USCIS Ask Immigration: 1-800-375-5283—Addresses and Phone Numbers
Forms Request Online: http://www.uscis.gov
Passport Agency: 202-647-0518 — Passport applications and information

Human Resources Development Canada
25 St. Clair Ave. East
Toronto, Ontario M4T 3A4
Phone: 416-952-1201
Fax: 416-954-3107

Traffic Control Group
476 Brook Street, 4th Floor
New York, NY 10013
Phone: 212-431-3700
Fax: 212-431-7107
Email: info@trafficcontrolgroup.com
Web: http://www.trafficcontrolgroup.com

Canadian Embassies In The U.S.

Canadian Embassy—Washington, D.C.
Visa Section
501 Pennsylvania Ave., N.W.
Washington, DC 20001
Phone: 202-682-1740
Fax: 202-682-7726
Cable: CANADIAN WASHINGTON
Telex: 0089664 (DOMCAN A WSH)
Web: http://www.canadianembassy.org

Canadian Consulate General—Detroit, MI
600 Renaissance Center, Suite 1100
Detroit, MI 48243-1798
Phone: 313-567-2340
Fax: 313-567-2164
Cable: CANADIAN DETROIT
Web: http://www.detroit.gc.ca
Territory: Michigan, Indiana, Kentucky, Ohio

Canadian Consulate General—Los Angeles, CA
550 South Hope, 9th Floor
Los Angeles, CA 90071-2627
Phone: 213-346-2700
Fax: 213-346-2767
E-mail: lngls@international.gc.ca
Web: http://www.losangeles.gc.ca
Territory: California, Arizona, Hawaii, Nevada, Utah

Canadian Consulate General—Atlanta, GA
1175 Peachtree Street, N.E.
100 Colony Square, Suite 1700
Atlanta, GA 30361-6205
Phone: 404-532-2000; Fax: 404-532-2050
Web: http://www.atlanta.gc.ca
Territory: Georgia, Alabama, Florida, Mississippi, North Carolina, South Carolina, Tennessee, Puerto Rico, U.S. Virgin Islands

Canadian Consulate Trade Office—San Diego, CA
4370 LaJolla Village Drive, Suite 620
San Diego, CA 92122
Phone: 619-597-7050; Fax: 619-457-2844
E-mail: cdntrade@cts.com

Canadian Consulate—Miami, FL
Suite 1600
First Union Financial Center
200 South Biscayne Blvd.
Miami, FL 33131
Phone: 305-579-1600
Fax: 305-374-6774

Canadian Consulate General—Boston, MA
Three Copley Place, Suite 400
Boston, MA 02116
Phone: 617-262-3760; Fax: 617-262-3415
Territory: Massachusetts, Maine, New Hampshire, Rhode Island, Vermont, St. Pierre-et-Miquelon

Canadian Consulate Trade Office—San Francisco, CA
580 California Street, 14th Floor
San Francisco, CA 94104
Phone: 415-834-3180; Fax: 415-834-3189

Canadian Consulate Trade Office—San Jose, CA
333 West San Carlos Street, Suite 945
San Jose, CA 95110
Phone: 408-289-1157; Fax: 408-289-1168
Web: http://www.sanfrancisco.gc.ca

Canadian Consulate General—Minneapolis, MN
701 Fourth Ave. South, Suite 90900
Minneapolis, MN 55415-1899
Phone: 612-332-4641; Fax: 612-332-4061
Territory: Minnesota, Colorado, Iowa (except the Quad-Cities), Montana, Nebraska, North Dakota, South Dakota, Wyoming

Canadian Consulate General—Buffalo, NY
HSBC Center
Suite 3000
Buffalo, NY 14203-2884
Phone: 716-858-9500; Fax: 716-858-9562
Territory: Western, Central and Upstate New York, West Pennsylvania, West Virginia

Canadian Consulate General—New York, NY
1251 Avenue of the Americas
New York, NY 10020-1175
Phone: 212-596-1628; Fax: 212-596-1793
Web: http://www.canada-ny.org
Territory: Southern New York State, Connecticut, New Jersey, Bermuda

Canadian Consulate General—Chicago, IL
Two Prudential Plaza
180 N. Stetson Ave., Suite 2400
Chicago, IL 60601
Phone: 312-616-1860
Fax: 312-616-1877 or 312-616-1878
Territory: Illinois, Missouri, Wisconsin

Canadian Consulate General—Seattle, WA
412 Plaza 600, Sixth and Stewart Streets
Seattle, WA 98101-1286
Phone: 206-443-1777
Fax: 206-443-9662 / 206-443-9735
Territory: Washington, Alaska, Idaho, Oregon

Canadian Consulate General—Dallas, TX
750 N. St. Paul Street, Suite 1700
Dallas, TX 75201
Phone: 214-922-9806
Fax: 214-922-9815
Cable: CANADIAN DALLAS
Territory: Texas, Arkansas, Kansas, Louisiana, New Mexico, Oklahoma

Commercial Bonding Agents:

Mendelssohn Commercial
69 Yonge St., Suite 400
Toronto, Ontario M5E 1K3
Phone: 1-800-665-4628
Phone: 416-863-9339; Fax: 416-863-5149
Web: http://www.mend.com

Clear Custom Brokers, Ltd.
240 Duncan Mill Road, Suite 404
Toronto, Ontario M3B 1Z4
Phone: 416-977-7821; Fax: 416-977-4930
Web: http://www.clearcustomsbrokers.com

Pacific Customs Brokers Ltd.
#101-17637 1st Avenue
Surrey, British Columbia V3S 9S2
Phone: 1-888-538-1566; Fax: 1-877-538-1166
Web: http://www.pcb.ca

Cleared and Delivered.com
Phone: 1-888-465-8865
Web: http://www.clearedanddelivered.com

Internet Currency Exchange Rate Sites:

Xenon Laboratories Universal Currency Converter
Web: http://www.xe.net/currency/

Currency Converter by Oanda, Inc.
Web: http://www.oanda.com

Currency Converter by Yahoo
Web: http://finance.yahoo.com/currency?u

Exchange Rate.com
Web: http://www.exchangerate.com

CHAPTER TEN
Managing The Road

"Any time you walk into a theater, a venue, an arena or a club, I don't care if it's as small as the Iron Horse or as large as Wolf Trap, you are really walking into someone's house. You don't walk into someone's house and rearrange their furniture without asking 'please' and 'may I.' Once you are kind and say 'please' and 'thank you,' they will hand you anything you want on a silver platter. It makes the day easier."

Mary Beth Aungier
tour manager,
Mary Chapin Carpenter

The challenges of touring as a self-booking artist require your expertise in many areas beyond your specific talent. Taking care of yourself and your business while touring is another area that demands your attention. Artists that have toured for many years have discovered helpful techniques to stay healthy, comfortable and performing at their peak. Many of these tips and suggestions are from long-time touring musicians and seasoned road managers.

The Road Manager's Role

Even though you may not have the budget to hire a professional road manager, the tasks and responsibilities of that position need to be taken care of by someone in the group.

"A road manager should be a helpful assistant, a guide and example to all, a leader of the pack, a superb logistician, a boss and a powerful negotiator, and most of all, a friend to artists and crew members alike."

Geoffrey P. Trump
tour accountant, ticketing,
Dave Matthews Band, Inc.
Strangely Brown, Inc.

> **HotTip:** Check with your bank and your promoter about Electronic Funds Transfers (EFT) of performance fees. Sign up for online banking to check all payments made to your account.

Add one more hat to the rack if you are a solo artist. Personally, I have found that the duties of the road manager, while sometimes overwhelming when you are in the middle of a tour, are very enjoyable for the most part. Knowing how to incorporate the "road manager" into all of your other personalities will help make your road trips run more efficiently.

The road manager is the caretaker, the overseer, the timekeeper, the business manager, the travel consultant, the go-between, the runner, the advance person and the person who makes contact with all the important people once at the performance venue.

The road manager is also the person in charge of getting the band where they need to be on time and in good shape. It is a job that requires knowledge of every aspect of the business. On the technical end, the road manager may serve as lighting and sound consultant, stage manager and/or visual consultant. They will make sure the food is on time, the water is on stage, and that the stage is ready for the artist. Often they will be the one to say when the show begins, when the intermission ends and for how long the artist will sign autographs. Before the tour begins, they advance the date—call ahead to alert the presenter of arrival time and check details regarding the rider and technical requirements.

There is a road-manager checklist that can be used for each performance on page 269. If you have a partner or a group, specific duties can be assigned to each individual so one person does not have the daunting task of doing it all. As a solo artist this list will help you take care of business efficiently and allow you to concentrate on the performance. Much of the checklist information may have already been gathered on the Information Form which was sent with your contract. If any items have not been finalized, this is a good reminder to do so. You may make multiple copies of this list for future use and add any items that are specific to your act.

"Advance your shows! That way you know what you're getting into and they know what to expect."

Alex Hofmann
tour manager,
BoDeans, Radiohead, P.J. Harvey, Samples

Life's Details On The Road

Dealing with life's details while on the road can often be a test of your creativity and stamina. The little things that we all take for granted when at home can take hours to accomplish. Banking and cleaning clothes need to be figured into a routine to be handled efficiently. Meals are another necessity that, left to chance, can throw your health and disposition off your normal track. Here are a number of suggestions that can help you deal with life's details on the road.

"Road managing is the most important thing—the details make all the difference and it's a ton of details. Get it together before you hit the road. It can mean the difference between a band staying together or breaking up."

Laurie Lewis
musician

Banking
While touring for any length of time, you are sure to accumulate cash and checks. You need some cash on the road but the bulk of the money should be sent to your bank. There are a number of ways to do this.

1. Ask your bank for pre-addressed envelopes and deposit slips for your account prior to the tour. Meet with your banker to notify them that you will be making deposits from the road on an ongoing basis. You might want to insure the letter at the post office when mailing. Keep accurate records of all deposit amounts and dates while on the road to check against your monthly statement.
2. Find a local bank while touring to change cash into a bank check to mail with your deposit. Not all banks will turn your small bills into a bank check without an account in their chain. Be prepared for this.
3. Change cash into a postal money order and then mail your bank deposit.
4. Wire cash to your bank account from any local bank. Your bank will charge your account a wiring fee and the local bank will also charge a fee. Each bank's charges differ and may range from $5.00 to $12.00. To wire money, you will need your account number, your bank's address and your bank's routing number. Your bank may be willing to discuss a discount wiring rate if they know you will be using this method often.
5. Change cash into American Express Traveler's Checks. If you are a AAA member, any AAA office can do this at no charge.

Who Holds The Money?

Solo performers have no problem answering this question: You collect it, you bank it, and you pay the bills. If you travel as a duo or a band without a road manager, designate one person to be in charge of all the money transactions and banking. Having one person be accountable is much easier than assigning different money tasks to various band members.

Unless otherwise designated, the road manager is usually the person in charge of collecting all fees, settling the box office, accounting for merchandise sales, paying per diems if they have not already been paid by management prior to the tour, paying for hotels, keeping petty cash for daily road expenses and sending the tour money to management for banking. Individual group members will deal with their own pay and personal banking.

Per Diems

A per diem is an amount of money paid to each individual group member for daily expenses, mostly food. Sometimes this amount is calculated for an entire tour, if under a month, and paid in a check to the group member prior to departing for the tour. For band members not used to budgeting or when tours are longer than one month, per diems may be paid a number of times during the tour. A per diem allows each group member to have the freedom to deal with their

> **HotTip:**
> "Salaries are fully taxable, per diems are not. It might be possible to pay a higher per diem and a lower salary in order to provide your band and crew the maximum benefit of your limited resources. (Check with a business manager or accountant first.)"
> **John Porter**
> manager, Nitty Gritty Dirt Band, Kris Tyler, Mike Robertson Management

"Make sure your tech rider is rock solid, air tight and current. Get it to the promoter as far in advance of the date as possible."
Paul Deiter
road manager

"If you leave cash in the hotel safe overnight write a large reminder on your bathroom mirror in erasable felt pen or lipstick. When you get up in the morning remember to clean your teeth. With a bit of luck you will see the reminder on the mirror!"
Geoffrey P. Trump
tour accountant, ticketing, Dave Matthews Band, Inc. Strangely Brown, Inc.

> **HotTip:** 🌶️
> "If you are in charge of making sure everyone else is on time, get a good alarm clock. Don't rely on the hotel's wake-up calls. Start calling everyone about 20 minutes in advance, just to remind them that it is about time to go. There is usually one guy in the band who's always late."
>
> Richard Battaglia
> road manager, sound engineer,
> Bela Fleck and
> The Flecktones

"Have a schedule and be able to tell everybody if you're leaving at 10 a.m. after breakfast or you're leaving at 10 a.m. and you'll stop and eat within an hour."

Laurie Lewis
musician

"Never eat at the same chain of fast-food restaurants twice in the same day."

Harvey Reid
songwriter, producer,
label owner,
Woodpecker Records

own meals and eat according to their personal eating habits. Once you achieve a certain level of recognition, you can often count on the hospitality of the presenter to provide one meal at the venue. This factor may also have been calculated into your original per diem amount.

For example:
❖ The tour is ten days long.
❖ You are performing eight shows each with dinner provided.
❖ Your per diem may be calculated for two meals per day for eight days and three meals per day for two days (the two travel days).

Meals On The Road
Whether touring solo or in a large group, allow enough time to eat. This seems a small thing. Yet when faced with long drives, weather, waking up later, and going to sleep late, taking care of yourself by eating according to your needs is often an afterthought. Get into a routine that is comfortable for you and stick to it. If breakfast is your preference, plan to stop for it each morning or schedule to have eaten before leaving. If you would rather eat lunch, make time to break for it each day. When touring in a group, get some consensus from the group prior to setting out on the tour as to how you will deal with meals.

Understand each individual's special dietary requirements ahead of time. If you have special needs, make sure you are prepared for them. Do not get caught on a stretch of road with nothing for miles around without your power bar and with an oncoming episode of low blood sugar. I have been there and it is not fun.

Granted, some days will offer more time to enjoy local cuisine, while other days may only allow for eating on the go. Considering all the important issues to deal with on the road, plan wisely to help avoid unnecessary stress among group members regarding meals.

Cleaning Clothes On The Road
Laundry becomes a necessity when touring for longer than one week. If you have one or two stage outfits, you may need to deal with cleaning your clothes sooner.

Many hotels offer overnight dry-cleaning services, so ask about this when advancing the tour. Knowing which hotels offer cleaning or where the closest laundromats are will aid in determining your laundry schedule. Plan a few hours to gather at a laundromat on off days. Group members should schedule this as one of those group activities for the sake of efficiency.

Tour Books
Managing your days on the road effectively means keeping all the tour details organized and accessible, especially when traveling with a band and crew. Major touring artists create

a tour book which details each day's travel and performance schedule. Once all of the tour schedule information has been gathered, you or the company creating your tour book compiles the information into a book format and allocates one page for each day of the tour. The book provides each member of the team with an at-a-glance overview of the day's activities.

A tour book provides the following information:
❖ Travel times and mode of transportation
❖ Load-in and performance times
❖ Accommodations and services provided at the hotels
❖ Contact information for each venue and hotel
❖ Special appearances scheduled
❖ List of contact numbers for tour team—agent, manager, label, publicist, road manager

Merchandise

The artist, road manager or someone in the band is usually responsible for making sure the artist's product arrives at the venue in good supply. If your mode of travel necessitates shipping your product ahead to each venue, the responsible person should make sure that all orders are placed in a timely manner with any suppliers—record company, t-shirt manufacturer, etc.—to guarantee timely arrival. Artists whose record companies do not allow them to sell their recordings at concerts and who are doing a high volume of business, may be in a position to use one of the major merchandise companies who make and sell t-shirts, sweatshirts and hats. These merchandisers will tour with the artist and take full responsibility for every aspect of ordering, selling, inventory and collection. Management works out merchandising deals prior to large tours. If this is your situation, you do not have to deal with the merchandise. Just pack the venues, put on a great show and collect your merchandise check. (See resources for lists of merchandisers.)

Instrument Insurance

Each artist is responsible for carrying their own instrument insurance. This is an optional expense. But, if you tour, it is highly recommended. I have seen a guitar lifted out of a parked car while the artist was unloading in one city. Taking up a collection for musicians who suffer such a situation is certainly one answer but having instrument insurance is a more reliable proactive plan. An artist I worked with received a brand new Taylor guitar by insured mail carrier with a broken neck. That artist also had the unfortunate experience of arriving at his destination by air while most of his luggage did not. It was never found and $3,000 later he was reimbursed by the airline. However, there was no guarantee of

> "The benefits seem obvious to anyone on the road, or anyone who has ever needed to reach someone on the road. The Tour Books have detailed phone information on the hotels and venues."
>
> **Lawrence Levy**
> Tour Books, Inc.

> "Never assume that the promoter will meet your specifications without your consistent and timely follow-up."
>
> **Paul Deiter**
> road manager,
> David Crosby

> "Have as much information as you can before you leave your home base, i.e., directions to the hotel or club, time schedule for sound check and performance, who is going to pay you and how (cash, check or beer). Know who the production contact is so you know who to deal with when you arrive. Get an inside phone to the club for emergencies."
>
> **Alex Hofmann**
> tour manager

> **HotTip:** 🌶
> "One thing I do that is really convenient—I record the directions sent by the concert organizer on a little SONY Walkman so that I can LISTEN to the directions instead of trying to drive whilst reading them."
>
> Peggy Seeger
> singer, song-maker

> "When getting directions, if the last phrase you hear is 'you can't miss it,' you probably will! Make sure you get more specifics."
>
> Kari Estrin
> former tour manager,
> 3 Mustaphas 3, Suzanne Vega, Tony Rice

being reimbursed. Having instrument insurance meant the equipment could at least be replaced. Instrument insurance is available from the resources listed at the end of this chapter.

The touring checklist beginning on page 269 will help you keep track of all of the details that need your attention before, during and after a tour or a single performance date.

Road Stories

This section will provide you with some situations often encountered while touring and the remedies chosen by road managers and artists. There are so many road stories one could write a very entertaining book on that alone. I have selected a number of topics which overwhelmingly challenge the touring artist and stories that were both entertaining and inspiring.

Life on the road is very different than anything you have known in your life at home. Traveling to various locales presents a touring artist with a number of challenges. Language tends to be a major factor adding interest and sometimes confusion to your day. Words and phrases that have one meaning in one part of the country may mean something totally different in another. The Nields offer these words of wisdom from a recent cross-country tour.

Road Wise, Road Wary

Sometimes:
- Being an opening act means you play before the audience gets there.
- Being the headliner act means you play after the audience leaves.
- "You are going to be on TV" means some local teenager brings his home video camera to film you for cable access.
- Making a left at the first light means go through the first light, make a right at the second light, pass the gas station and then find the club.
- When you smell smoke on the highway it really is your car.
- Even-tempered means evenly angry at all times.
- Beer is free but you have to pay for water.
- "No pizza" on your rider means you get *pizza* for dinner.
- A vegetarian meal means rabbit food.

And:
- In Kansas sometimes salad is Jell-O (plain or cherry).
- In North Dakota sometimes chicken is square.
- At Denny's, fruit cup means banana slices with strawberry sauce.

Patty Romanoff
road manager, The Nields, Bulletproof Artist Mgmt

The Topics
- Car trouble
- Travel problems
- Not getting paid/not receiving deposits on time
- Equipment trouble
- Lost, stolen or broken instruments
- Personnel problems—band, crew
- Venue problems

> **HotTip:**
> "Buy every gadget you can that plugs into a cigarette lighter."
> Harvey Reid
> songwriter, producer

Car Trouble

Greg Brown

This road story from Greg's very early touring days is a wonderful example of how we determine what we are meant to do in our lives and how often our commitment to our goals is tested. This also is a prime example of how so many of the situations we encounter are often simply out of our control.

" I was driving to one of my first coffeehouse gigs in southern Wisconsin in a VW squareback. I broke down in the middle of nowhere and still had another three hours to go to get to the gig with only two hours to spare. I remember saying to God or the sky or something, 'If I get to this gig, then I'm going to take it as an indication that I should get back into playing music. If I don't, which is fine too, then I'm going to take it as a sign the other way and I'm going to study forestry. So show me a sign! I had no more than said that when a farmer pulled over and said, 'What you got going on?' After telling him the car was stuck, he replied, 'I work on VWs, my place is two miles down the road.' So he put a chain on the car and changed the pump or something. An hour later I was back on the road. Well okay."

Greg Brown
singer, songwriter

10,000 Maniacs

Cars breaking down are a fact of life. When there is an audience waiting on the other end, the situation can be extremely costly as well as place undue stress on members of the group. Keep your cool, assess the most strategic method of getting help, make sure you, your vehicle and group members are safe and move forward with a plan of action to attempt to remedy the situation. It is not a bad idea to have a cell phone—for just these types of emergencies. Here is a story from Dan Griffin's early days of road managing the band 10,000 Maniacs—before the big deli trays.

" We were an entourage of six guys and one woman. Four of the band members rode in the passenger van with our gear. So, I drove my car with Natalie, the vocalist, and Jerry, the drummer. In the middle of nowhere, Pennsylvania (and in the middle of a rainstorm), my lights begin to fade on my 1980

"Get an AAA membership and a mobile phone. Both are business expenses that more than justify themselves for touring artists. The AAA membership will not only save you money on travel discounts available to members, it can also save your butt at 3:37 a.m. on the New Jersey Turnpike in January when Mother Nature is messing with the road conditions. Gotta have the phone to call AAA or the police if needed."

John Porter
manager

When driving, my six preferred methods for staying alive-awake-alert, in order of priority:
1. Stop, stretch every hour
2. Jumping jacks
3. Crunchy food
4. Facial calisthenics
5. Stop, take a nap
6. CAFFEINE!

Billy Jonas
singer, songwriter, performer, industrial re-percussionist

Dodge Omni. Of course, the guys had passed us in the van some miles back so I chose to walk to the next town to call a wrecker leaving Jerry and Natalie in the car. After a few miles, I came upon a garage where I found the band had pulled over to wait for us when they lost sight of us for a few miles. We called a wrecker and got in the van to go back and pick up Natalie and Jerry. The wrecker made it to the car first. As we were going over a long bridge we noticed the tow truck with my car in the opposite lane. Natalie was in the front seat between Jerry and a large, bearded, stogie-smoking, oily guy with a big smile on his face. The look on her face was one of shock and of being in another world. We did make it to the gig and the show was incredible. The promoter and audience were great to us, and the car breakdown was only remembered as humorous—not the crisis it seemed at the time."

Dan Griffin
former road manager,
10,000 Maniacs

Bill Monroe

Whether touring in your own car or in a professional tour bus, mechanical things break. If you lease a tour bus, the leasing company will find a replacement vehicle as quickly as possible and may even pick up the expenses incurred by the group as you attempt to make it to the gig from wherever the bus broke down. However, if you own your own bus, as Bill Monroe did some years ago, all repairs are the owner's responsibility. And if you have an old bus, you might want to have backup drivers on call for emergency pickups. Better yet, you might want to buy a newer model rather than waste time and money on constantly fixing an old one. Byron Berline offers this story from his days as one of Bill Monroe's Bluegrass Boys.

"Lease from an established tour-bus company that has numerous backup buses. If you break down, they will do their best to get a replacement as soon as possible. Don't forget that cell phone . . . it can save many hours of waiting for help."

Richard Battaglia
road manager,
sound engineer

" Bill Monroe had a 1946 GMC bus and every time we took it out it broke down. The worst time happened when we had to go to California. Doug Green was playing guitar with us at the time and we stopped in Nashville to pick him up when the third gear on the transmission went out. The bus stayed in the shop in Nashville since it wasn't fixed by the time we had to leave for California. Bill said, "I'll have to fly. I'll just take Doug with me and we'll pick up people to play with us until you get there."

When the bus was finally fixed the rest of us, James Monroe, Lamar Greer, Bill's girlfriend at the time, Virginia Stauffer and myself took off for California. We made it to Texas when the third gear went out again stranding us in Dallas for about three or four days because we couldn't get a part. (They didn't make parts for those things anymore.) Bill was already in California playing at the Ash Grove with the Kentucky Colonels and the Dillards. We called one of the bluegrass players we knew in Dallas, Mitchell Lan, who also worked in a machine shop. He made us a part on a lathe and put it in. We nursed the bus out to California and when we got into Indio, California, the lights wouldn't work. Once again, we got to a mechanic and as he starts to pull the front panel off, sparks and flames start flying out. He got the fire extinguisher and sprayed this powdered stuff all over the bus. You couldn't imagine what it looked like. We had made it to California about two weeks late and played the few gigs that were left. Bill, of course, had been playing all along while we were traveling.

As I look back on it now, Bill spent so much money on that bus he could have bought a new one."

Byron Berline
fiddler, former member,
Bill Monroe's Bluegrass Boys

> **HotTip:**
> Big truck stops have a good setup for phone calls with lots of phones, fax machines, desk space, privacy and quiet. Some even have phones at the restaurant booths.
>
> Liz Masterson and Sean Blackburn
> singers, songwriters

Travel Problems

Performers that use any variety of public transportation place their fate in someone else's hands as soon as they buy the ticket. Air travel is the performing artist's most widely used method of public transportation. Most times, it is reliable, fast and fairly convenient. Sometimes, it can ruin your whole day. If you travel by air, I suggest you do so armed with a heavy dose of humor and patience. If you can, carry your most important instrument and one change of stage clothes with you. There is an art to packing for a tour by air which takes some performers years to perfect.

Indigo Girls

As your touring entourage grows, keeping track of band members and crew can become challenging. Travel by air, bus or van requires that you create workable, consistent systems for all. When you have multiple vehicles and gear, the road manager must know that all members of the entourage are accounted for especially while en route between gigs.

Geoffrey Trump now serves as tour accountant for the Dave Matthews Band. He offers this traveling strategy and story from his days as tour manager for the Indigo Girls.

> The four rules of the road for traveling musicians:
> 1. Eat a salad every day.
> 2. Keep all your stuff in one place.
> 3. Make sure the keys are in your hand BEFORE you close the trunk.
> 4. Never, ever, under ANY circumstances, sleep on a sofa bed.
>
> Bernice Lewis
> singer, songwriter

" Always write the name of each person on the back of their laminated pass. If anyone leaves the bus to get something to eat while the driver is not around, they must leave their laminate on his seat. That way he knows to wait for them. Otherwise they will get "oil-spotted."

One time we stopped late at night at a truck stop to refuel. Several of us went into the truck stop to get a bite or have a bathroom break. Minutes after we got off the bus another band member woke up and, seeing the baked potato fast food joint, she went there to buy a snack. It was the middle of no-where—maybe in Nebraska. The driver finished fuelling and we all got back on the bus and left—except no one knew that the fiddle player had gotten off the bus. Half an hour later one of us noticed that her bunk was empty. Reluctant to turn around, the driver used his CB radio to see if the crew bus, (which was an hour behind us), could

When driving, my six preferred methods for staying alive-awake-alert, in order of priority:
1. Stop, stretch every hour
2. Jumping jacks
3. Crunchy food
4. Facial calisthenics
5. Stop, take a nap
6. CAFFEINE!

Billy Jonas
singer, songwriter, performer, industrial re-percussionist

"Lease from an established tour-bus company that has numerous backup buses. If you break down, they will do their best to get a replacement as soon as possible. Don't forget that cell phone . . . it can save many hours of waiting for help."

Richard Battaglia
road manager,
sound engineer

stop and pick her up. We sat and waited. Finally, she showed up in a Highway Patrolman's car, whom she had persuaded to give us chase."

Geoffrey P. Trump,
former tour manager
Indigo Girls

California

If you think touring by air within the continent is tricky, then touring in foreign countries on small airlines is downright adventurous. Flight schedules are flexible and the occurrence of a seemingly small event can throw flights off by days. When planning tours to out-of-the-way places, leave enough time on either side of the tour to reach and return from your destination. Even when you are fairly secure in your planning, be prepared for that unexpected fly in the ointment to add some excitement to an otherwise well-thought-out schedule. When problems occur, have the determination to make a situation work for you, try every conceivable avenue and then start on the inconceivable. I have found that most performers have an incredible commitment to fulfill their obligations and will go the extra mile. In the following story, the band went many extra miles. Byron Berline shared this travel miracle from the band California's South Pacific tour for the United States Information Agency (USIA).

"We had to leave Kwajelain Island for the Grass Valley Festival in California three days early in order to get there a day before the festival to rest. As we were supposed to leave for the states, the incoming evening flight could not land on the island because the lights at the airport were not working. They said, 'Sorry we can't take you.' So I called the festival and told them we probably weren't going to make it.

During all the confusion and phone calls to make alternate arrangements, there was one kid on the island who was on a ham radio to Guam. He found out that we could leave the next morning but had to travel in the opposite direction from where we needed to go. The flight stopped at three or four other islands before we could catch a flight from Guam to Honolulu. However, the flight from Guam to Honolulu was completely booked. With some discussion, some people were bumped off the flight from Guam so we could fly. We were told that the airline traveling that route might be two, three or four hours late and for us to get to Guam and make the flight to Honolulu everything had to be perfectly on time. Well, we tried it anyway. We took off from Kwajelain Island and finally made it to Guam. It was unbelievable that we actually made the connections to Honolulu. Everything was clicking.

We flew into LA and caught a plane to Sacramento. We were up for two days, flying forty-two hours. We were frazzled. At the Sacramento baggage claim, all that came off the conveyer belt were our instruments—no clothes. We rented a car and got to Grass Valley with twenty minutes to spare before we had to play our first set. We were shaken and running on fumes. And, our luggage arrived later, some pieces two weeks later."

Byron Berline
fiddler with the bluegrass band California

Bela Fleck & The Flecktones

Touring by air with instruments and gear can be a challenge before you even arrive at the gate. Here are some hard truths shared by Richard Battaglia after many years of touring with Bela Fleck and The Flecktones as both road manager and sound engineer.

> **HotTip:** While touring, have copies of contracts with you with contact numbers for all upcoming dates. Make sure you can contact presenters in case any travel delays occur.

"There are two hard-and-fast rules when flying with equipment. First, nothing over 100 pounds will get on as baggage. Second, every experience will be different. If a case is over 70 pounds, it is overweight and subject to excess-baggage fees. That could be anywhere from $30 to $200 or even higher. On a domestic flight (USA), each person is allowed three bags. So if there are six of you, that is eighteen pieces. If you are over your limit, they can charge you again. The system is incredibly arbitrary. If you fly overseas, it is okay to leave with three pieces each. Here is a good way to get around any hassles. Use curbside check-in. In order to do this, you need to have your tickets and everyone's photo ID. The porters will do all they can for a $50 or $60 tip. It might even be worth $100. Otherwise, it could cost as much as $400 to $600 for excess weight and bags. All you have to do is deliver the pieces to the curb and the porter takes it from there! Don't forget, every airline has different rules about size."

Richard Battaglia
road manager, sound engineer
Bela Fleck & The Flecktones

CATS

Touring is a challenge no matter what size of a production you are. The bigger the production, the bigger the problems, and the more expensive the solutions. Among theatrical agents, performers and performance venues, this road story about the touring production of *CATS* is legendary.

"*CATS* closed on a Sunday night in Seattle and we were supposed to open in Springfield, Missouri on Tuesday, election night 1992. While the trucks were driving en route they hit a snowstorm in Wyoming and one truck slid off the road and turned over. No help could get through because of the storm and then the state closed the roads after only one or two of our trucks were able to get through.

When the two trucks arrived for our load-in Tuesday morning, we had our electric package, all the lights, some of the carpentry, our truss, the pod (the unit upon which Grizabella, the lead cat, rides up to the heavens), the big tire, and basically that was it. By early Tuesday morning the snowstorm had subsided in Wyoming and they opened the roads. Our trucks were instructed to go to the Denver airport where our company's manager had chartered a cargo plane for $17,000. Having previously flown the show to Hawaii, they had a manifest listing everything that could fly—all their sets, props, costumes and makeup that would fit into a 747 jet. One of our prop men who made it to Springfield, flew into Denver to meet the trucks, get them loaded onto the plane and then was to fly back with them. However, not all the trucks made it to Denver in time to have their equipment loaded onto the plane. Unfortunately, this plane was smaller than a 747 and our prop man had to decide what was important to make a show happen and what wasn't. The important things that we loaded were the costumes, the makeup, and the musical instruments. The wardrobe is a pretty big department and that was almost a full plane right there. All the prop pieces and most of the set didn't make it to the plane in time—this included the walls and the set decorations.

All in all, we decided that we had enough to do a show. A local trucking company met the plane and got the stuff to the theater at about 3-4 o'clock in the afternoon. The decision was made that since this was a brand new market for *CATS* and it was a full-week run, that we would open the show as scheduled. When the cats came in for their regular sound check at 4 p.m. and saw no set, we explained the situation. We had our deck, which is the floor that goes on top of the stage and has a lot of marks on it for the cats to know where they need to be. We also had the costumes, the makeup and the orchestra—so we did a show.

I think it was probably one of the best shows ever done by *CATS*. The emphasis was strictly on the performance and the music, nothing else. *CATS* is a large visual show which relies a lot on spectacle. Without the spectacle there was nothing to look at but the performers and listen to the music. I asked the promoter how many complaints we got and he said none, no complaints and no requests for refunds. Later that day, the other trucks managed to get through and we put in the rest of the set. But when we actually did a show with just the tire, the pod and the flooring—no walls— we just went with the bare stage, the cast probably danced and sang better than they ever did because there was no place to hide. The audience was looking at you every second."

L.A. Lavin
former production stage manager.
touring production, *CATS*

"If you're in a position when you're not so sure you're going to get paid, you can go to the artist and say, 'What do you want to do?' The artist usually wants to play while touring and you often end up with something."

Bob Jones
former road manager,
Sarah Vaughan,
Duke Ellington, Buddy Rich

Not Getting Paid—No Deposit

Whether you are a solo performer or a major recording artist, every once in a while you might get "stiffed." Sometimes you enter into a situation and caution is your best friend. Other times you just didn't see it coming—the promoter leaves without paying you, the check bounces, you were too trusting or "the check is in the mail." Hopefully, this has not happened to you. If it has and you are a member of the AFM, you can call upon their legal staff to help you collect. For other performers, you need to assess the loss and weigh your options if you choose to seek compensation. (Refer back to Chapter Seven.) In some instances, a few heartfelt phone calls may clear up a misunderstanding and payment will be on its way. In other situations, your presence in the box office demanding your due may remedy the situation.

Paul Craft and Faron Young

There are those circumstances when, after all is said and done, you have been taken and there is just no way to find the folks who left with your money. Thankfully, these are few and far between—but not unheard of. Paul Craft, a publisher and songwriter in Nashville, Tennessee, related this tale of woe from his solo touring days in the 70's.

" My agency booked me to open four shows for Faron Young in Alaska. I was going to make $500 a night and all expenses. I flew up with Faron and his band. We did the four shows. I was advanced $60 cash. When it came time to get paid, I went into the guy's hotel room. They had the money all stacked up and they wrote me a check for $1940, which is what they owed me. I could have had them cash the check right there but I didn't think to do that. When I got back home nobody's check cleared. Faron's check bounced, my check bounced, everybody's check bounced and we never heard from them again. When I recently saw Faron's manager, Billy Deaton, at Faron's funeral, I asked Billy how he was doing. He replied, 'I'm still going to get our money.' It got to be a joke. But for some reason, I think he's still making efforts to get the money from these guys and it's been almost twenty years."

Paul Craft
songwriter, publisher

3 Mustaphas 3

You will run into all sorts of promoters when touring. Many of them have established their very particular methods of taking care of business. Some promoters have all of the accounting and receipts well organized in a folder showing exactly where every penny was spent. Others simply count out your pay and don't expect you to question the transaction. You have to be prepared for anything. Kari Estrin offers these unique encounters while tour managing/managing the world music band, the 3 Mustaphas 3.

" We were scheduled to play in some sparsely-populated southern town. When I advanced the date with the promoter, she told me how much she didn't like the band. She couldn't stand the music and she was only doing it as a favor, so could we cancel it now. I implored her and said, 'Look, they are really wonderful live, you will love them.' I thought great, the band is going to go in and sing in Bulgarian and these people are going to hate them. Well, we got to the gig and the audience drank a lot of beer and could not tell the difference between world music and bluegrass. The gig went very well and when I went to get paid, the

HotTips:

Check with the promoter to make sure all deposits are sent and checks have cleared prior to leaving on the tour.

When asked whether you want a check or cash, take the cash. You can always transfer the cash into a bank check or traveler's checks, or wire the cash to your own bank account.

"If you want cash on the night of the show, call the promoter and order it. He is unlikely to have an extra $1000.00 in cash in his pocket!"

Geoffrey P. Trump
tour accountant, ticketing,
Dave Matthews Band, Inc.
Strangely Brown, Inc.

promoter closed the door, opened the safe, laid a gun on the table and counted out the money. I decided against asking about percentages, took what I could get and left.

Another time, the 3 Mustaphas 3 played a very reputable club in a run-down section of Los Angeles. I checked with our agent each day for an accounting update of which promoters' deposits had arrived. At settlement, the management paid me half our fee. I asked if they could produce a bank receipt since we had not received their deposit yet. They couldn't and I convinced them in a firm but friendly manner that I could not leave without either payment in full or a half payment and a wire receipt. I also guaranteed that if they had sent their deposit, we would return it. I left with full payment. A week later their deposit came through. It was happily returned, but now I know why it took me an hour to get payment in full that night."

Kari Estrin
manager, tour manager,
3 Mustaphas 3

Lost, Stolen Or Broken Instruments

Some of the most frustrating experiences that touring artists can face are those involving problems with their instruments. Having anything happen to what you use to earn your living can be devastating, especially when you are in the middle of a tour or en route to your next gig. Theft always takes us by surprise and even though there have been stories with remarkable endings, where the instrument is recovered, many artists are left without their instrument or the resources to replace it.

Tom Paxton

Damaged instruments also catch many artists at the most inopportune times, like just before a performance. Often contacting the airline just flown on may provide some satisfaction and provide nominal compensation. But in many cases, the burden of proof leaves the artist with little relief and there is still a need to borrow a temporary replacement and eventually buy a new instrument. Instrument insurance can be useful in these situations as can be your homeowner's insurance with an attached rider to cover your instruments while touring. When all else fails, Tom Paxton's method of dealing with his broken guitar may at least bring you some solace.

"This would be about 1980. I had a fairly new Martin M38 which was a wonderful instrument. John Hammond had shown me his which I played at Mariposa and loved, so I bought one and was instantly happy with it. I had a Mark Leaf case for it—a big, heavily-padded, tough case. I flew up to Michigan to split a show with the Kingston Trio. When I got to the theater to do the sound check, I opened my case and the neck was broken up near the head which is where it usually happens. I was stunned. I couldn't believe it and immediately called Republic Airlines and said, 'You've broken my guitar.' They said, in effect, 'No we haven't, prove it.' I had to borrow one of the Trio's guitars to do my show.

When I got back to New York, I took my broken guitar to Matt Umanoff Guitars where I bought it. He fixed it, but I had to buy another guitar. I called Martin and they sold me another M38 for half price. But it really rankled me. It had to have been one hell of a drop to transfer the shock all the way through the neck of that guitar to snap it. It rankled me so much that I wrote a pretty funny but scathing song about Republic Airlines. It finishes with perhaps the favorite couplet I've ever written. 'There could be no greater satisfaction than if you should go the way of Braniff.' And they did—they went out of business and I like to think I had something to with it.

I didn't go after them. It would have taken more time and money than it was worth and I wouldn't have gotten any satisfaction. I still remember what the guy said. 'Well, how do we know it wasn't broken before you got on the plane.' Right—whenever I pack for a gig I make sure I bring the guitar with the broken neck to try to screw the airline. We're all in the business of screwing airlines with broken guitars and then by a clever ruse we borrow a guitar to do a show. But, they've caught on to us you see!"

Tom Paxton
singer, songwriter

> **HotTip:** ASCAP, BMI and the AFM all offer instrument insurance.

Laurie Lewis

The road can be a lonely and daunting place to live your professional life especially when you are operating as a small band, a solo or duo. It is important to establish and maintain a network of contacts along the way. Fans are often willing and able to lend a hand when problems arise. Laurie Lewis has experienced most trials of the road while touring with her band Grant Street as well as in other performing configurations. She offers this advice.

"So much has happened to us. We've had broken instruments, lost instruments, and luggage not show up. Once a bass didn't arrive when we flew up to Washington and luckily we had a friend who lived there and he wasn't working that night. He came down and loaned us the bass. Another time a guitar neck broke flying to the east coast. But we stopped at Tom's brother's house and we borrowed his guitar. And once I left my bow at a gig we played in Pasadena. Luckily, I always carry two bows with me. So, when I opened my case in North Carolina, I flipped out because I didn't have my good bow but I had another perfectly serviceable bow. It's networking.

If you're traveling, and I know it's really, really hard to do, but keep in touch with your road friends, people who you meet on the road, people who can help you out sometimes. One thing that's important to know is that there are people who offer to help on the road with all kinds of stuff. Often they're musicians and they know

"Leave as few loose ends at home as possible. They will be the first to greet you upon your return."

Judith-Kate Friedman
singer, songwriter

what it's all about. But, many times they're not. They just truly want to help but it's not just a one-way street. You need to nurture the relationships and keep them open so that if you need them they will be there for you. At the end of every year and sometimes twice a year, we send thank-you notes to every place that we played."

Laurie Lewis
musician

Personnel Problems—Band, Crew

Advice

Here is some sound advice on the topic of touring with others from manager, John Porter. His work with artists like Nanci Griffith, the Nitty Gritty Dirt Band, Kris Tyler, Los Lobos, Joe Ely, Steve Wariner and Foster & Lloyd gives him years of experience in all kinds of touring situations.

> "The bottom line in our organization is we have rules, and one of those rules is you never lose your temper. If you have to lose your temper, you go on the bus, lock it and then lose your temper."
>
> **Mary Beth Aungier**
> tour manager,
> Mary Chapin Carpenter

"First, make sure everyone understands the economics of your particular tour. Usually nobody's getting rich. Touring is difficult enough. Personalities, money and an individual's personal problems can all sideline a tour or make a difficult situation even worse. As you build the team that goes with you on the road, keep all these things in mind. If the side person you are thinking about hiring already has some problems at home—on the road they will be magnified (if not externally, internally) and they will affect the way he/she approaches your gig. Sit down with whomever you are thinking about taking on the road and discuss these issues—make sure your touring business and their role in it is understood. A touring unit quickly becomes family. Avoiding as much dysfunction as possible from the start can make your life much easier.

> "When you spend a long time touring with a band, there are times when things are not as sweet as you'd like. People get out of hand, some lose direction, personalities conflict, things rub. With Emmylou's band, personnel changes and long breaks between tours have done much to stop the pressure building up, but there have been times when I've had to let off steam."
>
> **Phil Kaufman**
> road manager,
> Emmylou Harris,
> author, *Road Mangler Deluxe*

Once you are out there, if problems develop, address them quickly, honestly and as rationally as possible. Agree to disagree. But before you pile in a car, van or bus—have an understanding about terms and what is expected of each member of the team. Always hold up your end (and be honorable). If you feel someone isn't holding up their end, warn them politely and in private. If the problem continues, sit them down (again in private) and provide them a written warning documenting your problems. At this point, you begin to passively search for a possible replacement. If the problem persists past this point (a three strikes and you're out policy), ask them to quit. If they refuse, actively find a replacement and then fire them in writing showing justifiable cause. Withhold all pay due until they agree to sign a waiver against possible future legal action, etc. Pay a two-week severance package. If you have hired the wrong person, you are at fault too and should shoulder that financial responsibility. Likewise, if all goes well and it is financially possible, bonus your band and crew at the end of a tour. It helps provide goodwill and a talent pool from which to draw for your next tour."

John Porter
manager, The Nitty Gritty Dirt Band, Kris Tyler,
Mike Robertson Management

Sarah Vaughan

Avoid problems before they occur by knowing what is important to you on the road such as your travel habits, creature comforts, etc. While Bob Jones was road managing for many of the jazz greats touring throughout the world, he made it his business to care for all the little details that made his artists comfortable.

> "One of the things of which I was very much aware was that for certain artists, there were always things that each artist was very particular about, and inevitably, those were the kinds of things that always screwed up at the last minute. Sarah Vaughan needed among other things, an air-conditioned car, an air-conditioned hotel and Kleenex—actual white Kleenex. It might say Kleenex but they might be imitations as far as she was concerned. She couldn't have cared less if there was caviar in the dressing room; she wanted these specific things. What I would have to do was send out a list of these kind of oddball requests to the promoters. When I would advance the dates, I would say there are three things that you need to have down solid—Kleenex, an air-conditioned car and an air-conditioned hotel. I would package four or five boxes of Kleenex in my bag just in case.
>
> To avoid last minute craziness, I would try to find out the specific wants and needs of each artist before I went on the road with them so that I would know what to stress. One of my little points was to buttonhole those four or five items that drove the artist crazy. Because if they were driven crazy, I was driven crazy. Make sure that those things are covered and if they aren't, figure out a way to cover them."

Bob Jones
former road manager,
Sarah Vaughan, Duke Ellington, Buddy Rich, Ella Fitzgerald

"As a road manager on a large tour always try and say "Hello" to each and every person at least once a week. You can't get to know everybody intimately, but they will really appreciate it if you acknowledge them."

Geoffrey P. Trump
tour accountant, ticketing,
Dave Matthews Band, Inc.
Strangely Brown, Inc.

Illness

Robin & Linda Williams

Performers are not immune to the frailties of the human body. They catch colds, get stomach viruses, and sometimes, have major medical problems just like everyone else. In general, though, most performers are incredibly resilient and will perform under the most adverse physical conditions. Performers seldom use the old "call in sick" option as so many nine-to-fiver's do. Most performers will go through extraordinary efforts to carry out their commitments to perform. I happened to be witness to one such circumstance while working with Robin & Linda Williams. This occurred on October 19, 1989, as told by Robin Williams.

> "This was the first tour with our dobro player, Kevin Maul. We were running around the house madly packing for this three- or four-week tour and there was one last chore to be taken care of. We had some workman making repairs on the roof and before leaving I needed to double check

"Be on time! Consideration for the other bands and house crews goes a long way. Let someone know if you're running late."

Alex Hofmann
tour manager

> "Leave your house as clean as possible before you leave on tour. This may seem like an unnecessary burden, but you will reap the rewards when you return home a month later after a hectic tour."
>
> Kari Estrin
> former tour manager,
> 3 Mustaphas 3, Suzanne Vega, Tony Rice

that they had done the work. I put a ladder on the deck and went up on the roof to inspect it. As I was coming down, the ladder gave way and I fell headfirst 30 feet onto the deck. I didn't land on my head, but I ended up with a shattered bone in my elbow and a shattered kneecap. This was Kevin's introduction to touring with Robin & Linda Williams—me lying on the deck, Linda next to me refusing to let me move and the rescue squad arriving to take me to the hospital. And, we had to perform at a benefit that night in Charlottesville.

I laid around the emergency room for a couple of hours. There was the question of whether I would be all right to work and then there was the more immediate problem of the gig that night. I knew I didn't have any serious injuries but I had an ache in my arm and an ache in my leg. So, Linda and the boys went over to Charlottesville to do the benefit without me. A friend sat with me while they put a cast on my leg. But they couldn't do anything to my elbow except eventually operate. They played the show with John McCutcheon sharing the bill. I was lying on the couch when they returned. I asked them about the gig and they said, 'It went really well, we got a standing ovation, it was a great night, everyone had a great time.'

The next day we were supposed to play in Richmond in the afternoon so the three of them had to leave really early again, without me. They got in the van about nine o'clock and then ten minutes later they came back and Linda said, 'Robin I know you have a broken arm and a broken leg, but the transmission just went out on the van and we've got to be in Richmond. You've got to find somebody to fix this transmission now because we've got to have it by Monday to go on tour.'

Now, I was still in my hospital gown but somehow I got upstairs with this huge cast, got some clothes on and called a neighbor. We got in the van to test the transmission. He drove me over to this mechanic's house who had just quit working for a dealer and was looking for work. They left me sitting on a kid's swing while they went out to test the vehicle. He said he could start working on it right away. I almost fainted from the pain and discomfort of sitting on the swing.

When Linda and the boys returned that evening, I asked them how it went and they said, 'It went great, we played the first set before anybody ever realized you were gone.' I thought, that's a fine how-do-you-do. I didn't work this hard all these years to be so easily forgotten. The next day when we were doing *Mountain Stage*, I decided I could travel. I had crutches, could move around a little and, at least, I could sing. We drove over to Charleston, West Virginia in Jim Watson's van. You should have seen their faces when we drove up. Me on crutches with my swollen elbow, unrecognizable as an elbow. I was looking bad and feeling weak from the ride over. I sat with an ice pack on my arm when I wasn't singing. They found a wheelchair and they rolled me out on the stage and I would sing and then they rolled me off again.

When we got back on Monday, the mechanic had the transmission fixed so we left on Tuesday morning and began our tour. I played every job on that tour. It was hard because I was on crutches, plus I had this shattered bone in my arm which made using the crutches really difficult. But there was nothing else to do. After about five jobs, the swelling had gone down and I could pick up the guitar and play a little rhythm. It was a hardship on the guys and Linda because they had to do all the driving. I went through the whole fall on crutches. After about six weeks, I got the knee taken care of. I finally got the bone taken out of my arm and that laid me up for another three weeks. But I was fine in time to play First Night that winter."

Robin Williams
singer, songwriter

Venue Problems, Technical Problems

Mary Chapin Carpenter

No matter how many dates you play and no matter how long you've been at it, each new date is its own adventure. Even when you have every detail carefully planned and your day is running like clockwork, surprises have a way of challenging you. Mary Beth Aungier has been the tour manager for Mary Chapin Carpenter since 1989. She offered this story about her very busy and committed group of artists.

"We were on the west coast scheduled to perform at Slims, a wonderful club. Earlier in the day we had to perform on the *Arsenio Hall Show*. The band, myself, and our sound engineer flew to L.A. to tape the show while our tech, monitor engineer and back line tech stayed in San Francisco and set up all the gear in preparation for our show that night at Slims. Everything went well. We taped the show at six o'clock, got to the airport by seven, arrived into San Francisco by eight, got to the club about eight-forty and hit the stage at nine. Everything was set up. We felt great. Everything was working and there, but for the grace of God, we could have been late but we weren't.

It was a sold-out show. Slims holds about 500 people and it was absolutely standing room only, packed. The band began and 20 minutes into the show, the entire block lost power. So, in the middle of a song, everything goes dark. The band is just standing there, no one knows what to do. So, Chapin has everyone calm down and she screams to the audience, 'Make an aisle to the bar.' And the band walks across the room and climbs on top of the bar. Chapin played her acoustic guitar, John Jennings played his acoustic guitar, John Carroll played his accordion and Robbie McGruder, our drummer, turned some ice buckets upside down and played ice buckets while J.T. Brown, our bass player, took a little shaker or a cup with ice cubes in it and played that. They were literally standing on top of the bar while the guitar tech and I held flashlights. It was the most magical and glorious night because less than 20 seconds after the entire block lost power, the band just proceeded with their show.

Those are the gigs where you are really tested. It would be easy to say, 'OK we're going to take a break until the power goes back on' But the band said, 'Hey, you know we can do this.' The audience quieted down and no one left. That was the true mark of

---

HotTip:

It is time to hire a road manager when:

1. You arrive at the venue and there is no one there to help unload your gear.
2. Your backline roadie refuses to make you tea during the show.
3. You spend so much time signing autographs for the fans after the show that the promoter leaves without paying you.
4. You stay up late after every show and miss your wake up calls.
5. You are checking into a hotel room reserved under a pseudonym, but the front desk will not give you your key unless you show a valid I.D.
6. You are playing shows in three different towns called Springfield in the same week.

Geoffrey P. Trump
Tour accountant, ticketing
Dave Matthews Band, Inc.
Strangely Brown, Inc.

Learn as much as you can about how a sound system works. They are all linear and sometimes even logical. It is not a sin to understand electronics and it may save your professional life on more than one occasion."

John McCutcheon
singer, songwriter,
from *International Musician*,
1992

really thinking quick on your feet. We opened up the doors of the club because the air conditioner was off. People were laughing and singing along. Chapin played that way for about forty minutes. Then, the power came back on, they ran back on stage and continued with the electric version of their set. I know the club owner at the time, Harry Duncan, was really appreciative because a week prior a very well-known band just packed up and left when a similar thing happened and he lost a lot of money.

Harry always talks about that night. He was a very important promoter for us and it's a very important club. He knew how much Chapin cared about the show and he appreciated how she really cared about people not demanding their money back. After that, he pretty much said you guys can have whatever you want. We got on his A-list.

Mary Beth Aungier
tour manager, Mary Chapin Carpenter

Ani DiFranco

Artists persevere in the face of all manner of technical situations. Most of the truly committed artists know that they will be faced with some performance situations where they must simply take charge of everything if they want the show to happen at all. For instance, I have witnessed sound engineer, Myrna Johnston, rewire a venue's electrical system so the sound system wouldn't hum. Here are a few stories from Scot Fisher, Ani DiFranco's manager.

"Our rider is many pages long. It used to be just a one page boilerplate thing. I would say be prepared to do everything yourself, like turning the lights on, taking tickets at the door, even cleaning up food in the cafeteria before you go on stage because the show is in the cafeteria and they forgot to tell the cafeteria staff to stop serving and everybody's eating their cherry pie looking at you sound checking.

There was one show in Ohio where we showed up and we had changed the rider from, 'A sound engineer is required' to 'A *professional* sound engineer is required.' So the professional sound engineer was a volunteer student who said, 'I've never really played the keyboard before.' The keyboard he was referring to was the sound board. So I, as a carpenter, swept that person aside and said, 'I'll play the keyboard.' There were two speakers on stage, one of which was blown. So she played her concert with the one good speaker.

Ani's had gigs where the sound was so bad that she turned off the system and told the whole audience of 150 people to come close to the stage. She sat on the edge of the stage and played acoustically.

Recently, Ani played in Texas and she said, 'Oh my God there's a mouse crawling at my feet, hang on, hang on.' She's one of the top touring artists in *Pollstar* and things like this can still happen."

Scot Fisher
manager, Ani DiFranco,
president, Righteous Babe Records

Touring Checklist

Advancing The Date
1. **One month to three weeks prior to the date or the entire tour, call the presenter to make final arrangements:**
   - ❏ a. Confirm hotel or housing—name, address, phone, confirmation #'s, directions to hotel/house and venue from the hotel. Make sure prepayments have been made as contracted. Ask if the hotel has a late-night restaurant, dry-cleaning service, exercise facility or pool and find out the check-in and check-out times. Find out in whose name the reservations are made and the hotel contact.
   - ❏ b. Send a rooming list to the hotel in advance for a speedy check-in.
   - ❏ c. Confirm sound and lights contact, business and cellular phone or pager, equipment review, sound-check time and load-in time.
   - ❏ d. Confirm hospitality arrangements—meals, dressing room and stage amenities.
   - ❏ e. Confirm travel arrangements—arrival times, pickup requirements, driver contact information.
   - ❏ f. Notify presenter of any merchandise shipments expected to arrive at the venue.
   - ❏ g. Get advanced ticket sales update.
   - ❏ h. Ask for nearby banks, restaurants, gas stations, laundry facilities and grocery stores when confirming hotel.

Travel And Final Tour Arrangements
2. **At least two weeks prior to leaving on tour:**
   - ❏ a. Check that all appropriate tickets have arrived and are correct.
   - ❏ b. Reconfirm any rental vehicles.
   - ❏ c. Reconfirm any rental equipment and arrange final pickup time and date.
   - ❏ d. Compile and send a complete tour itinerary to important people who may need to contact you on the road: family, friends, record company, publicist, office manager, pet caretaker, housesitter.
   - ❏ e. Check all of your equipment and instruments for condition. Make any repairs necessary and order any parts.
   - ❏ f. Check all of your instrument cases for road worthiness, especially flight cases.
   - ❏ g. Make sure your instrument insurance is up to date.
   - ❏ h. Check that all contracts are returned, signed and filed with the union if you are a member.
   - ❏ i. Gather appropriate papers, passport, visas, instrument lists and receipts, bonding agent contacts (where necessary), work permits (when appropriate) for international travel. Make sure all group members have appropriate papers especially if they are crossing borders separately.
   - ❏ j. Refill any prescription drugs necessary and update supplies for first-aid kit and emergency road kit for those driving.

3. **24-48 Hours Prior To The Date:**
   - ❏ a. Call presenter with approximate arrival time.
   - ❏ b. Call driver to confirm pick-up.
   - ❏ c. Check on any last minute details or updates.
   - ❏ d. Confirm arrival of merchandise shipment.
   - ❏ e. Reconfirm any press or radio interviews that are scheduled for day-of-show.
   - ❏ f. Get advance ticket sales update.

Day Of Show
4. **Arrive in town:**
   - ❏ a. Check into hotel, one person checks in all group members.
   - ❏ b. Check with hotel clerk for nearest gas stations, post office, grocery stores, restaurants and banks if you haven't previously.

- c. Check in with any media that are expecting day-of-show interviews.
- d. Arrange a meeting time and place with group members to assemble for a timely departure for the venue and sound check.
- e. Allow enough time for any meals especially when food will not be provided at the venue.

5. At The Venue:
- a. Check with tech crew to load-in.
- b. Meet presenter or presenter's representative.
- c. Check in with box office, get ticket update for advanced sales.
- d. Arrange for merchandise sales area and inventory review with venue representative. Choose an area conducive to meeting fans and signing product during intermission and after the show.
- e. Discuss lighting setup and complete stage focus during sound check.
- f. Distribute copies of set list to sound and lighting engineers between sound check and show.
- g. Get your final guest/comp list to the box office.
- h. Meet with stage manager and house manager to coordinate the show schedule.
- i. Check for all on-stage necessities: water, towels, etc.
- j. Do one final line check to make sure all mics and lines are on and working prior to being introduced. Either do it yourself or have a band member, tech person or crew member do it.

6. Getting Paid:
- a. Always have a copy of the signed contract with you along with any budget agreed to during negotiations. When settling the show, fill in the actuals column of your budget form. Be prepared to question any excessive expenses when fees include percentages over expenses and get receipts when necessary.
- b. Keep track of all deposits received, if applicable. If a club says they have paid and you have not received it, require them to produce a bank receipt or copy of the check. No receipt equals no deposit. Get full payment according to the contract during settlement.
- c. Always arrange to be paid in a private place away from any audience or staff.
- d. Arrange with the presenter exactly where and when to meet them to review the box office and get paid prior to going on stage. If you, as the artist, handle this yourself, it is easier to wait until after the show, unless it is a flat guaranteed fee. If you travel with a road manager, the presenter and road manager can begin settling the box office and final budget during intermission or just as the second half of the show begins. Again, if the fee is a flat guarantee, settle up anytime it is convenient.
- e. Have someone from your group present at the door to help keep count of the paying audience at club dates. Get into a system of having your own backup door count. It helps when it is time to settle the box office. At most clubs, it is not necessary—at some, it is. By doing this each time, you will never have to worry about inaccurate counts.
- f. Settle any merchandise percentage and double check your inventory and sales.

7. Load-out and departure:
- a. Check and double check all dressing rooms, backstage areas, bathrooms and showers for anything that belongs to you. If you are a group, assign one person to do this every time after everyone is out.
- b. Thank the stage crew, the staff, the technical crew and the promoter before leaving. This leaves a positive, lasting impression of your professionalism no matter how the show went.
- c. Leave with the review copy of any recording you had previously arranged for.

Travel Savvy

This section was written with the help of Nina Gorin, former travel agent with Airways Travel in Oklahoma City, Oklahoma.

Touring equals travel. One can travel smart or one can spend a lot of money attempting to get from one place to another and eat up your tour budget. Smart traveling means advance planning. This is not the area of your life that calls for spontaneity. Last-minute reservations will cost you more in most cases. Advance planning can get you fantastic deals on airfare, hotel and car rentals. If you plan far enough in advance you can take advantage of various memberships in travel clubs which offer half-price discounts and future travel bonuses.

Work With A Travel Agent

Finding a competent and creative travel agent is a priority. Not any travel agent will do. Find an agent who demonstrates an understanding for the needs of a touring performer who carries instruments. Oftentimes, an agency may have a group or corporate department. Many of the larger talent agencies and major record companies have in-house travel agencies that specialize in touring travel arrangements. You may have to test a few agents from a few different agencies. When you begin working with a new agent, explain your particular situation and the type of travel you are likely to be doing.

The Benefits Of Using A Travel Agent

Time is money. Your time is better spent promoting and booking your act rather than wasting time trying to figure out the maze of airline schedules and, worse, the absolute insanity of airline fares. A good travel agent frequently develops a good working relationship with at least one, if not more, carriers.

A travel agent can also:
- Negotiate special fares for groups or for major tours
- Book hotels
- Arrange tour buses (if a bus tour is preferred or more efficient)
- Rent cars, vans or shuttles to and from airports
- Pre-purchase foreign currency, traveler's checks
- Arrange for visas

Larger Travel Agent Versus Smaller Travel Agent

Large travel agencies have some advantages. Due to their volume, generally limited to a few very specific suppliers, they may be able to get upgrade certificates, or "special" deals. The

---

HotTip: Visas may not arrive until one or two days prior to departure. If official papers have been sent to the border crossing, you can call them directly to confirm their arrival. (See Ports Of Entry page 241-242).

"Work with a travel agent who understands your needs and can help you achieve your travel goals (usually getting from point A to point B and back without loss of shirt and firstborn). Once you find a great travel agent—love them, make them family and refer your friends. Such a partner in your career can save you money and headaches."

John Porter
manager

> **HotTip:**
> **Discount Airline Websites**
>
> http://www.bizrate.com
> http://www.cheaptickets.com
> http://www.expedia.com
> http://www.hotwire.com
> http://www.orbitz.com
> http://www.priceline.com
> http://www.sidestep.com
> http://www.ticketspinner.com
> http://www.travelocity.com

disadvantages are if they receive override commissions from specific airlines, there is a tendency to "overlook" other carriers which may have better schedules and/or fares. Unless you are working with a specific agent in the agency, you may be just another phone call. The special attention you may need may not be there. If your agent is away, who will be taking care of your account?

Small agencies also have advantages and disadvantages. The disadvantages are that those upgrade certificates, "special deals," might not be as available since the volume of business is not as great with individual carriers. The advantages to you are important. Your account and business are appreciated and desired. Individual accounts are obviously more significant to the bottom line of the smaller agency and will be serviced in a more personal manner. The agent might have more latitude to search for lowest fares and best routings than would be possible if she had to fulfill a quota.

Finding The Right Travel Agent

When personal interviews are not possible, a phone interview, not only with the agent but with some of her corporate accounts, is definitely warranted. Reliability is important when you have tour dates at stake.

What You Should Know About Your Travel Agent

- ❖ What other corporate accounts do they have?
- ❖ What is the ratio of corporate to leisure travel?
- ❖ Does this agency specialize in a specific market or type of travel (cruise only, bus tours only, senior citizens, students, domestic only, Europe, Asia, etc.)?
- ❖ Are they familiar with travel arrangements for touring performers?
- ❖ How long has this company been in business?
- ❖ Does the agency belong to any professional organizations (ASTA-American Society of Travel Agents), ICTA (Institute of Certified Travel Agents), franchises or consortiums (which might affect which carriers they promote)?
- ❖ How long has the agent been actively working in the travel business?
- ❖ What are business hours? Is this convenient to your time zone? Are there weekend hours?
- ❖ Does the company have a toll-free number?
- ❖ Is there an after-hours number (usually found in larger agencies/franchises) for emergencies? If not, is the home phone/pager of the agent available? (Emergencies are common and often the agent can help with rescheduling missed flights or more pressing questions like, "I left my passport/visa in my hotel room," or "I'm at the airport and they are trying to

> "Work with a travel agent who is attentive to the special needs of a touring artist. They must arrange efficient connections and logical routing for timely arrivals. Find an agent who also demonstrates concern for your travel budget."
>
> Sandy Goldfarb
> travel representative
> in association with
> Ladera Travel Service

charge me to send my bass." Or worse "I'm at the airport, and my equipment won't fit on the plane."
- How are tickets delivered—in person, regular mail, certified mail, express? Who pays for delivering tickets?
- Are boarding passes/seat assignments routinely provided?
- How do you pay for tickets—credit card at the time tickets are issued, check when tickets are issued or monthly? This can be a very touchy subject. A form of payment must be entered into the airline record when a ticket is issued. Once the ticket is issued it is almost impossible to change the form of payment. The ticket must either be voided and reissued (which means the fare could be gone) or the airline needs to give authorization, in which case, you can almost always count on some penalty/service charge from the carrier. The travel agency must report to the airline all tickets negotiable documents issued during the week on the next Monday. NO EXCEPTIONS. Non-reporting not only costs the agency a significant penalty from the airline but the agency forfeits its commission as well.
- Does this agency charge a service charge? Since Delta Airlines began limiting agency commissions in 1995 (everyone except America West, Southwest, TWA and Western Pacific have followed suit), many agencies have imposed service charges. These may be for tickets under a certain value, for tickets on carriers not bookable through their computer (Southwest for example), for non-air, hotel/car bookings and for any changes that are later made to a reservation. This service charge to the customer may be in addition to the mandatory imposed airline penalties.

What Your Travel Agent Must Know About You

Send your travel agent the following:
- Names, mailing addresses, phone numbers, fax numbers and frequent-flyer numbers for all artists who are traveling.
- Credit card information and who pays for tickets (frequently a signed charge form for "on-file" authorizations).
- Who is authorized to make changes and who pays for the changes? Is a band or crew member authorized to "bill" your credit card?
- Name and address, including zip codes, of person authorized to receive tickets.
- Airlines and hotel preferences and those to avoid.
- Seat preferences. Aisle, window, front, over wing or back. Realize the airlines block the "best seats" for their super-frequent flyers. The travel agent has a very limited selection available. Sometimes only middle seats are available, sometimes no seats are available, and passengers must get seat assignments upon check-in at the airport.

> **HotTip:** Request airline seating as far forward on the plane as possible. When changing planes, you will deplane more quickly.

> "I know our performers like to be seated nearest to the exits so they can get off the plane quickly and get their equipment."
>
> **Vickie Gee**
> owner, travel agent,
> World Travel

> "On an international flight, always check with each band member to see their passports before getting off the plane. Remind them to take their passports out of the seat back pocket and put them back in their jacket pockets!"
>
> **Geoffrey P. Trump**
> tour accountant, ticketing
> Dave Matthews Band, Inc.
> Strangely Brown, Inc.

> **HotTip:** 🌶
> Board flights when attendant asks for those passengers needing extra time. This assures ample space for carry-on instruments in the overhead bins.

- Car rental company preferences and car size requirements—economy, compact, mid-size, full size, luxury.
- Meal preferences for flights that still serve "food"—kosher, diabetic, fruit, vegetarian, no salt, low cholesterol. While the request should be made at time of reservation, it is the passenger's responsibility to reconfirm special meals no later than 24 hours prior to flight time.
- Instrument and equipment types, measurements and weights. It is critical that the travel agent know dimensions of carrying cases for instruments. As more and more markets are being served by commuter lines or feeder lines (also called puddle jumpers) cargo space is at a premium, and very restricted. An acoustic bass in a carrying case with wheels probably will not fit in an AT7 aircraft. Oversized instruments may be required to buy a ticket. Instruments may not be in the aisle, in emergency rows or in the rows immediately in front of or behind emergency rows. If at all possible, insist on bulkhead seating for the extra room.

The travel agent will keep this information in their computers so they can give you quality service without burdening you with the same questions again and again.

You want a travel agent who can help get you to the gig on time and is willing to advocate on your behalf should a problem arise during your travel. By using one agent, you will develop this advocacy relationship.

Contact your agent at the beginning of your tour planning, inform them of the approximate departure, return dates and the general routing. If this is a flying tour, they can be watching for any fare wars far enough in advance so you can take advantage of very low rates. If this is a driving tour with vehicle rentals or leases, they can assist in finding the best deals. Your agent can also help you take advantage of any hotel deals along the route especially if they can book hotels within one chain.

Information You Must Know About Travel

Airline prices are subject to change until the ticket is actually issued.
This cannot be stressed enough. No travel agent, unless working with a consolidator, can protect a fare. They may only "hold" a seat for 24 hours and, in some cases (special super sales, for example), tickets must be issued at the time reservations are made.

The farther in advance you book, the cheaper the fare.
This is basic airline economics. The closer to flight time, the more expensive the tickets.

> "Giving your cello a name and enrolling it in a mileage program won't work anymore, due to photo ID requirements. I've done this before for someone, "C. Smith," and the cello used to use its frequent-flyer miles for upgrades to first class!"
>
> Nina Gorin
> former travel agent,
> Airway Travel

> "Provide the promoter with the artist's travel plans as early as possible. Come to us with it in a reasonable and timely fashion."
>
> Christine Risatti
> director,
> Downtown Presents,
> Richmond, VA

The cheaper the ticket the more restrictive it is.
Generally a minimum of a Saturday night stay is required (anything that leaves after midnight Saturday on the return flight fulfills this restriction) and a maximum of 30 days is allowed. Any changes to this and you are looking at penalties of $50 to $60 per ticket plus the difference in what you paid and what the new fare costs.

Illegal Ticketing

Missing The Outbound Flight

If you miss the outbound flight, all down-line connections are automatically cancelled by the carrier. This situation frequently happens with "hidden cities." For example, from Oklahoma City to Albuquerque the fares are generally very reasonable. The fares to Denver are much higher. The passenger wants to go to Denver on United (the only non-stop in the market). The flight stops in Denver on the way to Albuquerque. The fare to Albuquerque is $180 round trip. The fare to Denver is $340 round trip. The passenger buys the ticket to Albuquerque and walks off the plane with carry-on luggage in Denver. So far so good. However, on the way back, the passenger does not board in Albuquerque. When he checks in at the Denver Airport, he finds that his reservation was cancelled by the airline as a "no show" and he must now buy a full-fare ticket one way from Denver to Oklahoma City. This type of ticketing is illegal.

Back-To-Back Tickets

You are coming from Nashville to perform in New York City on Monday, Tuesday and Wednesday. Due to time and hotel costs, you do not want to leave the preceding Saturday and spend the extra nights in New York. So you buy one set of round-trip tickets from Nashville to New York, departing Monday and returning the next week, and a second set of tickets originating in New York on Thursday and returning the next Sunday to Nashville.

If the carrier catches the agency issuing "back-to-back tickets" the following will most likely occur:
1. Your reservations will be cancelled.
2. You may be back-charged for a nonexcursion rate ticket (i.e. no Saturday stay).
3. Your travel agent will be billed for full fare of the tickets, fined, and may lose ticketing authorization.
4. If you buy one set of tickets on one carrier and a second set on another carrier the same applies, only doubled. Delta and Continental are leaders in the field of tracking used tickets. The other carriers are sure to follow. It is not worth the risks.

HotTip:
"Unless an absolute emergency, never change the outbound flight. This affects the entire ticket price. If you miss the outbound flight, all down-line connections are automatically cancelled by the carrier."
Nina Gorin
travel agent

"When you live on the west coast and have to travel anywhere to the east, remember you lose a couple of hours. This makes it hard to play on your travel day and if there is any travel problem at all, you may not arrive in time for the gig."
Byron Berline
fiddler

"Routing . . . We live in Denver and were booked in Boston. The airfare was sky high! We saved hundreds of dollars by driving 1000 miles to Phoenix, Arizona and flying to and from Boston. We booked a good tour in Arizona and came out way ahead!"
Liz Masterson and
Sean Blackburn
singers, songwriters

> **HotTip:** 🌶
> When driving to an airport for extended air tours, book a room at a nearby hotel on either the night before an outbound flight or the night of your return. Most hotels will include free parking for at least two weeks or more. The room price is often much less than airport parking.

Selling Unused Tickets

We have all seen the ads in the paper: "One-way to South Podunk, April 2—going cheap" or "Unable to travel will sell cheap round-trip to Miami." These actions are flagrantly illegal since the name on the ticket is not the name of the passenger. If you try it and are caught, you will be stopped by security. The airlines will make you pay a full fare, no-advance purchase, one-way ticket or they will deny boarding. In the old days, there was one thing that made this even worse—the person traveling did not show up on the passenger manifest, the person ticketed did. In case of an emergency, the wrong people got notified, and the other person goes unknown and his family is unable to take legal recourse because that person was not legally on the plane.

Due To The New Federal Anti-Terrorism Laws, The Following Is In Effect

Government-issued photo ID (passport, driver's license, alien registration card) must be presented at check-in by each passenger. If the names do not match the name on the ticket and the ID, the passenger does not get on the plane or on AMTRAK. If you use a nickname or stage name, the ID must be in that name. No excuses . . . no exceptions.

Traveling With Pets

Pets require advance notice to the airline carrier plus an extra 1 to 1½ hours for paperwork at check-in. Be sure to have a copy of the pet's vaccinations, a proper carrying case (animal must be able to turn around in it) as well as food and water. Each airline is different. Weather affects whether animals may travel. For this reason, travel as early in the morning as possible to avoid excess heat and avoid last flights of the day, in case of delays or flight cancellations.

Also, it is illegal to drive your pet across state lines in your vehicle without the proper temporary license. Check with your pet's veterinarian.

Frequent-Flyer Miles

For those who fly a great deal, membership in the frequent flyer mileage program of your most frequently-traveled airline is a must. Having cards for all of the airlines assures you of increasing your mileage when unable to fly your airline of choice. Mileage programs are free and one can sign up over the phone by calling the airline's direct reservations number or ask the ticket agent while you are waiting for the next plane. Sign up! Frequent flyer miles can accumulate quickly and you will appreciate those free flights in the future.

"When a performer is in an emergency situation and needs to get to a performance when there is engine trouble on the plane or bad weather, they know to call in and we make them a priority. We are a clearinghouse for problems. With performers, it is always a very immediate need and we are there for them."

Vickie Gee
owner, travel agent,
World Travel

Airline Frequent-Flyer Mileage Programs
- United Mileage Plus: http://www.united.com
- American AAdvantage: http://www.aa.com
- Delta Airlines SkyMiles: http://www.delta.com
- US Airways Dividend Miles: http://www.usairways.com
- Continental One Pass: http://www.continental.com
- Southwest Airlines: http://www.southwest.com

Credit Cards
You can add to your miles even when you are not flying. Airlines are offering credit cards that add miles. Unless you pay off your balance each time, the finance charges on these cards can reach as high as 19% and 21% so read the fine print. Many other credit cards have instituted mileage programs as well. They often have a yearly membership fee which can be as much as $50 or more along with a fairly high interest rate.

Rewards Network
Rewards Network offers cash reward discounts off hotels and your entire dining bill, including the food, drinks, tax and tips at participating merchants. Simply log on to their website and join. Register up to five credit or debit cards that you might use when paying for your meals or hotels.

You must make your hotel reservations through Rewards network to qualify for the 5% hotel savings. There is an annual membership fee of $49.00. They will apply the first $49.00 of savings to your membership fee,

For more information:
Web: http://www.rewardsnet work.com
Member Services at 1-877-491-3463.

Discount Travel Programs

Preferred Traveller
Preferred Traveller is another discount travel program that offers half-price hotel discounts, lowest-fare airline reservations, car-rental discounts, vacation-package discounts, theme-park and major-attraction discounts as well as restaurant discounts. There is a membership fee of $96.00 annually.

For more information:
Web: http://www.preferredtraveller.com

Travelers Advantage
Travelers Advantage offers half-price hotel discounts worldwide along with discounts on airlines, car rentals and vacation packages. They offer a three-month free trial membership. After the first three months, you can join for

---

HotTip: Check with your long distance phone provider for awards programs offering Frequent Flyer miles. Phone time may equal free flights.

"When flying, essential equipment: ear plugs and a sleeping mask; a sweatshirt to roll up for neck support; and I ALWAYS carry a long sleeved shirt, even in the summer— airplane air conditioners are fickle at best."

Billy Jonas
singer, songwriter, performer, industrial re-percussionist

> **HotTip:** 🌶
> The discount hotel plans may give their half-off rate on a full-price room. Check the prices carefully. AAA discounts on hotel rooms are often lower than the corporate rate.
>
> Discount Hotel Websites
>
> http://www.expedia.com
> http://www.hotels.com
> http://www.hoteldiscount.com
> http://www.hotwire.com
> http://www.orbitz.com

"Don't trash hotel rooms. That's not rock 'n roll, it's just stupid since it makes it difficult for the next band that comes through."

Alex Hofmann
tour manager

a low monthly fee, risk-free guaranteed. If at anytime you are not satisfied, you may cancel.

For more information: Travelers Advantage: 1-800-548-1116. Web: http://www.travelersadvantage.com

Organizational Memberships

When you join some organizations, you are entitled to certain discount programs from national companies as part of your member benefits package. For example, the IBMA has a discount program arranged with Alamo for their membership's car rental convenience.

AAA Membership

As a AAA member, always present your card or ask for the AAA discount price for car rentals and hotels when making reservations. The AAA discount is often lower than the corporate discount. The AAA discount card is also good for discounts at many oil change maintenance centers.

Aside from the towing privileges offered, AAA provides free trip-tik maps, free American Express Travelers Checks, regional guidebooks with recommended hotels and restaurants and knowledgeable travel agents.

AAA Plus offers free towing for 100 miles in most areas instead of the usual five miles (although cities like New York are exempt). For the few extra dollars a year it could save quite a bit on the road.

If you are planning tours, memberships in some of these discount programs can reduce your budget. Working with one of these programs instead of a travel agent simply requires getting used to using their hotline numbers and becoming familiar with any restrictions or advance-notice requirements.

Car Rentals

If touring requires that you rent a vehicle, rather than use your own, get acquainted with all of your local car-rental companies, even dealers who lease cars. If you tour more than 100 miles in a day, you can quickly eliminate the ones that do not include unlimited mileage. It will always be more expensive paying for the miles above the free per-day miles. Ask about drop charges if you rent in one city and return in another. If the drop charge is reasonable, it may be worth paying it rather than traveling back to the original rental dealer. Establish a relationship with one car company in your area and, if possible, with the manager of the office. If you anticipate renting often, consider signing up for their corporate program. By becoming a steady customer, you can expect premium service and the benefit of discount offers.

Need Larger Vehicles
Many car-rental companies have larger passenger vans, station wagons or cargo vans for rent. The charges are usually higher than economy car rentals, but may be cheaper than luxury car rentals. I have also found good deals on luxury cars, like Lincoln Continentals, in some big cities where vans are just not available. A luxury car often has very large trunk space and can accommodate six passengers and luggage comfortably.

Return With A Full Tank
Fill the tank before returning the car. This has often been the most inexpensive way of dealing with gas when returning a rental car. Recently, rental agents have begun offering a pre-purchase option at a very reasonable per-gallon rate. You can include a refill at the time of rental. I often refill my own tank simply because I do not know how much gas I will return with. Why pay for a full tank if you are close by and still have half a tank? I would rather gauge my own usage than be charged in advance. It is a convenience, though, especially in some cities where the surrounding gas stations are more expensive than the per-gallon charge the rental agency is offering.

Frequent-Flyer Points For Car Rentals
Rentals from cooperating airline partners may earn frequent-flyer points. Check your program and make inquiries when reserving your vehicle.

Rent Outside Larger Cities—Save Money
If you live in a large city like New York, renting the vehicle in a suburb outside of the city or even in New Jersey can save you money in taxes alone.

Off-Airport Rental Offices
When possible, renting a car from an office outside the airport can save the additional airport tax which at some airports is 12% or higher. Airport rentals without reservations are always higher.

Reservations With Discount Cards
Memberships in AAA, AARP, and Sam's Club offer the three best discounts. Advise the rental company that you are using a discount card when you make the reservation so the special fares may be found.

What Is Not Included In The Rate
Car rates do not include collision, damage waver, personal injury, or any other insurance. Nor are local access charges, sales taxes, state road taxes (Florida and Hawaii are good examples) included. These extra charges can double the base rate of the car.

HotTip:
"Buy AAA Plus. Trust me. When you are 99 miles away from home, you get to tow the car to your regular mechanic. When you're more than 99 miles from home, you get to have it towed to a AAA-certified mechanic."
Bob Franke
singer, songwriter

"If the hotel/motel or bed and breakfast doesn't have a fax machine or modem connection in the rooms, you're asking for communication problems."

John Porter
manager

> **HotTip:**
> The discount hotel plans may give their half-off rate on a full-price room. Check the prices carefully. AAA discounts on hotel rooms are often lower than the corporate rate.
>
> **Discount Hotel Websites**
>
> http://www.expedia.com
> http://www.hotels.com
> http://www.hotelsgo.net
> http://www.hoteldiscount.com
> http://www.huge-hotel-discount.com

"Don't trash hotel rooms. That's not rock 'n roll, it's just stupid since it makes it difficult for the next band that comes through."

— Alex Hofmann
tour manager

Car Rental Insurance

Most people are covered by their personal car insurance. Check with your insurance carrier to find out if you are covered, what the limits are and if there is a limit to the number of days you may use a rental car. Know what your insurance deductible is before rejecting the rental coverage. Some credit cards also provide coverage. The advantage of purchasing the rental company's coverage is in case of an accident. Generally, the only cost you incur is the deductible charged to your credit card until the insurance company settles. Your homeowner's/renter's insurance should cover your possessions if they are lost or stolen. Check with your carrier. Most rental companies have an additional charge for extra drivers. Some companies, like Hertz, do not charge spouses. Significant others are not included, although at this time, there are indications that this might be changing. Never let anyone who is not a signer to the rental agreement drive the car. Any insurance you have with the car company will be instantly void if there is an accident.

Using Credit Cards

All car-rental companies require a credit card to rent a car. Even if the rental is ultimately paid in cash, the credit card is basically collateral and, if anything happens to the car, the credit card is charged. For those who do not use credit cards, Hertz has a cash ID program. Plan this way in advance. It takes about four-to-six weeks for processing. You fill out the cash application, get a letter from your bank, and, once approved, you may rent at Hertz without putting up the hefty cash deposit (usually at least $500). If you do not use bank cards, Budget is owned by Sears and you may charge to your Sears card. Remember to let the car-rental agent see a flight receipt and get frequent-flyer miles for rentals with airline partners. Miles do not accrue automatically by your name. You must actively pursue that miles are given for each applicable transaction.

Hotels

Similar to car rentals, there is limited availability for discount rates when using AAA or AARP. Plan ahead. Be aware of hotel cancellation policies especially when guaranteed to a credit card for late arrival. Many popular locations, resorts, seasonal locations (Florida, Arizona, South Texas) may have 7 to 14 day cancellation penalties. Some locations have non-refundable deposits. Be sure you know what you are paying for.

If your presenting organization is booking and paying for your hotel, remind them to book the rooms far in advance of the date to avoid conflicts with other major events in town, i.e., sports events, homecoming weekends, graduations, conferences, etc. Even though they may be paying for the hotel, you should still be concerned with the convenience and proximity to the venue. Hotels more than 15 minutes from the venue are not convenient especially when you are playing in large cities with rush-hour traffic.

Hotel Telephones
Always check with the front desk about room charges for local as well as long-distance calls, access charges for long-distance phone service and toll-free calls. This is a way many hotels make a "killing." If you want to avoid the hotel's service charge, you can always use your cellphone.

Hotel Confirmations
Whenever possible insist on written confirmations. This protects you from sudden rate changes, as well as "I'm sorry the hotel is overbooked," or "We don't have a reservation for you." In the case of overbooking, try to insist on an upgrade to a better room at the rate you agreed to pay. In the event the hotel "walks" you to another hotel, be sure that the new hotel has space before you go and try to arrange some form of compensation from the hotel that is not honoring your reservation.

Overbooking
Hotel overbooking is not as serious as airline overbooking but it is more aggravating. After all, you are generally tired by the time you get to the hotel and not very patient. Hotel overbooking usually occurs because people stay longer than their original reservations. Be considerate of those coming after you and officially extend your stay with the management. If they cannot accommodate you, they will let you know and appreciate your desire to stay at their property.

Conclusion
Utilizing any of these travel tips will make your tours run more efficiently while saving your budget from going through the roof. Advance planning is the key to smart touring.

Summary
- Become familiar with the designated road manager's responsibilities to manage your tours efficiently.
- Do not leave the details of a tour to the last minute. It will cost you dearly.
- Smart touring takes advance planning, networking and using the resources available to you.
- Work with a travel agent that is familiar with artist touring habits, needs and problems.
- Take advantage of discount programs and frequent traveler programs.

HotTip:
"Buy AAA Plus. Trust me. When you are 99 miles away from home, you get to tow the car to your regular mechanic. When you're more than 99 miles from home, you get to have it towed to a AAA-certified mechanic."
Bob Franke
singer, songwriter

"If the hotel/motel or bed and breakfast doesn't have a fax machine or modem connection in the rooms, you're asking for communication problems."
John Porter
manager

Resources
Discount Programs:

Entertainment Book—Entertainment Publications
Phone: 1-800-374-4464
Web: http://www.entertainment.com

Preferred Traveller
Web: http://www.preferredtraveller.com

Rewards Network
Phone: 1-877-491-3463
Web: http://www.RewardsNetwork.com

Travelers Advantage
Phone: 1-800-548-1116
Web: http://www.travellersadvantage.com

Discount Airlines:

America West
Phone: 1-800-235-9292
Web: http://www.americawest.com

America Trans Air (ATA)
Phone: 1-800-435-9282
Web: http://www.ata.com

Frontier Airlines
Phone: 1-800-432-1359
Web: http://www.frontierairlines.com

Gulf Stream International Air
Phone: 1-800-525-0280
Web: http://www.gulfstreamair.com

Jet Blue Airline
Phone: 1-800-538-2583
Web: http://www.jetblue.com

Southwest Airlines
Phone: 1-800-435-9792
Web: http://www.southwest.com

Spirit Airlines
Phone: 1-800-772-7117
Web: http://www.spiritair.com

Frequent-Flyer Mileage Programs:
See page 277.

Instrument Insurance Providers:

AFM Local 1000
Phone: 212-843-8726
E-mail: local1000@igc.org
Web: http://www.afm.org/1000/
Members only benefit

American String Teachers Association (ASTA)
4153 Chain Bridge Road
Fairfax, VA 22030
Web: http://www.astaweb.com
Provided by: Merz-Huber Co.
630 Fairview Rd.
Swarthmore, PA 19081-2318
Phone: 610-544-2323
Web: http://www.merzhuber.com
Member's benefit

ASCAP—Music Pro Insurance
New York Office-membership
Phone: 212-621-6240; Fax: 212-724-9064
Los Angeles Office-membership
Phone: 323-883-1000; Fax: 323-883-1049
Nashville Office-membership
Phone: 615-742-5000; Fax: 615-742-5020
Web: http://www.ascap.com/benefits/musicpro.html
Provided by Sterling & Sterling
Members call Sterling & Sterling directly
Phone: 1-800-605-3187
Web: http://www.musicproinsurance.com
Member's benefit

BMI
Partnership with Gig America
Web: http://www.bmi.com

Clarion Associates, Inc.
Musical Instrument Insurance
1711 New York Ave.
Huntington Station, NY 11746
Phone: 1-800-VIVALDI (848-2534)
E-mail: clarion@clarionins.com
Web: http://www.clarionins.com

The Heritage Musical Merchandiser Insurance Program
Heritage Insurance Services
826 Bustleton Pike, Suite 203
Feasterville, PA 19053-9859
Phone: 1-800-289-8837
Fax: 215-322-5854
Web: http://www.heritage-ins-services.com

Merchandisers:

Giant Merchandising
5655 Union Pacific Ave.
Commerce, CA 90022
Phone: 323-887-3300
Fax: 323-887-3345
Web: http://www.giantmerchandising.com

Signatures Network
Two Bryant Street, 3rd Floor
San Francisco, CA 94105
Phone: 415-247-7400
Web: http://www.signaturesnetwork.com
Web: http://www.winterland.com

MusicToday.com
5391 Three Notchd Road
Crozet, VA 22932
Phone: 1-877-687-4277
Web: http://www.musictoday.com

Goldenrod Music, Inc.
Goldenrod Promotions
1310 Turner Street
Lansing, MI 48906
Phone: 517-484-1712
Fax: 517-484-1771
E-mail: music@goldenrod.com
Web: http://www.goldenrod.com

Services:

Tour Arts
2829 Bridgeway, Suite 205
Sausalito, CA 94965
Phone: 1-800-669-5566
Phone: 415-332-0410
Fax: 415-332-0430
E-mail: ajohnson@tourarts.com
Web: http://www.tourarts.com
Tour management and travel arrangements specializing in orchestras, dance companies, theater, opera companies and fundraising tours

International Talent & Touring Directory
Billboard
1515 Broadway
New York, NY 10036
Phone: 1-800-344-7119
Web: http://www.billboard.com
Listing touring services by city—charter and limousines, instrument rental, hotels, legal and financial services, sound and lighting, security, concert promoters

Software:

Tour Manager
Patten Sounds
Music Business Store
5198 Arlington Avenue, PMB 513
Riverside, CA 92504
Web: http://www.musicbusinessstore.com
Complete tracking of all facets of your tour

Travel Agents:

AAA
Road Service
Phone: 1-800-AAA-HELP
Web: http://www.aaa.com
For travel services contact AAA nearest you listed in Yellow Pages or in the back of the Tour Books provided by AAA

Travel Websites:

Cheap Tickets.com
Web: http://www.cheaptickets.com

Expedia.com
Web: http://www.expedia.com

Hotels.com
Web: http://www.hotels.com

Hoteldiscount.com
Web: http://hoteldiscount.com

Hotwire.com
Web: http://www.hotwire.com

Orbitz.com
Web: http://www.orbitz.com

Priceline.com
Web: http://www.priceline.com

Sidestep.com
Web: http://www.sidestep.com

Ticketspinner.com
Web: http://www.ticketspinner.com

Travelocity.com
Web: http://www.travelocity.com

CHAPTER ELEVEN

Trade Shows, Conferences And Industry Events

"Business conferences are the most efficient way to make that personal connection with people who are doing exactly what you do. Doing business face to face is an effective strategy. A personal interaction will always pay off even if it is somewhere down the road and not immediate."

Phyllis Barney
former executive director,
The Folk Alliance

One of the fastest ways to boost your career to the next level is to participate in an industry-related trade show or business conference. These events open doors to the world in which you want to play an active role. You are immediately surrounded with the movers and shakers of the industry. You have an opportunity to meet the people who have been in the business for years as well as those who, similar to yourself, are just becoming familiar with the business. Attend a trade show or conference and the manner in which you conduct business will change significantly.

"Conferences are about meeting people, creating relationships and absorbing the collective knowledge and energy of your peers."

Louis Jay Meyers
founder,
SXSW, LMNOP, A2A
Conferences

A Variety Of Conferences To Attend

There are conferences that cater to specific genres of music, different levels of music, varieties of performance types and

> "Each year, more than 3,500 performing arts professionals from around the world meet and network at the Arts Presenters Members Conference, enjoying performances, workshops and inspiring dialogue in addition to participating in a global trade show and marketplace. The Conference, the largest in North America, is an exciting opportunity to explore important arts industry issues, conduct business and gain professional and leadership development guidance."
>
> Sandra Gibson
> President, CEO
> Association of Performing Arts Presenters (Arts Presenters)

> "One of the biggest mistakes that I made in getting started was to go to one conference. I should have gone to six that first year. Now we go to 25 a year. You really should just jump in."
>
> Charlotte Britton
> former agent, owner,
> Britton Management

> "The Cutting Edge Music Business Conference, started in 1992 and is held annually, in New Orleans, Louisiana. It provides a forum for musicians, record executives, publishers, promoters, attorneys, managers and anyone interested in finding out more about the business and share information and ideas."
>
> Eric Cager
> executive director,
> Cutting Edge Music Business Conference
> Music Business Institute

specific performance venues. You can attend a conference geared to the college market, the rock genre, the folk genre, performance art, theater, children's performances, etc. Each conference offers the participating artists an opportunity to present themselves to the promoters, media or recording representatives. Selecting and attending an appropriately-suited conference will enhance your booking efforts.

When I first attended the Association of Performing Arts Presenters (APAP) conference in New York City, I was overwhelmed by the size. I quickly realized that my world—working in isolation while attempting to book my artists—was about to bust wide open. That one conference expanded my view of the new venue possibilities which existed for my artists. I began attending regional conferences as well as exploring other appropriate trade shows suited for the artists I represented. *The most important lesson I learned from my conference attendance was that I was not alone.* I had allies who were willing to share their information, their expertise and help me along my path. Just knowing that I no longer needed to operate in a vacuum was worth the registration fees.

Expanding Your Markets

As a self-booking artist, one of the toughest challenges to your career is to catch the attention of the promoters booking the venues you want to play. Many promoters booking the larger venues are wary of dealing directly with artists, especially unknown artists. This places you at a disadvantage. By attending a booking conference, an artist has the potential for personal contact and the opportunity to begin building a working relationship with some of these promoters. The conference allows a self-booking artist to begin to level the field with the other booking agents. Equalizing the competition is unlikely. But, personalizing the contacts may at least get your future calls answered or returned.

An artist need not be limited to only one type of conference. Many conferences overlap genres and purposes, concentrate on particular areas of the country or world, and may often target one specific aspect of an artist's career. For example, you may attend numerous regional conferences that focus on the college market and may also attend a genre-specific conference such as the International Bluegrass Music Association (IBMA) to reach those connected with that industry. By overlapping a variety of conferences, you expand your potential performance opportunities. It is not uncommon for promoters, media and industry representatives to also follow conferences that encompass all of their interests. The act they discover at one conference may not attend another. Artists and presenters alike take advantage of the opportunities that most directly address their concerns.

Their limitations to multiple-conference attendance are, like yours, often related to budget.

Once again, this discussion begs another review of your ten-year plan. Selecting conferences to attend and organizations to join will be logically directed by your long-term goals. Matching conference attendance with your event time line will enhance your experience. Attend a conference simply to understand all that it offers so that you might prepare properly for a future event. A first-time event will often help move you along your time line by providing important information and skills development.

Benefits Of Attending Conferences
- Workshops and panels provide you with an opportunity to address your current career challenges with those who have solutions.
- Industry professionals are available to enhance your skill level.
- Individuals working in your targeted area of interest become accessible for the first time.
- Targeted industry is introduced to your act for the first time.
- New information becomes available and knowledge of new contact lists expands your booking possibilities.
- Evaluate your position in the market by gauging your competition.
- Opportunities to develop new colleagues awaken possibilities for projects and collaborations.

Two Types Of Conferences
Conferences cater to many varieties of interests within the entertainment industry. There are essentially two categories of conference: Those requiring membership in the organization presenting the conference and those only requiring conference registration but no organizational membership.

Membership-Driven Organizational Conference
An organizational conference is usually held annually and provides the organization's membership with a fun and productive way to meet, learn from each other and conduct business. Attending one of these conferences generally requires membership in the organization. Conference-only attendance is possible in some instances but the attendee will be charged a nonmember registration fee which is higher than that of a member. Some examples of conference-sponsoring organizations are: International Bluegrass Music Association (IBMA), National Association of College Activities (NACA), Association of Performing Arts Presenters (APAP), the Folk Alliance and Canadian Arts Presenting Association/L'Association Canadienne des Organismes Artistiques (CAPACOA). Refer to the resource section for contact information.

> "For me, the best thing about the Folk Alliance conference was meeting, face-to-face, the radio DJs that I had corresponded with over time . . . I felt as if I was meeting an old friend for the first time in person!"
>
> **Lorin Grean**
> harpist, vocalist, composer,
> Silver Wave Records

> "I look at a conference from the standpoint of who is going to be there. What is my purpose in going? What do I hope to accomplish by simply meeting people? What seeds am I planting for longer-term relationships?"
>
> **Andrew McKnight**
> singer, songwriter

> "Most music industry organizations like IBMA are member led, and offer not only member services to the masses, but leadership opportunities. The routine benefits and services you receive through a trade organization are worth much more than your annual dues, but more important is the opportunity to work with others to help shape the future of the music and careers far beyond your own."
>
> **Dan Hays**
> executive director,
> IBMA

Membership in the organization entitles you to benefits that are geared towards enhancing your growth and participation in the field. Memberships may have dues structures based on various categories. Often these organizations will host either one annual conference or a series of regional conferences along with the annual event. As a touring artist, it is invaluable to become a member in a national organization which hosts regional events. Your access to those in your industry nationally, as well as regionally, can build your recognition on multiple levels.

Non-Membership-Driven Conference

These conferences exist as a business whose sole purpose is to present its conference, although some provide additional support activities. Examples of these types of conferences are South by Southwest (SXSW), North by Northeast (NXNE), MIDEM, and Association for the Promotion of Campus Activities (APCA) to name a few. All of these conferences are found in this chapter's resource section. Each conference functions on behalf of their targeted audience. There are no membership dues only the conference registration, exhibiting and showcasing fees where appropriate. By participating in one of these conferences, a performing artist has an opportunity to expand their current audience and broaden the scope of their current industry recognition.

Regional Events

As an artist who concentrates your touring in one particular region, attending one of the national conferences can put you in touch with a number of presenters who work within your region. These initial contacts can then open doors to regional events, conferences and showcases. I have attended a number of national organizational conferences which eventually led me to smaller regional conferences. The regional events were more closely suited to my artist's touring goals at that time.

If the conference is regional, it provides the perfect opportunity to expand within that region. At a national or international conference, the opportunities for expansion are multiplied. The efforts that would be expended in developing the contacts for these regions with individual mailings and phone calls are condensed physically and financially into a single event. The costs associated with registration and showcasing are often far outweighed by the value of the first-hand personal connections.

> "The Southern Arts Federation's Performing Arts Exchange, (formerly the Southern Arts Exchange), provides presenters with the methodology to present traditional performing art genres such as gospel, bluegrass, blues, traditional dance and storytelling. The PAE conference also provides traditional artists with the opportunity to showcase, attend professional development workshops and network with colleagues."
>
> **Teresa Hollingsworth**
> program coordinator,
> traditional arts,
> Southern Arts Federation

Memberships

Membership in one or more of these organizations can launch your career. Do not delay joining. The fees for memberships and conference attendance can vary from year to year ranging from very low to many thousands of dollars. After looking through the resource section, call those organizations that are of interest to get their current materials. Once you have examined each of the various offerings, you can determine which, if any, will suit your current level of development. Try one at a time and budget for the fees and the dues. View this as an investment in your business. Plan well in advance to take advantage of all the benefits membership offers.

Long-Time Attendees Reap Benefits

Make a commitment to attend a specific conference for at least two or three years. Long-time attendees often reap the rewards of their previous year's attendance the next year. Usually, newcomers need to prove their interest and commitment to the sponsoring organization and earn the respect and trust of the membership by attending for a few years. Attendance for just one year may not truly accomplish your potential goals. Conferences demand a longer-term financial and emotional commitment before realizing satisfactory booking returns. If the sponsoring organization gives you access to your target audience, they will take notice of your active participation.

It took two full years of attending APAP before I began to see the returns from my investment. The promoters that I met during the first year returned to my booth the second year and showed an increased interest. They were not only interested in the performers I represented but also showed an interest in my organization because I was there for a second year and third year. My continued attendance demonstrated stability and helped them to develop trust in my artists and my company. It is so important for presenters to have confidence in the acts they book and the agents with whom they work. They want to know that an act booked now will still be touring when their performance date comes around. Attending the same conference year after year reinforces that relationship.

Enhancing Your Conference Experience

Each conference offers its attendees a number of tools which will help in your self-promotion. Each new promotion tool carries with it an additional expense. Consider each of the promotional tools discussed below when gathering information for each conference. Weigh the costs of each tool and compare one conference's costs with another. If you have determined that a specific conference meets all of your career goals and gives you access to your market, take advantage of a multitude of opportunities at a single conference to enhance your visibility and your career's viability.

Showcasing

A showcase offers an artist the opportunity to demonstrate their talents to the people within their industry. They have

> "I get to hear what the hot-button issues are in education and cultural tourism and see ways that I can connect to them. I learn about potential alliances, relationships and presenters that I can interact with down the line."
>
> **Andrew McKnight**
> singer, songwriter

> "The best thing about showcasing is that it gives people a chance to see exactly what you do. Showcasing has been a great way for me to communicate with programmers. I would never have been able to alert people to my sound and quality of performance in any other way."
>
> **Greg Howard**
> composer, Chapman Stick performer

> "We recently showcased at the Northwest Presenter's Conference in Coeur d'Alene, Idaho. We paid for airfare and hotels. I paid the guys in my band and really made a commitment. I probably spent $1,000 for the possibility of getting some bookings in that region. It worked out really well for us. All of these northwest presenters were there to see us and now we have got at least three tours booked. That thousand-dollar outlay was really worth it."
>
> **Laurie Lewis**
> musician

> "Without the conference showcases, some groups may never have the opportunity to show their wares to presenters outside their home region."
>
> Dan DeWayne
> artistic director,
> Chico & California World Music Festivals

> "Laura Love showcased at the Folk Alliance. She did the best showcase she could do but the sound was awful and the show was running late. If an artist really has charisma and if it is something that is really true and genuine, it comes through. Bad sound is not going to keep a good artist down. And, as a direct result of that showcase, she got the Vancouver, Edmonton and Mariposa festivals and that just opened up all the touring possibilities for her. It was worth everything we spent emotionally and financially."
>
> Mary McFaul
> manager, Laura Love Band,
> McFaul Booking & Management

> "It's almost critical that the artist send a video, cued to the best piece, with their press kit when applying to a showcase. If the artist knows anyone on the showcase selection committee, they should send their information to that committee member."
>
> Maranne Welch
> International Showcase of Performing Arts For Young People

the chance to be seen by presenters, record companies, media, agencies and managers as well as fans.

Showcasing at a trade event can begin industry recognition of your act which is important when it comes time to actually do the bookings. Booking festivals, as well as most other performance venue types, is easier once the act has been seen. If an act impresses those in the industry who are seasoned in experiencing new talent, there is more of a chance that the act will impress a general audience. The promoter is more enthusiastic about giving the act an opportunity at their venue after they have witnessed an audience's reaction.

For example:
I had just begun working with Canadian artist Ferron. Previous to our working together, she was selected to showcase at a Folk Alliance Conference. Many who attended were familiar with her music and her songwriting but had not seen her perform live recently or at all. With just three songs, she presented a stunning showcase and it became the topic of discussion at the conference and on the Internet for many months to follow. Her showcase reintroduced her to an entire industry of professionals which then prompted multiple festival and venue bookings.

That is the upside. On the downside, I have also seen showcases where the performer has an off night or the sound is bad and the showcase does little for the performer. In one instance, an act had really poor sound and it seemed to ruin the showcase. It became an ongoing topic of discussion where most attendees felt the artist was a victim of the circumstance. The final result seemed to work in the artist's behalf anyway since the discussion about the event still helped to promote the artist. The situation enabled the artist to have a fabulous fall tour and continue to move forward in her career.

The Juried Showcase

Most conferences host juried showcases. Artists submit an application which a selection committee reviews. They choose artists which satisfy their showcase criteria. Those artists then have the opportunity to present their act before the conference attendees. All of the showcases throughout the conference will most often take place under the same showcase conditions, i.e., same hall, sound, lights, staging, etc. However, a number of conferences, such as SXSW, feature a variety of showcase venues. The performance environment may work for one artist and be detrimental to another. The key is to prepare for your showcase.

Some conferences, such as NACA and APCA, cater to the college market. While NACA showcases will include major acts presented by some of the larger agencies which command some hefty fees, the Association for the Promotion of

Campus Activities (APCA) focuses their attention on acts that command fees between $1,000 and $2,500 per night. They have devised a showcase plan that guarantees each exhibiting artist a showcase, if selected. This conference caters to a smaller group of attendees which reduces the competition among showcasing artists and increases the amount of business conducted.

Some conferences are specifically designed to showcase artists to the music industry and media. 2NMC, SXSW and NXNE are three examples of these showcase-focused conferences. Applications and showcase fees are submitted and then acts are selected by committee. Performance venues vary. Some performances take place in a club situation, some in ballrooms, others in theaters. Here again, the individual circumstance can make or break your showcase.

These showcase-focused conferences develop mainstream industry recognition by the media. Record companies and artist representatives look to sign new talent. The attendance by presenters has grown in the last few years, but these conferences are industry and media events rather than performance-booking events. These are the select conferences to attend when you are ready to shop for a label, an agent or a manager, and begin to create that media "buzz" for your act. *Success at one of these media conferences can increase your value in the marketplace and propel your career forward.*

Do-It-Yourself Showcases

Many conferences offer agents, artists, record companies and organizations the opportunity to schedule and plan their own showcase at a time specifically designated within the main body of the conference. The expense of arranging for the room, sound and lights (if any) and publicizing the event is left up to the showcase presenter, you. Most conferences promote the showcases in the conference program book. They may charge a nominal fee for this service. They charge a nominal fee for this service. Depending on the availability and variety of venues, these showcases can take place in hotel rooms, ballrooms, clubs, theaters, churches and, sometimes, even hallways. This type of presentation has enhanced the showcasing experience for both the artist and the industry representatives.

Present A Professional Performance

To benefit from any of these showcase situations, an artist must be prepared to perform in less than optimum circumstances. If you are presenting your own showcase and have control over the environment, you are at an advantage. The key here is not the performance environment but your performance. Since the variety of circumstances can present a challenge, it is up to you

"The APCA conference has, as one of its basics tenets, the concept of a showcase being offered to every booth sold. We have a formal screening process but anyone not accepted will receive a full refund of any fees paid. This approach helps artists that are new to the market, giving them an opportunity to submit for a college-market showcase without having to buy a non-refundable booth."

Eric Lambert
executive director, APCA

"SXSW is the sort of conference that you get out of it what you put into it. It is not a place where somebody is going to have something magical happen. Instead, SXSW is the kind of place where we provide the infrastructure and, if you provide an opportunity, you can make something happen. People who can make things happen for you will be here. What you do with that is up to you."

Brent Grulke
creative director, SXSW

"Play at a convenient time. Don't play at one in the morning. If you have a choice, play earlier rather than later. If you have a choice between playing at five in the afternoon or one in the morning, you might think it's cooler to play at 1:00 a.m., but agents, managers and A & R people are going to be tired and burnt out, get people when they're fresh."

Steve Martin
agent, partner,
The Agency Group

> **HotTip:** 🌶
> "Make sure you know who is coming, introduce yourself while you are there, and close the "sale" after you get back home. If you don't make those follow-up calls after the event, you have probably wasted the effort."
>
> Dan Hays
> executive director,
> IBMA

to have your showcase presentation tightly rehearsed and professionally presented. Crumbling under the strain of the adverse conditions says little for your performance durability. Everyone has an off time. Prepare yourself diligently to make the most out of every showcase opportunity. Select material that you are comfortable performing.

If you have a chance to do a sound check, meet the tech crew, adjust lighting or rehearse in the space, take it! The more comfortable you are with the situation, the better your performance will be.

I had such a chance during the Tucson Folk Alliance conference. I prearranged for my act to work with the sound technician during one of his down times in order to adjust their special stereo microphones. He was interested in the new technique. He had worked previously with my artist and gave us an extra hour with the hall and the equipment. The result—their sound was the best sound that entire night. The act's performance preparation and their technical excellence resulted in a record deal.

These opportunities are not always available. Whatever extra time you can get in sound check, use it to your greatest advantage. If there is no extra time on the technical end, plan ample rehearsal time to have your set down cold. Rehearse the entire performance, even the patter in between songs, so that it fits the available time for your showcase. Showcase times often run from ten to twenty minutes. Some events may even provide for a full forty-five minute set to one hour.

Promote Your Showcase

Even when the presenting organization publicizes your showcase in official conference material, it is your responsibility to enhance their promotions. You've gone to great efforts for this showcase opportunity, let those people you specifically want to attend know where and when you'll be performing. There's no guarantee that they'll show, but your chances are greater if they have received an invitation. These invites are taken seriously. Many presenters plan their days and evenings carefully to schedule each showcase. With the Internet, faxes and postcards, an artist can quickly and cheaply notify attendees of their event. The conference organizer often provides an advanced list of those attending. Look through the advance materials and target those individuals you want to receive notice of your showcase.

Prior to many conferences, I am inundated with postcards, flyers, faxes and, now, e-mail notices from artists, agents and showcase sponsors. The deluge usually begins a month before the conference. I keep all notices in a file and create a schedule, blocking out times and rooms where those I am interested in seeing will be performing. Most of us in the industry take note of new names, looking for the next

> *"This year we showcased unsigned artists from thirty-three states and four countries. After six years, quality over quantity is still our secret to success."*
>
> Mark Willis
> partner,
> Atlantis Music Conference

> *"The extra time and care afforded us by the sound technician allowed us to enter our showcase situation confident that our sound was under control."*
>
> Freyda Epstein
> violinist, vocalist, teacher, producer,
> formerly, Freyda & Acoustic Attatude

artist with that "buzz."

Exhibiting

Whether or not you are selected to showcase, or choose to do so privately, renting a space in the conference exhibition hall will enhance your conference experience. Again, there is usually an exhibit fee. Most conferences offer exhibit space in the form of a booth which is six feet by eight feet with a six foot draped table with two chairs. Some conferences offer exhibit space with just a six-foot draped table with two chairs at a reduced fee. This format is perfectly suited for the self-booking artist with a fixed budget.

The exhibit hall allows you to establish a home base and let those you want to meet know where you will be. Exhibit halls are designed to create a flow of people through the hall to sample the exhibitor's wares. It is a perfect opportunity to have brief introductory conversations. The exhibition hall provides a great promotional opportunity to distribute an informative showcase handout along with samples of music and press materials.

Examine The Displays

Exploring the exhibit hall allows a newcomer the chance to examine the other exhibitors' displays and promotional materials. Take notice of them—some are very elaborate and often costly, yet, others are simple and creative. What works for one exhibitor may not for another. The challenge for the first-time exhibitor is to witness the way in which others use their space to conduct business, socialize and display their products. Once you develop a feel for the space and the experience, you will be better able to use the format to its greatest affect. Generally, most get the hang of it after a day or two. These events might often last for three or four consecutive days.

Effective Exhibit-Hall Planning

The exhibit hall can be a demanding experience for those unprepared. If you choose not to exhibit the first time, make the most out of the exhibit hall by following these suggestions.
- Review the descriptions about the exhibitors once you have received the conference materials. Attendees receive a list of exhibitors and their corresponding booth or table numbers along with a map of the exhibit hall.
- Note any exhibitors that interest you, for whatever reason. You may want to visit agent booths to see how they represent their artists and note the most effective displays.
- Stroll through the entire hall. Note displays that interest you during the first exhibit-hall session and indicate their numbers in the program guide.

> **HotTip:** The expense of exhibiting is offset by the personal contact made with those in the industry. Exhibit halls provide a valuable space to conduct business and make introductory presentations.

"I would encourage artists to attend one year to simply see what others do that created the benefits that they would like to emulate."

Dan Hays
executive director,
IBMA

"In general, music conferences are of real benefit to independent artists because they get you directly in touch with a lot of people within a short amount of time. These people are often not very accessible and a conference is a great way to jumpstart the relationship. Because they are attending, they have more time to talk than normal."

Dave Hooper
co-organizer,
2NMC, New Nashville Music Conference

> **HotTip:** 🌶
> Use large graphics that can be viewed easily from a distance to create booth and table displays. Photo enlargements and poster displays are often very effective.

- Visit the displays that you have noted and spend some time at each of them during the second session. Note their graphics, their handouts, perhaps even their name to understand what attracted you to the display on your first walk through.
- Visit those exhibitors whose descriptions were of interest to you when first reading the conference materials during the next session.
- See as much of the rest of the hall as possible using the remaining exhibit sessions. Ask exhibitors if they would mind if you took a sample of their materials. I suggest asking for samples, because the materials were created at some expense and are for industry representatives, not other performers. When you have your exhibit, you will be very conscious of who takes your material. Some exhibitors, especially those representing merchandisers, records companies, festivals, promoters and organizations, are more than happy to freely share their materials. They are attending to specifically get the word out about their product or event.

Once you have experienced an exhibit hall as outlined above, you will be well prepared to create the display and handout materials for your own exhibit.

Creating Your Display

As you will notice at any conference that you attend, exhibit displays vary. They range from homemade to factory-made, from low-budget to extremely expensive. Depending on the type of conference or trade show that you are attending, the exhibits tend to match the trade show and the expected attendees. For instance, those exhibiting at the Folk Alliance, the IBMA and some of the regional NACA conferences tend to reflect a more homemade creativity and are often less costly productions. Those at APAP, for instance, are often displays purchased in part or in whole from exhibit-manufacturing companies. Some displays include lighting, shelves, banners and draperies. Almost anything goes and anything can make a creative, engaging exhibit.

I have seen very effective displays created with colorful blankets, tapestries and cloth. These elements lend a thematic flavor using colors and images from various regions of the country or from around the world. I have had quilts made to serve as a table drape and coordinated the colors to match all of my promotional materials. Some people enlarge photographs to life-size and mount them to stand next to their booths. Others play with lighting and three-dimensional displays, while others incorporate slide shows, video displays and audiotape playbacks. The options are endless.

Create your exhibit so that it is useful for a number of

> *"Pacific Contact is Canada's West Coast premier booking conference and trade show featuring over fifty main stage and independent showcases and sales spotlights for artists. It is a great way to network, book tours and learn about the business, all while having fun."*
>
> **Joanna Maratta,**
> executive director,
> British Columbia Touring Council

different conferences. Plan to spend some money when designing a booth display because you want your display to represent you well at all of the conferences you choose to attend. Decide which conferences you want to attend in the next two years after examining the materials from those organizations. For example, if you decide to attend the Folk Alliance and the IBMA, create one display that fits your budget now since it will work at both conferences. Be as elaborate as your budget permits. If, however, you decide to join the Folk Alliance and also want to join APAP, design a more upscale display to suit APAP's arts-presenter attendees. The display will then work well at every other conference.

Guidelines For Building An Effective Exhibit

- Design exhibit displays suitable for the most expensive conference you will attend. APAP, Association of Performing Arts Presenters is likely to be the most expensive of the performance-booking conferences. APAP exhibitors are some of the largest agencies booking theater, dance and the performance arts in the country, as well as smaller agencies along with individual artists.
- Create a color scheme.
- Incorporate bold graphics with word and photographic enlargements for visual impact. The distance from the backdrop to the front of the table is too far to read small-printed reviews or other matter.
- Use felt or felt-like materials as backdrops to make assembly and breakdown of displays quick and simple.
- Use Velcro tabs on enlarged photos or display items to hang easily on a felt backdrop.
- Use banners as a classy, effective method of creating a simple, yet attractive display.
- Offer giveaway items, such as buttons, pens, bumper stickers and, even, food to help attract attendees to your exhibit and keep them there for a few minutes. I became famous for my hazelnut coffee at the IBMA trade show. People flocked to my booth as the aroma wafted throughout the hall.
- Video- and audio-playback systems allow attendees to sample your performance and attract attention. Equipment rentals are often available from the exhibit hall company, the hotel where the conference is being held or, in some cities, from recommended local vendors. If you do not have your own portable equipment, these rental deals reduce your travel burdens while allowing you to present a professional display at reasonable costs.
- Mount photos and other graphics on lightweight materials such as foamcore or foam board. It keeps the photos from bending and is easily carried. These materials are readily available at art-supply stores for costs ranging from $4 up

HotTip: Add lights to a display to create a visual impact and attract attention.

"Everybody's giving the buyers their promo material and the buyers' bags get bigger and heavier and when they get home they throw it in a corner and don't even want to deal with it. I sent my press kit the next week, first class, and it is the only thing they got that day."

Mike Williams
singer, songwriter

"When dealing with conferences or conventions, keep your expectations realistic. Remember that a great number of the attendees have been there a long time and you must earn their respect before you can play their reindeer games. But, someday you will be the old-timer!"

Louis Jay Meyers
founder,
SXSW, LMNOP, A2A
Conferences

> **HotTip:** 🌶
> Create displays that are easily and quickly assembled and disassembled. Use felt and velcro to apply and remove graphic elements.

"Do anything to differentiate yourself—I used to skate around the exhibit hall on roller skates."

Mike Williams
singer, songwriter

"Patience on the artist side is important, especially after I return from a booking conference. Many fall conferences do not develop into to gigs until January. Some book a year in advance, so it takes awhile for them to plan their year."

Chris Fletcher
CEO, Coast to Coast Music Booking, manager, promotional consultant, instructor, Music Business

to $10 per sheet depending upon the size. I buy the larger sheets—20" x 32" or 20" x 42"—and then cut multiple boards to the appropriate sizes. Depending on the number of items intended for mounting, one large sheet is often enough.

❖ Size any display materials so they can be easily carried or shipped. If materials are carried, make sure they are packed to fit in an overhead airline bin or in a very sturdy case that you feel comfortable checking with your luggage. Arriving at the conference with a bent or destroyed display is not a good way to kick off your exhibit experience. I was able to pack all of my booth displays in a sturdy garment bag. It fit in the overhead bin when flying.

If you decide to have a display created for you by one of the many exhibit production companies, check your local phone book first. I have referenced some display manufacturers in the resource section of this chapter. If you notice a factory-made display at a conference that seems interesting, ask the exhibitor for the manufacturer's name.

Exhibiting at a conference has all the potential of boosting your career up another notch on your goal ladder. It requires planning and a certain amount of commitment to attend any of the conferences more than once. As you become more familiar with those who attend each conference, you are able to gear the displays and materials to that audience. The more conferences you attend, the more familiar you become to the attendees. That familiarity eventually leads to working relationships and performance dates.

Networking At Industry Events

Networking is one of the keys to your success. So many of us working outside major agencies have often experienced a sense of isolation because we work on our own. One of the greatest benefits that attending an industry trade show or event offers a self-booking artist is contact with others who are also developing their careers. Conferences provide the venue where artists like yourself can share your experiences, successes and challenges. It is in this environment that one person's triumph can be the answer to another person's most burning question. Finding others who have been where you are now and are willing to share valuable advice, contacts and information is why networking is so powerful. Where once you were reinventing the wheel, now you know someone who already has the exact information you need. That sense of having to work in isolation is diminished. You return from a conference with new resolve, new resources and a renewed enthusiasm for your work.

I have found that my conference plans kept me creative. Each year I would present my artists in a fresh light to attendees. Every new conference held promise of potentially new contacts and fresh opportunities as well as a way to help me determine exactly how my business was positioned within that market. Viewing my business in reference to similar operations kept me alert to new trends aware of my colleagues' advancements and my competitors' advantages. A conference opens a window to the industry in which you hope to thrive.

Guidelines To Effective Networking

Discovering other performers or agents who work in a similar genre or tour similar venues can open new collaborative possibilities. The ability to interact, in person, with all of those industry representatives and presenters in a comfortable, cooperative atmosphere is one of the prime benefits of networking. I offer some simple guidelines to making the most out of your conference opportunity to network.

- Be open and flexible to new opportunities.
- Be friendly.
- Have business cards available at all times and remember to keep them well stocked.
- Be prepared to learn and absorb as much new information as possible.
- Be prepared to trade information. You may have some very valuable insights to share.
- Learn the art of schmoozing. The term applies perfectly to these conference situations where you are always "talking shop." Finally you have a chance to talk about your field and your work with others that absolutely understand, can empathize and help.
- Be very courteous of the others attempting to accomplish agendas similar to yours.
- Be available for impromptu meetings, jam sessions and social gatherings.

After-Hours Socializing

The majority of the formal and informal business conducted at these industry events takes place in after-hours social settings. Seek out these informal situations and participate. You never know who might be listening or willing to share some new ideas over lunch or a drink. I have conducted more business in some of these informal meeting places where conversations flow more easily than in some of the more established sites like the exhibit hall.

Take advantage of:
- Meetings in hotel bars and restaurants. They are opportunities to break down the formal barriers and get to know those who share your business.
- Hospitality suites sponsored by an individual or company. They offer unique gathering spaces to meet and talk with

"To know the road ahead, ask those coming back."

Chinese proverb

"Conferences sponsored by the regional arts organization are outstanding places to network, both with presenters and with agents and artists. Through the exhibit hall and the many social events, you will have an excellent opportunity to 'get to know' each other and to talk about arts in both a professional and casual atmosphere. The value of networking cannot be overstated in this business."

I. B. Dent
interim director,
Gertrude C. Ford Performing
Arts Center

conference attendees. Sometimes impromptu jam sessions occur which add to the party atmosphere.

❖ Jam sessions which take place in hotel rooms as well as hotel hallways and lobbies. Be prepared to join in. Other musicians talk about with whom they have enjoyed playing. Word spreads among attendees about an artist from those listening on the sidelines or playing in the session. Interesting collaborations may surface between new acquaintances. I have seen songwriters form partnerships after an evening of song-swapping and musicians from one musical genre join forces with another to plant the seeds for a new album project.

> "There were a lot of artists who showcased and set up booths and were representing themselves. I spoke to one guy and he said he does it every year and it works out really well for him. He doesn't showcase anymore. He just goes to the conference and schmooses and gets hired."
>
> Laurie Lewis
> musician

Additional Promotional Tools

Within the framework of any conference, there are built-in conference amenities that you can also take advantage of to aid with your promotion.

Advertising

Every conference will provide its attendees with a conference program book as well as a directory of attendees. Advertising is often the source of funds paying for the printing of these conference books. Ad rates are offered by the conference organizer. Advertising your act in one of these conference books assures you of reaching everyone in attendance. If you know where your booth will be, include that in your ad. As a member of an organization, you may also use advertising to promote the act, even if you are unable to attend the conference that year. These books are referenced often by those you are attempting to reach. The costs for advertising in many conference books are usually reasonable. When budgets are tight and your personal attendance at a conference is hampered, a well-designed ad can serve as your emissary.

> "Become part of the culture in which you want to participate. It is not about where you are going to find this gig or that gig. You have to start figuring out who the people are, who the players are. You do that by attending conferences and going to showcases. That is where you will find everybody who is working professionally. As you go to these events and meet people, you become part of the fabric."
>
> Mary McFaul
> manager

Sponsorships

Many conferences seek donations in the form of sponsorships from its members to help pay for conference functions and amenities. The sponsor is given additional recognition for their event sponsorship—a benefit which creates multiple name recognition opportunities.

I served as sponsorship chair for the Folk Alliance conference for three years. During that time, I solicited organizations and individuals who wanted to promote their companies to those attending the conference in a more elaborate manner. Some companies sponsored major events attended by the entire membership, others sponsored events on a smaller scale. Each sponsor used their sponsorship dollar to buy themselves a larger presence at the conference while assisting the organization to pay the bills.

If you have the budget and the creativity, you can work

with the sponsorship chair at most conferences to design a program tailored to you while helping the organization with their necessities. The visibility of sponsoring a major conference event, such as a luncheon, cocktail party, showcase or workshop presentation, can establish your company's credibility within the industry. Your efforts will be appreciated by the organization and the industry will recognize your existence.

Item Inserts

For an additional fee, attendees can place giveaway items into an official conference bag that includes the program book and other important conference materials. This goodie bag insures that every attendee receives something from you. However, this can be a costly promotional tool. In the case of CDs or press kits, this could get expensive unless you work out a great deal with your manufacturer or record label. Some conferences hand out 5,000 bags. Consider your costs for each item placed in the bag as well as the insertion fees charged by the organization. Those fees alone may range from $300 to $1,000.

Speaker Or Panelist

Even though you may be new to the field, the industry and to conference attendance, you may have some expertise to offer other attendees. Workshops and panels often cover a broad spectrum of topics in an effort to address the many concerns of the attendees. Consider your background of experience. Perhaps you have something to offer. Ask for a copy of the previous year's program book and familiarize yourself with past offerings. Submit your ideas to the conference organizer. By participating in a workshop or panel, you can increase your visibility.

I participated in various panel presentations by discussing such topics of interest as how to create effective promotional packages and booking techniques. The workshops were appreciated and I was able to establish my place within the industry. The added recognition further helped my business grow.

Conclusion

Attending a conference can be a costly investment considering travel, hotel, meals and conference fees. However, it will be a worthwhile investment because it is one of the fastest routes to directly accessing the people who you need to know in order to advance your career. You may not land the record deal or book the tour of the century right away, but you will become familiar with the industry. You will create a network of contacts and increase your knowledge of how to conduct your business more efficiently and effectively.

HotTip: Design ads for their visual impact as well as their message content. This is your opportunity to reach all of the conference attendees. Let them know your booth number. Make it count.

"I love to speak on and moderate panels. It requires me to be extremely well informed about the current state of the industry, gives me the opportunity to share and give back, and also brings more attention to my work and career as an artist. Plus, it puts me right up there with the people that I want to meet, making my own conference goals much easier to achieve."

RAVI
singer, songwriter,
former guitarist for triple
GRAMMY nominee, Hanson

> **HotTip:**
> Ask those in attendance what kind of workshop they would like to see at next year's conference and organize a panel around that topic. Submit your workshop ideas early in the programming process.

Summary

- Conferences expand your resources, thereby expanding your career.
- Conferences enable you to target your best potential audience.
- Conference attendance requires advance planning and budgeting.
- Showcase opportunities enable you to demonstrate your performance to those professionals who have the potential to advance your career with bookings, media reviews, label signings, or possible agent and management deals.
- Showcase performances require your utmost attention to professionalism regardless of the performance environment or the challenges of the moment.
- Conference exhibit halls provide another tool which enables you to promote your act to those within your field.
- Networking offers you the chance to meet new colleagues, gain personal contact with those who can influence your career, and build upon your skills and knowledge of your field.

Resources

Books:

How To Work A Room: Learn Strategies of Savvy Socializing For Business and Personal Success
Susan Roane
Warner Books
ISBN: 0446390658

Make Your Connections Count:
The Six-Step System To Build Your Meganetwork
Melissa Giovagnoli
Dearborn Trade
ISBN: 079311151X

Power Schmoosing: The New Etiquette For Social and Business Success
Terri Mandell
McGraw Hill
ISBN: 0070398879
Phone: 1-800-262-4729
Phone: 212-512-4729

Networking In The Music Industry:
How To Open The Doors to Success In The Music Business
Jim Clevo
Rockpress Publishing Company
ISBN: 096270136X

Networking In The Music Business
Dan Kimpel
Writer's Digest Books
ISBN: 0898795974

Display Manufacturers:

Downing Displays
550 TechneCenter Drive
Milford, OH 45150-2785
Phone: 1-800-883-1800
Web: http://www.downingdisplays.com

Displays2go
55 Broad Common Rd.
Bristol, RI 02809
Phone: 1-800-572-2194
Fax: 401-247-0392
Web: http://www.displays2go.com

Nimlok Company
7420 North Lehigh Avenue
Niles, IL 60714
Phone: 1-800-233-8870
web: http://www.nimlok.com

Nimlok Canada Ltd.
315 Esna Park Avenue
Markham, Ontario L3R 1H4
Phone: 416-798-7201
web: http://www.nimlok.com/ca/

Skyline Displays
3355 Discovery Road
St. Paul, MN 55121
Phone: 1-800-328-2725
Fax: 651-234-6571
Web: http://www.skylinedisplays.com

Membership Organizations Presenting Conferences:

APAP—Association of Performing Arts Presenters
1112 16th Street NW, Suite 400
Washington, DC 20036
Phone: 202-833-2787
Fax: 202-833-1543
E-mail: info@artspresenters.org
Web: http://www.artspresenters.org
Mid-January—annual conference New York City.
Regional Conferences:
Late August—WAA, Western Arts Alliance
 Association
Mid-September—MAC, Midwest Arts Conference
Late September—PAE, Performing Arts Exchange
See Chapter 12, Funding, for regional organization contact information or call APAP for details on the current year's regional conferences.

Alberta Showcase
Arts Touring Alliance of Alberta
Arts Development Branch
901 Standard Life Centre
10405 Jasper Avenue
Edmonton, Alberta T5J 4R7
Phone: 780-420-0604
E-mail: info@artstouring.com
Web: http://www.artstouring.com
Mid-October—annual showcase, exhibit, artists' directory, presenters' profile.
Showcase music, theater, dance and performing arts.
Membership required.

Arts Northwest
P.O. Box 1354
Port Angeles, WA 98362
Phone: 360-457-9290; Fax: 360-457-9294
Web: http://www.artsnw.org
October-November—annual conference, trade show, showcases for theater, arts council presenters in Washington, Idaho and Oregon.
Showcase performing arts, theater, music, performance for children.
Membership required.

CAPACOA—Canadian Arts Presenting Association/L'Association Canadienne des Organismes Artistiques
17 York Street, Suite 200
Ottawa, Ontario K1N 9J6
Canada
Phone: 613-562-3515
Fax: 613-562-4005
E-mail: mail@capacoa.ca
Web: http://www.capacoa.ca
Annual arts presenters conference, showcases
Showcase music, theater, dance.

Cinars
International Exchange for the Arts
3575, Saint-Laurent #216
Montreal, Quebec H2X 2T7
Canada
Phone: 514-842-5866
Fax: 514-843-3168
E-mail: arts@cinars.org
Web: http://www.cinars.org
Late November-Early December—International conference, held in Montreal focusing on developing international performance markets.
Showcase dance, music, theatre, multimedia and multidiscipline.

CMJ Music Marathon, Music Fest & FilmFest
College Music Journal
151 W. 25th St., 12th floor
New York, NY 10001
Phone: 917-606-1908
Fax: 917-606-1914
E-mail: marathon@cmj.com
Web: http://www.cmj.com
Oct.-Nov.—conference, showcase in New York City.
Showcase all genres of music.
Subscription available to journal, college radio chart reports.

Folk Alliance
PO Box 285
Memphis, TN 38101
Phone: 901-522-1170
Fax: 901-522-1172
E-mail: fa@folk.org
Web: http://www.folkalliance.net
Mid-February—annual international folk music and dance conference in Memphis, TN.
Regional annual conferences: Northeast, Midwest, Southwest.
Showcase folk, acoustic, world, ethnic music and dance.
Membership required.

IAAAM—International Association of African American Music
P.O. Box 382
Gladwyne, PA 19035
Phone: 610-664-8292
Fax: 610-664-5940
E-mail: IAAAM1@aol.com
Web: http://www.IAAAM.com
June—annual conference, awards, Emerging Artist Showcase.
Presents series of educational seminars, conference, tour sponsorship, concert production.

IBMA—International Bluegrass Music Association
2 Music Circle South, Suite 100
Nashville, TN 37203
Phone: 1-800-438-4262
Fax: 615-256-0450
Web: http://www.ibma.org
Mid-October—annual week-long trade show, showcase and festival.
Regional annual conferences: West Coast, Southeast.
Showcase new and established bluegrass acts.
Membership required.

International Entertainment Buyers Association
P.O. Box 128376
Nashville, TN 37212
Phone: 615-463-0161
Fax: 615-463-0163
E-mail: info@ieba.org
Web: http://www.ieba.org
Annual conference and showcase.
Membership required.

International Festivals and Events Association
2601 Eastover Terrace
Boise, ID 83706
Phone: 208-433-0950
Fax: 208-433-9812
Web: http://www.ifea.com
Annual convention and seminars.

MENC-The National Association for Music Educators
1806 Robert Fulton Drive
Reston, VA 20191
Phone: 1-800-336-3768
Phone: 703-860-4000
Fax: 703-860-1531
Web: http://www.menc.org

Montana Performing Arts Consortium
Montana Arts
P.O. Box 1872
Bozeman, MT 59771-1872
Phone: 406-585-9551
Web: http://www.mtperformingarts.org
Early February—annual block booking conference and showcase.
Showcase music, theater, dance.
Membership required.

NACA—National Association for Campus Activities
13 Harbison Way
Columbia, SC 29212-3401
Phone: 1-800-845-2338
Phone: 803-732-6222
Fax: 803-749-1047
Web: http://www.naca.org
Mid-February—annual conference, showcase, exhibit hall.
7 Regional conferences throughout the U.S.—Mid-America, Northern Plains, Northeast, West, South, Central, Mid-Atlantic
Showcase music-all genres, comedy, theater, performance art.
Membership required.

Songwriters Guild of America
1506 Broadway
New York, NY 10036
Phone: 212-768-7902
Fax: 212-768-9048
E-mail: lasga@aol.com
Web: http://.songwritersguildofamerica.visualnet.com
Late October—annual conference, showcase; weekly Los Angeles Songwriters Showcase.
Showcase pop, rap, R&B, country, gospel, folk, Latin, world, dance, jazz, hip-hop, children's music.
Membership required.

NAMM—National Association Of Music Merchants
5790 Armada Drive
Carlsbad, CA 92008-4391
Phone: 1-800-767-6266
Phone: 760-438-8001
Fax: 760-438-7327
Web: http://www.namm.com
January and July—annual conference, trade show, concerts.

NARAS—National Academy of Recording Arts & Sciences
3402 Pico Blvd.
Santa Monica, CA 90405
Phone: 310-392-3777
Fax: 310-392-2306
Web: http://www.grammy.com
Showcase unsigned rock bands.

NARM—National Association of Record Merchandisers
9 Eves Drive, Suite 120
Marlton, NJ 08053
Phone: 856-596-2221
Fax: 856-596-3268
Web: http://www.narm.com
Mid-March—annual conference, trade show, showcase.
Showcases presented by member labels.

OAPN—Ohio Arts Presenters Network
P.O. Box 10606
Columbus, OH 43201
Phone: 614-299-0221
Fax: 614-291-3059
Web: http://www.oapn.org
October—annual conference, trade show, showcase.
Showcase theater, dance, all varieties of music.

Ontario Contact
Community Cultural Impresarios
215 Spidina Ave., Suite 125
Toronto, Ontario M5T 2C7
Canada
Phone: 1-866-209-0982
Phone: 416-703-6709
Fax: 416-504-2418
E-mail: info@ccio.on.ca
Web: http://www.ccio.on.ca
November—annual conference, professional development workshops, exhibit hall, showcases.
Showcase dance, theatre, music.
Produce the Ontario Touring Resources Guide.

Pacific Contact
BC Touring Council
P.O. Box 547
Nelson, BC V1L 5R3
Canada
Phone: 250-352-0021
E-mail: fyi@bctouring.org
Web: http://www.bctouring.org
Late March–early April—annual conference, professional development workshops, exhibit hall, showcase.
Showcase dance, theatre, music.

The Network of Cultural Centers of Color
1000 Richmond Terrace
Snug Harbor Cultural Center
Staten Island, NY 10013
Phone: 718-556-6282
Web: http://www.folkalliance.net/nccc

Women In Music—National Network
31121 Mission Blvd., Suite 300
Hayward, CA 94544
Phone: 510-232-3897
Fax: 510-234-7272
Web: http://www.womeninmusic.com

State Arts Councils often work with presenter consortiums within the state. See Chapter 12 for State and Provincial Art Council contact information.

Non-Membership-Driven Conferences:

APCA National Conference
Association for the Promotion of Campus Activities
P.O. Box 4340
Sevierville, TN 37862
Phone: 1-800-681-5031
Fax: 865-908-7104
E-mail: contact@apca.com
Web: http://www.apca.com
Late February-Early March—annual conference, trade show, showcase. November—Fall Programming Conference.
Showcase guaranteed with booth; all performance types interested in the college market.

Atlantis Music Conference
1339 Canton Road, Suite E
Marietta, GA 30066
Phone: 770-499-8600
Fax: 770-499-8650
E-mail: atlantis@atlantismusic.com
Web: http://atlantismusic.com
October—annual conference, workshops, panels and showcases.
Showcase all genres pop music.

Canadian Music Week
c/o P.O. Box 42232
128 Queen Streets
Mississauga, Ontario L5M 4Z0
Phone: 1-888-780-0663
Fax: 416-780-0290
Web: http://www.cmw.net
Early March—annual music conference, trade show, showcase.
Showcase all genres: acoustic, pop, rock, urban.
National songwriting competition

Cutting Edge Music Business Conference
Music Business Institute
1524 North Claiborne Ave.
New Orleans, LA 70116
Phone: 504-945-1800
Fax: 504-945-1873
E-mail: cut_edge@bellsouth.net
Web: http://www.jass.com
August—annual music business conference, trade show, showcase.
Showcase rock, alternative rock, funk, blues/roots, country rock, jazz, hip-hop, acoustic and electric folk rock, Latin, hard rock metal, R&B, and more.

East Coast Music Association
145 Richmond St.
Charlottetown, PE C1A 1J1
Phone: 902-892-9040
Fax: 902-892-9041
Web: http://www.ecma.ca
February—annual conference, concerts, showcase, awards show.
Showcase and concerts of all music genres.

IAJE International Conference
P.O. Box 724
Manhattan, KS 66505
Phone: 785-776-8744
Fax: 785-776-6190
Web: http://www.iaje.org
January—jazz educators conference, musicians, media, labels.

International Showcase Of Performing Arts For Young People
P.O. Box 5368
Clinton, NJ 08809
Phone: 908-328-8822
E-mail: info@ipayweb.org
Web: http://www.ipayweb.org
Mid-January—annual conference, showcase; Conference venue moves annually.
Showcase children's music, theater, storytelling, puppet shows, dance, etc.
Send letter of inquiry for information—Applications April through June.

Mid-Atlantic Music Conference
Wholeteam Enterprises, LLC
3364-A Chamblee Tucker Road
PMB #199
Chamblee, GA 30341
Phone: 1-888-755-0036
Web: http://www.midatlanticmusic.com
October-annual conference, showcases, all genres.

MIDEM
Reed Midem Organisation
BP 572
11 rue du Colonel Pierre Avia
75726 Paris
France
Cedex 15
Web: http://www.midem.com
Conferences:
January—MIDEM Europe-Cannes, France
Mid-May—MIDEM Asia
Mid-September—MIDEM Latin America and Caribbean Music.
International music licensing trade show with music showcases.

Millennium Music Conference
P.O. Box 1012
Harrisburg, PA 17108
Phone: 717-221-1124
Fax: 717-221-1159
Web: http://www.musicconference.net
June—annual rock music showcase and symposium.

NEMO Music Showcase & Conference
580 Harrison Avenue, 4th Floor
Boston, MA 02118
Phone: 617-275-7073
Phone: 617-275-7072, band information
E-mail: info@nemoboston.com
Web: http://www.nemoboston.com
September—annual music conference, showcase, trade show and Kahlua Boston Music Awards
Showcase all genres: rock, jazz, blues, hip-hop, bluegrass, country, rap, R&B, reggae, etc.

NXNE—North By North East
In Canada Contact:
189 Church Street, Lower Level
Toronto, Ontario M5B 1Y7
Canada
Phone: 416-863-6963
Fax: 416-863-0828
E-mail: info@nxne.com
Web: http://www.nxne.com
In the U.S. Contact:
NXNE
Box 4999
Austin, TX 78765
Phone: 512-467-7979
Fax: 512-451-0754
June—annual conference, trade show, showcase.
Showcase all music genres held in Toronto, Ontario.

SXSW—South By Southwest Music And Media Conference
P.O. Box 4999
Austin, TX 78765
Phone: 512-467-7979
Fax: 512-451-0754
E-mail: sxsw@sxsw.com
Web: http://www.sxsw.com
Mid-March—annual music conference, showcase.
Showcase international talent, all genres: rock, jazz, blues, hip-hop, bluegrass, country, rap, R & B, reggae, etc.

Colgate Country Showdown
Special Promotions, Inc.
63 Music Square East
Nashville, TN 37203
Phone: 615-321-5130
Fax: 615-320-1708
Web: http://www.countryshowdown.com
Annual local, state, regional and national winners compete for cash and a recording contract.
Showcase country music artists.

Winter Music Conference
3450 NE 12th Terrace
Fort Lauderdale, FL 33334
Phone: 954-563-4444
Fax: 954-563-1599
E-mail: info@wintermusicconference.com
Web: http://www.wintermusicconference.com
March-annual conference, showcases, workshops, trade show, award show.
Nightclub acts and DJs showcase.

WOMEX—World Music Expo
WOMEX
Bergmannstr. 102
10961 Berlin
Germany
Phone: 011-49-30-318-6140
Fax: 011-49-30-318-614-10
E-mail: womex@womex.com
Web: http://www.womex.com
Mid-October—annual European music conference, showcase, trade show.
Showcase all world, roots, folk ethnic, traditional.

CHAPTER TWELVE
Funding Sources

"Performers should not hesitate to contact their local and state arts councils to find out what resources exist for them and how they might work with these public funding agencies."

Peggy Baggett
executive director,
Virginia Commission for the Arts

Touring is expensive. Although you anticipate and plan for the income from guarantees and percentages to offset the expense of going on the road, there are outside methods of tour support that might be appropriate for your act. Hedging the budget with alternative revenue sources has helped many artists survive the rigors of the road. One example is merchandise sales. They play a large part to keep costs down on tour expenses as well as add a revenue stream that can sometimes double or triple your income on individual performance dates. Within this chapter, I will discuss grants, sponsorships, fund-raising projects, patrons and record company tour support. The resource section at the end of this chapter includes contacts for funding sources in the U.S. and in Canada.

Funding Resources

Although in the past submitting applications for grants to arts agencies was a fairly reliable avenue for funding, throughout the 90s the arts have been a consistent target of budget cuts within local, state and national government. However, arts agencies continue to survive and disperse funds

"The regional arts organizations are outstanding support systems for the presenter for a number of reasons: they sponsor regional conferences, provide performing arts grants, support regional art consortia and are a constant resource for information."

I. B. Dent
interim director,
Gertrude C. Ford Performing Arts Center

for various arts projects; some agencies do so with reduced government resources but many have found alternative private resources.

Vigorous lobbying at all levels of government has enabled agencies to maintain some support for cultural activities. Although the resources were never in abundance, available sources of funds were much higher in the 80s compared to where the support levels were in the 90s.

Within the last few years, bold new initiatives by arts organizations and private corporations have been rejuvenating the funding resources throughout the country. One such initiative was begun by Americans for the Arts, a recent reformation of the National Assembly of Local Arts Agencies and the American Council for the Arts. They have been creating arts partners throughout the country in an effort to increase funding sources available at the local level. Many other partnering programs are being developed to sustain cultural enrichment throughout the country. Thankfully, there are still grant sources available and with some research, you may be eligible to receive support for your project or touring endeavors.

Grants

Where Does The Money Come From?

Endowments for the arts begin at the national level. The most noted arts agencies funded by Congress are the National Endowment for the Arts (NEA) and the National Endowment for the Humanities (NEH). These agencies in turn grant funding to regional, state and local arts agencies, government agencies, and not-for-profit organizations. It is possible that one of your projects may be suited for funds granted directly from the NEH. But rarely would an individual qualify for grants directly from the NEA. The NEA awards grants directly to individuals in these three categories only:

❖ Literature Fellowships—applications required
❖ American Jazz Masters—nomination process
❖ National Heritage Fellowships in the Folk and Traditional Arts—nomination process

It is more likely that you will find resources available to you from a local or state arts council. The NEA awards grants to arts agencies and organizations for projects that fulfill the grant guidelines in the following categories:

❖ Heritage and Preservation
❖ Education and Access
❖ Creation and Presentation
❖ Planning and Stabilization

"The Louisiana Division of the Arts supports professional Louisiana artists through several grant programs. Louisiana-based artists with recognized artistic merit—either as a Louisiana Touring Directory artist, a Louisiana Fellow in one of the arts disciplines, or as evidenced by promotional materials—may seek funding in the following programs:"

- Project Assistance
- Arts in Education (AIE)
  Arts Basic (e.g. teacher training workshops)
  Artists in the Classroom (e.g. residency activities)
  AIE Projects (e.g. in-school touring)
- Director's Grant-in-Aid
- Individual Artist Mini-Grants

Dee Hamilton
program director,
Performing Arts,
Presenting & Touring
Louisiana Division of the Arts

During the last few years, the Endowment has been under the sharp knife of Congress as they continually seek to cut the NEA out of the national budget completely. Each year, supporters of the arts rally to defend the NEA's existence.

Within each state, there are regional and state arts agencies providing funding for cultural programs. In Canada, each province has its own arts council. These councils are funded through budget line items from the federal, state or provincial governments. In the U.S., arts councils may also receive a portion of their funding from grants provided by the National Endowment for the Arts.

The state arts agencies and provincial arts councils provide funds to local organizations and government agencies which carry out programming at the local level within the state or province. You can begin to see how major funding cuts at the national level takes their toll on local projects as less money makes its way down the line.

What Can You Do?

Where does this leave the individual touring artist? It leaves

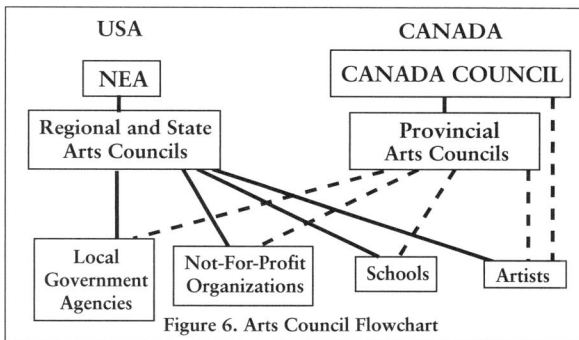

Figure 6. Arts Council Flowchart

you with a number of options and some specific tasks to add to the "to do" list.

1. Call or visit online websites for your state arts council and get a list of current programs. You are specifically interested in a touring program, but you may also determine that some of the other programs are appropriate for upcoming projects.
2. Request or download the appropriate application forms and deadline information. The decision to include grant funding in your plans definitely requires another review of your long-term goals since grant applications require a lengthy lead time.
3. Ask if they can suggest other organizations within the state, the region or even your own city that may have available grants if your state no longer has funding appropriate to your situation. I will discuss other resources further in the chapter.

HotTip:

For complete information about available grants, applications, guidelines and application deadlines, contact the NEA or the NEH.

NEA
Nancy Hanks Center
1100 Pennsylvania Ave., NW
Washington, DC 20506
Phone: 202-682-5400
Web:
  http://arts.endow.gov

NEH
1100 Pennsylvania Ave., NW
Washington, DC 20506
Phone: 1-800-NEH-1121
Phone: 202-606-8400
Phone: 202-606-8495
  Grants Office
E-mail: info@neh.fed.us
Web:
  http://www.neh.fed.us/

"With the controversy about the National Endowment for the Arts that has filled newspapers recently, many performers think that there is no longer subsidy from government to support artistic endeavors. However, the state and local arts councils around the country are continuing to see growth in their budgets and are continuing to support activities such as touring."

Peggy Baggett
executive director,
Virginia Commission
for the Arts

> **HotTip:** 🌶️
> Applying for a grant is a long-term process. Application deadlines are often set for the year prior to the funds being available for use. Example: Application deadline is December 2006—funds are available July 2007. Deadlines vary with each state arts agency as do deadlines for different programs within the same state arts agency.

"Most years, the California Arts Council publishes a collection of papers called "On the Road," which is a list of every organization that used the CAC program and who they booked. Look for organizations which booked similar styles of music and they will be your hottest prospects for booking. The next best resource for California gigs is the Western Alliance of Arts Administrators (WAAA) directory. Some of them will say to you, "What's your lowest price? Let's skip the paperwork and get on with the booking."

Nancy Carlin
agent,
Nancy Carlin Associates

Who Gets The Money?

Depending upon the type of program for which you have applied, the initial recipient of the money will vary. I will limit the discussion to touring grants. Artists with whom I have worked have received touring grants from the Virginia Commission of the Arts, the New York State Council on the Arts and the California Arts Council. In general, a touring grant will work in the following manner.

Steps to receive funding

- ❖ The artist applies to the state arts council for funding.
- ❖ Once the artist is approved to receive funding, the arts council determines the fund amount based upon the arts council's current total budget allocation from the state government, the NEA and other resources.
- ❖ The artist is notified of their grant award. This money is set aside for the artist to be dispersed by the arts council to organizations presenting the artist on the artist's behalf—the artist then receives their allocation from the presenter.
- ❖ The artist must arrange for performances with eligible presenting organizations.
- ❖ The presenting organization must apply to the state arts council for funds to present that specific artist.
- ❖ Most state arts councils provide matching funds towards the artist's performance. The presenter must contribute up to a specific percentage of the performance fee, sometimes 50%. The matching amounts vary from state to state.
- ❖ Once the arts council approves the presenter's request for the artist and the funds, the arts council pays the appropriate matching amount directly to the presenter, who in turn pays the performer their full fee.

As a touring artist, being included on the roster of funded performers gives you access to another level of presenter. These presenters are dependent upon grant money to carry out their programs and they often only select performers from the touring roster. Acceptance on a touring roster lends your act a new credibility and ultimately allows you to increase your guaranteed revenues within the selected touring region.

The Application Process

Many artists avoid applying to art councils for grants because they are daunted by the application process. Each state's application varies. Some states require lengthy information just short of writing a thesis, while others simply ask you to fill in forms. You will reap the benefits of being included on a touring roster for many years if you allow yourself to work through that first application.

Helpful Tips When Applying For Grants

- Set aside a specific time frame to work on a grant application. The process can be lengthy. Set aside a number of days depending on the complexity of the application.
- Read through the entire application at least three times. The first time will seem overwhelming. As you reread it, you will notice that you may already have many of the items required. Some thoughtful rewrites can transform your existing materials into the requested application formats. On the third read through, begin a list of items that need to be created from scratch or that may require some research.
- Use the granting organization as a resource. As a first-time applicant, council staff are available to answer questions and assist you to create an application worthy of their consideration.
- Request touring rosters from past years. You may recognize artists that you know. Those who have mastered the process are often willing to serve as mentors. Past rosters will also indicate the variety and type of performing groups that have been included. This helps you determine whether your act is appropriate for the touring roster. If there are no acts similar to yours on past rosters, check with the granting organization. Each year may bring new members to the selection committee and the selection criteria may broaden.
- Follow the directions explicitly. If they request material submitted in a specific order, submit your application in exactly that order. If they request 17 copies of each item, submit only 17 copies.
- Work with the organization to fulfill special requests. Some applications request an upcoming itinerary of performances so that one of their committee members may attend a show. Their report will be included in your application.
- Submit applications by the deadline. The next day is too late. All of your hard work will be returned and you will have to wait an entire year or two for the next round.
- Make sure your application is neat and organized. Both reflect on your organizational skills and the application committee tends to be very particular. You want them to make it through all the paperwork to judge your performance-worthiness.
- Always save copies of your application. If you reapply in the future, the previous application forms can often be reused with minor updates. If you are using a computer to generate your written material, the next application will be a breeze.
- Future funding requests are often based on the amount of money you were able to use during the previous funding

HotTip:
"Pay attention to application deadlines. Leave yourself enough time to use a professional application approach—organized, typed and well written. Incomplete, rushed or hand-written applications will rarely be considered."
Andy Spence
director,
Old Songs Festival

"PennPAT provides multiple layers of support for the artists, including grants to presenters for touring engagements; grants to the artists for print and electronic marketing materials; support for showcasing/conference attendance; training/networking opportunities such as an artist's retreat; and direct marketing support such as representation at booking conferences."
Katie West
director,
Pennsylvania Performing Arts on Tour

"Being listed in the roster means an artist has met strict selection criteria. It really says something about the artist."
Linda Bolton
agent,
Northern Lights Management

> "When applying for a grant, always be sure to proofread your application. Artists should make sure that their information is consistent from page to page and that the material is presented clearly and concisely. Try not to trip up the reviewer by using a lot of abbreviations or acronyms of which they may not be familiar."
>
> **Heather Lyons**
> individual artist program director,
> Kentucky Arts Council

> "Quite often presenters do not have the time for investigating a large number of performing groups or enough money to see a performance in another city. One method to overcome this is to rely on the artists that are published in the Regional Grant Booklet. *If an artist has the support of the regional arts organization then you know that professionals in the field have recommended this particular act and that they are quality.*"
>
> **I. B. Dent**
> interim director,
> Gertrude C. Ford Performing Arts Center

season. Once you have received a grant, always use up your funding allocation within the year that it is allocated. Example: The funding allocation is $5,000. If you only dispersed $4,500, next year's grant may only be $4,500. I have also seen applications turned down completely because all of the funds were not used. When faced with numerous applications, the grant committee considers awarding funds to those artists who are able to use their funds effectively. An artist who is capable of completely dispersing their funds is viewed more favorably than one who is not.

❖ Disperse your funds so that more presenters get smaller amounts. Example: Use $5,000 to fund five performances at $1,000 per presenter rather than $2,500 to fund only two. There are no written rules that specify this, but consider this—arts councils are in the business of making the cultural arts available to large numbers of people. If you are able to apply your funds to many performances, more people benefit from the arts council's work. It is a numbers game. When more people are served per dollar, more dollars are granted to reach more people. These audience-attendance numbers are the backbone of the arts council's applications for funding from their sources.

Each granting organization has developed numerous programs which promote and advocate cultural arts development within the state or local community. Along with touring programs which directly benefit touring artists, there are other programs that a performing artist can take advantage of even if they choose not to tour.

Touring Rosters

Many state arts councils support artist touring rosters along with other programs for individual performing artists. This model of funding may vary from state to state. The most common method for touring roster artists to receive funding is to have a presenting organization select a specific artist from the touring roster and apply to the arts council for tour support. Funds are awarded based on a formula of factors that will differ in each state.

Funding Factors:
❖ Amount of yearly funding received by presenting organizations in the area
❖ Availability of residency programs
❖ Whether the area is rural or inner city
❖ Regular availability of cultural arts programs in the area

The Canada Council for the Arts

The Canadian equivalent to the National Endowment for the Arts is the Canada Council for the Arts/Le Conseil Des Arts Du Canada. The Canada Council makes grants available to individuals in a number of categories.

The Canada Council offers a wide variety of assistance programs to touring, recording and developing Canadian artists. For applications, deadlines and a current presenters directory for jazz, folk and world music, contact:

The Canada Council for the Arts
Music Section
350 Albert Street
P.O. Box 1047
Ottawa, ON K1P 5V8
Canada
Phone: 1-800-263-5588, extension 5060 (in Canada)
Phone: 613-566-4414
Fax: 613-566-4390
Web: http://www.canadacouncil.ca

Here is a sample of some of the grant programs available from the Music Section of the Canada Council of the Arts.

Grants Available For Musicians
Grants for Individual Musicians: Emerging, mid-career and established professional musicians.
❖ Classical Music of All World Cultures
❖ Non-Classical Music
❖ Travel Grants

Composer/Composition Program-Commissioning of Canadian Compositions: supports Canadian composers and conductors.
❖ Classical Music
❖ Non-Classical Music

Small Ensembles/Bands/Groups Program: For those wanting to self-produce concerts in their town of residence.

Grants for Sound Recording: Assist with production and promotion costs of recording Canadian jazz, folk music, First Peoples' music, world music, musique actuelle, classical music and new music.

Music Touring, Presenting And Management Program
❖ *Music-Touring Grants:* Assistance for musicians, singers and ensembles to cover cost of interprovincial touring in Canada.
❖ *Festival Travel-Assistance Grants:* Travel assistance is available to professional Canadian artists performing at

---

"I started doing some stuff for the Iowa Arts Council. There was a very innovative woman who had started several programs. One was the Touring Artist Program which was a group of maybe eight or ten artists of different disciplines. In the summer we would tour the state and go to very small towns to teach and perform for a couple of days. It helped me get into performing because I had to loosen up and talk about the songs. I was playing for people who were actually listening."

Greg Brown
singer, songwriter

"When applying for a grant or a special program, artists should closely review the requirements and guidelines for the program. If you have a question, call the administrator of the program! It never hurts to establish a personal connection with the funding agency."

Heather Lyons
individual artist program director,
Kentucky Arts Council

"The Canada Council for the Arts has an enormous variety of programs to help people with their pursuit of a career in music. Canadian artists should explore all of the programs to find those most suited to their art form."

Gary Cristall
former director, music section of the Canada Council for The Arts

Canadian festivals not previously performed and that are outside their home province.
- *Music-Management Grants to Managers, Agents and Artists:* For Canadian professional music artists, managers and agents in the development of artists' careers.
- *Contemporary and New-Music Presenting Grants:* Available for interprovincial presenting projects.

Meet The Composer

This is another U.S. national granting organization receiving funds from the NEA and state arts councils. Their seven branch offices can be found in the resource section of this chapter.

With so many artists falling under the categories of songwriters and composers, Meet the Composer is an organization with which you ought to become familiar. They fund the presenter for programs by approved composers. Each branch of Meet the Composer has a different application and a variety of guidelines and requirements.

To receive funds, most Meet the Composer awards require that the artist be available to the public for some form of discussion about their compositions. Simply performing as you normally do may not meet the necessary requirements of the grant unless you include explanations about your songs, compositions and style within the context of your performance. Be prepared to do some additional work. All publicity must indicate that funds have been partially granted by Meet the Composer. Any additional media that can be arranged to promote the event must also indicate that Meet the Composer funds have helped make the appearance possible. It is worth these extra appearances and promotions to be a recognized Meet the Composer artist.

Funds will not be large in most cases, but may be able to offset the presenting organization's budget by a notable amount. When I have applied for funds for performances taking place in New York State, the presenter received amounts ranging from $150 to $300 per composer. With two recognized composers on the bill, this reduced their program budget by $600 on some occasions. In some instances, informing a presenter that you are eligible for funds from Meet the Composer may be the deciding factor for hiring you over another performer.

The Foundation Center

Located in Washington, DC and in New York City, the Foundation Center is a national resource for grants and funding by private and public foundations. Their main purpose is to provide information to nonprofit organizations about available funding resources. They offer minimal information for individuals about grants and scholarships but may

---

"In Canada, there is support to attend showcases on a national and provincial level. Be professional, be organized, be smart—take advantage of the dollars that are out there."

Rosalie Goldstein
management consultant,
Goldstein & Associates, Ltd.

"At the federal level, we have accessed Canada Council touring and travel grants; foreign affairs travel, showcase and prospection grants; money from the various consulates and the embassy; FACTOR and MUSICACTION for touring, showcase and album production."

Heidi Fleming
Fleming Artists Management

"Artists can help presenters who apply for grants by preparing their materials to meet the required criteria of the granting organization. If you are eligible for Meet the Composer, state it prominently in your material.

"Prepare: A one page bio, a one page list of compositions and recordings and return your signed contracts quickly."

Andy Spence
director,
Old Songs Festival

serve as a starting point for further research. However, the Foundation Center is invaluable for nonprofit groups seeking funding sources.

Sponsorships

Sponsorships are a resource of funding tapped heavily in the pop, country and jazz music genres as well as dance and theater. Major concert-presenting organizations, radio stations and public radio and television use the sponsorship method of subsidizing programs as a backbone of their fund-raising activity. Sponsorships, in many cases, provide a survival net for organizations unable to solicit advertising. Major corporations seeking alternative methods of pitching their products find sponsoring a major event or prominent sports or music personality invaluable.

Direct Sponsorships

As an individual artist or lesser-known group, you still have access to sponsorship dollars. You and your act can benefit from sponsorships in two ways.

1. *Event Sponsorship:* A single event in which you are a featured performer can be sponsored by a company, product or organization. Many concert series promoters court local businesses to sponsor individual events within the concert series. This helps to offset the costs of the concert. These sponsorships are sought after by the presenter.

2. *Tour Sponsorship:* An entire tour may be sponsored in part or in whole by a company, product or organization. Country music and pop music concert tours are known for their sponsorship deals. Notable examples include Michael Jackson's Pepsi Tour, and the Rolling Stones' 1997 tour sponsored by Sprint. As an individual self-booking artist, reality makes it unlikely that Pepsi or Sprint is about to knock on your door. However, if you are interested in adding sponsorship income to your tour, you will have to do some research and solicit appropriate individuals and companies.

How To Find Sponsors

Consider the products, equipment, and instruments that you use in your business and perhaps in your personal life. Look for a hook or interesting manner in which you can connect yourself with some of these items and the company that supplies or produces the item. In each case, find something unique about your connection to the product and how you can help promote it or the company. The National Association of Music Merchants (NAMM) is an organization whose members often partner with performers for instrument and equipment endorsements. This group would

"Let presenters know that you have received a Meet the Composer grant in the past. This alerts them to the fact that they can apply for a grant on your behalf and is a plus when considering who to hire.

Ginger Parker
founder, coordinator,
Kirkland Art Center

"Nowadays, whenever I present my own shows, I always get sponsorship from two or three local businesses to cover some, or all of the costs of theatre rental, sound man, musicians, printing, etc. I put the sponsor's names and logos on all printed materials, thank them publicly at the show and reserve prime seats for them (and perhaps two friends) at the show."

Lowry Olafson
Canadian singer, songwriter

> **HotTip:** 🌶
>
> "When looking for sponsors for my events or projects, I approach smaller businesses. It saves a lot of time and energy if you can deal directly with the decision-maker. You get a yes or no quickly, without having to wait for committee meetings or board decisions. It also makes it easier to get paid-they just write the check."
>
> Lowry Olafson
> Canadian singer, songwriter

be a likely place to begin your research. They host two conferences each year in Nashville and Los Angeles. Below is a list of logical items for you to consider.

1. *Musical instruments*—manufacturers, dealers, particular stores
2. *Instrument strings*—manufacturers of specific brands
3. *Gear and equipment including sound, lights and staging*—manufacturers, dealers of brands you use
4. *Personal health products*—specific brands of new or special products
5. *Travel companies*—airlines, car-rental agencies, travel agencies, hotel chains
6. *Touring vehicle; brand of gasoline*—manufacturer, specific dealer
7. *Food or beverage*—manufacturer, store, brand
8. *Clothing*—manufacturer, store, specialty item
9. *Exercise or hobby equipment*—manufacturer, dealer, store
10. *Office equipment*—manufacturer

Make a list of specific items or brand names you use that might provide a unique sponsorship opportunity to the original manufacturer or area distributor.

Performing instruments, equipment, supplies—list manufacturer's name

1. _____
2. _____
3. _____
4. _____
5. _____
6. _____
7. _____
8. _____
9. _____
10. _____

Transportation aids—list company or manufacturer's name

1. _____
2. _____
3. _____

4. _____
5. _____
6. _____
7. _____
8. _____
9. _____
10. _____

Personal and office products—include manufacturer or store name

1. _____
2. _____
3. _____
4. _____
5. _____
6. _____
7. _____
8. _____
9. _____
10. _____

Prepare A Proposal

Once you have identified a number of items, brands or stores, select one or two of the items with which you can most uniquely be identified. The key to getting sponsorship dollars is in establishing yourself with the company as a qualified spokesperson who will help promote the product to a targeted audience. If a manufacturer, dealer or store feels that you can best represent their product or company to a new or broader audience, then you may have the makings of a sponsorship deal.

Prepare a proposal that specifies the following:
1. Who are you and what is your unique relationship with the company's product?
2. What do you want from the company? i.e., money, product, services.
3. What will you do for the company? i.e., place their logo on all of your promo and advertising, record a commercial for the product, mention the product at all of your shows, display product banners or other signs at shows, etc.

HotTip: Consider all of the brand names, specific dealers and stores where you have purchased instruments, equipment or other merchandise. Develop ongoing relationships with specific dealers and stores that may lead to endorsements.

"Sponsorships and endorsements are a great way to augment the financial and publicity resources available to promote your career. However, when you enter into an endorsement deal, you have an obligation to service that endorsement, so only endorse products that you use and truly believe in. Just playing an instrument and a mention in your liner notes may not provide enough visibility to warrant free gear or tour support. However, to increase your value to potential endorsees: include their name in all outgoing emails and publicity, conduct "in-store" clinics, wear swag at industry conferences, and make product literature available at your shows."

RAVI
singer, songwriter,
former guitarist of triple
GRAMMY nominee, Hanson

FUNDING SOURCES

> **HotTip:** Support any proposal with audience-attendence and product-sales numbers along with a variety of press reviews from credible media to establish your notoriety.

4. Who is your audience? Companies like numbers. What is the average size of your audience? How many shows per year do you play? What is the average age of your audience? What are the general interests of your audience and their average income? As an artist, have some idea of who is attending your shows.
5. What is the time frame for the tour or individual event? Is this a three-month tour to ten states or is it one event in your hometown?

Make sure the proposal is well written. Include copies of your promotional kit along with any recorded material.

Contacting Sponsors

Sponsorships are generally handled by the advertising or public relations departments of most large companies. In some cases, all sponsorships are farmed out to the company's advertising agency. By calling the company's general number or customer-service number, you can acquire the necessary information and direct contact for the person handling sponsorships. The proposal needs to be addressed to that person or department in order to receive any consideration.

If you are serious about using sponsorship as a revenue resource, then the International Events Group, Inc. *IEG Sponsorship Report and Directory* is an industry resource. Subscriptions for the report (24 issues) are available to for-profit organizations or individuals and to not-for-profit organizations. The *IEG Sponsorship Sourcebook* is available for nonsubscribers as well as subscribers. It is geared toward the presenter seeking event sponsors and the sponsor seeking sponsorship opportunities. There are specific IEG SR Briefing Reports selling to nonsubscribers and subscribers dealing with specific sponsorship topics. One topic is *Music & Entertainment Tours: How To Package Them For Sponsorship*. Check within your community, at a local university, radio station, arts council and possibly the library for copies of IEG products before making this investment. Once you find a copy of the *Sourcebook*, one day of research may provide enough contact information to see how you fit into the sponsorship marketplace. See resources.

Securing sponsorship funding is not easy nor are there many success stories outside the realm of major sports figures or major-label recording artists. However, I believe that many artists have not considered this revenue source because it seems that sponsorship deals are only for the "big" acts. Try to find smaller companies with a more direct relationship to your hometown or your unique audience. This may prove to be more successful than attempting to attract nationally-known manufacturers who usually court the major stars.

"I ask people whose businesses I personally support and can happily recommend to my fans. They have included realtors, car dealerships, the local building supply company, my printer, my banker, cafes and a bakery. All of these people are trying to expand their visibility and I treat their sponsorship like a personal introduction to my fan base. It's important to me that the sponsorship be mutually beneficial. I have had many repeat sponsors over the years."

Lowry Oalfson
Canadian singer, songwriter

Indirect Sponsorships

As a touring artist, you might be able to benefit indirectly from sponsorship opportunities. In these cases, the presenter is the direct recipient of the sponsorship and must also acquire the sponsorship. Some savvy presenters may have sponsorship deals already in place with local businesses. During my years as an agent, I have suggested some of the following ideas to presenters when they were unfamiliar with the process.

1. *Hotel Sponsorship:* The performer's contract calls for hotel to be provided by the presenter. This is an item on the presenter's expense budget. The performer's percentage is calculated after expenses. Suggest that the presenter find a hotel to sponsor the rooms in exchange for the hotel's name and logo to appear on all advertisements and concert promotions. The addition of the hotel name costs the presenter nothing. The free rooms reduce the expenses on the budget. The artist's final payment increases.

2. *Media Sponsorship:* Presenters often find a local media sponsor for their series or event. As an event sponsor, the media outlet, radio, TV or print media, may provide actual funds to aid with some aspect of the event. More often than not, a media sponsorship is a direct trade of advertising. With a media outlet as a sponsor, the artist can be sure of maximum media exposure. Alert your record company to any media-sponsored events so they might supply appropriate product support. If you are an artist with your own label, use these media-sponsored events to get your releases recognized by a new audience. Plan to extend a few extra promo copies to the media sponsor. The extra mentions and airplay with be well worth your cost.

3. *Concession and Hospitality Sponsorship:* Many events have concession items which are donated by particular local or national businesses. These items are either for sale or free to the audience. Ongoing concession sponsorhip is a two-way street. In one direction, the sponsorship builds community support for events. In the other direction, the event or series builds community support for the sponsoring business. This mutual back-scratching broadens the audience and once again reduces the presenter's expenses for concession and potential hospitality items. If performer meals are provided by a specific restaurant, the restaurant's name and logo should appear on all promotions and advertisements. The reduction of presenter expenses is reflected in the artist's final payment.

Local Sponsorships

Earlier in Chapter Eight, we discussed the importance of developing a home base of support. If we use the term literally, we can create some basis of financial capital to launch

> **HotTip:**
> Suggest to the presenter that they find one hotel to sponsor the entire year's concert season and benefit from a year's worth of advertising.

> **HotTip:** Send promotional copies of a current CD to a local media or hospitality sponsor to boost media and community attention for an upcoming event.

a first-time lengthy tour or support for an upcoming project.

Here are a few ideas to consider:

- ❖ Invite family and friends who own their own business or work for a small business to become sponsors. Creating a variety of sponsorship levels can enable them to contribute to the tour comfortably. Their financial support entitles them to mentions on all related promotional materials. This method of sponsorship offers the people you know a way to support your career while realizing some personal or professional benefit. They have helped launch your success without the sense of having simply loaned you money.
- ❖ Invite local business owners with whom you are familiar to participate in a similar manner.
- ❖ Invite family or friends to become a sponsor. Create a variety of support levels. For each level, the sponsor receives something from you, i.e., a signed CD; your entire catalog of recordings; a private concert; a song written just for them. You get the idea. Once again, this allows those close to you to participate in your career development in a very positive way.

Record Company Tour Support

Record company tour support is a familiar item generally negotiated into a major label recording contract. Independent labels are less likely to provide tour support funding simply because the funds are not available. If you have an occasion to negotiate any record deal, think about including some of the following in the deal. It never hurts to ask and in some instances, variations on the request may prove helpful to some aspect of the tour.

Tour Support Suggestions: The Record Company

- ❖ *Travel assistance:* Contributes to airfares, touring vehicle, hotels, per diems (minimum daily expenses).
- ❖ *Band and crew support:* Covers the cost of additional band or technical crew members to make the show more representative of the new release.
- ❖ *Promotion assistance:* Hires a publicist at their expense to promote a new release and tour dates.
- ❖ *Radio-promotion assistance:* Hires a radio promotion company to promote a new release to increase radio airplay and get recognized on the radio charts.
- ❖ *Publicity-package assistance:* Produces new promotional package materials and photos to promote a tour and a new release.
- ❖ *Poster production:* Produces tour posters and ships them to all contracted presenters.
- ❖ *Co-op advertising:* Shares costs of ads with presenters throughout the tour.
- ❖ *Ticket buys:* Buys numbers of tickets at each tour date ensuring

> *"Be aware, tour support is often a recoupable expense, and sometimes the label might not go about things in the cheapest way. I'd rather rough it for a while on the road and wait until a really big tour, (like opening for a much larger act), comes along to hit them up for cash."*
>
> Andy Deane
> Bella Morte

that targeted media, merchandise buyers and other industry people attend the shows.

More suggestions about how to work with your record company will follow in Chapter 18.

Conclusion

As with so many aspects of maintaining a performing career, creative thinking plays an important part. If expanding your audience means increasing your financial resources, knowing about these funding sources may prove helpful.

> **HotTip:**
> Be creative and flexible when discussing record-company tour support. The record company may be interested in working with artists who present thoughtful proposals backed by a solid tour of meaningful performance dates in valuable media markets.

Summary

- There are grants available to touring artists throughout the U.S. and Canada.
- The rewards of receiving grant funding for a project or tour far outweigh the time required to successfully complete a grant application.
- Evaluate grant programs carefully to find the appropriate program suited to your goals.
- Prepare materials within your promotional packet that assist presenters who might apply for grants on your behalf.
- Eligibility to receive touring funds is an asset which artists offer to a presenter in an initial conversation since it ought to be a factor when considering whom to hire.
- Sponsorships can create funding partners who benefit from each other. Use sponsorship strategies to launch an upcoming tour, a special event or project.
- Make tour support part of any record contract you negotiate. Develop a tour-support package in which the record company can participate and that enhances your touring to promote new releases.
- Be creative when considering alternative methods of supporting your touring career.

Resources

Foundation Centers And Resource Organizations:

Americans For The Arts
1000 Vermont Avenue, NW, 6th Floor
Washington, DC 20005
Phone: 202-371-2830
Fax: 202-371-0424
Web: http://www.artsusa.org
Formerly The National Assembly of Local Arts Agencies and The American Council for the Arts. Incorporating: National Coalition of United Arts Funds and United States Urban Arts Federation.

Americans For The Arts
One East 53rd Street
New York, NY 10022
Phone: 212-223-2787
Fax: 212-980-4857

Foundation Center
1627 K Street, NW
Washington, DC 20006
Phone: 202-331-1400
Web: http://www.fdncenter.org/

Foundation Center
79 5th Avenue, 8th Floor
New York, NY 10003
Phone: 212-620-4230
Fax: 212-807-3677
Web: http://www.fdncenter.org

National Assembly of State Arts Agencies
1029 Vermont Avenue, NW, 2nd Floor
Washington, DC 20005
Phone: 202-347-6352
Fax: 202-737-0526
E-mail: nasaa@nasaa-arts.org
Web: http://www.nasaa-arts.org

Government Funding Sources On The Internet:

Federal Domestic Assistance Catalog
Web: http://www.gsa.gov/fdac/
Listing of government agencies in the U.S. that provide funding and assistance.

U.S. Non-Profit Gateway
Web: http://www.nonprofit.gov
Directory of information about grants, regulations, taxes and other government services.

National Funding Organizations For The Arts:

National Endowment for the Arts (NEA)
Nancy Hanks Center
1100 Pennsylvania Avenue, NW
Washington, DC 20506-0001
Phone: 202-682-5400
Web: http://www.nea.gov

National Endowment for the Humanities (NEH)
1100 Pennsylvania Avenue, NW
Washington, DC 20506
Phone: 1-800-NEH-1121
Phone: 202-606-8400
Phone: 202-606-8495-Grants Office
E-mail: info@neh.fed.us
Web: http://www.neh.fed.us/

Meet The Composer
75 Ninth Avenue, 3R Suite C
New York, NY 10011
Phone: 212-645-6949
Fax: 212-645-9669
Web: http://www.meetthecomposer.org

Meet The Composer Affiliate Network:
Meet The Composer—Arizona
Arizona Commission on the Arts
417 West Roosevelt
Phoenix, AZ 85003
Phone: 602-255-5882
Fax: 602-256-0282
Web: http://www.azarts.gov
Serving Arizona

Meet The Composer—Mid-America
Dir. Performing Arts Division
Mid-America Arts Alliance
2018 Baltimore Avenue
Kansas, City, MO 64108
Phone: 816-421-1388 ext. 226
Fax: 816-421-3918
E-mail: info@maaa.org
Serving AR, KS, MO, NE, OK, TX

Meet The Composer—Midwest
Arts Midwest
2908 Hennepin Avenue, Suite 200
Minneapolis, MN 55408
Phone: 612-341-0755, Ext. 23
Fax: 612-341-0902
E-mail: general@artsmidwest.org
Serving IL, IN, IA, MI, MN, ND, OH, SD, WI

Meet The Composer—New England
Dir. Creations and Presentations Program
New England Foundation for the Arts
145 Tremont Street, 7th Floor
Boston, MA 02111
Phone: 617-951-0010
Fax: 617-951-0016
Web: http://www.nefa.org
Serving CT, ME, MA, NH, RI, VT

Meet The Composer—New York and Mid-Atlantic
75 Ninth Avenue, 3R Suite C
New York, NY 10011
Phone: 212-645-6949
Fax: 212-645-9669
Web: http://www.meetthecomposer.org
Serving NY, DE, MD, NJ, PA, VA, WV, Washington, DC.
Also currently AK, CA, CO, ID, MT, NV, NM, VT, OR, WA, WY

Meet The Composer—South
Southern Arts Federation
1800 Peachtree Street, NW, Suite 808
Atlanta, GA 30309
Phone: 404-874-7244 ext. 16
Fax: 404-873-2148
Web: http://www.southarts.org
Serving AL, FL, GA, KY, LA, NC, SC, MS, TN

Regional Arts Organizations:

Arts Midwest
2908 Hennepin Avenue, Suite 200
Minneapolis, MN 55408
Phone: 612-341-0755, Ext. 23
Fax: 612-341-0902
E-mail: general@artsmidwest.org
Web: http://www.artsmidwest.org
Serving IL, IN, IA, MI, MN, ND, OH, SD, WI
Mid-September—annual conference, trade show, showcases

Consortium For Pacific Arts & Cultures
735 Bishop Street, Suite 310
Honolulu, HI 96813-4819
Phone: 808-946-7381
Fax: 808-955-2722
Serving AS, CM, GU

Mid-America Arts Alliance
2018 Baltimore Avenue, Suite 700
Kansas, City, MO 64108
Phone: 816-421-1388
Fax: 816-421-3918
Web: http://www.maaa.org
Serving AR, KS, MO, NE, OK, TX

Mid-Atlantic Arts Foundation
201 North Charles Street
Baltimore, MD 21201
Phone: 410-539-6656
Fax: 410-837-5517
Web: http://www.midatlanticarts.org
Serving DE, DC, MD, NJ, NY, PA, PR, VI, VA, WV

New England Foundation for the Arts
145 Tremont Street, 7th Floor
Boston, MA 02111
Phone: 617-0951-0010
Fax: 617-951-0016
Web: http://www.nefa.org
Serving CT, ME, MA, NH, RI, VT

Southern Arts Federation
1800 Peachtree Street, NW, Suite 808
Atlanta, GA 30309
Phone: 404-874-7244
Fax: 404-873-2148
Web: http://www.southarts.org
Serving AL, FL, GA, KY, LA, MS, NC, SC, TN
Late September—annual conference, trade show, showcases—Performing Arts Exchange

Western States Arts Federation
1743 Wazee Street, Suite 300
Denver, CO 80202
Phone: 303-629-1166
Fax: 303-629-9717
E-mail: staff@westaf.org
Web: http://www.westaf.org
Serving AK, AZ, CA, CO, HI, ID, MT, NM, NV, OR, UT, WA, WA

State Arts Agency Directory:

Alabama State Council On The Arts
201 Monroe Street, Suite 110
Montgomery, AL 36130-1800
Phone: 334-242-4076
Fax: 334-240-3269
Web: http://www.arts.state.al.us

Alaska State Council On The Arts
411 West 4th Avenue, Suite 1E
Anchorage, AK 99501-2343
Phone: 907-269-6610; Fax: 907-269-6601
E-mail: aksca_info@eed.state.ak.us/aksca
Web: http://www.eed.state.ak.us

American Samoa Council On Culture, Arts and Humanities
P.O. Box 1540
Office of the Governor
Pago Pago, AS 96799
Phone: 684-633-4347
Fax: 684-633-2059

Arizona Commission On The Arts
417 West Roosevelt Street
Phoenix, AZ 85003
Phone: 602-255-5882
Fax: 602-256-0282
E-mail: info@aaarts.gov
Web: http://www.azarts.gov

Arkansas Arts Council
1500 Tower Building
323 Center Street
Little Rock, AR 72201
Phone: 501-324-9766
Fax: 501-324-9207
E-mail: info@arkansasarts.com
Web: http://www.arkansasarts.com

California Arts Council
1300 I Street, Suite 930
Sacramento, CA 95814
Phone: 916-322-6555
Fax: 916-322-6575
Web: http://www.cac.ca.gov

Colorado Council On The Arts & Humanities
1380 Lawrence Street, Suite 1200
Denver, CO 80204-2059
Phone: 303-866-4353
Fax: 303-866-4266
E-mail: coloarts@state.co.us
Web: http://www.coloarts.state.co.us

Connecticut Commission On The Arts
One Financial Plaza, 755 Main St.
Hartford, CT 06103
Phone: 860-256-2800
Fax: 860-256-2811
Web: http://www.cultureandtourism.org

Delaware Division Of The Arts
Carvel State Office Building, 4th Floor
820 North French Street
Wilmington, DE 19801
Phone: 302-577-8278
Fax: 302-577-6561
E-mail: delarts@states.de.us
Web: http://www.artsdel.org

District Of Columbia (DC) Commission On The Arts And Humanities
410 8th Street, NW, 5th Floor
Washington, DC 20004
Phone: 202-724-5613
Fax: 202-727-4135
Web: http://www.dcarts.dc.gov

Florida Division of Cultural Affairs
500 S. Bronough Street
Tallahassee, FL 32399
Phone: 850-245-6470
Fax: 850-245-6497
Web: http://www.florida-arts.org

Georgia Council For The Arts
260 14th Street, NW, Suite 401
Atlanta, GA 30318
Phone: 404-685-2787
Fax: 404-685-2788
Web: http://www.gaarts.org

Guam Council On The Arts & Humanities Agency
P.O. Box 2950
Hagatwa, GU 96932
Phone: 671-646-2781
Fax: 671-648-2787
Web: http://www.nasaa-arts.org/asa/gu.shtml

State Foundation On Culture And The Arts (Hawaii)
250 South Hotel Street
Honolulu, HI 96813
Phone: 808-586-0300
Fax: 808-586-0308

Idaho Commission On The Arts
P.O. Box 83720
Boise, ID 83720-0008
Phone: 208-334-2119
Fax: 208-334-2488
Web: http://www.state.id.us/arts/

Illinois Arts Council
James R. Thompson Center
100 West Randolph Street, Suite 10-500
Chicago, IL 60601
Phone: 1-800-237-6994
Fax: 312-814-1471
E-mail: info@arts.state.il.us
Web: http://www.state.il.us/agency/iac

Indiana Arts Commission
150 W. Market Street, Suite 618
Indianapolis, IN 46204
Phone: 317-232-1268
Fax: 317-232-5595
E-mail: arts@state.in.us
Web: http://www.in.gov/arts

Iowa Arts Council
State Historical Bldg.
600 East Locust
Des Moines, IA 50319
Phone: 515-281-6412
Fax: 515-242-6498
Web: http://www.iowaartscouncil.org

Kansas Arts Commission
Jayhawk Tower
700 SW Jackson, Suite 1004
Topeka, KS 66603
Phone: 785-296-3335
Fax: 785-296-4989
Email: kac@arts.state.ks.us
Web: http://www.arts.state.ks.us

Kentucky Arts Council
21st Floor, Capital Plaza Tower
500 Mero Street
Frankfort, KY 40601
Phone: 502-564-3757
Fax: 502-564-2839
E-mail: kyarts@ky.gov
Web: http://www.kyarts.org

Louisiana Division Of The Arts
1051 North 3rd Street, #420
Baton Rouge, LA 70804
Phone: 225-342-8180
Fax: 225-342-8173
E-mail: arts@ky.gov
Web: http://www.crt.state.la.us/arts

Maine Arts Commission
193 State Street
Augusta, ME 04333
Phone: 207-287-2724
Fax: 207-287-2725
Web: http://www.mainearts.com

Maryland State Arts Council
175 West Ostend Street, Suite E
Baltimore, MD 21230
Phone: 410-767-6555
Fax: 410-333-1062
Web: http://www.msac.org

Massachusettes Cultural Council
10 St.James Ave.
Boston, MA 02116
Phone: 617-727-3668
Fax: 617-727-0044
E-mail: mcc@art.state.ma.us
Web: http://www.massculturalcouncil.org

Michigan Council For The Arts & Cultural Affairs
702 West Kalamazoo Street
Lansing, MI 48909
Phone: 517-241-4011
Fax: 517-241-3979
Web: http://www.michigan.gov/hal

Minnesota State Arts Board
Park Square Court
400 Sibley Street, Suite 200
St. Paul, MN 55101
Phone: 651-215-1600
Fax: 651-215-1602
Web: http://www.arts.state.mn.us

Mississippi Arts Commission
501 North West Street
Suite 701B Woufolk Bldg.
Jackson, MS 39201
Phone: 601-359-6030 or 6040
Fax: 601-359-6008
Web: http://www.arts.state.ms.us

Missouri Arts Council
111 North 7th Street, Suite 105
St. Louis, MO 63101
Phone: 314-340-6845
Fax: 314-340-7215
Web: http://www.missouriartscouncil.org

Montana Arts Council
City County Building
316 North Park Avenue, Room 252
Helena, MT 59620-2201
Phone: 406-444-6430
Fax: 406-444-6548
Web: http://www.art.state.mt.us

Nebraska Arts Council
Burlington Bldg.
1004 Farnam Street
Omaha, NE 68102
Phone: 402-595-2122
Fax: 402-595-2334
Web: http://www.nebraskaartscouncil.org

Nevada State Council On The Arts
716 North Carson Street, Suite A
Carson City, NV 89701
Phone: 775-687-6680
Fax: 775-687-6688
Web: http://dmla.clan.lib.nv.us

New Hampshire State Council On The Arts
2½ Beacon Street
Concord, NH 03301
Phone: 603-271-2789
Fax: 603-271-3584
Web: http://www.state.nh.us/nharts

New Jersey Council On The Arts
225 West State Street, 4th Floor
Trenton, NJ 08625-0306
Phone: 609-292-6130
Fax: 609-989-1440
Web: http://www.njartscouncil.org

New Mexico Arts Division
228 East Palace Avenue
Santa Fe, NM 87504-1450
Phone: 505-827-6490
Fax: 505-827-6043
Web: http://www.nmarts.org

New York State Council On The Arts
175 Varick Street, 3rd floor
New York, NY 10014
Phone: 212-627-4455
Fax: 212-620-5911
Web: http://www.nysca.org

North Carolina Arts Council
Department of Cultural Resources
221 East Lane Street
Raleigh, NC 27699-4632
Phone: 919-733-2821
Fax: 919-733-4834
Web: http://www.ncarts.org

North Dakota Council On The Arts
1600 East Century, Suite 6
Bismark, ND 58503-0649
Phone: 701-328-3954
E-mail: comserv@state.nd.us
Web: http://www.state.nd.us/arts

Commonwealth Council For Arts And Culture (Northern Mariana Islands)
P.O. Box 5553, CHRB
Saipan, MP 96950
Phone: 011-670-322-9982 or 9983
Fax: 011-670-322-9028
Web: http://www.nasaa-arts.org/aoa/nmar.shtml

Ohio Arts Council
727 East Main Street
Columbus, OH 43205
Phone: 614-466-2613
Fax: 614-466-4494
Web: http://www.oac.state.oh.us

State Arts Council Of Oklahoma
P. O. Box 52001-2001
Oklahoma City, OK 73152-2001
Phone: 405-521-2931
Fax: 405-521-6418
E-mail: okarts@arts.state.ok.us
Web: http://www.oklaosf.state.ok.us/~arts/

Oregon Arts Commission
775 Summer Street, NE
Salem, OR 97301-1284
Phone: 503-986-0082
Fax: 503-986-0260
Web: http://www.oregonartscommission.org

Pennsylvania Council On The Arts
Finance Building, Room 216
Harrisburg, PA 17120
Phone: 717-787-6883
Fax: 717-783-2538
Web: http://www.pacouncilonthearts.org

Institute Of Puerto Rican Culture
P.O. Box 9024184
San Juan, PR 00902-4184
Phone: 787-724-0700
Fax: 787-724-8393
Web: http://www.icp.gobierno.pr

Rhode Island State Council On The Arts
One Capitol Hill, 3rd Floor
Providence, RI 02908
Phone: 401-222-3880
Fax: 401-222-3018
Web: http://www.risca.state.ri.us

South Carolina Arts Commission
1800 Gervais Street
Columbia, SC 29201
Phone: 803-734-8696
Fax: 803-734-8526
Web: http://www.state.sc.us/arts

South Dakota Arts Council
South Dakota State Library Bldg.
800 Governors Drive
Pierre, SD 57501-2294
Phone: 605-773-3131
Fax: 605-773-6962
Web: http://www.sdarts.org

Tennessee Arts Commission
401 Charlotte Avenue
Nashville, TN 37243-0780
Phone: 615-741-1701
Fax: 615-741-8559
Web: http://www.arts.state.tn.us

Texas Commission On The Arts
P.O. Box 13406, Capitol Station
Austin, TX 78711
Phone: 512-463-5535
Fax: 512-475-2699
Web: http://www.arts.state.tx.us

Utah Arts Council
617 East South Temple Street
Salt Lake City, UT 84102
Phone: 801-236-7555
Fax: 801-236-7556
Web: http://www.arts.utah.gov

Vermont Arts Council
136 State Street, Drawer 33
Montpelier, VT 05633-6001
Phone: 802-828-3291
Fax: 802-828-3363
E-mail: info@vermontartsconcil.og
Web: http://www.vermontartscouncil.org

Virgin Islands Council On The Arts
P.O. Box 103
St. Thomas, VI 00802
Phone: 340-774-5984
Fax: 340-774-6206
Web: http://www.vicouncilonarts.org

Virginia Commission For The Arts
Lewis House
223 Governor Street, 2nd floor
Richmond, VA 23219
Phone: 804-225-3132
Fax: 804-225-4327
Web: http://www.arts.state.va.us

Washington State Arts Commission
P.O. Box 42675
Olympia, WA 98504-2675
Phone: 360-753-3860
Fax: 360-586-5351
Web: http://www.arts.wa.gov

West Virginia Division Of Culture and History
Arts and Humanities Section
1900 Kanawha Boulevard East
Charleston, WV 25305-0300
Phone: 304-558-0220
Fax: 304-558-2779
Web: http://www.wvculture.org

Wisconsin Arts Board
101 East Wilson Street, 1st floor
Madison, WI 53702
Phone: 608-266-0190
Fax: 608-267-0380
E-mail: artsboard@arts.state.wi.us
Web: http://www.arts.state.wi.us

Wyoming Arts Council
2320 Capitol Avenue
Cheyenne, WY 82002
Phone: 307-777-7742
Fax: 307-777-5499
Web: http://wyoarts.state.wy.us

Canadian Funding Resources:

Canada Council For The Arts/Le Conseil Des Arts Du Canada
350 Albert Street
P.O. Box 1047
Ottawa, Ontario K1P 5V8
Phone: 1-800-263-5588, in Canada
Phone: 613-566-4414
Fax: 613-566-4390
Web: http://www.canadacouncil.ca

FACTOR
355 King Street W, 5th Floor
Toronto, Ontario M5V 1J6
Phone: 416-351-1361
Fax: 416-351-7311
Web: http://www.factor.ca
Touring, showcase, album production.

Musicaction
432 rue Sainte Hélène
Montreal, Québec H2Y 2K7
Phone: 514-861-8444
Fax: 514-861-4423
Web: http://www.musicaction.ca
French language projects, instrumental and world music projects based in Québec.

Canadian Provincial Arts Councils:

Alberta Foundation for the Arts
901 Standard Life Center
10405 Jasper Avenue
Edmonton, AB T5J 4R7
Phone: 780-427-6315
Fax: 780-422-9132
Web: http://www.cd.gov.ab.ca

Arts Foundation of Greater Toronto
401 Richmond Street West, Suite 365
Box 124
Toronto, Ontario M5V 3A8
Phone: 416-597-8223
Fax: 416-597-6956
Web: http://www.artstoronto.com

British Columbia Arts Council
c/o Cultural Services Branch
800 Johnson Street, 5th Floor
Victoria, British Columbia V8W 1N3
Phone: 250-356-1718
Fax: 250-387-4099
Web: http://www.bcartscouncil.ca

British Columbia Touring Council
P.O. Box 547
Nelson, BC V1L 5R3
Phone: 250-352-0021
Fax: 250-352-0027
E-mail: fyi@bctouring.org
Web: http://www.bctouring.org
Pacific Contact—annual conference, trade show, showcase.

Conseil Des Arts & Lettres Du Québec
79, Boulevard. Rene-Levesque, East #320
Québec, Québec G1R 5N5
Phone: 418-643-1707
Fax: 418-643-4558

Conseil Des Arts & Lettres Du Québec
15e Ètage
500, Place d'Armes
Montreal, Québec H2Y 2W2
Phone: 514-864-2001
Fax: 514-864-4161
Web: http://www.calq.gouv.qc.ca

Department of Tourism and Cultural
P.O. Box 8700
St. John's, Newfoundland A1B 4J6
Phone: 709-729-0862
Fax: 709-729-0870
Web: http://www.gov.nf.ca/tcr

Manitoba Association of Community Arts Councils, Inc.
525-93 Lombard Avenue
Winnipeg, Manitoba R3B 3B1
Phone: 204-945-2237
Fax: 204-945-5925
Web: http://www.artscouncil.mb.ca

Montreal Arts Council
3450 St. Urbain Street
Montréal, Québec H2X 2N5
Phone: 514-280-3580
Fax: 514-280-3789
Web: http://www.artsmontreal.org

New Brunswick Arts Board and Arts Branch
634 Queen Street, Suite 300
Fredricton, New Brunswick E3B 1C2
Phone: 1-866-460-2787
Fax: 506-444-5543
Web: http://www.artsnb.ca

New Brunswick Arts Council
Level 3, Brunswick Square
39 King Street
Saint John, New Brunswick E2L 4W3
Phone: 506-635-8019
Fax: 506-635-8603
Web: http://www.nbac.ca

Newfoundland and Labrador Arts Council
P.O. Box 98
Newman Building
One Springdale Street
St. John's, Newfoundland A1C 5H5
Phone: 709-726-2212
Fax: 709-726-0619
E-mail: nlacmail@nfld.net
Web: http://www.nlac.nf.ca

Nova Scotia Department of Education and Culture
Cultural Affairs Division
P.O. Box 578
Halifax, Nova Scotia B3J 2S9
Phone: 902-424-5929
Fax: 902-424-0710

Ontario Arts Council/Conseil Des Arts De L'Ontario
151 Bloor Street West, 5th Floor
Toronto, Ontario M5S 1T6
Phone: 1-800-387-0058 in Ontario
Phone: 416-961-1660; Fax: 416-961-7796
E-mail: info@arts.on.ca
Web: http://www.arts.on.ca
Guide To Grants, Awards & Services.

Organization of Saskatchewan Arts Councils
Department of Community Service Arts and Multicultural Branch
1102 8th Avenue
Regina, Saskatchewan S4R 1C9
Phone: 306-586-1250
Fax: 306-586-1550
Web: http://www.osac.sk.ca

PEI Council of the Arts
115 Richmond Street
Charlottetown, PEI C1A 1H7
Phone: 902-368-4410
Fax: 902-368-4418
Web: http://www.peiartscouncil.com

Saskatchewan Arts Board
2135 Broad Street
Regina, Saskatchewan S4P 3V7
Phone: 306-787-4056
Fax: 306-787-4199
Web: http://www.artsboard.sk.ca

Toronto Arts Council
141 Bathurst Street
Toronto, Ontario M5V 2R2
Phone: 416-392-6800
Fax: 416-392-6920
E-mail: mail@torontoartscouncil.org
Web: http://www.torontoartscouncil.org

Yukon Arts Branch
P.O. Box 2703
White Horse, Yukon Y1A 2C6
Phone: 867-667-8589
Fax: 867-393-6456
Web: http://www.btc.gov.yk.ca

Sponsorship Directories:

IEG Sponsorship Report
IEG Sponsorship Sourcebook
IEG Legal Guide to Sponsorship
IEG Sponsordex
IEG Event Marketing Conference Series
IEG Consulting
IEG SR Briefing - Media, Supermarkets, Music & Entertainment Tours, Telecommunications, Beer, Financial Services
640 North LaSalle Street, Suite 600
Chicago, IL 60610-3777
Phone: 312-944-1727
Fax: 312-458-7111
Web: http://www.sponsorship.com

CHAPTER THIRTEEN
Marketing Your Act

"Everything your company does is marketing . . . and when entrepreneurs balance multiple roles, the marketing hat is often worn the least."

Alexander Hiam
author,
Marketing For Dummies

There is a science and an art to marketing any product or service. As a self-booking artist, the job of "selling" all aspects of your act, for the most part, rests squarely on your shoulders. I have always believed that marketing needs to be the main priority of any type of business, if that business plans to be successful. Whether you are developing a new business, a new product, a new act or a new recording, success is directly related to the marketing campaign that accompanies it.

Marketing And Business

Investing all your time and money in product development, and very little in marketing is a surefire recipe for failure. Few new businesses spend time testing in order to properly gauge the true value that their product holds within the market. Successful businesses often start marketing while the product is still in development. The information gathered from advanced marketing helps develop a better product while creating excitement for the product's eventual availability.

One of my favorite marketing success stories was the famous Pet Rock campaign. This was marketing in its finest

"You've got to market yourself. Ani's always realized she's a worker, she's got to market herself. You can market yourself very honestly and with integrity, but you still have to market yourself."

Scot Fisher
manager, Ani DiFranco;
president, Righteous Babe Records

> "Ten percent of your income should always be rolled over into your promotion. The promotions you place will invite your listeners to see you long before you step on stage. Don't assume they know you. Rather, assume they don't."
>
> Patrice McFarland
> graphic designer,
> New York State Museum

form. It proved you can sell anything if you market it properly. You may recall those well-boxed rocks destined for some anxious owner's shelf. Did anyone really need a Pet Rock? No! But everyone had to participate in the excitement generated by the campaign. And that is what marketing is all about—generating excitement. "Gotta have it! Gotta be there!"

Other examples of marketing genius were the Cabbage Patch Dolls, Tickle Me Elmo and yes, even the Beatles, Elvis and Billy Ray Cyrus. Whether it was a product, like a doll, or a new phase of music history such as the Beatles, a savvy marketing campaign was behind each success.

To effectively sell any product or service, you need to create a strategic plan of action. The tools with which you execute that plan of action are advertising and promotion. The following brief definitions describe the role each plays.

Marketing

Marketing is the overall plan to develop audience awareness. The tools you use to market your business vary depending upon your budget, target audience, product or service, and the various mediums to be used to carry your message.

Advertising

> "Marketing is most successful when it is most creative . . . Great marketers are part artist and part scientist."
>
> Alexander Hiam
> author,
> *Marketing For Dummies*

One aspect of a marketing campaign may be paid advertising. An advertising campaign is the strategic placement of paid display or classified ads that target your service or product to a specific audience. Most major companies create their campaigns with huge advertising budgets to back their products. Not every business is fortunate enough to have that kind of resource; yet incorporating strategic advertising into your marketing plan could be advantageous.

Promotion

On the other hand, promotion is free public notification of a product, event or service. The promotional portion of a marketing campaign manifests itself in many forms and may incorporate a variety of mediums, such as print, broadcast and electronic media.

This chapter, as well as the next four, focus on the tools in the advertising and promotion toolbox used to create and execute an effective and profitable marketing campaign.

Your Marketing Plan

> "Naturally, the marketing plan does identify the market. It lays out the framework for creating the advertising. It specifies the media to be utilized along with costs . . . The briefer your marketing plan, the easier it will be to follow."
>
> Jay Conrad Levinson
> author,
> *Guerrilla Marketing*

How does the above relate to you? Throughout this book, I have focused on long-term planning and assessing your career. Incorporating a marketing plan for each project must be a priority if you intend to achieve any level of success. Our earlier discussion of writing a business plan mentioned the importance of a marketing plan when attracting investors for outside funding (refer back to Chapter Three).

Here we set in motion the campaign that your business plan or long-term goals describe.

For the success of your business, marketing activities must coincide with your development as an artist. Your art is also your product and it will grow and develop throughout your career. This evolution provides ample opportunity to launch new aspects of your career while keeping your marketing campaign fresh. For example, you may use an upcoming tour for a new campaign by developing a distinct tour theme and name and by creating some new aspect of your promotional package to accompany it such as a poster, a flyer or a new photograph.

Since the purpose of this book is to build a successful touring career, the discussion of marketing focuses on promoting tours. By example, you will be able to translate the information given here to any other project, such as promoting a new release, a new show, etc.

> **HotTip:** Set aside some time to research and gather information pertinent to your specific act's marketing outlets. Advance planning for marketing campaigns and conference attendance can make a huge difference in your career's momentum.

Planning For A Marketing Campaign

A marketing campaign requires advanced planning and timely execution in order to take advantage of advertising and promotional deadlines. With some research, knowing which of the tools best fulfill your requirements can save you time and money with each successive campaign. Here is a pre-marketing campaign checklist—what you need to do prior to setting your plan in motion. At this point, this list is a general guide to be used when planning national, regional or local tours. As you plan tours encompassing more markets, the tools necessary for successful promotions change. Instead of using only local media, nationally-distributed magazines, trade papers, radio and TV outlets need to be incorporated into the plan. The following list provides an overview. Specifics for using each media outlet effectively will follow in chapters 14, 15 and 16.

"Be a marketing renegade. Don't be afraid to open new doors and look beyond the usual performance or retail venues. Comb newspapers, magazines, and other publications for leads and follow up!"

Dianne de Las Casas
professional storyteller,
director, Story Ballet Magic,
president, Independent
Children's Artist Network

Pre-Marketing Campaign Checklist

1. *Research:* Find magazines, trade papers, newsletters, directories, Internet newsgroups, websites, calendar listings, radio, television shows and conferences that are appropriate outlets for your act. (Incorporate the resource sections of this book.)
2. *Gather Information:* Collect samples, request catalogs, brochures, playlists, programming schedules, membership information and applications from appropriate resources.
3. *Note Deadlines:* Begin a list of deadlines which will grow as you accumulate additional media resources. Notice the lead time necessary for some print media outlets. Some magazines require two to three months lead time whereas some listings only require two to three weeks. Conferences can often require many months

> **HotTip:** 🌶
> Build a special-project savings account by setting aside a percentage of tour earnings for upcoming conferences and advertising. This is another creative use of money that might have gone towards agent commissions. Incremental savings for career-advancing events have a smaller impact on the overall budget than finding last minute resources to fund the full amount.

advance registration while rewarding you with discounted fees. By charting these deadlines, planning and budgeting your marketing campaign for the next two years becomes an exercise in creative decision making that impacts your future. Given time and budget, some deadlines may prove impossible to meet. Determining deadlines also provides momentum for future strategic marketing. This allows you to maintain the "big picture," or overview of your career so carefully constructed in Chapter One.

4. *Plan For The Next Two Years:* Work within a two-year time frame to take advantage of future deadlines for conferences and advertising and promotion for tours currently being planned. If you have completed a business marketing plan, detailing the next two years should be well within your capability. If you have not yet created a marketing plan, there is no time like the present. Planning a two-year campaign adds motivation to your career. (Refer back to Chapter Three, Business Plans.)

5. *Select Targeted Marketing Outlets:* When you complete the research and deadline evaluation, select the specific outlets that suit your campaign.

6. *Create A Marketing Budget:* Based on the selected outlets, create a working budget. Include advertising costs, printing costs, shipping costs, membership dues, conference registration fees and promotional product costs.

7. *Create A Marketing Time Line:* Based on the selected outlets and their deadlines, create a working target date calendar suited to your tour plans for the next two years. (See Chapter 21, page 446.)

8. *Target Funding Resources:* With a budget and target dates in place, begin to seek outside sponsorships before beginning the marketing campaign. Adding these support documents to any sponsorship proposal increases your validity and further identifies you as a marketing resource for the sponsor. (Refer to Chapter 12, Funding Sources.)

9. *Assess Your Promotional Materials:* Re-examine your current status on promotional materials. Do you have all the materials necessary to satisfy the promotional campaign you have planned? (Refer back to Chapter Five, The Promotional Package.)

10. *Create A Visible Graphic Reminder:* Transfer your target dates to a wall calendar as a separate visual reminder. Place it within easy reach of your desk and phone to insure timely adherence to your campaign deadlines. If you can set alarms on your portable computer for those times when you are away from the office, you will accomplish meeting deadlines with ease.

I offer these planning suggestions having had the unfortunate experience of missing too many deadlines in the past. When caught in the day-to-day chaos of running your business, a plan that is set out before you, with visual reminders, relieves the anxiety of playing catch-up. Having these long-range targets helps you plan for future expenditures like conferences and advertising.

You Are Your Own Publicist

The promotional aspect of the marketing plan involves contacting and disseminating appropriate promotional materials to select media in a timely manner.

Hiring a professional publicist for specific projects or a tour is certainly one option to relieve you of this meaningful endeavor. However, professional publicists can be expensive. Some publicists may charge a percentage of each project's or tour's revenues, but most publicists charge a monthly fee plus expenses. Fees range from $500 to $2,000 or more per month. Those companies charging higher rates justify their charges by touting their contact list and their track record of successful major publicity campaigns. Such agencies usually sport a client list of notables.

Similar to developing lasting relationships with presenters who eventually may book your act, developing lasting relationships with those in the media will get you interviewed, reviewed, and previewed. Just as artists may benefit from a professional booking agent with their many years of nurturing their booking contacts, those artists represented by a publicist benefit similarly from their media contacts.

Publicists do not necessarily take on a client simply because the client has the budget to pay. Careful consideration is given to whether or not the publicist can accomplish the artist's desired goals. Is the artist at a point in her career that justifies the expense? Is there a story? Will the media respond? Does the publicist have confidence in the artist to warrant attaching their reputation to them? These are the questions that a professional publicist must ask before committing to an association. As an artist seeking a professional publicist, your career must be at a point that they can produce the results for which you are paying.

If your budget and career are not at that point, the logical alternative is to do it yourself. Accept the job as a priority responsibility, and begin incorporating the following tasks into your daily routines.

What A Publicist Must Do

❖ *Develop a skilled and pleasant phone manner:* The phone personality developed for booking needs to shine as a publicist. You are out to befriend every media person with

> **HotTip:**
> Nurturing your media contacts requires time and a personable attitude.

"Plan a strategy . . . do you want to build a buzz in your own state, in the Northeast, Southeast, Midwest, etc.? Then talk with a publicist further about what makes sense for the artist and get a price for ongoing work."

Ellen Giurleo
publicist,
Full House Promotions

"To be effective, it helps to be persistent, but not pushy. Give people a chance to call you back, but if they don't, call them again. After you have sent your materials, follow up with another phone call—make sure they have received them, and ask if they need anything else."

Valerie L'Herrou
former publicist

"Price varies depending on the publicist's experience, on what the artist wants the publicist to do and what the publicist feels is important to accomplish."

Penny Parsons
publicist

> "Someone who represents you should be enthusiastic about your work. Their sincerity will far outweigh any other press materials!"
>
> **Sandy Goldfarb**
> publicist

> "Every venue should have a press list and be thrilled that the artist is smart enough to know to use it. The artist really needs to take responsibility for that. Your job does not end when you book the gig and learn the song."
>
> **Amy Kurland**
> owner,
> The Bluebird Cafe

> "Be your own best PR person. It's in everyone's interest for you to be as involved as possible in your business. You may be new to a market, but the person who booked you probably isn't.
>
> "Work with promoters to get a 'buzz' going."
>
> **Rebekah Radisch**
> former publicity director,
> Sugar Hill Records

whom you will be dealing. Media people are besieged by calls for stories and interviews, multiple offers to attend shows with free tickets to back up the offers, and piles of promotional materials and press releases to plow through. If you have any hopes of actually speaking with the features editor or calendar editor, your phone manner will be the final determinant. Unless you are a hot new artist with a "buzz" or represent a name artist that the writer has been dying to interview, you need to rely on your winning phone personality in order to introduce yourself.

- ❖ *Build relationships with the media:* This is the number one task of a publicist. Their success depends on their ongoing relationships with media contacts who will allot space for their clients in print and on broadcast media outlets.
- ❖ *Insure timely advance notice:* Keep in touch with appropriate media well in advance of an event or release to allow your contacts to work for you. Attention to media deadlines increases your chances of securing the appropriate advanced promotion.
- ❖ *Target the appropriate contact:* By developing a list of current contacts and their specific areas of expertise, your timely notifications have more opportunities of being included as planned. Each media outlet has its own hierarchy of jobs. Ask for the specific contacts in advance of sending materials. For example, send calendar listings to the calendar-listing editor and not to the features editor, unless so directed. It may be necessary to send one publication multiple press notifications. In most cases, the different departments do not share incoming notices.
- ❖ *Work with the promoters:* By working closely with the promoters who have booked your act, you can gauge how intense their promotional efforts to promote your show will be. Consult with them about promotion and advertising during your contract negotiation stages. The budget detailed in Chapter Seven includes line items for advertising and promotion. At this early stage of your partnership, evaluate how much the promoter is committing on your behalf and then what remains for you to complete an effective promotion for this date.
- ❖ *Use local promoters as a resource:* Timely advanced discussions with the promoter can provide current media contacts that address your type of act. The Information Form provided in Chapter Seven includes spaces for such requests.
- ❖ *Prepare interesting, well-written press releases:* Having worked on these when the promotional package was prepared, it is time to put them to use. If updates are necessary, now is the time to do it—before any mass mailing or fax campaigns begin. You will begin to appreciate those fill-in-the-blank press releases.

❖ *Schedule interviews:* Include information about the artist's availability for interviews on all releases. Strategic phone follow-up to confirm receipt of the press materials and discuss possible interview schedules must be timely and ongoing throughout a campaign. Not only does this effort demonstrate your professionalism, it continues to build your media relationships. If an interview is impossible, ask for some form of coverage, even a printed photo with a caption.

❖ *Double-team with the promoter:* Discuss the plans for contacting the media with each promoter. Make a list of tasks and determine who will be responsible for each and when each task will be accomplished. If the club does not have a publicist, let the promoter know when you will begin contacting the media to set up interviews and check on the timely arrival of your press materials. By augmenting the promoter's efforts, you can both be certain that the date will get the necessary promotion. By defining each of your roles early in the process, there can be some accountability and backup to insure that the date was promoted according to plans.

❖ *Work with the media while on tour:* Media contact may not always be completed prior to the start of the tour. Consistent follow-up is often required during the tour for dates towards the middle or end of the tour. Return media calls promptly. It may make the difference in having your event covered. Maintain a supply of extra photos and press materials to be sent or faxed while touring for a last minute boost to your promotional efforts. If you have a website, refer media contacts to the site for press kit and photos. Remain flexible when dealing with the media. Last minute interview opportunities are not unheard of even after having been told, "It is not possible." Attending to media formats, deadlines and requests has the ultimate result of getting your act covered.

Keep In Touch

Keeping up with the media is a full-time endeavor. Marketing and promotions are so important to career development that I hired an in-house publicist to exclusively work on promoting my artist's tour dates. The result was measured in the number of stories, cover photos, interviews, concert reviews and new product reviews that ran for every date she covered. We were able to efficiently conduct cooperative campaigns with the record company's public relations department. A publicist enhanced our efforts on all fronts. The most significant result was measured in increased attendance. (Hiring help is discussed in Chapter 20.)

"Keep your mailing list, e-mail addresses, phone and fax list scrupulously up-to-date.

"Describe who you are and what you do in a disinterested way; you are a singer/dancer/songwriter; you are NOT the next Beatles/Dylan/Baez. Do not lie or exaggerate in an unbelievable way."

Richard Flohil
publicist,
Richard Flohil & Associates

"So many talented musicians can't speak about their art as eloquently as they perform their art. Rather than doing interviews, they should turn to a publicist who can talk about their talent and represent them more adequately to the media."

Marika Partridge
former director,
All Things Considered

"Some of my favorite musicians don't have any concept of how to play the promo game. That's why there are publicists, managers, agents, promoters. So the musicians can do what they do best. Although some, like the Talking Heads, had a very clear vision of how to present their press materials."

Larry Kelp
host, *Sing Out*, KPFA,
freelance music writer

> **HotTip:** Allow six weeks prior to the first performance date to execute a successful tour publicity campaign.

> "A good publicist is not just a good noisemaker, but is a good storyteller . . . and should be able to convey the artist's story in an authentic and meaningful way."
>
> **Susan A. Martinez**
> Martinez Management and Media

> "Anytime you use a publicist, retail promoter or radio promoter, you compete with every other artist that you have admired in whatever format you are trying to compete. Unless your product looks, sounds and can be found almost as easily as your competitor's, it is an uphill struggle at best."
>
> **Michael Moryc**
> Matrix Promotions

> "An artist should strategize with his or her publicist way in advance to come up with a concrete publicity/marketing campaign. They should let the publicist know up front what they are willing to do, when they will make themselves available and whether or not they actually enjoy the entire press game. All aspects of press should be considered including print, broadcast, radio and online."
>
> **Alisse Kingsley**
> director of publicity, Warner Bros. Records

Working With A Publicist

If You Decide To Hire A Publicist

You have reached that point in your career where you have determined that working with a professional publicist is the next logical step to achieve specific marketing goals.

Here are a few other things to consider:

- *Know the scope of your touring:* Determine if you need a publicist to handle publicity for individual tour dates, short regional tours or to launch a national or international tour.
- *Determine your recording status:* When are you releasing a new recording? Know whether your record company support includes hiring a publicist in their promotional budget. Touring to support a new release needs to be your number one priority. Determine the length of the tour and which markets you intend to cover.
- *Create a budget:* Understand that the cost for a publicist may be quite expensive. Depending on the publicist, you may be able to work out a percentage deal or an hourly wage.
- *Be prepared to give interviews:* Once a publicist is on board, part of their job is to set up appropriate interviews with targeted media outlets. This means your time is being tapped heavily. An interview can last anywhere from ten minutes to an hour. A publicist will schedule blocked interview times when you will either call or be called. Several interviews can be conducted within a three-hour time block.
- *Determine what you want to accomplish:* It is important to set specific goals for any publicity campaign so that the campaign has focus and you can evaluate its effectiveness when completed. Was it worth the money you spent? Did the publicist achieve the goals set at the beginning? Has it made any impact on your career? Will you work together again in the future?
- *Give yourself and the publicist enough lead time:* Make sure you have enough time between hiring the publicist and the beginning of your targeted event(s) to launch, execute and complete your publicity campaign so that the money is well spent and your goals have a chance of being realized.

This will help determine your preparedness for working with a professional publicist. When the situation is right, the act is ready and the publicist is committed, working with a publicist can strengthen the work you are doing to market your act. An ongoing relationship with the right publicist can have a major impact on your career growth and market recognition.

Types Of Publicists

Not all publicists can help you achieve your goals. Know your goals prior to hiring a publicist. The following three types of publicists will accomplish tasks with respect to their particular focus and expertise.

Regional

Those artists whose careers are regionally based will strengthen their reputation by working with a publicist who concentrates in that region. These publicists have developed relationships with the various media outlets locally. When living within or traveling to a specific area, work with a strong regional publicist to benefit the outcome of the tour.

National

Work with a national publicist when you are ready to create a media blitz. If you are attempting to gain recognition in the major markets, nationally or internationally, then work with a publicist whose contacts are firmly connected with those media outlets. This is especially true when attempting to get articles in major trade and genre magazines, such as *Rolling Stone* or *Spin* or entertainment magazines, like *People* or *Star*. Your publicist's contacts can make a story happen if the act has the story to tell. They can pitch the story to the appropriate editors with whom they have developed long-term relationships. Often these major entertainment publicity companies are hired for a short time period to work on a specific project. A national company can also serve as full-time publicist handling general media contacts.

General

As a touring artist seeking media coverage to enhance performances and new products on an ongoing basis, work with a publicist who is committed to promoting your act for the long term. Their contacts are certainly important and will help get the media coverage for which you are looking. Your goals differ from the media-blitz type of coverage. You want to develop an ongoing relationship with the media in all of the markets intended for touring. Having a publicist work with you to promote all of your dates, year after year, may be one of the most beneficial situations you can develop while growing.

Whether this situation proves more cost effective when you hire an in-house publicist or whether you contract with a professional publicist, the benefit gained is the consistency of contact with a familiar person. Those in the media respond to consistency. Talking to the same person year after year about the same act builds a relationship between you and the media that eventually gets you coverage. It builds trust. When your representative is honest about who you are and is

---

"Look for somebody who understands what you are doing and who can translate that into language the press, the DJs, the public and the presenters will get excited about. Look for a track record. What do the publicist's clients say about the service they get? What exactly will be done to promote you?"

Sue Trainor
publicist

"A publicist doesn't have to have contacts in every city in which you want to work. As long as he/she is enthusiastic, reliable and resourceful, they can get that information."

Ellen Giurleo
publicist

"A publicist can be a critic's best friend or worst enemy. The friend makes sure we have the CD, the bio, the photo, the clips and the itinerary before we need them; quickly finds the answer to any question we might have and sets up the interview with one phone call. The enemy expects a long feature on every move his artist makes, never stops calling and then drops us from the mailing list."

Geoffrey Himes
music critic,
The Washington Post

> **HotTip:**
> Follow-up is the key to media coverage in any format.

> "Look for a publicist who has a wide range of contacts in both the media and the music industry, and who has both worked in and is trusted by the media. Make sure your publicist is someone who believes in your talent unreservedly and wholeheartedly."
>
> Richard Flohil
> publicist

> "Don't assume that I pay more attention to major label publicists, because I don't. It's okay to follow up mailings with a phone inquiry, but don't call editors of weeklies at the beginning of the week. Give me plenty of lead time."
>
> Philip Van Vleck
> arts editor,
> Sun–Herald

consistent about how they represent you, the media responds with belief in the publicist and in your act. When an interesting story is pitched by someone trusted and respected, the media is more eager to tell it.

Follow-Up

When you deal with any media, timely follow-up is a must if you want the contents of your promotional packet to eventually translate into preview articles, interviews, cover photographs and airplay.

Once your packet arrives at its destination you should promptly follow up to reap any benefits possible. If we analyze the costs, you will see how following up really does pay off.

Each completed promotional packet	$2.00 to $5.00
CD, video, DVD	$1.50 to $5.00
Shipping by two-day priority mail	$4.05 $4.05
Total investment for one packet	$7.55 to $14.05

From a financial standpoint, you already have invested in this one prospect. That investment has the potential to get you work and press, but only if you follow up.

When you send packets to presenters, record companies, newspapers, radio or television, call the next week and make sure it was received. Yours is only one of many hundreds of similar press kits received every week. I have seen the piles of unopened envelopes sitting in the offices of presenters, record company executives, publishers and radio stations. The numbers of artists all vying for the same attention is astounding.

Many of the artists with whom I have spoken have asked me when they should expect to hear back from the record company, magazine, or presenter. When I asked when they sent the packet and last spoke to them, their response was, "Two or three months ago." My heart sank. Any packet sitting in someone's office for two or three months is either lost, or buried in a pile in the corner of a back room, if it has arrived at all. When you send out a packet, assume that the recipient will *not* call you. Frankly, it is not their job. You are the one making the pitch and you have to follow through. Call the next week to make sure your packet arrived, then set up a time when you will call again to continue your discussions with this person.

Be Realistic With Your Mailings

With that in mind, I suggest you carefully consider, realistically, how much follow-up you can physically do on your own or with an assistant. Send materials out at a rate you can easily track. A general shotgun mailing of promotional packets may be an expensive way to get your name out, if you cannot follow up effectively. If you keep your large packet mailings under control, you can more easily track each one and gain value from each mailing.

Mailing Lists

This is one of my favorite topics. A mailing list is probably the single most rewarding promotional effort that an artist can make on their own behalf. A mailing list provides you with immediate feedback about your career. Although your list requires some maintenance and expense, it is easy to start and can be your career's most effective promotional tool.

Developing a mailing list is an essential ingredient to an artist's marketing program. It is your loyal fan base, whether you tour regionally or internationally. Beginning with the home base of support, your mailing list solidifies your relationship with your fans. It is one of the finest examples of direct marketing. Your mailing list directly targets those who have identified themselves as individuals interested in your career, so keeping those individuals informed of your developments is smart business. If you have not begun building your mailing list, here are some reasons why you should do so immediately.

Six Reasons To Start A Mailing List

1. *Easy to do:* In the simplest form, set out a blank pad of paper asking for name, address, zip code, e-mail address and occupation at each performance. A more professional approach would be to set out preprinted forms requesting the same information. Include the performance venue and date on each form. This information will be useful when making yearly evaluations which will be explained in Chapter 22. Once the information is entered into a database, an e-mail program, or sent to a mailing house for processing, a targeted audience is now available to you for all future marketing campaigns.
2. *Costs nothing to start:* This is the most inexpensive research you will ever encounter in your career. A mailing list identifies your target audience for performances and product sales and potential future project assistance.
3. *A minimal investment to maintain:* The costs to publicize events and career developments is minimal when considering that these notices are directed at your targeted audience. An artist who has maintained their mailing list for a long period of time can see their investments in printing, postage and maintenance pay off in loyal audience members returning to your shows and purchasing product.
4. *Builds an audience:* As an advertising tool, it takes the guesswork out of target marketing. Your mailing list

HotTip: Target five to ten venues or media outlets per week to contact. You can successfully follow-up on five to ten contacts in one week. You cannot follow up on a mailing of 300 or 3000. Plan to be successful!

"Since 1978, maintaining our mailing list has been the single most important thing we've ever done in terms of helping get crowds out to the gigs."

Robin & Linda Williams
singers, songwriters

"The most important thing is to identify your audience, collect them and communicate with them. They are the people who make it possible for us to do what we love to do by coming to the show, buying our CD and returning to our next show with a friend."

Bridget Ball
singer, songwriter

> **HotTip:** Add a column for "Occupation" to your mailing list sheet to help further identify your audience's demographics.

caters to *your* audience. Your committed fans help increase your audience better than any other form of advertising or promotion.

5. *A tool that you can use:* Your fans are committed to your act. Some may offer to help advance your career in various ways, such as contact referrals, promotion assistance, project funding sources, etc. Knowing who is on your mailing list can provide valuable resources when you need them. Your list may contain people in the media, in banking, in marketing or business. You may have lawyers and doctors and arts administrators on your list. Never underestimate its power. You never know what role someone already committed to you may play in your career.

6. *Inclusive:* A mailing list makes people feel included in your career. They are participating in your growth and development and that makes them part of something bigger than themselves.

E-mail And Your Mailing List

Conducting business by e-mail and making information available to large numbers of people at virtually no cost is one of the most inexpensive tools available. It is only a matter of time before the majority of individuals on your mailing list have e-mail. Begin now to build your e-mail address list for those currently receiving your mailings. For all newcomers, ask for an e-mail address. Sending e-mail postcards, flyers, merchandise catalogs and tour itineraries is a no-cost method of keeping in touch with your fans, venue bookers, the media and industry professionals as often as you like, offering timely career updates. (More about e-mail in Chapter 17, The Internet.)

Time Your Mailings Appropriately

Schedule mailings to coincide with news, major events, new releases or products, and tour-itinerary updates. You will be surprised at how dedicated your fans can be. Those on your list want to be kept informed, but not barraged. If your list is very large and you are not using email for your mailings, and you are concerned with costs, mail to everyone once per year. Depending upon how often and where you tour, schedule quarterly announcements to targeted touring regions. This is a manageable way to update those on your list. For shorter tours, consider bundling enough dates together to warrant the cost. Prepare mailings so that they arrive at least two weeks prior to the first date on the tour. Give yourself enough time to allow for holidays and weekends.

> "For gig announcements, which should be mailed as first-class postcards, use a mail house when you no longer can get your mailings out on a timely basis. Consider the revenue lost from not drawing fans to gigs as well as the other costs involved in doing mailings yourself."
>
> "For newsletters and CD announcements which are not time-sensitive, use a mail house for over 2,000 pieces. A mail house can mail barcoded bulk, whereas the new postal rules will prevent you from mailing other than at straight first-class rates."
>
> — Victor Heyman
> Heyman Mailing Services

Interviews

Anytime you give an interview, whether for print, radio or television, consider it a performance. Since you have been chosen for this interview, use it to your greatest advantage. Now that you have made the cut, leave the impression that you are "a good interview," and someone whom the interviewer would like to speak with again. A good interview should result in a better article and increased radio airplay.

The Art Of Interviewing

Not every performer is suited to be a good interview. Practice will certainly help. But, in some cases, speaking about your career, your projects or your performances may not be one of your hallmarks. Although I have not met too many performers who were at a loss for words when asked to talk about themselves, when given the added pressure of time and an unfamiliar interviewer, you may be uncomfortable. If you are uncertain about your interview skills, rehearse with a partner. Here are a few suggestions to build up your interview know-how.

Building Interview Skills

- Create a fact sheet that answers the more obvious questions—birthplace, musical influences, etc. so your interviewer can use your time to ask more provocative questions.
- Select a number of topics about your performance and career that are of particular interest to you or that are currently important to promote.
- Create your own set of questions that will lead you to talk about those topics.
- Practice answering these questions with a partner.
- Set interview time limits of varying lengths to practice both short, interesting, and long, enhanced answers. This will prepare you for quick phone or long in-studio interviews. These time limits help you cover all the important topics that you want to present as well as learn how to lead an interview if faced with an interviewer less adept than yourself. You still want to use the time to your advantage.
- Write out your set of topic questions and carry them with you to interviews. When faced with an inexperienced interviewer or someone unfamiliar with you, hand them your list of questions and both of you will sound informed and interesting.
- Be prepared for an interviewer who may challenge you and ask more intriguing questions. This situation often makes an interview much more interesting. Answering the same questions over and over can become rote. Allow yourself to stretch and share something deeper. Your fans appreciate those insights.

> **HotTip:**
> Create beautiful e-mail campaigns using one of the many internet services such as Constant Contact Vertical Response Topica

> "Interviews can help develop relationships with reviewers or DJs which not only helps for the one occasion but for the rest of your career."
>
> Ken Irwin
> co-owner,
> Rounder Records

> "When conducting interviews an artist should remember that journalists are usually dealing with a finite set of questions that they ask day after day for fear of wanting to stay within 'journalist protocol.' Anything that goes astray from these questions is a welcome addition. Interesting anecdotes, controversial issues and personal insights will make an interview and subsequent story a lot more entertaining. Humor is always a plus!"
>
> Alisse Kingsley
> director of publicity,
> Warner Bros. Records

> "Be at the phone at the appointed time for interviews. Then, approach your interview as a chance to let your personality shine in a way that will enhance the meaning of your music and make the reader curious to hear what you do, on record or on stage."
>
> **Jack Bernhardt**
> traditional and
> country music critic,
> *The News and Observer*

> "Something that tickles me is a thank-you note. It can be via e-mail or snail mail. If an artist learns that I am featuring his/her album, or have given him/her a favorable review, I am always pleased when the person is so thoughtful as to send me a thank-you note."
>
> **Rich Warren**
> host, *The Midnight Special*,
> WFMT Radio, Chicago, IL

> "After an appearance at a radio station, stay in touch with the DJ. I can't tell you how many artists that I've interviewed didn't get in touch with me the next time they were in town. I think it can be received as a slight."
>
> **Julia Mucci**
> Buzz Promotions

Once you are comfortable with the process and feel that interviews will enhance any promotional campaign you launch, include a simple line on all press releases stating that you are available for interviews and how to contact you. In most instances, you or your publicist will have to pursue potential newspaper writers and radio hosts to set up your interviews.

Interview Etiquette

The media is doing you a big favor by scheduling an interview. They have set aside valuable time, print space or air time to feature you. It is your responsibility to honor their efforts on your behalf. Increase your value as a prospective interviewee by following these interview etiquette suggestions.

- ❖ Contact media no less than two weeks in advance to set up an interview. If this is your first introduction to this media person, begin making introductory calls at least one month in advance.
- ❖ Reconfirm interview time, place or phone number no less than two days before the interview.
- ❖ Call immediately to make any changes in the schedule should they be necessary. Offer a number of rescheduling options.
- ❖ Be on time. When conducting a phone interview, be ready at the appointed number when they call you, or if you call them, be on time. When meeting an interviewer, plan to arrive a few minutes early. When conducting in-studio radio interviews, plan to arrive at least 15 to 30 minutes early to allow for microphone set up.
- ❖ Make sure you have accurate directions to any studio or meeting place. Get a phone number in case of emergencies so that you can contact the interviewer with your whereabouts and approximate time of arrival if delayed.
- ❖ Find a quiet place to conduct any phone interviews.
- ❖ Be prepared to focus your attention on the interviewer at that moment. Remove yourself from all other distractions.
- ❖ Be appreciative of the interviewer's interest in your career.
- ❖ Be charming. No matter what situations are infringing upon your world, if at all possible, make the most out of your interview time and exude that charming personality. An interviewer may see right through you if it is false so gather your sincerity and put on your best face. It will only benefit you in the long run.
- ❖ Thank all involved in making the interview happen including the interviewer and any technical staff. If you have promotional copies of cassettes or CDs, offering a copy to the staff is a wonderful way to win fans and get future airplay.
- ❖ Send a thank-you note, e-mail or make a phone call to the interviewer after you see the article in print or shortly after the interview takes place. Nothing makes an interviewer feel more appreciated than a "thank you." This wins friends and keeps you on the interviewer's "hot list."

❖ Contact that media person any time you return to the area with a new show or product. It is appropriate to offer the interviewer the first shot at another interview.

Getting Previews And Reviews

Timely follow-up is key to getting any notices in either print media or broadcast media. Remaining aware of what pieces of your promotional package were sent to whom or which press release was sent and when, is crucial to dealing with the media. Most writers and DJs are inundated by material from other artists, record companies and publicists. They are all vying for the same space. When left to an editor or music programmer, they will select stories, events or music that excites them, that they deem to be of interest to their audience or is of such great importance that they cannot ignore it. Your job is to convince those who have that decision-making power that your event or music is worthy of their attention.

If you sent music, for example, and the music is exciting enough to capture their attention, your battle is half over. Now to cinch the deal, you have got to follow up with a phone call and let them get just as excited about you, the artist who created the music. Making sure the proper person received the music or press material is a priority to getting any coverage. What materials are most important to send to each of the media outlets—print, radio and television—and what response can be expected, as well as how to use the Internet to your greatest marketing advantage, is discussed within the next four chapters.

Conclusion

Marketing who we are and what we do or sell is eighty percent of the game. Having quality presentations and products completes the picture. Strive for both in every aspect of your career. Devote a majority of your attention to marketing if you want public and media attention devoted to your act.

"People need to realize that most of us are doing a job two or three people should be doing, particularly depending on the size of the publication. I will eventually return everybody's phone calls. I keep everybody's name in my computer until I call them back and then I erase them. A lot of stuff comes up that may be more immediate. Most professional people don't mind being called back at a decent interval. If you call every day, most people are not going to respond to that."

Richard Harrington
pop music critic
The Washington Post

"Whomever is calling should throw me a good hook or interest me by telling a story about the band. There's got to be something that makes your pitch stand out from the pack whether it's visually, graphically, or just the name of the band."

Greg Haymes
music writer,
Albany Times Union

Summary

✧ Make marketing a priority in developing your career.
✧ Learn how the job of the publicist can enhance all of your media connections.
✧ Evaluate your projects and your position within your specific entertainment community to decide whether hiring a professional publicist is appropriate or an in-house assistant is what you need at each phase of your career.
✧ Create your own pre-marketing research plan.

Resources

Marketing Books:

Do It Yourself Advertising And Promotion
3rd edition
Fred E. Hahn and Kenneth G. Mangun
John Wiley & Sons, Inc.
ISBN: 0471273503

Guerrilla Marketing for the Home-Based Business
Jay Conrad Levinson and Seth Godin
Houghton Mifflin Company
ISBN: 0395742838
Web: http://www.hmco.com/trade/

Guerilla Marketing with Technology: Unleashing the Full Potential of Your Small Business
Jay Conrad Levinson
Perseus Publishing
ISBN: 0201328046

Guerilla Marketing Handbook: 201 Self-Promotion Ideas for Songwriters, Musicians & Bands
ISBN: 0971483809
Bob Baker
The Buzz Factor
P.O. Box 43058
St. Louis, MO 63143
Phone: 1-877-692-7999
Email: info@thebuzzfactor.com
Web: http://www.thebuzzfactor.com

Marketing for Dummies
Alexander Hiam
For Dummies
ISBN: 1568846991

Marketing Without Advertising
Michael Phillips and Salli Rasberry
Nolo Press Inc.
Phone: 1-800-955-4775
ISBN: 0873379306

Ogilvy On Advertising
David Ogilvy
Vantage Books
A Division of Random House
ISBN: 03947903X

Ruthless Self Promotion
Jeffrey P. Fisher
Hal Leonard
ISBN: 0872887146

The Complete Guide to Internet Promotion for Musicians, Artists & Songwriters
Tim Sweeney, John Dawes
Tim Sweeney and Associates
ISBN: 1929378017

The Self-Promoting Musician: Strategies for Independent Music Success
Peter Spellman
Berklee Press Publications
ISBN: 0634006444

Publicists:

See Appendix, Publicists, page 483.

CHAPTER FOURTEEN
Accessing The Media—Print

"What print media can do is to enhance and verify a 'buzz' or career growth. What it can't do is create it. People need to hear music. Of all the different kinds of support systems—audience, radio, and print—print media is the least important by itself. All it can do is enhance the power of any of the other support systems—it's like a booster."

Scott Alarik
music critic,
The Boston Globe

Beyond your mailing list, a well-developed, flexible promotional package, as covered in Chapter Five, is your main marketing tool. As you become familiar with the various media outlets, begin to tailor your press packet to the requirements of each outlet. It is important to have your contact information on everything you send, because there are times when you will mix and match what you mail and there is no guarantee a piece will not be misplaced in a busy media office. This chapter will help you target the appropriate print media person and increase your chances of getting your act covered.

"When you provide information to the media, be factual—who, what, where, when, why, how—straightforward and credible and, above all, interesting."

Richard Flohil
publicist,
Richard Flohil & Associates

Magazines—Genre Specific
Genre-specific magazines concentrate their stories and advertising on specific types of music or performance. Some

popular examples of these magazines are *Rolling Stone*—rock and pop music; *Sing Out!*—folk music; *Bluegrass Unlimited*—bluegrass music; *Living Blues*—blues music; *Jazz Times*—jazz music; *Performing Songwriter*—songwriters who perform in multiple styles; and *Guitar Player*—musicians who play guitar. These magazines are generally distributed nationally and internationally. As your career develops, contact these types of publications to become the subject of a feature article or cover story. Allow yourself a lot of lead time. Some magazines schedule stories a full year in advance. However, when something occurs in an artist's career that is newsworthy and timely, magazine schedules have a way of becoming flexible.

Many of these magazines incorporate itinerary calendar listings. Artists may list their upcoming tour schedules which enables them to gain name recognition by an international audience. By availing oneself of this medium, new artists can begin to broaden their following while developing new touring markets.

Often these magazines also include segments where brief notices of accomplishment may be offered by artists and agents. Without demanding large allocations of space, an artist can submit brief press releases which report current information about the act on a monthly basis. Examine these magazines by requesting a sample copy. They offer the self-promoting artist many opportunities to position their act within the appropriate genre.

What to send:
- Cover letter to introduce yourself and your act.
- Complete press packet including a number of photographs—different shots (if available), color slides and a copy of your current music or video. (Hard copy of Electronic Press Kit)
- Previous recordings, if they do not have any of your earlier ones.
- Monthly itineraries if a calendar section is included. (Check with the magazine for specific format.)
- Brief press releases of important career advances as they occur, especially if a bulletin-board section is included in the magazine. (Check with the magazine for specific format.)
- Frequent career updates and new-release announcements which may be suitable for the calendar and bulletin-board sections as well as for review. Send these on a continual basis.

Contact the magazine one week after sending materials to confirm that they received the packet and determine their interest in your act.

"Read the papers and magazines that you are writing to and see what they are looking for . . . Tell us what is different, give us a hook: Did someone study sitar under an Indian master? Does someone have a three-octave range? Does the band drive around to gigs in an old hearse? Whatever it is, tell us. And I am not saying to stress gimmickry—just your own distinct personality."

Jim DeRogatis
former pop music editor,
Chicago Sun Times,
former senior editor,
Rolling Stone

"Writing about music is like dancing about architecture. Sometimes it's really hard to get people excited about music by using black words on a white page. There is no substitute for hearing the music, whether it's live or on the radio. Print media used to be able to give you a visual image, and now MTV can do that. It is no longer the domain of print media."

Greg Haymes
music writer,
Albany Times Union

What to expect:
- ❖ The process of deciding which artist to cover in a feature may be lengthy. Some magazines have a six to nine month waiting list of performers that are slated for future magazine coverage.
- ❖ The materials you sent will be kept on file should there be interest in a future feature.
- ❖ They may include shorter pieces within appropriate segments of the magazine at first and will watch your development to lengthen additional coverage when appropriate.
- ❖ A feature article or interview is dependent upon the impact you or your act are making within the specific genre.

> **HotTip:** Electronic Press Kits (EPK) can include: Biography, press release, MP3s, photos, video-they can be emailed or downloaded from a website.

Trade Papers And Magazines

Billboard is probably the most significant music industry trade paper. The weekly reports about the business of the industry are read primarily by those within the industry. The radio chart reports included in each week's paper have an irrefutable impact on the music industry as a whole, radio airplay and ultimately the recording careers of soon-to-be and currently major artists. Similarly, *Radio and Records* and *Gavin*, along with a few others, need to be included in this category of trade paper.

On the live performance side of the trades, weekly magazines like *Pollstar* and *Performance Magazine* serve the touring music industry. They report significant news items and artist tour itineraries and are read by artists, agents, managers, promoters and club owners. The feature that makes these magazines significant is their box office reporting section. Here venues submit attendance figures for recently played dates. Promoters check this resource often when determining whether or not to book a specific artist. The box office report gives promoters an at-a-glance view of an artist's current drawing power. If you begin to draw significant crowds, ask your promoters to report your appearances. Nothing sells an artist to another promoter like a series of sellouts at previous venues.

These magazines also include artist tour itineraries as well as the results of their performances. These are probably the two most important pieces of information required by promoters who may book you. Multiple appearances in these magazines builds name recognition and informs those in the industry that you are touring.

These trades also focus on major news happenings within the industry. Items submitted for news sections will be judged for their relevance as they relate to the general industry.

What to send:
- ❖ Consistent press-release updates are appropriate for the *Billboard* group when accompanied by new CD or video releases. They are interested in your career as it relates to your recordings.

> "Rock journalism is people who can't write interviewing people who can't talk for people who can't read."
>
> **Frank Zappa**
> musician

> "Nothing is going to get the attention of a critic as quickly as GREAT MUSIC."
>
> **Jim DeRogatis**
> former pop music editor,
> *Chicago Sun Times*,
> former senior editor,
> *Rolling Stone*

> "I think all writers respond more to a contact they know well. I'll listen to something that a PR person pitches me if we've got a relationship where I can be honest about the project, about how I feel about it."
>
> Larry Kelp
> host, "Sing Out", KPFA-FM
> freelance music writer

> "I choose to write about what I think will be of interest to the reader and what I think will be interesting for me to write about, but the reader's consideration is the most important. Success is not the only reason to do a story. There has to be something more to it. The people have to be interesting but there has to be a story as well."
>
> Richard Harrington
> pop music critic,
> The Washington Post

> "Make your publicist's and your job easier by having **great photographs**. The decision to put a picture in the paper is often made by a photo editor rather than a music writer."
>
> Dick Renko
> manager,
> Trout Fishing In America,
> Muzik Management

❖ Watch *Billboard* for its thematic papers which spotlight certain trends within the market. Past themes included children's music as well as folk music. Check their scheduled dates for special issue themes. If you are appropriately suited for one of them, send a letter and packet and ask to be considered for the special issue.

❖ Send brief press releases regarding career news to *Pollstar* and *Performance Magazine*. You can mail or fax them to make their weekly deadline.

❖ Send tour itineraries to *Pollstar* and *Performance Magazine* that include dates as far into the future as possible.

❖ Ask the promoters from each venue to send your box-office score to *Pollstar* and *Performance Magazine*, especially if your shows have strong sales.

What to expect:

❖ To have an article written about you in the *Billboard* group of trade magazines depends upon your new release, your act's impact on the market and if it is news to the industry.

❖ Inclusion in one of *Billboard's* thematic papers depends upon the impact you have had within that specific market.

❖ Once your itinerary has been listed in *Pollstar* or *Performance Magazine*, it may be some time before you will be listed again. There will be reference made to the week that included your last full itinerary listing.

❖ Press releases may be included in an appropriate news brief section of *Pollstar* or *Performance Magazine*. If your news is significant to the general industry, it has more chance for inclusion.

Major Market Newspapers

Newspapers in major markets serve two functions as they relate to the arts. First, they are committed to informing their readers about current art trends. Therefore it is important to develop ongoing relationships with the arts-features editor. One of the ways that these papers function is to review new releases and feature articles on meaningful artistic career development. Many of these major-market newspapers are distributed worldwide—*The New York Times*, *The Boston Globe*, the *Chicago Sun Times*, *The Washington Post*.

Second, these newspapers also function as information resources within their own markets, i.e. *The Washington Post* in Washington, DC; *The New York Times* in New York City and *The Boston Globe* in Boston. Use these media to distribute information not only about new releases, but also about upcoming tour dates in their area of coverage.

There are a variety of editors covering different sections of the paper. The features editor is only one of many. You will be interested in getting materials to each of the following editors: The weekly calendar, the arts or music editor, the features editor, the event calendar (which is sometimes in addition to the weekly calendar) and, when appropriate, the news editor.

What to send:
- A short cover letter of introduction briefly describing the event or project you wish to have covered and why.
- A current press release including more details.
- The press packet which should include a photo and/or color slide, bio, quote sheet, information sheet, and two or three of your best recent reviews.
- A copy of the music or performance.

If they have need of any additional background material, they will ask for it.

What to expect:
- Once the material is sent, call to check that it was received and to discuss their interest in pursuing more in-depth coverage.
- It may take a number of calls to reach the editor. If your materials are of some interest to the editor, but you are not yet at the stage to warrant a feature, you may not hear back from them.
- If you continue attempting to reach them, eventually you might have a conversation to introduce yourself and begin establishing a relationship. If you have left a message once, try again next week.
- If your event is timely and fits within the scope of that editor's coverage, some form of coverage is likely: calendar listings, mentions in weekly-events listings and perhaps even a photo with a caption.
- Competition for space is fierce in these papers.
- Similar to the information above, feature coverage is usually dependent on the impact you and your act are making in the field.

Local Daily Newspapers

These papers are interested in reporting the events which impact the community on a daily basis. The arts usually fall into an entertainment section distributed weekly, on or near the weekend. Inclusion in this section is paramount to promoting your event. As an out-of-town artist, send materials to the entertainment editor as your primary source. Separate information should also be sent to the weekly-events-calendar editor.

Consider other areas where information about your appearance might fit within the general news categories of

> *"The music section of most city newspapers still regards itself as a news section, so they are looking for stories that are newsworthy—that are of interest to general readers—something new, or something that is being much talked about."*
>
> **Scott Alarik**
> music critic,
> *The Boston Globe*

> *"Finding a good, credible promoter who will help publicize your gig is crucial. If you're playing a venue with a solid reputation, you may have a chance at getting coverage."*
>
> **Mike Boehm**
> pop music writer,
> *Los Angeles Times/ Orange County Edition*

> *"Try to find some kind of hook that will make you interesting to the writer and readers. Non-mainstream music is fighting for a place in print with the mainstream or the major labels."*
>
> **Penny Parsons**
> publicist

> **HotTip:** When you present well-written press releases, you will find them reproduced verbatim when space allows.

"Writers don't want to spend a lot of time on the details of setting up and arranging an interview or tracking down last week's album review. The contact person should be ready to provide all of it."

Larry Kelp
host, "Sing Out", KPFA-FM
freelance music writer

the paper. If you are doing school performances, send material to the children's or family section; if your event has some charitable feature, discuss options with the news editor. Evaluate all of the aspects of your performance. How might they impact upon the various segments of the community? Target those newspaper sections specifically in addition to the arts section.

If you are a local artist, it is imperative that you develop a relationship with your local newspaper. Being a hometown artist has some advantages and disadvantages. Getting listed in the weekly calendar of events is a must and will likely be one of the sections that is available to you on an ongoing basis. Usually a special event spurs coverage in the form of a feature article. If you are offered a possibility to be featured without supporting a special event or occasion, try to suggest waiting until you book that special gig or concert. When your performance touches on various niche markets, avail yourself of the variety of sections within the paper which target those markets. Highlight aspects of your performance in relation to different interest groups to gain multiple opportunities for coverage. For example, performing at a banking conference may warrant a mention in the business section of the paper. Write your press release to emphasize that.

What to send:
To the weekly arts section
- A short cover letter of introduction briefly describing the event or project you wish to have covered and why.
- A current press release including more detail.
- A current black and white photo and a color slide. Most entertainment sections are produced in color, especially the cover. Without a color slide, you have lost your chance to even be considered for a cover.
- A press packet which should include bio, quote sheet, information sheet, and two or three of your best, most recent reviews.
- A copy of the music or performance.
- If they have need of any additional background material, they will ask for it.

For the calendar listing
- A short press release detailing the event: who, what, where, when, why and how.
- A black and white photo and/or color slide.

For the news editors
- A cover letter explaining the newsworthiness of this event and suggesting specific segments of the paper in which a story like this could be included.
- A black and white photo and color slide.

"I find it a little annoying when a band comes to town and they send me all their great press and don't enclose any music. I'm a music writer. I write about the music. I don't write about what other people wrote about."

Greg Haymes
music writer,
Albany Times Union

- A press release that talks specifically about how you are integrally associated with the event and what makes this news, as opposed to promotion. For example: You were invited to perform for the bankers' convention because your song about the recent stock-market fluctuations received attention on National Public Radio as well as some recent national talk shows. That is news because it deals with a current issue and it is promotion because it advertises an upcoming event. Pitch the news to the news editor, the promotion to the arts editor.
- Include your bio, a quote sheet and two recent reviews.

What to expect:
- Follow-up calls are necessary to each of the editors.
- If the calendar listing arrived within deadline, it is likely to get in.
- Depending on the event, who you are or your status in the community, a photo may be included and captioned.
- If your press releases have been written in a manner that allows the editors to pull pertinent paragraphs directly from it, your chances of coverage in the arts and news sections increase.
- When there is a story that is meaningful to the community, an editor may call you to confirm details or schedule an interview. Include information about your availability and interest to do an interview to help editors plan their schedules and copy space.
- Something very special or having impact upon the community must happen in order to get an interview or cover story.

Arts And Alternative Papers

Often distributed on a weekly basis, these papers cater to those whose interests follow the arts and alternative lifestyles. Targeting these community-based papers is likely to reach a large segment of your audience and should be high on your priority list. Also interested in events that impact upon the community they serve, these papers offer calendar and feature sections, as well as news segments. By pre-determining the extent to which your event can be placed in other sections, above and beyond the calendar listings, you may find these papers more open to an interesting twist to a story line.

Carefully adhere to deadlines when sending material to weeklies. While researching media outlets, it is to your advantage to find out all of the different departments these papers include. As an arts paper, there may be different types of calendar listings and your event may be suitable for multiple inclusion. Develop an ongoing relationship with the editors to help get coverage. As an out-of-town artist, you can lend

HotTip:
"For commercial print media, send stuff to everybody. The paper is dozens of different people doing different jobs that often overlap."
Scott Alarik
music writer,
The Boston Globe

"Electronic Press Kits (EPK™) are quickly becoming the new standard that both the professional and independent music industry is using to communicate the value and marketability of an artist. Real-time updates, richer information, cost-efficiency and increased effectiveness give the EPK™ a significant advantage over traditional paper press kits."
Panos Panay
founder & CEO,
Sonicbids

"It is certainly to a venue's advantage for you to get good press. If we send a picture in for every artist that plays here, the newspaper would say, 'Well she's sending me a dozen pictures this week, which one am I supposed to choose?' If the artist only sends a photo once every six months, they are very likely to get it in."
Amy Kurland
owner,
The Bluebird Cafe

some regional or national importance to your performance in town.

These types of papers are likely to support the hometown artists by extending coverage as the artist further develops their careers. Befriend these editors and writers. They can help build your local audience. Call them with information about new releases and include them on your mailing lists to receive every piece of mail. Invite the reviewers to shows with tickets waiting at the door. One day, they may just take you up on your offer.

What to send:
For the calendar listing
- A short press release detailing the event: who, what, where, when, why and how.
- A black and white photo and/or color slide.

For the editors
- A cover letter explaining the arts and newsworthiness of this event and suggestions for specific segments of the paper in which a story like this could be included.
- A press release that details how you are integrally associated with the event and what makes it newsworthy and arts-worthy. Include times that you are available for interviews.
- A black and white photo and a color slide.
- A copy of your CD if it is a new release not yet covered.

What to expect:
- If your information arrived on time, it is very likely that you will be listed in the calendar sections.
- If space allows, a photo and caption may also be included.
- If you perform in town often, your coverage will depend upon the scope of the event in light of your past performances and your competition during that week.
- A calendar listing can be ongoing.
- Stories and interviews may be less likely if you are a hometown artist. Schedule important events with enough time between them so you can take full advantage of media coverage. Unless something big, new and exciting is happening, papers are not inclined to offer print space. If you are the flavor of the month, they will write about you weekly. For example: My hometown alternative paper, the *C'Ville Weekly* will mention our hometown artist, Dave Matthews or the Dave Matthews Band often. Hometown papers enjoy participating in an artist's development. If you are the hometown-kid-made-very-good, you never have to worry about coverage.

> *"A telephone call gets my attention earlier and more intimately than any other form of communication. I especially like hearing about upcoming gigs in my area. And if I'm familiar with the artist, it gives me a chance to chat about current goings-on; if the artist is new to me, I can ask questions that may pique my interest and prompt me to give coverage that mail or a fax might not evoke."*
>
> **Jack Bernhardt**
> traditional and
> country music critic,
> *The News and Observer*

Wire Services

There are literally thousands of newspaper syndicates and independent wire services worldwide. Some of the most widely known syndicates which distribute entertainment news are mentioned here. Most notable among the familiar services are Associated Press (AP), Reuters and Knight Ridder. In Canada, add the Canadian Press & Broadcast News to the list.

Here is an example of how a local story can "make it" onto the wire. A local writer for a daily paper or a freelancer does a story about you for a local event. That paper is a member of a particular wire service, and your editor decides to send the story to the wire service to be further considered for release nationally. Once approved for national distribution, any affiliated paper can reprint the story in their paper.

Record reviews are also great space fillers, because they are often short and if it is a review of a nationally-touring artist, it can have meaning for readers in many cities. For instance, reviews written for the dailies in Nashville and St. Paul may be reprinted in papers in a number of other cities. When touring on a regional or national basis, local papers are more likely to pick up these stories for reprint in the tour markets where you will be appearing, especially if the local paper does not have the time or personnel to write their own story or conduct their own interview. With this in mind, include a tour itinerary with every press release you send to any print media.

"The criteria is the same as any other story consideration—the usefulness to the paper and how it fits the editor's theme. If I'm writing a story for St. Paul and we send it to Knight Ridder and they send it out on the wire, then it's up to the editor in Charlotte to decide if he wants to use my story instead of assigning one of his own guys. Editors pull stories off the wires all the time if we know an act is coming to town. However, stories only stay on the wire for about 72 hours. If you don't grab it when you can, then it's lost."

Jim Tarbox
*copy editor,
entertainment staff,
Showtime,
St. Paul Pioneer Press*

What to expect:
- This is a bonus. If a writer submits a story to a wire service and it is accepted, some of the advance work has been done for you since their story might appear in many different papers—often across the country.
- When multiple markets print a story about you, it signifies the impact you are making within the genre and that you are newsworthy. Accept this as a gift.

Newsletters

Group and organization newsletters are an often-ignored resource for direct promotion. Timing is critical when accessing newsletters. Many are either monthly, bimonthly or quarterly, with lengthy advance deadlines for advertising or article inclusion. Newsletters target a direct market whether it is genre specific, region specific, trade specific or interest specific—it is the perfect niche-marketing tool and should not be overlooked.

When planning regional tours, ask promoters which newsletters are circulated in that region that are appropriate for your act to target along with the newsletter of the organization for which you are working.

> **HotTip:** Find out from each interviewer or reviewer which wire service their paper is affiliated with. Once you know that an interview was picked up by a particular service, mention this when speaking with other papers affiliated with the same service.

First, contact the individual newsletters to get a copy of a recent issue. Check for advertising and classified ad rates (which are usually very reasonable); types of articles and deadlines for advance information on upcoming events—calendars, venue listings, artist listings.

Speak with the editor about their interest in doing an interview or writing a preview article for the upcoming tour date. Perhaps there are other areas of interest that could be incorporated into the issue, especially one whose issues take a thematic approach.

What to send:
- A press release.
- A black and white photo unless you know the newsletter prints color, then send a color slide as well.
- A biography.
- Current release for possible review.
- Your full press packet, if they would like, to keep on file.

What to expect:
- Decisions to include your information are based on how you or your show impacts upon the community of readers which the newsletter serves.
- Items that are suited to the newsletter's format and space constraints will most likely be included with the editor's prior agreement if you adhere to the deadlines.
- Feature articles are most often included when your performance is pertinent to that issue of the newsletter and you are appearing in their area.
- A display ad is a perfect substitute if you have missed article deadlines or the editor has chosen not to include an article.

> "Local newsletters are always desperate for material to fill up their white space. It's an excellent source for performers to directly target the audience that they're seeking. From the organization's standpoint, they want material that will benefit their audience. The rates are also very inexpensive if you decide to place an ad."
>
> Barbara Karol
> former chairfolk,
> San Diego Folk Heritage

There are literally thousands of newsletters which may be appropriate for you to use in a marketing campaign outside the regular entertainment-related organizations. The newsletter is the ultimate niche-marketing tool. If you determine your product or music has some significance to an organization, trade group, religious group, charity group, etc., consider advertising in its specific newsletter. Once you have identified specific niche markets to which you would like to become significant, inquire about their newsletter procedures and deadlines. A well-placed article or press release may create some interest on your behalf.

Lists of newsletters are available in directories in the library and are published by media services. (See this chapter's resource section for information.)

Conclusion

With the information and the tools provided in this chapter, you should have the capability to plan your print media campaigns more strategically. Similar to each presenter you work with, each individual that you encounter in the media has their own method of working with publicists and artists. Once again, this is the relationship game; developing a working, ongoing relationship with those in the media is your surest, most direct route to coverage next to having an artistic product worthy of notice. By targeting the specific outlets with the information they need and in the manner they are accustomed to working, access to print media can infuse new life into your career.

Summary

- Become familiar with the various forms of print media and how you can use them to your advantage in a variety of situations, for different purposes.
- Send appropriate material to each specific editor.
- Timely follow-up calls are imperitive if you want to receive attention from editors.
- Develop EPKs for easy access to your press materials.

> **HotTip:**
> *Gale Directory of Publication and Broadcast Media*
> Phone: 1-877-877-4253
> Phone: 248-699-4253
> Web: http://www.gale.com
> *Newsletters in Print* lists 11,000 newsletters found in libraries.
>
> **Online Newspapers Worldwide**
> http://www.onlinenewspapers.com
> free
>
> **Newspapers Worldwide**
> http://www.newspapers.com
>   free

Resources

Directories:

Musician's Atlas
38 Porter Place
Montclair, NJ 07042-2036
Phone: 973-509-9898
Fax: 973-655-1238
E-mail: MRGroup@aol.com
Web: http://www.MusiciansAtlas.com
Press, publicity resources.

Musician's Guide to Touring & Promotion
49 Music Square
Nashville, TN 37203
Phone: 615-321-4295
Fax: 615-327-1575
http://www.musicianmag.com
A&R directory, gigs, services, websites/band directory, tapes & disk services.

Genre Magazines:

Audiophile:

The Audiophile Voice
Production Offices
P.O. Box 43537
Upper Montclaire, NJ 07043
Phone: 973-509-2009
Fax: 973-509-2032
E-mail: epitts@ix.netcom.com
Web: http://www.enjoythemusic.com

Stereophile
261 Madison Ave.
New York, NY 10016
Phone: 212-886-3923
Fax: 212-886-2810
Web: http://www.stereophile.com

Bluegrass:

Bluegrass Now
P.O. Box 2020
Rolla, MO 65402
Phone: 1-800-736-0125
Phone: 573-341-7336
Fax: 573-341-7352
E-mail: bgn@fidnet.com
Web: http://www.bluegrassnow.com
Bluegrass, features, reviews, tour schedules, group news.

Bluegrass Unlimited
P.O. Box 771
Warrenton, VA 20188-0771
Phone: 1-800-258-4727
Fax: 540-341-0011
E-mail: info@bluegrassmusic.com
Web: http://www.bluegrassmusic.com
Bluegrass; features, interviews, band news, tour schedules.

Blues:

Blues Access
1455 Chestnut Place
Boulder, CO 80304-3153
Phone: 303-443-7245
Fax: 303-939-9729
E-mail: cary@bluesaccess.com
Web: http://www.bluesaccess.com
Features, reviews, festival listings.

Blues Revue
Route 1, Box 75
Salem, WV 26426
Phone: 304-782-1971
Fax: 304-782-1993
E-mail: info@bluesrevue.com
Web: http://www.bluesrevue.com
Features, reviews, radio charts.

Living Blues
Center For The Study Of Southern Culture
Hill Hall, Room 301
The University of Mississippi
University, MS 38677-9836
Phone: 1-800-390-3527
E-mail: lblues@olemiss.edu
Web: http://www.livingblues.com
Features, reviews, radio charts.

Classical:

BBC Music Magazine
North American Edition
Room A1004
Woodlands, 80 Wood Lane
London W1Z 0TT, Great Britain
Phone: 011-44-0181-576-3283 or 3693
Fax: 011-44-0181-576-3292
Web: http://www.bbcamerica.com

Fanfare
273 Woodland Street
Tenafly, NJ 07670
Phone: 201-567-3980
Fax: 201-816-0125
Web: http://www.fanfaremag.com

Gramophone
Gramophone Publications Limited
38-42 Hampton Road
Teddington
Middlesex TW11 0JE
Great Britain
Phone: 011-44-020-8267-5050
Fax: 011-44-020-8267-5866
E-mail: gramaphone@haynet.com
Web: http://www.gramophone.co.uk/recofthemonth.asp

Country:

Country Weekly Magazine
1000 American Media Way
Boca Raton, FL 33464
Web: http://www.countryweekly.com
Country music features, news, reviews, interviews.

Music Row
1231 17th Avenue South
Nashville, TN 37212
Phone: 615-321-3617; Fax: 615-329-0852
E-mail: news@musicrow.com
Web: http://www.musicrow.com
Country music news from Nashville, deals, features.

Country Music Media Guide
Talent & Booking
P.O. Box 14265
Palm Desert, CA 92255
Phone: 760-779-8056; Fax: 760-779-3568
E-mail: info@talentandbooking.com
Web: http://www.talentandbooking.com
Country magazines, radio, TV stations and shows.

Dance:

Dance Magazine
333 Seventh Avenue, 11th Floor
New York, NY 10001
Phone: 212-979-4803
Fax: 212-674-0102
E-mail: dancemag@dancemagazine.com
Web: http://www.dancemagazine.com

Dance Spirit
Lifestyle Media, Inc.
110 William Street
New York, NY 10038
Phone: 646-459-4800
Fax: 646-459-4900
Web: http://www.dancespirit.com

Early Music:

Early Music America
2366 Eastlake Ave. E.
Seattle, WA 98102
Phone: 206-720-6270
Web: http://www.earlymusic.org
Early music, features, reviews, instruments.

Entertainment News:

Variety
5700 Wilshire Blvd., Suite 120
Los Angeles, CA 90036
Phone: 323-965-4476
Fax: 323-857-0494
Web: http://www.variety.com
Film, TV, music; news, features.

Folk, Acoustic, World Music:

Dirty Linen
P.O. Box 66600
Baltimore, MD 21239-6600
Phone: 410-583-7973
Fax: 410-337-6735
E-mail: info@dirtylinen.com
Web: http://www.dirtylinen.com
Folk, world music, roots music, Celtic; features, interviews, tour schedules, new release and concert reviews.

Folk Roots Magazine/ Southern Rag Ltd.
P.O. Box 337
London, England N4 1TW
Phone: 44-20-8340-9651
Fax: 44-20-8348-5626
E-mail: froots@froots.demon.co.uk
Web: http://www.frootsmag.com
Folk, Celtic; features, interviews, reviews.

Old-Time Herald
P.O. Box 51812
Durham, NC 27707
Phone: 919-419-1800
E-mail: info@oldtimeherald.org
Web: http://www.oldtimeherald.org
Features, reviews, interviews, about Old-Time Music.

Sing Out! Magazine
The Sing Out Corporation
P.O. Box 5460
Bethlehem, PA 18015-0460
Phone: 610-865-5366
Fax: 610-865-5129
E-mail: info@singout.org
Web: http://www.singout.org
Folk music; features, reviews, regular columns.

Victory Review
P.O. Box 2254
Tacoma, WA 98401-2254
Phone: 253-428-0832
Fax: 253-428-8086
E-mail: victory@nwlink.com
Web: http://www.victorymusic.org
Folk, roots, acoustic music; features, reviews, area venue performance schedules and events, monthly columns.

Guitar:

Acoustic Guitar
P.O. Box 767
San Anselmo, CA 94979
Phone: 415-485-6946
Fax: 415-485-0831
E-mail: ag@pcspublink.com
Web: http://www.acguitar.com
Features, interviews, reviews, products.

Finger Style Guitar
21143 Hawthorne Blvd., #508
Torrance, CA 90503
Phone: 888-223-3340
Fax: 310-465-1788
E-mail: fsguitar@aol.com
Web: http://www.fingerstyleguitar.com
Features, reviews, news, products.

Flatpick Guitar Magazine
68 East Main
Pulaski, VA 24301
Phone: 1-800-413-8296
Web: http://www.flatpick.com

Guitar Player
2800 Campus Drive
San Mateo, CA 94403
Phone: 650-513-4300
Fax: 650-513-4642
Web: http://www.guitarplayer.com

Guitar World
1115 Broadway
New York, NY 10010
Phone: 212-807-7100; Fax: 212-627-4678
E-mail: editor@guitarworld.com
Web: http://www.guitarworld.com
Electric, features, reviews, products.

Maximum Guitar
Harris Publications
1115 Broadway
New York, NY 10010
Phone: 212-807-7100
Fax: 212-627-4678
E-mail: mail@maximumguitar.com
Web: http://www.maximumguitar.com
Rock, heavy metal, features, reviews, products.

Jazz:

Down Beat
102 North Haven Road
Elmhurst, IL 60126
Phone: 800-554-7470
Fax: 630-941-3210
E-mail: editor@downbeat.com
Web: http://www.downbeat.com

JazzImprove
E.S. Proteus, Inc.
P.O. Box 26770
Elkins, PA 19027
Phone: 1-866-493-7185
Web: http://www.jazzimprov.com

JazzInternet.com
Web: http://www.jazzinternet.com
links to internet jazz magazines, e-zines and resources

Jazz IZ
2650 N. Military Trail, Suite 140
Boca Raton, FL 33431
Phone: 561-893-6868, ext. 303
Fax: 561-893-6867
E-mail: mail@jazziz.com
Web: http://www.jazziz.com
Features, reviews, news.

Jazz Times
8737 Colesville Road, 9th Floor
Silver Spring, MD 20910-3921
Phone: 301-588-4114
E-mail: info@jazztimes.com
Web: http://www.jazztimes.com
Jazz and blues, features, reviews, news.

Keyboard:

Keyboard
2800 Campus Drive
San Mateo, CA 94403
Phone: 650-513-4300
Fax: 650-513-4661
E-mail: keyboard@musicplayer.com
Web: http://www.keyboardonline.com
News, features, reviews, products.

Musician General:

Performer (Northeast, Southeast, Southwest)
285 Washington Street
Sommerville, MA 02143
Phone: 617-627-9200
Fax: 617-627-9930
E-mail: info@performermag.com
Web: http://www.performermag.com

Opera

Opera America
330 Seventh Ave., 16th Floor
New York, NY 10001
Phone: 212-796-8620
Fax: 212-796-8631
e-mail: frontdesk@operaamerica.org
Web: http://www.operaamerica.org
Publications, meetings, resources, singer services, professional development

Opera News
The Metropolitan Opera Guild, Inc.
70 Lincoln Center Plaza
New York, NY 10023
Web: http://www.operanews.com

The Opera Quarterly
Duke University Press
Box 90660
Durham, NC 27708-0660
Phone: 919-687-3633

Rap, Hip-Hop:

The Source
215 Park Ave. South
New York, NY 10003
Phone: 212-253-3700
Web: http://www.thesource.com
Hip-hop, rap, features, reviews.

Vibe
215 Lexington Avenue, 3rd Floor
New York, NY 10016
Phone: 212-448-7300
Web: http://www.vibe.com

Rock, Alternative:

Rolling Stone
1290 Avenue of the Americas, 2nd Floor
New York, NY 10104
Phone: 1-800-283-1549
Phone: 212-484-1616
Web: http://www.Rollingstone.com
Features, reviews, music news.

Spin
205 Lexington Avenue
New York, NY 10016
Phone: 212-231-7400
Fax: 212-231-7312
Web: http://www.spin.com
Rock, pop; features, reviews, news.

Singer, Songwriter:

American Songwriter Magazine
50 Music Square West, Suite 604
Nashville, TN37203-3227
Phone: 615-321-6096
Fax: 615-321-6097
E-mail: info@americansongwriter.com
Web: http://www.americansongwriter.com

Backstage
5055 Wilshire Blvd.
Los Angeles, CA 90036
Phone: 323-525-2356
Fax: 323-525-2354
Web: http://www.backstage.com
Film and TV trade to get inside information on upcoming projects to pitch songs, performances.

Hollywood Reporter
5055 Wilshire Blvd., Suite 600
Los Angeles, CA 90036
Phone: 323-525-2000
Fax: 323-525-2377
Web: http://www.hollywoodreporter.com
Inside information on film and TV upcoming projects.

Performing Songwriter Magazine
P.O. Box 40931
Nashville, TN 37204
Phone: 615-385-7796
Fax: 615-385-5637
Advertising: 310-316-0069
E-mail: perfsong@performingsongwriter.com
Web: http://www.performingsongwriter.com
Features, mini-features, reviews, monthly columns.

Singer Magazine
2333 Rawley Pike
Harrisonburg, VA 22801
Phone: 540-438-7464
Web: http://www.singermagazine.com

Variety
5700 Wilshire Blvd., Suite 120
Los Angeles, CA 90036
Phone: 323-857-6600
Fax: 323-857-0742
Web: http://www.variety.com
Film industry trade, songwriters, composers get inside information on upcoming TV and film projects to pitch material.

Theatre:

American Theatre Guild
Theatre Communications Group
520 8th Avenue, 24th Floor
New York, NY 10018-4156
Phone: 212-609-5900
Fax: 212-609-5901
E-mail: tcg@tcg.org
Web: http://www.tcg.org
Plays, lectures, film, panels, other performances. October Issue—annual production schedules for theatres coast to coast.
American Theatre
ArtSearch
Dramatists Sourcebook
Show Business Weekly

Newspaper, Radio And Television Directories:
Found in libraries, online or for sale

Burrelle's Media Directories
Burrelle's Information Services
75 East Northfield Road
Livingston, NJ 07039
Phone: 1-800-876-3342
E-mail: directory@burrelles.com
Web: http://www.burrelles.com
Information available for U.S., Canada and Mexico.
Newspapers and Related Media—Daily Newspapers
Newspapers and Related Media—Non-Daily Newspapers
Magazines and Newsletters

Broadcast Media—Television and Cable
Broadcast Media—Radio
Available in print, CD-ROM, Internet, costs for the set, print and disks.

Gale Directory of Publication and Broadcast Media
Gale Research
27500 Drake Road
Farmington Hills, MI 48331
Phone: 1-800-877-4253
Web: http://www.gale.com
Annual Guide listing newspapers, magazines, journals, radio stations, television stations and cable systems.—Sold in 3 volume set, cost $460.00.
Newsletters in Print—lists 11,000 newsletters.
Encyclopedia of Associations—USA 3-parts, 23,000 associations.
International Associations—2-volume set.
Regional, State and Local Associations—one volume.
Available in libraries.

Editor & Publisher
770 Broadway
New York, NY 10003-9595
Phone: 1-800-336-4380
Fax: 646-654-5370
Web: http://www.editorandpublisher.com
Editor & Publisher International Year Book—U.S. Dailies, U.S. Weeklies and Special Newspapers, Canadian Newspapers, Foreign Newspapers, News, Picture and Syndicated Services. Annual
Editor & Publisher/Free Paper Publisher, Community, Specialty & Free Publications Year Book
Community Weeklies, Shoppers/TMC, Specialty and Niche Publications, Non-Daily Newspaper Groups
Database available on disk or labels, call for prices.
Editor & Publisher Syndicate Directory—list of syndicates, authors, byline features.

Newspapers Worldwide
Web: http://www.newspapers.com

Online Newspapers
Web: http://ww.onlinenewspapers.com
lists of the world's newpapers

SRDS Media Solutions
1700 Higgins Road
Des Plaines, IL 60018
Phone: 1-800-851-7737
Phone: 847-375-5000
Fax: 847-375-5001
Web: http://www.srds.com
Five directories with media data on 17,000 publications worldwide.
Business Professional: Asia Pacific/ Middle East / Africa.
Business Professional: Europe.
Business Professional: The Americas.

Consumer Magazines Worldwide.
Newspapers Worldwide.
Cost per guide.

Parrot Media Network
2917 North Ontario Street
Burbank, CA 91504
Phone: 818-567-4700
Fax: 818-567-4600
E-mail: info@parrotmedia.com
Web: http://www.parrotmedia.com
U.S. TV Station Directory—printed quarterly.
U.S. Cable TV Directory—printed semi-annually.
U.S. Newspaper Directory—printed semi-annually.
U.S. Radio Directory—printed semi-annually.
Directories priced per issue or packaged per year. Subscriptions available for online use, directories updated daily.

Organizations With Targeted Media Lists:

CMA
APAP
Folk Alliance
IBMA
See Resources in Chapter 11 for contact information. Lists available for sale.

Trade Magazines:

Billboard
1515 Broadway, 39th Floor
New York, NY 10036
Phone: 1-800-344-7119
Web: http://www.billboard.com
Charts: http://www.billboard.com/charts
Industry news, interviews, features, reviews.
Radio Charts: Pop, Country, Hits of The World, Contemporary Christian, Gospel, R & B, Rap, Dance Music, Latin, Blues, Reggae, World Music.
The Power Book—Fall and Spring Edition, guide to radio and record promotion.

Performance Magazine
International Touring Talent Weekly Newspaper
1203 Lake Street
Fort Worth, TX 76102-4504
Phone: 817-338-9444
Fax: 817-877-4273
Web: http://www.performancemagazine.com
Industry news, tour schedules, box office reports.

Pollstar
4697 W. Jacquelyn Avenue
Fresno, CA 93722
Phone: 1-800-344-7383
In California: 559-271-7900
Fax: 559-271-7979
E-mail: info@pollstar.com
Web: http://www.pollstar.com
Industry news, tour schedules, box office reports.
Pulse Charts: albums sales, radio plays.

Wire Services:

Listed in *Editor & Publisher,* hundreds of press networks exist worldwide.
Here are a few of the main networks:

Associated Press—Main Office
450 W. 33rd Street
New York, NY 10001
Phone: 212-621-1500
Web: http://www.ap.org

The Canadian News & Broadcast News
36 King Street East
Toronto, Ontario M5C 2L9
Phone: 416-364-0321
Fax: 416-364-0207
Web: http://www.cp.org
Web: http://www.canpress.ca

Catholic News Services
3211 4th Street NE
Washington, DC 20017-1100
Phone: 202-541-3250
Fax: 202-541-3255
Web: http://www.catholicnews.com

Reuters—New York Bureau
Three Times Square
New York, NY 10036
Phone: 646-223-4000
Web: http://www.reuters.com

Reuters-Canada
Suite 2000
Standard Life Centre
121 King Street west
Toronto, Ontario M5H 3T9
Phone: 416-941-8000

Knight-Ridder/Tribune Information Services
700 National Press Bldg.
Washington, D.C. 20045-1601
Phone: 202-383-6134
Web: http://www.knightridder.com
Subscriptions available.

CHAPTER FIFTEEN
Accessing The Media—Radio

"I remember a classic story of Web Wilder coming in to play at the club, QEII. Every one of the three daily newspapers did an interview with him, as well as the alternative weekly, the alternative music monthly and the school newspaper. He was prominently featured in each publication. I showed up at the gig, there's Web Wilder and his band and six people in the audience. The six people were the writers from each of the six papers. There was not a single paying customer there. All that blitz, all that publicity resulted in nothing. The problem—there was no airplay."

Greg Haymes
music writer,
Albany Times Union

When we are discussing music, radio is perhaps the most important of the media support systems in an artist's career. Music must be heard and radio offers an artist that opportunity. Getting your music to the medium and getting it played is the focus of this chapter. Regardless of your genre, there are some basics from which all artists can benefit when attempting to get airplay.

Radio Formats
Radio formats, for better or for worse, separate music into categories. They provide a system mainstream radio uses to streamline new releases. These stations can reach their target audiences and cater to their very particular musical tastes. If you want to reach a mainstream audience, pay attention to the var-

"While a lot of the stories about Windham Hill say that we were not created by airplay, I would argue that in the early days, while progressive FM still existed, airplay was terribly important to us. Geographically we were played on every station from KTWN in Minneapolis to stations in the Boston area and all up and down the west coast."

Will Ackerman
guitarist, founder,
Windham Hill Records;
Imaginary Road Records

ious radio formats to understand how your music may benefit by directing it towards a specific format. It will be advantageous for artists not concerned with mainstream attention to also understand radio formats and how they may even play a role in the creation and marketing of their own music. (See the resource section for websites and magazines with radio charts.)

Many times, an artist's music fits squarely in one specific format. However, their music may change and overlap formats, in an attempt to expand the artist's audience. When an artist's music has the ability to cross formats, the artist's recognition, record sales and audience have greater growth potential. Nanci Griffith is a great example of an artist who, remaining true to her music, found a home in a number of formats.

> "There are various formats today. Right now there are so many different format shades in adult contemporary that you need to know whether you are talking about Traditional Adult Contemporary, where you'll hear Celine Dion, Hot Adult Contemporary, where you'll hear Sister Hazel or a new format, Modern Adult Contemporary, now playing Sheryl Crow, Shawn Colvin, Wallflower and a lot of the hip new folks who got their toehold on Triple A."
>
> **Jessie Scott**
> program director,
> XCountry
> XM Satellite Radio

> "Nanci's music lent itself to multi-formats. We took her to Nashville radio when Nashville was going through some changes. It was the same time that Steve Earle, Lyle Lovett, and a variety of other edgier, outside-of-the-norm, traditional country artists were being signed. What we found was that country embraced them very briefly and then rejected anything that wasn't a little bit more traditional. Nanci kept doing what she did—making really great records, and we kept trying to find niches for her. We worked public radio a lot and some of the secondary country stations. At the same time, Triple A started being the new format which was almost like the rock formats of the late sixties, early seventies. It seemed like a natural home for her and she did very well there since Triple A was a format where people were willing to give great music a chance—fresh, strongly-lyrical music—and it worked. We took a multi-format approach to some of her music—some singles were released AC, some Triple A, and some were released pop. It really depended on the tune. Through Nanci's world travels, she involved a lot of guests on her records. Look at the Flyer album and there's everybody from the guys in U2 to Marc Knopfler to Adam Duritz from Counting Crows. By adding some of these core artists who were established in these formats to her recordings, it gave us some other opportunities for the Triple A market and other formats to embrace her."
>
> **Ken Levitan**
> former manager,
> Nanci Griffith

> "I wish artists would target their music and not be so scattershot. The reality is that there is more to getting on Triple-A radio than producing a recording with rock-and-roll instrumentation."
>
> **Rich Warren**
> host, *The Midnight Special*,
> WFMT Radio, Chicago, IL

Target the format which plays your music before you enter the recording studio. A recording that has focus and maintains that focus throughout is the first step in getting airplay in a specific format.

Radio Charts

The list of charts on page 365 demonstrates how the various radio trade magazines use a variety of labels to report airplay.

Each radio format has a radio "chart" associated with it. These charts help to register the amount of airplay any specific cut of a recording receives nationwide during a one week period. The cut is registered on the chart in numerical order

Billboard Charts	Radio & Records Charts	Roots Music Report
1. AC Adult Contemporary	1. AC Adult Contemporary	1. Roots
2. Pop	2. Hot AC	2. Bluegrass
3. Adult Top 40	3. Alternative	3. Roots Blues
4. Hot 100	4. Country	4. Folk
5. Country	5. CHR Rhythmic	5. Roots Country
6. Contemporary Christian	6. CHR Pop	
7. Gospel	7. Latin	
8. Jazz	8. NAC/Smooth Jazz	
9. Jazz/Contemporary	9. Active Rock	
10. Rock	10. Rock	
11. R & B	11. Triple A	
12. Rap	12. Urbana	
13. New Age	13. Urban AC	
14. World Music		
15. Latin		

according to which one received the most plays that week. Each chart may also focus attention on a particular segment of radio airplay. For example, *Billboard* tracks more mainstream stations in various formats while *CMJ (College Media Journal)* tracks college radio. You may be familiar with the *Billboard, Radio and Records* or *Roots Music* radio charts.

There are a number of other charts which register airplay in the above-mentioned formats. These alternative charts can open new possibilities for those of you who thought that there was no opportunity for national chart recognition because your music did not fit the *Billboard* formats. Among them, *Americana* charts airplay of contemporary acoustic music that draws in some way from the country music traditions; *Jazz* and *NAC (New Alternative Contemporary)/Smooth Jazz* charts airplay of instrumental and vocal recordings in jazz, world music, Celtic and New Age. Triple A or A3 format is a midway point between the acoustic music formats and Adult Contemporary formats. *New Age Voice* charts offer a flexible place for instrumental and vocal music to receive some national attention without having to fall firmly in the jazz category.

The *Americana* chart is geared to artists who record on independent labels. Artists from bluegrass labels and singer/songwriter labels are receiving recognition here as well as the *Roots Music Report*. You will see artists like Steve Earle, Greg Brown and Chesapeake having some success on the *Americana* chart.

As a recording artist planning a new project, careful consideration should be given to radio prior to making your recording. By listening to the various radio formats and studying the charts, you may be better prepared to create a recording that is well

> "When approaching the Triple A radio format, one must be aware that it is very diversified territory. Unlike formats that follow a formula, Triple A covers many styles of music. It is important to be familiar with the station's play list and understand their range of programming to know if your music is suitable for their air waves."
>
> **Louise Coogan**
> radio promotor,
> Songlines, Ltd.

> "If your music fits in a particular format, study who is successful and why. You can make your own music be individual and still have some of the familiar qualities that help it fit in a particular format."
>
> **Michael Moryc**
> independent radio promoter,
> Matrix Promotions

> **HotTip:** 🌶
> Read *Radio and Records* for in-depth information regarding reporting stations and radio charts.
> Read *Crossroads* for reporting stations in folk, roots and world music.

"If you look at what is happening on the AC charts in the last couple of years, it has become a lot more responsive to acoustic textures. Tracy Chapman's 'Give Me One Reason' was a huge song for her. Listen to the instrumentation on Sister Hazel or Matchbox 20—you're hearing acoustic guitar in there, there's an edge to it, but it's definitely rooted in the acoustic."

**Jessie Scott
program director,
XCountry
XM Satellite Radio**

suited to meet the competition head on. Your recording may have a stronger opportunity of receiving wider recognition from radio when strategically produced and recorded. If you know what is being played, you will know what works in a given format. However, there is no substitute for creative uniqueness. Emulate what works on the air, but strive to develop and maintain something fresh that is all your own.

I will discuss using independent radio promotions companies in Chapter 18, Working With Your Record Company. For now, if you are a recording artist, it is important to have some understanding of the role radio formats play in enhancing or hindering your radio experience.

Reporting Stations

There are stations throughout the country which are designated as "reporting stations"—they report their playlists to the various charts. For mainstream commercial radio, a reporting station is usually in a large enough market to influence the charts. The station must adhere to the format 100 percent. The station must be committed to having 60% to 75% of their playlist coming from new music. The two most important and influential systems are Broadcast Data Systems (*Billboard*) and *Radio and Records*. A reporting station whose playlists are accepted by these systems is part of a group of stations which influence the success or failure of a particular recording in a specific format.

Beyond Mainstream Radio

Radio charts for music outside of the mainstream formats have surfaced over the last few years. You can find bluegrass, world, roots and folk music reported by stations around the world. For artists whose careers gravitate towards these genres, establishing a radio presence outside the commercial radio market is becoming more feasible as these genres begin reporting airplay and tracking retail sales.

Reporting stations and charts for these music genres are growing and lists of stations can be found online on the *Roots Music Report*—reporting roots, bluegrass, blues, folk and country and *Americana*—reporting acoustic country-tinged music. In Canada, *Chart Attack* reports college radio charts, electronic, metal, hip-hop, world and jazz.

(See resource section for radio charts.)

Commercial And Non-Commercial Radio

Commercial radio is supported by paid advertising. Non-commercial radio is supported by public contributions, grants, fund-raising campaigns and local business underwriting (which often sounds like advertising). Non-commercial radio includes college radio (sometimes a college station may be supported by paid advertising), public radio and community radio.

Commercial Radio

Commercial radio most often supports radio formats such as adult contemporary, country, rock and alternative rock, etc. Radio programming caters to the dictates of the major record labels on their quest for making hits and defining current music-industry history. With major labels supporting their new artists' releases with many hundreds of thousands of promotion dollars, it is still very much a money game. Most independent labels and their recording artists cannot compete. This makes commercial radio often inaccessible to all but the major labels. Once in a great while, a renegade artist slips through the cracks, as in the case of independent bluegrass artist Alison Krauss and Union Station. They occasionally receive airplay on mainstream country, Americana, and A3 as well as NPR and college radio.

If you are on an independent label but suited for commercial radio formats, incorporating a professional radio promotion company into your marketing plan and having a sizable promotion budget is a must.

If it is radio, the music says it all. Know your format. Research some previous playlists of the stations you are targeting. Read *Billboard, Radio & Record, Americana* and *FMQB* to know which artists are currently being played. Check the resource section for directories of radio stations appropriate to your format to get music director contact information.

What to send:
- Send the latest CD, and include a one sheet introduction on the artist (this gives a short bio, a description of the music on the CD and contact information, see pages 79-80).

What to expect:
- Follow-up phone calls are a must. Whether you do it or whether you hire a radio promotion company, it is unlikely that you will get any attention on commercial radio without personal contact.
- It is difficult to get airplay unless you have major label support, a radio promotion company promoting the release, a previous push from college radio, a large regional fan base creating listener demand or influences from other mediums such as MTV.
- Attempt to gain some recognition by winning over individual stations beginning on the home front and expanding out. Often, hometown commercial stations program local acts into their playlists. Plan to use these opportunities to support new releases and release concerts. Schedule interviews in-studio or by phone when promoting these events.

Non-Commercial Radio

Non-commercial radio includes college radio, public radio and community radio. Each type of radio programming offers

---

"There are a lot of different paths where you might want to start. Years ago, if you could get a modicum of success on Triple A, you could parlay that to the Hot AC chart. Ninety-five percent of the artists being played on Hot AC came from Triple A. In deference to where one goes now, I would have to say that Alternative is the place where more new music is breaking."

Jessie Scott
program director,
XCountry
XM Satellite Radio

"Publicity is great but people are going to buy records from hearing it on the radio—not from reading a review. If there is an obvious radio cut or two, they should be sequenced in strategic places on the record such as cut one or two."

Roger Lifeset
independent radio promoter,
Peer Pressure Promotion

independent recording artists as well as non-music-related performers an arena in which to promote their music or their act.

College Radio

Most college radio stations have a general volunteer DJ staff hosting each show. The show formats cover a broad spectrum of tastes catering to those on campus and the community at large. Given the transient nature of a college community and the wide variety of show formats, accessing college radio takes persistence and commitment similar to booking performance dates on the college campus. Often independent radio promotion companies and radio promoters from major labels dedicate whole departments or specific individuals to deal with the college market. But if the college market is so transient and flexible, why devote so much promotional effort here? The college market is the proving ground for many new acts, especially in the pop, rock and alternative-rock genres. It is often on college radio that the next "superstars" are launched.

The variety of programming offered by college radio also opens many doors for independent music labels and independent artists. Thanks to the wide spectrum of tastes, college radio stations often have DJs whose musical preferences include, folk, world music, jazz, blues, Celtic, New Age, bluegrass, country, rock, alternative and hip-hop as well as classical and opera. It is on these segmented shows that contemporary independent artists find a home.

Because of the segmented nature of college radio, hosts of specialty shows might be on air once a week for an hour or two at a time. If that is the case, little room is left for repetition of a single cut from one specific artist. Therefore, most DJs opt to feature as many new artists as they can each show. This method of programming may make it difficult to build momentum for any one particular artist, one particular release or one specific cut. Especially affected by this phenomenon are most of the acoustic genres like folk, bluegrass, Celtic, and world music. It does, however, offer airplay opportunities to artists who might not otherwise have a radio venue.

What to send:
❖ Research some previous playlists of the stations you are targeting to become familiar with the artists played. This will save you from sending recordings to inappropriate stations.
❖ Find out who the show hosts are, their specific genre of interest and their show times.
❖ Target specific DJs if the station is broken into topical or genre shows.
❖ Target the music director on some stations.
❖ Send a cover letter introducing yourself.

"There are fewer and fewer stations in the country making their own programming decisions. As a result, those that are, are more and more important to the music industry. These are the stations where a new artist and new albums can get a start."

Phil Shapiro
advertising salesman, host, WVBR's *Bound for Glory*, Ithaca, NY

"I'd often get ten or more CDs a week and since I usually play 15 songs on a given one-hour show, it's almost impossible to play every new release even once—let alone multiple times."

Bob Blackman
host, *The Folk Tradition*, WKAR, East Lansing, MI

- Include the CD (very few stations will play cassettes), a short biography or "one sheet."
- Create a CD-sized typed list of the songs with the *exact* running times if the CD does not have the songs and song times listed on the back. Make this note legible and easy to read. Include the title of the CD, your name and contact information, including a phone number and e-mail address. This is a must!
- Print your name and title of the CD on the CD itself. Many times the CD gets separated from its box during a show.
- Create a self-addressed stamped postcard with survey questions about your CD and the response it is generating from the DJ as well as the listeners. Some DJs like survey cards and will answer them when they have a chance, others will not bother.
- Design lyric sheets or booklets to be included with the CD. Preprinted lyric sheets allow the DJs to check for inappropriate language which may be a problem on some stations as well as determining a song's suitability for specific topical shows.
- Place a sticker on the CD cover to indicate specific tracks which should be given airplay priority or which are particularly geared towards certain types of shows, such as a folk, Celtic or jazz show, if the CD is of a more eclectic nature.
- Remember the artist's itinerary and/or press release indicating upcoming dates in the vicinity of the station. DJs will mention upcoming appearances and play additional cuts closer to the performance date.
- Indicate in your cover letter your availability and desire for a possible live, in-studio, taped or phone interview to promote upcoming appearances. This requires your personal follow-up by phone or e-mail.

What to expect:

- With college radio, it is much more difficult to contact the specific show's host since they are mostly volunteer DJ's without regular office hours. However, many will answer e-mail.
- Some DJs may find the time to fill out the enclosed postcard questionnaire but the return rate is very low due to the DJs time constraints.
- Request to be placed on the station's mailing list of playlists or check the Internet and the station's website. Most stations are posting playlists.
- A CD can take anywhere from two to six weeks to get an initial review and then be included in an airplay rotation. For specialty shows, this can be longer due to the large volume of new releases and the shortage of air time.
- Follow-up with the station may confirm that the CD has been received. If you happen to catch the host of your targeted show, you might even get some feedback.

HotTip:
"Send a very simple, clear concert announcement that the DJ can read verbatim on the air. Use capital letters and double-space type. Don't use colored paper. Your announcement might be faxed to other DJs, colored paper faxes poorly."

Julia Mucci
Buzz Promotions

"Your record will get played on the radio if it is professionally performed, produced, packaged and promoted. If you sound like an amateur, then I sound like an amateur. That's not good for my career, not to mention yours."

Wayne Rice
host, *Bluegrass Special*,
KSON, San Diego

"All radio people have agreed upon one thing. We want either a CD-sized sheet inserted in a CD or a label on the front with the order of the songs numbered with exact timings. We are so adamant about this, we are in 100 percent agreement."

Rich Warren
host, *Midnight Special*,
WFMT Radio, Chicago

> **HotTip:** 🌶️
> As independent artists interested in feedback on your releases, hire someone in-house to make follow-up calls over a two- to three-week period if you are not quite ready to hire a radio promotions company.

❖ Record and radio promotion companies that offer stations regular service, such as continually sending new promotional releases, are more likely to have ongoing correspondence with the station and receive feedback about specific releases.

Public Radio

Public radio has a great deal to offer performers who do not fit the mainstream commercial radio model. As I mentioned at the beginning of this chapter, public radio is supported by underwriting, grants and donations from individuals—it is not supported by paid commercial advertising. A public radio station can be found catering to numerous communities throughout the country. Public radio carries programming fed by a number of the national programming providers such as National Public Radio, Pacifica Network, Public Radio International, as well as programming created at the local station. There are performance and airplay opportunities on both the national and local levels. An artist can participate in situations ranging from interview segments to feature performances on nationally-syndicated specialty shows. Many local public radio stations schedule specialty shows which play new releases in a variety of genres, air live performance shows, host interviews and produce local concerts. Performers can find a number of ways to access a large audience who are regular and committed listeners to public radio nationwide.

> *"Any time an artist approaches a radio station, it's important to follow the station protocol as far as whom to call and when. Should you be invited to the station for an interview, always remember you are a "guest in their home" and should act accordingly."*
>
> **Louise Coogan**
> radio promotor,
> Songlines, Ltd.

National Public Radio

National Public Radio (NPR) is one of the public radio programming organizations based in Washington, DC. NPR offers a number of programs from which a performing artist can benefit—most notably, *All Things Considered*, NPR's afternoon news and information program. Regular feature interviews are conducted with new musicians or established artists who have something new to say. This interview slot is highly competitive and is scheduled according to the subjective interest of the current host. An interview segment airing on *All Things Considered* may last for up to five minutes and gives an artist a national prime time audience. *Morning Edition* and *Weekend Edition* often have similar features with segments sometimes lasting up to 20 minutes.

NPR also features concerts and interviews in a variety of genres ranging from classical to jazz to opera to contemporary. Talk shows like *Fresh Air* can oftentimes include interviews with performing artists who have something extraordinary to share about their career or current project.

> *"Phone campaigns done in a consistent manner are effective. Even if initial airplay is light, look at it as seed work. Know when to take no for an answer. They will be more welcoming of your next CD or appearance."*
>
> **Julia Mucci**
> Buzz Promotions

What to send:
❖ Research each targeted show and get the name of that show's producer.

- Call first to establish a relationship with the producer, confirm what materials they accept and whether you are suited for their show.
- Then send the materials they have requested. Often they want a cover letter explaining why this music is special, the current CD, a biography and possible additional background information supporting the cover letter.

What to expect:
- Call within one week to confirm arrival of materials and set a time to discuss the material with the producer.
- Remember, if you are sending things to *All Things Considered, Weekend Edition* or *Morning Edition* or any similar show on the Pacifica Network, they are all news shows and news takes priority over any of the filler segments. Therefore, the producers are most concerned with getting the current happenings on and not your interview. It may take them some time to even listen to the material. Once they do and express interest in scheduling an interview, it may take some time to do the taping. Once the taping is done, it may be some additional time before it actually airs. Once in a while the turnaround is very fast. Even when a firm date is set, your segment can always be bumped for a news event. It will eventually be rescheduled.

Those who choose to explore public radio on a national level will find many career-advancing opportunities available to them.

Nationally-Syndicated Radio Shows

There are a number of shows that have reached a level of recognition by a national audience and which are carried by many stations. Some are live performance shows such as *A Prairie Home Companion, Mountain Stage,* and *E-Town.* Others are prerecorded and mix live in-studio performances with recorded music, like WFMT's *Midnight Special,* and WXPN's *World Café, Atlantic Crossing, Acoustic Cafe, Afropop Worldwide* and in Canada, *Saturday Night Blues* carried by CBC One.

Along with the larger nationally-syndicated shows, there are many shows which remain a mainstay within a specific geographic area. One such show is WBVR's *Bound for Glory* in Ithaca, NY. They have been on the air continuously for over 31 years. Shows like this feature recorded music, live-performance segments and interviews. They help create an awareness for new and established performers alike.

What to send:
- Send the best possible representation of your work. In most cases a current CD or electronic press kit with MP3 files of

"Laura Love's NPR interview was the most influential media event in her career since her Mercury record was released in May. She's been on CNN, Fox Cable News Network, reviewed in People, Time Magazine and The New York Times. But the single most visible result came from her interview with Scott Simon on NPR's Weekend Edition."

Mary McFaul
manager, Laura Love Band,
McFaul Booking and Management

"Unless an artist or a band has a very unique sound, or story, or both, as well as possesses some solidity to relate to the general public, they are not going to get any attention from either a host or a reviewer."

Marika Partridge
former director,
All Things Considered

"Public radio is a source that some artists might overlook in their attempts to get commercial airplay and it's a mistake. Public radio shows often have a very loyal audience of real music enthusiasts and they love to tell others about what they've discovered."

Chris Tschida
former producer,
A Prairie Home Companion

selected cuts. Some shows will listen to cassettes to determine who they are interested in booking. Some of these live shows do not play recorded music so a CD is not imperative. For the shows that play recorded music, a CD is a must.
- ❖ Submit materials to the proper person, whether it is the producer or associate producer—first find out to whom you should send your packet.
- ❖ A current press kit or EPK including photo. With many of these shows being marketed to a live ticket-buying audience, background biographical information and a promotional photograph help the show's promotion.
- ❖ A cover letter of introduction.
- ❖ An itinerary schedule. Some shows will consider bookings depending upon your tour schedule and others have the budget to fly you to the show.
- ❖ A video of a live performance or an EPK (electronic press kit) is important for some shows since these radio shows are presented to a live audience.

What to expect:
- ❖ Follow up your package with a phone call to insure the packet was received.
- ❖ It may take a while for the appropriate person to review your material. Being inundated by so many packets, it is unlikely that they will call you immediately and once again, the responsibility rests with you to keep in touch.
- ❖ The number of guests included on a single show may vary but is usually limited to a very small number. Some shows are thematic, offering performance slots for only those fitting that week's direction. Some shows are genre focused, again, limiting the selection of performers. Given the length of the production season, the number of guests per show and the show's focus, the chances for being included on a show are limited, but not impossible.
- ❖ Place appearing on these shows on your list of goals. Send the producer frequent career updates. Situations often arise where a guest cancels, an opening needs to be filled at the last moment or you are just what they were looking for.
- ❖ These shows are fun. They offer some national attention but they are only one aspect to consider in your radio marketing plans. As with some of the above print media, if you are making a particular impact in your specific genre, you will have more likelihood for consideration on some of these programs.
- ❖ Lastly, the host of each show definitely plays a major role in deciding who is booked. The producer or booking person, in most cases, refers any suggestions to the host who then has the final say.

Local And Regional Shows

> *"I received a call from John Diliberto, host of* Echoes, *an NPR radio show syndicated to over 135 stations nationwide, asking me for an interview. I was off and running on the airwaves, singing to many more people than I had ever been able to before. Somehow, throughout the year, my shyness toward radio interviews has dissolved into some sort of closet-chatty-stand-up-comedienne-persona!"*
>
> **Lorin Grean**
> harpist

> *"Mountain Stage reaches hundreds of thousands of listeners each week. Listeners have come to depend on us to deliver a quality package for their ears. For them to hear you on the show creates an awareness of your talents from Anchorage, Alaska to New York City."*
>
> **Andy Ridenour**
> producer,
> *Mountain Stage*

> *"A Prairie Home Companion is a very big public radio show that gets a lot of attention. But, there are many terrific programs on small local public radio stations with knowledgeable hosts and dedicated listeners."*
>
> **Chris Tschida**
> former producer,
> *A Prairie Home Companion*

There are an ever-increasing number of local and regional shows produced by public and community radio stations that include in-studio live performances and interview segments. Some programs may also be in front of a small studio audience and are often broadcast throughout the state or local region. These shows offer artists many chances to use radio to promote local appearances and new releases.

What to send:
- Research the station to find out the producer's contact information before sending any materials.
- A cover letter.
- A current CD.
- An itinerary of upcoming performance dates in the area.
- Song titles, exact timings on both the CD and CD box along with your contact information.

What to expect:
- You must follow up with a phone call.
- These programs are also highly sought after by touring performers. Therefore, available slots are limited.
- Once booked, performance times will vary from short interviews to interviews and live performances lasting sometimes up to an hour or more.

Community Radio

Community radio is often very similar to public radio and many college radio stations. Often operating with a community-based volunteer staff, the variety of programming that exists rests with the tastes and interest of the volunteer DJ staff. These stations will take news shows and other programming from satellite feeds offered by the various networks I spoke about earlier. A majority of their programming is generated locally, once again offering numerous opportunities for artists to use community radio to reach new audiences.

Recently, there have been a number of community radio stations programming large blocks of time that incorporate a mix of musical genres and formats. This method of programming introduces new music to a broader audience. While specialty shows segment the programming, mixed genre time blocks offer audiences variety and exposure to music they might not have ever heard. Scheduled at prime listening times like weekday drive time, more people are becoming familiar with new artists and their music. Accompanied by interview segments, this type of programming is a touring artist's promotional dream come true.

Contacting stations with this type of programming is often easier than those with specialty shows airing once a week. These stations will have a steady DJ hosting the show with regular on-air hours as well as office hours. Many of these

> "I think E-Town helps performers reveal themselves in a slightly different context than perhaps a more traditional interview. Yes, we definitely feature the music, promote new CDs, and reach a lot of people; this helps when artists tour towns where E-Town is heard—E-Town is part of the fabric of promotion."
>
> **Nick Forster**
> creator of *E-Town*

> "Competition to appear on A Prairie Home Companion is keen. We have weeks where demo cassettes and CDs come in by the boxful. I'd recommend really listening to the show to which you are submitting so that you know what the show sounds like."
>
> **Chris Tschida**
> former producer,
> *A Prairie Home Companion*

> "Right now we're very music-industry oriented. It's not a strong time for independent artists to get airplay during our weekday programming. But because there's so much variety in our weekend programming, almost everybody should send us an album. Chances are fairly good that somebody will be interested."
>
> **Phil Shapiro**
> host,
> WVBR's *Bound For Glory*,
> Ithaca, NY

> "Do offer your services to public radio. Offer to compose a jingle, promo or fund drive testimonial. Stations never have enough talent to help with these. Volunteer."
>
> Julia Mucci
> Buzz Promotions

stations also report to the appropriate trades which lends even more advantage to gaining access to these types of stations.

What to send:
- Research the station to find out the host's contact information before sending any materials.
- A cover letter.
- A current CD.
- An itinerary of upcoming performance dates in the area.
- Song titles, exact timings on both the CD and CD box along with your contact information.

What to expect:
- Follow up to make sure your materials have been received.
- Ask if they report to any trades or maintain playlists.
- Use these stations for interviews when appearing in the area.

Internet Radio:
Many stations stream their broadcast audio via their website. This expands opportunities to now reach a worldwide audience. Check http://www.internetradioindex.com for a comprehensive database of links to stations worldwide.

> "Radio today has to be accessible to people—to the lifestyles they live. Acoustic Sunrise airs every weekday morning—it is a part of people's lives. They wake up, they eat breakfast, and drive to work to it. It's popular because it's easy to find."
>
> "Listeners to non-commercial community radio get a much more interesting product born out of diversity and individual expression—it's not all coming from the top down, being homogenized."
>
> John Hill
> former host,
> WNRN's *Acoustic Sunrise*
> Charlottesville, VA

Conclusion
Radio airplay is imperative if you are a musical act. Accessing appropriate radio stations, individual shows and maintaining an ongoing relationship with radio hosts and DJs offers touring artists another method of broadening their audience.

Summary
- Research the various radio formats to help focus your recordings and enhance your airplay.
- Understand each type of radio station and how you can include them within your marketing plan to gain a radio presence.
- Be available for live in-studio and phone interviews.
- Attempt to gain recognition from some of the nationally-syndicated shows to build a national and international audience base.

> "Stations are posting playlists on their home page. Most stations have websites to tell you what kind of station they are, what they play and the programming schedule."
>
> Rich Warren
> host, *The Midnight Special*,
> WFMT Radio, Chicago, IL

Resources

Radio Trade Magazines and Online Sites:

Billboard
1515 Broadway, 39th Floor
New York, NY 10036
Phone: 1-800-344-7119
Web: http://www.billboard.com
Charts: http://www.bilboard.com/charts
Industry news, interviews, features, reviews.
Radio Charts: Pop, Country, Hits of the World, Contemporary Christian, Gospel, R&B, Rap, Dance Music, Latin, Blue, Reggae, World Music
The Power Book—Fall and Spring Edition, guide to radio and record promotion.

CCM Online
Web: http://www.ccmcom.com/
Christian Music magazine, radio charts, countdown, Christian stations reporting.

Chart Attack
41 Britain Street, Suite 20
Toronto, Ontario M5A 1R7
Phone: 416-363-3101
Fax: 416-363-3109
Web: http://www.chartattack.com
Canadian college radio charts, electronic, metal, hip-hop, world, jazz and alternative retail sales.

CMJ New Music Monthly
151 W. 25th Street, 12th floor
New York, NY 10001
Phone: 917-606-1908
E-mail: advertise@cmj.com
Web: http://www.cmj.com/newmm
Features, reviews—dance, Hip-Hop, metal, alternative, college radio charts.

Friday Morning Quarterback (FMQB)
Executive Mews, Bldg. F-36
1930 East Marleton Pike
Cherry Hill, NJ 08003
Phone: 856-424-9114
Fax: 856-424-6943
Web: http://www.fmqb.com
Send recordings to appropriate department: AC, Triple A, CHR, Modern rock, Rock.Rhythm crossover, metal.

Radio Television Interview Reporter
Bradley Communications
P.O. Box 1206
Landsdown, PA 19050-8206
Phone: 610-259-0707
Fax: 610-284-3704
Web: http://www.RTIR.com
Contacts to syndicated radio, TV and cable talk shows.

Radio and Records
2049 Century Park E., 41st Floor
Los Angeles, CA 90067-4004
Phone: 310-553-4330
Fax: 310-203-9763
Web: http://www.radioandrecords.com
Industry news, radio news, reviews.
Radio Charts: AC, Active Rock, Adult Alternative, Alternative, CHR/Pop, CHR/Rhythm, Country, Hot AC, NAC/Smooth Jazz, Rock, Urban, Urban AC.

Roots Music Reports
107 Blue Oak Lane
Wimberley, TX 78676
Phone: 1-877-532-2225
Web: http://www.rootsmusicreport.com

Singing News
P.O. Box 2810
330 University Hall Drive
Boone, NC 28607
Phone: 828-264-3700
Fax: 828-264-4621
Web: http://www.singingnews.com
Southern Gospel Music, features, charts, news.

Radio Lists and Directories:

College Radio Station Directory
Web: http://www.therecordindustry.com/collegeradio-AK.htm
Indie recording industry resources. U.S., Canada, Europe, Asia

Folk DJ-L
Web: http://www.folkradio.org
Lists folk stations, shows, DJs, playlists and charts.

Internet Radio Index.com
Web: http://www.internetradioindex.com
Links to over 1800 Internet radio stations

International Radio Station List
Web: http://www.radio-locator.com
Lists U.S., Canadian, European and other international stations.
Bitcasters—list of stations that broadcast on the Internet.

World Wide Web Virtual Library: Broadcaster
Web: http://archive.museophile.org
Radio station database, broadcast industry databases.

The Music Review
Web: http://www.musreview.com
Radio station search engine, access to radio charts.

Public Radio:

CBC
Canadian Broadcasting Company
P.O. Box 500, Station A
Toronto, Ontario M5W 1E6
Canada
Phone: 866-306-4636
Web: http://www.cbc.ca

The Christian Science Monitor
One Norway Street
Boston, MA 02115
Phone: 617-450-2000
Web: http://www.csmonitor.com

NPR
National Public Radio
635 Massachusetts Avenue, NW
Washington, DC 20001
Phone: 202-513-2000
Fax: 202-513-3329
Web: http://www.npr.org

PRI
Public Radio International
100 North Sixth Street, Suite 900A
Minneapolis, MN 55403
Phone: 612-338-5000
Web: http://www.pri.org

Radio Broadcast Organizations

Americana Music Association
P.O. Box 128077
Nashville, TN 37212
E-mail: info@americanamusic.org
Web: http://www.americanamusic.org

Association Of Independents In Radio (AIR)
328 Flatbush Avenue, #322
Brooklyn, NY 11238
Phone: 1-888-937-2477
Web: http://www.airmedia.org

Voice Of America
Office of Public Affairs
330 Independence Avenue, SW
Washington, D.C. 20237
Phone: 202-401-7000
Fax: 202-619-1241
Web: http://www.voa.gov

XM Satellite Radio
1500 Eckington Place, NE
Washington, DC 20002
Phone: 202-380-4000
Fax: 202-380-4500
Web: http://www.xmradio.com

Cable Radio:

MTV Radio Network
Web: http://www.mtv.com/music

VH1 Radio
Web: http://www.vh1.com/radio

Independent Radio Promoters:

See Appendix, Independent Radio Promoters, page 481

CHAPTER SIXTEEN
Accessing The Media—Television

"TV exposure is a good thing, if not indispensable, in taking a new artist's career to the next level."

Terry Lickona
producer,
Austin City Limits

A number of media opportunities for artists at all levels of their careers are provided by national and local network affiliates, public television, cable, public access and educational broadcasts. Becoming familiar with television opportunities offers an artist a means to access a larger general audience when incorporated within their marketing campaign.

"Broadcasting is really too important to be left to the broadcasters and somehow we must find some new way of using radio and television to allow us to talk with each other."

Anthony Wedgewood Benn
British Labour politician

Educational Access

The FCC dictates that cable companies must provide an educational-access channel to be available in the cable system's coverage area. This channel is available to public and private schools, colleges and universities. These institutions can create their own programming or access programming through downlink satellite feeds. Tutor programs are becoming widespread as a means to offer after-school help for students in need. Many university instructors can now conduct classes nationwide while remaining in their home facility.

If you have a program suitable for a school audience, educational access television may be another avenue for you

> "Public access provides any individual with the ability to be trained on equipment and to check out that equipment, to edit their film and then to be seen by the public, virtually with very little censorship."
>
> Chris Lunn
> president,
> CCAT Pierce County,
> City of Tacoma, WA

to develop. Local facilities offer the public the technical equipment and assistance necessary to produce your own educational programming. Many colleges and universities have broadcast studios where individuals may present program proposals to student classes in order to create an educational program. Once the program is completed, send notices to the target educational facilities you wish to approach. By working with the educational-access programmer, you can announce a scheduled airing of your program to those in your target audience. Various educators can plan to air your program in appropriate classrooms.

Performances are not the only presentation possible. Workshops, music instruction, storytelling, theater, topical discussions and educational games are all some of the ideas that can be brought to the classroom via educational access. This is another possible way to increase your audience in your local region.

Check with your local cable company for the contact person. Many of you may find a whole new world in which to be creative.

Public Access

Public-access television is becoming a more familiar format to many communities. The Federal Communication Commission (FCC) also dictates that cable companies must provide at least one channel in their service area. Depending on the area in which you live, there may be a number of public-access channels available for use. They may not, however, be in operation. Check with your cable provider for the public-access channels in your area. Ask the cable company about their current public-access programming.

Each cable company provides a public-access television studio facility to the local area. Many times a city will administer the program. A public-access program will often include qualified instructors teaching classes in the use of equipment and broadcast techniques. Any individual can be instructed in all phases of television production through their public access facility.

> "Music shows are quite prolific. Remember that quite often folks who create these shows are volunteers who participate without compensation in this glorified 'hobby.' There are many shows whose productions have proved so popular, they are aired in numerous other towns and provide far-reaching exposure."
>
> Robert Haigh
> general manager, WCAT TV
> producer,
> *The Acoustic Cafe* (TV)

You may choose to learn, firsthand, how to use the equipment and begin producing your own shows. For those of you not interested in that aspect of the production, crews of previously-trained individuals can be recommended to you by the cable company. Once you have put together your own crew of video, audio and lighting technicians, camera operators, a director and a producer, you can create a show or series of shows to be aired on the channel. I know the thought of producing your own television show may be more than you bargained for—but watch public access sometime. You would be surprised at how simply shows are put together and yet achieve a certain degree of high quality.

If you have any name recognition within your community, you may find that organizing a crew is fairly easy.

Those who have begun their own shows are often amazed at the number of people who tune in to their public-access channel. It is one way of consistently appearing in front of a large general audience. As public access becomes more popular, programming slots will be harder to procure. But at this time, many cable systems have available slots with multiple opportunities for your show to air.

Public Television

Public television offers yet another opportunity for up-and-coming performers to develop a television audience. Public television stations throughout the country have been instrumental in creating a wealth of arts-related shows that air locally, statewide, regionally and sometimes nationally or internationally. Public television is attentive to the audience they serve. The arts community has been insistent that arts-related programming remain a priority.

In the music arena, the ongoing *Austin City Limits* created by KLRU in Austin, TX, and the now discontinued *Lonesome Pine*, created by Kentucky Public Television, are just two examples of programming finding homes on public television.

On the state level, many public televisions stations, whether independent or associated with a college or university, have developed programming with formats suitable for interviews, performance or documentation of meaningful artistic endeavors. Many stations have funding designated for these types of programs. Others are open to programming suggestions, especially when a proposal is accompanied by a funding source.

Become familiar with local public television. Their existing resources may offer local, regional and visiting artists new opportunities for alliances. To access local public television production, research the types of programs currently being produced and who the producers are. Knowing the topics, formats, and recent guests will help determine whether your act is appropriate for consideration.

What to send:
For nationally- and internationally-distributed shows:
- Do the research first.
- It is best not to send anything until you are at the level in your career that suggests you can compete with those currently being programmed. Use recent press received from national and major-market media and, if you are recorded, the current level of airplay and the market where you are receiving airplay (especially important is any level of radio chart reporting, i.e., *Billboard, A3,*

HotTip:
Association of Public Television Stations offers links to U.S. stations.
http://www.apts.org

Canadian Broadcasting Company
http://www.cbc.org

"People who watch *Austin City Limits* are true music fans who respond (i.e., buy records) to something original, unique or edgy. Our show has built a tradition of showcasing new, up-and-coming talent, and many artists got their first national TV exposure here (George Strait, Lyle Lovett, Nanci Griffith, Stevie Ray Vaughan). Even established artists believe that their appearance on *Austin City Limits* brought them to an entirely different or larger audience (Leonard Cohen, Vince Gill)."

Terry Lickona
producer,
Austin City Limits

"Artists need to be more aggressive!"

Mark Foust
Iowa Public TV

Americana, NAC, etc.) to gauge whether you are ready or not.
- Once you feel confident that you are ready to compete, contact the producers first to introduce yourself and ask permission to send materials.
- Let them instruct you regarding their current criteria.
- Send a current CD and a complete press kit.
- Include a black and white photo and/or color slide.
- Send any recent quality video in any format—it will not be used for broadcast, only for review.

For local, state and regionally-distributed shows:
- Again, research is the key.
- Speak to the producers to determine which shows are suitable.
- Send a current CD.
- Include a complete press kit, EPK is helpful.
- Send black and white photos and color slide. If the show is a calendar type of show promoting local upcoming events, a color slide is important.
- Include any quality video available in any format. A segment of video may be used on air, in which case, sending the highest quality format video or digital files available is suggested.

There is less competition associated with most programming on this level unless a specific program becomes popular. Many programs are interested in working with developing artists to document their entry into the market and chronicle the impact the artist begins to make on a local, regional or state level.

What to expect:
- Acceptance on these nationally- and internationally-distributed programs once again depends upon your position in the market and the impact you or your act has made.
- Inclusion is based on a number of factors. Shows that have national distribution are themselves competing for funding as well as viewers. At the national level, it becomes a matter of playing the numbers game for survival. Therefore, programming moves beyond experimentation and often necessitates adhering to a proven formula that secures dollars and audience. Incorporating entry-level performers into programming happens when that artist is no longer able to be ignored and the "buzz" warrants the artist's inclusion. Until that point, producers will opt for proven artists to help hold and build audiences and respond to funding resource concerns.
- Response may not be immediate. Contacting the producers may not result in an immediate response unless the "buzz" scenario exists.
- Awareness of your career development helps producers judge when you might be ready for their show. Send updates once a

---

"Send some sort of video showing you performing live—no matter how crude the production—I can see through that. I need to know how you present yourself on a stage in front of an audience—that's what our show is all about! If I read a rave review in a respectable newspaper (as opposed to the hometown daily paper), music magazine or syndicated column, it'll definitely get my attention and whet my appetite for more."

Terry Lickona
producer,
Austin City Limits

"I hosted a seven-part series for PBS that has actually led to a number of things. It was a small production and low budget, but we went around the state interviewing old-time people and musicians. This was a statewide television show but it goes to other states over a period of time because they send it up on the satellite. Small shows, like mine, give you a wonderfully respectful notoriety."

David Holt
traditional musician,
storyteller, host,
Folkways on North Carolina
Public Television

year unless you are instructed otherwise, i.e., "Your act does not fit our format. Don't call us, we'll call you."

- ❖ Consideration for new programming ideas is more prevalent from stations that are local, state or regional. They offer more chance for experimentation and development unless there is a particularly popular regional show.
- ❖ Developing strategic partnerships can be instructive and beneficial when a producer chooses to incorporate you into current programming ideas or create a new program for the artist.
- ❖ Suggestions for programming that fulfill an identified concern and reach an audience segment not currently being served is one way to start an ongoing relationship with public television.

Accessing existing programming that caters to current and upcoming events like calendar-type shows will garner a timely and more immediate response from producers—your event either works into their program or it does not. The more you know about the show, the more you may be able to create a suitable story about your event that will work for the producer. Program development, however, requires research and a commitment of time and funding. This may result in a lengthy process but could eventually prove worthwhile.

> *"It's been years since I booked an artist who was truly undiscovered. You need to have SOME sort of career or track record to deserve one of the valued slots on our show: an independent record deal with at least regional distribution, a manager and booking agent (even if it's a relative), a band and/or experience playing before a live audience. Austin City Limits isn't a starting point—you need to build yourself up to that level first."*
>
> **Terry Lickona**
> producer,
> *Austin City Limits*

Cable Television

The number of networks accessed on various cable and satellite systems is growing as more channels become available. There are programmers catering to everything from numerous musical genres such as rock, country and jazz to classic and new independent films and from home shopping to the chef of the hour. Shows such as *Emeril Live* on the Food Network showcase musical acts regularly featured sitting in with the house band. Other shows offering a glimpse of foods around the world, often include music from the area featuring a local act.

Artists have the possibility of participating in some form of cable programming even when moving through entry career levels. There is a constant revolving door of programs being tried on cable.

With the growth of the cable industry, many networks which originally produced their shows in-house have now turned to outside production companies to supply their programming. This leaves less room for the network to book talent directly. Many programs come to the networks already packaged with talent, content and sponsor. If an artist had a show concept that included artists who would draw ratings and demographics, the network may put you in touch with one of the production companies with whom they work. Sometimes if it is an interesting concept, the network might consider producing it themselves. But currently, it is very difficult to find slots on some cable networks as a beginning artist.

Video Shows

Cable channels such as MTV, VH1, BET, CMT and in Canada, Much Music, which mostly present music videos have added well-made newcomer videos for artists who were at the beginning stages of their "buzz." These additions sometimes helped to move these artists from newcomer status to household names. As the medium developed, these once all-video cable channels have begun to add a variety of show formats to enhance the video presentations. For example: Much Music presents 24 hours of every genre of music broadcasting in Canada, the U.S. and countries in Europe and South America. Many shows on these channels focus their attention on artists who are already established or who have made a large enough impact on the industry that they are well on their way to becoming household names. Very few shows offer "baby bands" a venue until there is significant industry recognition.

Many of the current shows which air attempt to place known acts in comfortable live settings where they are seemingly one-on-one with their studio audience or up-close-and-personal with the television viewing audience. Shows like *Storytellers* on VH1 or *Musicians on BRAVO* give the viewer a personal sense of the artist in relation to their art. They attempt to demystify the "star" aspects of the artist. However, these shows are still using established artists who will attract viewers to the channel and are not offering many shows which introduce new talent.

Using the medium to your advantage requires some research to discover the best programmers on which to focus your attention. Consider where you are in your career. Are you ready for television? If you are, some programming exists which may be accessible to you.

In order to incorporate cable into your marketing plan you need to plan for the expenses involved and become aware of the resources available to make the most out of all cable has to offer. If your plans include cable, research partially involves watching what the programmers are programming. Become familiar with their formats, the content, who hosts the shows, the types of interview questions asked, who the newcomers are and how they compare with you and those familiar to the general public. What formulas are being used to create the programs that are on for more than a season?

What to send:

❖ Contact the programmers you have deemed appropriate to determine your next steps. For some, recording a video

---

"What the Nashville Network did was make me known to a certain segment of the population across the nation. Not enough people that you could attract a huge audience, but still enough that they might be 20% of any audience. It also gave the presenters something they could wrap their promotions around that had national credibility."

David Holt
traditional musician, storyteller, former TNN host,
Fire On The Mountain, The American Music Shop

"CMT has developed quite a reputation in the music industry for helping launch the careers of new artists. Oftentimes CMT will telecast great videos by artists who may be at an early stage in their career and may not be receiving a lot of airplay on the radio. We've had many instances where artists have told us that radio stations were receiving requests for their songs from viewers who had seen their video on CMT and were calling their local radio stations to ask them to play the song."

Chris Parr
program director,
CMT

may be the next step and, for others, simply sending a current CD and promotional package may suit.
- If creating a video is the next step, ask which production format they accept. Creating a video in the currently-accepted format will give you a fighting chance to, at least, have it reviewed.

What to expect:
- Keep in touch with the producers. Developing a relationship with them is key.
- For programs other than the video type, once your materials are on file, they may contact you when an appropriate situation arises.
- Update producers with new releases and career developments to help them determine when you are ready for their show.
- Timing the video with the release of the CD or single and the current level of airplay will impact on the programmer's decision to add the video or to increase the video's play.
- Selecting your video for airplay may again be determined by a number of factors—whether your video is consistent with the content format of the network, whether the artist has a recording being distributed nationally and whether the video is consistent with the on-air look of the network. Each network has their own standard guidelines. Ask for those guidelines before proceeding.

Local Network Affiliates

Within most major cities and certainly within a region, a major network NBC, ABC, CBS or FOX will be the main broadcast program provider for a local television station. The major network provides most of that station's programming, but not all. Programming slots are available for local news, and possibly, some locally-produced shows. Check with an area concert promoter to discover potential programs which you may access for promotion or performance purposes.

The most likely target programs are a morning or noon news segment devoted to upcoming events. As a news program, demonstrating the newsworthiness of your event will give you a better chance to be slotted into the show. If you are targeting a news show, send materials to the news department to the attention of the producer of that specific news show. When programs other than news are the target, send materials to the producer of that specific show.

Local network programs consider the following for inclusion on local news segments:
1. Local events or people that impact a wide segment of the broadcast coverage area.
2. Important community events or individuals who make an impact outside the broadcast coverage area.

HotTip: Film is the dominant video format. It is not worth the effort or the investment to record the video in another format to save money. Do your research before taping.

"When MTV actually did start, it was very much like early free-form FM radio. A lot of major labels were not submitting videos yet so MTV was forced to scour the earth for these quiet little indie labels to see if they could give them product. We had our video, 'I Want To Be a Life Guard,' in our hot little hands before MTV went on the air. We went into very heavy rotation right from the start."

Greg Haymes
formerly Sarge with Blotto

> **HotTip:** 🌶
> Television producers appreciate seeing any format of video available. It helps them evaluate how to present your video segment and whether it is suitable for their show.

3. Important events or people from outside the community who will make a significant impact on those within the broadcast coverage area.

What to send:

The timeliness of this kind of promotion requires advance contact with the producers prior to sending any materials. They can determine whether coverage of this event is suitable for their show's format and presentation. Once they agree to review your material send the following:

❖ A cover letter.
❖ A well-written press release focusing on the news about the event or person.
❖ A color slide.
❖ A video if available, preferably in the highest current format if it is intended for broadcast use. VHS format is fine for an introduction, depending on what was discussed in the advance call. A DVD is better and more versatile.
❖ A copy of the latest CD, if it is a musical act.
❖ A full press kit EPK and a current tour itinerary if touring. When considering inclusion in a news segment or entertainment segment, having pertinent information helps to formulate a more cohesive segment, especially if an interview is incorporated into the piece.

What to expect:

❖ Attempting inclusion on a news show may be subject to the current news of the day. Be prepared for emergency news to take precedence at the last minute.
❖ Follow-up is recommended until the segment has been approved or until they pass on it.
❖ Last-minute decisions are to be expected since this is a news show.
❖ Once the producer has agreed to include your segment, someone will contact you regarding the details of the setup, what will be included, timing, technical needs and interview material. Some details may be left for discussion once you arrive. On an average, the entire segment on-air may be as short as two minutes or as long as five depending on the show's format, length and whether or not you perform.
❖ Inclusion on another type of locally-produced show will be totally dependent on the producer, the show's general focus and the method of production. Some shows are taped live and others produced in advance, then edited to fit specific time formats.
❖ When scheduling a show other than news on a local network affiliate, the timeliness of the show's airing is important. Some shows that are recorded during a specific production time can be prerecorded while you are in the

"The media's interest is whetted by a community effort. When local performers work together with an area organization, the amount of clout that they have multiplies geometrically. Any local media station looks for the kind of project where different aspects of the community link together to accomplish something. It becomes a perfect source for a news story."

Barbara Karol
former chairfolk,
San Diego Folk Heritage

area and saved to air just prior to your next scheduled event since these shows' focus revolves around local happenings or noteworthy events.

- Prerecorded programming may have specific production periods during one time of the year. Shows taped during that period begin airing later in the season or in the next airing season. Use these programs to simply build your audience in the coverage area. Attempting to use this type of show to promote a specific event is difficult. Find out when they plan to air it to help you target performance dates and thus benefit from the recent publicity surrounding the show.

National Networks

It is unlikely that in the early stages of your career, national network programming will enter into your marketing plans. However, it is worth your while to at least explore the potential programming opportunities that do exist and target them if someday you want to be on those programs. Have a clear picture of what is available and the types of guests that are appropriate for performance or interview segments. This adds valuable information to your marketing strategies.

Television Contests

The Internet has leveled the playing field for independent artists to flourish on the world market. In response, major labels, film and television producers, are using their vast financial resources to access huge television audiences to develop the next superstars. Now shows like *American Idol; American Junior; Nashville Star; Born to Diva; Dance Fever; Fame* and *Star Search*, to name a few, are huge hits providing enormous financial rewards for the producers and the winners.

These showcase contests mix the vast audience building capabilities of television and the Internet. They create loyal fans for hometown talents at the local level, then build a national and international audience as the show progresses to the final winning episode. The beauty of these shows is, that the viewing audience votes for their favorites. Once the winner is selected, the label or producer knows they have a star with immediate selling power. The artist's development has already been done on television and the Internet. Whatever financial investment they've poured into the actual search and show production, is recouped by advertising and rewarded instantly by million-selling record sales and offers for film, television and Broadway starring roles. These shows offer virtual unknowns a shot at stardom on a level only TV can create.

Shows With Live Performance Segments

We are all familiar with *Saturday Night Live, The Tonight Show with Jay Leno, The Late Show with David Letterman*

> **HotTip:**
> Television Contests
>
> ABC
> Dance Fever
> http://abcfamily.go.com/dancefever/
>
> CBS
> Star search
> http://www.cbs.com/primetime/starsearch
>
> FOX
> American Idol
> American Juniors
> http://wwwidolonfox.com
>
> MTV
> Making The Band
> http://www.mtv.com/onair/makingtheband/
>
> NBC
> Fame
> http://wwwnmc.com/fame
>
> USA Network
> Nashville Star
> http://www.usanetwork.com/nashvillestar/
>
> VH1
> Born To Diva
> http://www.vh1.com/shows/borntodiva/series/jhtml

> **HotTip:** 🌶
> Remain open to media opportunities by having an awareness of the programming possibilities.

and *Late Night with Conan O'Brien*. Each presents a live-performance segment and works with their own set of criteria for deciding who gets the slot. The shows are highly competitive and almost all of them make selections based on current releases, radio-chart positions, sales and the impact the act is having on the music market at that particular moment. Very rarely do any of these shows introduce new talent that does not have one or all of the above criteria working for them. Record-company backing and support is also a major factor contributing to which act gets on and when. Personal preferences of the hosts play a small part in the decision process. It has more to do with which show will be first to get the newest act with a mainstream "buzz."

Daytime News And Entertainment Shows

Other potential shows are the morning news/entertainment shows like *The Today Show, Regis & Kelly, Good Morning America* and *The CBS Morning News*. Again most of the above criteria comes into play with a slight exception—if an act is newsworthy outside the normal music industry news, there may be an opening.

For example:

Singer/songwriter, Leslie Nuchow was selected for a showcase and major promotional effort sponsored by Virginia Slims. When she found out that they were essentially using struggling women musicians to promote smoking to young women, she turned them down based on her personal beliefs about tobacco and the fact that her grandmother died of emphysema.

Wanting to create a positive alternative to the Virginia Slim's event, she created Virginia Slam, a showcase for women singer/songwriters. Seeking help with the project, she contacted the National Coalition of Tobacco-Free Kids. They asked her to participate in a press conference at the National Press Club in Washington, DC and tell her story. *The Daily News* picked up the story and printed an interview. The media frenzy began. She was invited to perform on *Good Morning America* and talk about her experience and Virginia Slam I, which took place at The Wetlands in New York City on June 12, 1997. The event was so successful that follow-up events were planned. Other news shows followed.

Leslie's story clearly illustrates what can happen when you leave yourself open to possibilities. Her goal of a musical career was clear, but by standing behind her convictions she was able to make decisions based on the facts and how they impacted upon her goals. She stayed on a path that allows her to reach her musical goals on her own terms, resulting in a far better outcome than she ever imagined.

These situations are rare, but you must keep an open mind about what interests the media. You may not have anything that fits into television at this time. But, by being aware of what is promoted and what kinds of stories are programmed you have a better chance of recognizing the rare opportunity.

What to expect:
- Accessing the producers of notable shows is remarkably simple. Call the main network and ask for the specific show's producer. Any show will have a main producer and some may have a producer who specifically deals with hiring music talent.
- Some shows may have a producer specifically designated for hiring interview guests or guests that are topic related. This is the starting place.
- Make sure you are ready for the network shows. Your press, product sales and record company (if you have one) will help make this determination.
- If the producers determine that there is significant media attention surrounding your act, product or event and it is news appropriate to a national audience, you have an opportunity to use this media.
- National network television is not an easy outlet to break into and I would not place a major focus of attention here until all the indicators mentioned above are in place.

Conclusion

Television has the potential of boosting your career to the next logical level. Depending on your career goals, television may be the media outlet most important to positioning your act.

Summary

- Incorporate television into your marketing plans when ready. The medium offers opportunities at all levels of a performing career.
- Take advantage of some of the local television opportunities available such as public and educational access.
- When you are in a position to do so, use local news segments to promote an area event to a much wider audience.

Resources

Television Networks and Shows:

ABC
500 S. Buena Vista Street
Burbank, CA 91521
Web: http://abc.com

Austin City Limits
KLRU-TV
Terry Lickona, Producer
P.O. BOX 7158
Austin, TX 78712
Phone: 512-471-4812
Web: http://www.klru.org

BET—Black Entertainment Television
2000 M Street, NW, Suite 602
Washington, DC 20036
Phone: 202-533-1990
Web: http://www.bet.com

CBC Television and Radio
P.O. Box 500, Station A
Toronto, Ontario M5W 1E6
Canada
Phone: 416-205-3311
Web: http://www.cbc.ca

CBS News
524 West 57th Street
New York, NY 10019
Phone: 212-975-4321
Web: http://www.cbs.com

CBS The Early Show
CBS
513 West 57th Street, 7th Fl
New York, NY 10019
Phone: 212-975-2824

Late Show with David Letterman
CBS
1697 Broadway
New York, NY 10019
Phone: 212-975-5300

Sesame Workshop
Sesame Street
One Lincoln Plaza
New York, NY 10023
Phone: 212-595-3456
Web: http://www.sesameworkshop.org

FOX
Web: http://fox.com
Web: http://fox.com/links/affiliates.htm

Much Music
299 Queen Street West
Toronto, Ontario M5V 2Z5 Canada
Phone: 416-591-5757
Web: http://www.muchmusic.com

NBC
30 Rockefeller Plaza
New York, NY 10112-0194
Phone: 212-664-4444
Web: http://nbc.com
Late Night with Conan O'Brien
Saturday Night Live
The Today Show

Late Night with Conan O'Brien
Jim Pitt, Music Producer
30 Rockefeller Plaza, Room 901 West
New York, NY 10112
Phone: 212-664-3737

NBC Tonight Show with Jay Leno
Debbie Vickers, Producer
3000 W. Alameda
Burbank, CA 91523
Phone: 818-840-4444

PBS
1320 Braddock Place
Alexandria, VA 22314
Web: http://www.pbs.org

CMT
330 Commerce Street
Nashville, TN 37201
Phone: 615-335-8400
Web: http://www.cmt.com

Viacom
MTV Networks/ VH1 / Nickelodeon
1515 Broadway
New York, NY 10036
MTV
Phone: 212-258-8000
Web: http://mtv.com
VH1
Phone: 212-258-7800
Web: http://vh1.com
Nickelodeon
Phone: 212-258-7500
Web: http://www.nick.com

CHAPTER SEVENTEEN
Internet Marketing

"Internet marketing is a must-participate activity for any entity that wants to get and stay noticed. The Internet is causing the music industry to go through the most significant transformation since the advent of radio. No matter where the industry transitions to, the key to success is reaching your existing and future audience at a fraction of the cost of today's traditional models."

Mitchell Levy,
president & CEO, ECnow.com
author, E-Volve-or-Die.com

My discussion regarding the Internet is focused on how to market your act more effectively by incorporating this tool into your marketing plan. This section offers suggestions on how to use the Internet's resources to your advantage. I have listed many books, magazines, websites and software in the resource section of this chapter. You need to make Internet marketing part of your plan.

In a *New York Post* article, Prince discussed his strategy for releasing all of his future recordings. After completing his major-label contract with Warner Bros., Prince set up his own label and distribution network on the web stipulating that the CD would not be pressed until 100,000 orders had been confirmed. Not only was the cost risk for the CD diminished, but he was in direct communication with his fans. This was a significant breakthrough for a major performer to take control of his recording business utilizing grassroots methods of marketing and distribution. As an incredibly prolific artist, the restrictions placed on his creativity by the major label meant that he was only able to release one recording every 12 to 18 months. The Internet provided Prince with the means of creating as many recordings as he

"The new electronic interdependence recreates the world in the image of a global village."

Marshall McLuhan
Canadian sociologist

> **HotTip:** 🌶️
> Cable, wireless cable and cellphone technologies make online access affordable and always available.

"Disintermediation: The removal of the intermediary in business transactions using the conventional distribution model of the music business. Convention has the artist sign with a label, the label sells to the distributor, the distributor sells to the one-stop, the one-stop sells to the retailer and the retailer sells to the consumer. The Internet makes it possible for the artist to sell directly to his/her fan."

"Demassification. The Internet may become a medium that has mass use but it will never be a mass medium in the sense that radio and television are mass media. Radio and television represent a single point of origin with many points of reception. That process gives rise to the star-making machinery and the star-making mentality that drives our culture. The Internet represents a significant shift from that. Now you have many points of origin with many points of reception. It's harder to assemble a mass audience but it is easier to assemble a viable audience on a smaller scale."

— Paul Schatzkin
former president,
songs.com

could produce in whatever time frame his talent allowed and in whatever quantity his fans demanded.

Prince's entrepreneurship had a huge impact on the recording industry. The Internet provides the means for many more creative, enterprising individuals to succeed at maintaining a viable career.

Get Hooked Up And Logged On

As I mentioned earlier, e-mail is one of the least expensive and most useful tools you can incorporate immediately into your business. If you have not purchased a computer and added the Internet already, reading this section may provide the added incentive necessary to get you to think seriously about making the investment.

You need an Internet Service Provider (ISP). Today, new computers often come loaded with the necessary software and are equipped with a high speed modem. Your computer will have instructions for you to simply sign on. For those of you with older computers, you have a multitude of options when selecting your online service. In addition to the main providers such as America Online (AOL), Yahoo, Hotmail, Mindspring, and Earthlink, phone companies such as MCI, AT & T and Sprint, software companies such as Microsoft and local cable-television services provide e-mail. There are also numerous local ISPs.

Do some research. Find a company that is reliable, has local-access numbers easily available in most places where you will be touring and has a low-cost plan giving you as much or unlimited online time for one low price or for free.

If using a smaller, less in-demand provider suits your style, check them out and make sure that you will have speedy access and all of the bells and whistles you feel you need. Most importantly though, make sure that you can access them whether you are at home or anywhere on the road.

Modems/Cable/DSL/T1

When you are touring, time is more precious than ever. Even if you only send and receive e-mail, you want to do it quickly. Speed is a necessity online. Use a modem with the highest current baud available in your laptop. Not traveling with a laptop? Stop into one of the many Internet cafés to send and receive your e-mail.

While at home, Cable, DSL and T1 phone-line connections to the Internet provide instant access and high speed uploads, downloads and web surfing. Of course, constant access and speed come with a price, so check with your local television cable and phone companies for pricing and discount promotions.

E-Mail

E-mail offers a touring artist a no-cost method of contacting unlimited numbers of people in the media, within the industry and on your mailing list. Here are a number of ways to use e-mail effectively within your marketing plan.

❖ Include a signature at the bottom of each e-mail message—a signature is a block of type that includes your name, e-mail address, website address, mailing address, phone number, fax and a short descriptive line about your product, act or service. It is one method of advertising yourself to newsgroups, discussion groups and anyone you contact without blatantly advertising. Here is the signature I use:

```
* * * * * * * * * * * * * * * * * * * * * * * * * * * * * * * * * * * * * * * * *

The New Music Times, Inc.        How To Be Your Own Booking Agent
P.O. Box 1105                          THE Musician's and
Charlottesville, VA 22902         Performing Artist's Guide To
434-591--1335 * Fax: 1-866-874-9321   Successful Touring
E-mail: jg@performingbiz.com
Web: http://www.performingbiz.com—seminars
Web: http://www.managerinabox.com—consulting

* * * * * * * * * * * * * * * * * * * * * * * * * * * * * * * * * * * * * * * * *
```

❖ Create an Electronic Press Kit to email to prospective presenters; add a general cover letter that can be modified depending upon the recipient. Once you have made initial contact, your press kit can have an immediate impact on the recipient.

❖ Create an ongoing e-mail file of your tour dates that can be updated. E-mail press, presenters and people who need to know what you are up to at a moment's notice.

❖ Post messages to bulletin boards, user groups and newsgroups which give you a broader presence within your specifically targeted community.

❖ Keep in touch with any of your media and presenter contacts, unobtrusively, while providing pertinent updates about your career or a brief check-in to inquire about the status of a specific project or booking. E-mail makes communication quick and effective.

❖ Send a press release blitz to the media with some important late-breaking news about your act.

❖ Send itinerary listings to magazines. You can save a file for each magazine in their specific format and then update them as often as the magazine accepts updates, once a week, once a month, etc.

❖ Send direct e-mail letters to promote your act by collecting targeted e-mail addresses from membership lists, newsgroups, and bulletin boards that are pertinent to you.

❖ Negotiate booking dates with written copies of your transactions that can be saved for later reference.

HotTip:

Sonicbids has set the industry standard with its Electronic Press Kit (EPK™) platform that enables music industry professionals to send and receive press kits online. Used by thousands of musicians, Sonicbids' EPK™s offer an easy-to-use, web-based graphical interface containing all the basic information of a standard press kit, including music, bio, photos and date calendar. The Sonicbids EPK™ can be emailed to anyone with a click of the mouse or submitted in online promoter accounts through a virtual "Drop Box". Sonicbids partners with an ever-growing list of thousands of festivals, clubs, and events both nationwide and worldwide.
http://www.sonicbids.com

"E-mail makes road work more productive and helps end the huge glut of work you have to do before and after a road trip. However, it also prevents songwriting time and fills the downtime that you used to get only on the road, and those, oddly enough, were the most memorable parts of travel."

Harvey Reid
musician, label owner

> **HotTip:** Research any product that you are interested in before purchasing. Online products are no different than store-bought or mail-ordered products. Research before you purchase.

❖ Send copies of the contract and finalize details on e-mail before writing and sending the final paper copy to then be signed.

E-Mail Software

There are many sophisticated programs now available designed to make your e-mail correspondence quick and efficient as well as partially automated. As a touring performer not always able to get online to check your e-mail, install one of the e-mail data collection/response programs such as Eudora or Microsoft Outlook. These programs help you maintain e-mail contacts and stamp any outgoing e-mail with your contact information. (See resources for e-mail software.) The new programs allow you to create filters which direct certain types of incoming e-mail to be filed in predesignated folders for easy retrieval. Many provide security features to insure the privacy of your correspondence. Coupled with your online-service provider, these programs make managing your online communication easy and keep you looking professional.

Automated E-Mail Messengers—Auto Responders

Responding to numerous e-mail messages can also become an added burden while touring. By incorporating a program which automatically sends a return message to all of your incoming correspondence, correspondence can be semi-automated and data continually collected. This package sends a simple response to the original message sender notifying them that you have received their e-mail and will be contacting them shortly. A more sophisticated version of the auto responder software is an Infobot package which also allows an incoming request for specific information. It will select from your predesigned files appropriate information and automatically send it back to the correspondent. (See resources for software.)

Marketing With E-Mail

E-mail provides a method of always providing information about your act with each correspondence. Whether you are promoting tour dates, a new release or product, a new show or information about group members, your e-mail messages can include pertinent information which lets people in your targeted market group know about you. E-mail marketing websites provide templates to create graphically appealing easy to use e-mails at very low costs.

Websites

Once you are hooked on e-mail, you are a short distance away from creating a full Internet presence with your own website. Regardless of the quality or complexity of each site,

---

"A few years ago, the Internet was known as a great place to view dancing hamster web pages and college co-ed spycams, but wasn't regarded as a useful tool to further Indie music careers. What a difference a few years makes! These days, aspiring artists have access to powerful Internet resources that will help them sell their CDs, get booked, get promoted, get published and get signed."

Shawn Fields
founder, Getsigned.com

"Build a mailing list using Internet technology. Email lists are inexpensive and easy to set up. Collect email addresses following performances, when fans buy your merchandise, and from networking contacts. Add them to your list immediately. Then use the list. Send out a monthly email newsletter or performance schedule. There is a direct correlation between your attending audience and merchandise sales and how consistent you are with your mailing list."

Dianne de Las Casas
professional storyteller, director, Story Ballet Magic, president, ICAN - Independent Children's Artist Network

one fact remains, the web is the great equalizer. A small independent artist can exist equally in this medium with a large multinational corporation. Any single Internet user can access either site and purchase their products and gather their information. The Internet is the one marketing medium that is accessible to anyone regardless of money, experience or connections.

Creating your own website, like any other aspect of your career, also requires some degree of marketing to inform people of your website address. Once your site exists on the web, it is likely that some Internet surfers will stumble upon it. However, if you want your website to enhance your marketing efforts, you need to market the website.

Website Design Basics

Website marketing begins with the design. As you plan your site's design incorporate these five elements and techniques as offered by Mitchell Levy founder of ECnow.com:

1. Keyword-load your URL—Keywords make your site easy to find on the web.
2. Easily navigated—Make your site easy to use with easily accessible information while satisfying its intended purpose.
3. Optimize your site's positioning in the search engines—Select keywords and phrases that ensure your site will be found within the first two pages the search engine displays.
4. Provide something of value to your intended community—An informative site, kept current and fresh keeps your audience coming back.
5. Submit your sit to the top seven search engines—Once designed, you must alert the world about the site. Search engines help users find you.

For more design savvy techniques that will boost your site's effectiveness and efficiency see the resources on page 396 and visit (http://www.ecnow.com)

Marketing Your Website

Exchange Links

The Internet community is comprised of individuals like yourself, eager to exchange information and benefit from each other's successes. Submitting your web address (URL) to be linked on other related sites is a no-cost method of advertising to groups of people with similar interests.

A link is a highlighted word with imbedded URL codes. When you click on the highlighted word, it accesses the URL address and directly connects you to that specific site. Create a link section on your site offering to exchange links with sites of similar interests. Site links allow visitors to simply

---

HotTip:

Generate Income from your site.

E-commerce enabled site should deliver 5 customer-focused components:
1. Time-does it save time?
2. Attention-does it capture and keep my attention?
3. Trust-Does it establish trust?
4. Convenience-Is it convenient to conduct business?
5. Feel-Does it give the right feel for the products/services sold?

Mitchell Levy
author,
E-Volve-or-Die.com
CEO ECnow.com

"The most powerful technique for getting users to visit your site on a regular basis is to create interesting content that is updated on a regular basis."

Tom Vassos
IBM Internet
marketing director;
author,
Strategic Internet Marketing

click on the link and move to that new site. Yet, savvy web designers should realize that linking to other sites may drive viewers from your own.

In any web-surfing experience, exploring links expands your access to new and related information.

Self Promotion
Include your web address on all e-mails, business cards, stationery, promotional materials.

Newsgroups, Bulletin Boards
Include your signature on all postings to these groups. This accepted manner of providing contact information adheres to the Internet ethics code of proper behavior when interacting within these noncommercial groups. It keeps getting your name out there along with your site. When you participate in discussion groups, you have a chance to offer your expertise on familiar topics. Well-thought-out comments in newsgroups can entice new visitors to your site in search of other valuable information which you may have to offer.

Advertising
Website owners may offer individuals and companies opportunities to place both classified and display advertising on their sites. The advertising helps pay the site maintenance costs. If you have a site, consider offering advertising rates and space. More and more magazines and businesses related to your specific art form are beginning to offer advertising on their websites. The cost to advertise is often far more economical than the magazine's print advertising rates. You may find that advertising on the web suites your budget and allows you to incorporate a paid advertising campaign into your marketing plan.

Using Your Site Effectively
The most interesting sites are often the ones that provide information while also offering a certain degree of interactive opportunities. As a performing artist, your site can provide visitors with information about you and your products, recordings, videos or books. It can be used by the media and presenters alike who want to find out more about you before either writing a story or booking your act.

How you can make your site work for you
- ❖ Keep promotional materials and photographs available on your site for easy downloading by media and presenters.
- ❖ Have an updated press release available for downloading by press or presenters.
- ❖ Add sound clips and possibly a video.
- ❖ Keep schedule updates and tour itineraries accessible. Presenters, the media and your career-team members—

"The Internet is free marketing. Stay in touch with your fans on a monthly basis via newsletters, notes from the road, and your website. Keep them coming back for more."

Ericka Wilcox
founder, Virtual Associates,
executive director,
Berkshire Artists Group

"I learn new things every day from the folk music discussion groups on the Internet. It's one of the most interesting and valuable resources I have come across in a long time as a venue owner. As an artist, I can't think of any way to get better and more quickly connected."

Amy Kurland
owner,
The Bluebird Cafe

"You can update information from one minute to the next much more quickly than if you had to reprint brochures or catalogs."

Jay Conrad Levinson and
Charles Rubin
authors,
Guerrilla Marketing
Online Weapons

band members, publicists, record labels, agents or managers—can gain quick access to new tour information.
- ❖ Build your fan base by including a guest book or sign-in form for visitors to your site. These people can become recipients of e-mail newsletters and new product information.
- ❖ Create an order form where visitors can purchase your products.
- ❖ Provide links to other sites that are of interest to you and your site visitors.
- ❖ Provide your song lyrics or pieces of composed works or writings.
- ❖ Offer information about topics which interest or relate to you.

"It helps end this crazy constant mailing and faxing of information to journalists and promoters, who can just go to our websites and get our bio, pictures, stage plot, etc."

Harvey Reid
musician, label owner

Conclusion

By keeping your site updated and useful, visitors will return so that they may keep up with your career, buy your new products or use information you are making available for timely promotional purposes.

Used in conjunction with the other methods of support media, the Internet can become a tool which works for you 24 hours a day, seven days a week, no matter where you are.

Summary

- ❖ Participate in the online marketing revolution. The Internet offers individual performers a venue where they may compete equally with larger corporations.
- ❖ Use e-mail to reduce mailing costs and stay in close contact with your fans on a regular basis.
- ❖ Market your website and create a global presence previously unavailable to smaller businesses.
- ❖ Use your website to promote your act, sell your merchandise, and win new fans and customers.

"Web pages and the Internet are perfectly designed for music. All serious artists should have a well-maintained and creatively informative, yet simple, web page. Sell your records there, give current touring information, sound clips from your latest release and sell merchandise."

John Condon
former director A & R,
Asylum Records
Elektra Etertainment

Resources

Internet Magazines:

PC Magazine
Web: http://www.pcmag.com

Internet World
Web: http://www.IW.com

.net
Web: http://www.netmag.co.uk/

Smart Computing
131 W. Grand Drive
Lincoln, NE 68521
Phone: 1-800-544-1264; Fax: 402-479-2104
E-mail: editor@smartcomputing.com
Web: http://www.smartcomputing.com
Information on how to access and use the web.

Guerrilla Marketing Newsletter
Web: http://www.gmarketing.com/
Online subscription.

Internet Marketing Books:

Customer Service On The Internet: Building Relationships, Increasing Loyalty and Staying Competitive, 2nd Edition
Jim Sterne
John Wiley & sons
ISBN: 0471382582

E-Volve-or-Die.com
Thriving in the Internet Age Through E-Commerce Management
Mitchell Levy
New Riders
ISBN: 0735710287

Guerrilla Music Marketing Handbook
Bob Baker
P.O. Box 43058
St. Louis, MO 63143
Phone: 314-963-5296
Web: http://www.thebuzzfactor.com

Guerrilla Marketing Online Weapons
Jay Conrad Levinson and Charles Rubin
Marine Books
ISBN: 039577019X

Internet Marketing For Dummies
Frank Catalino, Bud E. Smith
For Dummies
ISBN: 0764507788

The Musician's Internet: On-Line Strategies For Success In The Music Industry
Peter Spellman
Berklee Press Publications
ISBN: 063403586X

NetResults.2
Best Practices for Web Marketing
Rick E. Bruner, Leland Harden, Bob Heyman
New Riders
ISBN: 0735710244

The Professional Musician's Internet Guide
Ron Simpson
MixBooks
ISBN: 0872887383

Internet Resource Directories:

The Indie Contact Bible
Big Meteor Publishing
P.O. Box 6043, Ottawa J
Ottawa, Ontario, K2A 1T1
Canada
Phone: 613-596-4996
E-mail: indiebible@rogers.com
E-mail: bigmeteor@rogers.com
Web: http://www.bigmeteor.com/icb
Features website listings only of reviews, radio stations, services, for independent music of all genres.

Musician's Atlas
38 Porter Place
Montclair, NJ 07042-2036
Phone: 973-509-9898
Fax: 973-655-1238
E-mail: MRGroup@aol.com
Web: http://www.MusiciansAtlas.com
Lists websites for artist development, webzines, web radio, web CD sales, resources and much more.

Internet Sites:

AudioSurge.com
Web: http://www.audiosurge.com
Submit your music, plays tracks, sells music.

CDBaby.com
Web: http://www.cdbaby.com
Online sales for Indie musicians.
Membership required

Jupiter Communications
Web: http://www.jupiterdirect.com
Online sales of books and other resources.

Liquid Audio
Web: http://www.liquidaudio.com
Digital solutions to promote and sell music online.

MP3.com
Web: http://www.mp3.com
Download music in MP3 format.

Online Switchboard
Web: http://www.switchboard.com/
Find people and businesses online.

Career Development Sites:

Getsigned.com
Web: http://www.getsigned.com

Gig Swap International
Web: http://www.gigswap.com

Indie-Music.com
Web: http://www.indie-music.com

Music Books Plus
Web: http://www.musicbooksplus.com

Music Link
Web: http://www.musiclink.com
Provides artists with new payment methods including contributions and grants.

Music Newswire
Web: http://www.musicnewswire.com

Music Registry
Web: http://www.musicregistry.com
Music business directories for film, TV, publishing, legal, and record labels.

The Musician's Assistant
Web: http://www.musiciansassist.com
Information packed site for musicians. Links to helpful sites on touring promotion, recording.

Nashville Music Network
Web: http://www.nashvillestar.com
Internet connection for latest information and voting for USA Network's Country Music star contest.

VH1 News
Web: http://www.VH1.com/news
Music industry news.

Web-Hosting for Musicians:

Hostbaby
Web: http://www.cdbaby.com
Template driven self-service host site. Very low cost. Guest books, sound clips, create email campaigns, online CD sales.

Totalband.com
Web: http://www.totalband.com
Hosting, site builder, email, gigbook, sound clips, musician resources, online CD sales

Artistopia
Web: http://www.artistopia.com
Hosting, resources, site building, email, artist development, CD sales

Nimbit
Web: http://www.nimbit.com
Hosting, email, CD Sales, e-commerce store

Self Service Direct Marketing:

Constant Contact
Web: http://www.constantcontact.com

Topica
Web: http://www.topica.com

Vertical Response
Web: http://verticalresponse.com
Publishes online newsletter and direct email advertising.

Free or Low-Cost E-mail Accounts:

Hotmail
Web: http://www.hotmail.com

Juno
Web: http://www.juno.com

Netzero
Web: http://www.netzero.com

Yahoo
Web: http://www.yahoo.com

Free or Low-Cost Internet Service Providers:

Juno
Web: http://www.juno.com

Netzero
Web: http://www.netzero.com

Internet Website Registration:

BuyDomains.com
Web: http://www.buydomains.com

Domain.com
Web: http://www.domain.com

Godaddy.com
Web: http://www.godaddy.com

Network Solutions, Inc.
Web: http://www.netsol.com

Auto Messaging Software:

AnsaBack
Web: http://www.ansaback.com

Site Marketing Companies:

The A1 Directory
Web: http://www.a1co.com/
Submit your site to directories one at a time.

Free Links
Web: http://www.freelinks.com
Free links to place your site.

HiPosition.com
Web: http://www.hiposition.com
Web positioning site.

NetPost
Web: http://www.netpost.com/
Links, ads, announcements.

Submit-It
Web: http://www.submit-it.com
Submit site to all major search engines, directories for one time charge.

Meta Search Engines:

AltaVista
Web: http://www.altavista.com

Dogpile
Web: http://www.dogpile.com/
Search many search engines at once using this web site.

Google
Web: http://www.google.com/
Search multiple search engines at once.

Essential Links
Web: http://www.el.com/
Now you can search through Yahoo, Excite, Alta Vista and mothers like Magellan and Hot Sheet with one click of your mouse. Very powerful search engine.

Mozilla
Web: http://www.mozilla.com

Netscape
Web: http://www.netscape.com

Yahoo
Web: http://www.yahoo.com

CHAPTER EIGHTEEN

Working With Your Record Label

"In promoting a new release, the artist's main job is to tour and perform as many live shows as possible along with doing interviews, in-store performances, and radio appearances. The artist should coordinate with the publicity department and ask what else they can do."

John Condon
former director, A & R, Asylum Records, Nashville,
Elektra Entertainment, New York

Congratulations! You landed a record deal. Do not think for a moment that you can kick back and relax. Your recording career is about to get a boost but you still have to play an active role in almost every phase. With a label on board, certain aspects of the process will be handled for you depending on the contract you negotiated. Other aspects will require your direct and constant participation if you plan on a successful release.

This chapter deals with how to make the most out of a working relationship with your label and how to help them promote your recording. Some of the suggestions may be more appropriately suited for those signed to major labels while other ideas will work with many of the independent

"Be a participant. Labels want to work with artists who participate actively in their own career. Learn as much as you can about the business. Labels prefer working with people who understand what it takes."

Barry Poss
founder,
Sugar Hill Records

labels. If you own your own label, you may be able to incorporate some of the suggestions into your future plans if your budget allows. Keep in mind that any of these suggestions can be carried out on a scale appropriate to your own situation. The key is to be an active participant, be receptive to new ideas pitched to you by your new team members at the label and remain creatively involved in the promotion of all of your products.

Working With A Team

Working with a team of professionals who are experts in promoting and selling recordings is the largest advantage you gain once signed to a label. An established label, whether major or independent, offers a newly-signed artist access to established systems and networks. Some of these include:

❖ Distribution
❖ Publicity
❖ Promotion, radio
❖ Sales
❖ Advertising
❖ Manufacturing
❖ Production
❖ Publishing

Each of these departments represent a team effort. Working with the label's publicity, sales and promotion departments can dramatically increase the distribution and sales of your recordings.

The publicity, sales and promotion departments work together to coordinate all of the details surrounding a new release. Meeting the heads of these departments should be one of your top priorities once signed to the label. They open doors to an entire sales force and a promotion and marketing machine that help to place your name and recording in front of the media, promoters, and retail buyers. Your partnership with these team members is paramount to the success of your release. Heed their advice, be available for their suggested projects and seek every opportunity to learn from them.

A note about record labels. Every label is working with specific budgets designated for each artist. Not every artist will receive equal attention from the label. Some major labels invest huge amounts of money on artist projects that sometimes fall short of their desired result. Once a label's sales expectations come close to approaching its goals, the label may choose to increase their investment in the artist's development. Some labels are committed to artist development because they simply believe in the artist. They may invest label time and money in that artist regardless of the

> *"It is important for the artist to discuss their overall career-development game plan with the label so that the promotional and marketing plans are focused and all are working for the same ends."*
>
> Ken Irwin
> co-owner,
> Rounder Records

> *"I think that success is going to come, not from the emulation of what is currently popular, but from hopefully finding an artistic voice that is unique and different. The industry is always looking for change and for something new, and I think that is one of the advantages the independent artist has."*
>
> Will Ackerman
> guitarist, founder,
> Windham Hill Records,
> Imaginary Road Records

number of units sold. Hopefully, the artist's career has longevity to offer the label rather than "flash-in-the-pan" sales. However, this is the exception rather than the rule.

The Publicity Department

The publicity department coordinates all efforts and pre-release materials involving the artist's image and the recording's entrée into the marketplace. Often this will involve creating new publicity materials that reflect a cohesive graphic look for the artist and the recording. It may mean writing new biographical materials and taking photos prior to the release. They may create electronic press kits or longer-format videos for release to targeted media or video-format shows.

Once the recording is released, the publicity department also coordinates all releases to the media, including press releases accompanying advanced copies of the recording. They schedule all interviews prior to and during the tours, and set up any radio or television shows.

The publicity department will also work with whomever is coordinating upcoming tour dates to insure important markets are targeted for performances. Touring in specifically-chosen markets enhances the labels efforts to hit certain necessary media outlets as well as designated retailers. For example: Touring in Boston or New York City allows the label to access major news media such as *The Boston Globe* or *The New York Times* and *The Village Voice*. Large retail stores such as Tower Records or Borders Books and Music are accessible for major promotional efforts. These efforts spark interest by retail buyers who can then influence nationwide sales. Smaller markets hold some media and retail value as well. But if you are determined to gain national presence, hitting the major markets such as New York, Boston, Philadelphia, Washington, DC, Los Angeles, Atlanta, Chicago and San Francisco are a priority.

The Sales Department

While the publicity department is beefing up your image in preparation for your market debut, the sales department is priming the retailers for the release of your new recording. Advance notice of all upcoming new releases is sent to the distributors and a release date is scheduled. Label sales representatives contact their prime accounts in an effort to generate excitement for the new release and to schedule specific programs with targeted retail outlets. The label works directly with their distributor to pitch upcoming releases. The distribution sales force then pitches the upcoming releases to the retail buyers at individual stores and chain-store accounts.

The sales and publicity departments will coordinate many of their efforts to take advantage of the artist's assistance in

> "The role of successful record labels that stay in business is to have catalog. The way to get catalog is to work with artists that can keep making records and have the potential of being productive. I'd rather sell 10,000 to 75,000 records progressively and have that catalog continue to sell over time. It's why record companies want to own masters."
>
> **Jon Grimson**
> former Americana radio promoter,
> founder,
> Americana Music Association

> "It is my personal belief that when a publicist or publicity department has passion for a project, a lot more gets done than if someone is merely 'assigned' an artist. A good publicist should be willing to walk the line for their artist (within reason of course) and speak eloquently and passionately about their artist's work."
>
> **Alisse Kingsley**
> director of publicity,
> Warner Bros. Records

> "In the current retail environment of inventory overload, retail buyers will not be impressed by telling them you have a great record. You must be prepared to specify the audience for the recording and how you plan to reach that audience. For each release they will want to know the artist's key markets, sales track record, tour dates, music type or genre, how much radio airplay is the artist receiving and in what formats. Finally, they want to know the label's support program (co-op and institutional advertising, etc.) for the release."
>
> **Barry Poss**
> president,
> Sugar Hill Records

> "The best promotion departments are those that can get your music played on as many stations as possible. They must be open to trying new ideas—not following trends. They must be bold."
>
> **John Condon**
> Asylum Records,
> Elektra Entertainment

promoting their new release. When artists tour in a specific market, the label will advance this information to key sales representatives. Then the retailers can set up appropriate store displays cross-promoting the performance with the new release. Often retailers may place a new release on special sale when the artist performs in the market. This may boost initial sales.

The Promotion Department

The promotion department of a label is primarily concerned with getting new releases played on the radio. The major labels often have staff that coordinate efforts for both commercial and noncommercial radio. As part of the team, the promotion department may be involved with the project early in the recording process to help determine towards what specific radio formats, if any, the album can be geared. (Refer back to Chapter 15 for information about radio formats.) Knowing which radio formats are targeted for the release helps the promotion department prime the appropriate radio programmers. The promotions department may work with outside radio promotions companies hired by the label, to create the recording's radio presence. That process is explained later in this chapter under Radio Promotions.

The promotions departments of most major labels are keenly aware of the impact radio has on making or breaking an artist and their current release. Work with your promotions department—be available for radio interviews and any type of radio promotions they may conjure up.

Sales, Publicity and Promotion Tools

There are a number of specific tools that labels use to increase the public awareness of the artist and the new release. Many of these efforts involve artist participation. The following are some of the most commonly used. Discuss the possibility of incorporating some of these tactics into your next promotional campaign with your label. If you own your own label, perhaps a few of these might be suitable to give your company a shot in the marketing arm.

Touring

Touring is the artist's most significant method of assisting with the promotion of a new release. Whether you are a solo artist who owns your label or an internationally-known artist promoted by a major label with sales in the millions, touring sells records.

When an artist tours, the label's publicity, sales and promotion departments have an opportunity to get key sales and marketing people to upcoming shows. By inviting these market representatives to see a show in their area, the artist has a chance to create enthusiasm for their act and the new release. The label will arrange for tickets by either planning a "ticket buy" with the promoter directly or arranging for guest tickets through the artist. Major labels will most often arrange for a ticket buy. They know that it is a small price to pay to ensure a retail buyer's excitement for an artist who will then stock more of that artist's product.

Touring will impact most of the following promotional tools used by labels. The possibilities of connecting with media outlets and your audience are enhanced by a consistent touring schedule.

Itineraries

Planning tours in tandem with the label will insure that you play in markets that the label has targeted as significant. Once you create a tour of appropriate cities, it is important that you send completed itineraries to the label so it can be distributed to all of their departments. Then, they send your itinerary to their distributors, special retail accounts and media outlets. By having an updated tour itinerary, the sales, publicity and promotion teams can begin to enhance your tour with interviews, in-store appearances, showcases at select conferences or district retail offices and stores.

Have your itinerary schedule set far enough in advance to allow the label to take advantage of some of these tools. When open dates are scheduled too close to the actual performance, promotion opportunities are more difficult to arrange. Planning to use these tools may require at least two months lead time, so finalize tour dates as quickly as possible.

Interviews

Once the tour dates are set and the press releases sent, the publicity department will schedule as many interviews with key media as possible. Often this will take place prior to leaving on tour. However, some interviews may have to take place from a hotel room while on tour.

The most efficient method of conducting interviews is to set aside blocks of consecutive hours on a few consecutive days. Schedule the interviews in twenty- to thirty-minute segments. If you schedule them tightly, you can manage quite a number of interviews in a short time. But, give yourself some breaks so you can sound fresh and interested to each new interviewer. It is very likely you will be asked similar questions throughout the day. If you are working with a really sharp publicity director, they may have created a set of specific questions or topics that they have forwarded to each of the upcoming interviewers in advance. (Refer back to the section on Interviews in Chapter 13.)

Most of the advanced interviews will be with some form of print media. Some radio stations may also conduct telephone interviews which may be taped for later broadcast on specialty shows or to take place during a live show.

"The record companies seem to be the end-all but they're just one step in the picture. Having the fans and people to sell records to is much more important. Create fans of a band as opposed to fans of a song."

Coran Capshaw
manager,
Dave Matthews Band,
Red Light Management

"Touring enables significant people who deal with the selling of records to see the act. About 90% of the recordings sold in the U.S. are sold through nine accounts. If the buyer or sales manager for one of these accounts loves your music, they can have a real impact on sales. But you must play in their market."

Ken Irwin
co-owner,
Rounder Records

"After show meet-and-greets are always a plus for key retailers, press, radio and label people."

Alisse Kingsley
director of publicity,
Warner Bros. Records

> **HotTip:** 🌶
> "A radio interview is the same as a concert performance. An artist must be professional. While an artist may face 50 to 500 people at most venues, they could be heard by 10,000 people on a radio broadcast."
>
> Rich Warren
> host, *The Midnight Special*
> WFMT Radio, Chicago, IL

Radio interviews most often take place at stations scheduled along the tour route. The label will arrange special times for shows that include a performance segment. Most radio interviews will intersperse questions and answers with cuts from the new release. However, be sure to ask the radio contact whether the music will be live or a selection from your CD.

Check your schedule carefully when making in-person radio station appearances. Make sure you have enough time to get to and from the station, especially on performance days. One time I agreed to a radio interview and later found that "We are not far from the venue" really meant the station was forty-five minutes out of town. Get directions to and from the radio station with realistic drive times from the hotel and the venue. In some cases, radio personnel or your publicist will be able to arrange your transportation.

Radio interviews are important. The more you assist the label in conducting radio interviews, the more airplay the release is likely to receive. Nothing sells records like radio airplay.

In-Store Appearances

The label will coordinate an in-store performance with key retail outlets in specific markets. Many retail stores are creating live performance spaces to accommodate this. Hear Music stores have modeled their entire store to enhance in-store artist appearances. Barnes & Noble Bookstores and Borders Books and Music have created effective in-store performance spaces as well.

> "Retail is oversaturated with releases. There is not enough shelf space in the store for all the product each month. One of the biggest challenges in this environment is getting your record in the store. The best ammunition an artist can give the label to accomplish this is tour dates."
>
> Alison Brown
> recording artist,
> co-owner, Compass Records

An in-store performance to promote a new release takes a great deal of advanced planning if it is to be effective and draw a crowd. The retailer usually designs cooperative ads (co-op ads) with the label and the local presenter to announce the release, the in-store appearance and the performance. This cross-advertising effort creates public and media awareness of the artist's appearances and promotes the new release. It gets people into the store to sample the artist's music. Hopefully, an in-store performance generates sales of both recordings and tickets to the performance or promotes a future dates which is scheduled within the upcoming month. If so, have tickets available for sale for the upcoming date.

> "Touch as many people with your music as you can and think big. Do the in-stores, play a club for a week and have some people sit in with you to get some press out of it. Take whatever opportunities are given, step back and see how you can make it bigger than what it is."
>
> Jessie Scott
> program director,
> XCountry
> XM Satellite Radio

In-store performances require equipment setup, sound check and, usually, the presence of the entire band. It is an extra performance on the tour schedule. Work with the label to schedule in-store appearances responsibly. Many stores attempt to take advantage of the largest flow of store traffic, usually after work, on weeknights or lunch hours. Whenever possible, schedule these additional performances on days off from regular shows or earlier in the day if it must be done on a concert day.

Store Visits

Visiting a retail store that carries your product is another effective way to get the retailers excited about you and selling your recordings. It is always great for a retailer to meet an artist and hear an artist offer a simple "thanks for selling my recording." It takes very little time to stop in to a store recommended by the label and meet the sales people and the manager. If the label plans the drop-in far enough in advance, co-op ads may announce the visit along with flyers posted in the store and around the area. When time permits, a table can be set up for a record signing for those who purchase the recording at that time. Have plenty of promotional items available such as t-shirts, hats, bumper stickers, promotional photos, key chains, etc. The retailer and the label may have arranged for a special sale price for that day only, which enhances sales and generates excitement about the store visit.

Opening Acts

Promoting a new release with a label may afford a developing artist the opportunity to open for other touring label-mates. The label often arranges for such support act slots with the main act's management and booking agency. By touring with a main act, the new artist gains access to the main act's audience. With the additional promotion and advertising provided by the label, the new act has a chance of developing first-time record buyers and fans. (Refer back to Chapter Eight for more information on opening acts, co-bills and multi-bill performances.)

Showcasing

Labels can often arrange for a new act to showcase at specific venues that draw both media and industry attendance. When a label is breaking a new artist, they may buy a large number of seats in the venue and invite key media and industry personnel to the show. By creating a 'buzz' within the industry, these key personnel continue to generate excitement for the artist within their own spheres of influence, enhancing the 'buzz.'

A few of the notable industry showcase venues around the country are: The Bottom Line and Tramps in New York City, The Bluebird Cafe in Nashville and The Troubadour in Los Angeles. These venues schedule new-act showcases to accommodate the media and industry personnel. There are many other venues that will work with your label to present a showcase. Discuss possible situations with your label suitable for your act when the time is appropriate. (Refer back to Chapter Eight for showcasing in clubs and Chapter 11 for showcasing at conferences.)

HotTips:

Keep in-store performances short, no more than half an hour when preceding a performance for which tickets are being sold.

Plan store drop-ins far enough in advance so that the key store personnel are available on that day. The advantage of a store drop-in is to meet the store manager and buyer, and increase their enthusiasm for buying and carrying your product.

"An artist can tell their label about acts they are friendly with or who came to their shows in the event openings or co-bills might be indicated at a later date."

Ken Irwin
co-owner,
Rounder Records

> "The realities of playing here is that the industry does like to come. They believe that the sound and lights are good so that they're going to get a good representation of the band."
>
> Lance Hubp
> general manager,
> The Troubadour

> "Promotion people are really in the business to create, disseminate and distribute information. This information helps artists to be taken seriously by larger labels, booking agents and other concerns. We give them a standardized report with a very standardized language which makes it easier to transfer information."
>
> Roger Lifeset
> Peer Pressure Promotion

> "Americana Radio is still growing, with most formats leveling out or losing Listeners, we are gaining, slowly but surely. 2003 was a banner year with the Americana Music Chart premiering in the number one radio trade magazine, R & R and getting a 24/7 Americana station in a major market, KCUV, Denver!"
>
> Leslie Rouffe
> Songlines Ltd.
> Americana/A3 Radio Promotion

Radio Promotions

As mentioned earlier, the promotion department helps raise radio awareness of your recording. To assist in that process, independent radio promotion companies exist whose sole purpose is to call radio programmers and make them aware of the project they are currently hired to promote. Independent radio promotions companies are specialists who work with small independent labels as well as major labels to promote music that fits into one of the radio formats—rock, alternative, adult contemporary, country, A3, jazz, NAC/Smooth Jazz, Americana, New Age. (Refer back to Chapter 15, radio formats.) A recording supported by a radio promotions company has a greater opportunity to receive chart recognition because of their constant contact with the music directors at each of the reporting stations.

Radio Charts

The purpose of a radio chart goes far beyond simply seeing what number your recording was that week. There is valuable information which a label or an artist can gain from having their recording receive chart recognition. The information is reported to you in the form of a tracking sheet. Record labels, large and small, should enter into a relationship with a radio promotions company determined to gather the following information:

1. In which markets did the recording receive airplay?
2. How much airplay was received in each market—light, medium, heavy?
3. Which markets have added the recording, which dropped it?
4. How long did it take for the recording to be added from the time it was received?
5. How many weeks was the recording receiving airplay in each market?
6. Which specific stations are playing the recording in each market?
7. What was the chart position of the recording when it entered, what position did it attain, how many weeks was it on the chart?

These seven pieces of information can help you and your label target markets for touring, schedule stations for interviews and market to specific retailers in strong airplay markets. It can also help you to prepare for the next recording project. By paying close attention to the cuts that received the greatest airplay, you can evaluate how well you planned your recording for radio and specifically for the format chosen.

Using Independent Radio Promotions Companies

If you or your label decide to hire an independent radio promotion company, here is some information that will help you determine which company is right for you, plan an appropriate budget and know what can be expected.

❖ First and foremost, determine whether or not you are ready to hire a promotion company—artistically and financially.
❖ Does your music as a whole, or just one song, comfortably fit into a particular format?
❖ Can your recording compete with every other recording you hear on the radio?
❖ Does your artwork compete with other recordings you see in the record bins?
❖ Are you prepared to make a commitment to this process?

The Nuts And Bolts Of Radio Promotions

1. *Budget:* Planning a radio promotion campaign will cost approximately $300 to $600 per week for a national promotion. Discuss this kind of promotion with your label during contract negotiations so a budget might be set in advance.
2. *Duration:* The campaign should last for a minimum of six weeks. If the results warrant it, weeks can be added, in two-week increments, for a total of twelve weeks.
3. *Benefits:* The greatest benefit of working with a promotions professional is that their opinions are trusted by the radio programmers. They access the radio programmers on a weekly basis and present them with new projects that they have been hired to promote. Promotions people have generally been involved in this business long enough to establish a track record and long-time relationships with radio programmers. This alone can often mean the difference between getting a new recording reviewed or not. It can further impact whether or not the programmer will play it on the air to gauge listener reaction.

   Another benefit is working with someone who understands the format that you are attempting to access. If your recording is suited to the format, the promoter will help your project get the airplay it deserves. If your project is not suited to the format, they will tell you so and then not waste your time trying to promote a recording that just does not fit.
4. *Expectations:* During your six- to twelve-week promotion, you will receive weekly tracking sheets that follow the progress of the recording. The sheets will tell you which stations in each market are considering the recording and which have added it. The sheets will

> *"The most common shortcomings of any project are: the music is not 'focused' enough to compete in an established format—it tries to cover too many sides of an artist's abilities; the CD artwork is not competitive with major label product; and perhaps the biggest—distribution for the product is not secure. If we do the hard work of getting airplay on radio stations and product is not available in markets playing it—it is a waste of your money."*
>
> **Michael Moryc**
> Matrix Promotions

> *"When promoting your CD to radio, know whether or not you want to promote nationally or just regionally. If you want to do a national promotion, make a splash, don't send your CD out piecemeal. It takes multiple impressions to have an effect. It's also important to follow up with publicity and use that to leverage your touring options. If you can accomplish moderate success on all those fronts, your profile will certainly increase—leading to higher fees, better venues and increased touring and CD sales."*
>
> **Kari Estrin**
> acoustic radio promoter

> "Much of the time, a relationship has been forged with the radio programmer that has taken years to establish and a degree of trust exists where recommendations by the promotions person on your behalf will be taken more seriously. Radio programmers receive 50 to 60 CDs per week—having someone call who can get your CD heard is step one."
>
> Michael Moryc
> Matrix Promotions

> "The first thing we need to do is understand the objectives for the project and provide for them, what I call, my radio reality check. I listen to the record and compare my reality with your objectives. . . . There are many records that were never created to be played on the radio. We've got to be real about what results we can expect from the charts."
>
> Roger Lifeset
> Peer Pressure Promotions

> "Listen to the format and caste what really works on that format. With something that's a little more edgy, it is lost on country radio. There are not a lot of chance takers out there. Whereas, Triple A, at the time it blossomed, was a total chance taker. Create something that really works within the format."
>
> Ken Levitan
> former manager,
> Nanci Griffith

update the level of airplay the recording is receiving—light, medium, heavy—and, finally, which cuts are receiving play. If the recording is doing exceptionally well, it may make it onto the format chart and begin jockeying for higher position. The weekly update allows you and the record company to plan targeted promotions in key areas which may boost the airplay according to your report results. After six or eight weeks a determination as to whether or not to continue your promotion efforts can be made based on the reports.

A personal example

Before realizing there were companies that specialized in radio promotions, I had hired someone in-house to conduct a fairly elaborate survey for one of my artist's recordings. It was made using a unique microphone system and it was important for us to determine if the sound of the recording had any impact upon radio programmers playing it.

We phoned every radio station in the genre across the country during a two-week period. Many stations had received the recording but had not listened to it. Many loved it while others were inspired to play it after hearing about it and being gently coaxed to listen. By the end of the two-week period, many of the original stations had added it and most were giving it medium to heavy airplay. The follow-up phone calls, additional information and invitations for the programmers to express their opinions, as well as the recording technique itself, increased radio awareness of the artist and the recording.

The artist and I had taken on this project outside of the regular marketing campaign conducted by the independent label. It was money well spent. But, it was labor intensive.

Marketing Your Recordings To Specialty Stores

Whether you are on a label or own your own label, the large chain stores are not the only avenue in which to market your recordings. Smaller independent record stores are often a viable source. As an independent artist, you have more opportunities to establish your own accounts with these smaller stores. Begin regionally. You will have more control over each account.

Beyond record stores, small mom-and-pop gift stores often will carry music. Stores better known for other items, like clothing, cards, books, jewelry and some restaurants may consider selling your recordings.

According to Richard Flohil, early in her career, Loreena McKennitt placed her recordings in restaurants in the towns where she was about to perform. Not only did the restaurants sell her music but they posted announcements of her upcoming shows and played the recordings over their sound systems. This became one of her very lucrative niche markets. To this day, Loreena's record deal with Warner Bros. stipulates that she continue to handle all of the niche market accounts through her own label, Quinlan Road.

When attempting to place recordings in some of these alternative markets, creating an attractive point-of-purchase display may prove effective. Putamayo World Music label did just this for their world music CD series. By taking a thematic approach to the music incorporated within each of the recordings, they are able to target the CDs to sell in specific types of retail markets. Putumayo CDs are featured in specialty clothing boutiques, book and gift stores and coffee shops.

As an independent record company you can create a similar type of display and target an appropriately-suited store where you can begin your alternative sales. This will take some additional time and money. However, the reward may be that you are the only record company selling in that store or chain of similar stores. Those having a regional following will find adding alternative stores to your marketing efforts also increases your regional reputation. If you are savvy enough to land a regional store within a national chain, sales can increase exponentially.

Niche Markets To Consider:
- Clothing stores and magazines
- Baby stores and magazines
- Specialty food stores and magazines
- Cooking supply stores and magazines
- Art galleries and magazines
- Plant nurseries and garden shops and magazines
- Bookstores
- Gift shops, card stores and gift mail order catalogs
- Regional information centers
- Museums and historical sites
- Coffee bars—local or chain
- Hospital gift shops
- Public radio or public television premiums

_____

_____

_____

Follow-up with these smaller individual accounts will take some time on your part. But, if you concentrate on a small regional area at first, you will be able to add other markets as you become comfortable.

"Artists should encourage the promotion department to court the smaller stations as well as the larger ones. The object here is to maintain growth for the artist and build a career. Artists should keep a list of the smaller stations that are big supporters and remind the promotion department of them."

John Condon
Asylum Records,
Elektra Entertainment

"We at Putumayo World Music are committed to finding creative ways to get our CDs played and positioned in our retail accounts. To reinforce our 'Travel The World With Putumayo' advertising thematic, we frequently conduct in-store sweepstakes where we give away trips to the countries from where the music from the featured CD originates. For our 'Putumayo Blend: Music From The Coffee Lands' CD, we developed cafe retail partnerships with Barnes & Noble and Timothy's who actually developed and sold a Putumayo blend of coffee."

David Hazan
sr. v.p. marketing,
Putumayo World Music

"I have learned to approach sales from a pull marketing perspective. I focus on specialty stores that are not traditional sites for music sales . . . stores that attract customers that ought to be attracted to my music were they ever to encounter it."

Ed Sweeney
president, artist,
Old Harbor Music
Crossroads, March/April 1997

> "When introducing George Winston's new release in 1980, I got names and addresses out of the phone book and spent a few days in New York City going around to fashion photographers with the records. I would say, 'Hi, here's a free record, you might like it.' Suddenly it was the 'buzz' in New York. That's how Chuck Young at Rolling Stone got it. There was a four-star review and we had our first national press."
>
> Will Ackerman
> guitarist, founder,
> Windham Hill Records,
> Imaginary Road Records

Conclusion

If you work with an independent label, budget allocations may not provide for additional marketing projects. As concerned artists with a creative streak, do not let that stop you from working something out with the label to take advantage of some of these tools. You might consider securing financing yourself if you believe your project is worthy of stretching the boundaries of your label's normal routines. Either challenge the label to try something new or decide to take it into your own hands while keeping the label informed. Recognize that any promotion, publicity and additional sales will eventually benefit you. Once the label realizes that something new is working, they may jump in and provide assistance after all.

Be prepared to become part of the team. The expertise a label can provide in selling and promoting your recording is invaluable. If you are one of those artists who finds themselves working with a label, expect to work hard to promote your recording along with those teammates.

> "The best example of niche marketing of classically-oriented music is that the last seven albums to go platinum (which is one million sales) were CDs that Victoria's Secret sold in their stores. Using some of our historic recordings from the Nimbus catalog, we put together a unique compilation specifically for Opera News. We offered the CD to their renewing members of the Opera Guild as a premium. This disk is not available in any retail outlet."
>
> Peter Elliott
> vice president,
> Nimbus Records

Summary

- Get to know the people in the publicity, promotion and sales departments.
- Be available to assist your label with special projects that will help market and promote your new release.
- Work with the label to ensure you have similar goals and work toward that end.
- Coordinate tour dates with the label to take advantage of publicity and marketing outreach projects.
- Send timely itinerary notices to the label.
- Become aware of the various promotion tools available and use them to suit your own situation.
- Challenge your label to be creative when promoting your release.
- Explore alternative markets in which to sell your product. If you are on a label roster, consult with them when developing alternative marketing ideas.
- Be a part of the team when working with a label.

Resources

Books:

All You Need To Know About The Music Business: Revised and Updated for the 21st Century
Donald Passman
Simon & Schuster
ISBN: 0684870649

How To Make & Sell Your Own Recording: A Complete Guide to Independent Recording
Diane Sward Rapaport
Prentice Hall, Inc.
Englewood Cliffs, NJ
ISBN: 0139239472

Label Launch: A Guide To Independent Record Recording Promotion And Distribution
Veronika Kalmar
Griffin Trade Paperback
ISBN: 0312263503

Music Business Handbook & Career Guide
David Baskerville
Sage Publications
ISBN: 0761916679
Guide to copyrighting, publishing, licensing, retailing, media, promotion and more.

Start and Run Your Own Label
Daylle Deanna Schwartz
Watson-Guptil
ISBN: 0823079244

How the Music Business Works
Larry E. Wacholtz, Ph.D.
Thumbs Up Publishing
Phone: 888-782-7857; Fax: 615-386-0407
ISBN: 0965234118

The Real Deal: How to Get Signed to a Record Label
Daylle Deanna Schwartz
Watson-Guptil
ISBN: 0823084051

The Self-Promoting Musician
Strategies For Independent Success
Peter Spellman
Berklee Press Publications
ISBN: 063400644

Tim Sweeney's Guide To Releasing Independent Recordings
Tim Sweeney and Mark Geller
TSA Books
ISBN: 0965131602
How to set up your own label and market your music on a national level.

CD and Cassette Manufacturers:

See Chapter 5 Resources.

Directories Of Record Labels:

AustralAsia Music Industry Directories
GPO Box 2977
Sydney, N.S.W.
Australia 2000
Phone: +61-02-9557-7766
Fax: +61-02-9557-7788
E-mail: directories@immedia.com.au
Web: http://www.immedia.com.au
Lists record labels, distributors, mastering, music licensing, publishers.

Billboard
1515 Broadway, 39th Floor
New York, NY 10036
Phone: 1-800-449-1402
Web: http://www.billboard.com
International Buyer's Guide—labels, publishers, wholesalers, distributors, manufacturers.
Record Retailing Directory—lists independent record retail stores, chains, contacts, specialty.
International Latin Music Buyer's Guide—Latin music venues, labels, artists, industry contacts.
Radio Power Book—Radio stations, music directors, contacts.

Record Company Roster
Pollstar
4697 W. Jacquelyn Avenue
Fresno, CA 93722
Phone: 1-800-344-7383
Phone: 559-271-7900; Fax: 559-271-7979
E-mail: info@pollstar.com
Web: http://www.pollstar.com
Record companies with A & R contacts/artist rosters, music publishers, distribution groups.

Talent & Booking Online
P.O. Box 14265
Palm Desert, CA 92255
Phone: 760-779-8056
Fax: 760-773-3568
Web: http://www.talentandbooking.com
Lists country music record labels, A & R contacts/artist rosters, public relations firms.

Musician's Atlas
38 Porter Place
Montclair, NJ 07042-2036
Phone: 973-509-9898
Fax: 973-655-1238
E-mail: MRGroup@aol.com
Web: http://www.MusiciansAtlas.com
Lists websites for artist development, lists labels, publishers, press, radio.

The Musician's Guide to Touring & Promotion
49 Music Square West
Nashville, TN 37203
Phone: 615-321-4295; Fax: 615-327-1575
Web: http://www.musiciansguide.com
Lists agents, bands, clubs, labels, lawyers, press, fanzines, radio stations, music stores and more.
Semi-annual directory: cost $10.95

The Music Business Registry
7510 Sunset Blvd., #1041
Los Angeles, CA 90046-3418
Phone: 1-800-377-7411
Phone: 818-995-7458; Fax: 818-995-7459
E-mail: info@musicregistry.com
Web: http://www.musicregistry.com
A & R Registry—6 issues, updated every 8 weeks, lists all major and independent labels, A & R staff, and regional A & R staff.
Music Publisher Registry—2 issues, updated twice a year, lists all major and significant independent publishers.
Film/TV Music Guide—directory of film/TV studios, music supervisors, composer, agents, managers, TV network and independent production music departments and more.
All directories also available on disk.

North American Folk Music Business Directory
Folk Alliance
510 South Main Street
Memphis, TN 38103
Phone: 901-522-1170
Fax: 901-522-1172
Web: http://www.folkalliance.net

The Recording Industry Sourcebook
ArtistPro
Web: http://www.artistpro.com
ISBN: 1931140332
Comprehensive directories, labels, managers, agents, attorneys, media contacts and more.
Also comes with Sourcebase CD-ROM or database on disk. New searchable online.

The Industry Yellow Pages, Vol. 6
The Complete Major & Independent Record Label Music Business Directory, International Edition
Platinum Millennium
ISBN: 0971339112

Master Tape Restoration:

A Gentle Wind Inc.
Donald Person
P.O. Box 3103
Albany, NY 12203
Phone: 518-482-9023
Analog tape recovery and restoration of reel-to-reel tapes at risk from deterioration.

Online Independent Music Sales:

Amazon Advantage Program
Web: http://www.amazon.com/advantage

CD Baby
Web: http://www.cdbaby.com

CD Now
Web: http://www.cdnow.com

CD Street
Web: http://www.backstagecommerce.com

Emusic
Web: http://www.emusic.com

CD Universe
Web: http://www.cduniverse.com

iTunes
Web: http://www.apple.com/itunes

Song Plugger for Independent Artists:

TAXI
5010 North Parkway, Suite 200
Calabasas, CA 91302
Phone: 1-800-458-2111
Web: http://www.taxi.com
Bi-weekly listing of those looking for songs.
Yearly subscription, cost $299

CHAPTER NINETEEN
Working With Professional Agents And Managers

"I think the value of a booking agent is their knowledge of the industry; they know who the competitors are and are aware of what's hot and what's not at any given moment. Their expertise is of great value to the artist."

Andrea Rounds
director, Dodger Touring Limited (D. Tours)

As mentioned in the introduction, you may have an opportunity to work with a professional agent during your career. Although the majority of this book provides you with the tools you need to work as your own booking agent, the information provided here will also enhance your working relationship with a manager or agent.

"The best way to know what to look for in a manager is to learn how to manage yourself. An artist that knows how to set short- and long-range goals and develop a plan to achieve those goals will be more prepared to look at prospective managers."

Dick Renko
manager,
Trout Fishing in America,
Muzik Management

Definitions Of Agent And Manager:
❖ *A booking agent books performance dates.* They are paid by taking a commission on each date they book and contract, and the performer completes. Commissions vary but most often range from 10% to 20%.
❖ *A personal manager helps direct an artist's career.* They often serve as the team leader coordinating all efforts between the artist, the booking agency, the record company, the publicist and any other professionals involved

> **HotTip:** 🌶
> Review your long-term goals. Evaluate the type and number of dates performed each year. Know every aspect of your business before pursuing a relationship with an agent or a manager.

"The management/artist and agent/artist relationship is essentially a parasitic relationship. The artist is the commodity and the manager or agent is taking a percentage of his or her work. I think an artist starting out is going to do much better to try to lay the foundation themselves. You need to have an audience before you need to have a manager."

Teddy Wainwright
former manager,
Loudon Wainwright III,
The Roches

with the artist's career. Managers are paid by commission on all of the artist's earnings including all performances, record deals, publishing deals or any other contracts the manager negotiates on the artist's behalf. Commissions vary with each manager and can range from 10% to 50% depending upon the manager's investment in the artist. Most often, commission fees range from 15% to 25%. These commissions are in addition to the agent's commissions.

Carefully Consider Who You Invite Into Your Business

Before you enter into a relationship with an agent or manager, be fully aware of your goals and expectations. Up until this point, you have worked very hard to develop your business. View working with an agent or manager as inviting a new partner to share in your business. The decision to take on a partner is never taken lightly by anyone. In business, a partner influences its direction—the way decisions are made, the manner in which business is conducted and the future of the business' success. An agent or a manager can have that kind of impact on your business. Are you willing to hand your business over to anyone who shows an interest? You shouldn't be!

So many artists have anxiously asked me if I am taking on new artists or can I recommend an agent, hoping that I might solve all of their booking concerns. My response is usually to ask why they want to work with an agent. Inevitably, I most frequently hear, "I can't keep up with all of the booking business and I need more time to practice." Sound familiar? However, the other response is, "I have more work than I can handle and I am ready to turn it over to an agent." For most artists having these problems, consider the suggestions I make in Chapter 20 very seriously. If you are in this enviable position of having too much work to handle, you may have a career that is ready for an agent. Finding the right agent to book your act may be your next logical step. Depending upon the type of act you present, the type of venues in which you perform and your act's audience, there may not be enough professional agents handling bookings for your situation. For instance, if you perform 200 dates in elementary schools, there may not be an agent booking those types of dates. However, if you have built an audience in colleges, nightclubs, performing-arts venues and community-concert organizations, the likelihood of finding an agent is much greater. The remainder of this chapter will help you determine if you are ready to work with a professional manager or agent. However, in most cases, your business is simply growing and in need of strategic expansion. Hiring an assistant to help you get your work done may be the best solution. It may not require you turning over the lifeblood of your business to someone else. After all, an agent or manager is in business for themselves. Their business is working with artists to build the artist's career. How do you know how well they run their business? How do you know that they will be successful on your behalf? How do you know they will be more successful for you than you could be for yourself?

Before trusting anyone with the business of your career:
❖ List specific situations or areas in which you feel you need help.
_____
_____

❖ What part of your business needs the most help?
  _____ office management   _____ the bookings
  _____ career direction   _____ goal setting
❖ What is your annual income from bookings alone?
_____

❖ How many dates per year do you perform?
_____

❖ What type of performance venues do you regularly play?
_____

❖ What touring acts are similar to your own?
_____
_____

❖ Are you prepared to spend ten to twenty-five percent of your income on commissions to agents and/or managers?
  _____ Yes   _____ No
  _____ If the results warrant it.
  _____ I will spend anything so I won't have to do my own bookings!

By answering the above questions, you will be better prepared to assess your position when considering working with an agent or a manager. However, do not make this decision to simply be relieved of the workload. Your answers will help you evaluate where you stand in relation to what the agencies are looking for when they consider new acts. As we continue, this chapter will broaden your perspective of what is involved when working in a relationship with an agent or a manager.

The Courting Stage

In an effort to make the best decision possible, interview any prospective agents or managers. They will certainly want to gather as much information about you and your career and you must allow yourself the same opportunities to examine a future work partner. Do not let the enthusiasm of an agent or manager's interest in your act cloud your decision making. Similar to a friendship or love relationship, some work and

"Relinquishing the day-to-day responsibilities to a manager, a publicist, a record company or an agent does not mean relinquishing control of your career. An artist should always keep abreast of how their interests are being represented."

Jim Fleming
agent,
Fleming & Associates

"An artist should know enough about all the particulars of every aspect of the business so they can collaborate with the manager's, publicists, labels, etc. They should be mini-masters of all aspects of their career."

Ralph Jaccodine
manager,
Ellis Paul & Flynn Management,
Black Wolf Records, Black Wolf Press,
Moody Street Pictures

"It's important that an emerging artist really wants to build a career, not just play dates, and that they've met with some success while doing their own bookings."

Harriet Kyriakos
agent,
Bookin'

some do not. Entering into a business relationship of this sort needs time to grow and develop. At the very least, it is necessary to spend some initial time getting to know one another and what each of you can offer the other.

Finding an agent or a manager who is interested in working with you, and visa versa, puts you into the "courting stage."

When considering a new relationship with an agent or a manager, do the following:

- Schedule a number of meetings to get to know one another while working on the list below. If you are new to them, schedule a number of times when they can see you perform so they can become familiar with your act.
- Send them a list of your long-term goals.
- Ask the agent or manager to provide a brief history of their agency or management firm and of their involvement in the industry, their longevity, their professional affiliations, etc.
- Ask for a current and past client list.
- Contact some of the clients and ask for their evaluations of the agent or manager.
- Contact other performers, agents and managers to get a sense of their industry reputation.

When considering a new relationship with a manager also:

- Ask them for an evaluation of your current materials after they have reviewed them.
- Ask them for a proposal of their suggestions for your career development based on your materials, goals and performance.
- Discuss commission fees based upon how they intend to work with you.

When managers provide you with an initial plan of action, their client list for your contact and career evaluation in your preliminary meetings, they demonstrate their interest in your act and their desire to create a mutually-beneficial working relationship. Take an active role in evaluating a future partner. After all, you are depending upon this person for the growth of your career. Call the client list and other industry professionals. Solicit their opinions about the manager. Complimentary comments about a manager's standing within the industry sheds some insight about how they will represent you. Concerned and off-handed remarks offer red flags and should be taken seriously before you find yourself locked into an unfavorable situation.

When considering a new relationship with an agent also:

- Send them a list of past performance venues if not already included in your promotional packet.
- Contact some presenters to get a sense of their working relationship with the agent or agency.

"It is like being in a relationship with a spouse or a lover. It's a daily, round-the-clock relationship, and you've got to trust your instincts . . . It's a very major commitment, you are putting your career on the line and putting a lot of responsibility in someone else's hands."

Tom Carrico
manager,
Steve Forbert, Jonell Mosser,
Studio One Artists

"New artists seeking management should first and foremost look for someone who absolutely believes in them. That belief and passion can overcome many shortcomings. A manager should also be reality based and not just seeking fame and fortune. Look for a manager who will pay attention to the bottom line and not get the artist into debt to look cool or travel in style."

Denise Stiff
manager,
Alison Krauss and
Union Station,
Gillian Welch,
DS Management

- ❖ Ask for a list of trade shows, booking conferences and other industry events which the agency attends regularly.
- ❖ Ask for a proposed strategic plan for booking your act based upon your long-term goals, input from management (if any) and the agency's intended market.
- ❖ Discuss the commission fee based upon the agency's involvement in your career.
- ❖ Negotiate your option to continue to book yourself at local or regional dates until the agency is working full steam for you. Establish a future date when the agency will actually commit to having some dates booked for you. Until that time, you can continue to book dates. This guarantees that you will continue to have some work until the agency dates kick in, which may be three to six months down the line.
- ❖ Create a test period prior to signing any long-term contracts for exclusive representation. (Many agencies will ask to represent your act exclusively, meaning that no one else may book your act, not even you. Suggest a three-to-six-month trial period to see if they will be able to book your act satisfactorily. This creates an incentive for the agency to get some work quickly to demonstrate their commitment to you. The agency can also test the act's potential marketability. It will always take some time for an agency to promote a new act on their roster. But if you sign an exclusive immediately, they have no real incentive to prove themselves. I have seen some artist's careers lose momentum rather than gain once signed exclusively.)

This plan will enable you to evaluate whether or not you can work with an agent or agency. Their flexibility in negotiating an agreement will give you an indication of how a long-term working relationship will be. Those interested in having your act on their roster will be considerate of your concerns regarding ongoing income during the start-up period. Each agency has their own criteria for accepting new acts and may suggest some alternatives to the above list. It is important for you to remain in control of your career and scrutinize each offer before signing with one agent or another.

Once again, depending on your standing within the industry, your leverage to negotiate terms will vary. An unknown, untested act may simply be glad to be signed. Whereas, a name act with a proven track record can be more demanding. New act or name act, remain true to your long-term goals. Sign with an agent or agency because you can envision a beneficial working relationship that will be successful for you both.

Which Comes First—The Manager Or The Agent?

Is this another chicken-or-the-egg riddle? Perhaps! I believe the answer to which comes first is firmly embedded within the goals you have set for your career.

"It is about managing expectations—the artist and the manager's expectations need to be on the same page. You do this with constant communication and the 'us against them' philosophy. The two parties need to know they are in this together."

Ralph Jaccodine
manager,
Ralph Jaccodine Management

"To be good at being a manager you have to have a 360 degree view of the music industry and you have to know how each element interacts with all the other elements."

Jim Mason
author, educator, songwriter,
record producer

> *"For artists who are locating a manager, the manager has to believe in the music. If they're not a songwriter, they have to believe in that artist's presentation, how they perform and what they're about. It has to be an honest relationship and you have to be able to be honest from the very get go."*
>
> **Joni Foraker**
> vice president,
> Borman Entertainment

> *"There's a misunderstood public perception that management is not much more than a glorified baby-sitting position. But the truth of the matter is that the really skilled managers are probably the single most powerful group in the music business."*
>
> **Jim Mason**
> author, educator, songwriter,
> record producer

The Manager

The need for a manager driving your career depends upon what vision you have for your career. Having the right management on your team can provide you with the necessary connections to push you to higher levels of visibility within the market. Working with management, in some cases, can even help formulate career goals if you have not done that on your own. Or, management may enhance those goals already set with a broadened perspective of what is possible.

A manager who has connections within your chosen market helps to maintain an overview of your career and serves as a sounding board for important decisions while lending their years of experience. In some genres of music, it is important to have management overseeing the business on the artist's behalf since the artist has become a business. Coordinating artist touring and recording schedules, all manner of personal appearances, side musicians, tour vehicles, crew, staff and merchandising are all handled by the management team rather than the agency who books the tour dates. At this level, management is necessary.

During the early stages of a career, an artist with experienced management may move more quickly through their career development and reach their goals more rapidly than an artist without. Management provides a committed individual with whom to brainstorm about new directions and attempts at advancement. It is management's responsibility to find the right booking agency and negotiate their commission. A well-connected manager remains current regarding agency rosters and potential strategic alliances such as co-bill or opening-act slots. Aligning yourself with the right management team can provide an artist with a partner who can help the artist achieve their goals. In the best of situations it can be one of the most important relationships of an artist's career.

The Agent

For an artist in need of intensive career development, finding a manager may well be the first move to make. For other artists who created their start-up career plans, management may not be as necessary as working with a booking agent.

In some cases, working with an agent may provide the necessary career direction because of additional bookings. An agent who can upgrade the level of the performance venues and increase the number of performance dates may be all the career boost necessary. A well-connected agent, current on other agency and management rosters, booking conferences, showcase opportunities and the other artists touring in the market can enhance an artist's bookings, co-bill and support-slot opportunities. All of these raise the artist's visibility. Viewed as a strategic career move, rather than an attempt to rid yourself of one of the undesirable aspects of your business, working with the right agent may be the next appropriate step.

So, which comes first for you, the manager or the agent? All of the previous chapters have provided you with insights on how to control your business and have an in-depth understanding of what is involved in creating a touring career that has the potential for success. The addition of one or both of these industry professionals may not be necessary at this point. If you are inclined towards working with an agent and/or a manager at some future time, the remainder of this chapter will help you make those decisions more effectively.

Experience Versus Inexperience

My association with the first act I booked began in college and continued for twenty years. Not all artist/manager relationships benefit from such a long-term association, but those that do have the opportunity to help each other realize their full potential.

I began my first booking relationship by testing a couple of regions where the artists had already developed a following. In the beginning, I just booked dates and later grew into my managerial role. We were all young in our careers and I was so new to the industry that I can recall one presenter asking me if I had the authority to book this act. After proving myself worthy with the presenters, the bookings increased, as did the number of regions I handled along with my responsibilities.

In my case, when I began working with artists, I was filled with energy and enthusiasm but had very few contacts and hardly any resources. My commitment to the artists led me to the contacts and the resources that I needed. My resolve to make all of our careers flourish was my greatest asset.

For artists who have chosen to work with a newcomer to the field of booking or management, the determination to work diligently on behalf of the artist's career is often reason enough to join forces. Contact lists are available and skills to become a savvy agent or manager are able to be acquired as you are learning. Would aligning yourself with a veteran agent or manager increase your chances for more rapid success? Probably, if your act has "got the goods" and an agency is interested. The chances are less likely that a veteran agent or manager will sign you without a track record or some inclination that the act will be worth their investment.

There are some benefits to working with an inexperienced person who will serve as a manager or agent for your act. As you learn the ropes together, you are more apt to incorporate new and innovative ideas when marketing the act. Unencumbered by the way it should be done, you are free to create new marketing strategies that specifically suit you. I often made calls to prestigious industry professionals at record

"You may not need a manager yet! Often building a team for a developing artist will mean getting a publicist and booking agent before a manager."

Dick Renko
manager

"Having kept my own band working and eating for many years was great schooling for my booking and agent duties of the past 15-plus years."

Scott O'Malley
agent,
Scott O'Malley
& Associates, LLC

"There have been plenty of cases of brilliant artists whose art is only appealing to a small segment of the population. Those artists are always better off representing themselves, to act otherwise inevitably ends in disappointment for everyone."

Jim Fleming
agent,
Fleming & Associates

companies and major venues not knowing the perceived stature the person held within the industry. My naiveté proved valuable and allowed me to venture where others might have been intimidated. My concern was to do the best work I possibly could for my artist, regardless of whom I called or met. The main benefit of working with someone new to the business is that their primary interest is helping the act succeed and they are willing to learn while doing. The secondary benefit is that they are likely to be very committed to your joint venture. Since you are the only act on the roster you get 100% of their time.

The downside of working with an inexperienced person is their lack of knowledge of the industry and their lack of experience working with others within it. It may take time to develop your list of contacts. Personally, I have found that the research portion of every task was the most interesting and it is what held my interest and spurred me along to accomplish an objective.

For those faced with the prospect of working with someone who cares about your act, even though they are new to the industry, I offer this comforting news. Many name acts, historically and currently, began their careers working with close friends or family members serving as their managers. Most knew little or nothing about the business and, similar to my own experience and to many of your own experiences, they grew into the role by doing it every day. Eventually, as their careers developed, they associated with professional management companies and major agencies.

One well known example is that of Loretta Lynn and her late husband/manager Mooney Lynn. The book and film, *Coal Miner's Daughter,* demonstrate perfectly the beginning stages of career development and how a committed, enthusiastic individual, void of industry know-how and armed with common sense and good instinct, can make a difference in an artist's career. Loving the way his wife sang, Mooney Lynn helped nurture Loretta's career by buying her her first guitar, taking her first promotional pictures and sending her first single to radio stations across the country. He nursed her career to the point where she gained national recognition from her performances on the Grand Ole Opry.

> *"One key to any long-term management relationship is effective communication. Another is similar goals. A manager should never have aspirations for the artist greater that what the artist has for himself—be aware of the possibilities, yes; force them on the artist, no. Other important factors: mutual respect, attention to details, looking at the big picture, sound economic decisions."*
>
> **Denise Stiff**
> manager

> *"The movie* Coal Miner's Daughter *depicts a youthful and earnest Loretta Lynn taking her records from one disc jockey to another until she cultivated enough airplay to have a national hit."*
>
> **Country Music Association**
> *Pickers, Slickers, Cheatin' Hearts & Superstars:*
> *Country: The Music and The Musicians*

Working With A Manager

Whether you work with an industry veteran or a temporary novice, it is important to create a relationship with a manager that fosters the growth of the artist and the artist's business.

Five Principles For A Successful Artist/Manager Relationship

1. Establish a relationship based on honesty and reality. Work with a manager who has a realistic sense of what

you can achieve together. Create and follow a realistic action plan to accomplish your short- and long-term goals.
2. Communicate openly and often. Remain an active partner in the business, fully aware of all deals and prospective arrangements made on your behalf.
3. Remain accessible and available to each other. The nature of this relationship is often as close as one can get without being intimate (although many artist/manager relationships are forged by spouses or life partners). Whether you conduct your business by phone or in the same household, the nature of the business requires each other's constant attention. It helps to work with someone whose company you enjoy since you will be in contact on a daily basis, if not minute by minute.
4. Be open to new ideas, methods and strategies. Shared innovations often produce results that can further a career. Work with a manager to see your potential through new eyes. Their original perspective can move your business in creative directions you have not even thought about. Scrutinize the ideas, yes, but entertain new possibilities.
5. Form a trusting relationship. You must believe that each of you will act for the good of the other. At stake is your business and each of your reputations. A business partnership was formed to share the best of what each has to offer the other—to develop your career to its greatest potential.

Any artist/manager relationship based on these principles has potential for success. Should there be a shred of doubt that either of you will attempt to uphold these precepts, the relationship may not be right for you. As the relationship grows, return to these five principles and re-evaluate your standings with each other on a yearly basis. Hold each other accountable to maintain these principles and ensure a healthy, productive, long-term artist/manager relationship.

What To Expect From Your Manager

Management relationships are very individual. Some artists require a manager who is present in their daily business dealings, while others may work with a manager in a consultant-like capacity. The majority of artist/manager relationships maintain a constant level of communication and a high degree of involvement in both the artist's business and personal life. As the leader of the artist's career team, a manager is involved with all aspects affecting the artist's ability to perform.

Managers are generally responsible for the following:
❖ *Career planning:* Helps the artist to establish short- and long-term career goals. A manager will create an action

> "Trust, communication, patience and success are key. Each must believe that the other will always act in the best interest of the artist and the artist's career. Sometimes that means acting on what you believe at the time (given the information and tools available) to be the right decision."
>
> **John Porter**
> manager, The Nitty Gritty Dirt Band, Kris Tyler
> Mike Robertson Management

> "A manager needs to keep in mind the special circumstances of the band being managed. For example, my clients, the Blind Boys of Alabama, are blind, diabetic, and in their 70's. Our only "drug problems" are in regards to getting insulin for their diabetes!"
>
> **Charles Driebe, Jr.**
> entertainment attorney, manager,
> Blind Boys of Alabama

plan and strategically implement it. In addition, management also establishes realistic time lines during which to accomplish each goal. Management provides a vantage point from which to assess career growth and determine the success of each attempted project.

❖ *Artistic development:* Works with the artist to help raise their level of performance. Management often becomes involved in repertoire selection, choice of side musicians, accompanists or troupe members, staging, including sound and lights design selection, stage clothes or costume suggestions.

❖ *Tour coordination:* Coordinates all aspects of the artist's touring schedule, modes of travel, housing and travel arrangements and maintains the necessary budgets with which to accomplish it all.

❖ *Booking coordination:* Finds a suitable agency to book the artist's performance dates and negotiates the agency's commission. Management helps establish the type of performance venue the artist should play and designs a touring timetable with the agent. Along with possible record company suggestions, a manager selects target tour markets with the agent. Managers remain in constant contact with agents as the tours develop, accepting or rejecting date offers coming to the agent.

❖ *Publicity coordination:* Works with the record company, in some cases, to find an appropriate publicist to help promote the artist. The manager helps establish a publicity campaign and manages its implementation. Also coordinates schedules for interviews with artist, record company and publicist. Coordinates publicity appearances.

❖ *Record-deal arrangements:* Promotes artist to appropriate record company to secure a label deal. Negotiates (often with a lawyer) all recording contracts on the artist's behalf.

❖ *Publishing-deal arrangements:* Seeks publishing companies appropriate for artist's music (when applicable) and negotiates deals on the artist's behalf.

❖ *Image coordination:* Defines, promotes and defends the artist's image as they are represented to the public and to the industry. All publicity materials are first approved by management, in consultation with artist, in an effort to present a cohesive and appropriate image to the public.

❖ *Dispute mediation:* All final decisions regarding any event, problem, situation of concern to the artist or the artist's career are made by the manager in consultation with the artist. The manager will intervene on the artist's behalf to settle disputes of any variety. When necessary, the manager will involve legal counsel if they themselves are not a lawyer. (Lawyers are often drawn to management positions. Having the advantage of a legal background helps when dealing with negotiations and contracts.)

> "The relationship that we've had for eight years is one which is based on trust and hard work. You have to have someone that you absolutely trust because that person is representing you to the world."
>
> Scot Fisher
> manager, Ani DiFranco
> president,
> Righteous Babe Records

> "I compare the job to that of a conductor of an orchestra. A manager builds a team (with the artist) and directs everyone to work hard, creatively and honestly, so the team is moving in the same direction—at the same time as the artist."
>
> Ralph Jaccodine
> manager,
> Ralph Jaccodine Management

> "Key factors to an artist/manager relationship: Trust. Belief. Respect. These rule—without them, no contract works."
>
> Rosalie Goldstein
> management consultant,
> Goldstein & Associates

Be sure to associate yourself with a manager who functions effectively on your behalf in these areas and it will make a difference in your career. Some managers may have greater strengths in one area over another. An artist who understands some of what to expect from management is better qualified to assess the value the manager brings to the relationship. If you are particularly strong in some of these areas yourself, working with a manager who compliments the partnership may be all that is necessary.

Working With An Agent

Contrary to the popular opinion of most artists currently booking themselves, an agent is not a miracle worker. They cannot conjure a full tour calendar by merely signing a contract or shaking hands with an artist. For the most part, agents are extremely hard working, underpaid industry professionals. They receive little thanks from the rest of the industry for their efforts to connect artists and presenters in appropriate performance situations. In reality, most agents, whether working in a large agency or working from their dining-room table, are genuinely interested in helping their artists find suitable performance venues. They are dedicated individuals who care about the artist's career development. They work to upgrade the types of venues booked and the number of dates played.

Similar to working with a manager, an agent becomes a partner in your business. Their task, however, directly reflects your income in its most basic form. All record deals, publishing deals, publicity and promotion are directly dependent upon your touring career. Touring generates interest from audiences as well as industry and media. Without the tour dates, most of these other areas of an artist's career have little chance of flourishing. Look long and consider carefully. Take time to evaluate a potential agent and do not sign with the first one who demonstrates interest in your act until you have completed the checklist on page 415.

An Agent's Reputation

Although a manager has a more pronounced influence upon your entire career, they are very much a behind-the-scenes person. Your agent, on the other hand, is the direct link between you and the presenter. You may be familiar with the expression "a person is judged by the company they keep." This is often true when an artist is booked by an agent of questionable reputation. It is the agent's reputation that precedes the artist to the gig and the agent's reputation that presenters talk about among themselves. An artist cannot afford to battle their own agent's reputation while building their career. Nor can an artist afford to defend their own reputation because they are associated with a disreputable

> "The time to get an agent is when you reach the point where you are touring so much that you no longer have hours in the day to do it yourself. Until then, you should consider self-booking to be your self-awarded degree in the independent music business. If you do eventually hire an agent, this experience will be invaluable as you work together to plot your career direction. Ultimately, you are always your own best agent, giving direction and guidance to your team."
>
> Pete, Maura Kennedy
> The Kennedys,
> singer, songwriters

> "Have regard for your name, since it will remain for you longer than a great store of gold."
>
> Ecclesiasticus,
> *Apocrypha*

> "The act must have a grip on the realities of the music marketplace. No agent can work magic on a career. I always stress that I can only do as much for an artist as they are willing to do for themselves."
>
> Mike Drudge
> agent,
> Class Act Entertainment

> "The agent is not your manager, your press person OR your mother. S/he books the gigs. If you want any of the above, you'll have to pay."
>
> Sharon Davis
> former agent,
> Schnieder/Davis Agency

> "You should investigate a potential agent's style, image and reputation in the industry before delegating your good name to someone."
>
> Joanne Murdock
> agent,
> Artists Of Note

> "We look to sign career-oriented artists who move us personally, who play music we believe in. A strong live performance, determination to success, a good manager and a supportive record label are also positive factors."
>
> Tom Chauncey
> agent,
> Rosebud US

agent. Choose your work partners carefully! Spend the time to get to know the intended agent and the reputation they sport within the industry. The relationships the agent has developed over the years are paramount to your future success.

Exclusivity

As previously mentioned, many agents want to sign exclusive agreements with their artists. I can appreciate that. I had exclusive agreements with most of my acts. It is much easier to coordinate an artist's schedule if you are the sole booking agent. Rather than vying for presenters with other agents who book the act, only one agent or one agency books the artist's dates.

However, many artists have non-exclusive agreements with a number of agencies. In some instances, one agent might book fairs and festivals while the other agent concentrates on nightclubs and theaters and still another may book corporate engagements. In this manner, the artist has covered multiple performance situations and the agents do not compete for presenters. There is still the matter of coordinating time schedules, however. The artist or the artist's manager would work with each agent to assign time periods or juggle dates as they come in.

In some instances, larger, main acts do work with multiple agents, each booking whatever date they can regardless of venue or situation. A manager or an artist would take the best offer and fit the date into their tour schedule as each is considered.

Most artists will be faced with the prospect of working with an agent on an exclusive basis. This situation offers an artist a working relationship that has potential to be long-term and much more manageable. It also allows the artist to hold the agent accountable to their commitment to book reasonable tours without the excuse of having to compete for available dates with another agency.

What To Expect From An Agent

Although an artist/agent relationship may not be as close as an artist/manager relationship, the five principles of a successful artist/manager relationship from page 420 apply here as well. Any partnership so intimately involved in developing an artist's career must be based in honesty, reality, open communication, accessibility, and remain innovative and trusting. It is hard to imagine trusting my livelihood to anyone who would question these concepts. Once you find an agent with whom you believe a strong working bond can be forged, look to that agent to do the following for your act:

Agents are generally responsible for:

- ❖ *Booking performance dates:* An agent works with the artist or manager to define the appropriate touring markets and book the venues in those markets. In coordination with management, the agent books all personal appearance performances, concerts, radio, television shows, benefits, showcases, and, often, recording sessions except for promotional dates set by the record company. The agent remains updated on all calendar changes and provides the artist and the artist's career team with the up-to-date bookings.

- *Negotiating performance contracts:* Agents will have pre-set parameters from management or the artist within which they can negotiate performance dates with presenters. If a manager is involved, the manager accepts, rejects or suggests alternatives to the offers presented by the agent. When the artist acts as their own manager, they have the opportunity to do the same.
- *Issuing contracts:* Contracts for each performance date are issued by the agent or issued to the agent if the venue provides their own. The agent signs the contract on behalf of the artist. A copy of the completed contract is issued to the artist, the presenter and the manager (if any). All contract riders are negotiated at the same time and sent to the presenter with the contract.
- *Providing presenters with promotional material:* Agents will provide each presenter with promotional materials, unless otherwise designated. The agency coordinates with the artist's publicist and record company to have additional materials sent to the presenters.
- *Contacting presenters:* If management is not involved and the artist does not assume the responsibility of advancing the tour dates, the task may fall to the agency to coordinate all aspects of the performance with the presenter and then relate any information to the artist.
- *Holding deposits:* When a presenter returns a completed contract with the deposit, the agency holds those deposits in an escrow account until the date is successfully completed by the artist. Once completed, the agent takes their commission from the deposit and pays the artist the remaining portion along with any balance issued to the agent for the date. Most agents work with deposits in this manner because it is the legal and proper way to do it. Variations to this method can be found among agents and artists. Ask the agent you intend to work with about their methods of dealing with deposits and payments.
- *Follow up:* As each date is completed, an agent will follow up with the presenter to make sure the date was satisfactory and to find out about any problems that might have occurred. With this feedback, an agent can judge whether the presenter upheld all of their commitments as well as whether the artist fulfilled theirs. It is important for an agent to have a sense of their artist's behavior at performance dates, how the audience reacted and how the presenter felt

"When I first started trying to book myself, somebody would say, 'Call these people.' I would put it off for days, then I'd go and sit by the phone for a while and look at the phone. At that point I was really shy, scared, nervous. Finally I would call but if the line was busy or no one was there, I had done the call and I would not call back. So having an agent just made all the difference for me. I would get booked."

Laurie Lewis
musician

"When the agent shows some interest, you've got to understand what that agent is going to bring to you. Ask how many people are on your roster. How many agents do you have working? How much time do you have to devote to me. If you're on a huge roster with only one or two agents, you may not be getting the kind of attention you feel like you need. What are you going to get for your 15%?"

Mary McFaul
manager, Laura Love Band, McFaul Booking & Management

"Regard your good name as the richest jewel you can possibly be possessed of—for credit is like fire; when once you have kindled it you may easily preserve it, but if once you extinguish it, you will find it an arduous task to rekindle it again. The way to gain good reputation is to endeavor to be what you desire to appear."

Socrates

about working with the artist. Once the artist is at the venue, then their reputation reflects on the agent. An artist with questionable behavior makes return bookings more difficult for the agent and filters throughout the industry. Presenters talk to other presenters about the artists they recently had. A questionable report makes future bookings at new venues more difficult for the agent.

❖ *Attending conferences:* It is the agent's responsibility to represent the artist at any booking conferences or to apply for showcase opportunities on the artist's behalf, with the artist's knowledge, approval and agreement to attend if selected.

❖ *Publishing itinerary schedules:* Agents send the artist's upcoming tour schedules to all of the appropriate publications and industry personnel.

Negotiating Agent Commissions

Each agency has their own method of operation. It is up to the artist to negotiate their individual relationship with the agency. Here again, artists with more market value have greater leverage negotiating commission percentages and exactly what tasks the agency will perform on the artist's behalf. For example: A name artist commanding large guarantees with box office sellouts will be able to negotiate a lower percentage, perhaps 10%. The agent can sell the act to large venues easily. In most cases, the bookings result from calls to the agent from the presenter. When an agent has to do more—make the calls for an untested artist, accept lower fees at smaller venues uncertain of a sell-out, the agent's commission is higher. Agents may begin a relationship requiring a higher commission percentage during the early stages of working with a new artist. As the artist's booking potential increases, new commission percentages may be negotiated.

Expenses

Some of the smaller agencies may also charge each artist on their roster for some expenses in addition to their commission percentage. Most major agencies absorb the expenses below as a cost of doing business. Each agency will vary. In some cases, artists may expect these following expenses to be charged on a monthly basis.

❖ *Shipping costs:* All shipping expenses on the artist's behalf or for only large mailings may be charged to the artist.
❖ *Phone costs:* Monthly calls may be divided among all artists on the roster or an account coding may identify each month's calls made for each artist individually.
❖ *Conference attendance:* Artists may be expected to participate in all costs to be represented by the agent including registration fees, hotel, travel, meals, exhibit hall, showcase, and conference-specific promotional materials.

> *"I don't know if I'd still be in the game if it weren't for working with those people at Fleming's. They'll try and get me to do as many gigs as they can but they know where the line is and they work with me."*
>
> Greg Brown
> singer, songwriter

> *"The industry rule is 10%. The more money a band makes, the more negotiating power they will have to alter that percentage. Baby bands have no negotiating leverage on it, more well-known bands have a lot of leverage."*
>
> Steve Martin
> agent, partner,
> The Agency Group

> *"What the booking agent wants to know, are people going to show up that night?"*
>
> Scot Fisher
> manager, Ani DiFranco,
> president, Righteous Babe Records

* *Travel:* Artist may be asked for travel expenses when the agent is expected to be present at significant performance dates, showcases or industry events to represent the artist.

The Agency's Cost To Represent An Artist

Now that you have a deeper understanding of what it costs to do the business of representing yourself, it will be easier to understand the investment that an agent makes to represent a new artist. The biggest difference here is that an agent will take longer to recoup their investment since they are getting paid back at ten, fifteen or twenty percent. An artist booking themselves gets one hundred percent return minus their cost of doing business. Once an agent signs a new artist, they must invest in promoting that artist.

An agent's investment includes:

* *Salaries and commissions to agents and staff:* This is the largest expense. Agents working on booking a newly-signed artist often have a reduced income potential for the agency until the artist's career builds.
* *General office overhead:* Rent, utilities, furniture, hardware, software, stationery, etc.
* *Adding artist to roster brochures:* Redesign and reprint brochures and mail new brochures to presenters.
* *Advertising new roster:* Create new ad designs and a strategic advertising campaign which incorporates any newly-signed artists.
* *Conference exhibit booth displays:* Design additional display item for the artist to be incorporated into booth display.
* *Phone calls:* Make strategic calls to presenters informing them of new artist addition in an effort to generate enthusiasm and bookings.
* *Material development:* Work with artist to create new promotional materials or a supply of promotional materials and artist-specific contract riders.
* *Conference attendance:* Attendance at additional conferences may be necessary to tap the artist's appropriate market. For example: If the agency has consistently attended the national APAP conference and has recently signed an act appropriate to bluegrass festivals, they may decide to attend the IBMA trade show to familiarize that audience with their agency. Or an agency that represents an unsigned artist may choose a number of other industry events and conferences such as SXSW in order to showcase their artist to labels and the media.
* *Updating website:* Design web page to update site with the new artist addition.

All of these costs are incurred by an agency before any bookings take place. This initial investment may not be

> **HotTip:** Agents applying to a showcase for an artist must have authority to represent the artist and submit an application on their behalf. The artist must be made aware of all possible costs involved for which they are responsible if selected.

> "It costs us about $15,000 a year to represent an artist. It would be misleading to say that every newly-signed artist earns enough of a gross income so that their percentage rate of commission offsets that $15,000 expense. We need to know that within a couple of years the artist has that potential."
>
> Jim Fleming
> agent,
> Fleming & Associates

> "Being signed to an agency is often an artist's goal but not always the answer. I've seen small in-house operations more effective than being lost on a large roster of a company with three or four famous initials."
>
> Scott O'Malley
> agent,
> Scott O'Malley & Associates

recouped for six months to one year or more. With this in mind, it is easier for you to understand why agents are so careful to consider taking on a new act.

Looking For An Agent

I cannot think of a single agent who relishes the thought of ending a day of phone calls with little or no bookings to show for their effort and expense. Yet, I know every agent loves hearing the phone ring with offers from presenters to book their artists. Unless there are some compelling circumstances to sign a developing artist without a track record, most agencies sign acts who are in demand and offer a relatively quick income potential. Even those who consider working with developing artists often select them because there is some indication that there is a market for the act worthy of the agent's investment.

The artist can present the agent with some proof of market interest by their past booking records, industry enthusiasm at recent showcases, and growing media attention. When an artist begins to develop that industry "buzz," agencies begin to notice. It is usually a sign that the artist is generating market-interest and has sales potential. If an artist generates enough attention, an agency may jump to sign a developing artist.

Most new acts are not in this enviable position. Most new acts need to keep working to build their reputation, their bookings and their position in their particular market. After speaking with agents representing all varieties of musical genres, I have compiled this list of general criteria required by most agencies when considering a new act. If you find yourself able to fulfill all of these criteria, you are well positioned to begin your search for an agent.

Agent's Requirements When Signing New Acts

1. Most agents need to believe in the artist and their music or performance—if they do not like it, they cannot sell it.
2. The artist must have a nationally-available recording either on a major label or an independent label and have sold a significant number of recordings independently. With label support, an agent can more easily build an artist's market value. If the label is assisting with radio promotions, new release publicity and advertising, the agent's efforts to support performance dates are enhanced, increasing box office success and the potential for higher fees and return engagements.
3. The artists must be working at their music or performing career professionally and touring is not hampered by juggling schedules with a day job. Many performers are successful at maintaining dual careers. Agents are concerned with the artist's flexibility to fulfill performance dates that have been booked. It is possible

---

"Jim Fleming drove down to Cleveland to see Ani in this little bar. I seem to remember there were only six people in the whole bar. But he was taken by her music. Fleming & Associates is very music driven—they weren't looking at sales figures. They saw Ani's audience as being potentially greater than it presently was."

Scot Fisher
manager, Ani DiFranco,
president,
Righteous Babe Records

"My agency specializes in women artists so that's a criteria for me. I also require that the performer has someone doing publicity for them so I don't have to hassle with sending out promotional materials, setting up interviews, etc."

Tam Martin
agent,
Beachfront Bookings/
Productions

to establish a strategic plan with an agent so they are able to work around your day job schedule. While working with guitarist and full-time professor Dr. Dan Crary, I was able to book a full summer schedule of festivals, during most college vacations and Thursday through Sunday. It is a bit more work but very doable. Another example of an artist managing a dual career is John Starling of the bluegrass group, the Seldom Scene. He maintained his medical practice throughout the group's performing career.

4. The artist should have management or serve as manager for themselves. Agents want at least one consistent contact person on whom they can depend to take care of the act's performance details. Most agents prefer that an artist have management in order for both management and the agent to clearly delineate responsibilities. These responsibilities might include advancing tour dates, sending publicity materials or coordinating public relations. Agents prefer that management handle these tasks.

5. Most agents prefer that the artist had also previously booked tours in regions beyond their home base in order to gauge interest from the general marketplace. Artists who have booked themselves are more aware of the work entailed and often have greater respect for their agent and the job they face every booking day.

6. The artist must have a fan base. It helps an agent to have a starting place from which to expand. This enables the agent to sell the artist to the presenter. Strong ticket sales mean the agent has represented the artist to the presenter honestly. The presenter makes money on the act by offering their audience an act which is in demand. The agent/presenter relationship is solidified by this success and earns the agent future opportunities to book this venue for this act and others. The act has another chance to perform for their fans.

Where Do You Need To Be?

If you are eager to explore the possibility of interesting an agent in your act:

❖ Realize that if an agent's commission is 10% and the total booking income for one act is $50,000, the agent gets $5,000—with a 15% commission, they get $7,500. View it from the agent's perspective. As one act on a large roster generating many times that $50,000 amount, an agent may be able to afford the developmental time and expense of working with a new act. As one act on a small roster of lesser-known artists the fees and commissions are considerably lower. Begin to understand how an artist's current earnings impact the agency's decision to sign an act before approaching an agency.

"It's possible to do both things and in some ways, particularly if you want to keep your music pure and you don't want to sell out at any cost, you are going to have to keep your day job."

John Starling
lead singer,
Seldom Scene

"When an artist can convey their material with commitment and passion and intelligence, that's what I look for."

Steve Martin
agent, partner,
The Agency Group

"The band has to have a fan base. A record that an indie or a major really promotes is essential. A manager is nice but a single, organized, thoughtful point man (manager or band member) is a must. We're good at maximizing an artist's value in the marketplace—we can't create it."

Bruce Houghton
agent,
Skyline Music

> "An artist (or better yet, someone else in the business—another musician or the record company) should be able to establish that there is an audience—hopefully a real one, but strong potential at least—for the artist's music."
>
> Mitch Greenhill
> agent, manager,
> Folklore Productions

❖ Target agencies that book acts similar to yourself. Decide what type of act you are and choose among agencies specializing in booking blues acts, bluegrass acts, country acts, folk acts, jazz acts, dance, theater, etc. Those agencies have relationships and experience with appropriate presenters and venues who book that type of act.

❖ Find lists of agencies in the following directories. All of them and more, are found in the resource section of this chapter:
  1. *Association of Performing Arts Presenters Agency Member List*
  2. *Billboard International Talent & Touring Directory*
  3. *Chamber Music America*
  4. *Folk Alliance Agency Member List*
  5. *IBMA Agency Member List*
  6. *Musical America, International Directory of the Performing Arts*
  7. *Musician's Atlas*
  8. *Performance Booking Agencies*
  9. *Pollstar Agency Roster*
  10. *Dance Directory*

To introduce your act, call the targeted agencies and ask if they are accepting new acts at this time or in the near future. Ask permission to send appropriate materials. After polling many agencies, it is generally agreed that most require the artist to send the following when considering a new act:

1. An introductory cover letter.
2. A current biography along with a complete promotional package including current photos (black and white and color, if available), a current recording, some of the earlier recordings, a video if available, a current poster or flyer.
3. A list of past dates demonstrating your touring history—venue, city, contact, fee.
4. A copy of the most recent tour schedule—venue, city, contact, fee.
5. Highlight upcoming dates or potential showcase opportunities close to the agent's location. Invite the agent to a performance. Let them know there will be guest tickets waiting at the door, or at "will call."
6. A brief description of the fees you are currently getting, how many dates per year you are performing and your total annual earnings from performing dates alone. (This is taken from the questionnaire on page 415.)
7. A short paragraph describing the reason you want to work with this agency. After being approached by many artists during my 20 years as an agent, I felt that any artist who took the time to research the type of acts I booked before calling me, deserved my attention. I

> "When you are looking for a booking agent, you've got to sell yourself to the agency. This is a business proposal. Go to these booking agencies and say, 'I'm making X amount of dollars touring by doing it myself. If we went out with the touring history we have right now, this much money would be going into your agency. If we were to work together, I'd like to see maybe a 20% increase over the next year.'"
>
> Mary McFaul
> manager, Laura Love Band,
> McFaul Booking & Management

could determine an artist's business savvy and commitment when they demonstrated that they knew who I was and who my artists were. I was more likely to direct them to a specific agent that might be interested in taking them on or at least give them some time and advice. Those acts who simply called unaware of the type of act I would consider were quickly told I was not interested. They wasted my time and they wasted theirs. When you know the acts that an agent is booking, you are able to make co-bill suggestions or opening-act offers helping the agent see potential booking opportunities. Knowing something about the agent or the agency shows that you are willing to work to make this a partnership and that you are not looking for a free ride while the agent does all the work.

Once you have sent the required materials to the agency, follow up within a week's time to make sure the packet arrived. If they express interest, set a time for your first lengthy discussion after the agent has had time to review the materials. Get a commitment for a date within the next two weeks. If a great deal of time goes by, you begin to get a sense that the agent is not really interested in representing the act and you can move on to explore another agency.

Explore a number of prospective agencies at the same time. This process will take a while. Give yourself six months to research agents and interview them. Some may respond more quickly than others. Meanwhile, keep up with your bookings and take care of your business.

Suggestion:

The time when you are searching for an agent is a great time to hire an assistant to help with shipping and publicity if you have not done so already. Train the assistant to take on many of the essential tasks outlined in the next chapter. If you sign with an agency, your assistant will help provide that necessary contact between the agent and yourself, manage the office while you are on tour and help present an efficiently-run artist's business. However, if you are unable to find an agency during this time frame, your trained assistant may now have enough experience that you can add making cold calls and follow-up calls to their responsibilities. The assistant may, in fact, be ready to take on some booking responsibilities. Your assistant may provide a head start to having an agent in your own office since you hedged your bets and were proactive in taking care of your business. Agent or no agent—your business is able to flourish since you strategically planned for your growth.

Conclusion

Agents are most interested in working with artists who are willing to be equal participants in their artistic careers. They

> **HotTip:** Finding an agent can become a time-consuming project. It may require six, eight or even twelve months time from the moment you decide you are ready to begin the search to actually being signed by an agency. Keep your business operating at full steam during the process.

"I need trust and openness about gigs and how we have developed their career. Twice a year we re-evaluate what has happened and what we are planning for the next year. I need the artists to not fight me on the expenses like postage, attending conferences and phone calls. If I know they have a budget to keep for a specific month, I keep within those parameters. Each of my artists need to have a promotional photo and package or they can pay me an hourly rate to develop one for them."

Chris Fletcher
CEO Coast to Coast Music Booking, manager, promotional consultant, instructor, Music Business

"Take your career seriously as working musicians. Don't wait to gig; go out and play, ply your trade. If that's what's in your soul, don't wait for people to come to you."

Steve Martin
agent, partner,
The Agency Group

are not looking for those artists requiring baby-sitters or those needing their hands held through every tour. The most successful artist/agent relationships are those whose participants share in the design and execution of the tours. With the information that this book affords you, you will become a more active partner with your agent and have a more productive and successful relationship and touring career.

Summary

- Managers help design and oversee an artist's entire career. Agents book performance tour dates.
- Working with a manager or an agent is taking a partner into your business. Be selective.
- Assess your current situation to determine whether you are ready for, or need, a manager, an agent or both.
- Incorporate the five principles of a successful artist/manager relationship when searching for a manager. They are: honesty and reality, open and timely communication, accesibility, innovation and trust.
- Take an active role to interview prospective managers and agents and request background information that allows you to become familiar with the manager or agent.
- A manager is responsible for career planning, artistic development, tour, booking, publicity, record and publishing deals, image coordination and dispute mediation.
- An agent is responsible for booking tours, negotiating contracts, issuing contracts, presenter contact and after-date follow-up, holding deposits and dispersing payments, attending conferences, publishing itinerary schedules.
- Create a convincing biographical package to present to a prospective agent.
- Keep up the level of your business during any agency search period.

Resources

Books:

All You Need to Know About the Music Business Revised and Updated for the 21st Century
Donald Passman
Simon & Schuster
ISBN: 0684870649

Booking & Tour Management for the Performing Arts
Rena Road Show Shagan
Allworth Press
ISBN: 1581150954

This Business of Music: The Definitive Guide to the Music Industry
M. William Krazlovsky
Watson-Guptil Publications
ISBN: 0823077284

Music Business Handbook & Career Guide
David Baskerville
Sage Press
ISBN: 0761916679

Music, Money and Success: The Insider's Guide to Making Money in the Music Business
Jeffrey and Todd Brabec
Schirmer Books
ISBN: 0825672821

Pickers, Slickers, Cheatin' Hearts & Superstars Country: The Music and The Musicians
Country Music Foundation
Abbeville Press
ISBN: 0896598683

How the Music Business Works
Larry E. Wacholtz
Thumbs Up Press
ISBN: 0965234118

Navigating The Music Industry: Current Issues & Business Models
Dick Weissman, Frank Jernance
Hal Leonard
ISBN: 0634026526

This Business of Artist Management
Xavier M. Frascogna Jr. and H. Lee Hetherington
Watson-Guptil Publications
ISBN: 0823077055

See Resources, Chapter 7, Contracts, for other music business books.

Directories:

AustralAsia Music Industry Directory
GPO Box 2977
Sydney, N.S.W.
Australia 2000
Phone: +61-02-9557-7766
Fax: +61-02-9557-7788
E-mail: directories@immedia.com.au
Web: http://www.immedia.com.au

Billboard Directories
1515 Broadway
New York, NY 10036
Phone: 1-800-344-7119
Web: http://www.billboard.com
Directories:
International Talent & Touring Directory
Listing artists and their management, performance venues, hotels, and services.
International Latin Music Buyer's Guide
"Yellow Pages" of Latin Music contacts in US, Mexico, Central and South America.

Chamber Music America
305 7th Avenue, 5th Floor
New York, NY 10001-6008
Phone: 212-242-2022
Web: http://www.chamber-music.org

Music Directory Of Canada
23 Hannover Drive #7
St. Catharine's, Ontario L2W 1A3
Phone: 905-641-3471
Fax: 905-641-1648
Web: http://www.musicdirectorycanada.com
Listing of managers, agents, artists, labels, attorneys, and other music business related resources in Canada.

Musical America
400 Windsor Corporate Center, Suite 200
East Windsor, NJ 08520
Phone: 1-800-221-5488, ext. 7783
Web: http://www.musicalamerica.com
Listing artist's managers in classical, jazz, dance.

Rap Directory
Web: http://www.rapdirectory.com

Hip-Hop Directory
Web: http://www.hiphopdirectory.com

Performance Magazine
International Touring Talent Weekly Newspaper
1203 Lake Street
Fort Worth, TX 76102-4504
Phone: 817-338-9444
Fax: 817-877-4273
Web: http://www.performancemagazine.com
Subscription: Includes 51 weekly magazines and ten yearly directories. Individual directories also available separately.
Talent/Personal Managers
Booking Agencies

Pollstar
4697 W. Jacquelyn Avenue
Fresno, CA 93722
Phone: 1-800-344-7383
In California: 559-271-7900
Fax: 559-271-7979
E-mail: info@pollstar.com
Web: http://www.pollstar.com
Subscription: Includes weekly magazine plus five bi-annual directories.
Individual directories also available separately.
Agency Roster
Manager's Directory—Priced separately from subscription.
Mailing labels available for additional fee.

Dance Directory
333 Seventh Avenue, 11th Floor
New York, NY 10001
Phone: 212-979-4803
Fax: 646-674-0102
Web: http://www.dancemagazine.com

Talent & Booking Online
P.O. Box 14265
Palm Desert, CA 92255
Phone: 760-779-8056
Fax: 760-773-3568
Web: http://www.talentandbooking.com
Talent & Booking Directories:
Official Country Music Directory
Includes booking agents, managers, artists, record companies and public relations firms.
Country Music Media Guide
Country Music Sponsor Guide

The North American Folk Business Directory
Folk Alliance
962 Wayne Ave., Suite 902
Silver Spring, MD 20910-4480
Phone: 301-588-8185
Fax: 301-588-8186
Web: http://www.folk.org

The Recording Industry Sourcebook
Artistpro
ISBN: 1931140332
Web: http://www.artistpro.com
Labels, managers, distributors, attorneys, media contacts and more.

Organizations With Agency Lists:

APAP—Association of Performing Arts Presenters

The Folk Alliance

IBMA—International Bluegrass Music Association

CMA—Country Music Association

NACA- National Association of Campus Activities

NAPAMA- North American Performing Arts Managers and Agents

See Chapter 8 or 11 for contact information.

Organizations Of Managers And Agents

Music Manager's Forum
P.O. Box 444, Village Station
New York, NY 10014
Phone: 212-213-8787
Fax: 212-213-9797
Web: http://www.mmfus.com
Web: http://www.ukmmf.net (UK)

International Artists Managers Association
23 Garrick Street, Covent Garden
London WC2E9BN
UK
Pbone: 011 44 20 7379 7336
Fax: 011 44 20 7379 7338
Web: http://www.iamaworld.com

NAPAMA
459 Columbus Avenue, #133
New York, NY 10024
Phone/Fax: 1-888-745-8759
E-mail: info@napama.org
Web: http://www.napama.org

CHAPTER TWENTY
Hiring Help

"The hiring process begins with the identification of an unmet need. An unmet need may be a task that needs to be accomplished."

Richard S. Deems, Ph.D.
author, *Managing Your Employees*

For many of you, the business part of your career has grown and bookings have been steady. The art needs tending to and dealing with the day-to-day business is taking you from it. Managing your business effectively is always a challenge when the artist is lost to phone calls and paperwork. The first alternative to finding that miracle-working booking agent is to consider hiring an assistant. I know many artists who believe that once they reach this crucial point in their career development, the next logical step is to find a booking agent. For some, this may be may be appropriate. But for many, it is not really the complete answer. Running a more efficient business may be more on the mark. At this time in your career, you may be ready to turn over many of your daily tasks to someone else, without turning over your means of making a living.

Remain In Control

When you hire an assistant be ready to delegate responsibilities and tasks, yet remain in control. Here are some concrete reasons why and how you could benefit from hiring someone to help you.

Remember, because you are overworked does not mean you are ready for an agent. It means you need to make some

"Start by working with someone who can do the things that you don't need to do yourself. Shipping product, making travel arrangements, working with promoters after you've finalized a date and contract. Gradually, they can take on more of your business responsibilities as you are comfortable."

Cathy Fink
singer, songwriter, producer

> **HotTip:**
> If you are at a place in your career where you truly need an agent, the agents will find you.

"Success is not so much achievement as achieving. Refuse to join the cautious crowd that plays not to lose; play to win."

David J. Mahoney
American business executive

"Surround yourself with a network of people who support you and your work. Friends, family, and fans are great people to help spread the word about your work. If they believe in you, put them to work promoting your work."

Dianne de Las Casas
professional storyteller, director, Story Ballet Magic
president, ICAN - Independent Children's Artist Network

adjustments in how the work gets done. The most important part of your work is booking performance dates—that is what brings in the money. In order for you to be more effective at that task, other tasks could be delegated to someone else.

Hire An Assistant

As I mentioned earlier in Chapter 13, hiring someone in-house to help you with publicity and promotion is a perfect entry-level job to train someone new. Short of doing the actual publicity when first starting, another person could help package and send promotional kits to prospective promoters while you continue making cold calls. Here is a list of jobs that could be done by someone else. Can you see your business becoming more efficient with someone helping you with these tasks?

An Assistant's Tasks
1. Package promotional kits
2. Research lists and directories for appropriate new venues
3. Call promoters to check on the arrival of mailings
4. Ship packages by appropriate carrier
5. Make travel arrangements
6. Begin to make publicity calls
7. Fax or e-mail press releases or send PR materials to media outlets
8. Manage office while you are on tour
9. Relay messages and handle immediate requests from media and promoters while you are on tour
10. Begin making cold calls to new venues
11. Complete an entire booking transaction
12. Become your in-house booking agent and/or publicist

This scenario of hiring and training an assistant has worked for me and for so many other self-booking artists. It is more immediately effective than searching for a booking agent. The process of hiring your own office manager keeps you in control of your business. You have an opportunity to instruct your assistant in the art and techniques of running your business. This person is there to assist you and insure that your business is taken care of according to your plans. You set the pace, create the time line and achieve your goals on your own terms.

Granted, you are still learning yourself, shaping your business skills as you go along. Your hired help will probably not bring any advantageous entertainment business connections with them. But you will also not find yourself on the bottom of a long roster of artists crying out for attention. At this stage, you have a greater opportunity to build your career to where audiences are demanding your performances by hiring someone to assist. Your assistant's attention will be totally focused on helping you accomplish your goals.

Where To Find Help

Once you make the decision to hire someone, where do you find them? Look close to home, consider family members with whom you might enjoy working. You will never know what life skills and previous business skills lurk in those close to you until you ask. Look at your personal pros and cons when hiring family members or life partners and decide if it will be a productive working situation. You may find that building this career together offers many additional benefits.

Family Members

As a note of interest, many performing artists' businesses are run in part or completely by family members, some serving as managers or as publicists, and others as business managers. When an arts business encompasses so much of one's life, it may make more sense to include family members, if they are interested, than to leave them out. Treat family members as valued partners or employees and present compensation packages commensurate with their duties as you would any other employee. There may be certain tax advantages to hiring family members. Consult with your accountant in order to establish how these advantages may serve you.

College Interns

College internships are often part of a student's curriculum. Check with a local college or university business department to find student interns at very reasonable hourly rates. The student benefits from real work experience and you benefit from their business perspective. The one disadvantage to the internship is the length of time that the student will be available. It may not be worth your time to train them only to have them gone within a semester. Find a freshman who will be around for at least three to four semesters and possibly during the summer. Finally, internships may be good for an interim period while looking for someone who will make a substantial time commitment to your career.

Arts-Related Businesses

Check with radio stations, local clubs and student activities offices at colleges. They may refer part-time workers who are already interested in the arts, and have extra hours for another part-time job in the arts. I caution you against hiring another artist that is building their own business. A conflict of interest may surface that would be detrimental to both of your purposes. On the other hand, you may find that pooling your resources to hire someone else to work for both of you, saves money and offers the employee better work hours and better pay.

"It's more important in the early stages of your career to find people who you can trust, who will work hard for you. I was interested in working with Ani because I thought her music was incredible and I still do. I never thought I would be making a living from working with Ani."

Scot Fisher
manager, Ani DiFranco
president,
Righteous Babe Records

"You will find that the business end takes a huge chunk of time away from working on your music. Many times friends and fans are willing to help with posters, calendars and mailing lists."

Terri Allard
singer, songwriter,
Reckless Abandon Music

> **HotTip:** 🌶
> If possible, leave Monday to plan your week, recuperate from weekend touring, and organize yourself and your office in advance for your assistant.

"Paying this person based on any form of percentage doesn't make sense. If you want good work from someone, be prepared to offer them a decent wage for the work, decent workspace (unless they have one), a monthly, weekly work plan, etc. Part-time or full-time doesn't matter, but reliability, honesty and efficiency do."

Cathy Fink
singer, songwriter, producer

Temp Service Agencies

Temporary employment services are another method of finding part-time workers. The hourly rates are fixed and you have very little flexibility in determining wages. Depending on your office setup, this may be more awkward than hiring friends or family members.

Advertise

Target your audience and advertise in the local arts-and-entertainment paper and classified section. Those working other arts-related jobs are more likely to answer ads from this resource.

SCORE

In Chapter Three, I mentioned SCORE, Service Corps of Retired Executives. Consult with your local branch for leads to prospective employable individuals whose business expertise will significantly enhance your own.

Working With An Assistant

When hiring someone to work with you, I suggest starting with a part-time position. I found that two to three days per week with three-hour time blocks works well in the beginning. This still allows you to have time in your office alone to plan and prepare. Use their time wisely—organize the tasks that you expect them to assist with in advance. Remember, this is your money. Spend it efficiently and effectively.

Qualities To Look For When Hiring Help

This is an objective area. Your particular personality preferences come into play. Here are a few specific qualities to consider when hiring someone as an assistant, someone who might become your personal booking agent. As you know from your own learning experience, skill and industry know-how can be attained over time.

As a performer, you understand what it means to communicate with an audience. This skill can also be used when booking performances on the phone. Hiring someone whose background does not include performance, requires that you assess their telephone personality in advance. This can be accomplished by conducting a series of phone interviews prior to meeting in person. You will discern immediately their gift for gab, both positive and negative. Once you have established their level of phone skills, conduct a face-to-face interview.

They also must:
1. Be organized and adaptable.
2. Be honest.
3. Be efficient.

4. Demonstrate a willingness to be trained by you.
5. Respect your efforts and demonstrate a concern for enriching them even if they do not necessarily know or love your art.
6. Deal comfortably with different personalities and be able to maintain their resolve regardless of with whom they are currently speaking.
7. Understand and accept rejection in a businesslike manner and move on.

And:

8. Speak on the phone in a conversational manner.
9. Think on their feet.
10. Listen well.
11. _____
12. _____
13. _____
14. _____

Please add to this list any specific qualities that you require.

The Co-op

There has been an exciting new initiative among artists of similar intent. Artist groups have begun to pool their resources to form co-ops. With this joint effort, they have hired one individual to work for a number of artists. By pooling their finances, the artists are able to pay their employee a decent wage which relieves any one artist of the sole financial burden. The co-op functions as a larger entity now capable of creating a more impressive presence. Together the artists can afford significant advertising, an Internet presence, and a unified presence at conferences. This full-time employee represents all of the co-op artists. Participating in a co-op effort undeniably lends additional clout to the individual artist's efforts.

As you network with other like-minded artists, consider this valuable business possibility. What one artist hopes to achieve alone within a given time frame, a few artists can accomplish together in a shorter period more effectively and efficiently. As a member of a currently-functioning co-op, if you have not hired someone yet to help conduct business, consider this option.

When you join together in your efforts to promote the co-op and its individual members, realize that you have created an entity somewhat similar to that of an agency. With the right person working for you, each member may enjoy the benefits of belonging to a manageable roster of artists whose group representation carries more weight with promoters than that of the individual artist.

> **HotTip:** Compatibility is essential when hiring an assistant who will share your workspace. Get to know a potential employee before making a lengthy commitment.

> *"We got together because we were all roughly at the same level in our careers and had the same basic goals. It was a support network—we shared mailing and brochure costs and information, did gigs together, and learned from each other."*
>
> **Geoff Bartley**
> guitarist, singer, songwriter, former member,
> Buck & Wing Co-Op

> *"I was hired to book our Night Of Reckoning Show with co-op members Kieran Kane, Kevin Welch, Mike Henderson, Tami Rogers and a bass player. What better way to get some attention and focus on our label then by taking the entire roster out and having them perform together as a band. That allowed us to sell records at that one show, but also promote the individual artists, the label and the concept of our independent company."*
>
> J.D. May
> former general manager,
> Dead Reckoning Records

Creating An Agent

If the co-op has hired a person whose personality traits match those listed above, there is every reason to believe that an agent may be within the new employee just waiting to be born. Here are some additional suggestions to help your employee work more effectively on behalf of the entire co-op.

1. Have each co-op member create a set of documents that describe their own personal booking methods, scripts with their specific lead-ins and questions, performance venue requirements, fee structure, travel modes and requirements, contracts, riders, hospitality forms and information forms, etc. The co-op may also create standard forms that each member uses with individual forms for technical and hospitality requirements.
2. Have each member's promotional material readily available at the co-op's office.
3. Discuss negotiation parameters with the employee. The co-op may benefit from a group discussion about negotiations. Decide, in advance, what authority you are willing to give the employee. By setting booking parameters in advance, negotiations can be accomplished more smoothly and quickly. If calls for confirmation need to be referred back to each artist, the negotiations will eventually become tedious for the employee and for you. However, in the short run, allowing your employee to negotiate an offer for your approval may give you both an opportunity to get to know each other's considerations and thought processes. If you are training them for agenting, allow them to participate in the process, gradually building comfort with their decisions over time. If you review the negotiations chapter together and create budgets and bottom-line requirements, your employee will have a dependable working knowledge of how to create the deals that best represent your concerns and interests. This process will take some time to develop.
4. Create a petty cash account for business phone bills, shipping and office supplies.
5. Create weekly and monthly planning goals that each individual and the co-op are working to accomplish.
6. Create a long-term plan for the co-op. This will keep members enthusiastic about building for the future and will ensure the employee job longevity.
7. Give them this book. Reading is part of their job description.

Conclusion

By practicing some of these suggestions, your business can breathe new life and realize its full potential. We are challenged by the complexity of financial survival. All businesses have the opportunity to create their own uniqueness and stand out in a marketplace vying for recognition. As artists, you are more than qualified to demonstrate your creative nature in your art and in your business. Do not stagnate in the pursuit of financial viability.

Summary
- Hiring someone may be the most efficient way to ensure the growth of your business.
- Help can often be found in family members, friends, college interns, by placing ads in local arts papers, temp services, SCORE, etc.
- Plan your work efficiently to realize the most benefit from your assistant.
- Networking with other artists to form a co-op is one innovative way to develop your business while gaining resources and leverage in the marketplace.

"If only for the duration of the project, people in Great Groups seem to become better than themselves. They are able to see more, achieve more, and have a far better time doing it than they can working alone."

Warren Bennis,
Patricia Ward Biederman
co-authors,
Organizing Genius

Resources

Books And Audio Cassettes:

The Art of Possibility: Transforming Professional And Personal Life
Rosamund Stone Zander, Benjamin Zander
Penguin, USA
ISBN: 0142001104

Ben Jerry's Double Dip
How To Run A Value Led Business And Make Money
Ben Cohen, Jerry Greenfield, Meredith Maran
Fireside
ISBN: 0684838559

Growing A Business (audio)
Paul Hawken
Simon & Schuster
ISBN: 0671646249

Growing A Business (book)
Paul Hawken
Fireside
ISBN: 0671671642

Hiring Independent Contractors
The Employer's Legal Guide
Stephen Fishman
Nolo Press Self Help Law
ISBN: 0873379187

Managing Your Employees
George Devine
Prentice Hall
ISBN: 0136033415

Take Time for Your Life: A Personal Coach's 7-Step Program for Creating the Life You Want
Cheryl Richardson
Broadway Books
ISBN: 0767902076

Teaming Up: The Small Business Guide to Collaborating With Others to Boost Your Earnings and Expand Your Horizons
Paul Edwards, Sarah Edwards, Rick Benzel
J. P. Tarcher
ISBN: 0874778425

365 Ways to Simplify Your Work Life: Ideas That Bring More Time, Freedom and Satisfaction to Daily Work
Odette Pollar
Dearborn Trade
ISBN: 0793122813

Refer to Resources in Chapter 3 for more help with employment, financial and legal services for your business growth.

Virtual Assistants:

Assist U
Phone: 866-829-6757
Web: http://www.assistu.com
This organization refers qualified VAs and offers training for virtual assistants.

International Association of Virtual Assistants
Phone: 1-877-440-2750
Web: http://www.ivaa.org
A non-profit organization dedicated to educating the public on the role and function of the Virtual Assistant.

Traditional Office Support and Professional Organizers:

International Association of Administrative Professionals
Phone: 816-891-6600
Web: http://www.iaap-hq.org

National Association of Professional Organizers
Web: http://www.napo.net

Coaching Organizations:

International Coach Federation
Phone: 1-888-ICF-3131
Web: http://www.coachfederation.org

Coach University
Phone: 1-888-857-6410
Web: http://www.coachu.com

Professional Coaches and Mentors Association
Phone: 1-800-979-7262
Web: http://pcmaonline.com

CHAPTER TWENTY-ONE
The One-Year Plan

"He who every morning plans the transaction of the day and follows out that plan, carries a thread that will guide him through the maze of the most busy life. But where no plan is laid, where the disposal of time is surrendered merely to the chance incidence, chaos will soon reign."

Victor Hugo
playwright

The circle is now complete. Chapter One laid the groundwork for this moment. All of the following chapters provided you with valuable information necessary to propel your career forward. This chapter demonstrates how to piece together a one-year plan that details your actions throughout the year. Select helpful information from the previous chapters to help piece your plan together. If some aspects of your year are already in place, this exercise will help to organize those existing plans more definitively and possibly broaden their scope. If you are just beginning to envision the next year, this exercise will help you focus your time and attention on details necessary to accomplish your one-year goals.

"I never considered my dreams wasted energy; they were invariably linked to some form of action."

Ray Kroc
restaurateur,
franchised MacDonald's

One-Year Plan

A one-year plan details the activities necessary to accomplish your goals for a twelve month period. Each goal can now be seen as a series of events, projects or tasks that once completed, will move you closer to your end result.

The most effective way to begin the one-year plan is to establish your final goal and give it a deadline. Work

> **HotTip:** 🌶️
> Always factor in more time for mailings and responses when booking during the November through January holiday season.

> "Make short-term goals attainable and attach a realistic timetable to them. Long-range goals can be much broader, but the timetable is still important."
>
> Dick Renko
> manager,
> Trout Fishing in America,
> Muzik Management

> "Time is totally perishable and cannot be stored."
>
> Peter F. Drucker
> author,
> The Effective Executive

> "When a thing is done, it is done. Don't look back. Look forward to your next objective."
>
> George C. Marshall
> U.S. general

backwards from the last goal and approximate the amount of time required to accomplish each task. Then, set the next start and end dates and continue this process until, eventually, you reach the first project at the beginning of your year.

Each target date gives you something to look forward to and keeps you moving from one task to the next. A one-year plan leaves little question as to what to do next. It is laid out before you in small incremental steps. The target dates provide momentum to accomplish each task in its turn. The nice thing about using this target-date format is that it is perfectly suited to be transferred to a yearly wall calendar. This offers a visual reminder of each specific daily goal while viewing the entire year.

Set Target Dates

Establish target dates to logically lead you to the main goal. Display the dates on a wall calendar or in your planning book. List the title of each individual target date along with the completion date.

Visual target dates are an effective way to track your progress. They are a clear reminder of what has already been accomplished and what is yet to be done. Uncluttered with detail, the target-date format creates a visual impact which drives you forward to each successive deadline.

Setting target dates is a technique that you can incorporate for all of your project planning. You will discover yourself moving through the day's tasks with greater efficiency. By breaking down your goals into a series of smaller action steps, each goal becomes less overwhelming. Everything you want to accomplish in your life suddenly becomes achievable. You just need to take the first step.

Target Date Format

To illustrate how a one-year plan laid out in the target-date format works, I will use our hypothetical musician, Jessie. Using the one-year goals established in Chapter One, page 9, we will create a complete one-year plan for her. Since this artist has just begun performing professionally, let us assume that she has established four main goals for the first year—to set up an office, to create a promotional package, to book and complete a fall tour and to begin booking a spring tour of club dates.

Begin At The End

The one-year plan will reflect all of the steps necessary in order to accomplish these four goals. To determine the amount of time each task requires, Jessie begins with the last goal and sets the target start and end dates. The last goal is to begin booking a regional spring tour of club dates. After examining the calendar, an ending date of December 14 was selected as the final date to make booking calls since the holidays make it difficult to reach most presenters. Jessie will begin her calls on November 8 after a well-deserved vacation. A one-week vacation is set to end on November 7 and begin on October 31 following the culmination of her four-week fall tour which ends on October 30. Since the fall tour is planned for four weeks, she places a start date on October 1. Once those dates are in place, every other event and time needed to accomplish each task leading up to those dates can be determined.

We now know that in order for a tour itinerary to arrive at least two weeks prior to the first date, it must be mailed at least two weeks before, or emailed two days before we want it to arrive. That sets our mailing date on August 27 and email date for September 10. We now also know that a good publicity campaign usually requires at least six weeks. If the tour starts on October 1, six weeks prior to that is August 23 and the start date for the publicity campaign.

The year continues in that vein determining target dates and the time frames necessary to complete each task. Once completed, an entire year's tasks are set. They are easily achievable and leave no question about what to do next. I will describe the thought process behind each target date as we go along.

Display The Target Dates

By displaying each target date and the goal associated with that date on a large wall calendar, you provide momentum to your daily routine with a bold, visual reminder of what is next. Jessie might create a calendar like those shown on the following pages. Include deadline dates for when itineraries must be sent to appropriate media outlets on your own calendar. Since schedules may vary, many dates will be scattered throughout the year—some weekly, some monthly, some bimonthly. Remember to include these deadlines on any computer scheduling programs which have pop-up alarms as a reminder to send itineraries when deadlines occur while on tour.

HotTip: Most photo reproduction companies offer a ten day turnaround once they receive your original photo. Many will provide rush service for an additional charge. Use a company that files your original photo in-house so you can call or fax or email your order.

"The real secret of how to use time is to pack it as you would your luggage, filling up the small spaces with small things."

Henry Haddow

"Allow yourself to rest and to take care of yourself, you will actually perform better, more effectively and for a longer period of time. Find ways to take momentary rests during the day—after completing a task, take five deep breaths before going on to the next thing. If you lengthen the exhale, it triggers stress release. The increased oxygen will give you energy and the longer exhale quiets the adrenaline stress reaction."

Debra Russell,
certified life coach

January

Sun	Mon	Tue	Wed	Thu	Fri	Sat
1	2 Set up office	3	4	5	6	7
8	9	10	11 Meet with graphic artist	12	13	14
15	16	17	18	19	20	21
22	23	24	25	26 Office Set-Up Complete	27	28
29	30	31				

February

Sun	Mon	Tue	Wed	Thu	Fri	Sat
			1 Photo Session	2 Gather, Write Press Kit Mat'ls	3	4
5	6	7 Get Proofs from Photographer	8	9	10 Get Custom 8x10 Prints	11
12	13 Send Photos for Reproduction	14 Materials go to Artist, Typesetter	15	16	17	18
19	20	21	22	23	24	25
26	27	28				

March

Sun	Mon	Tue	Wed	Thu	Fri	Sat
			1	2	3	4
5	6 Research Organizations, Conferences	7	8	9	10	11
12	13 Research Media Lists	14	15	16	17	18
19	20	21	22	23	24	25
26	27	28	29	30 Graphics, Typesetting Due Back	31	

Target Dates—Jessie's One-Year Plan

The following one-year plan starts in January 2006 and continues through December 2006. The plan was arrived at by setting the last target date and backtracking through the year.

Four Months Before Booking Tour: Set-Up Office ....January 2
Begin to set up the office space. This may require trips to office-furniture stores, ordering equipment, perhaps painting, and gathering the various supplies necessary to run an efficient office.

Three and a Half Months Before Booking Tour: Meet with Graphic Artist............January 11
Start discussing promotional packet designs with a graphic artist as early as possible. You will need their input to create a budget, establish a reasonable time line and get a view of all the possibilities. The graphic artist will need as much time as possible to design your package.

Three Months Before Booking Tour: Office Set-Up Complete..........................January 26
Now the office space is complete. Move in and begin work.

Three Months Before Booking Tour: Photo Session ....February 1
This will give the photographer time to print contact sheets and choose the shots for final printing. The photographer will then need time to make the prints and digitize the photos. Once the prints are in hand there is ample time to get reprints of the promo shot to include in the press kit and add digitized photos to website and EPK.

Three Months Before Booking Tour: Gather, Write Press-Kit Materials ....February 2
Allow enough time to gather and write the materials to be included in the press kit. When working with a copywriter, add some time to this date.

Three Months Before Booking Tour: Get Proofs from Photographer ....February 7
The proof sheets should be available from the photographer. Make selections of the one or two shots that will be reproduced for use as your main promotional photographs.

Two and One-Half Months Before Booking Tour: Get Custom 8x10 Prints ....February 10
Receive custom 8x10 prints and digital photo CD from the photographer.

Two and One-Half Months Before Booking Tour: Send Prints for Reproduction....February 13
Send the 8x10 custom prints to the photographic reproduction company. Orders may be lower with digital photos available for download from the website.

Three Months Before Booking Tour: Materials Go to Artist, Typesetter.........February 14
Have all written material and photos ready to go to the graphic artist and typesetter when using outside services. Once graphics are in place, create an Electronic Press Kit for web placement or ID-ROM.

April

						1
	2	3 Send Materials to Printer	4	5	6	7	8
9	10	11	12	13	14	15
16	17	18	19	20 Materials Due Back From Printer	21	22
23 / 30	24	25 Prepare Press Kit Materials	26	27 BEGIN TO BOOK FALL TOUR (THROUGH JULY)	28	29

May

	1 BOOKING FALL TOUR (THROUGH JULY)	2	3	4	5	6	7
8	9	10	11	12	13	14
15	16	17	18	19	20	21
22	23	24	25	26	27	28
29	30	31				

June

			1 BOOKING FALL TOUR (THROUGH JULY)	2	3	4
5	6	7	8	9	10	11
12	13	14	15	16	17	18
19	20	21	22	23	24	25
26	27	28	29	30		

Seven Months Before Fall Tour: Research Organizations, Conferences.................March 6
Begin gathering materials from various organizations and conferences for which you think your act might be appropriate. Make a note of membership fees, registration fees, conference dates, registration deadlines and showcase-application deadlines. Select a few that fit your first year's budget, schedule and goals.

Seven Months Before Fall Tour: Research Media Lists.............................March 13
Begin to gather newspaper, radio and TV mailing addresses and contact lists. Buy address labels from organizations appropriate for your act and incorporate the contacts into your database. Purchase current media databases to add to your own. Review online databases and add to favorites list on your computer.

Four Weeks Before Booking Tour: Graphics, Typesetting Due Back...................March 30
Plan on final artwork and typeset materials to be back from the artist and typesetter. Again allow some room for delays depending on the design complexity. Begin EPK production.

Three Weeks Before Booking Tour: Send Materials to Printer.................April 3
Plan to send the press kit materials to the printer and EPK producer/manufacturer.

One Week Before Booking Tour: Materials Due Back from Printer....................April 20
Leave at least a week's leeway for printer delays so that all materials for the press kit are due back from the printer in time for mailing. Press kit materials will be more complicated than a tour mailer. Therefore, allow a full two weeks for the printer to complete the job. Plan for that extra week to be right on target to send booking promotional materials.

Five Months Before Fall Tour: Prepare Press Kit Materials......................April 25
Target new promotional material to be ready to send to presenters for fall tour bookings.

Five Months Before Fall Tour: Begin to Book Fall Tour.................*April 27 through July*
Tour bookings begun April 29 may continue through July. For the purpose of this exercise, we are booking club venues. If we were booking arts centers and concert series performances, these bookings would have had to have been done during the previous fall or earlier.

Two Months Before Fall Tour: Update Press Kit......................................*July 5*
In July, update any press kit materials adding recent reviews.

Seven Weeks Before Fall Tour: Prepare Mailer...*August 8*
Again, allow two weeks to prepare and print the mailing if sending by snail mail.

Six Weeks Before Fall Tour: Mail/Email Press Releases..........................*August 22*
Mail/email press releases to fall tour dates and begin to set up interviews, again, allowing a six-week promotion window.

July

Sun	Mon	Tue	Wed	Thu	Fri	Sat
						1
2 BOOKING FALL TOUR (THROUGH JULY)	3	4	5 Update Press Kit	6	7	8
9	10	11	12	13	14	15
16	17	18	19	20	21	22
23 / 30	24 / 31	25	26	27	28	29

August

Sun	Mon	Tue	Wed	Thu	Fri	Sat
		1	2	3	4	5
6	7	8 Prepare Mailer	9	10	11	12
13	14	15	16	17	18	19
20	21	22 Mail Press Releases	23	24	25 Send Tour Mailer	26
27	28 Begin Media Calls	29	30	31		

September

Sun	Mon	Tue	Wed	Thu	Fri	Sat
				Register for Winter Conference (through December)	1 Attend Select Fall Conferences (through November)	2
3	4 Begin Fall Tour Interviews	5	6	7	8 E-mail Tour Itenerary	9
10	11	12	13 Begin Advancing Fall Tour	14	15	16
17	18	19	20	21	22	23 Tour Kickoff Concert
24	25	26	27	28	29 BEGIN FALL TOUR Atlanta, GA	30 Charleston, SC

Five Weeks Before Fall Tour : Send Tour Mailer..*August 25*
Send an announcement of the fall tour so that it arrives at least two weeks prior to the September 25th concert date.

Five Weeks Before Fall Tour: Begin Media Calls ....*August 28*
Allow one week for press kits and press releases to arrive. Begin follow-up calls/emails to connect with newspaper, radio and TV media contacts to set up interviews and secure preview articles, release reviews and calendar notices. These calls will continue throughout the five weeks prior to the tour. Some last minute contact may need to be made during the tour.

Winter Conferences: Select and Register for Conferences ....*September-December*
Having researched and found appropriate conferences and showcases to attend during the previous winter months, begin the registration process. Take advantage of any early-bird discounts. Mark discount registration deadlines on the wall calendar.

During Fall Tour: Attend Select Fall Conferences ....*September-November*
Many conferences and showcases occur in the fall. Include some of these conferences within your fall tour schedule. Surround conference dates with performance dates in those regions.

Two-Three Weeks Before Fall Tour: Begin Fall Tour Interviews........................*September 4*
Again, writers will begin scheduling interviews two weeks prior to the start of the tour. If an interview is scheduled, it is likely that the writer will want to conduct the interview closer to the event date. Some interviews may need to take place while on tour.

Two Weeks Before Fall Tour: Begin Advancing Fall Tour ....*September 13*
Begin making calls to all the presenters on the fall tour to check on final details. (Refer back to Chapter 10, Managing The Road.)

One Week Before Fall Tour: Hometown Tour Kickoff Concert......................*September 23*
Present a concert for all the hometown supporters to kick off the fall tour. It is a great way to provide momentum for the tour.

Begin Fall Tour ....*September 29*
This tour targets a region close to home in order to hit a number of markets not previously played before.

End Fall Tour ....*October 29*
The four week fall tour ends.

Vacation ....*October 30–November 5*
Having returned from the fall tour, insert a well-earned vacation beginning November 1. Even if it is just to sleep, write it on

October

1	*2*	*3*	*4* Columbia, SC	*5* Charlotte, NC	*6* Chapel Hill, NC	*7* Johnson City, TN
8	*9*	*10*	*11* Roanoke, VA	*12* Charlottesville, VA	*13* Richmond, VA	*14* Alexandria, VA
15 Asheville, NC	*16*	*17*	*18* Bethlehem, PA	*19* Philadelphia, PA	*20* Baltimore, MD	*21* Columbia, MD
22	*23*	*24*	*25* Fredericksburg, VA	*26* Orange, VA	*27* Norfolk, VA	*28* Williamsburg, VA END FALL TOUR
29 Washington DC	*30* Vacation!	*31* →				

November

			1 Vacation!	*2*	*3*	*4* →
→ *5*	*6* Start Booking Spring Tour	*7*	*8*	*9*	*10*	*11*
12	*13*	*14*	*15*	*16*	*17*	*18*
19	*20*	*21*	*22*	*23*	*24*	*25*
26	*27*	*28*	*29*	*30*		

December

					1	*2*
3	*4*	*5*	*6*	*7*	*8*	*9*
10	*11*	*12*	*13*	*14*	*15*	*16*
17	*18* End Booking Calls for Holidays	*19*	*20*	*21*	*22*	*23*
24 *31*	*25*	*26*	*27*	*28*	*29*	*30*

THE ONE-YEAR PLAN

the wall calendar and take a break. Time is needed to rejuvenate and get excited about the next phase of the year's plan.

Five Months Before Spring Tour: Start Booking Spring Tour ....*November 6*
Begin booking the spring tour in November after returning from the fall tour. Since this is a tour of club dates, many presenters tend to confirm bookings much closer to the performance dates. Bookings may have to continue through February. Many last minute details will be finalized just before you go to press with your mailer.

Final Goal Of The Year: Holiday Break from Booking ....*December 18*
Booking is difficult during the holidays. Plan to resume booking calls after January 3, for spring tour dates.

This is our musician's year set out in target date format. Specific details necessary to be undertaken in order to accomplish these tasks, can be included within the various blocks of time. (For example: January 2—Visit office supply stores to get prices on furniture and necessary supplies and equipment.) For each individual project within this year, continue to detail each day's activities to fit within the time allotted.

Filling In The Tasks
Once the target dates are in place, fill in the blocks of time with daily tasks necessary to reach each goal successfully. You may begin to notice that events do not always exist in isolation of each other. Each day will be filled with tasks that lead to accomplishing multiple goals.

For example:
During the six week time period when a publicity campaign is conducted, many other events need to happen as the beginning of the tour approaches. By constantly viewing all of the target goal dates, it is less likely that a date will be missed. While calls are being made to media contacts, the tour mailer is being prepared, contact with each promoter to advance their date is occurring, interviews are being conducted, etc.

Review The One-Year Goals
This is a great time to review your one-year goals and update or refine them after having read the bulk of this book. So much of the information represented in these pages may influence how you now view your performing career. It certainly may have an impact upon the goals which you laid out in Chapter One. Take some time now to re-examine your goals and make any necessary adjustments before beginning your one-year plan.

"Most of us are spending too many hours at the office and not enough time with our family and friends. So go through your daily planner and decide when you want to take a vacation. If you don't block out the time for yourself, there won't be any."

Jeffrey J. Mayer
author,
Time Management for Dummies

"We have to do a little planning, particularly if the task is large. Subdivide it into smaller segments. Schedule it in a realistic time frame and protect the blocks of time allocated to it."

Jack D. Ferner
author
Successful Time Management

"Intelligence, imagination and knowledge are essential resources, but only effectiveness converts them to results. By themselves, they only set limits on what can be achieved."

Peter F. Drucker
author,
The Effective Executive

"Nothing is particularly hard if you divide it into small jobs."

Henry Ford
inventor

"Having once decided to achieve a certain task, achieve it at all costs of tedium and distaste. The gain in self-confidence of having accomplished a tiresome labor is immense."

Arnold Bennett
English novelist

"It's persistence that makes you great. It's persistence that allows you to reach your dreams. It's persistence that enables you to perform at your fullest potential."

Rick Pitino
basketball coach, author,
Success Is A Choice

Exercise: One-Year Plan

With your one-year goals firmly established, you can easily break down each goal into small tasks and lay out your one-year plan of action. Begin your plan on page 455 or work directly in your planning book to include all of the details. Have fun!

Summary

- ◆ Your one-year plan details the activities necessary to accomplish your goals for the next year.
- ◆ Set target dates to start and end each task.
- ◆ Place target dates on a wall calendar near your desk as a constant visual reminder of the next task to be accomplished.
- ◆ Fill in the blocks of time between target dates with the daily tasks necessary to reach the target date.

My One-Year Plan
Date Recorded _____

Resources

Books:

Getting Things Done: The Art of Stress-Free Productivity
David Allen
Penguin
ISBN: 0142000280
CD
Sound Ideas
ISBN: 0743520343

Successful Time Management
Jack D. Ferner
John Wiley & Sons, Inc.
ISBN: 0471033928

The Effective Executive
Peter F. Drucker
HarperBusiness
ISBN: 006091209X

*The Power of Full Engagement:
Managing Energy, Not time, Is The Key To High Performance And Personal Renewal*
Jim Loehr, Tony Schwartz
Free Press
ISBN: 0743226747

*The Procrastinator's Handbook
Mastering The Art Of Doing It Now*
Rita Emmett
Walker & Co.
ISBN: 0802775985

Time Management For The Creative Person
Lee Siber
Three Rivers Press
ISBN: 0609800906

Time Management For Dummies
Jeffrey J. Mayer
IDG Books
ISBN: 0764551450

Time Management From The Inside Out
Julie Morganstern
Henry Halt & Company
ISBN: 0805004699

Time Management For Unmanageable People
Ann McGee-Cooper with Duane Trammell
A Bantam Book
ISBN: 0553370715

Review the resources in Chapter One.

CHAPTER TWENTY-TWO
When To Quit Your Day Job

"Always leave enough time in your life to do something that makes you happy, satisfied, even joyous. That has more of an effect on economic well-being than any other single factor."

Paul Hawken
founder, Erewhon Natural Foods;
founder, Smith & Hawken Garden Supply Catalog

As your business develops, you will face certain growing pains that will challenge you. If you perform part time, you may find yourself questioning whether or not to quit your day job to perform full time or remain juggling the two. In situations where you have done a particularly good job of booking your own dates, you might consider expanding your business and adding an employee. Perhaps you have fulfilled your performance dreams and now would rather return to a steady income and pursue other interests. Whatever your situation, there comes a time when we all must face these challenges head on and deal with them. This chapter will help you evaluate your own situation so you can make the changes that can no longer be avoided.

Tending to the business side of your art is not always the most desirable portion of the work, yet it is often the thing that cries out for the most attention. It has a way of nagging in the middle of the night. You clench your teeth tighter, having only completed a small portion of the tour's bookings or only sent one-third of the promoters press materials. There never

"Success is a ... trendy word. Don't aim for success if you want it; just do what you love and it will come naturally."

David Frost
actor, broadcaster,
British statesman

> "I encourage artists to stop worrying about everything. The audience is going to tell you when you're doing something right. The response that you get is your information. Pay attention! They will lead you to the next thing."
>
> Mary McFaul
> manager, Laura Love Band,
> McFaul Booking & Management

> "To gain what is worth having, it must be necessary to lose everything."
>
> Bernadette Devlin
> IRA activist,
> first woman president of Ireland

> "I laid out a stepwise plan of goals and objectives over the course of a couple of years to measure whether I was getting to a point where doing the music would be viable. Are the reviews good, are people coming to shows, should I record a CD because people are really interested? I could determine the progress each time I hit a milestone."
>
> Andrew McKnight
> singer, songwriter

> "The decision to do the singer-songwriter label was in part marketing and reading the writing on the wall. But it was every bit as important that I just wanted new challenges."
>
> Will Ackerman
> guitarist, founder,
> Windham Hill Records;
> Imaginary Road Records

seems to be a quiet moment when the business lets you rest to simply revel in your past accomplishments. There is always the next tour, the next recording, the next promotional campaign and the next phone interview at 10 a.m. on Thursday from the hotel in Dallas.

How Are You Doing?

Throughout your career, it is important to reevaluate your efforts. There may be times when you question whether all the work is actually paying off. When you began your business, you entered into it by assessing your strengths, your assets and your needs. It is no less important to continue that process once you are in the midst of your career. In fact, constant reassessment keeps you acutely aware of new opportunities and the need for change.

Yearly Evaluation

Scheduling a review of your past year is a good way to check yourself and your progress. Determine which goals were met and what is left on the time line. Evaluate each project, tour, or promotional campaign. Discover which of your efforts were successful, which require adjustments in the future and which should be replaced with a new strategy. Without a timely assessment of all that you have undertaken, how will you be able to measure your success?

When you rely on external feedback, you only get part of the story. Larger audiences, more reviews and bigger sales all indicate something is being accomplished. However, evaluating the procedures and the process tells you what caused the audience response. Scrutinizing your techniques and strategies for building your own business keeps your business healthy, thriving and alive.

Treat your business as a living entity. Once your business is planted, you need to feed and water it and as it grows, prune it and trim it back every once in a while. It is not a thing to let go wild. A business demands that someone take control and be ever in the present with a keen vision of the future and a constant awareness of the past.

Once again, this is the time to return to your long-range goals and use them as a benchmark to measure your progress, your successes and your motivation towards alternatives. The plans you have set for yourself can help to determine what is working and what needs to be changed. As I mentioned earlier, long-range plans are flexible, yet they provide you with a clear vision of your path. If that path needs to be altered, then this process offers you the opportunity to do so. If you have simply strayed momentarily, your long-range goals will get you back on track.

A year-end evaluation gives you the information needed to make future plans.

Here's what you need:

❖ Keep a record of each tour's expenses. By using the budget provided in Chapter Eight, you can track each category of expense throughout the year. As you become more tour savvy, certain expenses may decrease while others may increase. This depends on the nature of your act's needs and any money-saving tips you have picked up along the way.

❖ Keep a record of each tour's promotional campaign. Note what kind of mailings were sent and the response. For example: A postcard itinerary saved you money in printing and postage, but a flyer allowed you to include your mail-order catalog. The faxed-press-release campaign actually received attention from the media and you received coverage with some advance stories and a few reviews. Perhaps an e-mail campaign would generate a greater response and cost even less next time. When you mailed an announcement for your upcoming tour, you received numerous calls looking for available dates. Was hiring a professional publicist to promote the new release and the tour an expensive investment? Did it pay off? All of these methods were worth testing. Evaluating their success helps you decide which to continue using and which ones need to be changed.

❖ Keep some record of your time. This is not meant as a joke. Although, I guarantee a good laugh if you add the hours and divide by some reasonable hourly wage that a day gig might offer. This is meant to help you evaluate the effort required to accomplish specific tasks. For instance, in order to book a $300 gig you made 12 phone calls, sent your press kit twice (they lost the first one), and spent $100 on a hotel that night. Was it worth it? Check the audience numbers and product sales. Perhaps your time could have been better spent. This is the kind of evaluation necessary to help determine limits and bottom-line requirements.

❖ If you are in a band, check in with other group members. A once-a-year check-in gives individuals in a group the opportunity to discuss personal changes and how the group might be affected by them. It allows each member to offer their own assessment of how the past year's efforts affected them or how they might help effect future changes.

Suggestion:

If you are acting as the group's agent and/or business representative, a yearly discussion to get feedback from other members may prove helpful in fine-tuning the business. This is also the perfect time to discuss compensation for your extra work. Pay the group's "agent" a percentage off the top of every date booked—10% seems to be the norm. If the

---

"I had already accomplished lots of the goals that I had set for myself as a performer. I was looking for a way to combine my skills with a little more of my soul and spirit in something that was engaging and felt meaningful. I was ready for something a little different."

Nick Forster
musician, creator of *E-Town* radio show

"The roots of true achievement lie in the will to become the best that you can become."

Harold Taylor
time management consultant

"You have to have talent. You could work hard and have the biggest mailing list in the world and do everything by the book, but if you don't have the talent you're not going to go anywhere. Ask your friends and family to be brutally honest with you because they care about you. If you're writing songs that really aren't that good, and your musicianship is not really that good, you want to know that."

Scot Fisher
manager, Ani DiFranco
president,
Righteous Babe Records

> "Emmylou Harris' old bass player, Tom Gyderer, said it best, 'Music is a passion and you have to decide if you're going to succumb to it or not. That's the big question, and if you do, then you will somehow find a way to make time to do it.'"
>
> **John Starling**
> lead singer,
> Seldom Scene

> "Never continue in a job you don't enjoy. If you're happy in what you're doing, you'll like yourself, you'll have inner peace. And if you have that, along with physical health, you will have had more success than you could possibly have imagined."
>
> **Johnny Carson**
> actor

> "If you really want to do music and be in the business, follow your heart and keep believing in yourself. If you know you have the talent, if it's truly the passion that burns inside you, you've got to follow it."
>
> **Kari Estrin**
> management consultant

> "After quitting radio, I was able to live on the money I saved on aspirins."
>
> **Fred Allen**
> comedian

> "You may be disappointed if you fail, but you are doomed if you don't try."
>
> **Beverly Sills**
> opera singer

agent also handles the other business for the group, like publicity, travel arrangements, selling merchandise, etc., add another 5%. After those percentages are taken off the top, the rest of the money is split between the band members equally.

If jobs are distributed throughout the group evenly, you may want to find ways to offer members some additional compensation. Once the band has a life of its own, money laid out to take care of band expenses and group projects needs to be eventually reimbursed to those individuals. Create a band fund to finance expenses and special projects. Depending on your group's makeup, this is a way of keeping members engaged in the business while recognizing each individual's participation.

Analyzing The Evaluation
This evaluation sounds very calculating and, after all, we are talking about the arts here, are we not? The free-spirited artist bumping heads with the three-piece-suited entrepreneur creates an odd fellowship. Yet, creative survival demands that kind of accountability. Once you can account for your successes and your failures, you have the stuff to hold it all together for another year or two or five or ten. And, if the accounting tells a different story, the evaluation may suggest even more drastic changes. Face it now and avoid facing the inevitable in a few years. An open evaluation will show all sides of the picture, pretty or not.

Planning To Quit Your Day Job
Deciding when to walk away from stability and security is a very personal decision. What drives each of us to do it is rooted deeply in our commitment to fulfilling our dreams. You may experience a time in your career when you are faced with the situation.

A Personal Story
In 1985, I began preparing myself to quit my day job (in my case it was a night job). I worked as a television broadcast engineer from 3:45 p.m. to 11:45 p.m. while continuing to run my booking and management business during the day. I was booking only one act at the time. But I knew that I could do more for the artists if I worked full time.

I was earning good money in television and it was an imposing decision to make to give that up for the uncertain future of my own business.

During the planning time, I scouted for other artists in need of representation, reduced my expenses, saved as much money as possible and plotted my expansion. Having a lengthy lead time allowed me to transition comfortably in a well-thought-out and executed manner. I gave one month's notice at the television station which allowed them time to find my replacement.

I try to leave any situation with my relationships intact. One never knows when those contacts may play a role in some future endeavor. This holds true for bosses as well as promoters, record company executives, artists and agents.

Some people are comforted by a consistent source of income, knowing where they will be between certain hours of the day and that they will probably get money back from the IRS at the end of the year. Others of us like to stare into the abyss and actually listen to the little voice in our head that beckons us to jump. I'm a jumper! There is a thrill knowing that each day holds some new challenge to be met or problem to be solved without the security net below to catch a fall.

My art was in the management of other people's art and I derived my joy from seeing it done well. I knew I wanted to live in the service of art and my commitment to that end propelled me towards my transition.

There are jobs for those who seek them. But for those of us who need to make a place in our lives where we can pull out our creative soul and hold it before a willing audience, there may be only one time, one chance to attempt art. We need to take that chance.

Are You Ready To Quit?

In order to evaluate your own situation, consider this checklist below.

❖ Have multiple discussions with partners and family members who are supportive.
❖ Give yourself enough lead time.
❖ List all of the reasons why you should do it at this particular time.
❖ Be committed to the notion that your part-time performing career really does warrant your full-time participation.
❖ Consider ways of cutting back on your day job incrementally rather than "all-out" quitting.
❖ Assess your real cost necessities—include mortgage, car payments, loans, health insurance and capital investments for the business.
❖ Save six months to one year's income as backup.
❖ Explore health insurance plans for the self-employed.
❖ Have other savings and check on your employee pension savings. These can be rolled into a retirement savings plan.
❖ Complete your long-term goals plan, business plan and marketing plan.
❖ Commit to your art and be ready to work for it.

> **HotTip:** Check with your current employer about extending your health insurance coverage through a COBRA program. After one year, the insurance may be transferred to a personal plan.

"I had been in music before and quit to become a psychologist. I had lied to myself for years that I didn't want music because I was scared. Once I understood what I wanted, I couldn't run away any longer and I knew I needed to pursue it. As I began getting more gigs in music, I gradually dropped different parts of the psychology career. I was able to decide to do music full time when I was making enough money to pay my expenses with music. I just wouldn't have and couldn't have done it before."

Lucy Kaplansky
singer, songwriter

"We never had delusions of grandeur. Ani wanted to record her music, play her music and sell it to an audience so that she could pay the rent. She wanted a different job than waiting on tables. I was 30 years old and still had all my fingers so it was time to get out of the carpentry business."

Scot Fisher
manager, Ani DiFranco
president,
Righteous Babe Records

Add other considerations you may have to help complete your evaluation. Consider every aspect of your life. This kind of transition will affect everything.

A New Transition

I already made one transition when I quit my television job and went full time into artist management. But, I reassessed my goals years later, I realized that after 20 years of booking and management I wanted to do something new. At the time I gave notice to my artists, I had no idea what was next. I only knew that I needed a change. This was the biggest chasm I had ever faced. I planned a fifteen month lead time to wrap up all aspects of the business while discovering the new me. The process was invigorating as well as emotionally draining. It challenged me to my core. I would not have traded a moment on this path. This book would not have been written if I was not so enamored of risky business. And here we all are, determining our future in the service of art.

When Your Business No Longer Feeds You

I would like to examine the other side of the story, the one we dare not think, let alone speak. There is that remote possibility that you might decide to stop performing and do something else. Perhaps you might return to the day job you left originally. Whatever the next phase holds for you, allow yourself to ponder the possibility that the art is not serving you and it is time to redesign your life once again.

Those of us committed to our dreams sometimes forge blindly onward in a state of denial. We often refuse to believe that it is not working the way we had planned or dreamt that it could work. We refuse to accept the facts as they really are. After all, as artists, we are supposed to pay our dues and suffer appropriately.

The accounting of your business retells the gory details over and over. The audiences dwindle, sales are down, the market is no longer friendly. Perhaps changes in your personal life are a more convincing voice echoing reality. Whatever factors begin to surface, pay timely attention to them.

Your commitment to your art may be more productively served in other fashions. Reverting to part-time participation may once again renew the excitement and relieve the stress around the business. Practicing the art in a more hobby-like environment may relieve the business stresses all together. This is a deeply personal decision.

Conclusion

Revisit your long-term goals and match your life's desires with your current situation. If it no longer works for you,

---

"The thing that makes a difference in doing it, is how you feel inside, which you'll only find out by plugging away for a while. I knew inside that I wanted to try and write songs and sing. I knew that if I didn't do that, I was going to be, in some ways, unhappy."

Greg Brown
singer, songwriter

"Don't be afraid to take a big step when one is indicated. You can't cross a chasm in two small jumps."

David Lloyd George
British prime minister

". . . I learned you have to trust yourself, be what you are and do what you ought to do the way you should do it. You have to discover you, what you do and trust it."

Barbra Streisand
singer, actor, director, producer

"If it's not fun, why do it?"

Ben Cohen
co-founder, Ben & Jerry's;
co-author,
Ben & Jerry's Double Dip

face it, redefine it, and change it. And if the situation demands, let the final act of your business be to end the business so that the art can breathe again.

Summary
- Assess the growth of your business on an annual basis.
- Conduct an honest evaluation of your methods and strategies in order to plan future growth.
- Evaluate your business' growth. You can determine the level of participation necessary.
- Plan adequately before quitting your day job and examine how it affects your life and those around you.
- Face the facts and know when to quit your business and try something else.

"Musicians don't retire; they stop when there's no more music in them."

Louis Armstrong
Jazz trumpeter

"Keep changing. When you're through changing, you're through."

Bruce Barton
advertising executive, writer, creator of Betty Crocker

Resources

Books:

Before You Say 'I Quit': A Guide to Making Successful Job Transitions
Diane Holloway, Nancy Bishop
Wellness Institute
ISBN: 1587411172

Built To Last: Successful Habits Of Visionary Companies
James C. Collins, Jerry I. Porras
HarperBusiness
ISBN: 0887307396

Integrative Life Planning: Critical Tasks For Career Development And Changing Life Patterns
Lorraine Sundal Hansen, L. Sunny Hansen, Sunny Hansen
Jassey-Bass Publishing
ISBN: 0787902004

Leading Change
John P. Kotter
Harvard Business School Press
ISBN: 0875847471

Secrets Of Self-Employment: Surviving And Thriving On The Ups and Downs Of Being Your Own Boss
Sarah Edwards and Paul Edwards
J.P. Tarcher
ISBN: 0874778379

Succeeding In Music: A Business Handbook For performers, Songwriters, Agents, Managers, and Promoters
John Stiernberg
Backbeat Books
ISBN: 0879307021

The Lost Soul Companion: A Book Of Comfort and Constructive Advice for Struggling Artists, Black Sheep, Square Pegs, and Other Free Spirits
Susan M. Brackney
Dell
ISBN: 0440509211

CHAPTER TWENTY-THREE
Ethics And Attitudes

"Integrity is the cornerstone of our business. We will conduct our affairs in a manner consistent with the highest ethical standards. To meet our commitment, we will:
- *Engage in fair and honest practices.*
- *Show respect for each other, our consumers, customers, suppliers, shareholders and the communities in which we operate.*
- *Communicate in an honest, factual and accurate manner."*

**Excerpt from *Our Shared Values*
Kellogg's Company Philosophy ©1992**

After ending my business of 20 years and before beginning anything new, I read every book I could get my hands on that dealt with business, marketing, leadership and spiritual growth. I was on a quest, preparing my own version of an MBA degree in life, business and the pursuit of my new self. I soon discovered that many of the books I read included a discussion about ethics. Each focused on conducting your business and your life within the framework of a defined and boldly-stated code of ethics.

Entrepreneurs begin their business plans with a mission statement. These mission statements spell out simply and eloquently how the owners of companies plan to conduct their businesses. Interestingly, each business includes, somewhere within their guidelines, a dramatic statement explaining their code of ethics—how to interact with their own personnel,

"Never esteem anything of advantage to thee that shall make thee break thy word or lose thy self-respect."

**Marcus Aurelius
Roman emperor**

> "The best and brightest, of course, realize that putting ethical behavior first often results in better business."
>
> Seth Godin
> author,
> *Wisdom, Inc.*

their clients, other businesses and the community in which they operate. Reading some of these statements from large companies like Ben & Jerry's, Boeing, Smith Barney and Kellogg's, I could begin to imagine how creating their mission statement became the backbone from which the company truly operated. There were also those companies which used their mission statement as a mere exercise, only paying lip service to lofty ideals. Their ethical standards of behavior were not reflected in their actions within the company or to the communities which they serve.

Although you may not have written a mission statement for your business, conducting your business with the highest standard of ethical behavior will add years to your career. This chapter addresses some of the more common questions that arise between artists and those with whom they conduct business.

Ethics

> "We wish to focus on the essence, which is to be forthright and clear in all dealings with our colleagues."
>
> NAPAMA
> *Guidelines for Ethical Behavior*

Without realizing it, most of us operate our businesses and live our lives within a code of ethics governing all that we do. It is no different in the performing business. As a business driven by the manner in which we relate to one another, actions rising from a known set of ethical behaviors seems right.

So much goes unsaid as we move quickly from one date to the next, one tour to the next. There is so little time to accomplish what tasks we have set for ourselves as it is. Taking a few moments to actually acknowledge how we intend to behave is certainly one thing we willingly leave for the next "to-do" list.

The challenge is not so much recognizing that we all want to be treated fairly and justly in the course of interacting, but to state openly what that means to each other and know it means the same thing to me as it does to you. The industry's standards of ethics have been outlined in the *Guidelines for Ethical Behavior* created by the members of the National Association of Performers, Managers and Agents (NAPAMA).

> "My code in life and conduct is simply this—work hard, play to the allowable limit, disregard equally the good and bad opinion of others, never do a friend a dirty trick, . . . never grow indignant over anything. Live the moment to the utmost of its possibilities . . . and be satisfied with life always, but never with oneself."
>
> George Jean Nathan
> author, editor, drama critic

While some of us operate to benefit all concerned, others do not. Recognizing that is half the battle. The remaining half is up to you—to conduct your day-to-day business affairs in a manner that is honest and above-board.

This ethics and attitudes discussion is framed with the artist/presenter business relationship in mind. There are a few topics which are important to address—especially when it comes to honesty and loyalty. These are fairly broad topics. I will break them down into very specific areas which will be of concern during your performing career.

Honesty

It is no surprise that most of us enjoy being dealt with in a truthful manner, no matter what the situation. In our everyday booking calls, it is even more important. Since we can only hope that anyone with whom we deal expresses themselves and their situation honestly to us, we can be sure that we are dealing honestly with them. In our efforts to check ourselves and uphold our part, we must consider each of the following situations carefully.

Have Clear Intentions

Know exactly what you need to achieve with each interaction before entering the situation. Maintain clear ideas of what you really need and for what you ultimately will settle. By knowing this, you can truthfully represent yourself to the other person, in this case, the presenter. When we are unsure of our own situation, our business dealings can become cloudy and that is when we begin fishing for answers and making up numbers. If you plan your budgets and prepare for each call to a presenter, you will be able to honestly represent yourself. The presenter will appreciate it and most likely answer in kind.

Uphold All Commitments

If you sign a contract, intend to keep it. Extenuating circumstances arise that may cause you to cancel a contract now and then. Make sure those circumstances have credibility. Developing a reputation for canceling without real cause is not one you want to foster. (Refer back to Chapter 7, Contracts, Force Majeure clause.) There are many situations that fit and here are a few.

Causes For Cancellation

A death in the family:
Unfortunately we all must experience this at some point. Presenters are most often understanding and will be helpful in rescheduling the performance. I have had to cancel three dates on the last weekend of a tour when my artist's father passed away. I phoned each presenter and offered to reschedule a date at their convenience. All but one presenter rescheduled and were completely understanding and sympathetic. The other presenter, new to the business, was totally unreasonable about the circumstance and thought they had spent more than enough money to advertise the date. They were unwilling to play the artist again. In that case, there is nothing that can be done to make them understand. Move on and wish them well. If there had been a deposit, we would have returned it.

Real illness (not the, "I just don't feel like going to Indiana tonight" illness):
Performers get sick just like everyone else. However, it inconveniences a lot of people when they do. Somehow, illness

> "High ethical standards—business or otherwise—are, above all, about treating people decently. To me that means respect for a person's opinions, privacy, background, dignity and natural desire to grow."
>
> **Tom Peters**
> author,
> *In Search of Excellence*

> "Cancellations. The manager-presenter relationship is a partnership in the service of a larger cause—the bond between artists and audiences. The contract is a crucial link in that chain. If it is broken, far more is lost than what can be entered on a balance sheet."
>
> **NAPAMA**
> *Guidelines for Ethical Behavior*

> **HotTip:** 🌶
> When it is necessary to cancel a performance, be honest with the promoter and attempt to reschedule the date at a convenient time for you both.

seems much more questionable to presenters when they have a house that is mostly sold out. Presenters tend to feel slighted and put out when an artist calls in sick. The presenter has already spent much of their budget to promote the date, that often cannot be recouped by rescheduling the date. In fact, more money needs to be spent to promote the date's cancellation and rescheduling. Some presenters will go as far as requiring a doctor's note. Therefore, use illness as an excuse only when it really is one.

Cancellation for career advancement:
This begins to walk a fine line. Most presenters have been in the business long enough to realize that artists are always looking for opportunities that will enhance their careers. They are most often understanding of these situations. I have included a clause in my contracts that allows a 30 day cancellation for such situations. Spelled out, they include special radio or television tapings or performances with main acts either in concert or in recording sessions. I also include a line stating, "or any other career-advancing situation." This gives the artist some leeway.

Where this phrase becomes questionable is if you interpret it to mean that you will accept a better offer from one presenter even though you have a signed contract for that date from another. Canceling one date to take another because it pays more or is a better performance situation needs to be handled by the artist and presenter in a direct and honest manner. Have an open discussion about the particular situation and come to some resolution that is satisfactory to the presenter. The relationship with the presenter may be as important to your career as this one date. You might sweeten the pot when you reschedule the date by offering the presenter a few extra percentage points for helping you out in this situation. Unfortunately, there are agents who make a practice of booking, contracting and cancelling gigs once they have a better one. However, cancelling once in a while for special circumstances is sometimes necessary. Just do not make a habit of it.

For example:
One example of an understandable situation is when a band has one booked date and then gets an opportunity to open an entire tour for a main act and the tour includes the aforementioned date. This happens often and most presenters know that it is the nature of the entertainment business. Chuck Wentworth had to deal with such a situation a few years ago while presenting the "Big Easy" Festival in Rhode Island. He had booked the Iguanas, a Cajun, Cunjunto, pop band from New Orleans to play the festival. Then the band was asked to be the support act for a Jimmy Buffet tour.

They called to get out of their festival contract. Understanding the boost that a tour like this could give to an artist's career, Wentworth rescheduled the band to play the RI Cajun & Bluegrass festival two months later when Jimmy Buffet was touring in the area.

Booking Multiple Dates In One City

It is important to understand the audience potential of each market you book. Some cities, such as New York, offer an artist numerous performance venues and the ability to, in some cases, perform a number of dates during a short time frame. If you are still performing in small clubs, this can be a terrific opportunity to really get your name around. Each club may cater to their own clientele giving the artist a new audience each night. For example, Calgary, Alberta, Canada has a number of acoustic performance clubs. You can play to three different audiences the same weekend. However, for a larger-name act, performing at Carnegie Hall or Town Hall would preclude you from performing in any other local venue. In this case, the promoter would most likely place a mileage restriction clause in their contract.

Most presenters book an act with the understanding that they are the exclusive presenter of the act in that city. The presenter plans their budget with this in mind. Discuss the possibility of performing in another venue within the city with your presenter to determine how it will impact on their date. Some may discourage you from doing so because they know there is not enough of an audience to support both dates. In other cities, a presenter may encourage you to get whatever other gigs you can, fully aware that the audience in their area can support multiple dates.

In most cases, you are booking your own act. Many agencies, though, book multiple acts who draw similar audiences. There are situations when an agent will book two or more of their acts into a city at different venues on the same night and never notify any of the other presenters that they have done so. In many instances, each date is impacted by the division of the audience. These situations may leave the presenters with an unfavorable opinion of the agent. You may find yourself on a roster of similar acts someday, so be considerate of the presenters with whom you work and how your agent's behavior impacts upon them and you. You do want to return!

Scheduling Promotional Performances

Many artists, along with their record companies, schedule short mini-concerts to promote new releases. Often these performances take place at local record stores, some of the chain bookstores like Borders Books and Music, Barnes & Noble and local coffee shops like Starbucks. The promotional

---

"A couple of years ago The Nashville Bluegrass Band had to cancel out of a bunch of festivals because they got the opening slot on a Lyle Lovett tour. If they were scheduled to play my festival I would have understood. Down the line, if they got more exposure playing for Lyle Lovett audiences and could win over some converts, then those people would come to my show next year because they heard of the band. Broadening the audience is always something you should look for."

Chuck Wentworth
former director
The Big Easy; RI Cajun &
Bluegrass Festival

"Depend not on fortune, but on conduct."

Publilius Syrus
1st century Roman writer

> **HotTip:** Make sure everyone on your team is aware of any promotional dates planned. Maximize the individual efforts of the promoter, the record label, the merchandiser and the publicist by keeping everyone informed.

aspect of these bookings means that they are performed in advance of a regularly-scheduled concert performance to boost ticket sales. If you schedule a free promotional teaser concert in the same town as the main concert, do it with the presenter's full knowledge and participation, and do it prior to the paid concert. If you are working with a presenter, the presenter must be made aware of every promotional effort undertaken by either the artist, the publicist or the record company. Leaving the presenter out of the loop is foolish. Adding the presenter's show to all promotions and ads placed by either the record company or the venue where the promotional teaser is taking place is the proper way to maximize all of your efforts.

Merchandisers who are more concerned with selling product and are newcomers to the presenting world, may not always think to include a local presenter in the promotions. They may also not be aware of how a preconcert teaser may or may not impact on the ticket sales. You should be! It is up to you to take the initiative and inform the merchandiser or the record company about how they must work with your local presenter. Remember, a teaser is just that, a short show of 20 to 30 minutes to entice ticket buyers to attend the real concert. The preshow (in-store, etc.) is not an hour concert or two 45-minute sets. The fact that these promotional gigs are free causes audiences to begin questioning whether they need to spend the money to see the act in concert when they go too long. It is to your advantage to uphold your position with the presenter in these cases. You will make more money and probably sell more product.

I am sure there are many other situations where honesty between artists and presenters can turn a questionable situation into a favorable one for both partners. Consider how what you do to build your career impacts upon those with whom you work. Look at the circumstance from both sides before charging ahead with a decision.

Loyalty

This is an area that touches many aspects of a performer's career. Loyalty to band members, managers, agents, record labels, office workers, etc. Loyalty to presenters justifies an in-depth discussion.

> *"Unless you can find some sort of loyalty, you cannot find unity and peace in your active living."*
>
> Josiah Royce
> American philosopher

Support The Presenters Who Supported You

Artists who are serious about building their careers, dream of the day when they can play a particular venue or type of venue. It might be Lincoln Center, The Universal Amphitheater, The Bottom Line or The Troubadour, or it might be any number of performing-arts centers across the country.

To get there, you must first build your career to have the audience that will follow you to these venues. To do so, you begin working with various presenters who have taken an interest in your act. These presenters, in many instances, get you started and give you your first gigs. Essentially, they make an investment in you. They start you with a small guarantee or maybe even just a percentage. You do well and they book you again with a larger guarantee and you bring in a larger audience. Next time around you sell out the house. Everyone is happy and has made money. The investment was well worth it.

Right Of First Refusal

Now, you are feeling good about your growth in that town and decide it is time to move up and play a larger hall. Whom do you call? You should call the presenter who has worked with you from the beginning and ask them if they would like to promote you in a larger hall. They may suggest doing two shows in the same hall first. This suggestion is probably a worthwhile one. If you can sell two shows, then you may have built an audience that could support going to a larger hall the next time.

Make a commitment to the original presenter that they will be the first one to have the opportunity to present you in the larger hall. This is called "right of first refusal." It means that you will offer the original presenter first crack at the next gig. If they refuse to do it, you are justified in finding another presenter to do the show. Demonstrate your loyalty to the presenter who first took a chance with you by offering them the opportunity to recoup on their investment. They deserve the chance. If they do not feel comfortable with the increased budgets or the size of the production or their ability to promote it properly, you gave them the opportunity. You might even consider inviting them to participate in some aspect of the production as a co-promoter so they can continue their association with your act, if it makes business sense to all involved.

The right of first refusal also comes into play when a new presenter offers more money or a larger venue. Go back to your original presenter and ask if they would like to match the offer. Keep in mind the benefits for which the original presenter was chosen—their ability to access your audience. Weigh that against the new presenter's offer and make a realistic decision about which promoter to use. Base your decision on all of the information available to you, not just a larger fee or hall.

The presenter who has helped an act develop their audience is familiar with what it takes to reach that audience. Do not throw that very important piece of your audience development away by jumping ship and working with a new promoter entirely. I have seen this happen too often. The artists, managers or record company believe that the artist has reached a point in their career where they can work with the major promoters in the larger venues. Guess what? Unless the act is

"Dance with the one you came with."

Anonymous

"The secret of a good life is to have the right loyalties and to hold them in the right scale of values."

Norman Thomas
founder of National Civil Liberties Union

"Try not to become a man of success but rather to become a man of value."

Albert Einstein
physicist

> "Not respecting a presenter's abilities and previous investment can have disastrous results for an act. Agents who are greedy when they should be savvy will feel the effects in their own pocket. I once promoted an English folk/rock band which sold 1,800 seats. The next year the agent sold the same show to a major rock promoter without contacting me. He didn't know how to reach a grassroots audience and they only sold 600 seats. I happened to run into the band that afternoon and they asked why I didn't promote the show. All I could answer was, 'I wasn't asked to.'"
>
> Kari Estrin
> former promoter,
> Black Sheep Concerts,
> booking and special events director,
> Caffe Milano

getting major radio airplay, the major promoters do not know how to promote the act. Some of the more creative grass-roots methods of promotion benefit a new artist's audience development in ways that are so subtle they are only realized once they are no longer employed. The large promoters use mainly multi-performer strip ads and some individual ads to reach a broad general audience. Often, these promoters have ongoing arrangements with certain venues within a city or region. Many of these venues may be inappropriate for your type of act. Know your audience, how to reach them and what venues they are most likely to frequent. These are important factors to consider when working with a promoter. Selecting a promoter who can enhance your career should be your paramount concern. Let the presenter who gave you the first boost ride along for a while until you can really make the leap to the next level.

Not only is it right to offer your original presenter the first opportunity to do your next show, it is a strategic move in sustaining your career development.

Attitude

I have presented a lot of shows and worked with many artists both as a presenter, a manager, an agent and a consultant. One thing that always impresses me about an artist, is their attitude. If they promote a positive attitude about their life and work, it affects everyone around them. If, on the contrary, they present a negative attitude and allow every minute detail to add to their depressed behavior, it also affects everyone with whom they come in contact.

This life of a performer is not an easy one. There are certainly stresses which can keep you occupied from early morning until late at night. But if you are committed to this work, then relish the prospects of dealing with all the different situations you encounter with an attitude that welcomes the challenges.

> "My definition of professional is "going beyond what it takes to get the job done." Send out a professional confirmation packet, be on time, deliver a good show, be good to your fans, and thank your clients. That's a lot more than some other artists deliver and you will be remembered for that."
>
> Dianne de Las Casas
> professional storyteller,
> director, Story Ballet Magic,
> president, ICAN - Independent Children's Artist Network

Situations Where Attitude Makes A Difference

Here are a few situations in which paying attention to your conduct will benefit your career.

Phone Conversations With Presenters

As I mentioned in Chapter Four, it is inappropriate to bring your personal problems into your phone conversations. Any problems that potentially impact your attitude towards the business will be reflected in how you deal with the presenter on the phone. This is not the time nor place to foist that chip on your shoulder onto the person at the other end. They are not responsible for former injustices you might have endured and certainly do not need to be treated rudely on the phone. Ultimately, presenters do not need to do business with you if it will be unpleasant.

Arriving At A Venue

Yes, there was traffic from one end of the city all the way to the venue and now you are running a little late. No one that you are about to meet at the venue is to blame. They did not put the traffic there just for you, so do not treat them like they did. If anything, they will be understanding and go out of their way to help you settle in to prepare for the show. If you enter each venue with the attitude that they are there to help you do your best to put on a great show, you are bound to be able to rise above any inconvenience.

Dealing With Technicians

This is a classic situation which would give anyone reason to quit. Most of the time the technicians with whom you will be dealing know their jobs and execute them impeccably. There are those times when you are bound to run across inept, incompetent, late or lazy technicians who could care less about you or your performance. But you still have a show to do. Hold firm to your pleasant demeanor and attempt to win them over. If all else fails, offer to set the board yourself during sound check. You know what it should sound like and you, or a band member, probably have worked with more sound boards than you care to remember.

Sometimes you may also run across a technician who arrives with their own bad attitude and nothing will shake them of it. You wonder what you could have done to make this person so nasty towards you. You probably did not do a thing and you most likely will go through the entire show not changing the way they act. Do your job and maintain your pleasant demeanor. It will be over soon.

Dealing With A Questionable Presenter

There will be occasions when you meet a presenter who is nonchalant about you and your presence in their venue. They have been difficult to deal with while setting up the date and they continue to demonstrate their lack of interest to your face. You are there for your audience. The presenter, in this case, is just a vehicle to help you reach your fans. You are there to give the best performance you can. Maintain your positive attitude toward the presenter and staff, and give the audience what they paid for. When it is time to leave, collect your money and, if the presenter is actually still at the venue, make sure to thank them for everything. Be positive every chance you get. If the show goes well and you sold a good portion of the house, you will get another gig there. Whether you choose to take it is up to you. You should be able to deliver a great show in spite of most external situations.

HotTip: Copping an attitude with the technicians will get you nothing but bad tech during the show.

"The faultfinder will find faults even in Paradise. Love your life."

Henry David Thoreau
American author

"When you work with these stagehands and venue personnel, like the woman who cooks the popcorn in front of the venue who's been there for 20 years and you're kind to all of those people, they really and truly remember you. They go out of their way to make your day at the venue much easier."

Mary Beth Aungier
tour manager,
Mary Chapin Carpenter

"Don't treat the soundman like he doesn't know what he is doing. We do everything we can to make you sound your best. Help us by knowing the language—the technical terms. Knowing the difference between delay and reverb and how to describe the sound that you are going for in terms of high end, low end, midrange, etc."

Marcus de Paula
former production manager
Caffe Milano

> "Rule #1—as a musician, you are in the business of service—you are selling yourself. Always be gracious, courteous, professional and respectful. Send thank-you notes and keep your moods in check. Everyone with whom you deal is your customer. And you want your customer to give you another booking, to return to see you in concert or to buy your next release. Leave any bad attitudes in a small box in your closet at home."
>
> Deborah Liv Johnson
> singer, songwriter,
> label owner,
> Mojave Sun Records

> "Garth has a wonderful knack of making you believe there is no one else in the world he would rather be singing to or talking with. When signing autographs, he never appears rushed or preoccupied, maintains eye contact and always asks fans' names—he's a pro. He also is concerned in concert to make sure even the folks in the "nosebleed" section are feeling special and enthralled with the show."
>
> Pam Lewis
> former co-manager,
> Garth Brooks,
> manager, publicist, PLA Media

Meeting With Fans Or The Presenter After The Show

You have worked hard for two hours presenting your show. You have had a long day getting to the venue and you did not sleep well the night before. If you think you absolutely cannot meet people after the show, inform the presenter or stage manager before the show and explain that you simply need to get some rest. Thank the important people necessary before the show so you can slip out after you have been paid and packed up so that they do not think you are ungrateful.

If it is not your habit to meet and greet after any show, then put it in your contract rider and have your agent or yourself make that clear before you arrive or before the show. The folks who work on presenting performances, especially volunteer organizations and nonprofit groups, do this work for the love of it. Their only reward is often getting to see some performers whose work they enjoy with the possible added bonus of having the chance to meet them. Most of us, after all, got involved with this business because we loved music, theater or dance, not because we were going to get rich quick. You do not have to party with the staff or even have coffee discussing the state of the world. You might just have to say "Hello, nice to meet you and thanks for all the work you have done. It was a great show." You ought to be able to muster a little gratitude for those who volunteered ushering, placed flyers for the last two weeks, sold ads for the program, decorated the stage or provided the food backstage with exactly the right stuff as outlined in your rider. Even those who got paid and worked for twelve hours making the stage just right deserve a little thank you. Forget how tired and worn out you are for just a moment. A little gratitude and graciousness can go a long way to insure your future. It may pay off with another invitation to play the venue again.

I know too many presenters who will absolutely never book some performers again because they were rude and ungrateful even though they sold lots of tickets. You can be sure the presenter will relay these situations back to the agency. So hedge your bets and be accommodating for another fifteen minutes or so. It will do your career more good than you can begin to imagine.

In Front Of Your Audience

This is the clincher. No audience wants to pay to see a performer who does not enjoy performing for them. If you have had it bad up until now, lock your attitude in your dressing room before setting foot on stage. This may not need saying, yet we have all been bombarded with a bad attitude from the stage from time to time. Even if you have a sense of where it could be coming from, it makes the audience uncomfortable and they do not deserve it. Do whatever it takes to lose the chip and put on a great show. Delay the show a few minutes if you are really down about something. Demonstrate your respect for other band members on stage, even when the band is falling apart. When you hit the stage, make it another world. If you truly cannot, reconsider performance as your career.

I have been very fortunate to have worked with some performers who take this situation very seriously. No matter what personal trials have happened moments before going on stage, they have been able to rise to the situation and honor their audience with a great show. If you have any doubts about how to treat an audience when upset, I hope you will follow their lead and be able to give your audience the respect they are due.

> **HotTip:** Always thank the presenter, the tech, and while on stage, put in a good word for the waitstaff and the food. This extra kindness is often greatly appreciated.

Conclusion

This entertainment business is a funny business. Artists plan to perform in front of strangers many months into the future never knowing what that day may hold for them or how they will feel. Artists allow perfect strangers to conduct business using their good names in an effort to promote a concert for them. In return, the artist hopes that person will be honest with them in their dealings.

Maintain the highest ethical standards for yourself and conduct your business by making every effort to uphold those standards throughout your career. In the long run, you will be the winner no matter what obstacles you encounter. You are building a career built on your reputation. You cannot afford to cut corners when it comes to ethical behavior or presenting a positive attitude. No matter how successful you are at doing most of the business necessary to build your career, your ethics and your attitude will be the two most memorable things about you.

Food For Thought
Your reputation arrives before you do, remains long after you are gone, and follows you wherever you go throughout your life.

For those of you wishing to learn more about NAPAMA or their Statement of Ethical Behavior, their information is listed in the resource section of this chapter.

> *"When fate hands us a lemon, let's try to make lemonade."*
> **Dale Carnegie**
> American author

> *"Always have a "Plan B" and be flexible enough to use it. The performance is the most important thing; therefore, all of the little things that can go wrong before or during the performance are incidental. Your professionalism and ability to adapt will follow you wherever you go."*
> **Johnette Downing,**
> children's musician

> *"I was moved by how well the band treated each and every person in the crew and entourage. . . . Sure it is business, but the Stones proved to me that no matter how big it gets, you can still make it fun."*
> **Dan Griffin**
> tour assistant,
> Rolling Stones,
> *Bridges To Babylon* tour

Summary
- Operate your business with a code of ethics that respects those with whom you do business.
- Strive to be honest in all of your dealings.
- Maintain a sense of loyalty to those who have supported your original efforts.
- Maintain a positive attitude that you present in all of your public dealings.

Resources

Books:

Aiming Higher: 25 Stories Of How Companies Prosper By Combining Sound Management & Social Vision
David Bollier
AMACOM
ISBN: 0814403190

*Ben & Jerry's The Inside Scoop:
How Two Guy Real Guys Built A Business With A Social Conscience And A Sense Of Humor*
Fred Lagoer, Jerry Greenfield
Crown Publishing
ISBN: 0517883708

Business Briefs: 165 Guiding Principles From The World's Sharpest Minds
Russell Wild, Russ Wild
Petersons Guides
ISBN: 1560795956

Character Is Destiny: The Value Of Personal Ethics In Everyday Life
Russell W. Gough
Prima Publishing
ISBN: 0761511636

Ethics For Everyone: How To Increase Your Moral Intelligence
Arthur Dobrin
John Wiley & Sons
ISBN: 047145953

Say It And Live It: The 50 Corporate Mission Statements That Hit The Mark
Patricia Jones and Larry Kahaner
Currency Doubleday
Bantam Doubleday Dell Publishing Group, Inc.
ISBN: 0385476302

Wisdom Inc.: 26 Business Virtues That Turn Ordinary People Into Extraordinary Leaders
Seth Godin
HarperBusiness
A Division of HarperCollins Publishers, Inc.
ISBN: 0887307582

A Passion For Excellence
Tom Peters and Nancy Austin
Warner Books
ISBN: 0446386391

Organizations:

The Music Managers Forum (MMF)
Barry Bergman
P.O. Box 444, Village Station
New York, NY 10014
Phone: 212-213-8787
Fax: 212-213-9797
Web: http://www.mmfus.com

MMFUK
1 York Street
London, W1U6PA
UK
Phone: 011 44 870 8507 800
Fax: 011 44 870 8507 801
Web: http://www.ukmmf.com

International Artist Managers Association
23 Garrick Street, Covent Garden
London WC2E9BN
UK
Phone: 011 44 20 7379 7336
Web: http://www.iamaworld.com

NAPAMA
459 Columbus Avenue, #133
New York, NY 10024
Phone/Fax: 1-888-745-8759
E-mail: info@napama.org
Web: http://www.napama.org

EPILOGUE

Be Creative In Both Business And Art

"Be brave enough to live life creatively. . . . What you'll discover will be wonderful. What you'll discover will be yourself."

Alan Alda
actor

They really are not separate, business and art, at least not from my perspective. You and I thrive on creativity in whatever form, found in whatever we are doing. There is an art to most things in life if you take a moment to notice. There is an art to the businesses we build and the careers we shape. When we add that flourish, that spark of creativity into our daily dealings, we breathe enthusiasm into everything we do. Taking care of business does not have to be drudgery when approached creatively. As a performing artist, incorporate your own sense of creativity into the business that you have designed.

Every aspect of your business has endless opportunities for you to apply your creativity. You can turn the mundane into inspiration. You now have the tools to accomplish your tasks and reach the goals that fuel your dreams. What remains is to take it one step at a time. Use the "big picture" to keep you steadily heading towards success. Yes, there is a lot of work ahead, but it is work of your own design for your own benefit. Any milestones achieved are yours to celebrate.

We have been on a journey. For my part, I have spent two years working on this book. I made my outline and

Remember to bring a creative touch to each:

Phone call made
Press release written
Promotional packet designed
Cover letter written
Contract negotiated
Brochure designed
Exhibit booth created
Conference attended
Showcase performed
Office designed
Date booked
Off-day scheduled
Promotional event planned
Interview given
Marketing campaign created
Tour market chosen
Strategic alliance sought
Problem faced
Challenge met
Goal pursued

designed a wall chart filled with unrealistic time lines, enthusiastic deadlines and notations of what my year was about to look like. The deadlines passed and more realistic ones were set. I discovered patience along the way and I was awakened to my own creative nature. I experienced writer's block, fear of criticism, fear that I would never finish, elation at the completion of each chapter and of collecting the final resources. Above all, this project gave me insight into what performers face every time they go on stage. The feeling of all the practice, all the planning and hard work coming together for the moment most relished—sharing their art.

As a creative individual, you have the opportunity to bring that light which sparks your art into your business and fashion the career you have dreamed about. Every day you are rehearsing for success. Just as you would rehearse a new song or a new dance prior to performing it, each goal you set, each call you make, each contract you issue prepares you for success. The more creative you are with every aspect of your career, the more your level of enthusiasm will grow. With a heightened enthusiasm, your work has greater potential to make you successful.

Practice the art of doing business and your business will allow you to practice your art.

Good Luck!
Jeri Goldstein

Resources

Books:

Aha! 10 Ways To Free Your Creative Spirit And Find Your Great Ideas
John E. Ayan
Crown Publishers
ISBN: 0517884003

Managing Creativity and Innovation
Harvard Business School Press
ISBN: 1591391121

Success Intelligence: How Practical and Creative Intelligence Determine Success In Life
Robert J. Sternberg
Plume
ISBN: 52279062

Thinkertoy (A Handbook of Business Creativity)
Michael Michalko
Ten Speed Press
ISBN: 0898154081

*The Little Book of Big Ideas:
Inspiration, Encouragement & Tips to stimulate Creativity and Improve Your Life*
Harold R. McAlindon, Michael Michalko
Cumberland House
ISBN: 1581820542

*The Art Of Possibility:
Transforming Professional and Personal Life*
Rosamund Stone Zander, Benjamin Zander
Penguin USA
ISBN: 0142001104

Appendix

Names are listed below with the individual's permission. Individuals whose comments appear throughout the book and are not listed here or in a resource section have requested that their contact information be omitted.

Agents:

George Balderose
Music Tree
1414 Pennsylvania Ave.
Pittsburgh, PA 15233
Phone: 412-323-2707
Fax: 412-323-1817
E-mail: tradfolk@music-tree.com

Linda Bolton
Northern Lights Management
437 Live Oak Loop NE
Albuquerque, NM 87122-1406
Phone: 505-856-7100
E-mail: nlightsmgt@aol.com
Web: http://www.northenlightsmgt.com

Robyn Boyd
3 Library Place
Chatham, NY 12037
Phone: 518-392-5372
Web: http://www.woodenshipproductions.com

Nancy Carlin
Nancy Carlin Associates
P.O. Box 6499
Concord, CA 94524
Phone: 925-686-5800
Fax: 925-680-2582
Web: http://www.nancycarlinassociates.com

Mike Drudge
Class Act Entertainment
PO Box 160236
Nashville, TN 37216
Phone: 615-262-6886
Fax: 615-262-6881
Email: mike@classactentertainment.com
Web: http://www.classactentertainment.com

Jim Fleming
Fleming & Associates
733-735 N. Main Street
Ann Arbor, MI 48104
Phone: 313-995-9066
Fax: 313-662-6502
E-mail: jim@flemingartists.com
Web: http://www.flemingartists.com/

Hiedi Fleming
Fleming Artists Management
Web: http://www.famgroup.ca

Chris Fletcher
Coast to Coast Music Booking
P.O. Box 5336
North Hollywood, CA 91616
Phone: 818-760-4176
E-mail: ccmusic@pacbell.net

Mitch Greenhill
Folklore Productions
1671 Appian Way
Santa Monica, CA 90401
Phone: 310-451-0767
Fax: 310-458-6005
Web: http://www.folkloreproductions.com

Bruce Houghton
Skyline Music
P.O. Box 31
Lancaster, NH 03584
Phone: 603-586-7171
Fax: 603-586-7068
E-mail: bruce@skylineonline.com
Web: http://www.skylineonline.com

Jeff Laramie
SRO Artists Inc.
Phone: 608-664-8160
Fax: 608-664-8161
Web: http://www.sroartists.com

Mark Lourie
Skyline Music
32 Clayton Street
Portland, ME 04103
Phone: 207-878-2330
Web: http://www.skylineonline.com

Steve Martin
The Agency Group
1775 Broadway, Suite 430
New York, NY 10019
Phone: 212-581-3100
Fax: 212-581-0015
Web: http://theagencygroup.com
New York, Toronto and London

Tam Martin
Beachfront Bookings/Productions
P.O. Box 13218
Portland, OR 97213-0218
Phone: 503-281-3874
Fax: 503-281-3881
E-mail: tammartin@aol.com

Joanne Murdock
Artists Of Note
P.O. Box 11
Kaneville, IL 60144-0011
Phone: 630-557-2742
Fax: 630-557-2753
Web: http://www.artistsofnote.com

Scott O'Malley
Scott O'Malley & Associates, LLC
P.O. Box 9188
Colorado Springs, CO 80932
Phone: 719-635-7776
Fax: 719-635-9789
Web: http://www.somagency.com

Ericka Wilcox
Berkshire Artists Group
Phone: 413-243-6662
E-mail: bershireartists@aol.com
Web: http://www.berkshireartists-group.com

Artists:

Terri Allard
Reckless Abandon Music
P.O. Box 373
Batesville, VA 22924
Phone: 434-823-7726
Web: http://www.terriallard.com

Candace Asher
Web: http://www.candaceasher.com

Kevin Asbjörnson
PianoOne, LLC
9693 Las Colinas Drive
Littleton, CO 880124-4201
Phone: 303-768-8712
E-mail: Kevin.Asbjornson@PianoOne.com
Web: http://www.PianoOne.com

Bridget Ball and Chris Shaw
Twining Tree
P.O. Box 609
Averill Park, NY 12018
Phone: 518-674-8282
Web: http://www.chrisandbridget.com

Geoff Bartley
Web: http://www.geoffbartley.com

Byron Berline
Double Stop Fiddle Shop
121 East Oklahoma Ave.
Guthrie, OK 73044
Web: http://www.doublestop.com

Lou & Peter Berryman
Box 3400
Madison, WI 53704
Phone: 608-257-7750
Web: http://www.louandpeter.com

Greg Brown
c/o Fleming & Assoc.

Ken Brown
P.O. Box 292
Fergus, Ontario N1M 2W8
Phone: 519-787-1524
Web: http://www.kbrown.ca

Paul Craft
Paul Craft Publishing
401 Bowling Dr.
Nashville, TN 37205
Phone: 615-292-9788
Fax: 615-269-9294

Dan Crary
Web: http://www.dancrary.com

Jennifer Cutting
Web: http://kinesiscd.com/jennifercutting/

Andy Deane
Web: http://www.bellamorte.com

Johnette Downing
Phone: 504-861-2682
Web: http://www.johnettedowning.com

Dianne de Las Casas
Web: http://www.storyconnections.com

Cathy Fink & Marcy Marxer
Community Music
PO Box 5778
Takoma Park, MD 20913
Phone: 301-891-1228
Web: http://www.CathyMarcy.com

Bob Franke
Telephone Pole Music
106 Winona St.
Peabody, MA 01960
Web: http://www.bobfranke.com

Judith-Kate Friedman
Web: http://www.judithkate.com

Steve Gillette & Cindy Mangsen
Compass Rose Music
P.O. Box 1501
Bennington, VT 05201
Phone: 802-442-6846
Web:
http://www.compassrosemusic.com

Lorin Grean
P.O. Box 908.
Santa Barbara, CA 93102
Web: http://silcon.com/~lgrean

Barbara Higbie
Web: http://www.barbarahigbie.com

Greg Howard
Web: http://www.greghoward.com

David Holt
P.O. Box 28
Fairview, NC 28730
Phone: 828-628-1728
Fax: 828-628-4435
Web: http://www.davidholt.com

Deborah Liv Johnson
Web:
http://www.deborahlivjohnson.com

Billy Jonas
Phone: 1-800-476-6240
E-mail: billy@billjonas.com
Web: http://www.billjonas.com

Lucy Kaplansky
Web: http://wwwlucykaplansky.com

Maura & Pete Kennedy
The Kennedys
P.O. Box 533
New York, NY 10276-0533
Phone: 1-800-864-3962
Web: http://www.KennedysMusic.com

Bernice Lewis
E-mail: blewis@williams.edu

Rob Lutes
Web: http://www.roblutes.com

Liz Masterson & Sean Blackburn
P.O. Box 12699
Denver, CO 80212
Phone: 303-433-4949
Fax: 303-433-4744
Web: http://www.lizmasterson.com

John McCutcheon
Appalseed Productions
P.O. Box 156
Charlottesville, VA 22902
Phone: 434-977-6321
Web: http://www.folkmusic.com

Andrew McKnight
Southern Exposure Management
P.O. Box 481
Aldie, VA 20105
Phone: 540-687-6759
Web:
http://www.shenandoahacoustics.com/andrew

Leslie Nuchow
Virginia Slam
Web:
http://members.tripod.com/slammusic/

Lowry Olafson
River Records
Box 1884
Gibsons Landing, BC V0N 1V0
Phone: 604-886-5844
Web: http://www.lowryolafson.com

RAVI
Ravi Enterprises
Phone: 1-888-439-7284
E-mail: ravienterprises@heyravi.com
Web: http://www.heyravi.com

Harvey Reid
E-mail: hreid@woodpecker.com
Web: http://www.woodpecker.com

David Roth
Maythelight Music
Web: http://www.davidrothmusic.com

Peggy Seeger
Web: http://www.pegseeger.com

Greg Trafidlo
Web: http://home.att.net/~kirasongs/

Sue Trainor
P.O. Box 412
Columbia, MD 21045
Phone: 410-381-2834
Web: http://www.hotsouptrio.com

Arts Councils:

Dee Hamilton
Louisiana Division of the Arts
PO Box 44247
Baton Rouge, LA 70810
Phone: 225-342-8180
Fax: 225-342-8173
E-mail: dhamilton@crt.state.la.us
Web: http://www.crt.louisiana.gov/arts

Teresa Hollingsworth
Southern Arts Federation
1800 Peachtree Street, NW, Suite 808
Atlanta, GA 30309
Phone: 404-874-7244
Fax: 404-873-2148
Web: http://www.southarts.org

Katie West
Director
Pennsylvania Performing Arts on Tour
230 South Broad St., Suite 1003
Philadelphia, PA 19102
Phone: 215/496-9424
Fax: 215-496-9585
Web:
http://www.pennpat.orgIndependent

Independent Radio Promoters:

Buzz Promotions
Julia Mucci
31-20 41st St.
Astoria, NY 11103
Phone: 718-721-3347
E-mail: juliebuz@aol.com
Promotes folk, acoustic, world music

Jacknife Enterprises
Jennifer Sperandeo
Phone: 512-416-0003
E-mail: jdiva@io.com
Promotes college, Americana

Matrix Promotions
Michael Moryc
217 Silo Court
Nashville, TN 37221-3544
Phone: 615-662-1413
Fax: 615-662-0512
E-mail: mmmatrix@delphia.com
Promotes Jazz, NAC/Smooth Jazz, New Age

MelFarina Media & Productions
Melissa Farina
P.O. Box 651
Crozet, VA 22932
Phone: 434-823-1240
Fax: 434-823-5832
E-mail: melfarina@aol.com
Promotes Americana, Country, Folk, A3

Peer Pressure Promotion
Roger Lifeset
30844 Mainmast Drive
Agora Hills, CA 91301
Phone: 818-991-7668
Fax: 818-991-7670
E-mail: pppromo@webtv.net
Promotes Jazz, NAC/Smooth Jazz, New Age

Songlines
Sean Coakley, Louise Coogan
Phone: 914-241-3669
Fax: 914-241-3601
E-mail: coogan@verizon.net
Promotes A3, Americana

Songlines
Leslie Rouffe
2007 21st Ave. South, #202
Nashville, TN 37212
Phone: 615-298-2262
E-Mail: lrouffe@comcast.net
Promotes A3, Americana

Legal Counsel:

Leslie Berman
628 Cleveland St.
Lake Charles, LA 70601
Phone: 337-436-5568
Web: http://www.leslieberman.com
Entertainment law, intellectual property law, and non-profit corporation law.
Licensed to practice in Louisiana, New York, New Jersey

Suzette T. Becker
Becker Entertainment Law
215 Decatur Street, Suite 300
New Orleans, LA 70130
Phone: 504-525-2552
E-mail: suzette@suzettetbecker.com

Charles Driebe, Jr.
Entertainment Law
E-mail: driebe@mindspring.com

Managers:

Tom Carrico
Studio One Artists
P.O. Box 11111
Takoma Park, MD 20913
Phone: 202-723-8855
Email: studiotc@aol.com

Kari Estrin Management
P.O. Box 60232
Nashville, TN 37206-2533
Phone: 615-262-0883
Fax: 615-262-9885
E-mail: kari@kariestrin.com
Web: http://www.kariestrin.com

Rosalie Goldstein
Goldstein & Assoc. Ltd.
307 Park Blvd.
Winnipeg, Manitoba R3P 0G8
Phone: 204-888-9470
Fax: 204-896-6033
E-mail: rocknros@total.net

Charlie Hunter
Young/Hunter Management
350 Massachussettes Avenue, #230
Arlington, MA 02174-6720
Phone: 781-643-2773
Fax: 781-643-0416
E-mail: info@younghunter.com
Web: http://www.younghunter.com

Ralph Jaccodine
Ralph Jaccodine Management
P.O. Box 381982
Cambridge, MA 02238
Phone: 781-647-5646
E-mail: RalphBkWf@aol.com

Mary McFaul
McFaul Booking & Management
P.O. Box 46318
Seattle, WA 98146
Phone: 206-938-5754
Fax: 206-938-1045
Web: http://www.mcfaullivemusic.com

Dick Renko
Muzik Management Productions
25904 Freedom Road
Chester, AR 72934-9119
Phone: 501-369-2221
Fax: 501-369-2221
E-mail: drenko@muzikmgt.com
Web: http://www.muzikmgt.com

Patty Romanoff
Bulletproof Artist Mgmt & Booking
Easthampton, MA 01027
Phone: 413-527-3395
Email: patty@bulletproofartists.com
Web: http://www.bulletproofartists.com

Denise Stiff
DS Management
2814 12th Street, South
Nashville, TN 37204

Presenters:

Spike Barkin
Festival, Special Event Poducer
47 Villard Avenue
Hasting-On-Hudson, NY 10706
Phone: 914-478-3860
Fax: 914-478-3860 *51

Dan DeWayne
Director—University Public Events
CSU Chico
400 W. 1st St.
Chico, CA 95929
Phone: 530-898-5917

Michael Jaworek
3701 Mt. Vernon Ave.
Alexandria, VA 22305
Phone: 703-549-7500, ext. 14
E-mail: michael@birchmere.com

Bob Jones
Festival Productions Newport Festivals
311 West 74th Street
New York, NY 10023
Phone: 212-496-9000
Fax: 212-877-9916
E-mail: robert.jones@fpiny.com

Fred Kaiser
Philadelphia Folk Festival
306 Summit Avenue
Fort Washington, PA 19034
Phone/Fax: 215-641-0497
E-mail: fkaiser@verizon.net
Web: http://www.folkfest.org

Phyllis Kurland
College Center
Nassua Community College
Garden City, NY 11530
Phone: 516-572-7153

Amy Kurland
The Bluebird Cafe
4104 Hillsborough Rd
Nashville, TN 37215
Phone: 615-383-1461
Web: http://www.bluebirdcafe.com

Mary Leb
Carnegie Hall, Inc.
105 Church Street
Lewisburg, WV 24901
Phone: 304-645-7917

Ginger Parker
Kirkland Art Center Coffeehouse
Route 12B, East Park Row
Clinton, NY 13323
Phone: 315-734-0276
E-mail: gingerkane@aol.com

Andy Spence
Old Songs, Inc.
P.O. Box 307 Wormer Road
Voorheesville, NY 12186
Phone: 518-765-4193

Chuck Wentworth
Cajun Music Ltd.
255 Holly Road
Wakefield, RI 02879
Phone: 401-783-3926

Publicists:

Cash Edwards
Under The Hat Productions
1121-B Bluebonnet Lane
Austin, TX 78704
Phone: 512-447-0544
E-mail: CashEdwards@austin.rr.com

Lance Cowan
LC Media
P.O. Box 965
Antioch, TN 37011
Phone: 615-331-1710
Fax: 615-331-5547
E-mail: lcmedia@sprynet.com

Richard Flohill
Richard Flohil & Associates
60 McGill Street
Toronto, Ontario M5B 1H2
Phone: 416-977-4788
Fax: 416-351-1095
E-mail: rflohil@sympatico.com
Promotes Canadian clients internationally: music.

Ellen Giurleo
Full House Promotions
P.O. Box 34883
Los Angeles, CA 90034
Phone: 310-837-7513
E-mail: fhpromo@adelphia.net
Promotes regionally and some national: music, clubs, festivals

Pam Lewis
PLA Media
1303 16th Avenue South
Nashville, TN 37212
Phone: 615-327-0100
Fax: 615-320-1061
Web: http://www.plamedia.com
International promotions: artists, books, events

Jill McGuckin
McGuckin Entertainment Group
500 E. Riverside Drive, #160
Austin, TX 78704
Phone: 512-217-9404
Fax: 512-707-1439
E-mail: megjill@aol.com
Promotes nationally and regionally: music, books, festivals

Mark Pucci Media
5000 Oak Bluff Court
Atlanta, GA 30350
Phone: 770-804-9555
Web: http://www.marcpuccimedia.com
National publicity for roots music, alternative country, country, blues, jazz; independent and major labels

Ginny Sea
Mixed Media
P.O. Box 20568
Cranston, RI 02920
Phone: 401-942-8025
Fax: 401-942-5487
E-mail: Ginny@mixedmediapromo.com
National music industry consulting — artist/project shopping service, radio promotions, publicity urban, jazz, hip-hop, folk, Americana

Lisa Shively
The Press Network—Main Office
P.O. Box 176
Pleasant Shade, TN 37145
Phone: 615-677-6645
Fax: 615-677-6644
E-mail: lisa@pressnetwork.net
Web: http://www.pressnetwork.com
Publicity and marketing music for independent and major labels, individual projects

Tracy Mann Hill
The Press Network—New York Office
94 North Main Street, Room 4
Nyak, NY 10960
Phone: 914-348-0472
Fax: 914-348-0571
Web: http://www.pressnetwork.com

Natasia Emery
UpBeat Entertainment
1233 West 11th Avenue, Suite 204
Vancouver, BC V6H 1K6
Phone: 614-732-8153
E-mail: upbeat@io.org
E-mail: globalseme.net
Provides music management services including publicity, radio promotion, grant writing for folk, blues, world and roots music.

Carla Sacks
Sacks & Co.
46 West 83rd Street
New York, NY 10024
Phone: 212-362-1800
Fax: 212-724-1989
Promotes music nationally, works with independent and major labels.

Mailing Service:

Heyman Mailing Service Inc.
5609 Fishers Lane #3B
Rockville, MD 20852
301-881-4685
E-mail: victor@heymanmail.com
Web: http://www.heymanmail.com

Print Media:

Scott Alarik
The Boston Globe
183 Third Street, #5
Cambridge, MA 02141
Phone: 617-661-4708

Jack Bernhardt
4809 Pleasant Green Road
Durham, NC 27705
E-mail: jbernhardt@mindspring.com

Geoffrey Himes
The Washington Post
New Country, Request
8 East 39th Street
Baltimore, MD 21218-1801
Phone: 410-235-6627

Richard Harrington
Pop Music Editor
The Washington Post/The Style
1150 15th Street, NW
Washington, DC 20071
Phone: 202-334-7540
Fax: 202-334-5587

Larry Kelp
E-mail: lkelp@aol.com

Chris Lunn
Festivals Directory
P.O. Box 7515
Bonney Lake, WA 98390
Phone: 253-863-6617
Fax: 253-862-8668
E-mail: festivalsnw@wolfenet.com

Philip Van Vleck
Music Editor
Herald Sun
Durham, NC
E-mail: vanvleck@nc.rr.com
Web: http://www.herald-sun.com

Radio:

Nick Forster
E-Town Productions
P O Box 954
Boulder, CO 80306
Phone: 303-443-8696
Web: http://www.etown.org

Andy Ridenour
Mountain Stage
West Virginia Public Radio
600 Capital Street
Charleston, WV 25305
Phone: 304-558-3000
E-mail: aridenour@wvpubcast.org

Phil Shapiro
WVBR-FM
979 Harford Rd.
Dryden, NY 13053
Phone: 607-844-4535

Rich Warren
The Midnight Special
WFMT Radio
5400 North St. Louis Avenue
Chicago, IL 60625
E-mail: music@midnightspecial.org

Record Labels:

Will Ackerman
Imaginary Road Studios
Phone: 802-257-7007
E-mail: will@williamackerman.com
Web: http://www.williamackerman.com

Charlie Dehan
Oneonta State College
Phone: 607-436-2216
Web: http://www.larchmontrecordings.com

Scot Fisher
President
Righteous Babe Records
P.O. Box 95, Elliott Station
Buffalo, NY 14205
Phone: 1-800-On-Her-Own

David Hazan
Sr. V.P. Marketing
Putumayo World Music
Web: http://www.putumayo.com

Ken Irwin
Rounder Records
One Camp Street
Campbridge, MA 02140
Phone: 617-354-0700
Fax: 617-354-4840
E-mail: keni@rounder.com

Alisse Kingsley
Director of Publicity
Warner Brothers Records
3300 Warner Blvd.
Burbank, CA 91505-4694

Barry Poss
Sugar Hill Records
P.O. Box 55300
Durham, NC 27717-5300
Phone: 919-489-4349
Fax: 919-489-6080
Web: http://www.sugarhillrecords.com

Steve Szymanski
Planet Bluegrass
P.O. Box 769
Lyons, CO 80540
Phone: 1-800-624-2422
Web: http://www.planetbluegrass.com

Road Managers:

Richard Battaglia
Chard Stuff, Inc.
P.O. Box 210383
Nashville, TN 37221

Patty Romanoff
Bulletproof Artist Mgmt & Booking
E-mail: patty@bulletproofartists.com
Web: http://bulletproofartists.com

Geoffrey P. Trump
Strangely Brown, Inc.
Phone: 434-823-5100
Fax: 434-823-5500

Services:

Shawn Fields
Getsigned.com
Web: http://www.getsigned.com
Career assistance website

Panos Panay
Sonicbids
580 Harrison avenue, Fourth Floor
Boston, MA 02118
Phone: 617-275-7222
Web: http://www.sonicbids.com
Electronic Press Kit development

Corina Ribidoux
Supervisor, Artist Immigration
AFM Canada
E-mail: Corina@afm.org
Visa specialist for AFM members touring U.S.

Debra Russell
Certified Life Coach
Web: http://www.artists-edge.com

John Stiernberg
Stiernberg Consulting
15468 La Maida Street
Sherman Oaks, CA 91403
Phone: 818-784-8618
Web: http://www.stiernberg.com
business consultant

Margreta H. Swanson
Financial Advisor
Securities America
Phone: 434-979-4822
E-mail: info@mhswanson.com

Index

AAA membership, 278
Accounting software, 43
Adjusted gross income, 42
Advertising
 agents, 427
 conferences, professional, 298
 hiring help, 438
 Internet, 394
 marketing campaign, 330
Agents, working with
 commissions, negotiating, 426
 co-ops, 440
 courting stage, 415-417, 429-431
 definition of an agent, 413-414
 directories, 433-434
 exclusivity, 424
 expenses, 426-427
 experience vs. inexperience, 419-420
 goals and expectations, 414-415
 investment, agent's, 427
 listing of agents, 480
 managers contrasted with agents, 417-419
 reputation of agent, 423-424
 requirements, agent's, 428-429
 resources, informational, 433-434
 responsibilities of agents, 424-426
 summary, 431-432
 See also Assessing current career situation
Airline prices/restrictions, 274-275
Alternative performance markets
 examine your alternatives, 223-224
 marketing to a niche, 221-223
 target market suggestions, 220-221
 venues, new performance, 224-225
 what is right for you, 218-220
American Federation of Musicians of the United States and Canada (AFM), 138, 156, 236, 244, 247
American Federation of Television and Radio Artists (AFTRA), 138, 157
Americana charts, 365, 366
Americans for the Arts, 308
Anti-terrorism laws, 276
Application process for receiving grants, 310-312
Arbitration, 158-159
Artists, listing of, 480-481
Arts agency directory, state, 324-327
Arts and alternative papers, 351-352
Arts organizations, regional, 323
Arts-related businesses, 437
Assessing current career situation, 15
 forms, 27-28
 goals and assessment list, comparing, 17
 necessities, determining your, 16
 organization and stocking up, 19-26
 planning tools, 18-19
 resources, informational, 29-30
 skills *vs.* time *vs.* cost assessment, 16-17
 summary, 26
 workspace/creative space, 17-18
 See also Day job, when to quit your
Assistant's tasks, 436
Association for the Promotion of Campus Activities (APCA), 288, 290-291
Association of Performing Arts Presenters (APAP), 210, 286, 287
Attitude
 audience, in front of your, 474-475
 fans or presenter after the show, 474
 phone conversations with presenters, 472
 questionable presenters, 473
 resources, informational, 476
 summary, 475
 technicians, dealing with, 473
 venue, arriving at a, 473
Attorneys, 147, 482
Audience, attitude in front of your, 474-475
Audience development, 194-195
Audio duplication companies, 88
Automobiles, 255-257, 278-280

Back door method for reaching booking person, 56
Backgrounds in a promotional photo, 68
Banking, 250-251
Battle of the bands, 204
Bela Fleck & The Flecktones, 259
Bible, The, 8
Billboard, 347, 348, 365, 367
Biography in promotions, 63-64
Block booking, 206, 207
Bluegrass Unlimited, 366
Blue-line proofs, 83
Bonding agents, commercial, 248
Booking software programs, 22-23
Book store chains, 209-210, 227
Borders. *See* Canada and U.S., crossing border between
Bottom line, know your, 113-115
Breach of contract, 157-159
Break-even point, 120
Brochure form for promotions, 76-77
Budgets
 creating, 113-114, 122-123
 riders, contract, 149-153, 165-166
 terminology, 119-120
Bulletin boards, 394
Business skills. *See* Assessing current career situation
Business strategies
 consultants, 34-35
 entities, five types of business, 33-34
 groups, performing, 32-33
 income to be reported, 42
 plan, creating a business, 35-36
 resources, informational, 43-45
 retirement plans, 39-41
 solo and duo performers, 32
 structure, clarify your, 31-32
 summary, 42
 taxes, 37-39

Cable modem, 23, 390
Cable television, 381-383
Calculators, 116
Calendar, one/two or three-year, 19
California (group), 258-259
Call forwarding, 55
Call waiting, 54
Campus activities office, 211
Canada and U.S., crossing border between, 235
 Canadian artists touring the U.S., 244-246
 immigration regulations, 236-237
 resources, informational, 247-248
 summary, 246
 U.S. artists touring Canada, 238-244
Canadian Arts Presenting Association, 210
Canadian Embassies in the U.S., 243-244, 247-248
Canadian provincial arts councils, 313-314, 327-328
Cancellation, causes for, 467-469
Cancellation clause in complex performance contract, 146
Cards, business, 74-75
Caregiver niche, 219-220
Cars, 255-257, 278-280
Cash, accepting, 261
CATS, 259-260
C corporation, 34
Cellular phones, 24
Chamber Music America, 430, 433
Chain stores and national tours, 209-210, 227
Chieftains, 225-226
Clubs, 201
Coal Miner's Daughter, 420
Co-bills, 215-216
Cold calls, 47-51
College
 interns, 437
 market, 210-212
 radio, 368-370

College Media Journal (CMJ), 365
Commercial bonding agents, 248
Commissions, negotiating agent's, 426
Commitments, upholding, 467
Community radio, 373-374
Competitions, 204-205
Complete Idiot's Guide To Winning Through Negotiating (Ilich), 108
Computers and supplies, 21-23
Concession sponsorship, 319-320
Conferences, professional
 advertising, 298
 agent's investment, 427
 exhibiting, 293-296
 expanding your markets, 286-287
 expenses, 426
 item inserts, 299
 membership-driven organizational, 287-288, 301-303
 memberships, 288-289
 networking at industry events, 296-298
 non-membership-driven, 288, 303-305
 regional events, 288
 resources, informational, 301-305
 showcasing, 289-292
 speaker or panelist, 299
 sponsorships, 298-299
 summary, 299-300
 touring, the art of, 188
 variety of, 285-286
Confirmation
 deadlines for, setting, 199
 hotel, 281
 letter of, 133-135, 164
Consignments, 189
Consultants, business, 34-35
Contact manager software programs, 21-22
Contests, 204, 227-228
Contracts
 beginning, when you are just, 137
 changing, 129
 complex performance, 137-138, 141-147
 confirmation, letter of, 133-135
 details, spell out the, 127
 forms, 160-182
 individualized, 127
 information form, 135-137
 intent, letter of, 131-133
 offer sheet, 120, 131, 162
 questionable items, 129
 read all contracts carefully, 128-129
 resources, informational, 182-183
 riders, 148-156
 simple documents, creating, 127-128
 simple performance, 137, 139-140
 summary, 159
 they issue, when, 128
 three items included in all, 126-127
 track of, keeping, 130
 types of agreements, 131
 union, 156-157
 write it down for clarity, 125-126
Cooperative memberships, 190
Co-ops, 439-440
Copyrights, 70-71
Copy writers, working with, 81
Cost assessment, skills vs. time vs., 16-17
Cover letter in promotions, 76
Creativity
 booking person, attempts to reach the, 55-57
 endless opportunities to apply, 477-479
 surroundings, comfortable, 17-18
 tour planning, 187-190
Credit cards, 277, 280
Criteria in negotiations, establishing, 95, 96
Crossroads, 366
Custom and economy prints, 71-72
Customs stations *vs.* immigration, 241

Daily planning book, 18-19, 29
Dance Directory, 430, 434
Database programs, 22, 228

484   INDEX

Day job, when to quit your, 457
  evaluation, yearly, 458-460
  a personal story, 460-462
  resources, informational, 464
  reverting to part-time participation, 462
  summary, 462-463
  transitions, 462
  See also Assessing current career situation
Deals, negotiated
  guarantee plus bonus, 117
  guarantee plus percentage, 116-117
  guarantee vs. percentage, 117
  sample scenarios, 118-119
  straight guarantee, 116
  straight percentage, 115-116
Deductions, allowable, 37-39
Demo recording or video, 75-76
Deposits, 138
Discount airlines, 272
Discount hotels, 278, 282
Display manufacturers, 301
Disputes, 129, 147, 157-159
Dreams into reality, transitioning, 1
  dream list, 2-4
  goals, identifying long-term, 4-13
  resources, informational, 14
  summary, 10
Dress and focal point in a promotional photo, 69-70
Duo performers, business structure for, 32

Economy and custom prints, 71-72
Educational access, 377-378
Effective Executive, The (Drucker), 453
E-mail, 340, 391-393
Employment authorization/validation for Canada, 238-240
  See also Day job, when to quit your; Hiring help
E Myth, The (Gerber), 35
Encore card, 277
Engagement clause in complex performance contract, 144
Entities, five types of business, 33-34
Ethics
  honesty, 466-470
  loyalty, 470-472
  resources, informational, 476
  summary, 475
Evaluation, yearly, 458-460
Event sponsorship, 315
Everything's Negotiable When You Know How To Play the Game (Skopec & Kiely), 92, 110
Everything's Organized (Kanarek), 18
E-Volve-Or-Die, (Levy), 393
Exchange, tour, 216
Exchange links, 394
Exchange rates, 244, 248
Exclusive agreements, 424
Exhibiting at conferences, 293-296
Expenses, 119, 138, 426-427
Experts and negotiation process, 92

Facility directors, 210
Family and friends, 188, 189, 437
Fans, attitude towards, 474
Fax machines, 23
Federal Express, 21
Fees, 70-71, 102
Festivals, 202-203, 228-229
Fictitious name certificate, 33
File folder for promotions, 77-78
First encounters
  cold calls, 47-51
  creativity, 55-57
  familiar promoters, 51-52
  questions, art of asking, 47
  scripts, composing, 45-46
  summary, 57
  telephone techniques, 52-55
  two minutes to hook them, 46
  venue, knowing the, 46, 58
Flinch negotiating gambit, 111-112
Flyer slick, 73
Folder form for promotions, 77-78
Folk Alliance and Canadian Arts Presenting Association, 287

Follow-up, 51, 338, 343
Force majeure clause in complex performance contract, 146-147
Foundation centers and resource organizations, 315, 322
Four Bitchin' Babes Tour, 217
Framing in a promotional photo, 68
Frequent-flyer miles, 276-277
Full-time employment. *See* Day job, when to quit your
Funding sources, 307
  application process, 310-312
  Canada Council for the Arts, 313-314
  foundation centers and resource organizations, 315, 322
  grants, 308-310
  Meet the Composer, 314-315
  record company tour support, 320-321
  resources, informational, 322-328
  sponsorships, 315-320
  summary, 321
  Virginia Commission for the Arts, 312-313

Gambits, negotiating
  flinch, 111-112
  good-guy, bad guy, 112-113
  higher authority, 109-111
  splitting the difference, 111
Getting Past No (Ury), 100
Getting To Yes (Fisher & Ury), 93
Goals
  agents, working with, 414-415
  assessment list compared to, 17
  cold calls, 47-51
  decisions influenced by, 4-5
  five-year, 8, 12
  one-year, 9-10, 13
  photo, promotional, 67-68
  ten-year, 6-8, 11
  two-year, 8-9, 12
Gold's Gym, 190
Good-guy, bad guy negotiating gambit, 112-113
Government funding sources on the Internet, 322
Grants, 308-310
  See also Funding sources
Graphic artists, 79-81
Gross income, 42
Gross potential/revenues, 119
Groups, business structure for performing, 32-33
Guarantee plus bonus negotiated deal, 117
Guarantee plus/vs. percentage negotiated deal, 116-117
Guerrilla Marketing Online Weapons (Levinson & Rubin), 330, 394
Guerrilla Marketing Weapons (Levinson), 75
Guidelines for Ethical Behavior, 466

Hard split point, 120
Higher authority negotiating gambit, 109-111
Hiring help
  assistant's tasks, 436
  control, remain in, 435-436
  co-ops, 439-440
  qualities to look for when, 438-439
  resources, informational, 442
  summary, 440-441
  where to find help, 437-438
Hobbies, 189-190
Home base of support, 190-194, 320
Honesty, 466
  cancellation, causes for, 467-469
  commitments, 467
  intentions, clear, 467
  multiple dates in one city, 469
  promotional performances, scheduling, 469-470
Hospitality rider, 154, 155, 178-179
Hospitality sponsorship, 319-320
Hotels
  conferences, professional, 137-138
  managing the road, 280-281
  national tours aided by, 209-210
  sponsorship, indirect, 319

Hot tips
  agents, working with, 414, 431, 436
  alternative performance markets, 218, 219, 223, 224
  attitude, 473, 475
  biography in promotions, 64
  block booking, 207
  blue-line proofs, 83
  brochure form for promotions, 77
  calculators, 116
  Canada and U.S., crossing border between, 244
  cancellations, 468
  cash, accepting, 261
  conferences, professional, 292, 299, 300
  contracts, 131
  employment authorization/validation for Canada, 240
  exhibiting at conferences, 293-296
  expenses, 138
  fees, 102
  fictitious name certificate, 33
  flyer slick, 73
  follow-up, 51, 338
  goals, long-term, 5
  grants, 309-311
  hiring help, 439
  house concerts, 210
  information gathering in negotiations, 97
  intent, letter of, 132
  Internet, 392
  liquid assets, 41
  listening skills, 107
  mailing lists, 341
  managing the road, 252, 255, 259, 271
  marketing your act, 331, 336
  Mondays, 438
  multi-act shows, 216
  negotiations, 99, 103, 104, 108, 110, 112
  newspapers, 350
  opening acts, 213
  phone service, long-distance, 24, 25
  photographs, 78, 445
  Pollstar, 347
  posters, 74
  press kits, 62
  printers (companies), 82
  print media, 351, 355
  promotions, 52, 470
  radio, 366, 370, 404
  record company tour support, 321
  regional touring, 198, 199
  retirement plans, 39
  riders, contract, 154
  savings, 332
  showcasing, 427
  sponsorship, 316-319
  store visits, 405
  supplies, office, 20
  taxes, 37, 38, 42, 188, 251
  technical requirements, 145
  telephone techniques, 54, 55
  television, 76, 382-386
  travel savvy, 273, 274, 278-280
  truck stops, 257
  unions, 156
  venues, 144, 201
  wire services, 354
House concerts, 210
How to Make Money Performing In Schools (Heflick), 188
Human Resources Development Canada, 237

IEG Sponsorship Report and Directory, 318
IEG Sponsorship Sourcebook, 318
Illness, 265-267, 467-468
Immigration regulations between Canada/U.S., 236-237, 244, 245
  AFM, 244
  Citizenship Immigrations of Canada, 239
  P-2 application, 244
  United States Citizenship and Immigration Services, 236-237, 244
  work permits, 238, 239, 244
Income to be reported, 42
Indigo Girls, 257

Informal business contacts, 297-298
Information
    contract form, 135-137, 160-161
    negotiations and gathering, 95, 96-98
    promotions, sheet in, 64
    rider, form for contract, 154, 156, 180-181
    See also Resources, informational
In Search of Excellence (Peters), 467
Insert design strategies, 78-79
In-store promotions, 189, 404-405
Instrument insurance, 253-254, 282
Instruments, lost/stolen or broken, 262-264
Insurance and indemnity, 145-146, 253-254, 280, 282
Intent, letter of, 131-133, 163
Intentions, clear, 467
International Bluegrass Music Association (IBMA), 286, 287
International Events Group, Inc. (IEG), 318
Internet, 194
    DSL, 23, 390
    e-commerce, 394
    e-mail, 391-393
    electronic press kit, 346, 347, 351, 355, 391, 401, 441, 447, 449
    hooking up and logging on, 390
    magazines, 396
    management consultant, 488
    marketing books, 396
    marketing your website, 394-395
    modems, 390-391
    music sites, 396
    Prince, The Artist formerly known as, 389
    site marketing companies, 398
    software, 397-398
    summary, 395
    T1, 23, 390
    website design basics, 393-394
    website registration, 398
    See also Resources, informational
Interns, college, 437
Interviews
    art of interviewing, 341-343
    off-day scheduling, 189
    promotions, 65
    record label, working with your, 403-404
Item inserts, 299
Itinerary schedule, 403

Juried showcase, 290-291
Jurisdiction clause in complex performance contract, 147

Laundry on the road, 252
Lawyers, 147, 482
Legal resources, 147, 182-183, 482
Lilith Faire Tour, 217
Limited liability company (LLC), 33-34
Liquid assets, 41
Listening skills, 106-107
Litho quantity prints, 72
Litigation, 159
Location shoots in a promotional photo, 69
Logos, 74
Long-distance phone service, 24-26, 29
Loyalty, 470-472

Magazines, genre specific, 345-347, 356-360, 396
Mailbots, 392-393, 398
Mailing labels, 20
Mailing lists, 338-341
Mail order catalogs, 29-30
Makeup in a promotional photo, 72-73
Managers, working with
    agents contrasted with mangers, 417-419
    courting stage, 415-417
    definition of a manager, 413-414
    directories, 433
    experience *vs.* inexperience, 419-420
    goals and expectations, 414-415
    Internet, 488
    listing of managers, 482
    resources, informational, 433-434
    responsibilities of manager, 421-423

successful relationship, 420-421
    summary, 432
Managing the road
    car rentals, 278-280
    checklist, touring, 269-270
    hotels, 280-281
    life's details on the road, 250-254
    resources, informational, 282-283
    road manager's role, 249-250
    stories, road, 254-268
    summary, 281
    travel savvy, 271-278
    See also Touring, the art of
Managing Your Employees (Deems), 435
Marketing for Dummies (Hiam), 329
Marketing your act, 329
    alternative performance markets, 221-223
    follow-up, 338, 343
    Internet, 394-396
    interviews, 341-343
    mailing lists, 338-340
    plan, your marketing, 330-333
    publicist, working with a, 336-338
    publicist, you are your own, 333-335
    resources, informational, 344
    specialty stores, 408-409
    summary, 343
    touring, the art of, 225-226
    See also First encounters; Promotions
Masters of Bluegrass Tour, 225
Meals and hospitality, 138, 252
Media, dealing with the
    follow-up, 338
    a full time endeavor, 335
    off-day scheduling, 189
    publicist, working with a, 336-338
    publicist, you are your own, 333-335
    sponsorship, 319
    See also Print media; Radio; Television
Mediation, 159
Meet the Composer, 314-315
Merchandise, 144-145, 253, 282
MIDEM, 288
Modems, 23, 390-391
Mondays, 438
Money
    Canadian/U.S., 244
    cash, accepting, 261
    exchange rates, 244, 248
    expenses, 119, 138, 426-427
    fees, 70-71, 102
    liquid assets, 41
    negotiations, 99-102
    salaries, 260-262
    savings, 332
    who holds the, 251
    See also Taxes
Multiple-act tours and performances, 216-217
Multiple dates in one city, 469
Multiple performances in one venue, 188
Music & Entertainment Tours: How to Package Them for Sponsorship, 318
Musician's Guide to Outrageous Success, Making and Selling CDs and Cassettes (Stanfield), 222
Music sites on the Internet, 396
Music store chains, 209, 227
Music videos, 382

National Association of Campus Activities (NACA), 211, 287, 290
National Association of Music Merchants (NAMM), 316
National Association of Performers, Managers and Agents (NAPAMA), 466
National Endowment for the Arts (NEA), 308-309, 322
National Endowment for the Humanities (NEH), 308-309
Nationally-syndicated radio shows, 371-373
National Public Radio (NPR), 370-371
National tours, 206-210
Necessities, determining your, 16
Negotiating Game, The (Karrass), 95
Negotiations

assumptions, 106
bottom line, know your, 113-115
in your daily life, 91-92
deals, types of, 115-119
experts, 92
gambits, 109-113
listening skills, 106-107
main steps in, 95-99
no is just the beginning, 105
open-ended questions, 100-101
positive responses, questions resulting in, 101
pressure situations, 107-108
price issues, 99-102
relationships, building, 92-94
resources, informational, 124
set-aside technique, 108-109
summary, 120-121
terminology, basic budget, 119-120
trade, the, 109
value, establishing, 102-103
walk away power, 103-105
win-win negotiating, 94-95
writing, put it in, 103
Net potential/revenues, 119
Networking at industry events, 296-298
New Age Voice, 365
Newsgroups, 394
Newsletters, 353-354
Newspapers
    arts and alternative papers, 351-352
    directories, 360-361
    local daily, 349-351
    major market, 348-349
    underused resource, 194
Niche marketing. *See* Alternative performance markets
No as the beginning in negotiations, 105
North by Northeast (NXNE) Conference, 288, 291

Off-day scheduling, business/personal, 189-190
One-year plan, 443
    laying out your, 454, 455
    resources, informational, 456
    reviewing the, 453
    summary, 454
    target date format, 444-453
Open-ended questions, 47, 100-101
Opening acts, 212-213, 405
Open mic performance situations, 217-218
Organizational memberships, 278
Organization and stocking up
    computers and supplies, 21-23
    phones and supplies, 24-26
    shipping supplies, 19-21
    stationery and supplies, 23
Overage, 120
Overbooking, hotel, 281
Overhead, office, 427

Paid, not getting, 260-262
Panel presentations, 299
Partnership, general, 33
Percentage amount, 120
Per diems, 251-252
Performance contract, complex, 137-138, 141-147, 169-171
Performance contract, simple, 137, 139-140, 167-168
Performance magazine, 347, 348
Performing arts centers, 201-202
Performing Biz Seminar, 489
Personal needs, 189-190
Personnel problems, 264-265
Pets, traveling with, 276
Phones. *See* Telephones
Photo, promotional
    backgrounds, 68
    choosing a photo, 71
    custom and economy prints, 71-72
    digital, 72
    dress and focal point, 69-70
    fees and usage rights, 70-71
    framing, 68
    goals for the photograph, 67-68

location shoots, 69
makeup, 72-73
photographer, finding a, 67, 68
replacing photographs, 78
reproduction companies, 89, 445
retouching, 73, 89-90
storytelling, 68
time, 69
Pickup dates, 188
Plan, creating a business
benefits of, 35-36, 330, 333
checklist, pre-marketing, 331-332
tools for, 18-19
touring, 187-190
See also Business strategies; One-year plan; *various subject headings*
Pleasure, mixing business with, 188, 189-190
Pocket folder for promotions, 77-78
Pollstar, 347, 348
Ports of entry into Canada, 241, 242-243
Postage scale/meter, 20, 30
Posters, 73-74
Presenters, attitude towards, 472-474
Presenters, listing of, 483
Press releases, 62, 65-67, 85-87
Pressure in negotiations, 107-108
Preview articles, 65
Price and negotiation process, 99-102
Printers, computer, 23
Printing, promotional, 78, 82-83
Print media
arts and alternative papers, 351-352
listing of, 484
magazines, genre specific, 345-347, 356-360, 396
newsletters, 353-354
newspapers, major/local daily, 348-351
resources, informational, 356-362
summary, 354-355
trade papers and magazines, 232-233, 347-348, 361, 375
wire services, 353, 361-362
Promoter profit/fee, 120
Promotions
biography, 63-64
brochure, the, 76-77
cards, business, 74-75
conferences, professional, 298-299
copy writers, working with, 81
cover letter, 76
defining promotion, 330
demo recording or video, 75-76
electroinc press kit, 50, 51, 76, 80
flyer slick, 73
folder form for, 77-78
functions of, three main, 61-62
graphic artists, working with, 79-81
honesty, 469-470
information sheet, general, 64
insert design strategies, 78-79
logos, 74
mp3, 80
one sheet, 79
photographic experience, 67-73
posters, 73-74
press release, 65-67
printing, 78, 82-83
quote sheets, 64
radio, 406-408, 482
record label, working with your, 402
resources, informational, 88-89
reviews/interviews and preview articles, 64-65
sample publicity releases, 85-87
showcasing, 292
store visits, 189
summary, 84
television, 76
See also First encounters; Marketing your act
Public access television, 378-379
Publicists
listing of, 483-484
record companies, 401
working with, 336-338
you are your own publicist, 333-335

Public radio, 370-371
Public television, 379-381

Questionable items on a contract, 129
Questions, art of asking, 47, 101
Quote sheets, 64

Radio
Americana charts, 365, 366
charts, 364-366, 406
college, 368-370
commercial, 367-368
community, 373-374
directories, 360-361, 375-376
formats, 363-364
interviews, 404
listings, 484-485
local and regional, 373
mainstream, beyond, 366
nationally-syndicated, 371-373
non-commercial, 368
promotions, 406-408, 482
public, 370-371
reporting stations, 366
resources, informational, 375-376
summary, 374
Radio and Records, 347, 365, 367
Record company tour support, 320-321
Record label, working with your, 399
directories, 411-412
interviews, 403-404
itineraries, 403
listing of labels, 485
opening acts, 405
promotion department, 402
publicity department, 401
radio promotions/charts, 406-408
resources, informational, 411-413
sales department, 401-402
showcasing, 405
specialty stores, marketing to, 408-409
store visits, 404-405
summary, 410
team, working with a, 400-402
touring, 402-403
Refusal, right of first, 471-472
Regional touring, 195-200, 288
Relationship building and negotiation process, 92-94
Rentals, car, 278-280
Reporting stations, 366
Reproduction companies, 89, 445
Resolution stage in negotiation process, 95, 98-99
Resources, informational
agents and managers, 433-434
assessing current career situation, 29-30
attitude, 476
business strategies, 43-45
Canada and U.S., crossing border between, 247-248
conferences, professional, 301-305
contracts, 182-183
day job, when to quit your, 464
dreams, 14
ethics, 476
funding sources, 322-328
hiring help, 442
Internet, 396-398
managing the road, 282-283
marketing your act, 344
negotiations, 124
one-year plan, 456
print media, 356-362
promotions, 88-89
radio, 375-376
record label, working with your, 411-413
television, 388
touring, the art of, 227-233
underused, 194
Retirement plans, 39-41
Retouching photos, 73
Reviews, 64-65
Riders, contract
budgets, 149-153, 165-166
explaining, 148
forms, 172-179

hospitality, 154, 155
information form, 154, 156, 180-181
technical, 154
Right of first refusal, 471-472
Riverdance Tour, 225
Road manager, 249-250, 485
See also Managers, working with; Managing the road
Road stories, 254
car troubles, 255-257
illness, 265-267
instruments, lost/stolen or broken, 262-264
paid, not getting, 260-262
personnel problems, 264-265
travel problems, 257-260
venue and technical problems, 267-268

Salaries, 42, 260-262, 427
Sales department in record company, 401-402
Savings, 332
School assembly programs, 188
S corporation, 34
Scripts, composing, 45-46
Secrets of Power Negotiating: You Can Get Anything You Want (Dawson), 91
Security. *See* Day job, when to quit your
Service Corps of Retired Executives (SCORE), 35, 438
Set-aside technique in negotiation process, 108-109
Sharing stage with other artists
co-bills, 215-216
exchange, tour, 216
multiple-act tours and performances, 216-217
opening acts, 212-213
open mics, 217-218
support act, 213-215
Shipping expenses/supplies/carriers, 19-21, 30, 426
Showcasing, 205, 230-231, 289-292, 405, 427
Sightseeing, 189
Skills *vs.* time *vs.* cost assessment, 16-17
Slides for demo, color, 72
Small Business Administration (SBA), 35
Small claims court, 158
Small-Time Operator (Kamaroff), 34
Software programs, 21-23, 30, 43-44, 397-398
Sole proprietorship, 33
Solo performers, business structures for, 32
South by Southwest (SXSW) Conference, 288, 291
Specialty stores, marketing to, 408-409
Split point, 120
Splitting the difference negotiating gambit, 111
Sponsorships
conferences, professional, 298-299
contacting sponsors, 318-319
direct, 315
how to find sponsors, 316-317
indirect, 319-320
local, 320
proposal, preparing a, 317-318
Stability. *See* Day job, when to quit your
State arts agency directory, 324-327
Stationery and supplies, 23
Stocking up tips, 26
See also Organization and stocking up
Store visits, 189, 227, 404-405
Storytelling in a promotional photo, 68
Straight guarantee/percentage negotiated deal, 115-116
Structure in which you operate your business, 31-32
Successful Time Management (Ferner), 453
Supplies, office. *See* Organization and stocking up
Support, home base of, 190-194, 320
Support act, 213-215

Target date format, 444-453
Target market suggestions, 220-221

INDEX 487

Taxes
  deductions, allowable, 37-39
  income to be reported, 42
  salaries vs. per diems, 251
  state, 145
  touring, 188
Technical problems, 267-268
Technical requirements clause in complex performance contract, 145
Technical rider, 154, 175-177
Technicians, dealing with, 473
Techniques of Effective Telephone Communication (Lovgren), 46
Telephones, 30
  agent's investment, 427
  attitude with presenters, 472
  expenses, 426
  hotel, 281
  long distance service, 24-26, 29
  off-day scheduling, 189
  techniques when using, 52-55
Television
  cable, 381-383
  contests, 385
  directories, 360-361
  educational access, 377-378
  listing of programmers, 388
  local network affiliates, 383-385
  national networks, 385-387
  promotions, 76
  public, 379-381
  public access, 378-379
  resources, informational, 388
  summary, 387
Temporary employment services, 438
10,000 Maniacs, 255-256
Terminology, basic budget, 119-120
Terrorism, laws against, 42
3 Mustaphas 3, 261-262
Tickets, 144, 275-276
Time issues
  mailings, 340
  negotiations, 107-108
  photos, promotional, 69
  skills and cost assessment vs., 16-17
  venue-booking, 199-200
Time Management for Dummies (Mayer), 19, 21, 23, 453
Tips. *See* Hot tips
Touring, the art of, 185
  alternative performance markets, 218-225
  audience development, 194-195
  block booking, 206
  books, tour, 252-253
  college market, 210-212
  directories, 231-232
  home base of support, 190-194
  house concerts, 210
  market your act for success, 225-226
  national tours, 206-210
  planning, creative, 187-190
  reasons for touring, 186-187
  record label, working with your, 402-403
  regional touring, 195-200
  resources, informational, 227-233
  sharing the stage, 212-218
  sponsorship, 315
  summary, 226
  venue types, 199-205
  See also Managing the road
Tracking contracts, 130, 182
Trade papers and magazines, 232-233, 347-348, 361, 375
Trade technique in negotiation process, 109
TRANSMEDIA, 277
Travelers Advantage, 277-278
Travel savvy
  agents, travel, 271-274, 283
  discount travel programs, 277-278
  expenses, 138, 427
  frequent-flyer miles, 276-277
  illegal ticketing, 275-276
  information you must know, 274-275
  pets, 276
  problems, 257-260
  websites, 283

See also Managers, working with; Touring, the art of
Truck stops, 257

Unions, 156-157, 183
University graduate business programs, 35
University graduate special interest groups, 35
UPS account, 20-21

Vacation while touring, 190
Value, establishing, 102-103
Venues
  alternative performance markets, 224-225
  attitude when arriving at, 473
  battle of the bands, 204
  chain store, 227
  clubs, 201
  competitions, 204-205
  contests, 204
  festivals, 202-203
  Internet, 228-229
  knowing the, 46, 58, 144
  listing of, 229-230
  multiple performance in one venue, 188
  performing arts center, 201-202
  problems, 267-268
  seasons, presenting, 200
  showcase clubs, 205
  time frames for different, 199-200
Video formats, 76, 382-386
  See also Television

Walk away power in negotiation process, 103-105
Warehouse club stores, 30
Websites, 393-395
  See also Internet; Resources, informational
Winter's Night Tour, 217
Winter Solstice Tours, 217
Win-win negotiating, 94-95
Win-Win Negotiating (Jandt), 94
Wire services, 353, 354, 361-362
Workshops, 300
Workspace, 17-18
Writing, putting negotiations/contracts in, 103, 125-126

Yearly planner, 18
YMCA and YWCA, 190

Index of Authors

Ackerman, Will, 400, 410, 458
Addison, Joseph, 195
Alarik, Scott, 345, 349
Alda, Alan, 477
Allard, Terri, 195, 196, 437
Allen, Fred, 460
Anderson, Muriel, 189
Armstrong, Louis, 463
Arnett, Ramona E. F., 33
Asbjörnson, Kevin, 219
Asher, Candace, 221
August, Rick, 126
Aungier, Mary B., 249, 264, 268, 473
Aurelius, Marcus, 465
Ausonius, 9

Bacon, Francis, 113
Baggett, Peggy, 307, 309
Balderose, George, 238, 244
Ball, Bridget, 195, 339
Barkin, Coleman "Spike," 53, 65, 200
Barney, Phyllis, 285
Bartley, Geoff, 189, 439
Barton, Bruce, 463
Battaglia, Richard, 252, 256, 259
Beck, Stevie, 63, 93
Becker, Suzette, T., 131
Benn, Anthony W., 377
Bennett, Arnold, 454
Bennis, Warren, 441
Berline, Byron, 257, 259, 275
Berman, Leslie, 158
Bernhardt, Jack, 342, 352
Berryman, Lou, 127,
Blackburn, Sean, 186, 189

Blackman, Bob, 368
Boehm, Mike, 64, 191, 349
Bolton, Linda, 311
Boyd, Robyn, 237
Braunfeld, Andrew L., 128, 157
Britton, Charlotte, 286
Brown, Alison, 404
Brown, Greg, 191, 255, 313, 426, 462
Brown, Ken, 32, 235, 241
Browning, Robert, 9
Burnham, Daniel H., 6

Cager, Eric, 286
Capshaw, Coran, 193, 403
Carlin, Nancy, 63, 243, 310
Carnegie, Dale, 475
Carpenter, Mary C., 267-268
Carrico, Tom, 416
Carson, Johnny, 460
Carswell, Ron, 35
Carter, Rosalyn, 9
Casey, Caroline W., 1
Casey, Susan, 126
Chauncey, Tom, 213, 424
Chopra, Deepak, 15, 45
Christina (Queen of Sweden), 15
Clark, Michele, 407
Cohen, Ben, 33, 462
Cohen, Herb, 106
Cohen, Jeff, 204
Condon, John, 393, 399, 402, 409
Coolidge, Calvin, 56
Cougan, Louise, 365
Craft, Paul, 261
Crary, Dan, 101, 216
Cristall, Gary, 313
Cutting, Jennifer, 71

Dahan, Charlie, 100, 102, 196, 197
Daniels, Chris, 47, 198, 209
Davis, Sharon, 424
Dawson, Roger, 91, 92
Deane, Andy, 191, 196, 209, 320
Deems, Richard S., 435
Deiter, Paul, 251, 253
de Las Casas, 71, 97, 331, 392, 435, 472
De Mille, Cecil B., 4
Dent, I. B., 149, 210, 297, 307, 312
de Paula, Marcus, 473
DeRogatis, Jim, 75, 346, 347
Devlin, Bernadette, 458
DeWayne, Dan, 202, 290
DiFranco, Ani, 268
Disraeli, Benjamin, 128, 194
Downing, Johnette, 475
Driebe, Charles, Jr., 127, 421
Drucker, Peter F., 445
Drudge, Mike, 49, 103, 423

Ecclesiasticus, 423
Edwards, Cash, 127
Einstein, Albert, 41, 471
Elliott, Peter, 410
Epictetus, 2
Epstein, Freyda, 6, 292
Estrin, Kari, 135, 207, 254, 262, 266, 281, 407, 460, 472

Fields, Shawn, 389
Fink, Cathy, 19, 105, 114, 187, 435, 438
Fisher, Roger, 93
Fisher, Scot, 193, 268, 329, 422, 426, 428, 437, 459, 461
Fleming, Heidi, 241, 244, 314
Fleming, Jim, 94, 103, 105, 107, 125, 415, 419, 427
Fletcher, Chris, 211, 296, 431
Flohil, Richard, 200, 202, 335, 338, 345
Foraker, Joni, 418
Ford, Henry, 454
Forster, Nick, 5, 373, 459
Foust, Mark, 379
Franke, Bob, 48, 208, 250
Franklin, Benjamin, 20, 36, 40
Friedman, Judith-Kate, 99, 185, 263
Frost, David, 457

Gee, Vickie, 273, 276
George, David L., 462
Gerber, Michael E., 35
Gibson, Sandra, 286
Gillette, Steve, 199
Giovanni, Nikki, 2
Giurleo, Ellen, 333, 337
Givens, Charles J., 6
Godin, Seth, 466
Goethe, Johann Wolfang von, 3
Goldfarb, Sandy, 272, 334
Goldstein, Rosalie, 203, 236, 240, 314, 422
Goodman, Joel, 222
Gorin, Nina, 274
Grean, Lorin, 287, 372
Grecion, Baltasar, 100
Greenfield, Jerry, 33
Greenhill, Mitch, 430
Griffin, Dan, 206, 256, 475
Grimson, Jon, 365, 401
Grulke, Brent, 291
Guerin, Pierre, 241, 245

Haddow, Henry, 445
Haggman, Karen, 126
Haigh, Robert, 378
Hannan, Kathleen, 220
Harrington, Richard, 69, 343, 348
Hawken, Paul, 39, 457
Haymes, Greg, 68, 194, 343, 346, 350, 363, 383
Hays, Dan, 288, 292, 293
Hazan, David, 409
Heflick, David, 188
Herold, Jordie, 214, 215
Heyman, Victor, 340
Hiam, Alexander, 329, 330
Higbie, Barbara, 217
Hill, John, 374
Himes, Geoffrey, 63, 337
Hirsch, Jim, 94, 148
Hofmann, Alex, 250, 253, 265, 278, 280, 281
Hollingsworth, Teresa, 286
Holt, David, 50, 380, 382
Hooper, Dave, 293
Horace (Roman poet), 17
Houghton, Bruce, 429
Howard, Greg, 289
Hubp, Lance, 406
Hugo, Victor, 443
Hunter, Charlie, 213, 214

Iacocca, Lee, 26
Ilich, John, 108
Irwin, Ken, 341, 400, 403, 405

Jaccodine, Ralph, 415, 417, 422
Jandt, Fred E., 94
Jaworek, Michael, 65
Jinnett, Jerry, 36
Johnson, Deborah L., 7, 210, 474
Jonas, Billy, 256, 277
Jones, Bob, 202, 258, 260

Kaiser, Fred, 200
Kamaroff, Bernard, 34
Kanarek, Lisa, 18
Karol, Barbara, 354, 384
Karrass, Chester, L., 95
Kaufman, Phil, 264
Kelp, Larry, 65, 335, 348, 350
Kennedy, John F., 18
Kennedy, Maura, 198, 423
Kennedy, Pete, 198, 423
Kennedy, Rod, 200, 203
Keynes, John M., 41
Kiely, Laree S., 92, 110
Kingsley, Alisse, 336, 341, 401, 403
Kaplansky, Lucy, 461
Kroc, Ray, 443
Kurland, Amy, 2, 205, 334, 351, 394
Kurland, Phyllis, 211, 212, 225
Kyriakos, Harriet, 53, 415

Lake, Tracey A., 35
Lambert, Eric, 206, 291
Landers, A., 7

Laramie, Jeff, 98, 115, 119
Laurie, Mark, 105
Lavin, L. A., 260
Leb, Mary, 201
LeBoeuf, Michael, 23
Levinson, Jay C., 75, 330, 394
Levitan, Ken, 364, 408
Levy, Lawrence, 253
Levy, Mitchell, 389
Lewis, Bernice, 257
Lewis, Laurie, 190, 250, 252, 263, 264, 289, 298, 425
Lewis, Pam, 474
L'Herrou, Valerie, 80, 333
Lickona, Terry, 377, 379-381
Lifeset, Roger, 367, 408
Lincoln, Abraham, 157
Lloyd, David, 126
Lovgren, Laura J., 46
Lunn, Chris, 217, 224, 378
Lynn, Loretta, 420
Lynn, Mooney, 420
Lyons, Heather, 312, 313

Mahoney, David J., 436
Mancuso, Joseph, 31
Mangson, Cindy, 252
Maratta, Joanna, 294
Marshall, George C., 444
Martin, Steve, 291, 426, 429, 432
Martin, Tam, 186, 428
Martinez, Susan A., 336
Marxer, Marcy, 190
Mason, Jim, 417, 418
Mason, Tim, 51, 117, 213
Masterson, Liz, 65, 185, 199
May, J. D., 440
Mayer, Jeffrey J., 19, 21, 23
McCutcheon, John, 64, 66, 207, 268
McFarland, Patrice, 62, 67, 80, 81, 330
McFaul, Mary, 104, 115, 193, 194, 290, 298, 371, 425, 430, 458
McIntyre, Deni, 69
McIntyre, Will, 69
McKnight, Andrew, 18, 31, 38, 287, 289, 458
McLuhan, Marshall, 389
Mears, Henrietta C., 19
Melba, Nellie, 32
Meyer, Paul, J., 2
Meyers, Louis, Jay, 285, 295
Miller, Cathy, 126
Monroe, Bill, 256
Morley, Christopher, 52
Moryc, Michael, 336, 365, 407, 408
Moss, Mark, 68
Mucci, Julia, 342, 369, 370, 374
Murdock, Joanne, 424
Murrow, Edward R., 91

Nathan, George J., 466
Newborough, Lord, 96
Nicholas, Ted, 101

Okrent, Brendan, 204
Olafson, Lowry, 315, 316, 318
O'Malley, Scott, 419, 427

Panay, Panos, 80, 351
Parker, Ginger, 315
Parr, Chris, 382
Parsons, Penny, 333, 349
Partridge, Marika, 335, 371
Pavlova, A., 7
Paxton, Tom, 262-263
Peters, Tom, 467
Peterson, John, 104
Pinson, Linda, 36
Pitino, Rick, 454
Pole, Laura, 219-220
Pope, Alexander, 20
Porter, John, 158, 255, 264, 271, 279, 421
Poss, Barry, 402
Prince, 389
Pulitzer, Joseph, 61

Rapaport, Diane, 62
RAVI, 208, 299, 317
Reagan, Ronald, 40
Reichman, Steve, 113, 196
Reid, Harvey, 37, 190, 252, 391, 395
Renko, Dick, 8, 45, 215, 348, 419, 444
Ribidoux, Corina, 236
Rice, Wayne, 369
Ridenour, Andy, 372
Risatti, Christine, 96, 154, 274
Rizzo, Jeanne, 102, 110, 114
Rockefeller, David, 34
Romanoff, Patty, 254
Ronstadt, Linda, 4
Rotella, Bob, 1
Roth, David, 205, 222
Rouffe, Leslie, 406
Rounds, Andrea, 413
Rousseau, Jean J., 61
Royce, Josiah, 470
Rubin, Charles, 394
Russell, Debra, 4, 10, 445

Samuels, Frederick N., 70
Schatzkin, Paul, 21, 390
Schwarz, Bob, 222
Sciaky, Carla, 187, 188
Scott, Jessie, 364, 366, 367, 404
Seeger, Peggy, 254
Shapiro, Phil, 368, 373
Shaw, George B., 16
Sills, Beverly, 460
Skopec, Eric W., 92, 110
Snadowsky, Stanley, 149
Sockman, Ralph W., 109
Socrates, 425
Spence, Andy, 130, 311, 314
Stanfield, Jana, 218, 221
Starling, John, 197, 429, 460
Steadham, Charles, 211
Stiernberg, John, 36
Stiff, Denise, 416, 420
Straw, Bill, 125
Streisand, Barbara, 462
Swanson, Margie, 39
Sweeney, Ed, 409
Syrus, Publilius, 469
Szymanski, Steve, 203

Tarbox, Jim, 353
Taylor, Harold, 459
Tec, Leon, 10
Thomas, Norman, 471
Thoreau, Henry D., 3, 473
Trafidlo, Greg, 212, 219-220
Trainor, Sue, 10, 67, 337
Trump, Geoffrey, 249, 251, 257-258, 261, 265, 267, 273
Tschida, Chris, 371, 373

Ungar, Stuart, 67
Ury, William, 93, 100

Van Vleek, Philip, 338
Vassos, Tom, 393
Vaughan, Sarah, 265

Wadsworth, Susan, 204
Wainwright, Teddy, 414
Warren, Rich, 342, 364, 369, 374, 404
Welch, Maranne, 290
Wentworth, Chuck, 148, 469
Wernick, Peter, 53, 54, 258
West, Katie, 311
Wilcox, Ericka, 394
Williams, Linda, 265, 339
Williams, Mike, 295, 296
Williams, Robin, 265, 267, 339
Willis, Mark, 292
Wilson, Susan, 70

Young, Faron, 261
Young, Irene, 67, 69

Zappa, Frank, 347

About The Author

Jeri Goldstein was the agent and manager for some of the top touring acoustic artists on the circuit including Robin & Linda Williams and Garrison Keillor & The Hopeful Gospel Quartet. Goldstein has booked national and international tours for artists performing in country, folk, gospel, bluegrass, contemporary, classical and children's music. She has also booked tours for theater and dance. After 20 years of working as an agent and manager, Goldstein authored the award-winning book, *How To Be Your Own Booking Agent, A Performing Artist's Guide To A Successful Touring Career*. Goldstein partnered with The Southern Arts Federation and Carnegie Mellon Arts Management Program, to produce an E-SeminArts, three-hour workshop CD-ROM, *Marketing Your Act*. Goldstein's articles for the self-managed artist can be found on Getsigned.com, and have been published in *Indie Magazine*, *Music Biz Magazine*, and *GiG Magazine*.

Goldstein created two innovative programs as a resource for performing artists—Manager-In-A-Box, a consultation program, is designed to help performing artists, agents and managers enhance their career development. The Performing Biz is Goldstein's seminar that is presented at universities, festivals, conferences, and for art councils or to individual groups of performing artists.

Complimenting her 30 years as president of The New Music Times, Inc., Goldstein's background runs the gamut working inside the entertainment industry as concert promoter, tour coordinator, commercial television production engineer for an NBC affiliate station, commercial country radio DJ, photographer and graphic artist. She has also served as President and member of the Board of Directors of the Folk Alliance. Goldstein coordinates the Folk Alliance's Booking Agent Training School for the annual conference. Currently, she makes her home in central Virginia.

Goldstein has conducted seminars for:

Arts Councils:
Arts Council of the Blue Ridge
Arts Midwest
Arts North Carolina
Arts Northwest
British Columbia Touring Council, Canada
California Arts Council
Indiana Arts Commission
Louisiana Division of the Arts
Mississippi Arts Commission
Missouri Folk Arts Program
New Orleans Arts Council
Ohio Arts Presenter's Network
Ontario Arts Council, Canada
Pennsylvania Arts Council, PennPat
Southern Arts Federation
Tennessee Arts Commission
Virginia Commission for the Arts

Organizations:
The Music Business Institute/Cutting Edge
Enoch Pratt Free Library
Folk Alliance
Independent Children's Artist Network
International Bluegrass Music Association
Louisiana Music New Orleans Pride-LMNOP
Music Entertainment Industry Educators Association
 —MEIEA

Schools:
Belmont University- School of Business
Carnegie Mellon University
Colorado University at Denver—Music Industry
Loyola University—Music Business Department
Music Tech College
New York University—Music Department
University of Kansas—Music & Dance Department
University of Virginia—McIntire Department of Music
Univeristy of Virginia—School of Continuing & Professional Studies

To order additional copies of this book, contact The New Music Times, Inc.
Phone: 434-591-1335   Fax: 1-866-874-9321
E-mail: jg@performingbiz.com   Web: http://www.performingbiz.com

Manager-In-A-Box®
Your On-Line Management Consultant

As a self-booking, self-managed artist, situations and questions may challenge you on occasion. Whether they are matters concerning career development or specific problems you have encountered while dealing with a performance date, *wouldn't it be great to consult with an industry professional?*

Now you can access someone with the experience and the connections to answer those questions—questions that do not warrant the cost of a lawyer but are beyond your current level of experience.

Advantages

Work with a 30-year veteran agent, manager and promoter familiar with:
- The independent and major label record industry
- National and international touring
- Festival, club, college, arts council and large venue promoters
- Resource recommendations, directories, conferences
- Business skills and promotion savvy

As-You-Need-It-Availability

Manager-In-A-Box® Programs

1. **Phone Consultation.** One 60-minute consult, set up in advance by e-mail. Contact Jeri at jg@performingbiz.com and suggest three times convenient to your schedule. Please select times that are at least one week from the date of your request. You will be contacted within 24 hours with the confirmed time and phone number to call. Send your check to The New Music Times, Inc. as soon as you receive confirmation or use your credit card on the day of your consultation.

2. **Premium Membership** includes:
   Six (6) e-mail questions answered
   Two 60-minute phone consultations
   Free promotional materials review

3. **Gold Membership** includes:
   Seven (7) e-mail questions answered
   Four 60-minute phone consultations
   Free promotional materials review

4. **One-Year Monthly Membership.** Your ongoing commitment to your developing career may require ongoing support. The One-Year Monthly membership provides you with multiple monthly consults that you can count on from one month to the next for a full year.

   Four 60-minute consults/ month + 5 emails   OR
   Three 60-minute consults/ month + 5 emails   OR
   Two 60-minute consults/ month + 3 emails   OR
   One 60-minute consult per month + 3 emails
   Free promotional materials review

The Performing Biz
Techniques, Hot Tips and Savvy Advice for a Successful Performing Career

Based on Goldstein's book, *How To Be Your Own Booking Agent,* her experience in the entertainment business offers participants first-hand knowledge of each topic discussed. She presents step-by-step methods of creating, developing and maintaining a successful performing career.

Who Should Attend?
- Performing artists
- Agents and managers
- Music students
- Presenters
- Theater students
- Arts administrators

Attendees Will Learn How To:
- Save time and money
- Plan your career for success
- Be creative in your business
- Focus on your goals

Available For Conferences, Lecture Series, Schools, Organizations, Arts Councils, Festivals, and Performing Artist Groups

Design A Seminar To Suit Your Group
- Half-Day Seminar (Four Hours):
- One-Day Seminar (7-8 Hours)

For more information contact Jeri Goldstein at
The New Music Times, Inc.
P.O. Box 1105, Charlottesville, VA 22902

Phone: 434-591-1335   Fax: 1-866-874-9321
E-mail: jg@performingbiz.com   Web: http://www.performingbiz.com

About The Editors

Kari Estrin—Editor

Kari's musical background encompasses a wide scope of the music business. In the 80s Kari formed Black Sheep Concerts & Publications, Inc., where she both published a folk music magazine and promoted her concerts at Harvard University's Sanders Theatre, Symphony Hall, The Berklee Performance Center and at area clubs. Kari also has extensive artist and tour management experience—her past management clients include guitar legend, Tony Rice and world music band, The 3 Mustaphas 3, who placed Number One in Billboard's World Music Charts. Kari currently manages Montreal-based roots artist, Rob Lutes. She has toured with Suzanne Vega and with other world music bands, such as Papa Wemba and Kanda Bongo Man.

Kari's event experience includes both the Newport Folk Festival and Merlefest as Assistant Festival Director. At MerleFest, Kari was Associate Producer for their series and home video, "Pickin' For Merle," in 1992 and while there, co-founded the prestigious Chris Austin Songwriting Contest.

As co-chair of The Folk Alliance's local committee for their 2002 Nashville conference, Kari produced a Woody Guthrie Tribute concert at the Ryman Auditorium in conjunction with his daughter, Nora Guthrie, and the Woody Guthrie Foundation. She preceded the concert with "Woody Month," a series of seminars, art and museum exhibits, book signings, and a film festival. Other event experience includes: co-producing All Star Guitar Night at the Ryman, booking Nashville's city-wide festivals, Summer Lights (1997) and Fest de Ville (2001), as well as booking area venues and co-producing the first Americana Music Association Conference in 2001.

Known for her unique, holistic and motivational approach to music business consulting, Kari specializes in coaching musical and other artists through her Career Assessment System—career planning tailored to the individual. Kari also offers other follow up consulting programs. Some of her other services include acoustic radio promotion and national publicity.

Deborah Liv Johnson—Copy Editor

Deborah Liv Johnson is the owner/artist of Mojave Sun Records. Her eight CDs include the critically acclaimed *The Cowboys of Baja Have Stolen My Heart*, *Across the White Plains*, *Softly and Tenderly* and *The Good and Bad of It*. Johnson's music is also now being distributed across Asia by Enrich Music which is based in Taiwan. Johnson is the former editor of Adventure 16's outdoor publication FOOTPRINTS and has a B.A. degree in creative writing from St. Olaf College. In addition to managing her record label, Johnson frequently tours the U.S. and handles her own booking and promotion.

Libby Post—Copy Editor

Libby Post is the President of Communication Services, an Albany, New York-based marketing and communications firm. Post writes and edits copy for clients including direct mail solicitations, brochures, newsletters, annual reports and other marketing materials. Her firm specializes in direct mail fundraising and program marketing for not-for-profit organizations, tourism marketing, economic development market research and political communications. Post holds a Master's in Political Communication and recently managed a successful race for Albany's Common Council President.